An Introduction to Early Childhood Special Education

LINDA L. DUNLAP

Editor

Marist College

ALLYN AND BACON

Boston   London   Toronto   Sydney   Tokyo   Singapore

Executive Editor: Raymond Short
Editorial Assistant: Christine Svitila
Marketing Manager: Kris Farnsworth
Editorial Production Service: Chestnut Hill Enterprises, Inc.
Manufacturing Buyer: Suzanne Lareau
Cover Administrator: Suzanne Harbison

Copyright © 1997 by Allyn & Bacon
A Viacom Company
Needham Heights, MA 02194

Internet: www.abacon.com
America Online: keyword: College Online

Library of Congress Cataloging-in-Publication Data

Dunlap, Linda L.
    An introduction to early childhood special education / Linda L. Dunlap.
      p.   cm.
    Includes bibliographical references and index.
    ISBN 0-205-18440-5 (case)
    1. Handicapped children—Education (Early childhood)—United
States. 2. Handicapped children—Services for—United States.
3. Handicapped children—United States—Development. 4. Special
education—Activity programs—United States.   I. Title.
LC4031.D696   1997
371.9'0472'0973–dc20   96-41886
                                         CIP

Printed in the United States of America

10 9 8 7 6 5 4 3 2   02 01 00 99 98 97

Photo Credits:
Special thanks to all the individuals who agreed to be in the photographs included in this book. Special thanks also goes to the children and their parents/guardians for allowing their photographs to be taken. In addition, thanks goes to Dr. Fred Attanasio and the staff of the Department of Communications of the Saint Francis Hospital in Poughkeepsie, New York, for allowing photographs to be taken at the preschool sites. Also, thanks to Melinda Sage, Allyson Burns, Nancy Pate, Eileen Taylor Appleby, Sherry Dingman, Awilda Velez, and Melanie Gardner for making arrangements to have their photographs taken by Jennifer McHale.

To the children, family members, and staff of the St. Francis Hospital Special Needs Preschool Program in Poughkeepsie, New York

CONTENTS

**CHAPTER 15   TRANSITIONS:
PREPARING FOR THE NEXT STEP   300**
Linda L. Dunlap, Ph.D.

PREFACE

The field of early childhood special education has undergone major changes during the past decade, resulting in an increase in the number of books on the topic. The language used to describe children with special needs has also changed. The term *handicap* has been replaced with the phrases *special need* and *developmental disability or delay*. Children with special needs are described as "children with disabilities" rather than "disabled children" to focus on the child rather than the disability. This book introduces the reader to the terminology needed to effectively interact with parents and providers of services for children with special needs.

This book is unique because it is written by professionals who work with young children with special needs. The authors have directly experienced the many changes that have occurred in early childhood special education over the past few years. It is valuable to have experts in several core disciplines write about the various disciplines. The majority of books on special education mention only briefly the variety of disciplines and instead focus primarily on specific types of special needs. A focus on specific needs emphasizes children's specific disabilities rather than the types of early childhood services necessary to meet their needs.

Through working with young children who have special needs, the contributors to this book have learned that each child's uniqueness creates special challenges. However, all children share many common characteristics and needs. Children with special needs love to play and to be assured that they are in a safe environment with people who value them. Family members want their children to receive the best services available, but each family group has its own special needs. Most parents want to be actively involved in their child's education, but many do not know how to contribute effectively. These issues provide the basis for this book.

Special education teachers and therapists are dedicated individuals who know a great deal about their disciplines. They are willing to work cooperatively with other professionals, but they frequently struggle to do so. Many professionals do not know the terminology associated with disciplines other than their own and frequently have little specific training in the area of early child development.

Many professionals recognize they have limited knowledge about each other's disciplines, yet such knowledge is crucial for providing an optimal level of service for young children with special needs. In most cases, regardless of a young child's specific, special need, there will be a core group of specialists involved in programs for each child.

Day care providers and teachers of regular preschool-aged children are likely to have children with special needs in their care. It is valuable for these individuals to become familiar with attributes associated with a variety of disabilities and early childhood special education services.

Federal laws require professionals to collaborate in evaluation and service delivery. Most professionals acknowledge the importance of parents' involvement in children's education but often are not trained in how to create successful partnerships. This book addresses the importance of collaborating with other professionals and developing effective parent/professional partnerships.

Federal laws emphasize the importance of early identification of and intervention for infants, toddlers, and preschoolers with special needs. The result of this emphasis is that many teacher education programs have added course work in developmental psychology and early childhood special education. There is a growing trend toward states' requiring certification in preschool special education for teachers who work with children younger than school age who have special needs.

This book begins by providing an overview of early childhood special education laws, assessment, and a description of some of the many professionals who may collaborate to provide services to children with special needs. This chapter also provides a brief overview of attributes typically found in early childhood special education programs.

Chapter 2 provides a discussion of typical early childhood development including cognitive, speech and language, physical, and social-emotional development. It is important to understand the theories and sequences of typical development to provide an effective and "least restrictive" environment for children with special needs.

Many books on special education focus on specific developmental delays and provide a chapter for each major type of delay. In contrast, Chapter 3 provides an overview of the variety of special needs of children, reasons a child may be at risk, and a brief discussion of how people may react to children with special needs. Early childhood educators need to have an awareness of the wide variety of special needs a child may have. For most types of disabilities, many similar features and service providers are incorporated into early childhood special education. Chapter 4 provides a discussion of AIDS, cocaine, and alcohol, which are contemporary factors that may place children at risk and in need of early intervention services.

An important characteristic of this book is its extended discussion of the importance of professional collaboration and service coordination provided in Chapter 5 and continued in Chapter 6, with an emphasis on parent/professional partnerships.

Chapters 7 through 11 are devoted to providing further discussion of major areas of development, assessment of developmental levels, and the types of services provided to enhance the development of those areas. Services discussed include special education speech and language, hearing, and occupational and physical therapy.

Each chapter demonstrates how various disciplines enhance the development of the whole child including cognitive, speech and language, physical, and social-emotional areas. The most effective collaboration will occur when special education teachers and therapists have a basic understanding of each other's disciplines. These chapters provide a description of these services and the terminology used in the major disciplines that commonly provide services to a variety of young children with special needs. Each chapter also provides practical suggestions for intervention strategies for children with specific needs.

Distinct from other books on early childhood special education, Chapters 12 and 13 describe the value of play and art activities for assessing children's abilities, as well as for integrating intervention services into play and art activities. Chapter 15 describes behavior management techniques and the book concludes with a discussion of the importance of designing effective transition plans and methods of helping children with special needs develop positive self-esteem. The book is based on the belief that all forms of early intervention must be centered on the philosophy that children must be valued and that all children can grow and learn. The entire book is built on the premise that children must be nurtured.

Each chapter begins with key points, provides a chapter summary, and includes review questions, suggested student activities, and additional readings and resources. Throughout the book there are examples of services provided for young children with special needs.

I am indebted to the children, parents, and staff of the Saint Francis Preschool Program in Poughkeepsie, New York, for being my "teachers" and providing the inspiration for this book. On behalf of all of the contributors, I want to thank our families and colleagues who provided encouragement during its preparation. Special thanks go to Mr. Randy Hayman, an instructor at Marist College, for the extensive editing he provided. Thanks also to Kim Kelly, Jo Anna Maldanis, and Beth Fox, who contributed to many aspects of this book, including the teacher's manual, and to Jennifer McHale, who took photographs at the Saint Francis Preschool Program. I want to thank Dr. Fred Antannasio and the staff of the Department of Communication Disorders of the Saint Francis Hospital for allowing photographs to be taken at the preschool sites. This book would not have been completed without the long hours of work and technical assistance from Dr. Gregory L. Dunlap and the patience and support of Jason and Jennifer Dunlap. They gave new meaning to collaboration.

In addition, reviewers made helpful comments which were incorporated as much as possible: Marie Fritz, Indiana State University; Mary D'Zamko, University of North Florida; Michaelene Ostrosky, Northeastern Illinois University; and Janet Lerner, Northeastern Illinois University.

CHAPTER 1

EARLY INTERVENTION SERVICES FOR INFANTS, TODDLERS, AND PRESCHOOLERS

LINDA L. DUNLAP, PH.D.

ABOUT THE AUTHOR

Linda Dunlap has taught psychology and education courses since receiving her Ph.D. from the University of Iowa in 1980. She served as a part-time faculty member at State University of New York at New Paltz and Dutchess Community College and Ulster Community College in New York from 1980 to 1984. Since 1984 she has served as a full-time faculty member and chair of the psychology department at Marist College in Poughkeepsie, New York. She served as a psychologist for the Saint Francis Hospital Preschool Program in Poughkeepsie from 1986 to 1994. This program provides services for children two to five years old who have developmental delays. Dr. Dunlap is currently a board member for the Dutchess County Child Development Council. She frequently contributes to articles about child development and parenting issues and serves as a consultant for local school districts. Dr. Dunlap is married and has a son, Jason, and a daughter, Jennifer.

CHAPTER KEY POINTS
- Early childhood intervention programs are available for children from birth through school age, are mandated by federal laws, and have demonstrated their effectiveness.
- Children who are believed to have special needs need to go through a screening and full assessment process.
- Parents and many different types of professionals are members of teams that provide services for children with developmental delays.
- Services may be provided within the child's home, a clinic, or a regular or special education classroom.
- Effective center-based programs have several common attributes.

This chapter provides an overview of federal laws that determine the basic characteristics of early childhood special education programs. It also describes the roles of various members of the collaborative team, discusses common attributes of early intervention programs, and concludes with a brief overview of one model of intervention.

OVERVIEW OF PROGRAMS FOR YOUNG CHILDREN

The National Association for the Education for Young Children (NAEYC) has provided guidelines for early childhood programs for all young children, those with and without **developmental delays.** The guidelines remind educators and parents that their most important responsibilities are to keep children safe and healthy and provide a nurturing and responsive setting for them. These responsibilities include recognizing and respecting the uniqueness of each child. NAEYC also emphasizes that family members should play a major role in the development of a child (McEvoy, 1990).

Early identification of children with developmental delays is vital. It may help prevent the developmental delays from becoming more serious or leading to additional problems (Odom & McEvoy, 1988). Most families of children with special needs do not resist services and are relieved to

learn that services are available (Erwin, 1996). Early intervention programs are designed to meet the child's and family members' need for support, information, and training (Bagnato & Neisworth, 1991).

Ultimately, society also benefits from early intervention programs because they have been shown to be cost-effective. Children who receive early intervention are more likely to attend **regular education classes** once they are school-age and often require fewer or less intensive special education services (Bailey & Wolery, 1992). This reduces the total cost of education during the child's school years (Bennett & Guralnick, 1991). One of the most important effects of early intervention is that it often helps children with special needs and their families adjust more effectively to day-to-day living, allowing these children to develop to their fullest potential (Burton, Hains, Hanline, McLean, & McCormick, 1992; Bowden, Black, & Daulton, 1990).

OVERVIEW OF FEDERAL LAWS

Several federal laws outline the services that state agencies are required to provide for children with special needs. The federal government provides supervision and partial funding for these required programs, which reach more than 4 million children nationwide (Bowden et al., 1990).

History of Special Education

Special education has changed a great deal over the last 100 years. In the late 1800s and early 1900s, children with special needs were often pushed aside as "lost causes." In the early history of special education, use of stigmatizing terms such as *idiot, moron,* and *dummy* was common. By the early 1900s, most states had established at least one residential institution for individuals with disabilities. During this time, there was a very limited number of classrooms located in public school buildings where a child with special needs could attend classes.

In the 1950s, only 12 percent of all children with developmental disabilities received special education services. As late as 1962, only sixteen states included children who were classified as "educable" under mandatory school attendance laws. During this time, even children with mild disabilities were not allowed to attend public schools. As recently as the early 1970s, children with severe disabilities did not receive a free public education (Gallagher, 1989). Children with special needs were taught in classrooms or other buildings set aside just for them. In some cases these classrooms resulted in the children being isolated and stigmatized. These children often were not provided opportunities to participate in many activities that occurred in regular classrooms such as art, music, and field trips.

Federal Laws Related to Early Childhood Special Education

In 1968 the **Handicapped Children's Early Education Assistance Act (Public Law [PL] 90–538)** established the **Handicapped Children's Early Education Program (HCEEP).** This program is now called the **Office of Special Education Programs (OSEP).** The act provided funding for identifying model programs and for disseminating information about these model programs. In 1969, **PL 91–230** combined all previous special education laws into one act.

More specifically related to early childhood education, in 1972, **PL 92–424,** the **Economic Opportunity Amendments,** required that not less than 10 percent of Head Start enrollment slots for preschoolers be available for children with special needs. In further support of the need for early intervention, **PL 93–380,** enacted in 1969, required states to establish the goal of providing full educational opportunities for all children with special needs from birth through age twenty-one.

In 1975, **PL 94–142,** the **Education for All Handicapped Children Act (EHA),** was designed to provide children who have developmental disabilities with a **free appropriate public education (FAPE).** Based on this law, states are mandated to provide identification programs that locate and evaluate all children, three to five years old, with special needs (Saranson, 1990). The law described due process procedures, including informed parental consent, and required **multifactored evaluation (MFE)** to determine if children were eligible to receive free intervention services (Meisels & Shonkoff, 1990).

Children must be evaluated in all areas of development including cognitive, speech and language, physical, social or emotional, and self-help skills. If significant delays are noted in any of these areas, which may negatively affect a child's ability to learn, special education services must be designed and put in place to meet the child's needs. These services are to be provided in such a way that the child maintains, as much as possible, a "normal" lifestyle (Farran, 1990). That is, whenever possible, children should engage in the same type of activities children without special needs experience, such as going on a field trip to a zoo. The law states that children should be educated in the **least restrictive environment (LRE).** The LRE is not always in a regular classroom, but children should be segregated as little as possible.

Because free preschool programs are generally only provided to children who have developmental delays or are **at risk** of developing delays, those children are often educated at special early childhood programs. At the preschool level, inclusion (children with special needs educated in regular education classrooms) is likely to occur only when special education programs are located within buildings that also provide preschool programs for children who do not have developmental delays (Carta, Schwartz, Atwater, & McConnell, 1991).

Many preschool classrooms designed for children with special needs are still **segregated** even when they are located in public school facilities. The idea of inclusion is slowly moving into the preschool special education system (Guralnick, 1996). Some special education programs are designed to include child care centers that provide day care and special and regular preschool programs within the same facility. Since, in most cases, toddlers and preschoolers spend only a small portion of the day attending **early childhood intervention programs,** there is generally time for parents to create **inclusion** experiences for their own child. These experiences may include attending a regular day care or preschool program in addition to the program for special needs (Carson, 1991).

PL 94–142 also mandates other services that must be provided, including transportation, testing, diagnosis, and therapy, as needed to every child with special needs. These types of services are referred to as related services. The law also guarantees parents the right to a due process hearing, which provides for a judicial hearing if parents disagree with the **Committee on Preschool Special Education (CPSE)** decisions regarding services provided for their child (Smith, Finn, & Dowdy, 1993). **Due process** ensures the parents' right to be fully informed, to fully participate in education decisions regarding their child, to mediation with an independent disinterested party, to challenge the school district's decisions, to appeal decisions before an impartial hearing officer, and to have access to their child's school records (Thurman, Cornwell, & Gottwald, 1996).

In 1986, the federal government made a more specific commitment to providing early intervention services with the passage of **PL 99–457,** the **Education of Handicapped Act Amendment.** This law mandates comprehensive services for infants and toddlers who have developmental delays or are **at risk** of developmental delays, as well as for their families. PL 99–457 was the first to focus on children from birth through two years old. It extended the provision of PL 94–142 to this age group. It requires family members to be involved in making decisions and to be able to receive direct services, such as counseling. It also requires the coordination of services for children and their family members and that plans be created for the transition to a preschool special education program (Salisbury & Vincent, 1990).

The **Technology-Related Assistance for Individuals with Disabilities Act** was established in 1988. This public law required that assistive and adaptive technology be provided as a part of related services for students who require them in order to benefit most fully from special education. Assistive devices include wheelchairs, artificial limbs, hearing aids, computers, and so on. (A detailed discussion of assistive devices can be found in Chapters 9 and 10.)

In 1990, **PL 101–476,** the **Individuals with Disabilities Education Act (IDEA),** re-authorized and extended PL 94–142. Language in the law was changed from use of the term *handicapped* to "children with disabilities," and autism and traumatic brain injury were added as classification categories. In 1991, **PL 102–119** was issued as an amendment to IDEA. It outlined specific services that must be made available for infants, toddlers, and preschoolers with special needs and their families. Additional services specified in this amendment include special instruction and therapy, assistive technology services and devices, family training, counseling, and home visits, and medical diagnostic, nursing, nutritional, transition, and recreation services.

Referral for Developmental Assessment

An initial screening of abilities of children should reveal whether they have special needs. In most cases, delays of more than six months in one or more areas of development indicate a need for further **evaluation** by appropriate specialists (Hartup, 1988). Table 1.1 provides a list of specialists to

TABLE 1.1 Specialists to Whom Referrals May Be Made Classified by Area of Concern

Physical Heath
- Pediatrician, M.D.—A medical doctor skilled in diagnosing and treating childhood diseases and in caring for children's health.
- General Practitioner, M. D.—A medical doctor who specializes in treating and caring for patients who have general health problems.
- Public Health Nurse—A registered nurse (RN) who surveys, screens, and manages family and community health care.
- Dentist, D.D.S.—A person licensed to practice dentistry (teeth and oral cavity).
- Orthopedist, M.D.—A medical doctor who diagnoses and treats bone and skeletal disorders.
- Cardiologist, M.D.—A medical doctor who diagnoses, treats, and manages heart disorders.

Speech and Language
- Speech and Language Pathologist—A professional who screens, diagnoses, and treats communication disorders related to voice, language, articulation, oral–motor skills, and hearing.
- Audiologist—Professional who screens and diagnoses hearing problems, evaluates hearing aid fittings, and may provide therapy relating to language development and hearing aid use.
- Child Psychologist—A specialist who focuses on understanding and treating the behavioral and emotional problems of children.
- Special Education Teacher—A teacher with special training and experience in educating children with special needs.
- Public Health Nurse

Hearing
- Audiologist
- Speech and Language Pathologist
- Otologist, E.N.T., M.D.—A medical doctor who diagnoses, treats, and manages physical disorders relating to the ear, nose, and throat.
- Pediatrician, M.D.
- Public Health Nurse
- Teacher of the Deaf and Hearing Impaired—A teacher with special training and experience in educating children who are deaf or hearing impaired.

Vision
- Ophthalmologist, M.D.—A medical doctor who screens, diagnoses, and treats eye disorders.
- Optometrist—A therapist skilled in assessing visual acuity, adapting corrective lenses, and assessing and managing visual perception and related difficulties.
- Pediatrician, M.D.
- General Practitioner, M.D.
- Public Health Nurse

Motor
- Occupational Therapist—A therapist who tests and suggests programs for perceptual problems, gross and fine motor difficulties, and suggests methods to teach skills needed for activities of daily living.
- Physical Therapist—A therapist who tests and suggests programs for gross and fine motor difficulties, walking problems, and methods to teach activities of daily living.
- Pediatrician, M.D.
- Neurologist, M.D.—A medical doctor who screens, diagnoses, and treats nervous system disorders such as paralysis, reflex coordination, epilepsy, and perceptual problems.
- Child Psychologist
- Speech and Language Pathologist
- Special Education Teacher
- General Practitioner, M.D.
- Public Health Nurse

Social and Emotional
- Child Psychologist
- Psychiatrist, M.D.—A medical doctor who specializes in treating mental disorders.
- Social Worker—A professional with special training and experience in helping people interact with society, family, and co-workers, and with financial difficulties. This professional also refers people to other specialists.
- Special Education Teacher
- Speech and Language Pathologist
- Audiologist
- Public Health Nurse

whom referrals should be made based on the area of concern. Several professionals are listed under multiple roles and, therefore, are only described when they are first listed.

Teachers, daycare providers, and parents of young children should not hesitate to seek referrals for developmental evaluations simply because a pediatrician or other medical professional has not initiated the referral. Medical professionals focus on maintaining a patient's good health and treating the person's illness rather than on making referrals for developmental evaluations. When children are seen by a physician, they are often only examined for a few minutes and at a time when they are not feeling well. This is not the type of setting where developmental delays are likely to be noted. Many physicians initiate referral, but if they do not and the parent or teacher is concerned about a child's rate of development, the parent should discuss this concern with the child's physician (Heisler, 1972).

THE ASSESSMENT PROCESS

The process of identifying a child with special needs and providing special education services involves several steps (Peck, Odom, & Bricker, 1993). The child must first be referred to a department of health, a CPSE, or some other agency or program that handles early intervention referrals. Once a referral has been made, the child's strengths and needs must be evaluated to determine if the child is eligible for services and what types of services the child may need (Bagnato, Neisworth, & Munson, 1996).

For a child to qualify for federally mandated early intervention services, the child's developmental level must be evaluated. The parents' written consent is required for an evaluation to be conducted. The evaluation should be conducted in the child's **dominant language.** The assessment must be performed by trained professionals, such as a special education teacher, psychologist, or speech and language pathologist. In most states, there is no direct cost to children or families for a screening, evaluation, or for services (Smith, Finn, & Dowdy, 1993).

Types of Assessment

Assessment refers to gathering and analyzing information for instructional, administrative, and guidance decisions. **Formal testing,** one aspect of

assessment, uses **standardized assessment** devices. Standardized assessments are often **norm-referenced,** which involves comparing the performance of an individual child to other children of the same age group (Hebbeler, Smith, & Black, 1991).

Diagnostic testing involves a more in-depth analysis of a child's strengths and weaknesses in a particular area. This data may be collected in the child's natural environment. Diagnostic testing is often **criterion referenced,** which involves determining whether a child's performance meets pre-established criteria or levels of mastery (Gullo, 1994). This type of assessment often does not emphasize the child's relative standing but instead provides a measure of the level of progress toward mastery (Smith, et al., 1993). This form of assessment aids teachers in designing individual instruction with a focus on specific skills. Although standardized criterion-referenced tests can be used, many criterion-referenced assessments are designed by the teacher or are built into the program (Slentz & Bricker, 1992).

Ecological assessment may also occur and involves evaluating how children function in the various environments in which they interact and assessing the settings themselves. Using ecological assessments, a parent may be asked about how a child responds to various situations and the child may be observed interacting with peers, parents, and teachers in normal daily settings. This type of assessment evaluates how the child functions in the current environment, as well as predicts how the child may function in other environments (Karnes & Stayton, 1988). Ecological assessments are designed to provide information about the child's strengths within natural settings in order to develop intervention methods based on those strengths.

Arena assessment is one form of ecological assessment used by **transdisciplinary teams.** These teams include professionals from several disciplines working together during assessment. All members of the team, including parents and professionals, should be available for the assessment session. One or more of the team members may interact with the child during the assessment process while other team members observe. Generally, one team member is designated as team leader and organizes the assessment process. **Play-based assessment** is another form of ecological assessment and is discussed in Chapter 12.

Developmental Screening

Typically, an initial screening is conducted to determine if the child needs a full evaluation. For children less than five years old, a screening is frequently completed by a special education teacher or speech and language pathologist. If a screening suggests the likelihood of a developmental delay, the child should undergo a formal evaluation. The formal evaluation, or "testing," is most often completed by a team of qualified professionals from several disciplines. They collaborate to determine the child's eligibility for early intervention services (Slentz & Bricker, 1992). A full evaluation generally includes:

- Review of the child's health records and medical history;
- Determining the child's current level of functioning in major developmental areas;
- Assessment of the child's needs;
- Making recommendations for appropriate early intervention services, if any.

There is a wide variety of developmental screening instruments available to determine if children have developmental delays. These tests evaluate one or more areas of skills development including adaptive or self-help, general cognitive or intellectual, gross and fine motor, and speech and language. Several assessment instruments used to evaluate these skills are listed in Table 1.2.

If the child being assessed is less than three years old, an assessment of the family is also mandated to determine the resources, priorities, and concerns the family has relating to the child's development. A more detailed discussion of the assessments social workers, special education teachers, speech and language pathologists, occupational and physical therapists, and other professionals use is provided in later chapters.

TABLE 1.2 Tests that May Be Used to Evaluate the Development of Children, Birth through Four Years

Birth to Six Months
Brazelton Neonatal Behavioral Assessment Scale
Cattell Infant Intelligence Scale
Gesell Developmental Scales
Infant Temperament Scale
Kent Infant Scale
Neurobehavior Assessment of Preterm Infants
Parent Behavior Progression
Play Interaction Measure
Uzgiris–Hunt Infant Psychological Development
    Scales

Six to 12 Months
Bayley Scales of Infant Development
Cattell Infant Intelligence Scale
Early Coping Inventory
Infant Learning
Memphis Comprehensive Development Scale
Parent Behavior Progression
Transdisciplinary Play-based Assessment

12 to 24 Months
Brigance Diagnostic Inventory of Early
    Development
Griffiths Mental Development Scales
Hawaii Early Learning Profile
Infant Daycare Rating Scale
Toddler Temperament Scale

24 to 36 Months
Autism Screening Instrument for Educational
    Planning
Bracken Basic Concepts Scale
Child Behavior Checklist
Childhood Autism Rating Scale
Cognitive Abilities Scale
Developmental Indicators for Assessment of
    Learning (DIAL-R)
Early Screening Profile (ESP)
Family Needs Survey
Griffiths Mental Development Scales
Hawaii Early Learning Profile
Leiter International Performance Scale (LIPS)
Transdisciplinary Play-based Assessment
Preschool Mullen Scale of Early Learning
Stanford–Binet Intelligence Test
System to Plan Early Childhood Services

continued

TABLE 1.2   Continued

36 to 60 Months
Adaptive Behavior Scale
Attention-Deficit/Hyperactivity Disorder Test
Battele Developmental Inventory
Bracken Basic Concepts
Child Behavior Checklist
Detroit Test of Learning Aptitude
Differential Abilities Test (DAS)
Early Childhood Environment Rating Scale
Gilliam Autism Rating Scale
Goodenough–Harris Drawing Test
Help for Special Preschoolers
Kaufman Assessment Battery for Children
Leiter International Performance Scale (LIPS)
McCarthy Scales of Children's Abilities
Preschool Mullen Scales of Early Learning
Porteus Mazes
Slosson Essential Skills Screener: "At-Risk"
    Identification (ESS)
Slosson Intelligence Test
Social Skills Rating System
Survey of Early Childhood Abilities (SECA)
System to Plan Early Childhood Services
Wechsler Preschool and Primary Scales of
    Intelligence (WPPSI-R)

Birth to Four Years
Birth to Three Assessment and Intervention System
Carolina Curriculum
Developmental Assessment for the Severely
    Handicapped
Developmental Observation Checklist System
Home Observation for Measurement of the Home
    Environment (HOME)
Mullen Scales of Early Learning
Preverbal Assessment Intervention Profile
Vineland Adaptive Behavior Scales

Individualized Family Service Plan and Individualized Education Program

After the child is evaluated, a meeting is held to review the results of the evaluation and to determine if the child is eligible to receive early intervention services (Ensher, 1989). If the child is classified as eligible for services, a written plan called an **individualized family service plan (IFSP)** for children from birth through two years old or an **individualized education program (IEP)** for children three years of age and older is developed based on the evaluation and assessment information (Slentz & Bricker, 1992).

IFSPs and IEPs should include the child's parent(s), a service coordinator, one or more members of the evaluation team, and any other person the parent wishes to invite, including anyone who may already be providing services to the child or family. The IFSP and IEP goals are discussed with the parent(s) at a planning conference. The IFSP or IEP should be presented to the parent(s) in nontechnical language. IFSPs are evaluated twice annually and IEPs once annually. See Table 1.3 for information that should be included within an IFSP.

An IEP has many of the same components found in an IFSP although there is often a reduction in the required services provided to the child's family in an IEP (Keogh & Glover, 1980). See Table 1.4 for the first few pages of a sample IEP form. Team members write a specific instruction plan for the child that would typically be found in additional pages of an IEP and would contain a detailed description of long- and short-term goals for various areas of development.

The IFSP or IEP must be implemented based on the approval of the local school district, which

TABLE 1.3   Information that Should Be Included in an Individualized Family Service Plan (IFSP)

An IFSP should include:

- The child's present level of functioning;
- Information about the family's resources, priorities, and concerns;
- Name of the service coordinator;
- Specific early intervention services being recommended;
- Expected outcomes and timeline for early intervention services;
- Projected dates for services to begin;
- Methods for transition into the next program.

TABLE 1.4   Sample Form for an Individual Education Program (IEP)

Service provider:_____   Meeting date:_____

Date of evaluation/report: _____

Child's name:_____

Mother's name: _____

Mother's address: _____

Mother's daytime telephone number:_____

Mother's evening telephone number:_____

Father's Name:_____

Father's Address: _____

Father's daytime telephone number:_____

Father's evening telephone number:_____

Purpose of meeting: ___Develop IEP   ___Review of IEP   ___ Develop Transition Plan

Child's present level of performance: _____

Child's placement status: _____

Cognitive:

verbal score: _____

performance score: _____

full scale: _____

Speech/Language:

articulation skills: _____

receptive language skills: _____

expressive language skills: _____

Physical:

fine motor: _____

gross motor: _____

vision:_____

hearing: _____

Self-help skill:

eating:_____

using the toilet: _____

dressing: _____

bathing: _____

continued

TABLE 1.4   Continued

Social/Emotional:

relationship with peers: _____

relationship with adults: _____

self-concept: _____

adjustment to school and community: _____

attention span: _____

Primary classification: _____

Secondary classification: _____

Status: ___eligible   ___ineligible   ___exit (no longer eligible for services)

Case Coordinator: _____

Placement location: _____

Program type: _____

Maximum group size:____   Student/teacher ratio:____   Program length:____months

Projected starting date: _____

Committee meeting date: _____

Review by: _____

Re-evaluation date: _____

(Note: Additional relevant goals and objectives for each child would also be stated on the IEP form.)

must place the child in the least restrictive program. If the child is not recommended for services, the family may be assisted in finding other programs or services that may benefit the child and family. If the parents do not agree with the recommendations in the IFSP or feel the child should be eligible for services that are not being recommended, the parents have the legal right to **due process.** That is, the parents have the right to appeal the decision in a hearing before a judge (Wasik, Ramey, Bryant, & Sparling, 1990). In most states, a wide variety of potential services are available to children and their parents through early intervention programs (Slentz & Bricker, 1992).

The IFSP and IEP are modified whenever necessary. See Table 1.5 for a list of services available for children with developmental delays.

SERVICES FOR INFANTS, TODDLERS, AND PRESCHOOLERS

Toddlers and preschoolers with special needs often benefit from attending programs designed and staffed with their needs in mind. In most infant and preschool special needs programs, there are many specialized professionals who have gone through extensive training to work with such children.

In some cases, children may be provided services at home (Schweinhart, et al., 1986). This is

TABLE 1.5 Services for Children with Developmental Delays

Early interventions services provided for young children with developmental delays include:

1. Early identification, screening, and assessment services
2. Medical, diagnostic, and evaluation services
3. Service coordination
4. Special educational instruction
5. Speech and language pathology and audiology
6. Physical therapy
7. Occupational therapy
8. Psychological services
9. Social work services
10. Counseling
11. Vision services
12. Nursing services
13. Nutrition services
14. Health services
15. Assistive technology devices and services
16. Transportation and related costs
17. Family education programs, support groups, and home visits

more often true for children less than two years old or those who are severely physically impaired. Many home-based services are parent-oriented and emphasize professional staff who train parents how to interact most effectively with their children. Some home-based programs are child-oriented and emphasize professionals who provide **direct intervention** with the child. Sometimes, these children may also receive therapy services at a regular daycare or preschool program (Wasik, Ramey, Bryant, & Sparling, 1990).

There is a growing trend for **home-based** and **center-based programs** to be **family-systems oriented.** This orientation is child-centered and parent-centered when the entire family system is provided intervention services. Individualized service plans for each child are developed based on each child and family member's needs within a family ecology context. In all types of early intervention programs it is necessary to help the child adapt to fit the environment and to change the en-

vironment to fit the child's needs. This process is referred to as ecological congruence (Thurman, 1977).

One advantage of receiving services within a daycare or preschool environment is that children frequently benefit by interacting with other children. They learn a great deal from observing and modeling the behavior of peers and adults. Children who have developmental delays benefit from opportunities to interact with children who do not have delays (Johnson, Pugach, & Devlin, 1990). They also need opportunities to gain confidence in their abilities and strengths within the context of the real world and through interactions with a variety of people (McDonnell & Hardman, 1988).

Therapy services may be provided at sites designed specifically for children with special needs, called **self-contained classrooms,** or in a setting with children who have special needs and those who do not, referred to as an **inclusion classroom.** Self-contained classrooms typically include a special teacher who provides most of the daily instruction to students who are segregated in a special class. For these children it has been determined that a self-contained classroom provides the **least restrictive environment.** Children with moderate to severe delays may learn most effectively in self-contained classrooms, although the ultimate goal is to integrate these children into regular classes.

In all forms of service delivery parents should be important contributors to their child's education. Parents benefit from opportunities to meet and interact with other parents of children with special needs. Programs designed to meet the needs of children who are developmentally delayed should provide the help needed to create these opportunities (Guralnick, 1991).

In a **center-based program,** children may receive therapy intervention within the classroom or may be **pulled out** for therapy outside of the classroom. Therapy is also provided within the context of classroom activities (Johnson et al., 1990). For example, occupational therapy goals could be practiced while the child is playing at a sensory table, physically exploring different materials such as sand or rice. Speech therapy could occur during an informal child–adult play interaction.

All children need a chance to achieve basic **problem-solving skills,** acquire tools for effective communication, develop a capacity to persist at tasks, and acquire a positive attitude about the process of learning. Research indicates that a center-based program is helpful because learning is often maximized when children are interacting with each other (Dunst, Snyder, & Mankinen, 1989).

DESCRIPTIONS OF TEAM MEMBERS

For the education of children with special needs to be effective, many individuals must **collaborate.** Team members working within an early intervention program should have an understanding of typical and atypical development, knowledge about family support, competency in child and family assessment, the ability to conduct program evaluations, and knowledge about proper professional conduct (Gallagher, 1992). Three important attributes of team members are:

- Having training and experience related to early childhood;
- Having a professional license or certification in a specific discipline;
- Having the ability to work effectively as a member of a team.

Several team members are discussed in detail in subsequent chapters including **social workers, parents, special education teachers, speech and language pathologists, teachers of the deaf and hearing-impaired,** and **occupational** and **physical therapists.** In addition to these individuals, several other specialists also provide services in early education programs for children with special needs. The next sections describe the roles of these individuals as members of the service team.

Psychologists

Frequently, parents and children are referred to a **psychologist** for a general developmental evalua-

tion. Psychologists either have a doctorate or master's in counseling, clinical, or school psychology. In most states they are either licensed or certified. Those who have a master's degree are usually supervised by a psychologist who has a doctorate. A psychologist may work in a program full-time, or provide part-time consultation.

In most early childhood programs, psychologists focus on assessing children's intellectual level, psychological and emotional status, and level of adaptability. Psychologists often administer standardized assessment instruments (tests) and evaluate concept development, and verbal, perceptual, social-emotional, self-help, and motor skills. Psychologists classify or diagnose the child based on the results of a formal assessment and observation (Hebbeler, et al., 1991). For example, the evaluation may include classifying a child as autistic or autistic-like.

In addition, psychologists often evaluate the emotional needs of the child and child's family to determine whether psychological support services are needed. These judgments are frequently made by interviewing the parents and observing the child. The data is often combined with additional data a social worker or other staff member provides. The psychologist may provide counseling for the child and family members as well as appropriate referrals for counseling services.

Counseling may be provided for the child in the form of **play therapy.** Play therapy involves using puppets or toys to help children deal with traumas such as abuse or the death of a family member. This type of therapy is often inappropriate for preschool children because it requires verbal comprehension and symbolic play skills. Many preschool children with special needs have delayed verbal skills, which further limits the usefulness of play therapy (Gallagher, 1992).

In some cases, a **developmental psychologist** is a team member in a program designed to provide services to a child with special needs. A developmental psychologist has a doctorate or master's in psychology or education and focuses on child development or education/special education. Often, this person is *not* licensed as a counselor or trained to administer formal psychological evaluations.

Developmental psychologists focus on the developmental stages of childhood, learning theories, and methods of instruction. They often interact directly with children, teachers, or therapists within the classroom to help determine appropriate developmental goals and intervention strategies. They may be asked to help solve **behavior management problems** or determine the types of instructional methods that could be used to meet each child's needs. For example, a developmental psychologist may help a child with a high level of **separation anxiety** adjust to being away from his or her parent during the child's first few days of attending a new class.

Psychologists may recommend to other service providers methods of interacting with children and their families to achieve a desired educational goal. Psychologists can participate in designing and implementing evaluation instruments used to assess the effectiveness of various types of interventions, as well as assess the overall program effectiveness. Psychologists often provide **in-service training** (lectures or workshops) to staff and/or parents on a variety of topics, including discipline, appropriate expectations, and transitions to other programs.

Nurses

Nurses who work in programs with children who have special needs may be **licensed practical nurses (LPNs)**, requiring a two-year degree, or **registered nurses (RNs),** requiring a four-year degree. Although most nurses do not have formal training in the specific needs of the developmentally disabled, most nursing degree programs require coursework in developmental psychology. Some nurses complete a master's in education in addition to a nursing degree and may be referred to as "nurse–educators."

Nurses often serve as consultants rather than full-time members of service teams in an early childhood special education program (Karnes & Stayton, 1988). Nurses tend to focus on the health of the child and family. They can conduct basic health assessments, especially those related to the child's special needs, and provide instruction to staff and parents regarding methods to adequately care for a child's health needs, including how to use **assisted ventilation** (e.g., oxygen therapy), **catheters** (e.g., elimination of body waste), or **feeding tubes,** and how to administer medication.

Nurses could also demonstrate to children, teachers, and parents proper hygiene techniques such as methods of bathing and brushing teeth. Nurses often help develop preventive healthcare plans by teaching parents and staff about ways to reduce the spread of infection and sickness among children and adults. LPNs and RNs could instruct staff and parents about how to deal with seizures or medical emergencies by providing in-service training. They may also offer referrals to other healthcare providers.

Pediatricians

Pediatricians are licensed physicians who specialize in medical care of children. They may serve as part-time staff to an early intervention program, but in most cases parents choose their child's pediatrician (Heisler, 1972). The pediatrician's role is crucial because a pediatrician's referral is often required for a child to receive assessments, such as a neurological or an audiological (hearing) evaluation, or therapy such as occupational or physical therapy.

Pediatricians focus on the child's health condition, including assisting family members to serve the child's health needs or helping children regain their health after an illness. Pediatricians assess children's physiological state as part of the general health evaluation and provide information about how a physical condition could affect the child's rate of development. They also provide information about the benefits and side effects of prescribed medications. Because some medical conditions require a restricted diet and/or activities, pediatricians may recommend a specific diet and/or appropriate activities. With the parents' approval, pediatricians could also help early childhood staff members learn how to provide for a child's special health needs and request information from school staff members about the child's health status.

Audiologists

Audiologists provide and coordinate services for children with auditory disabilities. They typically have a master's in audiology and are certified by the state. They evaluate the level of auditory functioning. If a child has a hearing loss at a particular frequency, audiologists can provide information about the types of sounds that could be difficult for the child to hear. They also recommend specific types of amplification or assistive devices that could enhance the child's hearing (Shonkoff & Hauser–Cram, 1987).

Nutritionists

Within an early childhood program, **nutritionists** help assess and implement plans to meet the nutritional needs of young children. They may provide general nutritional information to parents and staff. The primary goal of a nutritionist is to maximize the health and nutritional status of children. This role could be filled by a nurse, but most nurses are not specially trained in understanding the nutritional needs of young children. Nutritionists often work with other staff members regarding feeding problems or help find ways to facilitate the use of oral feeding mechanisms (e.g., food tubes). They also help plan diets for children with metabolic disorders (e.g., hormonal or blood sugar imbalances), severe allergies, diabetes, or other special medical conditions.

Early Childhood Educators

Individuals trained specifically in the field of early childhood education are often staff members at programs servicing young children with special needs. **Early childhood educators** may have an associate's, bachelor's, or master's degree in education, daycare services, or early childhood. They receive training focused on the typical stages of development and regular early childhood curriculum. Therefore, they are especially well prepared to help create the least restrictive environment, which involves including children with special needs in as many typical daily activities as possible.

Because most special education educators do not receive special training for teaching children younger than school-age (five years old), early childhood teachers help fill knowledge gaps (Deiner, 1993). Early childhood educators often work as co-teachers with a special educator or other staff member, such as a speech or language pathologist, teacher of the deaf or hearing impaired, and occupational or physical therapist.

Music Therapists

Music therapists are trained in an approved music therapy program at the undergraduate or graduate level. These degrees require completing a clinical internship, as well as coursework. Music therapists have skills in piano, voice, and guitar and are knowledgeable in music composition, theory, and history. Music therapy is provided in groups or individually. Although the value of music has long been acknowledged, only recently has music therapy been recognized as particularly useful in educating children with special needs (Wolery, 1991).

Music therapy typically includes various musical activities such as listening, singing, clapping, tapping, dancing, walking, moving, and playing various instruments. Music therapists choose songs that are age-appropriate and adapt their use to meet children's specific needs. At the preschool level, folk songs for children, standard nursery rhymes, and adaptations of contemporary songs are often selected that support classroom themes (Bayless & Ramsey, 1991). For example, if children are learning about farm animals, "Old McDonald" and "Bingo" might be selected to support the farm animals theme.

Music therapy often is especially useful for children with special needs. Music often helps to facilitate vocalization and increase the number and spontaneous use of vocabulary words through songs. Music therapy could be used to increase social, attending, and turn-taking skills and may help to develop fine and gross motor skills (Bricker, 1986).

Music therapy is often useful for children with behavioral problems. For example, children who have difficulty maintaining attention at **large group activities** may be motivated to attend and wait their turn by being allowed to play a drum. Music therapy activities are usually perceived as "nonthreatening" by most children and are an enjoyable way for children to receive instruction. During music activities, children are often unaware that certain skills are being "worked on" because they are having so much fun. Even when children are unwilling to participate in other activities, they are likely to participate in music activities (Haines & Gerber, 1996). Music therapy often provides children with positive experiences within a school setting, which helps to create a positive orientation toward school (Lepper, 1981).

Teacher Assistants

Teacher assistants often function much as teachers do, and are typically called teachers, but they may not necessarily be certified as teachers or therapists. They often have a two-year degree in childcare or early childhood education, but this degree is usually *not* required. Teacher assistants often supervise many of the classroom activities but do not conduct formal assessments and are not responsible for writing IFSP or IEP reports. Often, though, they attend meetings for planning the child's goals.

Daycare Providers

A large number of young children are cared for during part of the day by adults other than their parents. Sometimes **daycare providers** are extended family members but more often they are not. In either case, daycare providers frequently spend more time with children when they are awake than any other person. Therefore, it is often useful for them to be included as members of a child's service team.

TEAM COLLABORATION

Often, a single individual cannot provide all the services a child with developmental delays need. Team members have varied expertise and philosophies that should be combined to develop the most effective educational plan. Although involving a variety of professionals makes the process more complex and difficult to coordinate, the more professionals represented on a team, the more complete the service becomes (Schweinhart, Weikart, & Larner, 1986). (See Chapter 5 for further discussion of team collaboration.)

To develop an overall philosophy on how best to provide services to each child, it is often necessary for staff members to modify or compromise their personal philosophies to meet a child's needs (Karnes & Stayton, 1988). Individuals often must relinquish their "professional turf" to develop a true respect for all areas of expertise, including colleagues and parents, and have an effective team. (Chapters 5 and 6 provide further discussion of the need for collaboration.) The **Council for Exceptional Children (CEC)** has developed a **Code of Ethics and Standards for Educators** that are useful for all individuals who work with children (Salisbury & Vincent, 1990). These guidelines are summarized in Table 1.6.

It is important that no member of an early intervention team should attempt to "take over" a parent's responsibilities. It is imperative that they do not undermine the role of a parent because the parent is an integral part of planning and implementing the child's educational plan. Families should develop their own competencies and learn to be as self-sufficient as possible (Slentz & Bricker, 1992). Team members should *not* act as experts in areas outside their expertise. For

TABLE 1.6 Guidelines for Early Childhood Educators

Early childhood educators should:

1. Select and use age-appropriate instructional material, equipment, supplies, and resources;
2. Create safe and effective learning environments;
3. Maintain appropriate class size and workload;
4. Use assessment materials that are not discriminatory;
5. Maintain confidentiality of information about the child;
6. Respect parents and include them in the decision-making process;
7. Serve as advocates for children with special needs;
8. Obtain and maintain appropriate credentials.

example, families should be referred to psychologists or social workers when counseling is needed, rather than seeking counseling from a teacher.

Because the parents and child often receive intervention services, professionals must recognize the parents' role as services recipients and members of the team planning the child's services. In addition, parents can serve as board members, participate in advocacy and lobbying, act as classroom therapy aides, help raise money for toys, equipment, and special events, write or help to produce newsletters, build equipment, or do clerical or office work. Parents who become more involved usually improve their parenting skills, feel more confident, are more accepting of the child's developmental level, and become better advocates for their child (Goodman, 1992). (See Chapter 6 for a discussion of parents and professionals in collaborative partnerships.)

EARLY INTERVENTION PROGRAM ATTRIBUTES

Programs for young children vary greatly but should always involve a combination of education and care. As Abraham Maslow's hierarchy of needs (an order of needs that should be met to ensure the development of a person's potential) suggests, the basic needs of physical safety, emotional

security, sense of belonging, and **self-esteem** each need to be met before higher levels of intellectual skills can develop (Thiele & Hamilton, 1991).

Nurturing and educating a child involve simultaneous commitments to social, emotional, and physical growth, as well as cognitive development. For example, a child who is experiencing the death, divorce, or separation of a parent or interacting with a parent who has recently lost a job often has special emotional needs associated with these events. This child is likely to have "mood swings" and act more aggressively. These types of events are likely to interfere with learning (Bricker, 1986). Teachers should be sensitive to the emotional states of the children with whom they work.

Effective Interaction with Parents

An effective early childhood program also usually enhances parents' competency and confidence. It acknowledges that parents of all economic levels share common concerns, but each family also has individual needs that must be met (Krakow & Kopp, 1983). This may require individual or group counseling. Early childhood programs should include counseling services or, if they do not, should offer assistance in finding appropriate counseling services (Deiner, 1993).

Staff members must develop cultural sensitivity, which includes becoming aware of communication styles, values, and customs of families with different cultural and linguistic backgrounds. Service providers should understand that children and their families frequently have had experiences that could lead to skepticism and aloofness regarding whether services will be useful (Bornstein, 1991). Service providers should share their ideas with the family but should not attempt to change the value system of the family.

Providing Programming for Varying Needs

Ideally, an early childhood program serves children with a broad range of disabilities rather than a narrow range of classifications, such as only children with attention deficit hyperactivity disorders or autism (Bailey & McWilliams, 1990). Typically, when children with varying disabilities are learning together, a wider range of activities is provided. Also, staff are less inclined to develop a rigid format of how to care for a particular type of child, but instead must adjust the curriculum to meet the variety of needs (Bailey & Wolery, 1992).

Ideally, a center-based program provides contact between children without disabilities and their families and children with special needs and their families. Services must be provided in the least restrictive environment, under conditions that are as normal as possible (Casto & Mastropieri, 1986). Typically, special education programs strive to create a careful balance between accepting children as they are and helping them learn to "fit in." The desire for happy, well-adjusted children is appropriate but should not be achieved by attempting to fashion the child into a likeness of the "ideal" child. It is inappropriate to try to change a four-year-old with special needs into a "typical" four-year-old if the child's skills are at the typical two-year-old's level. If the child can only perform at the cognitive level of a two-year-old, it is likely this child will also behave similarly to a typical two-year-old, both emotionally and socially.

Recognizing Each Child's Individuality

Each child needs to be viewed as a unique individual, which includes recognizing varying levels of abilities (Halford, 1989). Adults should expect different abilities and learning styles from different children, accept them, and use them to design the appropriate learning experiences. Not all children should be expected to perform or enjoy the same experiences. Activities should be designed that help develop a child's positive self-esteem and feelings toward learning (Goodman & Bond, 1990).

Children should not be required to participate in all activities to obtain adult approval or **extrinsic rewards,** or to avoid punishment. Again, it is important to respect individual needs and preferences. Children with special needs frequently require that

the pace of the curriculum to be modified. Teachers often worry these children will fall further behind if instruction is not designed to "push" the child. In fact, it is more likely they will fall further behind when they are forced to deal with material they are not yet developmentally ready to process. They may also come to dislike learning or develop a **self-handicapping strategy,** such as is demonstrated when a child says, "I can't do anything well," and ultimately completely resists learning.

Adults should avoid introducing activities to a child when the child is not ready to grasp them. Children often become discouraged and avoid certain activities if they experience excess amounts of failure. Children may interpret frequent failure as their being unable to learn. Children are more likely to be unsuccessful when they believe they lack competency or when adults send them messages that suggest they are unlikely to succeed (Hanson & Lynch, 1989).

Too frequently, activities and stories used in preschool classrooms have themes that are too hard or boring for children at a particular developmental level. There needs to be a middle ground between modifying the child to fit the environment and modifying the environment to fit the child. Conformity and self-expression are both desirable outcomes. It is inappropriate to try to turn toddlers into students.

Goals and **objectives** must be determined for each child who is classified as having special needs and stated in an IFSP or IEP. Goals and objectives are generally most useful when they are stated in terms of outcomes adults would like to see the child achieve such as, "Jill will be able to catch, unassisted, a six-inch ball thrown from three feet away, on four of five trials." When objectives are stated in this manner (in behavioral terms), adults know what to teach and when the objective is reached (Egan, 1988).

Children as Active Participants in Learning

Children should be actively engaged in learning, frequently referred to as **active learning,** rather than allowed to remain passive by being lectured to or taught in a **rote** fashion (Halford, 1989). Young children can be actively involved in learning by making and building things. They should have an opportunity to observe and experience events around them. They need opportunities to talk about what they see and draw pictures representing their experiences or act out experiences through dramatic play. Young children benefit from interacting with adults and other young children, as well as with materials and their surroundings.

The younger children are, the more informal the learning environment should be (Kamii & DeVries, 1977). Children need ample time for informal play during which materials, props, and equipment are readily available for them to play with spontaneously. Children need opportunities to work together to make things or to pursue a topic or project (Kohlberg, 1968). Teachers and parents should strive to encourage children to develop an interest in learning. This interest seems to be present at birth, but there are many obstacles to maintaining and strengthening this disposition (Johnson–Martin, Jens, & Attermeler, 1986).

When children are given opportunities to understand concepts through observation and interaction with other people, these experiences are more meaningful and likely to be retained. Children should have opportunities to discover or invent solutions to concrete problems rather than simply being encouraged to memorize information. **Activity-based instructions,** such as measuring the ingredients for cookies, working with wood and tools, sorting objects, playing with gears and wheels, and working with clay, are all meaningful discovery or hands-on activities (Malone & Stoneman, 1990). (Refer to Chapter 12 for discussion of play activities that encourage children to be active participants in learning.)

There should be a balance between **teacher-guided instruction** and less structured learning, frequently called **discovery learning,** and opportunities for quiet as well as more active events. The daily schedule should not interfere with children's spontaneous activities. Children may be

pulled out during any of these periods for more intense therapy. Generally, it is inadvisable to remove a child during snack time or once the child has become involved in an activity. Whenever possible, movement to individual therapy should occur during a **transition** between activities (Salisbury & Vincent, 1990).

Development of Attitudes and Emotions

Early education involves helping children acquire knowledge skills, habits, and tendencies used in responding to situations in certain ways. Specific attributes children should acquire include curiosity, creativity, cooperation, and being friendly, helpful, hard working, and resourceful. These skills are most frequently acquired by being around people who have these behaviors and model them to children (Carson, 1991). Children are most likely to acquire and demonstrate these dispositions when they know adults value them (Goodman & Bond, 1990).

Early childhood education also contributes to the development of feelings or emotions about events. Emotions often developed through school experiences include feelings of confidence, competence, and security. Children's feelings of belonging, acceptance, or rejection are important for lifelong growth and development (Halpern, 1985).

Providing Experience with Pre-Academic Activities

An effective early childhood program avoids pressuring children to learn a large number of **academic skills** or to acquire a large number of specific pieces of knowledge (for example, memorizing the alphabet). It is unlikely to be useful to try to develop these skills if, in the process of acquiring them, the child's desire to use them diminishes. Educators should help children acquire skills and strengthen their desire to use them. Generally, the best way to do this is to employ a variety of teaching methods.

Children receive services to develop many skills areas. Children are provided many opportunities to discover or observe how reading and writing are useful before they are instructed in letter names, sounds, and word identification. These skills develop only when they become meaningful to children. Meaningful experiences include listening to and reading stories and poems, taking field trips, seeing classroom charts and other print material, participating in **dramatic play** and other experiences requiring communication, and experimenting with writing by drawing and copying. Reading and writing instruction stresses isolated skills such as recognizing single letters, reciting the alphabet, or coloring within the lines. These activities are not meaningful or useful for young children (Mahoney, O'Sullivan, & Fors, 1989).

Providing Activities That Enhance Physical Development

In addition to cognitive, communication, and social skills, each day children should have opportunities to use their muscles. Children learn as they move. Running, jumping, and balancing provide large-muscle practice. Children should go outdoors as often as the weather permits to allow for freedom of movement. In addition, there should be opportunities for children to be loud and spontaneous in their verbal expressions. Outdoor time should not be stringently limited or viewed as interfering with "real" instructional time or as a "recess" from learning. Outdoor time involves learning, and children also need daily small-muscle activities, such as playing with puzzles, art supplies, and pegboards (Spiker, 1990). Small-motor activities should not be limited to writing with pencils or coloring within the lines. (See Chapters 10 and 11 for a discussion of **fine** and **gross motor development.**)

Children also need a chance to experience music and art on a regular basis. They should be allowed to experiment and explore during these activities. Art and music should not be considered extra activities or used just as special "treats."

Music includes movement and art self-creation, and not merely replicating a model. Children are naturally creative and should be encouraged to use their creativity. Often, preschool children who hesitate to carry on a conversation or answer questions may sing words to a song. Some children who hesitate to participate in other activities often participate in art or music. (See Chapter 13 for further discussion of the importance of art in providing learning experiences.)

The classroom should be a place where the child can have fun and learn. Ideally, certain areas of the classroom are designed for specific activities. Generally, three to four major areas are found in most preschool classrooms. (See Chapter 12 for a discussion of these major areas typically found within a preschool setting.)

Daily Schedules

Children appear to be most comfortable when the daily routines are about the same. Children learn to expect certain things to occur at specific times or in a particular order. A daily schedule is also desirable because it may help avoid wasting time with spur-of-the-moment decisions. The schedule, however, should be flexible enough to "seize the moment," such as allowing time for the child to see an unexpected visitor, gaze at a rarely occurring rainbow, read a second book, or watch a fire truck out the window.

Children should not constantly be hurried to complete one task in order to move on to another. A schedule that rigidly allocates a specific amount of time for each activity is likely to result in fragmentation (not enough time to engage fully in an activity) and frustration for the child. The daily time allocated for various activities must be flexible. When children find an activity engaging, teachers should lengthen the planned amount of time for the activity, even if it means there may not be time to do something else that was planned. If a planned activity is scheduled to take thirty minutes, but children cannot be successfully engaged in the activity, it should be abandoned.

Adults should be guided by the philosophy of "seize the moment." Children need opportunities to engage in activities that interest them, require sustained effort, and are extended over time (Lee, O'Shea, & Dykes, 1987).

Each day's schedule should include a large amount of time for free play, which allows children to select from several activities set up by the teacher. These activities include puzzles laid out on tables, easels and paint, a sensory table, and dress-up clothes. (See Chapter 12 for a discussion of the importance of play.)

Time should be provided for **small** and **large group** activities. There should be fine and gross motor activities, as well as opportunities for art and music activities. Some children with special needs cannot spend an extended amount of time in structured activities; therefore, the amount of time children are encouraged to stay at a particular task may vary. As the year progresses, expectations for the length of attending is likely to increase (Thiele & Hamilton, 1991). Table 1.7 provides an example of a daily classroom schedule.

Cleanup, a cooperative opportunity, occurs at each transition period. Some children have great difficulty with transitions. They may not want to change activities because they are not ready to, or they may not want to clean up. It is important to

TABLE 1.7 Sample Daily Classroom Schedule

A sample daily schedule

- 8:30–9:00—Free play with at least three options for activities
- 9:00–9:15—Large group/circle time review of the day's activities
- 9:15–10:10—Outdoor play activities.
- 10:10–10:30—Snack in groups of three to five students
- 10:30–10:50—Small group activities such as art or cooking activities
- 10:50–11:00—Large or small group review of day and dismissal

provide children with advanced notice that a **transition** will soon occur. This notification could be accomplished by ringing a bell or dimming the lights and announcing, for instance, "In five minutes, we will be cleaning up so that we may go outside." It is desirable to indicate to children that the reason they should clean up is to do something else they enjoy.

There are many excellent programs available for young children with special needs. Many of these programs are based on curriculum and **good/ best practices** of regular early childhood special education (programs for children without special needs). (See Chapter 7 for a discussion of integrating regular and special education practices.) The last section of this chapter provides a brief discussion of one program model that has proved effective for regular and early childhood special education.

HIGH SCOPE: ONE PROGRAM MODEL

Many different curriculum or program models are available that may be useful for preschool-aged children with or without developmental delays. Several methods are readily adapted to meet a wide variety of needs. **The High Scope model** is one example. This method focuses on the importance of **active learning** (Hohmann, Banet, & Weikart, 1979). Active learning is affected by how the room is set up, what materials are made available to the child, and the child's daily schedule.

The High Scope philosophy is, in part, based on the work of Jean Piaget, a developmental psychologist. The following statement by Piaget (1945/1951) suggests the basic underlying philosophy of the High Scope method: "When the active school requires that a student's efforts come from the student himself instead of being imposed, and that his intelligence undertakes authentic work instead of accepting predigested knowledge from outside, it is simply asking that the laws of all intelligence be respected" (p. 56). (Piaget used the term "active school" to refer to a child being involved in active exploration of and experimentation with the environment rather than the child passively listening to a teacher provide instruction.)

The High Scope method has been accepted as effective practice for early childhood education (ages two to six years) for many years. More recently, it has also been shown to be very useful for preschool children with special needs. The basic premise of the High Scope method is that children are "active learners" and best learn from activities they plan and do themselves. The teacher's role is to ensure that children become involved in the activities. Children are also encouraged to organize their own "work."

Each day, children have daily opportunities to choose what they want to do. The teachers often help in developing a plan. Very young children or children with developmental delays may have difficulty planning where they will play and reviewing where they played. Older children may plan where they want to play, provide details on what they plan to do in the chosen area, and gather materials needed to complete the plan.

The need for consistent daily routines is stressed in the High Scope method. Planning time is also an important component. During planning time, children describe their plans to the adult and other children in the group. The adult responds to the children's ideas and may suggest ways to enhance their plans. After discussing their plans, children are given ample time to "work" on them. All children actively participate in cleaning up. They explain what they did, how they did it, with whom they worked, and discuss any problems they might have had. Table 1.8 provides an outline of the major goals of the High Scope method (Berrueta–Clement, Schweinhart, Barnett, Esptein, & Weikart, 1984).

The program's approach to teaching children with special needs is based on the philosophy that it is unnecessary to assume that a child should be motivated by adults, but rather that adults should promote learning that extends the child's present level of functioning. The adult's function is to help children to develop their own interests and

TABLE 1.8 Major Goals of the High Scope Method

The High Scope method is designed to:

1. Help children develop the ability to make choices;
2. Help children develop self-discipline by carrying out plans;
3. Develop children's ability to cooperate with others;
4. Increase children's knowledge about objects and skills;
5. Increase children's ability to express thoughts, ideas, and feelings;
6. Help children better understand verbal and nonverbal communication;
7. Develop children's ability to apply reasoning skills to a variety of situations;
8. Further develop children's creativity, initiative, and openness to learning.

learn to build on their own strengths rather than focusing on what they cannot do. The focus is *not* on deficits but on a child's current level of functioning. The adult matches learning activities to a child's skills.

High Scope stresses that children benefit most from more free play and least from formal lessons or structured therapy. Projects should be selected that provide different demands for "time-on-task" (how long a child participates in an activity) and that allow for different skill levels. The underlying goal of early childhood education should be to provide the same ladder, but allow children to be on different rungs. It is also best to have fewer periods and longer periods of activities, thereby reducing the number of changes or transitions for younger children, two to four years old, in particular. Children need advanced warning when it is time for transitions. Teachers should allow children to find their own way as much as possible and do no more **redirecting** than is necessary. It is particularly important for teachers to develop activities such as art and music, which are more likely to engage children. Children's choices should *not* be limited any more than is necessary.

CONCLUSION

The earlier that intervention occurs, the better. Early intervention provides an important foundation for later learning. It also provides support for children and their families, which may help prevent additional types of problems. Early intervention also helps family members adjust to a child's special needs by providing training to develop specific methods for working with the child.

Adults should *guide* young children rather than *lead* them. In fact, children should be encouraged to do the leading whenever possible. Early childhood education programs must present children and their parents with a sense of hope and warmth. Instead of viewing families and children as victims, service providers should view them as capable of making decisions and creating their own solutions to problems. Early childhood programs are most successful when most of the credit toward meeting the special needs of children goes to the children and their families.

The next chapter contains a discussion of theories regarding why developmental changes occur and provides an overview of typical stages and rates of development for children from infancy through age six years. Understanding why developmental changes occur and the typical stages and rates of development may provide help in the design of services for children with special needs.

CHAPTER SUMMARY

- Adults must keep children safe and healthy, and provide nurturing and responsive environments, including recognizing and respecting the uniqueness of each child.
- Services for children with special needs are provided in clinics, homes, or center-based or inclusion programs.
- If a child is believed to have a developmental disability, the child's needs should be assessed by a team of professionals.
- Adults working with children should receive training about how to work with those children who have special needs. They must also

have the ability to work effectively as members of a team.
- Team members often include a variety of professionals as well as parents.
- Effective early intervention programs provide services to children and parents with a variety of needs, recognize and value each child's individuality, view children as active participants in learning, and provide environments that enhance all major areas of development.

REVIEW QUESTIONS

1. What are several important features of effective early intervention programs? Why are they important?
2. What requirements are stated in the major federal laws that directly affect early intervention services for infants, toddlers, and preschool children, each of whom has special needs?
3. What are the responsibilities of a psychologist and nurse who are members of a program that provides services to young children with special needs?
4. What is the major philosophy of the High Scope program?

SUGGESTED STUDENT ACTIVITIES

1. Visit a special needs preschool classroom. Determine the age and special needs of the children who attend. Ask the staff to explain the rationale for the classroom daily schedule.
2. Find out what types of early intervention program are found in your community. Describe the basic philosophy of one or more of these programs and determine the type of children each program is designed to serve.
3. With a group of your peers, discuss potential pros and cons of using inclusion for early childhood special education programs.

ADDITIONAL READINGS

Guralnick, M. J., & Band, F. C. (Eds.). (1987). *The effectiveness of early intervention for at-risk and handicapped children.* New York: Academic Press.

Mitchess, D., & Brown, R. I. (Eds.). (1991). *Early intervention studies for young children with special needs.* New York: Chapman and Hall.

Ordover, E. L., & Boundy, K. B. (1991). *Educational rights of children with disabilities: A primer for advocates.* Cambridge, MA: Center for Law and Education.

Peck, C. A., Odom, S. L., & Bricker, D. D. (Eds.). (1993). *Integrating young children with disabilities into community programs:* Ecological perspectives on research and implementation. Baltimore, MD: Paul H. Brookes.

Rosenkoetter, S. E., Hains, A. H., & Fowler, S. A. (1994). *Bridging early services for children with special needs and their families: A practical guide for transition planning.* Baltimore, MD: Paul H. Brookes.

ADDITIONAL RESOURCES

Academy for Education Development
1255 23rd Street, N.W., Suite 400
Washington, DC 20017

Council for Disability Rights
343 S. Dearborn, No. 318
Chicago, IL 60604

High Scope Foundation
600 N. River Street
Ypsilanti, MI 48198

National Center for Clinical Infant Programs
733 15th Street, N.W., Suite 912
Washington, DC 20001

National Consortium for Child Mental Health Services
3615 Wisconsin Avenue, N.W.
Washington, DC 20016

National Council of Community Mental Health Centers
12300 Twinbrook Parkway, Suite 320
Rockville, MD 20852

National Institute of Mental Health
5600 Fishers Lane
Rockville, MD 20857

National Mental Health Association
1800 N. Kent Street
Alexandria, VA 22209

National Organization for Disability
910 16th Street, N.W., Suite 600
Washington, DC 20006

National Head Start Association
1220 King Street
Alexandria, VA 22314

Office of Special Education Programs
U.S. Office of Special Education and Rehabilitative Services
U.S. Department of Education
Washington, DC 20202–2641

President's Committee on Mental Retardation
Department of Health and Human Services
Office of Human Development Services
Washington, DC 20201–0001

Special Olympics
1350 New York Avenue, N.W., Suite 500
Washington, DC 20005

REFERENCES

Bagnato, S. J., & Neisworth, J. T. (1991). *Assessment for early intervention: Best practices for professionals.* New York: Guilford Press.

Bagnato, S. J., Neisworth, J. T., & Munson, S. M. (1996). *LINKing assessment and early intervention: An authentic, curriculum-based approach.* Baltimore, MD: Paul H. Brookes.

Bailey, D. B., & McWilliams, R. A. (1990). Normalizing early intervention. *Topics in Early Childhood Special Education, 10*(2), 33–47.

Bailey, D. B., & Wolery, M. (1992). *Teaching infants and preschoolers with disabilities.* Columbus, OH: Merrill.

Bayless, K. M., & Ramsey, M. E. (1991). *Music: A way of life for the young child.* Columbus, OH: Merrill.

Bennett, F. C., & Guralnick, M. J. (1991). Effectiveness of developmental intervention in the first five years of life. *The Pediatric Clinics of North America, 38,* 1513–1528.

Berrueta-Clement, J. R., Schweinhart, L. J., Barnett, W. S., Epstein, A. S., & Weikart, D. P. (1984). Changed lives: The effects of the Perry Preschool Program on youths through age 19. *Monograph of the High Scope Educational Research Foundation* (No. 8). Ypsilanti, MI: High Scope Press.

Bornstein, M. H. (1991). *Cultural approaches to parenting.* Hillsdale, NJ: Erlbaum.

Bowden, J., Black, T. L., & Daulton, D. (1990). *Estimating the costs of providing early intervention and preschool special education services.* Chapel Hill, NC: University of North Carolina, National Early Childhood Technical Assistance System.

Bricker, D. D. (1986). An analysis of early intervention programs: Attendant issues and future directions. In J. R. Morris & B. Blatt (Eds.), *Special education: Research trends* (pp. 28–65). New York: Pergamon Press.

Burton, C. B., Hains, A. H., Hanline, M. F., McLean, M., & McCormick, K. (1992). Early childhood intervention and education: The urgency of professional unification. *Topics in Early Childhood Special Education, 11*(4), 53–69.

Carson, M. (1991). *A guide for friends, neighbors and relatives of retarded children.* Chicago: Claretian Publishing.

Carta, J. J., Schwartz, I. S., Atwater, J. B., & McConnell, S. R. (1991). Developmentally appropriate practice: Appraising its usefulness for young children with disabilities. *Topics in Early Childhood Special Education, 11,* 1–20.

Casto, G., & Mastropieri, M. A. (1986). The efficacy of early intervention programs: A meta-analysis. *Exceptional Children, 52,* 417–424.

Deiner, P. L. (1993). *Resources for teaching children with diverse abilities.* Ft. Worth, TX: Harcourt Brace Jovanovich.

Dunst, C. J., Snyder, S., & Mankinen, M. (1989). Efficacy of early intervention. In M. Wang, M. Reynolds, & H. Walberg (Eds.), *Handbook of special education: Research and practice* (Vol. 3, pp. 259–293). New York: Elmsford.

Egan, K. (1988). *Primary understanding: Education in early childhood.* New York: Routledge, Chapman, and Hall.

Ensher, G. L. (1989). The first three years: Special education perspectives on assessment and intervention. *Topics in Language Disorders, 10*(1), 80–90.

Erwin, E. J. (Ed.). (1996). *Visions for a brighter future for young children and their families.* Baltimore, MD: Paul H. Brookes.

Farran, D. C. (1990). Effects of intervention with disadvantaged and disabled children: A decade review. In S. J. Meisels & J. P. Shokroff (Eds.), *Handbook of early childhood intervention* (pp. 501–539). New York: Cambridge University Press.

Gallagher, J. J. (1989). A new policy initiative: Infants and toddlers with handicapping conditions. *American Psychologist, 44,* 387–390.

Gallagher, J. J. (1992). The role of values and facts in policy development for infants and toddlers with disabilities and their families. *Journal of Early Intervention, 16*(1), 1–10.

Goodman, J. F. (1992). *When slow is fast enough: Educating the delayed preschool child.* New York: Guilford Press.

Goodman, J. F., & Bond, L. (1990). *The individual educational program: A retrospective critique from an early intervention perspective.* Unpublished manuscript, University of Pennsylvania, Graduate School of Education.

Gullo, D. (1994). Understanding assessment and evaluation in early childhood education. NY: Teachers College Press.

Guralnick, M. J. (Ed.). (1996). *The effectiveness of early intervention.* Baltimore, MD: Paul H. Brookes.

Guralnick, M. J. (1991). The next decade of research on the effectiveness of early intervention. *Exceptional Children, 58*(2), 174–183.

Haines, J. E., & Gerber, L. L. (1996). *Leading young children to music.* (5th ed.). Columbus, OH: Merrill.

Halford, G. S. (1989). Reflections on 25 years of Piagetian cognitive developmental psychology, 1963–1988. *Human Development, 32,* 325–357.

Halpern, A. S. (1985). Transition: A look at the foundations. *Exceptional Children, 51,* 479–486.

Hanson, M. J., & Lynch, E. W. (1989). *Early intervention: Implementing child and family services for infants and toddlers who are at-risk or disabled.* Austin, TX: Pro-Ed.

Hartup, R. M. (1988). The role of maternal emotions and perceptions on interactions with their young handicapped children. In K. Marfo (Ed.), *Parent–child interaction and developmental disabilities* (pp. 32–46). New York: Praeger.

Hebbeler, K. M., Smith, B. J., & Black, T. L. (1991). Federal early childhood special education policy: A model for the improvement of services for children with disabilities. *Exceptional Children, 58*(2), 104–112.

Heisler, V. (1972). *A handicapped child in the family: A guide for parents.* New York: Grune and Stratton.

Hohmann, M., Banet, B., & Weikart, D. P. (1979). *Young children in action: A manual for preschool educators.* Ypsilanti, MI: High Scope Press.

Johnson, L. J., Pugach, M. C., & Devlin, R. (1990). Professional collaboration. *Teaching Exceptional Children, 22,* 9–11.

Johnson-Martin, N., Jens, K., & Attermeler, S., (1986). *Carolina curriculum for handicapped infants and infants at risk.* Baltimore, MD: Paul H. Brookes.

Kamii, C., & DeVries, R. (1977). Piaget for early education. In M. C. Day & R. K. Parker (Eds.), *The preschool in action: Exploring early childhood programs* (pp. 363–420). Boston: Allyn and Bacon.

Karnes, M. B., & Stayton, V. D. (1988). Model programs for infants and toddlers with handicaps. In J. B. Jordan, J. J. Gallagher, P. L. Hutinger, & M. B. Karnes (Eds.), *Early childhood special education: Birth to three* (pp. 67–106). Reston, VA: Council for Exceptional Children and the Division for Early Childhood.

Keogh, B. K., & Glover, A. T. (1980). Research needs in the study of early identification of children with learning disabilities. *Thalamus,* November (11), 59–68.

Kohlberg, L. (1968). Early education: A cognitive-developmental view. *Child Development, 39,* 1013–1062.

Krakow, J. B., & Kopp, C. B. (1983). The effects of developmental delays on sustained attention in young children. *Child Development, 54,* 1143–1155.

Lee, J., O'Shea, L. J., & Dykes, M. (1987). Teacher wait-time: Performance of developmentally delayed and non-delayed young children. *Education and Training in Mental Retardation, 22,* 176–184.

Lepper, M. R. (1981). Intrinsic and extrinsic motivation in children: Detrimental effects of superfluous social controls. In W. A. Collins (Ed.), *Aspects of the development of competence* (pp. 155–214). Hillsdale, NJ: Erlbaum.

Mahoney, G., O'Sullivan, P., & Fors, S. (1989). Special education practices with young handicapped children. *Journal of Early Intervention, 22,* 261–268.

Malone, D. M., & Stoneman, Z. (1990). Cognitive play of mentally retarded preschoolers: Observations in the home and school. *American Journal of Mental Retardation, 94,* 475–487.

McDonnell, A., & Hardman, M. (1988). A synthesis of best practice guidelines for early childhood services. *Journal of the Division for Early Childhood, 12*(2), 328–341.

McEvoy, M. A. (1990). The organization of care-giving environments: Critical issues and suggestions for future research. *Education and Treatment of Children, 13,* 269–273.

Meisels, S. J., & Shonkoff, J. P. (1990). *Handbook of early childhood intervention.* NY: Cambridge University Press.

Odom, S. L., & McEvoy, M. A. (1988). Integration of young children with handicaps and normally developing children. In S. L. Odom & M. B. Karnes (Eds.), *Early intervention for infants and children with handicaps: An empirical base* (pp. 241–268). Baltimore, MD: Paul H. Brookes.

Peck, C. A., Odom, S. L., & Bricker, D. D. (1993). *Integrating young children with disabilities into community programs: Ecological perspectives on research and implementation.* Baltimore, MD: Paul H. Brookes.

Piaget, J. (1945/1951). *Play, dreams, and imitation in childhood.* New York: Norton.

Salisbury, C. L., & Vincent, L. J. (1990). Criterion of the next environment and best practices: Mainstreaming and integration 10 years later. *Topics in Early Childhood Special Education, 10,* 78–89.

Saranson, S. B. (1990). *The predictable failure of educational reform.* San Francisco: Jossey-Bass.

Schweinhart, L. J., Weikart, D. P., & Larner, M. B. (1986). Consequences of three preschool curriculum models through age 15. *Early Childhood Research Quarterly, 1,* 15–45.

Shonkoff, J. P., & Hauser–Cram, P. (1987). Early intervention for disabled infants and their families: A quantitative analysis. *Pediatrics, 80,* 650–658.

Slentz, K. L., & Bricker, D. D. (1992). Family-guided assessment for IFSP development: Jumping off the family assessment bandwagon. *Journal of Early Intervention, 16*(1), 11–19.

Smith, T. E. C., Finn, D. M., & Dowdy, C. A. (1993). *Teaching students with mild disabilities.* Ft. Worth, TX: Harcourt Brace Jovanovich.

Spiker, D. (1990). Early intervention from a developmental perspective. In D. Cicchetti & M. Beeghly (Eds.), *Children with Down syndrome: A developmental perspective* (pp. 424–448). New York: Cambridge University Press.

Thiele, J. E., & Hamilton, J. L. (1991). Implementing the early childhood formula: Programs under Public Service Law 99–457. *Journal of Early Intervention, 15,* 5–12.

Thurman, S. K. (1977) The congruence of behavioral ecologies: A model for social education programming. *Journal of Special Education, 11,* 329–333.

Thurman, S. K., Cornwell, J. R., & Gottwald, S. R. (1996). (Eds.). *Contexts of early intervention: Systems and settings.* Baltimore, MD: Paul H. Brookes.

Wasik, B. H., Ramey, C. T., Bryant, D. M., & Sparling, J. J. (1990). A longitudinal study of two early intervention strategies: Project CARE. *Child Development, 61*(6), 1682–1696.

Wolery, M. (1991). Instruction in early childhood special education: "Seeing through a glass darkly...know in part." *Exceptional Children, 58*(2), 127–135.

Chapter 2

TYPICAL STAGES OF EARLY CHILDHOOD DEVELOPMENT

MELINDA A. SAGE, M.A.

ABOUT THE AUTHOR

Melinda Sage received her bachelor's degree in psychology from Armstrong State College in Savannah, Georgia. She received her master's in psychology from Marist College, in Poughkeepsie, New York. While at Marist, she served as a graduate assistant, worked with the Peer Support Line, and was president of the Graduate Psychology Association. Ms. Sage is a member of the national psychology honor society, Psi Chi. She completed an internship at the West Point Mental Health Center, West Point Military Academy in West Point, New York. She is planning on pursuing her Ph.D. in clinical psychology. Ms. Sage is currently providing counseling services for school-aged children at McQuade Children's services in New Windsor, New York.

CHAPTER KEY POINTS

- Child development is the study of human growth and changes from conception through adolescence.
- Theories of development may be classified as organismic (e.g., Piaget) or mechanistic (e.g., Skinner) and continuous or discontinuous.
- Basic cognitive processes include perception, attention, reasoning, and memory.
- Heredity and environment appear to play a role in development of skills.

- There are typical sequences and ages at which most children acquire cognitive, speech and language, gross motor, fine motor, and social and emotional skills.
- Communication includes speech and nonspeech skills.
- Motor development includes fine and gross motor skills.
- Social-emotional development includes self-concept, self-esteem, emotions, and morality, and their development may be enhanced and evaluated during play interactions.

This chapter provides a description of typical sequences of development from infancy through age six. Although children with developmental delays do not progress at the same rate in one or more areas of development, as is typical for most children the same age, they do typically acquire skills in the same order or sequence (Black & Puckett, 1996). Therefore, an understanding of typical patterns of development is useful when designing or providing services for children with special needs.

This chapter begins with an overview of the field of **child development.** This overview is followed by a brief discussion of theories of development and the roles **heredity,** often referred to as nature, and environment, often referred to as nurture, play in development. In addition, major areas of development are discussed and each area is followed by a list of ages during which the majority of children acquire various skills.

THE FIELD OF CHILD DEVELOPMENT

Studying children and evaluating rates of development fall within the scope of the field of child development. Child development is a field of study dedicated to understanding all aspects of human growth and changes from conception through adolescence (Berk, 1994). Child development is a part of the broader study of human development, which involves changes experienced during a lifetime. Professionals whose interests focus on human development are often referred to as **developmentalists** (Bertenthal & Campos, 1987).

The tasks developmentalists perform include describing, explaining, and predicting how individuals at different stages typically think, feel, and behave (Horowitz, 1990). They often summarize sequences and rates of development in charts, called **developmental charts.** These charts are frequently referred to as **universal norms** (Thelen, 1989).

Universal norms suggest that development unfolds through a series of sequences or patterns. Universal norms provide an estimate for when a certain level of development will be reached. This method is referred to as the **normative approach** to child study (Brofenbrenner, 1989). Most children begin sitting, standing, walking, and talking at about the same time while growing emotionally, cognitively, and socially. In most cases, **milestones** at an earlier age set the foundation for more complex skills later in life (Thelen & Adolph, 1992).

Children with special needs often do not develop at the rate indicated by universal norms in one or more of the major areas of development. Concerns about children's rates of development occur when skills are significantly delayed in one or more areas (Kuhn, 1992).

There are no fixed, agreed-on criteria for determining whether children have significantly delayed rates of development. Children may be classified as having a developmental delay when they are several months behind in acquiring skills than is typical for their age or they are unable to perform tasks that 90 percent of children of equivalent age can perform. Even when the rate of acquisition of skills is slower than is typical, **developmental charts** are useful for tracking skills acquisition (Lewis & Miller, 1990).

Several different perspectives or **theories** attempting to explain and predict behavior have been suggested by developmentalists. These theories suggest how and why development occurs. Understanding various theories guide individuals who work with children in determining what should be done to help maximize development. Developmental theories are frequently classified according to two different criteria. Theories are classified as **organismic** or **mechanistic** and **continuous** or **discontinuous** (Berk, 1994).

Theories having an **organismic orientation** view children as active participants in their own development. An organismic theoretical orientation, as found within **cognitive theories,** including the theory of Jean Piaget (1950), assumes that there are certain structures within children that underlie development and that development is affected by experiences. **Organismic theories** also view children as active and purposeful. Children are believed to determine their own learning, but environments must be designed that support their development. The organismic perspective views the environment as supporting of growth rather than causing growth to occur (Flavell, 1992).

Mechanistic theories, in contrast, view children as passive recipients of environmental experiences. One example of a mechanistic theory, **behaviorism,** argues that patterns of **rewards** and **punishments** may be used to control children's behavior. A mechanistic theory suggests that the environment determines growth and development. Children are seen as passive recipients of experiences provided by the environment (Horowitz, 1992).

Theories may also be classified on the basis of whether development is viewed as being **continuous** or **discontinuous.** Theorists who view

development as continuous believe that young children respond to the world in basically the same way as adults although generally in a less complex way. The **continuous perspective** suggests that children have less information available to them. Over time, children are viewed as gradually acquiring an increasing amount of information and number of abilities through experiences (Flavell, 1992). For example, children and adults can remember events. The number of events (**stimuli**) that are remembered varies by age, with children typically remembering fewer stimuli than adults.

Other theories view development as being a **discontinuous process.** Development is presented as occurring in distinctly different stages, which is found in Piaget's theory. That is, children reason, think, and feel differently from adults. This view further suggests that new ways of understanding, behaving, and thinking emerge at different stages. The discontinuous perspective argues that it is necessary to accomplish the milestones of prior stages before moving on to more complex stages of development. It also suggests that change may be sudden rather than gradual at certain points in time (McHale & Lerner, 1990).

The **discontinuous perspective** stresses that stages of development are in the same sequence for all children. This perspective suggests that knowledge about stages of development is crucial when developing appropriate services for children (Berk, 1994). One of the most influential and frequently cited theorists who had a discontinuous perspective regarding development was Jean Piaget.

Piaget's Theory

Piaget's research focused on understanding the development of children's cognitive skills. Piaget's theory supports the **organismic** perspective and views development as being **discontinuous.** He believed that between birth and adolescence children progress through four distinct stages of development, including the **sensorimotor, preoperational, concrete operational,** and **formal operational stages.** These stages are summarized in Table 2.1.

TABLE 2.1 Piaget's Stages of Development

STAGE	AGE	DESCRIPTION
Sensorimotor	Birth to 2 years	Infants and toddlers learn through their senses and body movements. They develop the ability to imitate others and a sense of object and person permanence. Actions move from reflexive (automatic) to purposeful (intentional).
Preoperational	2 to 7 years	Preschool-aged children interact with the environment by using symbols. Thinking is often illogical. Development of language and use of imagination occurs.
Concrete Operational	7 to 11 years	Children's thought is logical, flexible, and operationally organized. Children cannot think abstractly or use rules of logic.
Formal Operational	11 years and older	Adolescents use abstract and scientific reasoning, including rules of logic.

Piaget (1950) described infants and toddlers as acquiring information through their various senses, including sight, sound, and touch. He labeled this first stage, which includes children from birth to two years, the **sensorimotor stage.** He viewed information processing in young children as initially being limited to use of their senses and physical movement rather than involving thinking, which occurs inside the head. Toddlers' competence increases as they develop the ability to imitate others.

An understanding of **object permanence** gradually develops during the sensorimotor stage. For example, children at four months of age do not look for an object placed out of sight. Two-year-olds search for objects placed out of sight because they know those objects continue to exist even though they cannot see them. As language is acquired, children move from being primarily dependent on physical movements to internalized thought for their interactions with the environment.

Most children two through six years are classified as being at the **preoperational stage.** According to Piaget, even though internalized thinking skills have developed, a preschool child's thinking is often rigid and illogical at this stage. That is, thinking is frequently limited to one aspect of a situation at a time. Thinking is also strongly influenced by how a particular object looks at any particular moment in time. For example, a piece of clay may appear big when rolled into a ball. The same amount of clay may be seen as small when flattened into a pancake. This tendency to center on one aspect of a situation and neglect other aspects is referred to as **centration.**

Children at the preoperational stage also lack **reversibility,** the mental ability to move through a series of steps and then reverse direction to move back to the starting point. During the preoperational stage, children gradually begin to use symbols and develop concepts or ways of classifying objects. The classification system is often incomplete. These pre-concepts limit children to making simple classifications.

Another characteristic of children at the preoperational level is that they are often egocentric. Piaget used the term **egocentrism** to describe preschoolers' self-centered view of the world. Egocentrism refers to children's inabilities to recognize other people's perspectives that may be different from their own. This lack of awareness of other perspectives leaves children to focus on their own perspectives.

For example, imagine a three-year-old facing the teacher while showing the teacher a picture. The child is likely to hold the picture facing toward himself or herself rather than toward the teacher. In this case, it is not that the child refuses to recognize another's perspective or is selfish or inconsiderate, but that he or she is unable to consider another's perspective. Preoperational children typically believe others perceive, think, and feel the same way they do (Piaget, 1952).

Other researchers (Gelman, 1972; Wooley & Wellman, 1990) suggested that Piaget underestimated the cognitive abilities of infants and preschoolers. These researchers demonstrated that when materials and language are less confusing, children are often able to perform more complex tasks and demonstrate more mature reasoning than was suggested by Piaget's research. For example, when children are told, "Remember to hold the picture so I can see it," young children are more likely to accommodate another's perspective rather than responding in an egocentric fashion, holding the picture toward themselves so that the adult cannot see it.

Frequently, adults expect children to think in ways that are much more typical for older children. Piaget describes two later stages of thinking skills not acquired until the school-aged years. The concrete operational stage spans the ages of six to eleven years, and the formal operational stage includes the ages of eleven years and above. Reasoning at these stages is governed by the principles of logic, but it is not until the formal stage of development that children are able to think abstractly and use **deductive** and **inductive** methods of **reasoning.**

The **constructivist perspective** grew out of Piaget's theory (Thomas, 1990). Constructivists suggest that children construct their own understanding of the world by actively seeking understanding of their environment through exploration. In contrast to Piaget and the constructionists, the behaviorist perspectives of theorists such as B. F. Skinner (1957) suggest that new skills, including cognitive skills, are acquired through experiences and hold a continuous perspective.

The Behaviorist Perspective

Behaviorists view behavior from a **mechanistic** and **continuous perspective.** Skinner saw learning as occurring through **operant conditioning.** This type of learning is affected by **reinforcements** and **punishments** that follow behavior. Reinforcement is defined as something that increases the likelihood that the behavior will occur again (Berk, 1994).

Consider the situation in which a parent praises a child for fitting a piece into a puzzle. **Praise** would be considered a **reinforcer** if the child increases attempts to fit other pieces into puzzles. Punishment refers to something that decreases the likelihood of the behavior that it follows occurring in the future. A parent may take a toy away from a child because the child grabbed it away from another child. After consistently responding in this fashion, if the child decreases grabbing toys away from others, then taking the toy away from the child is considered a form of punishment.

Another major type of learning suggested by behaviorists is **classical conditioning,** which involves associating a **neutral stimulus** (a stimulus that does not initially elicit a particular response) with another stimulus that leads to a particular response. For example, if each time a child gets a painful shot the nurse giving the shot wears a white coat, the child may learn to be afraid of anyone in a white coat. The neutral stimulus, the person in the white coat, becomes a negative stimulus because the child has learned to associate pain with white coats. The child may cry not only while being among medical personnel in white coats but also among checkout clerks or anyone wearing a white coat. These processes are discussed in the next section.

ROLES OF HEREDITY AND ENVIRONMENT

Development begins at the moment of conception and changes in all areas of development throughout life. During the first few years of life, a tremendous amount of growth occurs (Nilsson, 1990). The first few years of life are considered to be critical for development (Maxim, 1993). The early years are viewed as critical, in part, because brain growth is greatest during the first three years of life. Theorists continue to debate what specific factors contribute to development and the level at which **genetic** and **environmental factors** influence development and behavior (Greenough, 1991).

Genetic endowment, often referred to as **nature** or **heredity,** is believed to play an important role in development. This factor refers to the code for development received from parents at conception. Hereditary information signals the body to grow and is believed to contribute to characteristics, such as eye color, and skills, such as musical aptitude. Many early psychologists who studied child development believed that development was primarily based on a genetically determined series of events that unfolded automatically as a child matured (Loehlin, 1992). Those theorists believed that heredity was the primary determinant of behavior and that each child has an inborn clock guiding growth.

As research continued, evidence suggested that **environmental factors** also influence development (Spitz, 1946). Environmental influences include events that children experience in their homes, communities, and schools. Theorists who believe that the environment has a major influence on development came to be called **environmentalists.** They believe that parents, siblings, teachers, friends, and society create events that guide development (Plomin, 1989).

Many modern educators and psychologists believe that the environment and heredity contribute to development (Plomin & McClearn, 1993). These individuals are often referred to as **interactionists** (Scarr & Kidd, 1983). They argue that, although genetic information may establish potential, the environment has an effect on whether development reaches full potential. For example, most theorists would agree that heredity plays a major role in determining a person's height, but if a child is undernourished, the child is not likely to grow to full stature. Most modern researchers believe that heredity and environment contribute to the major areas of development (Smith & Luckasson, 1995).

The remainder of this chapter provides descriptions of the major areas of development. Lists of major milestones are provided for each area of development. These milestones may be used to help determine a child's stage of development. Milestones also are used to help determine which activities are developmentally appropriate. For example, most children do not learn to tie their shoes until age six. Therefore, it would be inappropriate to have an activity designed to develop this skill in two-year-olds. On the other hand, such an activity might be appropriate for five- and six-year-olds, depending on their developmental levels. The first major area of development to be discussed is cognitive development.

COGNITIVE DEVELOPMENT

Acquiring **cognitive skills** is one of the major areas of development. **Cognitive development** refers to the development of thinking skills. Development of cognitive skills directly relates to the development of other skills, including communication, motor, and social-emotional skills.

Most theorists believe cognitive skills are acquired through the interplay of neurological structures that include the brain and nervous system, as well as cultural-environmental influences. This is why each child's development is unique (Ginsburg & Opper, 1988). Similarities, however, do exist among children, making it possible to predict the general sequence (order of development) in which children typically develop. Children with **cognitive developmental delays** generally follow the same sequence of development although the rate of development for specific skills is slower than is typical (Illingworth, 1987).

Basic Cognitive Processes

Basic cognitive processes, including **perception, attention, reasoning,** and **memory.** These form the basis on which other cognitive skills grow. Deficits in any of these areas may contribute to cognitive delays, as well as delays in other areas of development. Perception, the ability to become aware of **stimuli** (events), is the first level of cognition.

Perception. **Perception** involves the ability to make sense of information provided to the brain from the sense organs, for seeing, tasting, touching, hearing, smelling, and physical movement of one's own body. Everyone processes and interprets sensory information differently. Therefore, each person experiences unique reactions to the environment based on varying perceptions (Gibson & Spelke, 1983). Knowledge about early perceptual abilities is used to develop environments that enhance learning.

Perceptual development begins as early as seven to eight weeks after conception (Bornstein, 1992). During this time, the **fetus** responds to tactile stimulation of the oral-nasal region of the face. Infants are born with perceptual abilities that allow them to begin learning immediately. Initially, newborns **reflexive responses** (automatic) to certain kinds of stimulation (Berk, 1994).

One example of a **reflexive response** is the newborn's pupils reacting to light. Newborns' (and everyone's) eyelids shut reflexively in response to intense light. Another inborn tendency is to usually turn the head toward the source of light. Turning toward stimuli increases the number of experiences for **newborns.** Although **visual acuity** is limited, most newborns can see objects relatively well when the objects are presented within eight to twelve inches from their faces. Newborns also track or follow objects held within this distance (Aslin & Smith, 1988).

Evidence suggests that newborns gaze longer at patterns than at solid forms and prefer a human face to other forms of visual stimulation. They can see colors and differentiate patterns soon after birth. In addition, by the time most infants begin to crawl, they typically have well-developed **depth perception** (Gibson & Walk, 1960). Visual acuity gradually improves and is believed to be similar to adult level by about age one (Aslin, 1987a).

Most newborns have well-developed **auditory** (hearing) **abilities.** Newborns listen longer to the human voice than to any other sound, prefer music to noise, listen longer to sounds that vary than those that stay the same, and frequently cry when they hear high-pitched loud sounds. By eight to ten months, infants pay more attention to speech sounds occurring in their **native language** (Elbers & Ton, 1985). For example, babies of parents who speak English focus on sounds used in English and begin to ignore sounds unique to other languages (e.g., Japanese limited use of "r's").

At birth, tactile perception, such as touch, is not as well developed as auditory abilities. About one week after birth most newborns respond to skin irritation. In most cases, tactile interactions appear to serve the very important purpose of providing a sense of security through touch. Some babies are overly sensitive to touch (respond excessively, move a great deal or atypically, such as pulling away). They do not appear to find touch comforting and may not react positively to rocking and hugging (Aslin, 1987b).

When **sensory delays** exist, they most frequently are visual or auditory (U.S. Department of Education, 1995). Impairments may be due to the inability to receive stimuli. Damage to one or more of the sensory nerve routes may prevent messages from reaching the brain. **Sensory impairment** could also include the inability to sense, understand, or process **perceptual information.** Sensory impairments limit the amount of information available for processing by the brain, and lack of information may contribute to delays in **intellectual functioning.**

Perceptual abilities also allow children to learn from active exploration of their environment. In addition to supporting intellectual development, perceptual abilities allow children to learn to recognize familiar people. This is believed to contribute to the level of trust that emerges and motivates the child to communicate with others. Children who are blind or deaf can communicate and learn to trust others by using alternative sensory information. If children can perceive a stimulus it is then necessary for them focus their attention on that event.

Attention.   For children to learn, they must be able to focus their attention on the most relevant information and learn to ignore less relevant information. This ability is known as **selective attention,** the ability to focus on specific stimuli over a period of time. Typically, even young children without developmental disabilities have difficulty focusing on details, are easily distracted, and do not engage in one activity for long periods of time (Stodolsky, 1974). As children mature, however, they gradually become more purposeful in their activities.

Children with **learning disabilities** who have **sensory impairments** or who are classified as having **attention deficit hyperactivity disorder (ADHD)** are often unable to focus or retain attention on specific stimuli. Children classified as ADHD typically have significantly shorter attention spans than most children similar in age (Stodolsky, 1974; Wellman, Somerville, & Haake, 1979). The ability to attend allows for the next crucial step in cognition, which includes reasoning about events.

Reasoning.   The ability to reason is another important area of cognitive development. As mentioned earlier in this chapter, different theories have varied perspectives about cognitive skills acquisition. Explanations of how children solve problems (reason) are of particular interest to theorists. Stage theorists, such as Piaget, believe that children move through distinct stages of reasoning abilities (Piaget, 1965).

Children who have not reached more advanced levels of reasoning are at the **sensorimotor stage** of development. During this stage, babies and toddlers use their senses to explore the environment physically. While exploring the environment, children discover ways to solve problems (Aslin, 1987b). For example, while an infant is investigating a toy piano, the child is likely to touch one of the piano keys, causing the piano to

play music. In this example, the child discovers that touching a key makes music and may receive reinforcement from the pleasing sound.

The thinking processes of preschool-aged children are *not* typically governed by logical qualities (Gelman, 1972). Children may solve many problems correctly, but they often use intuition rather than logic. They may solve the problem but cannot explain why the solution is correct. Children appear to use rules to govern their behavior but may not use them consistently (Piaget, 1965). This type of reasoning is demonstrated when children use limited and changing rules to group objects. For example, when a child is asked to group objects that go together, a brush may go with a doll one time. In this case, the brush was grouped with the doll because the child has learned that it is used on the doll's hair. In another case, a brush may be classified with a hammer. This time, the brush and hammer were seen as types of tools.

Although reasoning abilities in young children are limited, their reasoning is governed by rules. It also follows the principle of looking for simple and direct causes (Piaget, 1965). Preschoolers also tend to use **transductive reasoning,** to reason from one instance to another. This type of reasoning is less complex than **inductive reasoning,** reasoning from single instances to **generalizations,** or **deductive reasoning,** reasoning from general instances to particular ones.

Often, this tendency to look for simple and direct causes results in children attributing human qualities to nonliving objects. This tendency is referred to as **animism.** For example, a four-year-old may believe that a stone feels pain when someone kicks it and that the beans will be sad if you do not eat them. This type of immature reasoning limits the ability of young children to process certain types of information.

Piaget's theory set the stage for the belief that children are active learners and, therefore, should be provided with **discovery learning** and direct contact with the environment. He believed the environments in which children interact should include areas designed to stimulate thinking skills. Piaget's theory would *not* support attempts to accelerate development but rather would support developing environments that provide each child with opportunities to build on the child's own current level of reasoning. The ability to reason affects the way children store and remember events.

Memory. Another important area related to cognitive development is **memory** ability. The memory process involves the ability to store and retrieve information (Schneider & Pressley, 1989). Memory is complex and depends on the processes of attention and perception. Potential information, which is perceived and remembered only momentarily, is presented constantly inside and outside of the body. Information from these types of stimuli is ignored, forgotten, or stored in short-term memory. **Short-term memory** storage lasts less than sixty seconds and allows for storage of about seven items, give or take two, for adults and less for children (Lipsitt, 1990). Information is generally not placed into short-term memory unless it is interesting or important and the individual is purposely attentive.

Long-term memory may store information permanently and is limitless in capacity. Information is stored in long-term memory after being processed by short-term memory. Intent to remember is often aided by **rehearsal** (repetition). Information from short-term memory is most effectively transferred into long-term memory using some form of rehearsal (DeLoache & Todd, 1988).

Most preschoolers do not spontaneously rehearse information to aid memory. Presenting information repeatedly, providing rehearsal strategies, and encouraging rehearsals may help children to remember certain information. A child might be able to remember a telephone number after being encouraged to repeat it many times (Lange & Pierce, 1992).

Children's rehearsal strategies are limited and often ineffective when they are very young (Carr & Schneider, 1991). This limits the amount of material stored in long-term memory and how easily the stored material may be retrieved. **Constructivists,** discussed earlier in this chapter, suggest that much of the information encountered by children is selected and interpreted on the basis of already existing knowledge. See Table 2.2 for a list of cognitive development milestones for children from birth through age six who do not have developmental delays.

TABLE 2.2 Typical Cognitive Development Milestones

Newborns
- Prefers sweet; can distinguish sweet, salty, sour, bitter
- Responds to certain smells
- Prefers complex sounds and higher-pitched voices
- Scans visual field but tracking and color vision are not yet well developed; limited acuity

1 to 4 Months
- Performs simple actions focused around own body
- Demonstrates limited anticipation of events

4 to 8 Months
- Repeats interesting events
- Imitation of familiar behavior

8 to 12 Months
- Intentional goal-directed behavior
- Improved anticipation of events
- Imitation of more complex behaviors

12 to 18 Months
- Exploration of environment
- Combination of skills to obtain goals

18 Months to 2 Years
- Delayed imitation
- Engages in make-believe play

Age 2 Years
- Knows own first and last name
- Completes three-piece puzzles
- Points to various doll parts when asked

continued

TABLE 2.2   Continued

- Recognizes many objects and pictures
- Matches objects by color
- Understands the concepts "more" and "less"
- Points to actions in pictures

Age 3 Years

- Answers questions about the functions of objects
- Can use concepts "same" and "different"
- Distinguishes different sizes
- Shows interest in "why?" and "how?"
- Points to a picture that does not logically fit with others in a set.
- Knows own gender
- Counts up to five objects
- Sorts objects by colors into two or three sets

Age 4 Years

- Matches colors and shapes
- Names four colors
- Classifies objects by size
- Counts up to ten objects
- Matches (at least ten) common words to pictures
- Follows directions such as "come in"
- Understands the meaning of more abstract words such as *cold* and *tired*
- Relates experiences in sequence

Age 5 Years

- Identifies a penny, nickel, and dime
- Identifies the numbers one through ten
- Groups pictures by use
- Performs simple subtraction
- Spends an increasing amount of time attending to tasks
- Knows all basic colors
- Puts small (eight-piece) puzzles together

Age 6 Years

- Understands the concepts "first," "middle," and "last"
- Understands cause and effect
- Interprets feelings of story characters
- Predicts a story's outcome
- Recognizes basic shapes
- Tells a short story in sequence

To some extent all areas of development are affected by the development of cognitive skills. Communication skills are believed to be directly linked to cognitive skills. In most cases, when children have delays in general cognitive abilities, they also have delays in communication skills.

COMMUNICATION SKILLS

Skinner (1957) believed that language is acquired through the process of **operant conditioning.** An example of operant conditioning is when a child says, "juice," the child's mother is likely to respond by offering the child a drink. The child learns that being provided with juice is more likely to occur when saying *juice* than when not saying anything or crying. Behaviorists believe that a child's speech and language development is affected by hearing other people use speech and then imitating them, a process called **imitation.** It appears that reinforcement and imitation play a role in speech and language development (Bates, Bretherton, & Snyder, 1988).

Contrary to the behaviorist perspective, nativist Noam Chomsky (1957) believes that language skills are innate and naturally occur as the child matures. He referred to this natural ability as the **language acquisition device (LAD).** According to Chomsky, LAD allows children to combine words into grammatically correct phrases. Supporting the nativist perspective are data indicating that children across all cultures develop language in the same general manner (Bates, O'Connell, & Shore, 1987).

An example of LAD is found when children who live in English-speaking families learn to use *-ed* to indicate the past tense even on words that have an irregular past tense. For example, they might say "He runned" instead of "He ran." This is an example of **overregularization** (Marcus, Pinker, Ullman, Hollander, Rosen, & Fei, 1992). The tendency to use regular rules of **grammar** in situations that do not follow the rules is found in nearly every language. Because adults do not typically say *runned,* it is not likely that children learn to say *runned* based on **imitation** or **reinforcement** (Harris, 1992; Cromer, 1991).

Constructivists suggest that when children begin to acquire language it is based on expressing concepts that are already meaningful to them (Bowerman, 1985). Children with delayed speech and language skills are often also delayed in symbolic play and imitation skills (Fosnot, 1996). In contrast, children who are the first to use several gestures in sequence of pretend play are typically the first to speak two-word sentences (Bates, 1993).

In general, the majority of developmentalists make an appeal for the **interactionist perspective.** Interactionists believe that innate and environmental influences play roles in language development (Reznick & Goldfield, 1992). They suggest that children need sufficient time to mature to allow the natural ability to evolve. Children also need to have the opportunity to observe and imitate language (Goldfield & Reznick, 1990). Children's rate and quality of language development are also influenced by reinforcement and punishment, which may follow their use of speech (Bates, 1993).

Understanding the typical progression of language development may be used to determine a child's stage of development to create appropriate activities for the child (de Villiers & de Villiers, 1992). See Table 2.3 for a summary list of speech and language milestones. (Chapter 8 provides additional information on speech and language development.) The ability to communicate effectively may be limited by delays in motor development. The next section provides a brief discussion of motor development.

MOTOR DEVELOPMENT

Motor ability appears to be related to cognitive development (Aslin, 1987a). Initially, the human infant is dependent on adults for survival. During the first month, infants gradually adjust to life outside the womb. They develop regular rhythms of eating and sleeping. Children's physical development progresses remarkably during the first few years of life.

TABLE 2.3   Typical Speech and Language Development Milestones

Birth through 2 Months
- Cries to express need

2 to 6 Months
- Cooing

6 to 12 Months
- Babbling

12 to 18 Months
- First word
- Uses one-word sentences (*holophrases*)

Age 1 Year
- Uses words and gestures
- Imitates animal sounds
- Repeats words
- Looks at pictures of objects as they are named
- Recognizes names of body parts
- Points to nose, eyes, hair, and mouth

Age 2 Years
- Uses two-word utterances
- Vocabulary increases dramatically, expanding to about 25 to 300 words
- Shows effective communication skills such as taking turns to speak
- Able to relate experiences using words
- Verbalizes needs, such as for food and drinks
- Begins using pronouns

Age 3 Years
- Uses three- to four-word sentences
- Answers questions about the function of objects
- States own full name
- Uses past and present tenses
- Uses internal (private) speech to guide behavior when working on challenging tasks
- Asks for "more"
- Recites simple rhymes
- Names at least one color accurately
- Requests things by name
- Often overextends grammatical rules to exceptions

continued

TABLE 2.3 Continued

Age 4 Years

- Links phrases into causal relationships ("The baby is crying because he needs his mom.")
- Names primary colors
- Counts to five
- Recites rhymes and sings
- Uses verbs and plural nouns
- Uses many consonant sounds

Age 5 Years

- Asks what words mean
- Notices objects missing from a picture, such as no roof on a house
- Defines simple words
- Counts to ten
- Uses grammatically correct complex sentences
- Recites familiar stories by memory

Age 6 Years

- Predicts how a story will end
- Recites own telephone number and address
- States own age
- Tells a short story in a logical sequence
- Reads simple words

Piaget argued that children initially learn about their environment almost exclusively through physical exploration. Play abilities are also affected by motor development. For example, if children cannot run and kick a ball, they often are excluded from a social experience if the other children are playing kickball. Likewise, children unable to catch a ball will probably not be invited to play catch with other children. As mentioned earlier, the level of cognitive development directly affects motor development. The inverse is true as well—motor development directly contributes to acquisition of cognitive, as well as social-emotional skills. Two major types of motor skills development are **gross motor** and **fine motor.**

Gross Motor Development

Gross motor development refers to how children learn to move the large muscles in their bodies. The sequence of gross motor skills development is similar for all children, but the rate of growth may vary greatly. One aspect of gross motor skill is the **cephalocaudal trend,** which is characterized by children developing motor control over their heads and trunks before their arms and legs. Another pattern of gross motor skill is the **proximodistal** trend in development, which is displayed when children begin to gain control over their heads, trunks, and arms before they gain coordination over the extremities. These two trends of development appear to be genetically programmed patterns of development (Mathew & Cook, 1990).

In addition to genetic influences, the environment also appears to influence the rate of gross motor development (Thelen, 1989). Toddlers with frequent ear infections may have difficulty maintaining their balance while learning to walk. Likewise, children who have few opportunities to climb stairs or use play equipment may not independently master climbing stairs as quickly as those who do have these experiences. Research indicates that once children have these experiences, they often acquire the skills typical for children of the same age quickly (Illingworth, 1987).

A detailed discussion of motor development is presented in Chapters 10 and 11. See Table 2.4 for a list of the milestones of gross motor development for children from birth through age six years.

Fine Motor Development

In contrast to gross motor development, **fine motor development** involves smaller muscle groups and includes movements such as reaching, grasping, waving, and writing. Similarly to gross motor development, fine motor development drastically improves during early childhood (McHale & Lerner, 1990). Chapter 10 provides further discussion of fine motor development. See Table 2.5 for a list of the typical sequence of fine motor development. Cognitive, speech and language, and motor

TABLE 2.4 Typical Gross Motor Development Milestones

Birth to 6 Months
- Sits upright with prop
- Supports own head when in a sitting position
- Lifts head and supports self on arm when on stomach
- Raises arms and legs when placed on stomach
- Rolls over

6 Months to 1 Year
- Sits alone
- Crawls
- Pulls self from a sitting to standing position
- Stands without holding on to an object or person

Age 1 Year
- Walks unassisted
- Climbs onto low furniture
- Climbs stairs with assistance
- Pulls or pushes toys with wheels
- Kicks ball holding on to support
- Catches rolling ball between legs while sitting

Age 2 Years
- Runs very stiffly on toes
- Jumps using both feet simultaneously
- Walks upstairs holding the bannister
- Walks on tiptoes
- Pedals a tricycle while adult pushes
- Kicks a ball forward without losing balance
- Plays on a rocking horse
- Throws a ball overhanded five to seven feet
- Hangs from a bar

Age 3 Years
- Throws a ball to adult standing five feet away
- Runs without falling
- Hops on alternating feet
- Stands on one foot
- Walks backward for several feet
- Moves a chair to reach for an object
- Rides tricycle using pedals, unassisted by an adult

- Walks backward easily
- Walks on balance beam with one foot on the floor and the other on the beam

Age 4 Years
- Walks upstairs like an adult by alternating feet
- Runs smoothly with changes in speed
- Skips using alternate feet rather than galloping
- Bounces a ball
- Catches a ball with arms and body
- Jumps up and down on the floor several times
- Bounces playground ball
- Catches beanbags with hands

Age 5 Years
- Hops on one foot
- Performs jumping jacks and toe touches
- Walks up and down the stairs while carrying objects
- Catches a ball with two hands
- Bounces a ball in place
- Skips rope

Age 6 Years
- Jumps over objects ten inches high
- Does somersaults and cartwheels
- Performs headstand
- Rides a bicycle with training wheels
- Walks securely on balance beam
- Balances on roller skates
- Throws with accurate placement
- Dribbles ball
- Kicks rolling ball

development directly affect children's social and emotional development. The next section provides an overview of social-emotional development.

Social-Emotional Development

Newborns who do not have developmental disabilities are capable of responding to most **social experiences.** They initially respond reflexively to

TABLE 2.5 Typical Fine Motor Development Milestones

6 to 9 Months
- Grasps and holds objects
- Holds one object while looking for another
- Pokes at objects with index finger
- Puts objects in mouth
- Feels and explores objects with mouth
- Holds bottle
- Squeezes and shakes toys
- Plays with own hands

9 to 12 Months
- Feeds self by picking up food with fingers
- Uses thumb and index finger (pincer grasp) to grasp objects
- Transfers objects from one hand to another
- Holds two small objects in one hand

12 to 18 Months
- Builds tower of two cubes
- Claps hands
- Waves "bye-bye"
- Scoops with spoon or shovel
- Bangs together two objects held in hands
- Puts small objects into containers
- Scribbles

18 Months to Age 2 Years
- Puts rings on pegs
- Removes pegs from a pegboard
- Marks or scribbles with pencil or crayon
- Builds tower three to four blocks tall
- Opens loosely wrapped small objects (e.g., candies)

Age 2 Years
- Manipulates clay
- Turns doorknobs
- Picks up small objects with pincer grasp
- Completes three-piece puzzle
- Scribbles
- Cuts paper with scissors
- Strings large beads

- Opens and closes large zippers
- Uses spoon effectively
- Nests objects (inserts one inside the other) graduated in size

Age 3 Years
- Draws circle after being shown model
- Strings half-inch beads
- Cuts along a line
- Makes clay flat "cakes," rolled "ropes," and balls
- Sorts objects
- Fastens and unfastens large front buttons

Age 4 Years
- Traces vertical and horizontal lines
- Cuts while moving paper
- Completes puzzles with four to five pieces
- Uses fork effectively
- Dresses and undresses unassisted
- Draws cross (+) when shown an example

Age 5 Years
- Grasps pencil correctly
- Prints simple words
- Cuts circle
- Opens lock with key
- Makes recognizable objects with clay
- Draws diamond when shown an example

Age 6 Years
- Copies first name
- Builds structure with small blocks
- Completes a puzzle with sixteen to twenty pieces
- Dials telephone
- Uses knife to cut soft foods
- Draws person with six or more parts
- Draws line with ruler

physical stimulation. For example, when the newborn's cheek is stroked from the corner of the mouth toward the ear, the infant turns toward the stroking hand. Newborns grasp a finger placed in their palm. Most infants appear to gain a sense of security when they are held. Infants also respond positively to seeing a human face and hearing a person's voice (McHale & Lerner, 1990).

During the first six months of life, most infants begin to smile and laugh when another person is present. Over time, infants begin to smile more at familiar people. When infants (without hearing disabilities) cry, they are likely to stop crying when someone begins speaking (Grusec, 1988).

Nine-month-olds also respond positively when someone speaks to them. They often continue an activity in which they were losing interest after receiving encouragement from another person. They listen to what other people say and appear to understand much of what is said (Gunnar, 1990).

By age one, interactions with other people include give-and-take situations. Play becomes more social, or people-oriented. One-year-olds appear to prefer to be around "familiar" faces. The children display emotions such as fear, anger, and jealousy and develop a sense of humor (Harris, 1989). They begin to display an awareness of other people's feelings and needs and appear to want to please others. One-year-olds are more willing to cooperate but also demand to be independent, and that demand is called **autonomy.** The desire for autonomy and the need to cooperate are often in conflict (Erikson, 1950).

Children two to six years begin to learn the ways adults expect them to behave. The children's **emotions** now include modesty, guilt, shame, and sympathy. Empathy for other children in distress, cooperation, and helping others increase during the preschool years (Zahn–Waxler, Radke–Yarrow, & King, 1979). For example, two- and three-year-olds give gifts and share toys with others but also at times refuse to share. At two to three years, giving a gift is often used to initiate social contact. As children mature, their social skills develop and they demonstrate greater levels of generosity, cooperation, **empathy,** and helpfulness (Eisenberg & Miller, 1987).

As children mature, their social-emotional development becomes much more complex and often less predictable (Klimes–Dougan & Kistner,

1990). It is not unusual for three-year-olds to develop fears not previously present. Four-year-olds' mixture of self-reliance and assertiveness frequently results in aggressiveness or bossiness. Four-year-olds often want to choose clothes and food by themselves. Five-year-olds typically are more culturally conforming and begin to show "manners." (Grusec, 1992) Emotions now include pride, self-satisfaction, and persistence. Six-year-olds tend to be lively, energetic, and enthusiastic. They often become frustrated, angry, or quarrelsome when they are not succeeding at a task. Jealously is frequently displayed, and they may refuse to cooperate (Harter & Whitesell, 1989).

Research indicates that preschoolers who have developed a strong sense of trust, perceiving the world as dependable and safe because adults adequately provide for their needs, more readily learn how to give and take and accurately interpret the needs of others (Mahler, Pine, & Bergman, 1975). As a result, these children are more likely to welcome social experiences, and by the time they are four to five years old, they typically have a well developed set of social skills (Lewis, Sullivan, & Vasen, 1987).

Kindness is a social skill mastered through imitation. Grusec (1988) found that preschoolers who had observed an adult sharing, helping, and being sympathetic were more likely to demonstrate these attributes. Furthermore, the children in this study who were exposed to extensive **modeling** of the attributes reflected those attributes for an extended duration of time. Children, however, who received only limited modeling did not demonstrate retention of the attributes for an extended period of time (Eisenberg, 1992).

Play

Opportunities to play with others are important during infancy and the preschool years. Young children play by exploring their environment. They usually enjoy having other people interact with them (Howes & Matheson, 1992). These interactions include tickling and playing peek-a-boo, as well as shaking a rattle or demonstrating how to make a toy piano create sound. As children mature, their play becomes more active and often is self-initiated.

"The play years" characterize two- to six-year-olds because play is the major activity of children during this time. During the preschool years, play is an important experience aiding in the child's social, emotional, physical, and cognitive growth. Children learn to share, lead, follow, and solve problems. For example, when children experience aggression during play, they learn about bullies and self-protection (Black, 1992).

Children also learn about themselves through play. They learn about what they like to do, with whom they like to play, and what skills they have developed (Brownell & Brown, 1992). Play is one way for children to express their emotions, build relationships, and develop imagination (Connolly, Doyle, & Reznick, 1988). Play not only provides a mechanism for cognitive growth but also provides opportunities for children to develop friendships. Chapter 12 provides a more detailed discussion of the importance of children's play.

Self-Concept

Research by Lewis and Brook–Gunn (1979) indicates that by fifteen months toddlers recognize themselves in a mirror. By age two years, children spend more time looking at photographs of themselves than at photographs of other children. Two-year-olds also say, "That's me" or "That's Chris," using their own name when looking at a photograph of themselves. A sense of self lets children begin to compare themselves to others (Lewis, 1990).

Between eighteen and thirty months, children begin to use labels to describe themselves and others (Bullock & Lütkenhaus, 1990). These labels are often created on the basis of age such as "That's a baby" or "That's a man." They also classify people on the basis of gender (Fagot & Leinbach, 1993). It is during this period that children are more likely to select toys considered gender

appropriate. For example, a little girl is more likely to pick a doll than a truck during play.

A sense of self, or **self-concept,** includes a set of beliefs about one's own characteristics. Preschoolers often behave much like the important adults in their lives such as mom, dad, siblings, teachers, and care-providers. Often they are separated from these adults for part of the day. As a result of this separation, they begin to develop an awareness of their own uniqueness (Keller, Ford, & Meacham, 1978).

Adults learn about preschoolers' self-concepts when these children describe themselves. They often describe themselves based on observable characteristics such as their names, things they have or play with, physical characteristics, and everyday behavior. Preschoolers' self-concepts are not as well defined as those of older children or adults. A preschooler who is asked, "Tell me about yourself," is likely to say, "Hi, I'm Sara. I'm 4½ years old. I can brush my hair all by myself. See my new pink dress? I can color pretty pictures! My mom and I baked cookies. My dad works in his office."

Sara's statements include very concrete descriptions of herself, typical of preschool-aged children (Keller, Ford, & Meacham, 1978). Self-descriptive lists of attributes tend to include age, name, physical appearance, possessions, family members, and daily occurrences. Preschoolers may express their emotions when these are connected with specific occurrences. For example, if Sara had been asked if she had a good time at school today, she might respond, "Yes, we made a snack it was good." Describing feelings or values typically does not occur until children have reached greater cognitive maturity during middle childhood (Elder, 1989).

Self-esteem, directly related to self-concept, involves judging self-worth or goodness. Most preschoolers have relatively positive self-esteem. That is, they generally like themselves and feel competent. They generally know whether they are liked by others and how well they can do certain tasks (Harter, 1983). Positive self-esteem lets young children attempt new tasks during a period in which they are required to learn many new skills. Young children often rate their ability to complete tasks as extremely high and often underestimate the difficulty of tasks. Chapter 15 emphasizes the importance of the development of positive self-esteem.

Emotions

As young children's self-concepts become more well developed, the children typically become increasingly sensitive to praise and criticism (Thompson, 1990). At the same time, preschoolers' vocabularies expand rapidly, letting them verbally describe their emotions (Hyde & Linn, 1988). Their understanding of various **emotions** improves over time. Between years four and five, children can judge the causes of many basic emotional reactions such as happy, sad, scared, angry, and surprised (Lewis, Sullivan, & Vasen, 1987). They can also predict what a playmate may do next based on the emotion the playmate shows (Gnepp, 1983).

One limit of young children's emotional understanding is their inability to grasp complex emotional terms such as gratitude, envy, and pity. They are also unable to make sense of a situation with conflicting cues (Graham, Doubleday, & Guarino, 1984). For example, when four- and five-year-olds are asked what is happening in a picture showing a happy faced girl with a broken doll, they tend to focus on emotional expression and respond, "She's happy because she has a doll."

During the preschool years, children are generally better able to control their emotional outbursts due to an increased awareness of how their behavior affects themselves and others (Hyson, 1994). Between years three and four, children use many strategies for changing their level of emotional response to a more comfortable level for themselves. For example, they try to control their emotions through limiting sensory input by covering their ears when they hear a scary sound (Thompson, 1990).

As children mature, they begin to observe how adults handle their own feelings. This allows children to pick up strategies for regulating their own emotions. When adults have difficulty controlling and expressing their anger, children tend to imitate this response (Gottman & Katz, 1989). Therefore, it is important for adults to help children prepare for difficult experiences by modeling and creating coping strategies children may later use. For example, in addition to remaining calm themselves, parents may prepare children for the first day of school, which is often a difficult experience, by describing what to expect and how to handle their anxiety.

Morality

Psychologists, such as Piaget (1965) and Kohlberg (1969), report that **moral beliefs** change as children's cognitive abilities become more complex. Preschoolers first form concepts about morality during interactions with other children and adults (Kurtines & Gewirtz, 1991). A child might be heard expressing a sense of morality when commenting, "I naughty, I spill milk" or "Tommy not nice to me." In the late preschool years, children gradually become concerned with moral rules and may be heard to say, "You didn't share" and "It's not fair. He got more."

According to Piaget (1965), preschoolers often cannot make moral judgments or determine what is right or wrong based on their own concepts of fairness and justice. For example, seven-year-olds frequently report a child who intentionally pushed a friend off the merry-go-round as naughtier than a child who did so accidentally. Three-year-olds are less likely to make a judgment based on intentions. [Piaget believed that children recognize that adults may respond differently to violations of moral rules such as, "Be nice to others," than to breaks in rules such as forgetting to say "Please" and, "Thank you."] For example, parents are more likely to discipline a child for grabbing a toy than for not saying "Please."

Kohlberg (1969) classified moral development into three levels, in which each level is qualitatively different from and more advanced than each previous one. During childhood, children reason at the **preconventional level.** At this level, children decide what is right or wrong based on external, physical events rather than on society's standards. When faced with a moral dilemma, children at this level do not ask themselves whether something is right according to society's standards but instead focus on the consequences. They are likely to ask themselves, "Will I get in trouble?" rather than "What is the right thing to do?" Before elementary school age, children have not had adequate experience to learn the roles people play and the rules of society, nor are they cognitively mature enough to process a complex set of rules and information.

Although preschoolers do not reason at a **conventional** or **post-conventional** level, understanding these stages allows for a comparison between young children's and adolescents' and adults' levels of reasoning. The conventional level of moral reasoning focuses on conforming to social rules to ensure social order. The post-conventional level focuses on abstract principles and values related to social justice. All too frequently, adults expect young children to respond at conventional or post-conventional levels of moral reasoning, an unreasonable expectation based on children's level of cognitive development. The conventional and post-conventional levels require reasoning more complex than is found in most young children.

Preschoolers display more **prosocial** (positive) **behavior** when they have frequently experienced positive interactions with others. Young children often imitate the behavior of others they observe in everyday activities. For example, if they see others being honest and helpful, they are more likely to behave in this fashion (Zahn–Waxler, et al., 1979). When children's prosocial behavior is followed by a reinforcer, such as praise, they are more likely to repeat prosocial behavior in the future. Chapter 14 provides a more detailed discussion of behavior management. See Table 2.6 for a list of social-emotional development milestones.

TABLE 2.6   Typical Social-Emotional Development Milestones

Birth to 6 Months
- Smiles at familiar people
- Often stops crying when someone begins to speak
- Cries when caregiver leaves the room

6 to 9 Months
- Uses vocalizations to gain social contact
- Enjoys play with others
- Attempts to imitate others

9 Months to 1 Year
- Responds to others by vocalizing
- Shy when among strangers
- Focuses on conversations

Ages 1 to 2 Years
- Cooperates with familiar people
- Demands own way

Age 2 Years
- Wants to please others
- Shows love and affection
- Shows more empathy
- Shows patience
- Listens to the meaning of conversations

Age 3 Years
- Willing to take turns
- Does not like to share toys
- Willing to ask for help with personal needs
- Likes to listen to music and sing songs
- Plays more in areas where other children are playing
- Experiences shame, guilt, and pride
- Knows own gender
- Enjoys people and company

Age 4 Years
- Expresses humor
- Engages in pretend play
- Helps others
- Participates in group play
- Able to cross the street alone

- May have imaginary friends

Age 5 Years

- Realizes parents' demands
- Usually happy and self-confident
- At times shows fears
- Plays competitively and cooperatively
- Shows an awareness of other people's feelings
- Sometimes lies and steals small objects

Age 6 Years

- Able to choose friends
- Comforts playmates who feel sad
- Initiates conversations with children and adults
- Has acquired many morally relevant rules and behavior
- Tells lies
- Wants to finish tasks

CONCLUSION

Understanding the typical sequences of development is necessary to help ensure that a positive environment for development is created and for early detection of developmental delays. Understanding developmental sequences may aid in planning developmentally appropriate classroom activities. Growing up is full of challenges. Those children who do not develop at the rate expected face even greater challenges in meeting their potential. This makes early intervention critical. Knowledgeable adults can help plan an easier path for children with developmental delays. The next chapter provides an overview of developmental delays.

CHAPTER SUMMARY

- Developmentalists focus on describing, explaining, and predicting sequences of each major area of development.
- Theories of development may be classified as continuous or non-stage theories (e.g., behaviorism) and discontinuous or stage theories (e.g., cognitive) and mechanistic (e.g., behaviorism) or organismic (e.g., cognitive).

- Children with developmental delays usually follow the same sequence of development as those without developmental delays, but their rate of development is significantly slower.
- Cognition involves perception, attention, reasoning, and memory.
- Language development includes verbal and nonverbal skills. Speech includes communication with others and self-talk.
- The two majors areas of motor development are gross motor and fine motor skills.
- Concepts related to social-emotional development include play, self-concept, emotions, and moral development.

REVIEW QUESTIONS

1. What are the varying explanations regarding why and how development occurs?
2. What are the major attributes of the four major components of cognition?
3. How well-developed are infants' early perceptual skills?
4. What are the characteristics of Piaget's four major stages of cognitive development? How may teachers of young children use this information to develop classroom activities?
5. What are overgeneralization and overregularization? Explain how they provide evidence for the language acquisition device (LAD)?
6. What are the differences between gross motor and fine motor development?
7. Why is social-emotional development crucial during the early years of childhood? How might children's social-emotional development be evaluated?
8. What is the relationship between self-concept and self-esteem?

SUGGESTED STUDENT ACTIVITIES

1. Visit a childcare facility that has children of different ages. Observe how cognitive, speech and language, fine motor, gross motor, and social-emotional skills vary between children of different ages.

2. Interview children at various ages. Observe how language skills, moral reasoning, self-concept, or play skills are different at various ages.

3. Read a story that demonstrates a moral issue to a four- or five-year-old. Ask the child to discuss the dilemma. Evaluate how the child's viewpoint compares to your own. Evaluate the content of the child's response and the type of language used.

4. Show young children of various ages pictures with two to seven common items. Remove the picture and ask them to name the items in the picture. Note their strategies and number of correct responses.

ADDITIONAL READINGS

Hart, B., & Risley, T. R. (1995). *Meaningful differences in the everyday experiences of young American children.* Baltimore, MD: Paul H. Brookes.

Illingworth, R. S. (1987). *The development of the infant and young child: Normal and abnormal* (9th ed.). New York: Churchill Livingstone.

Thain, W. S. (1980). *Normal and handicapped children: A growth and development primer for parents and professionals.* Littleton, MA: PSG Publishing.

White, B. (1984). *The first three years of life.* Englewood Cliffs, NJ: Prentice-Hall.

ADDITIONAL RESOURCES

Association for Childhood Education International
   (ACEI)
11141 Georgia Avenue, Suite 200
Wheaton, MD 20902

Child Care Information Exchange
Box 2890
Redmond, WA 98052

National Association for Family Day Care
815 15th Street, N.W., Suite 928
Washington, DC 20005

REFERENCES

Anselmo, S. & Franz, W. K. (1995). *Early childhood development: Prebirth through age eight* (2nd ed.). Columbus, OH: Merrill.

Aslin, R. N. (1987a). Motor aspects of visual development in infancy. In P. Salapatek & L. Cohen (Eds.), *Handbook of infant perception, Vol. 1. From sensation to perception* (pp. 43–113). Orlando, FL: Academic Press.

Aslin, R. N. (1987b). Visual and auditory development in infancy. In J. D. Osofsky (Ed.), *Handbook of infant development* (2nd ed., pp. 5–97). New York: Wiley-Interscience.

Aslin, R. N., & Smith L. B. (1988). Perceptual development. *Annual Review of Psychology, 39,* 435–473.

Bates, E. (1993). Commentary: Comprehension and production in early language development. *Monographs of the Society for Research in Child Development, 58* (3–4, Serial No. 233), 222–242.

Bates, E., Bretherton, I., & Snyder, L. (1988). *From first words to grammar: Individual differences and dissociable mechanisms.* Cambridge: Cambridge University Press.

Bates, E., O'Connell, B., & Shore, C. M. (1987). Language and communication in infancy. In J. D. Osofsky (Ed.), *Handbook of infant development* (2nd ed., pp. 149–203). New York: Wiley-Interscience.

Berk, L. E. (1994). *Child development* (3rd ed.). Boston: Allyn and Bacon.

Bertenthal, B. I., & Campos, J. J. (1987). New directions in the study of early experience. *Child Development, 58,* 560–567.

Black, B. (1992). Negotiating social pretend play: Communication differences related to social status and sex. *Merrill-Palmer Quarterly, 38,* 212–232.

Black, J., & Puckett, M. (1996). *The young child: Development from pre-birth through age 8* (2nd ed). Columbus, OH: Merrill.

Bornstein, M. H. (1992). Perception across the life span. In M. H. & M. E. Lamb (Eds.), *Developmental psychology: An advanced textbook* (3rd ed., pp. 155–210). Hillsdale, NJ: Erlbaum.

Bowerman, M. (1985). Beyond communicative adequacy: From piecemeal knowledge to an integrated system in the child's acquisition of language. In K. E. Nelson (Ed.), *Children's language* (Vol. 5, pp. 369–398). NJ: Erlbaum.

Brofenbrenner, U. (1989). Ecological systems theory. *Annals of Child Development, 6,* 187–249.

Brownell, C. A., & Brown, E. (1992). Peers and play in infants and toddlers. In V. B. V. Hasselt & M. Hersen (Eds.), *Handbook of social development: A lifespan perspective* (pp. 183–200). New York: Plenum Press.

Bullock, M., & Lütkenhaus, P. (1990). Who am I? Self-understanding in toddlers. *Merrill-Palmer Quarterly, 36,* 217–238.

Carr, M., & Schneider, W. (1991). Long-term maintenance of organizational strategies in kindergarten children. *Contemporary Educational Psychology, 16,* 61–75.

Chomsky, N. (1957). *Syntactic Structures.* The Hague: Mouton.

Connolly, J. A., Doyle, A. B., & Reznick, E. (1988). Social pretend play and social interactions in preschoolers. *Developmental Psychology, 9,* 301–313.

Cromer, R. F. (1991). *Language and thought in normal and handicapped children.* Oxford: Basil Blackwell.

DeLoache, J. S., & Todd, C. M. (1988). Young children's use of spatial categorization as a mnemonic strategy. *Journal of Experimental Psychology, 46,* 1–20.

de Villiers, P. A., & de Villiers, J. G. (1992). Language development. In M. H. Bornstein & M. E. Lamb (Eds.), *Developmental psychology: An advanced textbook* (3rd ed., pp. 337–418). Hillsdale, NJ: Erlbaum.

Eisenberg, N. (1992). *The caring child.* Cambridge, MA: Harvard University Press.

Eisenberg, N., & Miller, P. A. (1987). The relation of empathy to prosocial and related behaviors. *Psychological Bulletin, 101,* 91–119.

Elbers, L., & Ton, J. (1985). Play pen monologues: The interplay of words and babbles in the first word period. *Journal of Child Language, 12,* 551–565.

Elder, R. A. (1989). The emergent psychologist: The structure and content of 3½–5½, and 7½-year-olds' concepts of themselves and other persons. *Child Development, 60,* 1218–1228.

Erikson, E. (1950). *Childhood and society.* New York: Norton.

Fagot, B. I., & Leinbach, M. D. (1993). Gender-role development in young children: From discrimination to labeling. *Developmental Review, 13,* 205–224.

Flavell, J. H. (1992). Cognitive development: Past, present, and future. *Developmental Psychology, 28,* 997–1005.

Fosnot, C. T. (Ed.). (1996). *Constructivism: Theory, perspectives, and practice.* NY: Teachers College Press.

Gelman, R. (1972). Logical capacity of very young children: Number invariance rules. *Child Development, 43,* 75–90.

Gibson, E. S., & Spelke, E. S. (1983). The development of perception. In J. H. Flavell & E. M. Markman (Eds.), *Handbook of child psychology: Vol. 3. Cognitive development* (4th ed., pp. 1–76). New York: Wiley.

Gibson, E. J., & Walk, R. D. (1960). The "visual cliff." *Scientific American, 202,* 64–71.

Ginsburg, H. P., & Opper, S. (1988). *Piaget's theory of intellectual development* (3rd ed.). Englewood Cliffs, NJ: Prentice-Hall.

Gnepp, J. (1983). Children's social sensitivity: Inferring emotions from conflicting cues. *Developmental Psychology, 19,* 805–814.

Goldfield, B. A., & Reznick, J. S. (1990). Early lexical acquisition: Rate, content, and the vocabulary spurt. *Journal of Child Language, 17,* 171–183.

Gottman, J. M., & Katz, L. F. (1989). Effects of marital discord on young children's peer interactions and health. *Developmental Psychology, 25,* 373–381.

Graham, S., Doubleday, C., & Guarino, P. A. (1984). The development of relations between perceived controllability and the emotions of pity, anger, and guilt. *Child Development, 55,* 561–565.

Greenough, W. T. (1991). Experience as a component of normal development: Evolutionary considerations. *Developmental Psychology, 27,* 11–27.

Grusec, J. E. (1988). *Social development: History, theory, and research.* New York: Springer-Verlag.

Grusec, J. E. (1992). Social learning theory and developmental psychology: The legacies of Robert Sears and Albert Bandura. *Developmental Psychology, 49,* 920–923.

Gunnar, M. R. (1990). The psychobiology of infant temperament. In J. Colombo & J. Fagen (Eds.), *Individual differences in infancy: Reliability, stability, prediction* (pp. 387–410). Hillsdale, NJ: Erlbaum.

Harris, M. (1992). *Language experience and early language development: From input to uptake.* Hove, England: Erlbaum.

Harris, P. L. (1989). *Children and emotion: The development of psychological understanding.* Oxford: Basil Blackwell.

Harter, S. (1983). Developmental perspectives on the self-system. In E. M. Hetherington (Ed.), *Handbook of child psychology: Vol. 4, Socialization, personality, and social development* (4th ed., pp. 275–385). NY: John Wiley & Sons.

Harter, S., & Whitesell, N. (1989). Developmental changes in children's understanding of simple, multiple, and blended emotion concepts. In C. Saarni &

P. Harris (Eds.), *Children's understanding of emotion* (pp. 81–116). Cambridge, England: Cambridge University Press.

Horowitz, F. D. (1990). Developmental model of individual differences. In J. Colombo & J. Fagen (Eds.), *Individual difference in infancy: Reliability, stability, prediction* (pp. 3–18). Hillsdale, NJ: Erlbaum.

Horowitz, F. D. (1992). John B. Watson's legacy: Learning and environment. *Developmental Psychology, 28,* 360–367.

Howes, C., & Matheson, C. C. (1992). Sequences in the development of competent play with peers: Social and pretend play. *Developmental Psychology, 28,* 961–974.

Hyde, J. S., & Linn, M. C. (1988). Gender differences in verbal ability: A meta analysis. *Psychological Bulletin, 104,* 53–69.

Hyson, M. C. (1994). *The emotional development of young children.* NY: Teachers College Press.

Illingworth, R. S. (1987). *The development of the infant and young child: Normal and abnormal.* New York: Churchill Livingstone.

Keller, A., Ford, L. H., & Meacham, J. A. (1978). Dimensions of self-concept in preschool children. *Developmental Psychology, 14,* 483–489.

Klimes–Dougan, B., & Kistner, J. (1990). Physically abused preschoolers' responses to peers' distress. *Developmental Psychology, 26,* 599–602.

Kohlberg, L. (1969). Stage and sequence: The cognitive-developmental approach to socialization. In D. A. Goslin (Ed.), *Handbook of socialization theory and research* (pp. 347–480). Chicago: Rand McNally.

Kuhn, D. (1992). Cognitive development. In M. H. Bornstein & M. E. Lamb (Eds.), *Developmental psychology: An advanced textbook* (3rd ed., pp. 211–272). Hillsdale, NJ: Erlbaum.

Kurtines, W. M., & Gewirtz, J. L. (Eds.). (1991). *Handbook of moral behavior and development* (Vol. 1, *Theory;* Vol. 2, *Research;* Vol. 3, *Application*). Hillsdale, NJ: Erlbaum.

Lange, G., & Pierce, S. H. (1992). Memory-strategy learning and maintenance in preschool children. *Developmental Psychology, 28,* 453–462.

Lewis, J. M. (1990). Social knowledge and social development. *Merrill-Palmer Quarterly, 36,* 93–544.

Lewis, J. M., & Brook–Gunn, J. (1979). *Social cognition and the acquisition of self.* New York: Plenum Press.

Lewis, J. M., & Miller, S. M. (Eds.). (1990). *Handbook of developmental psychopathlogy.* New York: Plenum Press.

Lewis, J. M., Sullivan, M. W., & Vasen, A. (1987). Making faces: Age and emotional differences in the posing of emotional expressions. *Developmental Psychology, 23,* 690–697.

Lipsitt, L. P. (1990). Learning and memory in infants. *Merrill-Palmer Quarterly, 36,* 53–66.

Loehlin, J. C. (1992). *Genes and environment in personality development.* Newbury Park, CA: Sage.

Mahler, M. S., Pine, F., & Bergman, A. (1975). *The psychological birth of the human infant.* New York: Basic Books.

Marcus, G. F., Pinker, S., Ullman, M., Hollander, M., Rosen, T. J., & Fei, X. (1992). Overregularization in language acquisition. *Monographs of the Society for Research in Child Development, 57*(4, Serial No. 228).

Mathew, A., & Cook, M. (1990). The control of reaching movements by young infants. *Child Development, 61,* 1238–1257.

Maxim, G. W. (1993). *The very young: Guiding children from infancy through the early years.* (4th ed). Columbus, OH: Merrill.

McHale, S. M., & Lerner, R. M. (1990). Stages of human development. In R. M. Thomas (Ed.), *The encyclopedia of human development and education* (pp. 163–166). Oxford: Pergamon Press.

Nilsson, L. (1990). *A child is born.* New York: Delacorte Press.

Piaget, J. (1950). *The psychology of intelligence.* New York: International Universities Press.

Piaget, J. (1952). *The origins of intelligence in children.* New York: International Universities Press.

Piaget, J. (1965). *The moral judgment of the child.* New York: Free Press.

Plomin, R. (1989). Environment and genes: Determinants of behavior. *American Psychologist, 44,* 105–111.

Plomin, R., & McClearn, G. E. (Eds.). (1993). *Nature, nurture & psychology.* Washington, DC: American Psychological Association.

Reznick, J. S., & Goldfield, B. A. (1992). Rapid change in lexical development in comprehension and production. *Developmental Psychology, 28,* 406–413.

Scarr, S., & Kidd, K. K. (1983). Developmental behavior genetics. In M. M. Haith & J. J. Campos (Eds.), *Handbook of Child Psychology. Vol. 2. Infancy and developmental psychobiology* (5th ed., pp. 345–433). New York: Wiley.

Schneider, W., & Pressley, M. (1989). *Memory development between 2 and 20.* New York: Springer-Verlag.

Smith, D. D., & Luckasson, R. (1995). *Introduction to special education: Teaching in an age of challenge.* (2nd ed.). Boston: Allyn and Bacon.

Spitz, R. A. (1946). Anaclitic depression. *Psychoanalytic Study of the Child, 2,* 313–342.

Skinner, B. F. (1957). *Verbal behavior.* New York: Appleton Century Crofts.

Stodolsky, S. S. (1974). How children find something to do in preschools. *Genetic Psychology Monographs, 90,* 245–303.

Thelen, E. (1989). The (re)discovery of motor development: Learning new things from an old field. *Developmental Psychology, 25,* 946–949.

Thelen, E., & Adolph, K. E. (1992). Arnold L. Gesell: The paradox of nature and nurture. *Developmental Psychology, 28,* 368–380.

Thomas, R. M. (1990). Basic concepts and applications of Piagetian cognitive development theory. In R. M. Thomas (Ed.), *The encyclopedia of human development and education: Theory, research, and studies* (pp. 53–55). Oxford: Pergamon Press.

Thompson, A. (1990). On emotion and self-regulation. In R. A. Thompson (Ed.), *Nebraska Symposia on Motivation* (Vol. 26, pp. 383–483). Lincoln, NE: University of Nebraska Press.

U.S. Department of Education, National Center for Educational Statistics. (1995). *Digest of educational statistics 1995.* Washington, DC: U.S. Government Printing Office.

Wellman, H. M., Somerville, S. C., & Haake, R. J. (1979). Development of search procedures in real-life spatial environments. *Developmental Psychology, 15,* 530–542.

Wooley, J. D., & Wellman, H. M. (1990). Young children's understanding of realities, nonrealities, and appearances. *Child Development, 61,* 946–961.

Zahn–Waxler, C., Radke–Yarrow, M., & King, R. M. (1979). Child-rearing and children's prosocial initiations toward victims of distress. *Child Development, 50,* 319–330.

CHAPTER 3

INFANTS, TODDLERS, AND PRESCHOOLERS WITH DEVELOPMENTAL DELAYS

LINDA L. DUNLAP, PH.D.

CHAPTER KEY POINTS

- There are many environmental and genetic reasons young children have developmental delays.
- Children who qualify for special education services may have developmental delays in the areas of cognitive, speech and language, motor, and social-emotional development or have health impairments.
- Specific labels or classifications are related to the major areas of development and may be used for children who have developmental delays.
- Lack of understanding about the needs of children with developmental delays may prevent necessary services from being provided and often leads to prejudices toward these children.

The underlying philosophy of this book is that all individuals who work with children with developmental delays or special needs must nurture these children "with open arms." That is, all adults should interact with these children in a warm and positive manner. Whatever special needs children have, they are more like other children than they are different. All children should be accepted and cared for and have opportunities to experience success.

This chapter provides a discussion of possible causes for developmental delays and descriptions of the characteristics and needs of children with developmental delays, birth through preschool years. It concludes with a discussion of reactions people may have toward children with developmental delays.

POSSIBLE CAUSES FOR DEVELOPMENTAL DELAYS

About 10 percent of all infants, toddlers, and preschool children are classified as developmentally delayed (U.S. Department of Education, 1995). Possible causes for developmental delays are numerous. They are categorized as **genetic influences** inherited from biological parents and **environmental influences,** including accidents, exposure to toxins, illnesses, and cultural disadvantages such as being raised in poor living conditions. Delays based on genetic influences are estimated to account for about 15 to 25 percent of developmental disorders. About 75 to 85 percent of these cases are linked to effects of the environment or the reasons for developmental delays remain unknown (Bee, 1995).

Factors that affect **physiological causes** may be referred to as **biological causes.** Biological factors may be based on environmental or genetic influences. Infections, lead poisoning, head injuries, and prenatal exposure to toxins are a few of the many possible environmental effects that may result in physiological abnormalities. Inherited disorders such as metabolic conditions (e.g., PKU) or syndromes (e.g., fragile-X) are examples of genetic factors that contribute to biological changes.

Although causes for developmental delays often are *not* clearly determined and every child has a unique pattern of delay, certain characteristics are associated with particular disabilities. These characteristics are described in this chapter. To help prevent developmental delays from occur-

ring, it is first necessary to develop an understanding of factors that place children **at risk.**

While children from all socioeconomic groups of society are known to have developmental delays, some children appear to be more vulnerable than others (Kendall, 1996). Children who live in environments believed to lower the likelihood of reaching maximum levels of development are often referred to as at risk or **high risk.** These children have a higher than normal probability of having a developmental delay. Although there is no single set of indicators identifying children as being at risk for a developmental delay, there are several situations or characteristics that suggest children are at risk (Ramey & Campbell, 1984). See Table 3.1 for a list of environmental conditions that may place children at risk.

Prenatal factors, conditions that occur during pregnancy such as **Rh incompatibility** (blood incompatibility), viral infections, **toxemia** (toxic substances in the blood), and exposure to drugs may place children at risk. **Perinatal factors,** conditions that occur during the birth process, including labor and delivery, may also contribute to

TABLE 3.1 Environmental Factors that May Place a Child at Risk

Factors that may place a child at risk include:

1. Living in families that are at lower socioeconomic levels;
2. Living in families with varied cultural backgrounds;
3. Living in families classified as dysfunctional;
4. Being born to teenage mothers or mothers more than forty years old;
5. Growing up in homes where English is not the primary language spoken;
6. Being exposed prenatally to viruses, drugs, or alcohol;
7. Being born into families with other children who have developmental delays;
8. Being born to mothers who were malnourished during pregnancy;
9. Being born to mothers who have diabetes, thyroid disorders, syphilis, or other viral infections.

abnormal development. Prolonged labors lasting more than twenty-four hours or difficult labors may lead to head injuries or lack of oxygen for the child. In addition, children with low birth weight and who are born prematurely, after less than thirty-seven weeks in the womb, are also considered to be at risk for developmental delays (Thurman & Widerstrom, 1990).

After birth, a number of medical complications or **postnatal factors** may place a child at risk. One postnatal factor is maternal deprivation. It occurs when mothers or mother figures behave in an emotionally unresponsive fashion toward their children. In the case of maternal deprivation, children often receive very limited stimulation. Sensory stimulation is crucial for optimal development of the infant.

A mother who does not appear to respond to her child's cries or smiles is one example of unresponsive behavior that may affect the level of infant stimulation. This type of response is more likely to occur after an unwanted pregnancy, when the mother has a serious or chronic illness, or while the mother is addicted to alcohol or other drugs (Evrand & Scola, 1990). It is also likely to occur when a infant has a disability that lowers the child's level of responsiveness, which in turn leads to the adults being less responsive. See Table 3.2 for a list of postnatal medical complications that also place children at risk.

Many environmental conditions believed to contribute to developmental delays are related to the **socioeconomic status (SES)** of children's families (Wachs & Gruen, 1982). That is, children from lower SES families are believed to be more vulnerable or more at risk than other children. This risk status may occur because low SES mothers often lack adequate prenatal care and are more likely to give birth to low birth weight children. Children with exceptionally low birth weight tend to have lower **intelligence quotient (IQ)** scores when evaluated later in life. Low birth weight is also related to higher rates of **seizures, mental retardation, cerebral palsy, and deafness** (Bennett, 1984).

TABLE 3.2 Medical Complications that May Occur During the First Month of Life

Medical complications that may occur during the first month of life include:

1. Hypoglycemia—low blood sugar;
2. Hypocalcemia—low blood calcium;
3. Hyperbilirubinemia—a jaundiced/yellow color due to abnormal blood pigments;
4. Respiratory distress syndrome—breathing difficulties that may be caused by immaturity of the lungs, infections, etc., and that may damage vital organs, especially the brain, heart, and kidneys, due to lack of enough oxygen;
5. Traumatic disorders—injuries to the head, spine, hands, feet, or legs;
6. Infections of the brain—conditions caused by viruses or bacteria, such as meningitis or encephalitis;
7. Degenerative diseases—conditions that affect the nervous system and cause gradual deterioration of it;
8. Metabolic and genetic disorders—conditions that affect the brain because the child's body either does not make or destroys some substances it needs; these traits are usually inherited;
9. Brain tumors—growths on or within the brain;
10. Drug-induced delays—prenatal exposure to prescription drugs, sedatives, vitamins, alcohol, or drug abuse;
11. Seizure disorders—conditions that can indicate epilepsy or other brain diseases;
12. Injuries due to battered child syndrome—conditions caused by neglect or abuse.

Children from low SES families are also less likely to have adequate medical care, including lack of **immunizations,** and may be **malnourished.** Lead poisoning, which is linked to mental retardation and learning disabilities, is more likely to be found in the homes of low SES families. These children are also more likely at risk because of the increased likelihood of having family members with histories of diabetes, muscular dystrophy, epilepsy, or hearing problems. Children from low SES backgrounds are more likely to be exposed to drugs, alcohol, and **human immunodeficiency virus (HIV)** prenatally, which also places them at risk (Herbst & Baird, 1983). Chapter 4 provides a detailed discussion of the risk factors associated with exposure to HIV, alcohol, and cocaine use.

Many children classified as developmentally delayed come from diverse cultural backgrounds and may be exposed to **bilingual** home environments (Hakuta & Garcia, 1989). Often, it is difficult to provide a nonbiased assessment of children from **diverse backgrounds.** This may be because it is difficult to find professionals who speak English as well as the language most often spoken in the child's home. Research indicates that children from varied cultures may be labeled as developmentally delayed, even when they are not, based on **aptitude tests** that are often biased against children from minority cultures (Capron & Duyme, 1989).

It is often difficult to separate effects of multiculturalism from effects of poverty. A disproportionate number of **culturally diverse** children live in poverty. The National Council on Disability (1993) reported that 53 percent of African American families and 40 percent of Latino families live in poverty. This is in contrast to this organization's estimate that about 22 percent of all American children live in poverty.

There are many factors that place children at risk of developmental delays. The goal of **early intervention programs** is to help prevent delays from occurring by providing proper nutrition, medical care, and healthy learning environments. Data from several infant and preschool intervention programs suggest that these programs are one of the most successful ways to compensate for the effects of poverty on children's later development (Campbell & Ramey, 1991).

INDICATORS OF DEVELOPMENTAL DELAYS

Most often, no single characteristic may be used to reveal that children are developmentally delayed or at risk of becoming developmentally delayed. There are common signs for developmental delays and the more quickly adults recognize these signs, the sooner children begin receiving medical and educational evaluations and intervention (Bailey & Wolery, 1992).

When children are not at developmental levels typically found in the majority of children their age, they often are classified as either having a developmental delay or at risk of developing a delay. Additionally, when children do not acquire skills such as performing, speaking, and perceiving new experiences as quickly as do other children the same age, they often are classified as **developmentally delayed.** A third indicator of a developmental delay is based on physical appearance. That is, if children's height or weight is not appropriate for their age or if their head growth, facial features, body proportions or shapes do not appear to be typical, children typically are considered at risk (Bagnato & Neisworth, 1991).

The most frequently noted developmental delays during infancy are **motor delays.** For example, a child who cannot grasp objects or first rolls over several months later than is typical may have a motor delay. In contrast to infancy, during preschool years the most frequently noted delays are **speech and language delays** (Thurman & Widerstrom, 1990). Chapter 2 provides a discussion of typical **developmental milestones** for children from birth to age six years. These milestones may be used to help determine whether children are progressing at expected rates or might be developmentally delayed.

Following a **developmental screening,** children evaluated as having a delay of six months or more in any area of development are generally referred for a more in-depth evaluation. Children who respond in ways that suggest they have hearing or sight impairments should also be referred for in-depth evaluation. The majority of children from birth through five years old who receive early intervention services have moderate to severe levels of developmental delays (U.S. Department of Education, 1995).

Developmental delays are classified within the areas of **cognitive, speech and language, physical, social-emotional development,** or **health impairments.** In some cases, a specific delay may be classified under one category by educators and under a different category by psychologists and medical personnel. Combining all categories, children with developmental delays comprise about 7 percent of all children through age twenty-one years (U.S. Department of Education, 1995).

Children younger than school age are often referred to as developmentally delayed rather than using specific category labels. Many characteristics used to describe children as having specific types of developmental delays are seen in all young children. These characteristics are possible signs of developmental delays only when they continue to exist for an extended length of time or are extremely rare. The next section provides a discussion of cognitive delays.

COGNITIVE DELAYS

Cognitive delays include the inability to develop thinking skills at a typical rate of development. Cognitive delays are observed in the majority of children who receive early intervention services. Children who are younger than school age typically are *not* classified using specific categories unless they have severe delays. Children who are classified as having cognitive delays make up the largest number of children receiving special education services in elementary and secondary schools. Cognitive delays often affect other areas of development including speech and language, motor, and social-emotional skills. The following section describes classifications that may be used as labels for children who have cognitive delays.

Low birth weight, poor prenatal care and nutrition, parental use of alcohol and drugs, smoking, exposure to infections such as rubella and meningitis during pregnancy, and birth traumas are related to higher incidences of cognitive delays. Accidents resulting in head injuries or lack of oxygen to the brain are also associated with cognitive delays. Environmental factors that *decrease* the likelihood of cognitive delays include adequate medical care and immunizations, good nutrition, household safety, use of car seats, use of bicycle helmets, parent education programs, proper sanitation, reducing exposure to lead, and reducing child abuse (Cravioto & DeLicardie, 1975).

Children living in low SES families are more likely to be classified as cognitively delayed. Additionally, children from minority groups (e.g., black, Latino) are more likely than children from the majority group (i.e., white) to be classified as cognitively delayed. This may be because children from minority groups are more likely to live in poverty. They are also more likely to be inaccurately assessed because of language or cultural differences. In addition to environmental contributors of cognitive delays, more than one hundred different hereditary conditions are known to be related to cognitive delays (Monolascino & Stark, 1988). **Chromosomal abnormalities** associated with incidences of cognitive delays include **Down syndrome, Turner syndrome, Klinefelter syndrome,** and **fragile-X syndrome** (Carr, 1995; Cicchetti & Beeghly, 1990).

Tay-Sachs disease and **phenylketonuria (PKU)** are **metabolic disorders** linked to cognitive delays. Many state departments of health routinely test for PKU disability at birth. Intervention with a special diet may prevent cognitive delays linked to PKU. In fact, researchers have estimated that more than 50 percent of all cases of cognitive delays may be preventable (Batshaw & Perret, 1986).

Children who are cognitively delayed often have delayed speech and language development. They tend to develop speech at a slower rate, have difficulty understanding **symbolic concepts,** and have inadequate **syntactic structure** and vocabulary, as well as severe articulation problems (Deiner, 1993). Specifically, speech patterns of preschoolers with moderate to severe levels of cognitive delays are often limited to one-word phrases. They often have difficulty responding to verbal requests and may avoid eye contact and appear to ignore others who attempt to interact with them. Preschoolers with cognitive delays often have delayed motor abilities including difficulty with balance and coordination. These children more frequently have hearing and visual impairments and are more susceptible to infections.

Additionally, children who have cognitive delays often have difficulty applying what they learn in one situation to another situation. They are also less likely to acquire information through **incidental learning.** This type of learning involves gaining skills as a result of experiences not specifically designed to teach that skill. Such children often need more **direct instruction** and more repetitive instruction (Polloway & Patton, 1993). These children have difficulty selecting and focusing on tasks. For example, many of these children have difficulty selecting a toy with which to play. They are likely to play with any one toy for a very limited amount of time before moving on to a new one.

Most children with cognitive delays need only limited or intermittent support for regular daily functioning. These children are classified as mildly delayed and comprise about 89 percent of all individuals classified as cognitively delayed. Only a very limited number of young children have cognitive delays at such a level that they need extensive or regular daily aid at home and school (Smith, Finn, & Dowdy, 1993).

Mental Retardation

Children classified as **mentally retarded** consistently demonstrate general intellectual functioning that is significantly below the level found in the general population. Based on an average intelligence quotient (IQ) of 100, children classified as mentally retarded have an IQ below 70 (Patton, Payne, & Beirne–Smith, 1990). See Table 3.3 for a summary chart of IQ scores, their frequency of occurrence, and the descriptive labels normally applied to different levels.

It is often difficult to accurately assess children's IQ when they are younger than four or five

TABLE 3.3 Percentage Occurrence of Various Levels of Intelligence Score

INTELLIGENCE SCORE	DEGREE OF INTELLIGENCE	PERCENT
85–115	normal intelligence	68
70–84	borderline normal intelligence	14
55–68	mild mental retardation	2
40–54	moderate mental retardation	0.13
25–39	severe mental retardation	<0.1
less than 25	profound mental retardation	<0.1

years old. The classification "mentally retarded," therefore, is generally not used to classify children less than six years old. Children severely or profoundly disabled may be classified earlier. For example, a three-year-old who has an exceptionally small head (**microcephaly**) would likely receive an extensive evaluation. Severe forms of mental retardation identified before age six are generally related to biological causes due to genetic conditions or the environment that result in physiological damage.

In some cases, preschool-aged children may be classified as mentally retarded if they are severely delayed in skill acquisition such as walking or saying their first word (Beirne–Smith, Patton, & Ittenbach, 1994). For example, a three-year-old might be classified as mentally retarded if the child is unable to perform skills most one-year-olds could perform. Guidelines listed in PL 99–457 state that the classification developmental delay rather than mental retardation is generally most appropriate for preschoolers. Table 3.4 provides a list of early indicators of possible mental retardation in infants and young children.

Heredity and environment are believed to have an effect on cognitive development. In most cases, though, reasons for cognitive delays are *not* known (Capron & Duyme, 1989).

TABLE 3.4 Early Indicators of Possible Mental Retardation

Indicators of possible mental retardation include:

1. Being very irritable or "too good" (such as being quiet for many hours);
2. Being difficult to feed;
3. Having an abnormally high-pitched cry;
4. Showing little recognition of parents after four months old;
5. Being unable to track objects visually;
6. Having abnormal muscle tone—either very floppy or very spastic;
7. Slow to reach developmental milestones (see Chapter 2);
8. Not smiling by two months;
9. Not babbling by six months;
10. Not sitting unsupported by seven months;
11. Not saying single words by eighteen months;
12. Not walking by eighteen months.

Learning Disabilities

Another class of cognitive delays is learning disabilities. Children classified as learning disabled have achievement levels below their measured level of aptitude. Preschool children are usually *not* classified as learning disabled because it is very difficult to accurately assess their aptitudes. During the first few years of life, children display tremendous variations in growth and maturation. This limits accuracy in assessing IQ (Mercer, Algozzine, & Trifiletti, 1979). Children diagnosed with brain injuries, however, may be classified as learning disabled before entering elementary school (Lovitt, 1989).

The classification **developmental learning disability** is more frequently used with preschool children. Children with developmental learning disabilities have difficulty acquiring the prerequisite skills needed for later academic tasks. Table 3.5 provides a list of early warning signs for learning disabilities.

Learning disabilities may accompany conditions such as **perceptual disabilities, brain injuries, neurological impairments, minimal brain dysfunction, dyslexia,** and **developmental apha-**

sia. Children who have learning problems that are primarily the result of visual, hearing, or motor delays, mental retardation, emotional disturbance, or environmental, cultural, or economic disadvantage are *not* classified as learning disabled (Bender, 1992).

Prenatal exposure to alcohol and cigarettes and traumas during birth are possible causes for learning disabilities. Learning disabilities have also been linked to postnatal events such as high fevers, meningitis, and head traumas. In some cases, learning disabilities are believed to be linked to genetic abnormalities (Mercer, 1992). Children with learning disabilities are more likely than children without learning disabilities to have family members with learning disabilities. The next section discusses traumatic brain injury and attention deficit hyperactivity disorder.

Traumatic Brain Injury

Traumatic brain injury (TBI) is often cited as a cause of cognitive delays (Savage, 1988). TBI often

TABLE 3.5 Early Warning Signs for Learning Disabilities

Early warning signs for learning disabilities include:

1. Having a short attention span; by five years cannot sit long enough to listen to a short story;
2. Being easily distracted;
3. Having poor listening skills; difficulty following directions;
4. Appearing not to be trying; acting lazy or defiant;
5. Using immature speech and language;
6. Confusing left side and right side;
7. Being awkward or clumsy in movement; cannot button, hop, etc.;
8. Exhibiting immature behavior for age;
9. Being generally disorganized;
10. Having difficulty with paper and pencil tasks;
11. Not being able to put words into sentences by 2½ years;
12. Using speech that cannot be understood 50 percent or more of the time.

also leads to other classifications, including health impaired, mentally retarded, or emotionally disturbed. TBI is not degenerative or congenital. It is caused by an external physical force such as might occur from a car accident or physical abuse. It may be temporary or permanent. Long-term effects of TBI include reduced stamina, **seizures,** headaches, excessive levels of activity, and a sense of helplessness or apathy. Additional problems may affect hearing and vision, memory, attention, IQ, reasoning, problem-solving, word retrieval, motor speech, language comprehension and acquisition, and concept acquisition (Bigge, 1991).

Attention Deficit Hyperactivity Disorder

Children with **attention deficit hyperactivity disorder (ADHD)** generally display cognitive delays. ADHD, historically referred to as attention deficit disorder (ADD), may be viewed as a form of learning disability by educators. In contrast, ADHD is classified as a behavioral disorder in the **Diagnostic and Statistical Manual** of the American Psychiatric Association (DSM-IV, 1994), used by most medical personnel and psychologists for classifying disorders (Forness, 1992; Zentall, 1993). The U.S. Department of Education is considering listing ADHD under a distinct category.

Common characteristics of children with ADHD are serious and persistent difficulties in three specific areas: (1) **attention span,** (2) **impulse control,** and (3) **hyperactivity** (not always present). According to the DSM-IV, for a child to be classified as having ADHD, the child must display for a minimum of six months and by seven years old, at least eight of fourteen specified characteristics. These characteristics are listed in Table 3.6. Classifications range from mild, involving displaying only eight symptoms, to severe, displaying most or all of the symptoms.

Depending on the classification criteria used, between 3 and 20 percent of children are classified as ADHD. It is estimated that ADHD is diagnosed six to nine times more often in boys than in girls (Kauffman, 1989). The most frequently cited

TABLE 3.6 Common Characteristics of Children Classified as Having Attention Deficit Hyperactivity Disorder (ADHD)

Children with ADHD display some or all of these behaviors:

1. Fidget, squirm, or seem restless;
2. Have difficulty remaining seated;
3. Are easily distracted;
4. Have difficulty waiting their turn;
5. Blurt out answers;
6. Have difficulty following instructions;
7. Have difficulty sustaining attention;
8. Shift from one uncompleted task to another;
9. Have difficulty playing quietly;
10. Talk excessively;
11. Interrupt or intrude on others;
12. Do not seem to listen;
13. Lose things;
14. Engage in dangerous actions.

indicators of ADHD for preschool children are excessive levels of activity, such as frequently shifting from one activity to another and talking when they are expected to be quiet. It is estimated that about half of all ADHD cases are diagnosed before the age of four (Dowdy, Patton, Smith, & Polloway, 1995).

ADHD is a long-term disorder that may begin in infancy and extend through adulthood (Sandburg, 1996). Predisposing factors include central nervous system disorder, **cerebral palsy, epilepsy,** and family members who have ADHD or other specific developmental disorders, or who abuse drugs.

Children with ADHD often have problems with organization, have a difficult time following rules, and are often easily distracted. In some cases, though, children with ADHD may be quiet and passive. This type of ADHD is believed be underdiagnosed because it is not disruptive for teachers and parents although it interferes with children's ability to learn. ADHD has negative effects on a child's life at home, school, and within the community (Resnick & McEvoy, 1994). Most children with ADHD have difficulty with academic activities and in interactions with peers and family members.

COMMUNICATION DISORDERS

Communication disorders include **speech and language disorders.** These two major types of communication disorders have distinct characteristics. A child with a speech impairment exhibits one or more of the following disorders:

- **Voice disorders,** including abnormal vocal quality, pitch, loudness, resonance, or duration;
- **Fluency problems,** including interruptions in flow, rate or rhythm of verbal expression (often referred to as **stuttering** or **dysfluency**);
- **Impaired articulation** or abnormal production of speech sounds.

Language disorders include delayed development of comprehension or expression of spoken, written, or signed language. For children to qualify for early intervention services an impairment must exist at such a degree that it adversely affects skills believed to be related to later educational performance. In general, speech disorders require less time in therapy as compared to language delays (McReynolds, 1986). Chapter 8 includes a detailed discussion of speech and language disabilities.

About 72 percent of preschoolers with developmental delays have a speech or language disorder as their primary disability (U.S. Department of Education, 1995). Many preschool children whose primary disability is initially speech or language are reclassified as learning disabled once they enter elementary school. In other cases, preschoolers classified as speech or language delayed do not have a significant speech or language delay by the time they enter elementary school (Lindfors, 1987). Often, it is not possible to determine why a child exhibits a speech or language delay.

SOCIAL-EMOTIONAL DISABILITIES

Children with social-emotional disorders exhibit one or more identifying characteristics over an extended period of time, which are manifested in various environments and include:

1. Difficulty developing or maintaining interpersonal relationships with peers or teachers;
2. Displaying inappropriate types of behavior or feelings;
3. Acting generally unhappy or depressed;
4. Developing physical symptoms or fears related to personal or school problems.

The Council for Exceptional Children (CEC) uses the term **emotional behavioral disorder** (EBD) to classify these children. Fortunately, very few children classified with social-emotional delays are classified as **seriously emotionally disturbed** (U.S. Department of Education, 1995).

Emotional and behavioral disorders are often difficult to identify. There is no single measure or test used to classify children as emotionally or behaviorally disabled. The classification often involves subjective judgments. It is often very difficult to determine which preschool-aged children need intervention because from time to time nearly all children display behaviors not typically found in children their age. In addition, cultural standards vary regarding which types of behavior are appropriate (Kauffman, 1993; Rogoff & Morelli, 1989).

Some children have **transient behavioral disabilities,** behavior patterns that come and go. These behavior types appear to be related to children's reactions to their environment. For example, a child may seem anxious, have trouble sleeping, be tense, or seem depressed. The child has physical problems such as skin reactions, stomach pains, and respiratory disorders. Many things could contribute to such behavior, including separation from a parent, the birth of a sibling, or the death of a family member or close friend. In some cases, a much less significant event may hold great importance for a child and leads to temporary behavior disabilities. For example, children often become depressed or angry after their favorite toy is lost or broken.

Heredity and environment are believed to contribute to occurrences of **social-emotional disorders.** Although causes for these disorders are not always known, evidence suggests that negative family interactions, such as child abuse, are associated with children developing these disorders (Kauffman, 1976).

Parents who abuse alcohol or other drugs are more likely to treat their children aggressively and may result in social-emotional disorders. Children who are victims of sexual abuse are particularly prone to emotional disturbances (Gallico, Burns, & Grob, 1991). Inconsistent or ineffective discipline techniques are also related to incidences of behavioral disorders (Sameroff, Seifer, & Zax, 1982). In addition, children are more likely to display behavioral disorders that other family members also exhibit, which suggests the possibility that some behavioral disorders are inherited.

Social-emotional disorders include behavior that is disruptive to oneself or others. Children with social-emotional disorders tend to have poor impulse control and more frequently become angry. A child who almost always gets into fights when playing with other children is not behaving in a typical fashion. This child is likely to be classified as being socially immature or as having a social-emotional delay. Although there is no single agreed-on strategy for dealing with social-emotional disorders, several methods of behavior management that often are helpful are discussed in Chapter 14.

Children who have behavioral disorders also frequently exhibit an inability to learn, which cannot be explained by known cognitive delays, hearing impairment, learning disability, or **autism** (White, Pillard, & Cleven, 1990). For example, a child who cannot sit at a table during an art activity without grabbing objects away from other children or fighting over materials will often be asked to leave the table. When children behave in ways that result in adults removing them from activities, they frequently miss out on activities designed to enhance learning and miss positive social interactions.

Children with behavioral disorders often have negative **self-esteem,** as compared to other children. Attributes related to negative self-esteem may be seen in their indecisiveness, lack of self-reliance, and inability to accept being wrong. Children with negative self-esteem frequently do *not* attempt activities until they are given specific instructions on how to complete the task. They often blame themselves for mishaps or disappointments and frequently are shy and hesitant in new situations. They may think they cannot handle problem-solving situations (Patterson, Kupersmidt, & Griesler, 1989). Methods designed to help children develop positive self-esteem are discussed in Chapter 15.

Frequently, children with behavioral disorders also manifest speech delays that are directly attributed to the disorders. For example, stress related to these negative patterns may lead to children developing articulation problems or excessive **stuttering (dysfluency).** More extreme language problems may surface, including **echolalia** (repeating back words used by another person) or bizarre speech (making up words or jumbling words in sentences). These language problems interfere with effective communication, creating further difficulty for these children. In some cases, children use these methods to call attention to themselves (Martin, D. A. 1992).

Conduct Disorders

Conduct disorders include intense and consistent hitting, temper tantrums, disobedience, defiance, destruction of property, lack of cooperation, resistance to new experiences or people, being inconsiderate or disruptive, interrupting, being negative, and seeking undue attention. Conduct disorders comprise about 4 to 10 percent of children classified as having a behavioral disorder. Boys are about eight times more likely than girls to be classified as having a conduct disorder (Brandenburg, Friedman, & Silver, 1990).

Anxiety Disorders

Anxiety disorders are another form of behavioral disorder and include being anxious, fearful, tense, timid, bashful, withdrawn, depressed, sad, disturbed, reluctant to participate in activities, easily brought to tears, secretive, and unresponsive to peers or adults. Inadequate or immature behavior types include an overdependency on others that are manifested as delays in self-help skills and interpersonal relationships. Other inappropriate behavior patterns associated with anxiety disorders include disregard for the consequences of one's actions, self-destructiveness, compulsive behavior, and **perseverance** (Walker & Severson, 1990).

Pervasive Developmental Disorders

Another form of behavioral disorder is **pervasive developmental disorder (PDD).** PDD includes impairment in development of social interactions and verbal and nonverbal communication skills. The most severe forms of PDD are **neuroses** and **psychoses,** including **schizophrenia.** Although children are rarely classified using these terms, neuroses and psychoses infrequently are used to describe preschool children.

Psychologists classify autism as a form of behavioral disorder and consider it to be similar to psychoses. Autism is classified under its own category by the U.S. Department of Education (1995) and has been classified under "other health impairments" in the past. Autism is discussed separately later in this chapter. The next section discusses two forms of PDD, neuroses and psychoses.

Neuroses.   Children classified with a **neurosis** appear to have inner conflicts and therefore often have difficulty getting along with other people. These children frequently appear anxious. Their anxieties may be exhibited in the form of a **phobia,** which is an irrational, persistent, and overwhelming fear.

Children with phobias fear objects or situations that present no actual danger, or if there is some danger, it is magnified out of proportion. There are many different phobias, including fear of high places, water, animals, being alone, thunder, or darkness. It is not unusual for children to

have mild fears, but phobias are unusual and are rarely used to classify children before school age (Quay & Werry, 1986).

Neurotic children tend to react to stressful situations with more than a typical amount of sadness and dejection. The child may appear to be dejected, discouraged, and sad for relatively long periods of time. Other forms of neurosis include compulsive or obsessive behavior. These reactions include persistent intrusions of unwanted thoughts, urges, or actions the child is unable to stop. Children are often aware of these thoughts but cannot stop them from occurring. These children appear to be forced to think about something they do not want to think about, such as a fire that nearly got out of control. They carry out behavior they do not really want to do such as constantly checking for smoke or saying they smell smoke (Haring, 1987).

Psychoses.   Preschool-aged children are also rarely classified as having a **psychotic disorder.** Psychotic disorders include loss of contact with reality. Children with a psychotic disorder cannot handle the typical daily demands of childhood. Most children who are psychotic are labeled **schizophrenic.** These children misinterpret reality and sometimes have **delusions** (false, fixed ideas) or **hallucinations** (false sensory impressions). They will withdraw, regress to use immature behavior, or act in some unusual way (Newcomer, 1993).

Oppositional Defiant Disorder

Oppositional defiant disorder (ODD) is a relatively new classification within the DSM-IV. ODD is used to describe children who are often noncompliant and angry (Newcomer, 1993). To be classified as having ODD, the behavior must exist for at least six months, and at least five of the conditions listed in Table 3.7 must consistently occur.

PHYSICAL DISABILITIES

Physical disabilities include perceptual or sensory, and motor disabilities and directed impact self-help

TABLE 3.7 Attributes of Oppositional Defiant Disorder (ODD)

Children with ODD:

1. Readily lose tempers;
2. Frequently argue with adults;
3. Actively defy or refuse adult requests or rules;
4. Deliberately behave in ways that annoy other people;
5. Blame others for their own mistakes;
6. Are easily upset by others;
7. Are angry and resentful;
8. Are vindictive;
9. Use obscene language.

---

and adaptive skills. Children born with physical disabilities are said to have **congenital disabilities.** Some disabilities occur because of accidents, illnesses, or child abuse and are referred to as **acquired disabilities.** Physical disabilities vary from mild to severe and may be transitory (temporary), progressive (gradually becoming more severe), or static (remaining the same). Physical disabilities, in the most severe cases, interfere with even the most simple tasks and may lead to premature death. Several types of physical disabilities are discussed in the next section.

Deafness and Hearing Impairments

Hearing impairment is a sensory, physical disability. Children with hearing impairments comprise about 1.3 percent of all children receiving special education services (U.S. Department of Education, 1995). About 94 percent of all children with hearing impairments have or acquire the disability before age three years.

Hearing impairments range from mild to severe. Children classified as deaf have a severe hearing impairment and cannot process linguistic (language) information through hearing, with or without amplification. Children classified as **hard-of-hearing** or **hearing impaired** have a permanent or fluctuating loss of hearing that adversely affects their children's abilities. For example, a

child who is hearing impaired may not clearly hear some words, which may interfere with the child's ability to say those words correctly.

Most children with moderate to severe levels of hearing impairment require some form of **amplification** to hear most sounds. They often use **sign language** or other alternative communication modifications or require the presence of an interpreter to function successfully in a regular classroom. Most children who are deaf or have hearing impairments manifest language delays during the preschool years (Gatty, 1992). Chapter 9 provides a detailed discussion of children who are deaf or hearing impaired.

Visual Impairments

Children are classified as **visually impaired** when the visual disability adversely affects normal development, even with correction. This classification includes children who have low vision or partial sight and children who are legally blind. Children with visual impairments comprise less than 0.5 percent of all children receiving special education services (Greenwald, 1990).

The prevalence of visual impairments increases with age. It is estimated that 4 of every 10,000 children are visually impaired. About 1 percent are classified as having severe visual impairment. Visual impairment is more prevalent in children from culturally and linguistically diverse backgrounds (Heiner, 1986). In these cases, poor nutrition and infection are believed to contribute to the larger number of incidences of visual impairment (Kirchner & Peterson, 1989). Because this book does not provide a separate chapter dealing with visual impairment, this topic is discussed in greater detail in this section and in Chapter 10.

Children born with visual impairments are referred to as blind or **congenitally visually impaired.** Children who develop visual problems after birth are referred to as **adventitiously visually impaired.** Visual impairments may have genetic causes or may result because of accidents or illnesses. Exposure to drugs and diseases prenatally increases the likelihood of the child being born with or developing a visual impairment. Half of all visual impairments in children are linked to prenatal or genetic factors.

Unlike children who are born blind, children who lose their sight after the age of two generally retain some memory of visual experiences. The later sight loss occurs, the more visual memory of prior images remains. Visual memory appears to enhance the development of concepts and other areas of learning (Warren, 1984).

Children who complain about scratchy or itchy eyes or headaches, rub their eyes excessively, or sit or move unusually close to objects might have a visual impairment. Children with visual impairments frequently exhibit **stereotypic** or odd movements of their hands or have eyes that are watery, red, inflamed, crusty, dull, wrinkled, or cloudy, or have pupils that look gray or cross-eyed. Children who are socially immature, overly self-conscious, withdrawn, overly passive, or overly dependent may behave in such ways because of a visual impairment. Children displaying one or more of the attributes listed above should be referred for an eye examination.

If a disease or abnormality related to the eyes is suspected, the child should be evaluated by an **ophthalmologist,** a medical doctor specializing in eye disorders. Children often receive routine visual evaluations by optometrists. Although **optometrists** are not medical doctors and cannot treat diseases, they can measure vision and prescribe corrective lenses. Optometrists make referrals to ophthalmologists when a disease is suspected (Maloney, 1987). Because occupational therapists frequently provide services to infants and preschool children with visual impairments, a more detailed discussion of visual impairment is provided in Chapter 10.

Orthopedic Impairments

Another major area of physical disability is or-**thopedic impairment,** which hinders development of motor skills, and may negatively affect self-help, adaptive behavior speech and language, and cognitive development. Orthopedic disabilities encompass problems with structures or functioning of the body, and include congenital anomalies (e.g., clubfoot), and impairments caused by disease (e.g., bone tuberculosis) and from other causes (e.g., cerebral palsy, amputation, fractures, burns).

Physical disabilities include impaired neuromuscular development such as **polio, muscular dystrophy,** and **multiple sclerosis.** They also encompass neurological impairments such as spinal cord or brain damage, including **spina bifida, cerebral palsy,** and **seizure disorders.** Children with orthopedic impairment comprise about 1 percent of all children receiving special education services (U.S. Department of Education, 1995).

Many physical disabilities related to injury could be prevented. These include spinal cord injuries most often occurring because of automobile accidents or child abuse. Brain injury or illness may result in tense and inaccurate muscle coordination, nearly constant movement of extremities, lack of muscle tone, and trouble with balance resulting in lunging and lurching while walking.

Children with motor impairments may need orthopedic devices and **physical** and perhaps **occupational therapy.** Frequently, motor disabilities result in speech disorders or delays in acquiring cognitive skills leading to misdiagnosing children as mentally retarded when they are not. Children with physical disabilities may have other disabilities such as mental retardation that lead to a classification of **multiply disabled.**

Children with an unusual physical appearance in the form of orthopedic impairments often suffer the most prejudice and discrimination by society in general because these types of disabilities may be easily seen. People are often embarrassed or uncomfortable when interacting with children who have physical disabilities (Goldfarb, Brotherson, & Summers, 1986). Chapter 10 provides further discussion of types of physical disabilities. Chapters 10 and 11 provide further discussion of services for children with motor delays.

HEALTH IMPAIRMENTS

Children described as **other health impaired** have physical needs that interfere with their development and require ongoing medical attention. These children comprise about 1 percent of all children who receive special education services (U.S. Department of Education, 1995). They have limited strength, vitality, or alertness due to **chronic** or **acute health problems** that interfere with development related to academic abilities.

Health impairments include **heart conditions, tuberculosis, asthma, hemophilia, sickle cell anemia,** cancer, epilepsy, and **diabetes.** (Chapter 4 provides further discussion of the **acquired immunodeficiency syndrome (AIDS),** another major area of health impairment.) It should be noted that many health impairments do *not* interfere with ability to learn, but some health impairments negatively affect development.

Children with health impairments often experience chronic fatigue or suffer from seizures. They frequently miss school due to illness, medical appointments, or special medical treatment. They often are viewed as fragile and adults frequently hesitate to place demands on them (Hutchins & McPherson, 1991; Brown, 1993). For example, asthma frequently causes coughing, shortness of breath, and wheezing. Some children with severe cases of asthma cannot participate in school activities that include outdoor field trips or play.

Children with health impairments often require special methods of teaching, therapy, and equipment (Hobbs, Perrin, & Ireys, 1984). For example, a child with asthma may be provided with opportunities for physical movement indoors rather than outdoors and require a nurse to be on staff to administer medicines.

Medications designed to help control symptoms related to various health impairments may result in troublesome side effects including headaches, tremors, stomach aches, lethargy, and reduced ability to concentrate (Martin, R. P. 1992). For example, allergies may be aggravated by environmental conditions such as presence of animals, chalk, molds, plant, soap, clay, certain dyes in paint, chemicals, and foods (Kauffman & Lichtenstein, 1986). A child might not be able to attend school unless modifications are made that eliminate many of the substances to which the child is allergic. Individuals who interact with children who have health impairments should obtain as much information about the child's specific health needs as soon as possible.

The next section describes some of the many health impairments that may negatively affect development. It should be noted that a variety of illnesses or diseases have similar symptoms and certain symptoms occur when there is no illness or disease. For example, a child who has been jogging may experience leg cramps, flushed face, and rapid pulse. These reactions are also symptoms of a diabetic coma.

Epilepsy

Epilepsy is a health impairment consisting of recurrent seizures or convulsions. It is the most common neurological impairment of children. Many different types of seizures may occur, and some are more likely to occur when the child has high fevers.

Major seizures are referred to as **grand mal** and may cause children to fall, lose consciousness, become stiff, drool, urinate, or have bowel movements. Breathing may be irregular, causing a pale or bluish skin color. Seizures generally last only a few minutes although they may last much longer. After this type of seizure children are often confused or complain of a headache and want to go to sleep. Parents should be notified when these types of seizures occur and should have the child seen by a medical doctor as soon as possible (Girvin, 1992).

Minor seizures are referred to as **petit mal** and include staring spells lasting a few seconds. During this type of seizure eyes blink rhythmically and the child responds as if the seizure never occurred. The seizures occur frequently and give the appearance that the child is momentarily "day dreaming." In most cases, both types of seizures can be fully or partially controlled with anticonvulsant medication (Sillanpaa, 1992).

Cystic Fibrosis

Cystic fibrosis, a genetic disorder, primarily involves the lungs and digestive tract. Children who have cystic fibrosis may live to early adulthood although this disease is eventually fatal. Most preschool children with cystic fibrosis appear normal except for a slight cough, although a more severely involved child may cough regularly, breathe hard, and tire easily.

Children with cystic fibrosis frequently have thin arms and legs, a barrel chest and an abdomen that protrudes. They often eat more and are more susceptible to bacterial infections such as pneumonia and bronchitis than are other children. Their cough is not contagious, but they are very susceptible to other children's infections (Hobbs & Perrin, 1985). Children with cystic fibrosis take antibiotics, pancreatic enzymes before each meal, intermittent aerosol therapy to aid breathing, vitamins, and receive physical therapy. Most children with this disease may engage in typical daily activities but should be allowed to rest if they become fatigued.

Cancer

Fortunately, the incidence of cancer during infancy and preschool years is very small. Next to medical care, the greatest need for families and children who experience cancer is emotional support. Families often react with shock, disbelief, denial, and fear. They frequently respond, "This can't be happening to my child" or "My child is too young to die." Family members often need help maintaining a positive and hopeful attitude.

Children who have cancer may frequently miss school because of numerous trips to doctors and hospitals. They may receive painful medical treatments that have negative side effects, including loss of speech or motor abilities that may require speech and language, occupational, or physical therapy. Children who suffer from cancer should be treated as normally as possible.

Congenital Heart Defects

Congenital heart (cardiac) defects are a major cause of death in early infancy. Fortunately, though, many defects may be corrected or improved with surgery. Heart defects are frequently found in combination with other conditions such as **Down syndrome** or **congenital rubella syndrome.** Heart defects are often abnormal openings between the two sides of the heart that result in poorly oxygenated blood mixing with freshly oxygenated blood. This means the heart must work harder to provide enough freshly oxygenated blood to the body. Heart defects may be related to narrowing of major blood vessels.

Children with heart conditions tend to have poor weight gain, irregular breathing patterns, unusual fatigue, and a bluish tinge to the skin, especially around the lips, fingers, and toes. Most children with heart diseases can be allowed to lead relatively normal lives (Irvin, Kennell, & Klaus, 1982).

Diabetes

Diabetes is related to the inability of an individual to use the body's sugar. It is controllable but not curable. Control is achieved by striking a balance between receiving insulin, eating the right foods, and exercising. Treatment includes eliminating foods high in sugar or starch content such as cake, candy, sugarcoated cereals, cookies, jellies, syrups, puddings, and sodas. Fortunately, very few young children have diabetes, but those who do need appropriate substitutes for many of the refreshments served at preschools and events such as parties. They often also need to eat at specific times of the day.

Two serious situations associated with diabetes are **insulin reaction** and **diabetic coma.** An insulin reaction is due to a lack of enough blood sugar. A diabetic coma occurs when there is too much sugar. Service providers should watch for signs of an undiagnosed case of diabetes: extreme thirst, frequent urination, and excessive appetite without weight gain. More severe symptoms include nausea, vomiting, abdominal pain, and apathy. A diabetic coma could occur if the child does not receive insulin or has a resistance to insulin. Stresses on the body such as infection, injury, diarrhea, or emotional upset may contribute to a diabetic coma (Association for the Care of Children's Health, 1984). Early warning signs of insulin reactions and diabetic coma are provided in Table 3.8.

Hemophilia

Hemophilia is a bleeding disorder most frequently affecting boys and occurring because there is not enough clotting factor (a substance that stops bleeding) in the body. It is not curable but can be controlled by replacing the clotting factors. Children with hemophilia bleed a great deal even from minor accidents. Children with hemophilia more readily bleed internally, including in the area of the brain. In this case, the child may have a severe headache or mental confusion. In the most severe cases, bleeding internally around the brain leads to death. Children with hemophilia should not play with toys or objects with sharp edges, should be encouraged to play in grassy rather than hard surface areas, and should avoid intense physical contact.

Asthma

Asthma is one of the most common chronic health impairments and the leading cause of school absences. It is related to difficulty in breathing because of narrowing of the bronchial tubes or airways. Asthma attacks often are physically painful and frightening. Asthma attacks usually occur after children are near something to which they are allergic, expose themselves to cold air, or experience a stressful event. Fortunately, relatively few preschool children have severe asthma attacks.

Cytomegalovirus

The **cytomegalovirus (CMV)** is a form of herpes, a **venereal disease,** that could lead to brain damage, blindness, and hearing loss. About 1 percent of all fetuses contract this disease and 10 to 15 percent of these develop CMV, which is transferred through bodily fluids. To help prevent spread of the disease, child care providers should frequently wash their hands, dispose of diapers in sanitary ways, and keep toys and play areas clean (Children's Hospital of St. Paul, 1984). There are many other potential health impairments not covered in this chapter that could affect development. The next section provides a discussion of autism, which was classified as a health impairment, as well as a social-emotional disorder, in the past but is now classified separately.

AUTISM

While *autism* was recognized in 1990 by the U.S. Department of Education as a separate category, psychologists and many medical professionals view autism as a behavioral disorder.

TABLE 3.8 Early Warning Signs of an Insulin Reaction and a Diabetic Coma

INSULIN REACTION	DIABETIC COMA
dizziness	extreme thirst
shakiness	dry tongue
trembling	fruity odor to the breath
nervousness	deep and labored breathing
hunger	loss of appetite
excessive perspiration	blurring of vision
nausea	cramps in the legs or stomach
headache	a flushed face
fatigue	dry skin
drowsiness	rapid pulse

Autism affects verbal and nonverbal communication and social interactions. It is generally manifested within the first three years life and occurs at all intellectual levels (0.2 percent of children, with occurrence in boys three times more likely). Children with autism often engage in repetitive activities (e.g., staring or excessive blinking) and movements (e.g., spinning wheels on a toy, flapping hands), resist changes in routines, and have unusual responses to sensory stimuli (Cohen & Donnellen, 1987).

About half of all children who are autistic do not speak. Those who do speak typically have immature patterns of speech, limited understanding of ideas, and frequently use words without the attachment of their usual meaning (Lovaas, 1977). Children who are autistic often demonstrate unusual ways of relating to people and objects. More specifically, they may act deaf, resist learning, show a lack of fear of real dangers, resist changes in routine, be unreceptive to physical affection, avoid eye contact, sustain repetitive action patterns such as rocking, head banging, and hand twisting, and may bite, scratch, or hit themselves (Batshaw & Perret, 1986). Chapter 14 includes a section on methods for working with children who are autistic. The next section provides a description of the last major category, multiple disabilities.

MULTIPLE DISABILITIES

Children with **multiple disabilities** have two or more disabilities resulting in multisensory or motor deficiencies and developmental lags in the cognitive, social-emotional, or motor areas, the combination of which interferes with learning. Evaluation of children with multiple disabilities is complex and often involves many different specialists. About 2 percent of all children receiving special education services are classified as multiply disabled (U.S. Department of Education, 1995). Multiple disabilities causing such severe educational problems that a child cannot be accommodated in special education solely for one

impairment are referred to as concomitant impairments. Children with multiple disabilities typically suffer the most from negative reactions of others.

INTERACTIONS WITH CHILDREN WHO HAVE DEVELOPMENTAL DELAYS

Parents whose children do not develop at the normal rate frequently ask themselves, "What went wrong?" Disabilities are rarely expected and no family is immune. Children with disabilities place extra demands on the family in terms of time, social stigma, psychological well-being, family relationships, economic resources, and freedom of movement (Seligman & Darling, 1989). Families often need financial support and physical help caring for these children. They need help not only from their families but also from the entire community (Swan & Morgan, 1993).

Parents often blame themselves for their child's disability. Self-blame is natural but not helpful because causes of disabilities are complex and rarely due to a single factor. Parents frequently rush from doctor to doctor subjecting their child to a never-ending set of assessments in an attempt to "know" what caused the developmental delay. In some cases, evaluation leads to a diagnosis, and this diagnosis may be helpful in providing optimal intervention for the child. In most cases, reasons for delays are not determined (Thurman & Widerstrom, 1990). It then becomes more important to focus on accurately assessing the child's level of functioning and finding ways to provide experiences that may aid the child's development rather than focusing on why the delay occurred.

Parents' reactions to the realization that their child is delayed is highly individualistic. Parents, however, at some point typically respond to feelings of denial, anger, grief, guilt, and shame (Drotar, Baskiewicz, Irvin, Kennell, & Klaus, 1975). These parents had dreams of the perfect family, and these dreams probably did not include a child with a developmental delay. Children who are developmentally delayed are slower at reaching developmental milestones, and some may never achieve them. Coming to terms with this is extremely difficult for many families. Chapter 5 provides further discussion of these reactions.

People may stare at or avoid children who have special needs or make comments such as, "How sad?" "What do they have?" "It must be very hard for you," "What's wrong with him?" or "I don't know how you do it." Other children may avoid or laugh at these children or make cruel remarks or jokes about them (Darling, 1983). These interactions frequently result in children with special needs and members of their family being sad or angry. These feelings may lead children with disabilities to isolation just at the time they need the most support.

Lack of knowledge about children with developmental delays often results in negative and prejudicial reactions. Frequently, people fear they will offend or physically hurt a child who is developmentally delayed. Individuals often avoid interactions rather than taking such a risk. It is important that people are honest with themselves about their own stereotypes, prejudices, and fears. In doing so, they are better prepared to understand and accept people who have disabilities. For example, a child who is in a wheelchair makes some people uncomfortable and they may avoid interaction with this child. These feelings are real and understandable but lead to less interaction with a child who really needs guidance and care.

Children with special needs and their families have feelings and needs similar to other children or families. They need an opportunity, for example, to talk about the way people react to them and to learn effective strategies for dealing with these people and their reactions (Gargiulo, 1985).

It is important to avoid using labels that degrade or lead to discrimination. Some labels are helpful because they provide common language with which to categorize needs. These categories help determine appropriate services. Children, however, must always be seen as children first. They need to be viewed as children with a disability rather than "disabled" children.

CONCLUSION

Children have a variety of special needs. Delays in one area often impact development in other areas. To adequately meet needs of children with developmental delays it is important to become familiar with the various types of disabilities and the characteristics associated with each. Education is crucial for eliminating misconceptions about certain disabilities. It is important to avoid using labels to stereotype children. Appropriate use of labels often allows for assessment of the most appropriate services. Educators should seek information about various types of disabilities and available therapies or intervention strategies.

The next chapter provides discussion of growing areas of concern, including cocaine and alcohol abuse, and HIV/AIDS. These environmental effects often result in developmental delays in all majors areas. Lack of knowledge and misconceptions about these environmental factors prevents appropriate early intervention for children who are affected.

CHAPTER SUMMARY

- When working with children who have special needs, it is important to remember that they require special services, but in most cases they are more like other children than they are different.
- Development is affected by genetics, such as chromosomal abnormalities, and by environmental factors, such as accidents, health problems, and parental behavior.
- Signs of developmental delays include slower rates of skills acquisition and atypical physical characteristics.
- Developmental delays occur in cognitive, speech and language, motor (including self-help and adaptive behavior), and social-emotional areas.
- Interactions with children who have special needs affects the development of these children. Education is key to relieving misconceptions about certain disabilities that often

lead to discrimination toward individuals with special needs.

REVIEW QUESTIONS

1. What are the major signs of developmental delays?
2. How might lower socioeconomic status contribute to developmental delays?
3. What are the characteristics of major areas of developmental delays?
4. Under which major classifications are children who are autistic and ADHD found? What characteristics do children with ADHD have in common?

SUGGESTED STUDENT ACTIVITIES

1. Contact your local school district, department of health, or state education department and request information regarding services for children with special needs.
2. Interview a parent of a child who is developmentally delayed. Ask the parent about the effect the disability has had on the child and family.
3. Volunteer your time in a program designed to meet the needs of preschool-aged children with special needs.

ADDITIONAL READINGS

Batshaw, M. L. (Ed.). (1991). *Your child has a disability.* Boston: Little, Brown and Company.

Seligman, M., & Darling, R. B. (1989). *Ordinary families, special children: A systems approach to childhood disability.* New York: Guilford Press.

Simpson, R. L., & Zionis, P. (1992). *Autism: Information and resources for parents, families, and professionals.* Austin, TX: Pro-Ed.

Stowe, R. (1991). *Not the end of the world.* New York: Pantheon/Random House.

ADDITIONAL RESOURCES

American Academy of Child and Adolescent Psychiatry
3615 Wisconsin Avenue, N.W.
Washington, DC 20016

American Academy of Pediatrics
P.O. Box 927
Elk Grove Village, IL 60007

American Association on Mental Deficiency
1719 Kalorama Road, N.W.
Washington, DC 20009

American Association of Psychiatric Services
   for Children
2075 Scottsville Road
Rochester, NY 14623

American Cancer Society
1599 Clifton Road
Atlanta, GA 30329

American Diabetes Association
National Service Center
P.O. Box 25757
1660 Duke Street
Alexandria, VA 22313

American Heart Association
7320 Greenville Avenue
Dallas, TX 75231

American Pediatrics Society
450 Clarkson Avenue
Brooklyn, NY 11203

American Psychological Association (APA)
1200 17th Street N.W.
Washington, DC 20036

Association for the Care of Children's Health (ACCH)
3615 Wisconsin Avenue, N.W.
Washington, DC 20016

Asthma and Allergy Foundation of America
1717 Massachusetts Avenue, Suite 305
Washington, DC 20036

Autism National Committee
7 Tereasa Circle
Arlington, MA 02174

Children's Defense Fund
122 C Street, N.W.
Washington, DC 20001

Children with Attention Deficit Disorders (Ch.ADD)
499 N.W. 70th Avenue, Suite 308
Plantation, FL 33317

Child Welfare League of America, Inc.
440 1st Street, N.W.
Washington, DC 20001

Council for Children with Behavioral Disorders
Council for Exceptional Children
1920 Association Drive
Reston, VA 22091

Cystic Fibrosis Foundation
6931 Arlington Road, Suite 200
Bethesda, MD 20814

Epilepsy Foundation of America
4351 Garden City Drive
Landover, MD 20785

March of Dimes Birth Defects Foundation
1275 Mamaroneck Avenue
White Plains, NY 10605

National Alliance for the Mentally Ill: Children's and
    Adolescent's Network
2101 Wilson Boulevard, Suite 302
Arlington, VA 22314

National Association of Developmental Disabilities
    Council
1234 Massachusetts Avenue, N.W.
Washington, DC 20057

National Council on Disabilities
800 Independence Avenue, S.W., Suite 814
Washington, DC 20591

National Cystic Fibrosis Research Foundation
3379 Peachtree Road N.E.
Atlanta, GA 30320

National Down Syndrome Congress
1800 Dempster Street
Park Ridge, IL 60068

National Down Syndrome Society
70 W. 40th Street
New York, NY 10018

National Federation for Asthma
P.O. Box 30069
Tucson, AZ 85751

National Hemophilia Foundation
35 West 39th Street
New York, NY 10018

National Society of Autistic Children
169 Tampa Avenue
Albany, NY 12208

National Society for Children and Adults with Autism
1234 Massachusetts Avenue, N.W., Suite 1017
Washington, DC 20005

REFERENCES

American Psychiatric Association. (1993). *Diagnostic and statistical manual of mental disorders* (4th ed.). Washington, DC: Author.

Association for the Care of Children's Health (ACCH). (1984). *Home care for children: An annotated bibliography.* Washington, DC: Author.

Bagnato, S. J., & Neisworth, J. T. (1981). *Linking developmental assessment and curricula: Prescriptions for early intervention.* Rockville, MD: Aspen.

Bagnato, S. J., & Neisworth, J. T. (1991). *Assessment for early intervention: Best practices for professionals.* New York: Guilford Press.

Bailey, D. B., & Wolery, M. (1992). *Teaching infants and preschoolers with disabilities* (2nd Ed.) Columbus OH: Merrill.

Batshaw, M. C., & Perret, Y. M. (1986). *Children with handicaps: A medical primer* (2nd ed.). Baltimore, MD: Paul H. Brookes.

Bee, H. (1995). *The developing child* (7th ed.). New York: Harper Collins.

Beirne–Smith, M., Patton, J. R., & Ittenbach, R. (1994). *Mental retardation* (4th ed.). Columbus, OH: Merrill.

Bender, W. N. (1992). *Learning disabilities: Characteristics, identification, and teaching strategies.* Boston, MA: Allyn and Bacon.

Bennett, F. C. (1984). Neurodevelopmental outcomes of low birth weight infants. In V. C. Kelley (Ed.), *Practices of pediatrics* (pp. 1–24). Philadelphia, PA: Harper and Row.

Bigge, J. L. (1991). *Teaching individuals with physical and multiple disabilities* (3rd ed.). Columbus, OH: Merrill/Macmillan.

Brandenburg, N. A., Friedman, R. M., & Silver, S. E. (1990). The epidemiology of childhood psychiatric disorders: Prevalence findings from recent studies. *Journal of the American Academy of Child and Adolescent Psychiatry, 29,* 76–83.

Brown, R. T. (1993). An introduction to the special series: Pediatric chronic illness. *Journal of Learning Disabilities, 26,* 4–6.

Campbell, F. A., & Ramey, C. T. (1991). *The Carolina Abecedarian Project.* Paper presented at the biennial meeting of the Society for Research in Child Development. Seattle, WA.

Capron, C., & Duyme, M. (1989). Assessment of the effects of socio-economic status on IQ in a full cross-fostering study. *Nature,* August 17, 552–553.

Carr, J. (1995). *Down's Syndrome: Children growing up.* NY: Cambridge University Press.

Children's Hospital of St. Paul. (1984). *CMV: Diagnosis, prevention and treatment.* St. Paul, MN: Author.

Cicchetti, D., & Beeghly, M. (1990). *Children with Down Syndrome.* NY: Cambridge University Press.

Cohen, D. J., & Donnellen, A. M. (Eds.). (1987). *Handbook of autism and pervasive developmental disorders.* Silver Springs, MD: Winston.

Cravioto, J., & DeLicardie, E. R. (1975). Environmental and nutritional deprivation in children with learning disabilities. In W. M. Cruickshank & D. P. Hallahan (Eds.), *Perceptual and learning disabilities in children. Vol. 2: Research and theory.* Syracuse, NY: Syracuse University Press.

Darling, R. B. (1983). *Families against society: A study of reactions to children with birth defects.* Beverly Hills, CA: Sage.

Deiner, P. L. (1993). *Resources for teaching children with diverse abilities.* Fort Worth, TX: Harcourt Brace Jovanovich.

Dowdy, C. A., Patton, J. R., Smith, T. E. C., & Polloway, E. A. (1995). *Attention deficit disorder: Practical considerations.* Austin, TX: Pro-Ed.

Drotar, D., Baskiewicz, A., Irvin, N., Kennell, J. A., & Klaus, M. H. (1975). The adaption of parents to the birth of an infant with a congenital malformation: A hypothetical model. *Pediatrics, 56,* 710–717.

Evrand, J. R., & Scola, P. S. (1990). Preparation for parenthood. In S. M. Pueschel & J. A. Mulick (Eds.), *Prevention of developmental disabilities* (pp. 27–35). Baltimore, MD: Paul H. Brookes.

Forness, S. R. (1992). Attention deficit disorders, academic functioning and stimulant medication. *School Psychology Review, 21,* 12–20.

Gallico, R. P., Burns, T. J., & Grob, C. S. (1991). *Emotional and behavioral problems in children with learning disabilities.* San Diego, CA: Singular Publishing Group.

Gargiulo, R. M. (1985). *Working with parents of exceptional children: A guide to professionals.* Boston: Houghton Mifflin.

Gatty, J. C. (1992). Teaching speech to hearing-impaired children. *The Volta Review, 94,* 49–61.

Girvin, J. P. (1992). Is epilepsy a progressive disorder? *Journal of Epilepsy, 5,* 94–104.

Goldfarb, L. A., Brotherson, M. J., & Summers, J. A. (1986). *Meeting the challenge of disability or chronic illness: A family guide.* Baltimore, MD: Paul H. Brookes.

Greenwald, M. J. (1990). Visual development in infancy and childhood. *Pediatric Clinics of North America, 30,* 977–993.

Hakuta, K., & Garcia, E. E. (1989). Bilingualism and education. *American Psychologist, 44,* 374–379.

Haring, N. (Ed.). (1987). *Assessing and managing behavior disabilities.* Seattle, WA: University of Washington Press.

Heiner, D. (1986). *Learning to look: A handbook for parents of low vision infants and young children.* East Lansing, MI: International Institute for the Visually Impaired.

Herbst, D. S., & Baird, P. A. (1983). Nonspecific mental retardation in British Columbia as ascertained through a registry. *American Journal of Mental Deficiency, 87,* 506–513.

Hobbs, N., & Perrin, J. M. (1985). *Issues in care of children with chronic illness.* San Francisco, CA: Jossey-Bass.

Hobbs, N., Perrin, J. M., & Ireys, H. T. (1984). *Chronically ill children and their families.* San Francisco, CA: Jossey-Bass.

Hutchins, V., & McPherson, M. (1991). National agenda for children with special health needs: Social policy for the 90's through the 21st century. *American Psychologist, 46,* 141–143.

Irvin, M. A., Kennell, J. A., & Klaus, M. H. (1982). Caring for the parent of an infant with a congenital malformation. In M. H. Klaus & J. H. Kennell (Eds.), *Parent infant bonding* (2nd ed., pp. 227–258). St. Louis, MO: Mosby.

Kauffman, J. M. (1976). Nineteenth century views of children's behavioral disorders: Historical contributions and continuing issues. *Journal of Special Education, 10,* 335–349.

Kauffman, J. M. (1989). *Characteristics of behavioral disorders of children and youth* (4th ed.). Columbus, OH: Merrill.

Kauffman, J. M. (1993). *Characteristics of emotional and behavioral disorders of children and youth* (5th ed.). New York: Macmillan.

Kauffman, J. M., & Lichtenstein, K. A. (1986). *The family as care manager: Home care coordination for medically fragile children.* Millersville, MD: Coordinating Center for Home and Community Care (CCHCC).

Kendall, F. E. (1996). *Diversity in the Classroom: New approaches to the education of young children.* NY: Teachers College Press.

Kirchner, C., & Peterson, R. (1989). Estimates of race: Ethnic groups in the U.S. visually impaired and blind population. In C. Kirchner (Ed.), *Data on blindness and visual impairment in the U.S.: A resource manual in social demographic characteristics, education, employment and income, and service delivery* (2nd ed.). pp. 101–109. NY: Foundation for the Blind.

Lindfors, J. W. (1987). *Children's language and learning* (2nd ed.). Englewood Cliffs, NJ: Prentice-Hall.

Lovaas, O. I. (1977). *The autistic child: Language development through behavior modification.* New York: Irvington.

Lovitt, T. C. (1989). *Introduction to learning disabilities.* Boston, MA: Allyn and Bacon.

Maloney, P. L. (1987). *Practical guidance for parents of the visually handicapped preschooler.* Springfield, IL: Chas. C. Thomas.

Martin, D. A. (1992). Children in peril: A mandate for health-care policies for low-income children. *Family and Community Health, 15*(1), 75–90.

Martin, R. P. (1992). Child temperament effects on special education: Process and outcomes. *Exceptionality, 3,* 99–115.

McReynolds, L. V. (1986). Functional articulation disorders. In G. H. Shames & E. H. Wiig (Eds.), *Human communications disorders* (2nd ed.). Columbus, OH: Merrill/Macmillan.

Mercer, C. D. (1992). *Students with learning disabilities.* New York: Merrill.

Mercer, C. D., Algozzine, B., & Trifiletti, J. (1979). Early identification—an analysis of the research. *Learning Disability Quarterly, 2,* 12–24.

Monolascino, F. J., & Stark, J. A. (Eds.). (1988). *Preventive and creative intervention in mental retardation.* Baltimore, MD: Paul H. Brookes.

National Council on Disability (1993). *Meeting the unique needs of minorities with disabilities.* Washington, DC: Author.

Newcomer, P. L. (1993). *Understanding and teaching emotionally disturbed children and adolescents* (2nd ed.). Austin, TX: Pro-Ed.

Patterson, C. J., Kupersmidt, J. B., & Griesler, P. C. (1989). *Self-concepts of children in regular education and in special education classes.* Unpublished

manuscript, Virginia Behavior Disorders Project, University of Virginia, Charlottesville, VA.

Patton, J. R., Payne, J. S., & Beirne-Smith, M. (1990). *Mental retardation* (3rd ed.). Columbus, OH: Merrill.

Polloway, E. A., & Patton, J. R. (1993). *Strategies for teaching learners with special needs.* Columbus, OH: Merrill.

Quay, H. C., & Werry, J. S. (Eds.). (1986). *Psychopathological disorders of childhood* (3rd ed.). New York: Wiley.

Ramey, C. T., & Campbell, F. A. (1984). Preventive education for high-risk children: Cognitive consequences of the Carolina Abecedarian Project. Special Issue: *Journal of Mental Deficiency, 88*(5), 515–523.

Resnick, R. J., & McEvoy, K. (1994). *Attention deficit/hyperactivity disorder: Abstracts of the psychological and behavioral literature, 1971–1994.* Washington, DC: American Psychological Association.

Rogoff, B., & Morelli, G. (1989). Perspectives on children's development from cultural psychology. *American Psychologist, 44,* 343–348.

Sameroff, A. J., Seifer, R., & Zax, M. (1982). Early development of children at risk for emotional disorders. *Monographs of the Society for Research in Child Development, 47,* serial no. 199.

Sandberg, S. (Ed.). (1996). *Hyperactivity disorders of childhood.* NY: Cambridge University Press.

Savage, R. C. (1988). *Introduction to educational issues for students who have suffered traumatic brain injury. An educator's manual: What educators need to know about students with traumatic brain injury.* Southborough, MA: Author.

Seligman, M., & Darling, R. B. (1989). *Ordinary families, special children: A systems approach to childhood disability.* New York: Guilford Press.

Sillanpaa, M. (1992). Epilepsy in children: Prevalence, disability, and handicap. *Epilepsia, 33,* 444–449.

Smith, T. E. C., Finn, D. M., & Dowdy, C. A. (1993). *Teaching students with mixed disabilities.* Fort Worth, TX: Harcourt Brace Jovanovich.

Swan, W. W., & Morgan, J. L. (1993). *Collaborating for comprehensive services for young children and their families.* Baltimore, MD: Paul H. Brookes.

Thurman, S. K., & Widerstrom, A. H. (1990). *Infants and young children with special needs.* Baltimore, MD: Paul H. Brookes.

U.S. Department of Education (1995). *17th annual report to congress on the implementation of IDEA.* Washington, DC: U.S. Government Printing Office.

Wachs, T. D., & Gruen, G. E. (1982). *Early experiences and human development.* New York: Plenum Press.

Walker, H. M., & Severson, H. H. (1990). *Systematic screening of behavior disorders (SSBD): A multiple gating procedure.* Longmont, CO: Sorpis West.

Warren, D. H. (1984). *Blindness and early childhood development* (2nd ed.). New York: American Foundation for the Blind.

White, D., Pillard, E. D., & Cleven, C. A. (1990). The influence of state definition of behavioral disorders on the numbers of children served under PL94–142. *Remedial and Special Education, 11,* 17–22.

Zentall, S. S. (1993). Research on the educational implications of attention deficit hyperactivity disorder. *Exceptional Children, 60*(2), 143–153.

CHAPTER 4

DEADLY EPIDEMICS:
FETAL ALCOHOL SYNDROME,
COCAINE, AND AIDS

SHERRY DINGMAN, PH.D.
AWILDA VELEZ, M.A.
MELANIE A. GARDNER, B.A.

ABOUT THE AUTHORS

Dr. Sherry Dingman is a full-time faculty member in the psychology department at Marist College in Poughkeepsie, New York. She received her Ph.D. in 1991 from the University of Montana from the Department of Psychology where she conducted research in biopsychology. While at the University of Montana, she also completed coursework for certification in early childhood intervention. She is currently involved in research with the local health department on topics that include the HIV epidemic, public nursing interventions for at-risk newborns, and Lyme disease vaccine trials. In addition, she studies language disorders and conducts cross-cultural studies. She is the mother of six children.

Awilda Velez received her bachelor's degree in May, 1994 and her master's in May 1995, in psychology from Marist College. She was the college's nominee for a Truman Scholarship. Although she is interested in making a contribution to the Hispanic community as a counselor and researcher, she first plans to pursue post-doctoral training in clinical neuropsychology. She worked

as a research assistant for the New York State Institute for Basic Research in Developmental Disabilities and as an intern at a center for individuals with developmental delays. She is currently employed as a family advocate at a home for children with special social and emotional needs.

Melanie Gardner received her bachelor's degree in psychology and special education in January 1994 from Marist College. She plans to pursue a Ph.D. in the area of biopsychology and is interested in the neuropathology of learning disorders. She is currently employed as a special education teacher working with students who have learning disabilities.

CHAPTER KEY POINTS

- Mothers who consume alcohol, use cocaine, or have human immunodeficiency virus (HIV) increase the risk of developmental delays in their unborn child.
- Exposure to fetal alcohol syndrome (FAS), cocaine, and pediatric AIDS affects children's development in certain characteristic ways.
- There are specific criteria for classifying children as having FAS and fetal alcohol effects (FAE).
- Children exposed to cocaine may be born prematurely and have long-term developmental delays.
- Certain precautions must be taken to help children with pediatric acquired immunodeficiency syndrome (AIDS) avoid other illnesses. These children often fail to thrive and have progressive infections of the brain.
- Specific early intervention practices help enhance the development of children exposed to alcohol or cocaine prenatally or who are at risk of developing pediatric AIDS.

Earlier chapters provided descriptions of federal laws, typical developmental delays, services related to children, and the importance of collaboration of services for children with developmental delays. Children exposed to **cocaine,** alcohol, and the **human immunodeficiency virus (HIV)** prenatally are likely to have developmental delays and will need case coordination and services (Levine, 1992). They will also need their care providers to

work effectively with the professionals who provide services for them and their families.

OVERVIEW OF PRENATAL EXPOSURE TO ALCOHOL, COCAINE, AND HIV/AIDS

As discussed in Chapter 3, there are many environmental reasons why children are at risk for acquiring developmental delays. This chapter provides information about the impact of alcohol, cocaine, and the human immunodeficiency virus (HIV). The children and their families discussed in this chapter will almost certainly need service coordination and effective parent–professional relationships as discussed in Chapters 5 and 6.

An increasing number of children are affected by controllable environmental factors that include cocaine, alcohol, and HIV. Children born with HIV or intrauterine exposure to cocaine tend to come from the ranks of the "underclass." Many are the children of poor and minority families. Only recently have enough data been compiled regarding these environmental factors for society to begin to recognize the profound consequences of such factors (Groze, Haines–Simeon, & Barth, 1994; Zuckerman & Bresnahan, 1991). Knowledge about these environmental influences help service providers more adequately meet the needs of children and family members influenced by them. The discussion of these factors begins with prenatal exposure to alcohol.

PRENATAL EXPOSURE TO ALCOHOL

Alcohol, a legal and socially acceptable drug, takes its toll across all socioeconomic classes and ethnic groups. About 6 million women in the U.S. are **alcoholics** or **alcohol abusers**—far more than those who use cocaine. Children exposed to alcohol prenatally are placed at developmental risk.

Developmental Disabilities Related to Prenatal Exposure to Alcohol

Exposure to alcohol prenatally may result in **fetal alcohol syndrome (FAS)** or **fetal alcohol effects (FAE).** FAS was first used in 1973 to describe a collection of mental, physical, and behavioral characteristics of children born to mothers who consumed alcohol during their pregnancies (Jones, Smith, Ulleland, & Streissguth, 1973). The probability that the child of a woman who is an alcoholic will be born with FAS ranges from 2 to 8

percent in most studies (Zuckerman & Bresnahan, 1991). Today, about one to two of every 1,000 infants born in this country suffers from FAS. It is estimated that another three to five of every 1,000 infants have symptoms of FAE.

These statistics for the rate of incidence of FAS and FAE may underestimate the extent of the problem. Untrained observers often notice the unusual facial features of children with FAS, but they either do not correctly diagnose the condition or do not record their observations. One investigation using the medical records of infants born to alcohol users revealed a 100 percent failure rate in diagnosing FAS though the features of FAS were present (Clarren & Smith, 1978).

About 25 percent of women in the U.S. report drinking during the first few months of their pregnancy. Another 6 percent report drinking an average of two or more alcoholic beverages daily throughout their pregnancy. A concerted effort has been made to warn women of the dangers of drinking while pregnant. These warnings, however, may not be presented in the settings where they would be most effective.

A survey of New Jersey physicians revealed a reluctance to discuss alcohol consumption with pregnant patients. This reluctance was related to the physicians' own use of alcohol, lack of training in discussing the problem, poor awareness of the problem, denial that FAS occurs in private practice, disinterest, time limitations, fear of offending the patient, and the belief that patients will not be honest about their alcohol consumption even when the issue is raised (Donovan, 1991).

Regardless of her past drinking history, a woman who abstains from alcohol throughout her pregnancy is not likely to give birth to a child with FAS or FAE. Recent investigations have revealed, though, that alcohol consumption by fathers before conception may influence fetal development. Male alcoholics could have toxic substances present in their semen, which may cause abnormal development of their child. Paternal alcoholism has been linked to low birth weight and might result in the father transmitting damaged genetic material to his offspring (Anderson, 1982).

Characteristics of Children with FAS and FAE

Criteria for diagnosis of FAS include a minimum of three symptoms to be present in the child. These are central nervous system dysfunctions, growth retardation, and facial abnormalities (Clarren & Smith, 1978; Cooper, 1987; Overholser, 1990). The related syndrome, FAE, may occur if the developing fetus is exposed to intermittent use or lower levels of alcohol. FAE manifests itself in learning or behavioral problems but does not include structural abnormalities. Although FAE is related to developmental delays, FAS is believed to create far more serious outcomes.

FAS and FAE result from parts of the body and brain failing to develop normally because of exposure to alcohol prenatally. As with other drugs, alcohol is not easily eliminated by the body systems of the unborn child. The alcohol consumed by a pregnant woman crosses the placenta and enters the body of her developing offspring within minutes, where it will be present in trace amounts up to twenty-four hours (American Academy of Pediatrics, 1993).

The cells of the developing brain begin to form during the first few weeks of pregnancy and the brain continues to mature throughout pregnancy. Therefore, exposure to alcohol can affect the developing brain at any time during prenatal development. Infants with FAS tend to have very low birth weight and a small head circumference for their gestational age. These children are sometimes diagnosed with **failure to thrive** and could remain significantly below the norm in height and weight throughout their lives (Jones, Smith, Ulleland, & Streissguth, 1973).

Many children with FAS have below average cognitive functioning because of brain damage. The degree of physical manifestations of the syndrome is highly correlated to the severity of brain damage. That is, children with more severe physical abnormalities generally function at lower cog-

nitive levels than children with less severe physical attributes (Streissguth, Clarren, & Jones, 1985). Children with FAS frequently lag behind other children of the same age in social and motor skills because of delayed mental development. See Table 4.1 for a list of characteristics associated with FAS.

POSSIBLE EFFECTS OF COCAINE USE

Children are often affected by the actions of the adults in their lives. Adult cocaine use has become an all too familiar behavior for the children who have become its victims. To understand the effects of cocaine use it is helpful to consider the types of individuals who are likely to use cocaine and the rate and effects of use on children's development. Although the influence of other types of illegal drugs are not specifically discussed in this chapter, many of the outcomes associated with cocaine use are relevant for understanding the outcomes of using other drugs.

Use of Cocaine

Whether snorted, taken intravenously, or smoked, cocaine creates an intense feeling of euphoria that has been called "the 30-minute thrill of a lifetime" (Craig, 1993). The extremely pleasurable, short-lived high of cocaine is often followed by an uncomfortable rebound effect. Users tend to turn to other drugs such as alcohol to deal with this discomfort.

Injecting the drug or smoking **crack,** a cheaper form of cocaine, causes it to reach the brain rapidly. This turns the euphoria produced by the drug into an ecstatic rush that often lead to physical effects similar to those experienced during an anxiety attack. These effects include increased blood pressure, racing or irregular heartbeat, anxiety or paranoia, nausea, headaches, and rapid, shallow breathing (Chasnoff, Landress, & Barrett, 1990).

Chronic users frequently reach a state where they engage in meaningless, repetitive activities,

TABLE 4.1 Attributes Associated with Fetal Alcohol Syndrome (FAS)

Central Nervous System
- mental retardation
- difficulty understanding abstract concepts
- difficulty understanding cause and effect
- difficulty with generalizations
- easily distracted
- difficulty perceiving social cues
- motor skills delays
- hyperactivity

Growth Retardation
- low birth weight
- small head size
- small brain mass
- below normal height and weight

Facial Abnormalities
- short eye slits
- droopy eyelids
- widely spaced eyes
- small, upturned nose
- a flattened mid-face
- small chin and jaw
- malformed ears
- lack of indentation in the upper lip
- thin lips
- cleft lip or palate

Other Physical Characteristics
- abnormalities of fingers and toes (small, bent, or joined)
- abnormal palm creases
- hip dislocations at birth
- club foot
- heart and kidney defects
- genital abnormalities
- unusual skin pigmentation
- strawberry birth marks
- excessive hair growth on body other than head

experience insomnia and hallucinations, lose their appetite, and even deplete the brain's supply of the chemical messenger dopamine. This chemical is believed to affect many areas of the brain, including those parts that contribute to feelings of pleasure (Chasnoff, Bussey, Savich, & Stack, 1986).

Chronic cocaine users often "crash" into a depressed state within a couple of hours after using the drug. This state is just the opposite of the pleasant and aroused state first produced by the drug (Kalat, 1995). Over time, users may come to see the drug as the solution to all of their problems because cocaine initially alleviates their depression. This makes it difficult to persuade them to seek help for their addiction.

Use of cocaine before the mid-1980s was limited to a class of individuals who could afford a very expensive high. Cocaine is now mass-marketed in the cheaper crack form, which is smoked. The number of users has vastly increased since 1975, as shown in Figure 4.1.

Crack users now include many women of child-bearing age. Published estimates of the number of crack- or cocaine-exposed infants born each year ranges from 30,000 to 100,000, or between 2 to 3 percent of all newborns (Gomby & Shiono, 1991).

To obtain cocaine, female users frequently become involved in prostitution, exchanging sexual favors for cocaine, or in selling drugs. One survey of pregnant substance abusers found that 36 percent of these women exchanged sex for drugs or for the money to buy drugs (Gomby & Shiono, 1991). Clearly, women involved in this lifestyle are poorly prepared for motherhood.

Direct Impact of Prenatal Exposure to Cocaine

Premature delivery, intrauterine growth retardation, and oxygen deprivation are factors associated with cocaine that place children at developmental risk. The experience of living with a mother who uses cocaine also places children at risk. The long-term developmental outcome for "crack babies" is under investigation, but the data are far from complete. The first generation of children exposed to cocaine prenatally is still growing up.

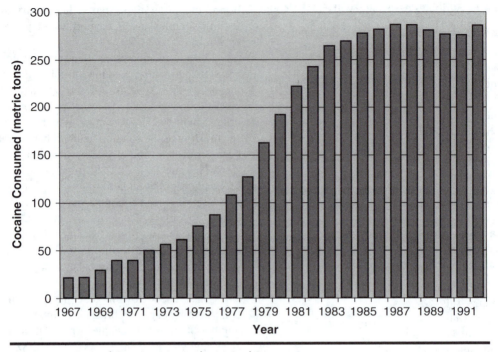

FIGURE 4.1   Rate of Cocaine Use in the United States

It is simply too soon to know what the full range of outcomes will be.

Prenatal cocaine exposure is associated with impaired fetal growth and smaller-than-normal head circumference at birth. Small head circumference appears to be due to a smaller-than-normal brain mass, which is related to a higher probability of later learning disabilities. Impaired growth and smaller-than-normal head size are thought to be caused by cocaine by constricting blood vessels in the **placenta,** the organ that provides nutrition and oxygen to the developing fetus (Gomby & Shiono, 1991). Chronic prenatal exposure to cocaine can also alter the functioning of the chemical messenger systems in parts of the developing brain that regulate state and orientation to stimuli (Chavkin & Kandall, 1990).

Pregnant cocaine users may experience premature and very rapid labor. Rapid deliveries are stressful and typically increase fetal heart rates and can even tear the placenta from the uterine wall (National Association of State Directors of Special Education [NASDSE], 1989). Cocaine crosses the placenta and accumulates in the body of the developing child. It takes longer for the drug to be eliminated from the still developing fetal system than it does from the mother's system. Children may be born addicted to cocaine and if they are will suffer withdrawal effects.

In 1989, 4.5 percent of all babies born in New York City tested positive for drug exposure. About a third of the babies exposed to drugs prenatally go directly from the hospital into foster care. The vast majority of them go home, many to live with parents who use drugs. These children often enter the foster care system at a later date after falling victim to physical child abuse or neglect. Others enter the foster care system because they are abandoned (Groze, et al., 1994; Groze, Haines–Simeon, & McMillen, 1992).

The popular media have painted a gloomy picture of the plight of babies exposed to crack

(Mayes, Granger, Bornstein, & Zuckerman, 1992). These infants have been portrayed as severely and irrevocably brain damaged. They are often seen as damaged to the point that they will never become functional members of society. Current scientific evidence, however, simply does not support this media image (Mayes, Granger, Bornstein, & Zuckerman, 1992). Oversensationalization of the plight of babies exposed to crack is as harmful to the children as the drug exposure itself. Misconceptions about their development make it more difficult to find foster care and other services for these children (Waller, 1993).

Unfortunately, even the scientific community does not seem to be immune to **self-fulfilling prophecies** about children exposed to cocaine prenatally. Evidence suggests that scientific articles are more likely to be accepted for publication when they report adverse effects of cocaine exposure. Studies that failed to find negative effects have been rejected for publication even when they were scientifically sound (Mayes, et al., 1992).

By focusing on the potential biological damage of intrauterine cocaine exposure, we avert our focus from the environmental impact this drug has on children. Many high-risk premature and chronically ill newborns do develop into healthy toddlers. Such instances provide ample reason for discarding a deterministic position (e.g., belief that developmental delays will always result when exposed to cocaine prenatally) on human development. Additionally, the effectiveness of early intervention has been repeatedly documented (Gallagher, 1989; Klein, 1988). We should *not* concede defeat for this particular group of children just because their mothers exposed them to cocaine in the womb, nor should we ignore the ongoing effects of cocaine in their lives.

Studies have reported that children exposed to drugs prenatally often differ from their peers in several ways. As infants they are more likely to appear insecurely attached to their primary care provider. As toddlers they are more likely to be restless, aggressive, and to have less mature play skills. As preschoolers they tend to require more

adult direction to cooperate and are less attentive and more restless than their peers. They also appear to struggle more with tasks that require self-organization (Beckwith, Crawford, Moore, & Howard, 1995).

One study found that prenatal cocaine exposure is related to less positive home environments, smaller than normal head size, and reduced levels of perseverance (the ability to attend to a task for extended periods of time). Together, these three variables accounted for about half of the variation between children's scores on the Stanford-Binet Intelligence Test. Level of perseverance during testing had the greatest influence on **intelligence quotients (IQ).** Reduced levels of perseverance were associated with lower IQ scores and had twice as much effect as the other two factors (Azuma & Chasnoff, 1993).

To date there have been no published studies that have followed children who were prenatally exposed to cocaine from birth to elementary school. Early reports linked cocaine exposure to moderate to severe developmental delays across developmental domains (Mayes, 1992). More recent studies report mild or no impairments in overall developmental functioning (Mayes & Bornstein, 1995; Scherling, 1994; Zuckerman & Frank, 1992).

Indirect Impact of Cocaine Use on Children

Before a particular developmental outcome is attributed to cocaine exposure, it is necessary to rule out the effects of other variables known to place children at developmental risk. Determining the specific effects of cocaine means ruling out the effects of exposure to multiple drugs, premature delivery, poor prenatal care, and socioeconomic status. It would be very difficult to evaluate the impact these other variables and the prenatal effects of cocaine have without very large numbers of subjects.

Studies investigating the effects of cocaine exposure on children have been based on relatively small numbers of subjects. A review of the primary literature published between 1982 and 1989 indicates that research was limited to only six geographical areas. In addition, the investigators were from ten academic institutions, all affiliated with clinical services (Lindenberg, Alexander, Gendrop, Nencioli, & Williams, 1991).

These findings suggest that much of the existing scientific literature on intrauterine cocaine exposure is primarily a set of multiple reports on the same groups of children. Many of these children were born to urban minority women receiving public assistance. Therefore, these children are likely to be at risk for developmental delays for multiple reasons. As a sample, they are probably *not* representative of all children who are exposed to cocaine.

The timing, quantity, and duration of exposure to cocaine almost certainly plays a major role in any effects it has on the developing brain. It could take years to disentangle any unique chemical effect of cocaine because this thread is one part of a web of effects cocaine has on the child's family and community. In addition, family drug abuse intensifies developmental risks associated with poverty, violence, abandonment, homelessness, multiple, short-term foster care placements, and inadequate parenting (Chasnoff, 1988).

The crack epidemic has transformed some neighborhoods into war zones. Abusers are often short-tempered. When these individuals are involved in minor family arguments, the arguments are more likely to explode into violence. This violence is often directed toward the children in the household. Parental substance abuse, including alcohol and cocaine, plays a role in about 70 percent of all child-abuse fatalities. When the victim is less than a year old, substance abuse is involved in 90 percent of child-abuse fatalities (Groze, et al., 1994).

Cocaine has another effect on children as well. Children as young as four years are being recruited to serve as lookouts and drug carriers. Dealers eventually introduce many of these children to the drug's euphoria. The care-providers of these children often look the other way as the children earn money in the crack economy. For intervention efforts to be most effective they will need to address the environmental as well as the intrauterine effects of cocaine (Oro & Dixon, 1987).

In many cases, the mother's addiction often impairs her ability to bond with her newborn infant. She may be insensitive to the needs and responses of her child. Addiction also drastically affect her ability to care for the child. For example, if the mother has gone without sleep, she is more likely to be irritable or aggressive toward her child. If she experiences a lack of appetite (a typical side effect of cocaine), she may not think that her child is hungry either and may fail to feed the child.

Many of the reported effects of cocaine exposure results from a breakdown in communication between a mother who uses cocaine and her offspring. Human infants are helpless at birth. Their survival depends on communicating their needs to adults who care for them. Infants typically use the full range of emotional signals at their disposal, from cries to chuckles, to communicate how they feel and what they need. Under normal circumstances, a mother uses these messages to guide her actions to help the infant achieve goals. Normally, care providers bring desired objects closer and provide comfort when infants signal distress. Mothers addicted to drugs, however, do not seem to respond appropriately to their infants' signals (Tronick, 1989).

Attentive, perceptive care providers are crucial for all infants. Perhaps they are even more crucial for infants whose developing brains have been exposed to cocaine. Women addicted to cocaine often are unable psychologically or physically to read their infants' messages. Studies of mothers who used cocaine report lack of back-and-forth interactions between these mothers and their infants. These studies also reveal a lack of mutual enjoyment in the relationships. Additionally, these mothers demonstrated less social initiative and resourcefulness in the relationship with their infants than mothers who did not use drugs. Infants of mothers who used drugs showed fewer positive responses such as smiling, laughing, and prolonged eye contact than did infants with mothers who did not use drugs (Gilbert, 1989).

Infants who chronically fail to obtain adult help in modifying their emotional states have only limited resources on which to fall back. Babies have very few patterns of responses at their disposal for regulating their emotions. When confronted by a stimulus that causes strong emotions, infants can only turn away to escape. Continual use of this strategy leads to frequent problems interacting with objects and people. Mothers who use cocaine are more likely to have infants who develop these strategies (Azuma & Chasnoff, 1993).

A preschooler who has difficulty playing in unstructured environments may have been an infant who learned to turn away from "overly exciting" objects. Habits formed in infancy frequently interfere with the exploratory behavior a toddler needs for normal cognitive development. Children who rarely succeed in engaging their mothers in emotional communication are likely to view themselves as ineffective and other people as unreliable (Tronick, 1989).

Children born to mothers who use cocaine reputably have difficulty organizing their experiences, understanding cause-and-effect relationships, and controlling mood swings. These difficulties might *not* be caused by the intrauterine cocaine exposure. They may be caused by interacting with a mother addicted to cocaine. The effects of a mother who is physically or psychologically unable to provide critical learning experiences may be far more enduring than any direct damage from the drug. See Table 4.2 for a list of possible effects of exposure to cocaine on children.

Studies published in the 1980s investigating the effects of intrauterine exposure to cocaine should be considered in light of the magnitude of the overlap between maternal cocaine use and HIV infection. Women who use drugs expose their unborn children to a far more serious risk than cocaine. By using needles to get high or by exchanging sex for drugs, women may expose

TABLE 4.2   Effects of Exposure to Cocaine

Effects on the Mother:
1. increased blood pressure
2. irregular heartbeat
3. anxiety and paranoia
4. nausea and headaches
5. rapid, shallow breathing
6. insomnia and hallucinations
7. loss of appetite

Effects on the Infant:
1. increased risk for spontaneous abortion
2. oxygen deprivation during gestation
3. premature birth
4. growth retardation
5. small head circumference
6. hypersensitivity to stimuli
7. irritability
8. withdrawal from stimuli

Effects on the Child:
1. impulsive
2. instability of mood
3. difficulty with concentration and lack of perseverance
4. difficulty with peer interactions
5. difficulty engaging in unstructured play
6. lower intelligence test scores

themselves to HIV. The next section describes factors associated with HIV/AIDS.

THE EFFECTS OF PEDIATRIC HIV/AIDS

The new picture of the HIV/AIDS epidemic is filled with drug users who share infected needles or have sex with multiple partners in exchange for crack ("New Picture," 1995). When people are intoxicated on cocaine or alcohol, they are more likely to engage in unprotected sexual intercourse. Unprotected sex with multiple partners may be deadly because it facilitates the spread of HIV, which causes the **acquired immunodeficiency syndrome (AIDS).**

Progression of the HIV Epidemic

During the first decade of the HIV epidemic, the majority of women diagnosed with AIDS became infected through intravenous drug use (Rubinstein, 1986). In the 1980s, a team of investigators found that 98 percent of mothers who had children with pediatric AIDS said they had used drugs during their pregnancy (Oller, 1995).

Pregnant cocaine users were 4-½ times more likely than nonusers to have a sexually transmitted disease (New York State Department of Health, 1990). Most of the children diagnosed with pediatric AIDS during the 1980s were born to such women (Childhood AIDS, 1991). The rate of HIV among injecting drug users continues to rise, but the overall pattern of the epidemic appears to be changing.

In 1992, heterosexual contact overtook injecting drugs as the major risk factor for HIV infection for women in the United States. A slow and steady rise in heterosexual transmission of HIV has already become apparent in poverty-stricken neighborhoods of cities. An increase in levels of HIV outside urban areas has also been documented. A number of scientists believe that this reflects the early stages of a widespread epidemic among heterosexuals. About a quarter of all new HIV infections are now being acquired through heterosexual contact. Between 70 to 80 percent of those infected through heterosexual contact are women who had sexual contact with men who inject drugs (Blatt & Miller, 1990).

In 1993, more than 75 percent of the new HIV cases among women and 84 percent among children occurred in minority populations, particularly within African American and Latino communities. Tragically, this means that the risk of infection for an African American woman is now fifteen times greater than that of a white woman (Jessee, Nagy, & Poteet–Johnson, 1993)

HIV may be the most serious epidemic ever to confront the human race. HIV poses a serious threat to most sexually active adults and infants born to infected mothers (Anderson & May, 1992). Every woman who becomes infected with the virus risks transmitting it to her unborn child. Medical authorities believe counseling and voluntary testing should be routine for all women of

childbearing age with any identifiable risk for HIV infection. Unfortunately, the vast majority of women with HIV are unaware of their health status. Therefore, it is unlikely that they suspect their children are at any risk (Cohen, 1992).

Through 1984, a total of 232 pediatric AIDS cases were diagnosed in the U.S. By 1991, that figure jumped to 4,249 pediatric AIDS cases. By the early 1990s, in some New York City hospitals more than one of every twenty-five women giving birth were infected. By 1994, an estimated 80,000 women in the U.S. had contracted the virus. In 1994, about 1,800 infants infected with HIV were born. By the year 2000, it is estimated that between 5 and 10 million infants worldwide will be born infected with the deadly virus (Jessee, et al., 1993).

About 25 percent of children born to women with HIV contract the virus from their mother, either across the placenta or while passing through the birth canal. Aggressive treatment with the drug zidovudine/azidothymidine (AZT) for infected pregnant women is believed to substantially reduce the infant's chance of infection (Connor, Sperling, Gelber, Kiselev, Scott, O'Sullivan, Van Dyke, etc., 1994). This occurs because AZT interferes with the virus replicating itself.

To date, there is no way to predict whether a woman with HIV will transmit the virus to her unborn child, but the odds are she will *not*. HIV is one of many conditions that can be passed from mother to unborn child. Some less stigmatized conditions (such as birth defects linked to maternal diabetes) are even more likely to affect the unborn child and are also costly to society. Many state health departments have gone beyond the recommendations of the Centers for Disease Control (CDC) and have suggested that women with HIV should not bear children. The underlying presumption of this policy is that children infected with HIV should not be born. This presumption, however, colors the ecological context for children with HIV.

In some cases, women with HIV calculate the costs and benefits associated with reproduction. Their perception of the risk of transmitting the virus to an unborn child is evaluated against other risks and alternatives they face. For many of these women, the better than 75 percent odds of having a healthy baby represents the best odds they have ever faced. Women infected with HIV who choose to have children do not intend to create harm. Quite the contrary, they usually intend to bring good into their world (Levine & Dubler, 1990).

Women do not need to be injecting drug users to be exposed to HIV. They may simply be unfortunate enough to live in poverty-stricken neighborhoods with a high local infection rate. Poverty and geography have placed these women in the path of the HIV epidemic often because their neighborhoods have been overcome by the cocaine economy (Heagarty, 1991).

Direct Impact of HIV on Children

HIV may lead to pediatric AIDS, a chronic childhood illness alternating between periods of progression and stability. HIV destroys cells that play a crucial role in the immune defense system (Levin, Driscoll, & Fleischman, 1991). The incubation period for the virus is generally much shorter in children than it is in adults. Life-threatening infections and central nervous system damage may appear in children in just months after infection rather than over years, as is the case for most adults.

Clinical symptoms of pediatric HIV include failure to thrive (failure to develop at the expected rate), recurrent bacterial infections, chronic or recurrent diarrhea, disease of the lymph nodes (lymphadenopathy), rare varieties of chronic pneumonia, viral infections, enlargement of the liver and spleen, and developmental delays. It is of paramount importance that people who work with children, especially in areas of high infection rates, be alert for symptoms of the illnesses afflicting children with HIV. Prolonging the lives of children with pediatric AIDS requires aggressive medical intervention against a host of pathogens that may invade their bodies (Childhood AIDS, 1991; Rudigier, Crocker, & Cohen, 1990).

The course of the illness in a given child depends on a number of factors, including the stage of immune system development at the time of exposure and the general status of the child's immune system. For example, if a mother's prenatal diet is low in protein or B vitamins, a child's immune system may be compromised even before exposure to the virus. The human immune system begins developing before the twelfth week of fetal life and remains immature for some months after birth. Maternal antibodies cross the placenta and are also present in a mother's milk to provide immunities to her developing child (Heagarty, 1993).

Infants born to mothers with HIV may test positive for the presence of HIV **antibodies** because their mother's antibodies cross the placenta. This does not mean that all infants who test positive for HIV antibodies at birth also have the virus. The child's own immune system becomes mature enough to manufacture antibodies in response to the presence of the virus after about fifteen months of age. At this time an HIV antibody test may detect whether a child has contracted the virus (Childhood AIDS, 1991). Figure 4.2 provides an overview of outcomes for infants born to women with HIV.

The first diagnosed pediatric AIDS cases in the U.S. were infants, which fostered the perception that infected children always died of AIDS within a year or two of birth. The prognosis is poor for infants who develop an HIV-related illness before their first birthday (Lockhart & Wodarski, 1989). Infants infected before birth may be born small for their gestational age and may not thrive after birth (Czarniecki & Dillman, 1992; Dokecki, Baumeister, & Kupstas, 1989). Many children who are infected are not even likely to be tested for the presence of HIV antibodies until they come down with an illness recognized as being related to HIV infection.

Based on more information, experts now estimate that 20 to 27 percent of children born to women with HIV will develop AIDS by their tenth birthday. The median age of diagnosis for pediatric AIDS was about five years of age in the

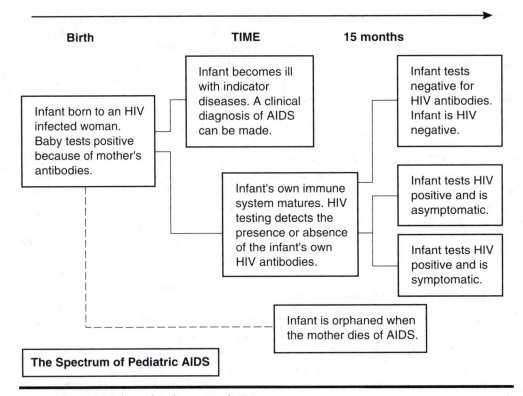

FIGURE 4.2 A Timeline of Pediatric HIV/AIDS

mid-1990s, which means that about half of the children who are infected will begin kindergarten before they are diagnosed with AIDS (De Gruttola, Ming Tu, & Pagano, 1992).

In 1987, the CDC developed a classification system for categorizing children affected by the HIV epidemic (Czarniecki & Dillman, 1992). Some infants are born with full-blown cases of AIDS and will die before their first birthday. Children more than fifteen months old born to women with HIV are classified as being of an **indeterminate infection status** if they show no symptoms of HIV infection. Children over fifteen months old who test positive for HIV antibodies but do not show clinical symptoms of AIDS are classified as **asymptomatic,** although they have abnormal immune system functioning at times.

The CDC collects statistics on AIDS cases and establishes the criteria that medical doctors use for reporting AIDS cases. These criteria are modified as more is discovered about the illness. Medical doctors diagnose pediatric AIDS when a child develops one of the opportunistic infections that signals a breakdown of the immune system (immunodeficiency), suffers from failure to thrive, or has a progressive infection of the brain (encephalopathy) because of the virus (Roth, 1992).

Opportunistic infections account for most AIDS-related deaths. These types of infections do not ordinarily occur in people with properly functioning immune systems. Opportunistic infections may be caused by bacteria that normally live in soil, water, organic matter, and the bodies of plants and animals. Recurrent bacterial infections are often the first indication of HIV infection in children. They include chronic and severe ear infections (otitis media), inflamed sinuses (sinusitis), inflammation of the digestive tract (gastroenteritis), and inflammation of the linings of the central nervous system (meningitis). Many children with HIV infections come down with a rare form of pneumonia caused by a protozoan (Scherer, 1991).

Children with HIV have a difficult time fighting off viral infections and should avoid close contact with people with contagious illnesses, including colds and flu. People who work with children should receive a flu shot each year, keep their own immunizations up-to-date, and be vaccinated against hepatitis B. These precautionary measures help keep providers from transmitting illnesses that are life-threatening to children with compromised immune systems. The herpes simplex virus, which causes boils, cold sores, and fever blisters, is life-threatening to children with HIV. It is very important to avoid exposing them to people with those conditions.

Common childhood viral illnesses such as chicken pox and measles may cause the death of children with HIV. Medical treatment within seventy-two hours of exposure to these common childhood illnesses may prevent children with HIV from becoming critically ill (Czarniecki & Dillman, 1992). It is, therefore, extremely important that daycare providers and preschool personnel inform all parents about any chance of exposure to these common illnesses. Parents need to be afforded the opportunity to protect their children by seeking prompt medical care.

Childhood immunizations may not afford the normal measure of protection for children with HIV. Their immune systems may simply not be capable of mounting a defensive response or producing antibodies. For a child with a weakened immune system, a vaccine made of a live virus could cause the disease it was intended to prevent. Live, oral polio vaccines given to household members pose a threat to a person with HIV. If a child with HIV is one of those household members, the child might contract a life-threatening case of polio from the person who received the live virus vaccine (New York State Department of Health, 1990).

The central nervous system is a primary site of HIV infection for children. Current data suggest that 80 to 90 percent of children with HIV will suffer some degree of central nervous system impairment over the course of their illness due to strokes, tumors, meningitis, and encephalitis. HIV is already one of the most common infectious causes of mental retardation and encephalopathy in children under the age of thirteen (Armstrong, Seidel, & Swales, 1993). Unfortunately, powerful drugs used to treat opportunistic infections in people with HIV have major side effects including neurological symptoms that may mimic developmental problems (Scherer, 1991).

Children with HIV are now surviving for longer periods of time, however, because of advances in medical treatments for opportunistic infections. Many children who do not suffer an early death from AIDS, though, will suffer from some degree of brain damage. HIV leaves the brain vulnerable to opportunistic infections, and the virus itself may invade the brain. Nutritional deficiencies, shortage of oxygen in the blood, and drug side effects may also affect central nervous system functioning in these children. Treatment with AZT appears to provide some relief from cognitive symptoms (Wilfert, 1994).

Pediatric HIV infection of the central nervous system include global developmental delays, abnormal motor functioning, cognitive disorders, sensory impairments, and impaired brain growth (Diamond, 1989). Two patterns of central nervous system involvement have been identified among children with pediatric AIDS (Fletcher, Francis Pequegnat, Rawdenbush, Bornstein, & Schmitt, etc., 1991).

One pattern of central nervous system involvement occurs in about 25 percent of all children with HIV, and the damage appears to be limited to certain areas of the brain. This form is known as a static pattern of infection. If abilities associated with the affected parts of the brain have already developed, effects will be noticeable. Deficits may also be masked until a later developmental stage and often are not noticed until a function fails to emerge on time (Armstrong, et al., 1993). For example, if the affected area of the brain controls the ability to walk, this impact might not be noticed until the child should be walking.

Children with a static pattern of infection may not achieve expected developmental milestones such as walking or talking. Additionally, the rate of development is likely to be slower compared to healthy children of similar ages. It is very unlikely that children with the static pattern of HIV will lose previously attained abilities in other functional areas. Unfortunately, this pattern of infection is often characterized by severely delayed cognitive functioning. These children have difficulties thinking and reasoning. Motor abnormalities, which vary in severity, frequently accompany these cognitive deficits (Armstrong, et al., 1993).

The more common pattern is **progressive infection** of the central nervous system. This pattern is caused by a primary and persistent infection of the brain resulting from HIV. It resembles the AIDS-related dementia found in adults. Children with this pattern not only fail to achieve developmental milestones, they also deteriorate in functioning over time (Armstrong, Seidel, & Swales, 1993).

Individual children experience different cycles of progression of the infection. Some experience a relentless deterioration in functioning while others experience times of relative stability between periods of deterioration. Ultimately, progressive infection results in cognitive and motor abnormalities, which are typically much more severe than those seen in the static pattern. The majority of children with HIV experience a progressive pattern of infection of the central nervous system.

A few children with HIV escape with only minimal functional problems from the virus. These children show selective impairment of perceptual/visual integration and poor visual organization on measures such as the Kaufman–ABC test (Diamond, 1989). Some seem to have attributes associated with attention deficit hyperac-

tivity disorder and a few may display autistic-like withdrawal (Levenson & Mellins, 1992; Levin, Kairam, Bartnett, & Mellins, 1991).

Indirect Impact of HIV on Children

Children with HIV face developmental risks apart from the risks caused by pathogens that invade their bodies. Children with this chronic illness must endure frequent and sometimes painful medical treatment, disruption of their daily routine for periods of hospitalizations, and side effects from medication. Adults need to be alert for signs of pain in children who may *not* be able to explain how they feel. Inattention to their pain leads to suffering and delay treatments for life-threatening infections.

The emotional impact of the infection may be as severe as the developmental delays it inflicts. Children with HIV frequently are placed in isolation wards while hospitalized and examined by gowned medical personnel. Even their own family members appear to be fearful when around them. Normal socialization experiences typically are lacking. They may develop negative self-esteem, loss of emotion, depression, and defense mechanisms for dealing with the situation. Children often interpret pain as punishment, attribute illness to family interactions, or blame themselves or other family members for their illness (Wiener, Moss, Davidson, & Fair, 1993).

Children with HIV also face risk factors inherent in their home environments. They may suffer from adjustment difficulties as they go in and out of the hospital or are moved from household to household. Intervention efforts targeted toward these children must take into account all of the neurological, medical, and social factors that may contribute to their developmental status. Table 4.3 provides a list of characteristics commonly found in infants and young children infected with pediatric AIDS.

Many millions of children, in addition to those infected with HIV, will be affected during the course of the HIV epidemic. It is estimated

TABLE 4.3   Possible Effects of Pediatric AIDS

1. Chronic and recurring childhood illnesses (e.g., diarrhea)
2. Life-threatening bacterial and viral infections
3. Diseases of the lymph nodes
4. Enlargement of the liver and the spleen
5. Central nervous system damage
6. Impaired brain growth
7. Failure to thrive
8. Abnormal motor functioning, including spasticity
9. Sensory impairments, including hearing and visual impairments
10. Impairment of perceptual and visual integration
11. Attention deficit hyperactivity disorder
12. Loss of affect, including depression
13. Severe withdrawal, which resembles autism
14. Psychotic behavior
15. Negative self-esteem
16. Cognitive delays, which may include loss of skills

that, by the year 2000, more than 125,000 children in this country will be orphaned in the wake of this epidemic. At least 40 percent of infected adults will suffer from an **AIDS-related dementia,** which includes the gradual deterioration of mental, physical, and psychological functioning (New York State Department of Health, 1990). A parent's dementia, chronic illness, and death associated with AIDS are usually very frightening experiences for children. Children who are affected need intervention services that address their emotional and social needs as they attempt to cope with the devastating infection, and ultimate loss, of their siblings and parents.

Impact on the Families of Children with HIV

The social environment of children affected by the AIDS epidemic is of special concern. Children most often contract the virus from their mothers. Mothers may have contracted it from the children's fathers. Additionally, more than

one child in a family might be infected. The social and emotional costs to a family affected by AIDS are immeasurable.

The psychological impact of pediatric HIV infection, superimposed on a family's existing problems, such as drug addiction, are devastating. Psychological issues confronting infected families include the stress involved in coping with the chronic illness of mothers and children, grief and mourning as children's levels of function deteriorate, and guilt and self-blame on the part of mothers who transmitted the virus to their children. Family members often experience feelings of isolation if they do not tell people in their family and social networks about the child's health status, but fear stigmatization if they do tell others. Denial is a common coping strategy for dealing with such pervasive problems. As families attempt to cope with anxiety, guilt, and grief over the impending loss of a beloved child, family members may withdraw from each other.

To date, the majority of pediatric HIV cases have occurred in families suffering from poverty, chronic unemployment, racial discrimination, homelessness, and welfare dependency (Task Force on Pediatric AIDS, 1989). Such circumstances often lead to confrontational relationships with various agencies and mistrust of authority figures. This makes it difficult for these families to follow the advice of early educators or medical personnel.

The magnitude of problems, physical and psychological, confronting families who have children with HIV may be overwhelming. Other existing problems will be compounded if a parent develops AIDS-related dementia. Parents might be too sick or dysfunctional to take care of a child who is chronically ill. If a child is removed from the home to live elsewhere, the child is likely to experience an overwhelming sense of loss.

The normal dynamics of the interactions of parents and children focus on the future. This focus includes urging children to eat their vegetables, do their schoolwork, and behave in ways that prepare them for adulthood. In contrast, children with HIV are unlikely to survive to their adult years, and this reality affects the foundation of many family relationships (Lipson, 1993). Adults may be reluctant to discuss their child's fatal infection because this brings the prospect of the child's premature death to mind.

In most cases, children with HIV are precious to their families. Family members need to feel that their hopes are shared by the professionals caring for their child. Special training can help providers become skillful in working more effectively with families that are experiencing extreme emotional stress.

Impact of HIV on Society

Costs to society from the pediatric AIDS epidemic include the direct costs of medical care and hospitalization, foster care services, and early intervention services, as well as the enormous indirect cost of the loss of children. Children with AIDS often spend longer periods of time in hospitals, need a greater number of services, and contribute to greater financial losses for hospitals than do adult patients with AIDS (Tokarski, 1990).

Pediatric AIDS has primarily been a disease of the urban poor. Public general hospitals in major cities have provided most of the medical care for these children. Many of these hospitals were already underfinanced before being besieged by the cocaine and AIDS epidemics. One New York City hospital, from 1981 to 1987, spent $34 million caring for thirty-seven abandoned infants who tested positive for HIV at birth (Dokecki, Baumeister, & Kupstas, 1989).

A shortage of foster parents and understaffed child welfare agencies contribute to babies remaining in expensive hospital environments even after they are medically ready to be discharged. Uncertainties surrounding the HIV status of infants exposed to drugs contributes to the problem of finding foster care for them. About 75 percent of children born to mothers with HIV do not contract the virus, but these children are placed at de-

velopmental risk when abandoned to institutional care (Childhood AIDS, 1991).

Several thousand children, including 25 to 33 percent of all children with HIV, will enter the child welfare system as a result of the AIDS epidemic (Groze, Haines–Simeon, & McMillen, 1992). Only a few of these children are placed in adoptive homes. The financial burden, including medical costs, of caring for children with AIDS falls heavily on the adoptive parents. Most state Medicaid programs do not cover treatments considered experimental, as many current treatments for pediatric HIV/AIDS are. Adoptive parents often report being provided with too little information about how to deal with children's developmental delays.

Another cost of this epidemic must be measured in terms of its impact on people in the helping professions including social workers, doctors, nurses, and educators. One study found that medical staff decisions to withhold treatment from infants were influenced *not* only by the infant's HIV status but also by the mother's HIV status. In this study, staff members justified withholding life-saving medical treatment from infants born to women with HIV on the grounds that the mother was going to die and the infant would have a poor social environment (Levin, Driscoll, & Fleischman, 1991).

The stress experienced by professionals who work with these children might be reduced if intervention efforts are focused on promoting the quality of life remaining for the children rather than on their impending death. Programs have been developed for nurses who work with children suffering from other fatal illnesses and should be used as models for working with children who have HIV (Rushton, Chapman, Hogue, Greenberg–Friedman, Billett, Joyner, & Park, 1993).

It may also be helpful to adopt the perspective that everyone ultimately dies. People find value in their own lives in spite of this truth, and so they should find value in the lives of children with

HIV/AIDS, however brief. In contrast to the cocaine and HIV epidemics, the negative effects of alcohol abuse have been of concern for a longer span of time.

EDUCATIONAL NEEDS AND INTERVENTION SERVICES

A child is a child within an ecological context. The ecology of a child born with cocaine exposure, pediatric HIV infection, or FAS is one of social interest, social construction, judgment, and evaluation. Providing services for these children occurs against a backdrop of social values such that blame is often ascribed to women who bear children impaired by their addictions or infected through actions related to their lifestyles.

Federal law PL 99–457 mandates that early intervention services be provided for infants, toddlers, and preschoolers who are developmentally delayed. Mandates include providing services for children who have been impaired from intrauterine exposure to alcohol, cocaine, or HIV (Gallagher, 1989). The developmental delays experienced by these children are compounded when parents use drugs or experience financial hardship or chronic illness, or when deaths of family members occur. The child's experience with intervention providers may be a welcome and reassuring addition to the child's life. Intervention has also been demonstrated to be effective in changing developmental outcomes for children at developmental risk because of prenatal exposure to cocaine, alcohol, or HIV.

In most cases, developmental services for children born infected with HIV or exposed to alcohol or cocaine resemble those for children with other functional needs. These services include addressing educational, medical, and psychosocial needs for the children and their families. There are a number of obstacles that are encountered in providing services to children who suffer because of their mothers' behavior. Supportive services provided to nuclear and extended families, however,

should be seen as the first and best option for serving these young children.

Written intervention plans, **individualized family service plans, (IFSPs)** and **individualized education programs (IEPs),** required by federal laws include the potential for intruding into the privacy of the family (Gallagher, 1989). Families affected by cocaine, alcohol, or AIDS are often concerned about confidentiality factors. For example, children with HIV often need medication administered during the day. The nature of the medication indicated on an IFSP or IEP may identify the child as HIV-infected. Therefore, it is important to use appropriate measures to protect and respect the family's privacy.

In cases of HIV and cocaine exposure, interventionists and educators frequently are unaware of a child's status unless a parent or guardian chooses to reveal this information. The child may simply be labeled as at risk. It is sometimes argued that specific knowledge of the child's status is unwarranted because such knowledge is *not* likely to affect the educational plan. While this line of reasoning might have validity in the elementary and secondary school setting, it may not be true in the early intervention setting.

Meaningful intervention for children who have been victimized by these epidemics includes providing individuals with whom these children may form enduring relationships. These individuals need to communicate emotionally with the children, helping them to learn how to regulate their emotions to achieve goals before other types of intervention strategies are likely to be effective.

Children afflicted with FAS generally require varying degrees of supervision throughout their lives, including special education (Cooper, 1987). The majority of the children's functioning will be limited to between only a second and fourth grade level. Children with FAS often have difficulty with abstract concepts such as time and space, cause and effect, and generalizing from one situation to another. Distractibility and difficulty perceiving social cues are also common. Therefore, special services need to be designed that help them develop these skills (Anderson, 1982). Unlike children exposed to cocaine and alcohol prenatally, children with pediatric AIDS are particularly vulnerable to environmental conditions. Therefore, a more in-depth discussion of several of their specific needs follows.

Although society tends to be sympathetic toward children with pediatric AIDS, some people argue that children with fatal illnesses should *only* be given the care needed to make their lives comfortable (Rushton, et al., 1993). This line of reasoning leads to the denial of services for children who are *not* deemed worthy of societal investments. It also rests on the underlying premise that experiences that are generally valuable to children are somehow *less* valuable to children born with severe disabilities or life-threatening illnesses. This assumption must be dispelled before early intervention services can be successful.

Some children with HIV are taken into state custody and put into foster care before a diagnosis of infection because of child abuse or neglect. Professionals working with foster families of these children need to afford them the same degree of respect they would extend to biological parents. Failure to accept and interact with the adults in a child's life, whether or not they are legal guardians, may leave the child feeling alone and resentful.

Often, family members who have children with pediatric AIDS view their children as fragile and in need of close protection. Their efforts to protect their children, however, often creates an emotional isolation chamber. Children benefit from normal social interactions. Therefore, families need guidance regarding safe and unsafe child care practices. This information helps encourage them to let their children experience most social interactions.

Building a sense of competency helps family members cope with the responsibility of caring for a child who is chronically ill. For example, family members may need help in discovering their own strengths and their child's strengths.

These discoveries can then be used to help plan and implement developmentally appropriate and safe activities for the children.

Simple modifications of the environment reduces children's exposure to environmental pathogens, thus improving their quality of life. Reduction of environmental pathogens includes ensuring that children with HIV do not take part in cleaning animal cages, tanks, or litter boxes, since these contain bacteria (New York State Department of Health, 1990). The children are also vulnerable to microorganisms living in the soil. Therefore, children should always wash their hands after playing outside. Staying clean is an imperative preventive health measure for these children. They should shower or bathe frequently and always wash their hands carefully after using the bathroom.

Molds and fungi could also be dangerous for children with compromised immune systems. Since kitchens and bathrooms provide environments where these organisms readily grow, these areas need to be well ventilated. Garbage containers should be covered and bleach solution should be used as a disinfectant (New York State Department of Health, 1990).

It is important *not* to expose children with HIV to raw food that may harbor microorganisms. Unpasteurized dairy products carry a risk of salmonella infection and undercooked meats carry the risk of toxoplasmosis. Children with HIV should *not* be served raw eggs in any form, including homemade mayonnaise, hollandaise sauce, mousse, or homemade ice cream. Vegetables should always be served cooked or peeled. Children with HIV often fail to thrive and may need special high-calorie diets. Nutritionists, nurses, or medical doctors should be contacted for information on appropriate dietary plans (New York State Department of Health, 1990).

In many cases, parents and guardians are *not* aware of their child's HIV status. Early childhood educators should be alert for hearing or visual impairments, unexplained gaps in development, repeated bouts of infection that precede a change in a child's developmental status, and the developmental delays that may signal HIV infection of the brain.

Children at risk of HIV infection should have developmental screenings similar to those for other children who are at risk for other developmental delays. Children should be referred for a comprehensive assessment if delays are detected. Early identification of HIV may directly benefit children by affording them the opportunity to receive aggressive medical intervention (Coleman, 1991; Crocker, 1989; Mayers & Spiegel, 1992).

The fluctuating course of HIV infection means that children require frequent reassessments of their developmental and neurological status. Educators should *not* assume that items passed during an earlier assessment still remain in the child's repertoire of functional skills. Reassessments at three to six month intervals have been suggested for toddlers and preschoolers with HIV (Byers, 1989). Assessments help determine how effective medical treatments are for these children and could be used to chart the progression of the illness. For example, assessment results may be used to evaluate how AZT treatment influences a child's cognitive development.

Children change as they develop and the effects of HIV interact with this process. Instruments sensitive to developmental changes provide significant information for monitoring interventions with these children. Developmental models that depict typical growth curves can be used to estimate the course of development for a child. By comparing the results of frequent assessments to projected development, it becomes obvious how a child is changing.

Raw scores rather than **standard scores** should be used for children with HIV. Using standardized scores may indicate that the child is declining in intelligence between assessments, while using raw scores may indicate that improvement is occurring but at a delayed rate. Assessment instruments need to be carefully selected and used with consistency. This helps to avoid the appearance of sudden changes in development that might

occur when using a variety of assessment instruments. Tests that are either too difficult or too easy also create a false picture of a child's development. The range of measurement of any instrument should be carefully considered before using it to track developmental changes in children with HIV (Levenson, et al., 1991).

The extended family is an often overlooked support system for children with developmental delays and their families. A significant proportion of the African American community, especially hard hit by the cocaine abuse and the HIV epidemics, lives in extended families (Wilson, 1989). This type of household comes into existence as one family absorbs another often because of lack of adequate resources in a single-parent household. Extended family members should be encouraged to help with childcare, household tasks, and transportation. They can also provide emotional support or instruction. The qualities and resources available within extended families must be understood by those who provide services.

Growing up in families headed by grandmothers provide children with resources and material and emotional support that often are in short supply in single-parent, impoverished households (Wilson, 1989). Even the detrimental influences of a parent's AIDS-related dementia, chronic illnesses, or addictions may be buffeted by these types of families. Unfortunately, grandmothers may already be exhausted from spending months or years caring for their adult children with AIDS before taking on the additional responsibility of grandchildren who are also chronically ill (Roberts, Severinsen, Kuehn, Straker, & Fritz, 1992).

Service providers must also carefully consider the ethnic and cultural environments of individual families to assure that treatment plans are appropriate and meaningful for the families. Whenever possible, "normal" experiences consistent with their cultural backgrounds must be provided for all children.

The potentially isolating implications of HIV infection make it especially important to create an environment in which children with HIV and their families may playfully interact. A child with HIV is, first and foremost, a child. Opportunities for play, creative arts, recreation, and field trips appropriate to the child's age and developmental level are important parts of an intervention program. Given the variable nature of the child's medical condition, flexible alternatives easily accessible to the child and family are essential.

The Developmental and Family Services Unit (DFSU), Children's Evaluation and Rehabilitation Center, Rose F. Kennedy Center, Bronx, New York, developed a model program for improving the quality of life for children infected with HIV and their families. This program provides therapy, referrals for education and preschool placements, home-based instruction, individualized occupational and physical therapy, feeding therapy, supportive counseling to help parents care for and cope with a child who is chronically ill, and advocacy in obtaining other services (Rudigier, et al., 1990).

Another model program, Opportunities for Parents and Children Together (O-PACT), was developed by researchers at a federally funded, university affiliated program. The O-PACT model of intervention focuses on parent and child interactions and is family centered and family driven (Forest & Libscomb, 1994). O-PACT provides services for parents accused of child abuse and neglect, parents with developmental delays and mental illness, teen parents, low income families, and for children with developmental delays or at risk of delays.

Parents who engage in behaviors that have harmed their child need to develop a sense of competence if they are to successfully provide care for the child. The O-PACT model offers a means of providing early intervention services while reducing the need for out-of-home placements, improving parenting skills, decreasing the family's social isolation, and monitoring child/family development. Methods of intervention provided in these two model programs and other similar programs may be useful for early childhood service providers.

CONCLUSION

Children who are infected or orphaned by the HIV epidemic and who are exposed to drugs prenatally or grow up in families where parents abuse drugs must be provided appropriate intervention services. These children should be viewed as the innocent victims of their environments. Children do not choose the family into which they are born. To avoid further victimization, prejudices about these children must be put aside.

The environmental influences, recently referred to as the "new morbidities," described in this chapter are leaving in their wake a multitude of children in need of human affection. Providing someone to love and care for these children may be the most difficult intervention service to provide because it does not consist of implementing a model curriculum or refurbishing a classroom. Curriculum and furnishings can be purchased, but love always has to be given as a gift. This special gift of love most certainly includes nurturing with open arms.

The road that must be traveled will be difficult for service providers, children, and their families. Everyone must travel it together, set priorities, and determine how best to serve these children.

The next section of this book describes various types of services that are provided for children who have special needs. The discussion begins with a description of the role of special education teachers and the types of services they provide.

CHAPTER SUMMARY

- Exposure to alcohol, cocaine, and pediatric AIDS prenatally and postnatally are likely to affect children's development in negative ways.
- Women who use intravenous drugs risk exposing their unborn children to HIV and to the effects of the drugs they use.
- Federal laws require that early intervention services be made available for these children, and these services appear to be effective.

- Society bears many costs as a result of FAS/FAE, cocaine use, and pediatric HIV/AIDS, but affected children carry the greatest burden.

REVIEW QUESTIONS

1. How have the abuse of alcohol and cocaine and the HIV epidemic affected children?
2. What are the clinical symptoms associated with intrauterine exposure to cocaine, HIV, and alcohol?
3. Why are early intervention services important for children with AIDS, FAS, and prenatal exposure to cocaine?

SUGGESTED STUDENT ACTIVITIES

1. Collect local data on the number of children infected with HIV/AIDS.
2. Develop a list of local organizations that provide services to children with pediatric HIV/AIDS, FAS, and those suffering from the effects of exposure to cocaine.
3. Visit an early intervention program that provides services for children exposed to cocaine or who are classified with FAS or FAE.
4. Volunteer to work for a community organization serving families affected by HIV.

ADDITIONAL READINGS

Boyd–Franklin, N., Steiner, G. L., & Boland, M. G. (Eds.). (1995). *Children, families, and HIV/AIDS: Psycho-social and therapeutic issues.* New York: Guilford Press.

Byron, E., & Katz, G. (Eds.). (1991). *HIV prevention and AIDS education: Resources for special educators.* Reston, VA: Council for Exceptional Children.

Chasnoff, I. J. (Ed.). (1988). *Drugs, alcohol, pregnancy, and parenting.* Boston: Kluwer Academic.

Leone, P. (1991). *Alcohol and other drugs: Use, abuse, and disabilities.* Reston, VA: Council for Exceptional Children.

Lewis, M., & Bendersky, M. (Eds.). (1995). *Mothers, babies and cocaine: The role of toxins in development.* Hillsdale, NJ: Erlbaum.

ADDITIONAL RESOURCES

American Academy of Pediatrics
141 Northwest Point Blvd.
Elk Grove Village, IL 60007

American Red Cross
AIDS Education Program
430 17th Street, N.W.
Washington, DC 20006

Developmental Disabilities and HIV Infection Project
AAUAP
8630 Fenton Street, Suite 410
Silver Spring, MD 20910

The Foundation for Children with AIDS
77B Warren Street
Brighton, MA 02135

National AIDS Hotline
(800) 342–2437

National Association of People with AIDS (NAPWA)
2025 I Street, N.W., Suite 415
Washington, DC 20006

Pediatric and Pregnancy AIDS Hotline
(212) 430–3333

Note: Current demographic information about AIDS may be obtained by calling the USA Centers for Disease Control at (404) 330–3020, 3021, 3022. Each taped message lasts for about three minutes and addresses a different aspect of the spread of AIDS.

REFERENCES

American Academy of Pediatrics Committee on Substance Abuse and Committee on Children with Disabilities. (1993). Fetal alcohol syndrome and fetal alcohol effects. *Pediatrics, 91,* 10004–10006.

Anderson, R. M. (1982). The possible role of paternal alcohol consumption in the etiology of the fetal alcohol syndrome. In E. Abel (Ed.), *Fetal Alcohol Syndrome, Vol. III: Animal Studies.* Boca Raton, FL: CRC Press.

Anderson, R. M., & May, R. M. (1992). Understanding the AIDS pandemic. *Scientific American,* May, 58–66.

Armstrong, F. D., Seidel, J. F., & Swales, T. P. (1993). Pediatric HIV infection: A neuropsychological and educational challenge. *Journal of Learning Disabilities, 26*(2), 92–103.

Azuma, S. D., & Chasnoff, I. J. (1993). Outcome of children prenatally exposed to cocaine and other drugs: A path analysis of three-year data. *Pediatrics, 92*(3), 396–402.

Beckwith, L., Crawford, S., Moore, J. A., & Howard, J. (1995). Attentional and social functioning of preschool-age children exposed to PCP and cocaine in utero. In M. Lewis & M. Bendersky (Eds.), *Mother, babies and cocaine: The role of toxins in development* (pp. 287–303). Hillsdale, NJ: Erlbaum.

Blatt, R. J. R., & Miller, W. A. (Eds.). (1990). (Special issue on AIDS). *The Genetic Resource, 5*(2).

Byers, J. (1989). AIDS in children: Effects on neurological development and implications for the future. *Journal of Special Education, 23*(1), 5–15.

Chasnoff, I. J. (1988). Drug use in pregnancy: Parameters of risk. *Pediatric Clinical Neurology of America, 35,* 1403–1412.

Chasnoff I. J., Bussey, M. E., Savich, R., & Stack, C. M. (1986). Perinatal cerebral infarction and maternal cocaine use. *Journal of Pediatrics, 108,* 456–459.

Chasnoff, I. J., Landress, H., & Barrett, M. (Eds.). (1990). The prevalence of illicit drug or alcohol use during pregnancy and discrepancies in mandatory reporting in Pinellas County, Florida. *New England Journal of Medicine, 322,* 1202–1206.

Chavkin, W. I., & Kandall, S. R. (1990). Between a "rock" and a hard place: Perinatal drug abuse. *Pediatrics, 85,* 223–225.

Childhood AIDS. (1991). *Pediatric Clinical Neurology of America, 38*(1), 1–16.

Clarren, S. K., & Smith, D. W. (1978). The fetal alcohol syndrome. *New England Journal of Medicine, 298*(19), 1063–1067.

Cohen, H. J. (1992). Pediatric AIDS vaccine trials set. *Science, 258,* 1568–1570.

Coleman, M. (1991). Pediatric AIDS: The professional responsibilities of child caregivers to children and families. *Early Childhood Development Care, 67,* 129–137.

Connor, E. M., Sperling, R. S., Gelber, R., Kiselev, P., Scott, G., O'Sullivan, M. J., Van Dyke, R., Bey, M., Shearer, W., Jacobson, R. L., Jimenez, E., O'Neill, E., Bazin, B., Delfaissy, J. F., Culnane, M., Coombs, R., Elkins, M., Moye, J., Stratton, P., & Balsley, J. (1994). Reduction of maternal–infant transmission of human immunodeficiency virus type 1 with zidovudine treatment. *New England Journal of Medicine, 331*(18), 1173–1225.

Cooper, S. (1987). The fetal alcohol syndrome. *Journal of Child Psychology and Psychiatry, 28*(2), 223–227.

Craig, A. (1993, September 6). Cocaine: Thrill carries high price tag. *Poughkeepsie Journal,* 3B.

Crocker, A. C. (1989). Developmental services for children with HIV infection. *Mental Retardation, 27,* 223–225.

Czarniecki, L., & Dillman, P. (1992). HIV/AIDS. *Critical Care Nursing Clinics of North America, 4*(3), 447–456.

De Gruttola, V., Ming Tu, X., & Pagano, M. (1992). Pediatric AIDS in New York City: Estimating the distributions of infection, latency, and reporting delay and projecting future incidence. *Journal of the American Statistician Association, 87*(419), 633–640.

Diamond, G. W. (1989). Developmental problems in children with HIV infection. *Mental Retardation, 27*(4), 213–217.

Dokecki, P. R., Baumeister, A. A., & Kupstas, A. (1989). Biomedical and social aspects of pediatric AIDS. *Journal of Early Intervention, 13*(2), 99–113.

Donovan, C. L. (1991). Factors predisposing, enabling, and reinforcing routine screening of patients for preventing fetal alcohol syndrome: A survey of New Jersey physicians. *Journal of Drug Education, 21*(1), 35–42.

Forest, S., & Libscomb. S. (1994). Opportunities for parents and children together (O-PACT): A dynamic model of intervention for at-risk infants and toddlers. 52 Corbin Hall, University of Montana, Missoula, MT 59812.

Fletcher, J. M., Francis, D. J., Pequegnat., W., Raudenbush, S. W., Bornstein, M. C., Schmitt, F., Brouwers, P., & Stover, E. (1991). Neurobehavioral outcomes in disease of childhood: Individual change models for pediatric human immunodeficiency viruses. *American Psychologist, 46*(12), 1267–1277.

Gallagher, J. J. (1989). A new policy initiative: Infants and toddlers with handicapping conditions. *American Psychologist, 44*(2), 387–391.

Gilbert, P. (1989). *Human Nature and Suffering.* Hillsdale, NJ: Erlbaum.

Gomby, D. S., & Shiono. P. H. (1991). Estimating the number of substance-exposed infants. *The Future of Children, 1*(1), 17–25.

Groze, V., Haines–Simeon, M., & Barth, R. P. (1994). Barriers in permanency planning for medically fragile children: Drug affected children and HIV infected children. *Child Adolescent Social Work Journal, 11*(1), 63–84.

Groze, V., Haines–Simeon, M., & McMillen, J. C. (1992). Families adopting children with or at-risk of HIV infection. *Child and Adolescent Social Work Journal, 9*(5), 402–426.

Heagarty, M. C. (1993). Day care for the child with acquired immunodeficiency syndrome and the child of the drug-abusing mother. *Pediatrics, 2* 199–201.

Heagarty, M. C. (Feb. 1991). Pediatric AIDS, poverty and national priorities. *American Journal of Disabilities in Childhood.* (Atlantic Information Services 1123, June 1991).

Jessee, P. O., Nagy, M. C., & Poteet–Johnson, D. (1993). Children with AIDS. *Child Education, 70*(1), 10–14.

Jones, L. J., Smith, D. W., Ulleland, C. N., & Streissguth, A. P. (1973). Patterns of malformation in offspring of chronic alcoholic mothers. *Lancet, 1,* 1267–1271.

Kalat, J. W. (1995). *Biological psychology.* New York: Brooks/Cole Publishing.

Klein, N. K. (1988). Children who were very low birth weight: Cognitive abilities and classroom behavior at five years of age. *Journal of Special Education, 22*(1), 41–49.

Levenson, R. L., Kairam, R., Bartnett, M., & Mellins, C. A. (1991). Equivalence of peabody picture vocabulary test-revised, forms L and M for children with acquired immune deficiency syndrome (AIDS). *Perceptual and Motor Skills, 72,* 99–102.

Levenson, R. L., & Mellins, C. A. (1992). Pediatric HIV disease: What psychologists need to know. *Professional Psychologist: Research and Practice, 23*(5), 410–415.

Levin, B. W., Driscoll, J. M., & Fleischman, A. R. (1991). Treatment choice for infants in neonatal intensive care unit at risk for AIDS. *Journal of the American Medical Association, 265*(22), 2976–2981.

Levine, A. J. (1992). *Viruses.* New York: Scientific American Library.

Levine, C., & Dubler, N. N. (1990). HIV and child bearing: Uncertain risks and bitter realities: The reproductive choices of HIV-infected women. *Milbank Quarterly, 68*(3), 321–349.

Lindenberg, C. S., Alexander, E. M., Gendrop, S. C., Nencioli, M., & Williams, D. G. (1991). A review of the literature on cocaine abuse in pregnancy. *Nursing Research, 40*(2), 69–75.

Lipson, M. (1993). What do you say to a child with AIDS? *Hastings Center Report, 6*–12.

Lockhart, L. L., & Wodarski, J. S. (1989). Facing the unknown: Children and adolescents with AIDS. *Social Work, 8,* 215–221.

Mayers, A., & Spiegel, L. (1992). A parental support group in a pediatric AIDS clinic: Its usefulness and limitations. *Health Social Work, 17*(3), 183–191.

Mayes, L. C. (1992). The effects of prenatal cocaine exposure on young children's development. *The Annals of the American Academy of Political and Social Science, 521,* 11–27.

Mayes, L. C., & Bornstein, M. H. (1995). Developmental dilemmas for cocaine-abusing parents and their children. In M. Lewis & M. Bendersky (Eds.), *Mother, babies and cocaine: The role of toxins in development* (pp. 251–272). Hillsdale, NJ: Erlbaum.

Mayes, L. C., Granger, R. H., Bornstein, M. C., & Zuckerman, B. (1992). The problem of prenatal cocaine exposure: A rush to judgment. *Journal of the American Medical Association, 267*(3), 406–408.

National Association of State Directors of Special Education (September, 1989). *Action Seminar: Infants exposed in utero to AIDS, Alcohol, Drugs.*

National Institute of Child Health and Human Development, National Institutes of Health. (1990). *The new face of AIDS: A material and pediatric epidemic.* (Atlantic Information Services, 125, August).

New picture of who will get AIDS is crammed with addicts. (1995, February 28). *The New York Times,* 4.

New York State Department of Health. (1990). *Prehospital Care Provider's Guide to AIDS.* Author. Albany, NY.

Oller, D. K. (1995). Personal communication at February, 1995 American Association for the Advancement of Science Annual Meeting.

Oro, A. S., & Dixon, S. D. (1987). Perinatal cocaine and methamphetamine exposure: Maternal and neonatal correlates. *Journal of Pediatrics, 1111,* 571–578.

Overholser, J. C. (1990). Fetal alcohol syndrome: A review of the disorder. *Journal of Contemporary Psychotherapy, 20*(3), 163–175.

Roberts, C. S., Severinsen, C., Kuehn, C., Straker, D., & Fritz, C. J. (1992). Obstacles to effective case management with AIDS patients: The clinician's perspective. *Social Work Health Care, 17*(2), 27–40.

Roth, E. F. (1992). The nature of AIDS and babies. *Child and Adolescent Social Work Journal, 9*(5), 373–379.

Rubinstein, A. (1986). Pediatric AIDS. *Current Problems in Pediatrics, 6,* 363–409.

Rudigier, A., Crocker, A. C., & Cohen, H. J. (1990). The dilemmas of childhood HIV infection. *Child Today, 2,* 26–29.

Rushton, C. H., Chapman, K., Hogue, E. E., Greenberg–Friedman, D., Billett, C. A., Joyner, M., & Park, C. D. (1993). End of life care for infants with AIDS: Ethical and legal issues. *Pediatric Nursing, 19*(1), 79–83.

Scherer, P. (1991). How AIDS attacks the brain. *American Journal of Nursing, 4,* 44–53.

Scherling, D. (1994). Prenatal cocaine exposure and childhood psychopathology. *American Journal of Orthopsychiatry, 64,* 9–19.

Streissguth, A. P., Clarren, S. K., & Jones, K. (1985). Natural history of the Fetal Alcohol Syndrome: A 10-year follow-up of eleven patients. *Lancet, 2,* 85–91.

Task Force on Pediatric AIDS: American Psychological Association. (1989). Pediatric AIDS and Human Immunodeficiency Virus Infections. *American Psychologist, 1,* 258–264.

Tokarski, C. (1990, April). Higher costs of pediatric AIDS care documented. *Modern Health Care,* 16–17.

Tronick, E. Z. (1989). Emotions and emotional communication in infants. *American Psychologist, 44*(2), 112–119.

Waller, M. B. (1993). Helping crack-affected children succeed. *Educational Leadership, 50*(4), 63–66.

Wiener, L., Moss, H., Davidson, R., & Fair, C. (1993). Pediatrics: The emerging psychosocial challenge of the AIDS epidemic. *Child and Adolescent Social Work Journal, 9*(5), 381–407.

Wilfert, A. (Ed.). (1994). *Pediatric AIDS: The challenge of HIV infection in infants, children, and adolescents.* Baltimore, MD: Williams and Wilkins.

Wilson, M. N. (1989). Child development in the context of the Black extended family. *American Psychologist, 44*(2), 380–385.

Zuckerman, B., & Bresnahan, K. (1991). Developmental and behavioral consequences of prenatal drug and alcohol exposure. *Pediatric Clinics of North America, 38*(6), 1387–1406.

Zuckerman, B., & Frank, D. A. (1992). Prenatal cocaine and marijuana exposure: Research and clinical implications. In I. S. Zagon & T. A. Slotkin (Eds.), *Maternal substance abuse and the developing nervous system* (pp. 125–154). Boston: Academic Press.

CHAPTER 5

SERVICE COORDINATION
AND THE ROLE OF THE
SOCIAL WORKER

EILEEN TAYLOR APPLEBY, PH.D.

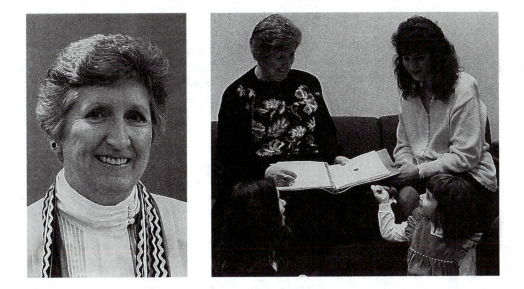

ABOUT THE AUTHOR

Dr. Appleby received her doctorate in clinical social work from New York University School of Social Work, her master's of social work from Adelphi University School of Social Work in Garden City, New York, and her bachelor's degree in music from Lycoming College in Williamsport, Pennsylvania. She is a member of the social work faculty at Marist College in Poughkeepsie, New York. Dr. Appleby was the social worker for one of the first community-based group homes in New York State for children who are mentally retarded.

She was the first professional to be asked to serve as an officer in the Parent–Teacher Association for Exceptional Children in Rockland County, New York. She also served on the Board of Directors of the Dutchess County Task Force for Child Protection. Dr. Appleby has received two formal recognitions from the Marist College Office of Special Services for her outstanding service to students with disabilities. She is married and enjoys pursuing musical activities in her limited free time.

CHAPTER KEY POINTS

- Federal laws relating to early childhood special education mandate that a plan for service coordination is developed.
- Many different types of professionals serve as service coordinator.
- A social worker often acts as service coordinator.
- Service coordinators may assess families' needs, social networks, and social services and aid in planning and coordinating services, provide direct and indirect intervention services, and monitor and evaluate service plans.
- Service coordination activities should result in families being empowered to become their own service coordinators.

The previous chapter provided an overview of developmental delays in infants, toddlers, and preschool children. This chapter discusses **service coordination** and describes the role of a **social worker** in coordinating many different types of services that young children and their families may need. It also provides a discussion of the emotional reactions family member may have when learning a child in their family has a developmental delay.

SERVICE COORDINATION FOR CHILDREN WITH SPECIAL NEEDS AND THEIR FAMILIES

The federal legislation in **Public Law (PL) 99–457, Part H,** the **Education for All Handicapped Children Act Amendment** of 1986, now referred to as the **Individuals with Disabilities Education Act (IDEA),** directs that services be provided to all children from infancy to five years old with special needs. Federal laws stress all services are to be family-centered and community-based. Essential aspects of children's service plans are coordination of services (Able–Boone, Sandall, Stevens, & Frederick, 1992).

In the past, "service coordination" was referred to as "case management," "case coordination," or "service management." Kirst–Ashman and Hull (1993) noted that it is not the family being managed but the services received by the family, which helps explain why, since 1991, case management came to be called service coordination in the later reauthorization of **IDEA (PL 102–119). Part H of PL 99–457** allows professionals from one of fourteen disciplines to serve as service coordinators (e.g., social workers, psychologists, occupational therapists, special education teachers).

The **individualized family service plan (IFSP)** must have "the name of the case manager from the profession most immediately relevant to the infant's or toddler's or family's needs who will be responsible for the implementation of the plan and coordination with other agencies and persons (100 Stat. 1150). The law is not specific on the standards for determining "the profession most immediately relevant" (Woody, Woody, & Greenberg, 1991). The IFSP must be evaluated at least once per year. In addition, the family must receive a review every six months.

Primary Focus of Service Coordination

The primary role of the service coordinator is to assist the family in identifying and accessing appropriate services. The service coordinator may or may not be involved in providing direct services. Service coordination is one of many types of professional social work activities. A service coordinator is sometimes referred to as a case manager or case coordinator. They organize, coordinate, and sustain a network of formal and informal support systems and activities designed to enhance the functioning of people with special needs.

Role of the Social Worker as Service Coordinator

Social workers are often in the best position to provide service coordination, because of their emphasis on **client empowerment,** competence to perceive the relatedness of the individual, family, and community, and counseling skills (Fiene & Taylor, 1991). Traditionally, the social worker is the **"family-centered" professional** on the collaborative team (DiMichele, 1993). Service coordination is within the knowledge and skill base of all four practice levels of social work, as designated by the **National Association of Social Workers (NASW).** A social worker has a college degree at the bachelor's level or higher. The four practice levels designated by NASW are provided in Table 5.1.

Major Tasks of the Service Coordinator

The purpose of service coordination is to increase the family's knowledge of and ability to use social services and supports. Very young children with special needs often require services from many

TABLE 5.1   The Four Basic Principles of Social Work

1. Basic professional—requires a baccalaureate from a program accredited by the Council on Social Work Education (CSWE).
2. Specialized professional—requires a master's from a CSWE accredited program.
3. Independent professional—requires two years of post-master's experience under suitable professional supervision.
4. Advanced professional—typically requires a doctorate in social work or a related social science field.

based on Morales & Sheafor (1992)

parts of the care system including medical care, rehabilitative services, financial assistance, special equipment, educational planning, and family counseling. When services are not coordinated, the effectiveness of services may be restricted. Gaining access to and coordinating these services may become an overwhelming task (Dennis, Williams, Giangreco, & Cloninger, 1993; Hanson & Lynch, 1992; Freedman & Clarke, 1991).

Few families are naturally equipped to manage the wide array of social services. The initial purpose of service coordination is to ensure that needs are identified and services are obtained, coordinated, sustained, and updated, and that the family is then empowered to become the primary service coordinator (DuBois & Miley, 1992). This description suggests that the service coordinator is working toward the competency of the family. The family can expect the service coordinator to perform four major tasks: assessment of needs, planning and coordinating services, providing direct and indirect intervention, and monitoring and evaluating the service plan. The first task of the service coordinator, assessment of needs, is crucial and directly affects the remaining three tasks.

ASSESSMENT OF NEEDS

According to Kirst–Ashman and Hull (1993), "Assessment refers to defining issues and gathering relevant information about a problem so that decisions can be made about what to do to solve it" (p. 25). In actuality, many types of assessment take place simultaneously and on several different levels. Assessments are generally conducted by several if not all of the professionals working with the child, including service coordinators, teachers, speech and language pathologists, psychologists, medical personnel, and occupational, physical, music, and art therapists. The role of the service coordinator is to facilitate interactions among all members of the assessment team. In addition, the service coordinator directly assesses the family needs, support networks, and social services.

Special education laws focus assessment involving families on identifying their resources, priorities, and concerns. Assessments focus on the immediate and long-term developmental needs of the child and also includes assessment of the needs of the child's family.

Family Needs

Federal laws mandate that direct family services be provided for families of children with special needs aged two years or younger. Assessment of the family needs involves examining the strengths and capabilities of the family, the childcare ability of the **informal support system** of the family, and resources available in the **formal support system.**

Assessment requires collaboration of the service coordinator and other team members, including family members. They must work together to compile, evaluate, rank, and combine various factors found within the family's environment. This process is designed to help create possible solutions for the identified needs of the family. The needs noted by the service coordinator and family must be considered in relation to the assessments of needs made by other professionals (Moxley, 1989). Seligman and Darling (1989) developed the **Parent Needs Survey (PNS),** which is frequently used by professionals to assess the needs of families of young children with disabilities. The major areas of assessment on the PNS are listed in Table 5.2.

Based on the combined assessments of entire teams of professionals, the parents of children with special needs often receive a tremendous amount of information. Parents often find the information to be confusing or contradictory. Service coordinators and the families must work together to use all the information effectively. Service coordinators evaluate this information at two levels: assessing the ability of families to understand the information provided by members of the service team, and assessing the capability of families to implement recommendations from team

TABLE 5.2 The Six Major Areas of the Parent Needs Survey (PNS)

The Parent Needs Survey includes information about:
1. Diagnosis, prognosis, and treatment;
2. Medical, therapeutic, and educational services;
3. Formal support from public and private agencies;
4. Informal support from relatives, friends, neighbors, co-workers, and other parents who have children with special needs;
5. Material support, including financial support and access to resources;
6. Competing family needs including the needs of other family members (usually parents and siblings) that may affect the family's ability to attend to the needs of the child with special needs.

from Seligman & Darling (1989)

members. While these two areas may seem similar, they are actually quite distinct.

Initial assessments of children with special needs are designed to discern their needs and determine areas of delay. Assessment involves family interviews, case histories, and observations, in addition to the use of various needs assessment instruments. A social worker frequently also assess the cognitive strength of the family and, perhaps more importantly, the emotional strength and functioning of the family (Buckley, 1983).

A disability that emerges during the development of a child generally evokes a wide range of emotional responses from family members (Hughes & Rycus, 1983). After first learning of their children's special needs, most families respond with varying levels of mobilization while at the same time experiencing emotional and functional turmoil. It is vitally important for families and professionals to understand the emotional "merry-go-round" many families experience. Overwhelming amounts of insensitively transmitted information may devastate them (Rolland, 1994).

Featherstone (1981) describes being on this "merry-go-round" while receiving information about her son shortly after his birth:

The doctor who had delivered Jody called to say that routine examination revealed a placenta infected with a disease called toxoplasmosis... Over the next year we learned that Jody was blind, hydrocephalic, retarded, and that he suffered from cerebral palsy and from seizures...Each week after that first telephone call brought new calamities... We were almost numb with the pain (p. 4).

It is important for service coordinators and families to assess their emotional ability to deal with this type of information. Families are capable of effectively dealing with unanticipated information but to do so often need the support of service coordinators.

Professionals sometimes respond as if the delivery of the content of the material is more important than considering how well families will be able to deal with the information. When this happens, conflict might arise between families and professionals. Therefore, assessments of the emotional strength and functioning of the family are crucial and, once completed, family members are generally better prepared to identify potential difficulties in handling certain kinds of information. Being able to identify the family's emotional status becomes an important strength of the service coordinator.

Service coordinators often assist families in identifying the types of information they are best and least able to manage. It is often useful for families to identify past crises and feelings associated with these events so that the service coordinator can better analyze how they cope with stress. For example, a service coordinator was working with the family of a four-year-old boy diagnosed as having fragile-X syndrome. Family members had become quite distraught when they received information about the boy's cognitive delays. Based on the family's reaction, it became more crucial for the service coordinator to prepare the family to manage the information than merely to present it to the family.

The service coordinator began interactions with the family by discussing the meaning and importance of cognitive development and its relationship to developmental disabilities. The service coordinator knew that the father in particular had very high expectations for himself, his employees, and for his sons. Although this father acknowledged his son's diagnosis, he was not prepared to accept the ramifications of the diagnosis.

The service coordinator discussed the importance of the family creating realistic expectations regarding the boy's development. The service coordinator also provided the family with a description of services available for him. After a few days, the father began to come to terms with the information and could begin dealing with the ramifications of the diagnosis. In fact, he became an effective advocate for his son.

The second level of assessment performed by service coordinators involves assessing the ability of a family to implement recommendations from various professionals. For example, a team of service providers might recommend that parents spend thirty minutes a day reading to their children. This recommendation might have be made without first assessing whether the parents could read at the necessary level.

Families' abilities to implement intervention recommendations is often directly related to their skill levels and emotional strengths. If families are not cognitively or emotionally able to handle certain issues, they are put under additional stress by being asked to implement treatment recommendations. Also, if specific skills are not developed within the family units, the families may not be able to meet their children's needs until they acquire the necessary skills. When children with special needs are involved, families must frequently be taught many new skills, including how to dispense medication, deal with mechanical devices, and/or implement complex behavioral regimens.

Social Networks

Before the needed support networks can be developed, an assessment of available networks is necessary. After the assessing the **support network,** service coordinators assists in designing support systems that integrate skills development with them. One aspect of a support system is the social network (Brill, 1976). **Social networks** include the total set of individuals and institutions with whom families connect and maintain relationships.

Social networks are particularly important for the families of children with special needs because often the support and influence of these networks sustain the family in coping with the demands of daily living with a child who has special needs. Social networks help strengthen the family's individuality, provide dependable communication and feedback regarding the child's development, provide emotional support and assistance with specific tasks, as well as direct them toward valuable resources (Bishop, Rounds, & Weil, 1993).

Research confirms the beneficial effects of social networks on families' abilities to cope with the demands of dealing with the needs of children who have a developmental disability (Moxley, 1989). For example, Biale (1989) found that adjustments to the birth of such a child were more positive when families consistently used network resources, especially extended family networks. Helping family members to gain support through their social network provides an important supplement to services available through formal networks.

Informal support systems include the nuclear and extended families, neighbors, friends, and work colleagues. The service coordinator and family work together to assess the accessibility of social network members and the degree of informal support available. The assessment centers around the number, proximity, and capabilities of the individuals in the social network, how often they have contact with the family, and the significance of the relationship with the family (Dudley, 1987).

To identify individuals who would be most supportive to the family, Moxley (1989) developed an interview system designed to explore the range of social relationships available. He recommended asking clients to list individuals with whom they have been in contact during the past year and to state how they are related, based on six categories that include household, primary kin, extended kin, work, neighbors, and informal relations in the community. Service coordinators use this or a similar system to help families identify support networks.

An example of the importance of assessing social networks involved a young couple whose son needed to be physically active or stimulated for as much of the day as possible. Providing physical stimulation and movement was not a problem when the child was in school, but it was problematic on weekends and holidays. This family needed a large support system of individuals who lived nearby, who had the time to help, and who were physically able to help. The couple had a positive relationship with their own parents, but their parents were elderly and lived several hundred miles away. This couple needed to enlist the support of friends and neighbors to become part of their support network. The service coordinator's role was to guide the couple in recognizing and planning their need for support.

It is often valuable to assess the support network system before burdening families with a program they might not be able to use (Early & Poertner, 1993). For example, families may not be able to use services because of the lack of adequate childcare. Appropriate childcare is needed on a regular basis and for emergencies by nearly all families, but adequate childcare for children with special needs is often difficult to obtain. These children could have needs requiring that all care providers receive specific training on proper care. In many cases, families will not be able to attend parenting classes or receive counseling services until appropriate childcare is found.

Social Services

Even though care provided by professionals might not be the first choice for families of children with special needs, at some point professionals will enter the picture. Most service coordinators and **social service** agencies have lists of resources available to families of children with special needs. These lists typically include information about mental health, medical care, transportation, daycare, legal help, and respite services (temporary relief from caring for the child). Providing families with lists of services that contain addresses, telephone numbers, contacts, eligibility requirements, and fees, however, may not be enough. Service coordinators also evaluate the adequacy of available services. Moxley (1989) suggested "five A's" of assessing the adequacy of professional care. The "five A's" are described in Table 5.3.

PLANNING SERVICES

In addition to assessing service needs, the service coordinator develops a comprehensive service plan that includes professional involvement and maximum family participation. Teamwork is generally considered the best model to use for developing a comprehensive service plan. The team approach is characterized by several professionals with various areas of expertise sharing their perspectives and suggesting treatments or services for children and, in some cases, for the children's families (Thomas, Correa, & Morsink, 1995).

Types of Teams

Three types of team approach are typically utilized, including **multidisciplinary, interdisciplinary,** and **transdisciplinary teams.** Family members, social workers, psychologists, physicians, speech and language pathologists, audiologists, nurses, teachers, daycare providers, and occupational, physical, art, and music therapists may all be members of teams.

Multidisciplinary Teams. A multidisciplinary team is one in which the professionals act as consultants, but they often do not provide hands-on treatment themselves. Each professional is responsible for assessment of a child and family needs related to each professional's own area of expertise. One

TABLE 5.3   The Five A's for Assessing Professional Care

Availability

- Does the service exist? Is there a service gap, a lack of an available service, needed by a child who has special needs or by the child's family?
- Example: There are respite services for school-aged children but not for preschool-aged children.

Adequacy

- Can the service be offered at a level that adequately meets the needs of the child and family?
- Example: A family needs meals delivered five days a week, but an agency was only able to deliver meals three days a week.

Appropriateness

- Does the service meet the specific needs of the child?
- Example: A policy exists allowing for placing a child in a play group based solely on age rather than also considering medical, therapeutic, social, or other needs.

Accessibility

- Are there geographical, financial, sociocultural, psychological, temporal, or physical barriers to delivering a service?
- Example: Affordable, wheelchair-accessible transportation, with car seats for young children, is necessary but not available.

Acceptability

- Does the service meet the preferences of the child and family?
- Example: A child is placed in a play group more than one hour's distance from the child's home. Although a service is recommended, in this case it may not be acceptable to the family because of the traveling time. A service may not be acceptable merely because the family deems it inappropriate. The case coordinator may step in, perhaps to convince the family of the importance of the child receiving the benefits of the service. Also, because this may be the family member's first experience with professionals, they may think they are obligated to accept, without question or comment, the services offered them. This should not be the case.

adapted from Moxley (1989)

individual, who could be the service coordinator, is responsible for summarizing the information. Often the various professionals who provide input do not come to a consensus because they do not spend time together discussing the child and the family's needs. Recommendations or findings may contradict each other using the multidisciplinary team approach because consensus is not the focus.

Interdisciplinary Teams. In contrast, an interdisciplinary team consists of those professionals who work directly with the child and family. Interdisciplinary teams typically place greater emphasis on communication among team members. Each member of the team may complete assessments independently but meet to discuss their findings and recommendations. Team members provide each other with feedback and then final recommendations are developed through consensus. Each child's individualized plan (IFSP or IEP) integrates team members' recommendations.

Trandisciplinary Teams. A transdisciplinary team approach is designed to reduce the fragmentation of services. This type of team involves a group of individuals including parents and various professionals, that assesses the child's and family's needs and plans and provides early intervention services. Team members train each other in their area of expertise and may assess a child or interview the family together. For example, a speech and language pathologist, a special education teacher, and occupational and physical therapists might all observe the child at the same time during "free play," and record their own specific observations as one of them takes the child through a set of predetermined tasks. Using a transdisciplinary team approach, one member of the team is usually designated as the team leader for a particular child and family. This method requires a major commitment of time and coordination of schedules.

Regardless of the type of team approach, service coordinators are needed to ensure continuity, feedback, and to establish a system of accountability to guarantee appropriate services. See Fig-

ure 5.1 for a description of the interdisciplinary team process provided through a story analogy.

Major Team Goals

The goal of the team is to formulate an organized evaluation and develop a service plan for the child. The plan would also include the needs of the family when children are less than three years old. The success of the plan relies in part on the communication level of all the participants. While professionals, such as educators, psychologists, social workers, and therapists, often have training and experience working in teams, this may be a new experience for family members. An important aspect of the service coordinator's role is to assist the family members in understanding their roles as part of the team and participating as effective members of a team. Duwa, Wells, and Lalinde (1993) list delineation of roles, respect, and effective communication as the factors they believe contribute to an effective team approach.

Team Members' Roles

Kirst–Ashman and Hull (1993) identified time, leadership, and communication as factors contributing to team building. They stated that the team leader should be qualified and experienced in working with teams. Additionally, team members should familiarize themselves with the **jargon** (terminology) of other disciplines, although professionals from different disciplines need to communicate in a jargon-free manner as frequently as possible. Often this is difficult, however, because one of the attributes of a profession is its specialized language. Family members are usually the least likely to understand and ask about professional jargon and acronyms. Therefore, the service coordinator must be prepared to translate and interpret professional jargon and try to curtail those who use jargon excessively.

Parental Involvement

One of the six major principles of PL 94–142 (the Education for All Handicapped Children Act,

An adaptation of *The Blind Men and the Elephant*

Six members of the interdisciplinary team gathered to discuss the elephant.

The teacher looked at the elephant's head. "We must deliberate how much it can be expected to learn."

The speech therapist looked at the elephant and seeing the trunk said, "This is clearly going to interfere with communication; we should direct our attention here."

The audiologist looked at the elephant's huge ears. "I'm sure this is causing the problem; we will put our attention on the ears."

The nutritionist looked at the elephant and saw how enormous it was. "Obviously, it eats too much. We will concentrate on its dietary needs."

The physical therapist looked at the elephant and saw the tusks. "They lack flexibility and they are going to interfere with socialization. This is where we will focus."

The art therapist looked at the elephant and said, "It's all one color; we should focus on the introduction of shade and nuance."

The team members argued from their individual perspectives. Enter the case coordinator, of course, who explained that the elephant is a large animal. "Each of you with your specialized training and perspective tends to 'see' the animal in terms of your area of expertise. We all must put the parts together to obtain an authentic picture of the elephant."

In Lillian Quigley's retelling of the old story from India, the blind men agree that the Rajah (case coordinator) is right and that they can discover the whole truth about the elephant by putting all of the parts together.

Also in Quigley's account, it is interesting to note that the blind men were able to get to the Rajah's palace to "see" the elephant and return home only through cooperation. They lined up from shortest to tallest and each man put his hand on the shoulder of the man in front.

FIGURE 5.1   The Interdisciplinary Team and the Elephant

1975) addressed parent participation (Turnbull, 1983). It mandated that parents have access to information, due process, and encouragement to participate in public hearings, advisory panels, and advocacy groups. PL 94–142 also mandated that parents be designated as members of the committee that develops their child's individualized education program (IEP) or individualized family service plan (IFSP) (Cone, Delawyer, & Wolfe, 1985; Bishop, Rounds, & Weil, 1993). The service coordinator is responsible for assuring that appropriate procedures are followed for developing an

IFSP or IEP and that services listed on the IFSP or IEP are provided.

Duwa, et al. (1993) cautioned that family involvement should not be considered synonymous with **family-centered programming.** They described family-centered involvement as including family members as decision, policy, and program participants and recipients of support, whereas family involvement suggests that parents help their children but the parents themselves do not receive services. A substantial amount of literature indicates that there are often complications in parent–professional relationships. (See Chapter 6 for further discussion of parent–professional relationships). The service coordinator must ensure that families be allowed and encouraged to participate in planning services.

Sheehan (1988) reviewed the research on parental involvement in early childhood assessment and planning of services and found that parents' evaluation of their children's accomplishments varied from those of other team members. That is, parents tended to rate their children's accomplishments at a higher level than did other team members or than test scores indicated. In addition, parents often reported dissatisfaction with the parent–professional relationships, stating that they felt blamed, suspected, ignored, and patronized by professionals, while also being viewed as uncooperative and angry (Smith, 1992).

Duwa, et al. (1993) cautioned that families should not be criticized, put at a disadvantage, or glorified as exemplary because of their decisions regarding the amount or degree of investment in the decision-making process. Again, it is the service coordinator's responsibility to ensure that families receive the services they need.

It is critical to determine the type of parent–professional relationships that will best serve children's needs. Mulliken (1983) asserts that a team approach, with parents as full members, is most beneficial for children since parents generally know a great deal about their children. Drawing from her experience as a parent, Alexander (Alexander & Tompkins–McGill, 1987) makes several suggestions to professionals regarding effective methods for working with parents of children with special needs. These suggestions are listed in Table 5.4.

INTERVENTION SERVICES

In addition to assessment and planning services, the service coordinator provides intervention services for the family. These services include **direct** and **indirect intervention.** Direct intervention services include teaching parents effective communication skills, making suggestions for methods to solve problems, and providing family counseling. Indirect intervention includes the service coordinator acting as a **broker,** who locates services, and an **advocate,** who acquires needed services.

Direct Intervention

The service coordinators intervene directly to help families strengthen skills and capacities for self-care. Summers, Dell'Oliver, Turnbull, Benson, Santelli, Campbell, and Siegel–Causey (1990) reported that families often need assistance in developing skills to work with professionals and service delivery systems. Modeling and coaching are often helpful techniques for teaching family members new skills, demonstrating problem-solving, and developing an inventory of responses that might be used in difficult situations.

Modeling Skills for Parents.   **Modeling** requires service coordinators to call attention to the behavior they are modeling for the parents and to explain why the modeled behavior is useful. In some cases, modeling behavior through role-play is very helpful. **Coaching** involves service coordinators encouraging family members to share their concerns or observations with other team members. It also involves providing opportunities to practice methods of sharing these concerns (Kirst–Ashman & Hull, 1993).

Shy or reticent family members need help learning how to participate or ask for clarification at team meetings. Using **role-playing** and coaching

TABLE 5.4   Suggestions to Professionals

When working with parents who have children with special needs:

1. Remember to view the child as a whole person. Although the evaluations of each individual professional in various disciplines are important, data must be processed together to provide appropriate intervention.
2. Judge each child on individual progress rather than merely against a set of universal norms. For example, there are expected standards or developmental milestones that may be used for evaluation of skills, such as sitting and walking, but the child should also be evaluated on individual progress toward achieving those goals.
3. Include parents' observations about the child's health, eating, and sleeping habits, for example, as important data. Listen with professional respect to parents.
4. Create a comfortable environment (time, space, attitude) for parents to speak. Listen to and value their contributions. Parents often approach professionals in fear. Professionals should not use fear to create or maintain an unequal relationship.
5. Help parents and professionals come to an agreement on a common language that will be used. Avoid jargon.
6. Consider the implications of a child as a member of a family. For example, if specific physical equipment is prescribed for a child, family members will need to know how it works and to understand that they should follow through on recommendations for its use.
7. Differentiate between fact and opinion. It is important that families have the facts. When professionals express an opinion, it should be identified as such.
8. Work toward solutions and resources. Parents need direction beyond a diagnosis. If printed resources are available regarding the child's type of disability, provide these resources to the family or tell parents how to get such material.
9. Provide a ray of hope. Remain optimistic about the child's progress. Remember that, after parents spend time with professionals, parents go home and must interact with other family members. Try not to send them away in despair.

adapted from Alexander & Tompkins–McGill (1987)

helps them become more assertive. For example, a service coordinator might ask a parent to participate in a role-play in which the service coordinator takes the role of special education teacher. During this role-play, the service coordinator, in the role of special education teacher, would create a variety of situations and the parents would practice responding to these situations. After each scenario, the service coordinator and parent would discuss the interactions and note effective and ineffective strategies. When parents successfully use effective strategies, the service coordinator should acknowledge these strategies.

Families with young children who have special needs are often reluctant or too inexperienced to share their thoughts, experiences, and observations of their children with professionals. In many cases, family members must interact with many different types of professionals throughout the child's educational experience and beyond.

There is a strong possibility that less assertive parents will quickly become frustrated and even angry because they believe their perspective is not being considered. It is nearly impossible for professionals to meet parents' needs if those needs have not been effectively communicated. For this reason, it is important for parents to learn to represent themselves and their present perspectives clearly and as soon as possible. Coaching and modeling are often effective strategies for developing this skill.

The need for parents to be able to learn to speak out is demonstrated in the following situation. A group of preschool personnel speculated about why a child arrived at school acting very tired. The staff discussion took place in the presence of the child's mother. They spoke about the seizure medication regime, speculated about bedtime routines at home, and were concerned about the effects of the long bus ride to the school. The mother, a shy young woman, became agitated while listening to the staff talk about her child, but said nothing.

Several days later, the service coordinator shared the mother's feelings with the staff and went on to explain that the child typically slept for only four hours each night, often waking up and screaming for more than an hour. The mother, feeling responsible, guilty, and exhausted, did not share this behavior with the staff. After practicing communication skills, though the use of modeling and coaching opportunities the service coordinator provided, the mother could describe her child's behavior to the team and participate in formulating treatment recommendations.

Much of the direct work with families centers around very specific incidents such as this one. The service coordinator, though, is also often involved in providing counseling services to families of children with special needs. Parents' emotional needs must be met before they can adequately meet the needs of their children. Children may also require counseling services that may be provided in the form of play therapy. Social workers often provide this type of child counseling therapy, which involves using toys to reenact situations or express feelings.

Dealing with Family Members' Emotional Needs. Parents of children with special needs often have direct service and emotional needs. Many of these emotional needs emerge during the service coordinator's assessment of the family's emotional functioning. Even if family members have many formal and informal social networks, there often is no one with whom family members may freely discuss their feelings of shock, denial, bargaining, anger, guilt, and depression.

The analogy of the **snow dome,** a small winter scene with snowlike flakes in liquid encased by a glass dome, is useful to illustrate the emotional ups and downs families of children with special needs often experience. When the snow dome is moved, the snowflakes fly around in the liquid but ultimately settle down only to wait again for the next movement of the dome. Just like the snowflakes in the dome, families often find themselves at the mercy of movement that are precipitated by any number of events over which they have little or no control. See Figure 5.2 for an illustration of the **snow dome effect.**

These successive events involve meeting the basic and specialized needs of the child and family and include medical, financial, educational and developmental services, and respite care. The snowflakes symbolize a wide range of emotional and coping skills, and there is no way to determine where, when, or how the emotional and coping "snowflakes" will fall. Families and professionals should consider this analogy to understand the various emotional reactions and coping skills of families. The feelings include shock, denial, sadness, anger, rage, anxiety, pain, bargaining, acceptance, and adjustment.

Contributing to the snow-dome effect is an often neglected but critical aspect of helping the family of a child with special needs deal with the feeling of "chronic or recurrent sorrow or grief" (Davis, 1987; Willner & Crane, 1979). This grief occurs because of the loss of the "ideal" child, the one without disabilities. This sense of grief also occurs when the child's disability is first diagnosed. Hughes and Rycus (1983) listed time, financial stability, person freedom, and mobility as attributes that often disrupt family equilibrium and contribute to the snow dome effect.

Use of Stage Theory to Understand Family Emotional Responses

Frequently, stage theories are used to understand and cope with loss. Stage theories generally imply that, with the passage of time, the loss is resolved and acceptance follows.

Seligman and Darling (1989) report on composite studies that draw varying conclusions about the number of stages of dealing with loss and whether the stages are sequential. It is important for parents and professionals to be aware of these feelings of loss. This awareness facilitates understanding a family's emotional reactions during transitions and crises.

Many families experience shock when the child's disability is first diagnosed. This is particularly true of a family that had no prior warning of a possible disability. Most families spend between seven and nine months expecting and planning for

FIGURE 5.2   The Snow-Dome Effect

a "normal" baby. In spite of a diagnosis that suggests that a disability exists, families may deny that there is an impairment. Kübler–Ross (1969) includes **bargaining** in her proposed stages of how an individual faces imminent death. The bargaining stage is useful when describing one reaction parents of children with specials needs exhibit. These parents often seek the miracle cure, "bargain" for a cure, or believe that if they, the parents, work extra hard, the child will improve or be cured.

While it is assumed that most parents will diligently seek every possible resource for their child, they should be encouraged, insofar as possible, to view the child realistically. For example, some years ago, when organ transplants were emerging as viable methods of treatment for certain health problems, the father of a young girl with a rare genetic disorder asked the service coordinator to assess the possibility of a brain transplant for his daughter.

The service coordinator acknowledged this father's Herculean effort, on behalf of his daughter, while explaining that a brain transplant was not available in the foreseeable future. Initially, the father became angry and blamed his wife, God, and his daughter's caretakers, including the service coordinator, for less than miraculous progress. Often, such anger is projected onto professionals. While it is disturbing, it is also understandable when put in the chronic mourning context.

Allowing parents to express anger frequently has a purifying or cleansing effect. The father was able to come to terms with his daughter's special needs, perhaps in part because he was allowed to vent his frustration and anger. He could then meet his daughter's needs in a more effective fashion, such as finding appropriate therapy.

In addition to the reaction of anger, parents may express feelings of guilt. Harris (1983) reports on a study by DeMyer (1979) in which two-thirds of the mothers of children diagnosed as autistic expressed guilt over having caused the impairment of the child, even though there was no evidence that they caused the autism. In some cases, the guilt is tied to the mother's behavior, including smoking, consuming alcohol, taking medication, or living near a chemical factory during pregnancy. Parents often feel guilty for not doing enough for the child before the child's birth, including such things as not getting enough rest or not eating the right foods.

As family members move toward acceptance of the chronic nature of the child's impairment, they may become depressed. Kratochvil and Devereux (1988) report that the literature regarding the length of the grieving process does not provide conclusive knowledge regarding the grief experienced by parents of children with special needs. They do, however, conclude that, while the grieving process for the parents might have closure, it is more likely to be recurrent and to extend over time.

Family members need to understand that their opposing feelings regarding the child's disability are legitimate and normal, and need to be prepared to have those feelings resurface from time to time (Biale, 1989; Kratochvil & Devereux, 1988). Davis (1987) suggested that service coordinators should be aware of predictable times when grief is likely to reemerge. Wikler, Wasow, and Hatfield (1983) identified major stress points as: the first time the child is diagnosed, atypical achievement at various developmental stages, educational placement or discussion of placement, and on the child's twenty-first birthday.

Wikler, Wasow, and Hatfield (1981) found that parents of children with special needs often experienced stress and sadness at several different times, and the researchers concluded that sorrow is often recurrent. Dane (1985) asserts that the mourning process often reemerges at "each developmental stage and when milestones of societal expectations are not attained by the child" (p. 507). In any case, it is understood that this mourning and the form it takes, for the most part, does not signify a dysfunctional family system but rather a normal grieving process.

The ambiguity of the mourning process has a direct impact on parent–professional interactions and relationships because there may be a resurgence of mourning brought on by various educational and rehabilitation evaluations. Parents and professionals alike often are not prepared to cope with the parents' extreme emotional outbursts, leading both parties to feel misunderstood and unappreciated. For example, Wikler, et. al. (1983) found that social workers tended to miscalculate how disconcerting later life experiences were to the parents of children who are mentally retarded. This suggests that the role of the service coordinator should also include educating families and professionals about **chronic mourning** and the possible outcomes.

The mourning process may be further complicated and exacerbated by the level of careprovider responsibilities. These responsibilities are often very demanding when they include caring for a child with special needs. Family members might not permit themselves or may be too busy to think or talk about the "perfect" child they anticipated but did not receive. A skilled social worker can assist the family members in talking about their expectations of the "perfect" child, facilitating and legitimizing this aspect of the grieving process. Table 5.5 provides a summary of Seligman and Darling's (1989) description of attributes that may affect the ability of parents to accept their child's special needs.

It is important to remember that families are not homogeneous in emotional reaction or structure. Each family member reacts differently at different points in time. Nonetheless, "each family member is personally affected by the developmental disability; each struggles with his/her own adaptation" (Daniels, 1982, p. 27). For example, while siblings (i.e., brothers and sisters) of children with special needs typically are very accepting and cooperative at a young age, the same siblings often have different reactions during adolescence. During adolescence siblings may begin to act resentful toward their brother or sister who has special needs.

TABLE 5.5 Attributes that Affect Parents' Acceptance of Their Child's Special Needs

Following are factors that may affect parents' acceptance of their child's special needs:

- The ability to discuss the child's weaknesses with relative comfort;
- The ability to maintain a balance between encouraging independence and being over-protective;
- The ability to work with professionals in preparing practical short- and long-term goals;
- The ability to follow personal pursuits that are unrelated to their child;
- The ability to discipline the child without guilt.

adapted from Seligman & Darling (1989, p. 87)

Bishop, Rounds, and Weil (1993) suggested that service coordinators encourage parents to discuss the expectations they have of their child. They observed that acceptance of the child's condition is enhanced when family members can view the child as having a condition rather than the condition being the sum total of the child. Denial most often results when the condition is used to describe the child and family.

Parents will benefit by learning to view their child as a child with a disability rather than seeing their child as a disabled child. When parents focus on the disability, the child's condition "becomes the focus for resentment, guilt, blame, and hopelessness" (Bishop, et al., 1994, p. 209). Appleby (1994) reported finding more positive self-concept evaluations in college-aged students with disabilities who had developed a more "philosophical" view of their disability. That is, these students saw themselves as a student with a disability. Students who had a less positive self-concept appeared resentful and were inclined to focus on their disability by viewing themselves as "disabled" students.

Lendrum and Syme (1992) addressed the needs of counselors who were involved in bereavement. The researchers pointed out that it may be difficult to accept the display of strong feelings that parents of children with special needs often show without attempting to try to make things better for the parents. They further suggested that, "it is a counsellor's task to help a client give words to his sorrow" (p. 83). They proposed, however, that counselors may not be able to help clients with this task until they come to terms with their own feelings. These observations seem applicable when working with parents of children with special needs. Counselors may feel very sad or be overwhelmed with a sense of hopelessness regarding the diagnoses of children who have developmental disabilities. Lendrum and Syme (1992) believe that it is important for counselors to understand their own feelings about loss because they could influence the effectiveness of their intervention.

This section has focused on ways that service coordinators provide direct services to assist families in coping with the emotional stress brought on by the variety of issues families of children with special needs face. While direct services are crucial, indirect services that encourage service providers or organizations to be sensitive to a family's needs are also important. Indirect services that are related to service coordination are delivery system knowledge development, staff supervision, staff deployment, dispute resolution, program development, staff information exchange, and organizational maintenance (Morales & Sheafor, 1992).

Indirect Services

Indirect services includes the two social work roles of broker and advocate. Very few individual programs are capable of meeting all of the needs of the child with disabilities and the child's family. The broker links families with a variety of necessary resources (Kirst–Ashman & Hull, 1993). The long-term goal of the broker is to enable families to deal with systems themselves once the connections have been made (Popple & Leighninger, 1993).

Service Coordinator's Role as Broker.   An example of the role of service coordinator as a broker involves finding a pediatric dentist who is familiar with, trained, and able to treat children with special needs. The service coordinator must model and coach the family about methods for finding an appropriate dentist. In the situations where the service coordinator initially contacts the dentist on behalf of the family, the family should be informed about all the steps taken to find the dentist and to establish a union between needs and services. This will help the family to meet subsequent needs without the assistance of the service coordinator. It is generally best if family members observe the service coordinator engaging in this process. For example, the service coordinator could invite the parents to sit and listen as the service coordinator talks with the dentist.

Another example of indirect services involves finding additional support networks. Families often require direction toward new support groups, such as may be found in interactions with other parents who have children with special needs. Families of children with special needs may share similar circumstances and feelings. The value of parent groups in providing support and education is somewhat neglected in the literature. Even though parent groups have received limited attention, research has suggested a number of important aspects of parent support groups for families of children with special needs.

Daniels (1982) studied parent groups to learn about the needs parents identified for themselves. Collins and Collins (1990) began parent support groups at parent's requests, and Alexander and Tompkins–McGill (1987) initiated parent groups to encourage leadership. These researchers reported that parents indicated that parent support groups were beneficial for four main reasons:

1. The groups provided opportunities to associate with other parents who had comparable needs;
2. They increased parents' abilities to face their feelings about their child;
3. They provided advice and support for how to deal with difficult situations;
4. They provided a mechanism for sharing information about community resources.

When providing suggestions to professionals who work with families who have children with special needs, Alexander and Tompkins–McGill (1987) recommend bringing together families with children who have similar diagnoses to share information and lend support to each other. Ferris and Marshall (1987) reported on a family support project in which a crisis group for families was used for effective emotional outlet, identification with other families, and distinguishing feelings.

Friesen (1989) reported that about half of the respondents to a national survey of parents of children with serious emotional disorders and who were attending support groups with other parents of children with special needs found this involvement helpful. In another study involving families of young children with special needs, Petr and Barney (1993) reported that parents cited emotional support as their most crucial need. The authors of this study further reported that "the most reliable and inspirational source of support was other parents of children with similar disabilities" (p. 250).

Professionals should be aware of and direct family members to family support groups. Many community newspapers periodically publish a comprehensive list of support groups. In addition, local United Way offices and Departments of Social Services often provide listings of support groups. If, however, there are not appropriate parent support groups available, the service coordinator should consider helping to organize them.

Service Coordinator's Role as Advocate. Additionally, the role of advocate helps to ensure that service providers are responsive to the family's needs (Morales & Sheafor, 1992). For example, a pediatric dentist might be found, but the dentist could initially refuse to take the child's case for any number of reasons. An advocate would speak on behalf of the family while at the same time modeling advocacy and assertion skills that the family members will need to access services for themselves in the future. This advocacy process lays the groundwork for children with disabilities to learn to be advocates for themselves later in life. Families unable to advocate for themselves will perhaps be less able to teach their children to advocate for themselves.

MONITORING SERVICE PLANS

In addition to assessment, planning, and intervention, the service coordinator monitors the service plan. Three aspects of monitoring include: confirming that agreed-on services are being provided, analyzing the level of success of the service delivery systems, and evaluating the level of commitment of social network members.

Using Organizational Skills

Service coordinators must have good organizational skills. They will often need to monitor many services provided by many individuals. To be most constructive, the service coordinator must understand and value the expertise of the other members of the team, including family members. The service coordinator must have well-developed organizational skills to guarantee that details of the intervention plan are conveyed to all parties.

The need for attention to details can be seen in the following example. A service team agrees that a child should learn to assist in getting dressed. After several weeks, the child is no closer in meeting this goal and often seems confused by the task. In this case, the service delivery providers are not completing the service plan and the child's status is problematic. It would be appropriate for any member of the team to contact the service coordinator about this difficulty because the service coordinator should have an overview of all aspects of the case. It might be determined that the service plan was not specific enough. That is, the plan did not state which items of clothing would go on first. If this were the case, the plan would need to be modified. The service coordinator would direct this modification process.

Often service coordinators are responsible for scheduling, leading, and generating the reports for team meetings. Usually, the most efficient way to monitor the service plan is for each member of the team to prepare a written report that is shared at the team meeting. It is often problematic and less productive when service coordinators lead the team meetings and also take responsibility for writing the entire report. It is difficult for service coordinators to state specific objectives for areas in which they are not experts. When each team member prepares a written report there is generally more time for productive discussions that lead to well-thought-out recommendations.

Careful program monitoring tends to advance the identification of additional needs as they arise and contributes to a smooth progression for the child and family (Moxley, 1989). Monitoring requires that all aspects of the service plan be recorded in detail, including who is responsible for affecting the plan, what implements are needed, and how soon the goals should be completed. Monitoring primarily involves service delivery and evaluating the usefulness of those services.

Determining Service Productivity

Service coordinators also monitor service plans by evaluating the productivity of the service plan, its bearing on the functioning of the child and family, the social network's ability to reinforce the family, and the capacity of the social service professionals to work with the family. Evaluation focuses on whether the plan achieves the sought-after outcome (Moxley, 1989).

During the **evaluation phase,** outcomes related to intervention are examined. The service coordinator should make certain that the projected goals are achieved. For example, it could be important to determine if the child is able to self-feed or if the home or service providing facilities are wheelchair accessible. These types of evaluations help determine whether service plans are resulting in the desired results.

Evaluation Tools

A vital aspect of evaluation includes deciding how to best gather data to draw accurate conclusions. In some cases, informal observations of children are sufficient. In other cases, detailed data gathered from daily or hourly observations or standardized assessment instruments are needed. It is also valuable to attempt to determine why plans or methods of intervention were or were not effective.

For example, a certain behavioral plan may work with a child in one family but not with another child in another family. Evaluation should also include the various service delivery systems and their ability to continue to provide needed services for the child and family. Additionally, since

children **age out** (no longer qualify because they are too old) of preschool services, it is important to determine if there are appropriate services available to the child and family during the transition to the next school situation. See Chapter 15 for a discussion of transitions.

Moxley (1989) developed a helpful introduction and questionnaire for securing professional reaction to the service plan and its effectiveness (p. 128). The results of questionnaires could be summarized at or before the team meeting and provide necessary evaluations of the service plans. Moxley (1989) believes that a part of the assessment process should include the family's evaluation of the service coordination. This evaluation should indicate the attitudes of the family regarding service coordination as well as empower the function of the family as more than service consumers. This evaluation directly evaluates the worth, significance, and benefit of the service coordination for the family.

CONCLUSION

Moore (1990) aptly points out that, "case management is not a panacea for the problems of social service delivery" (p. 447). DuBois and Miley (1992), however, make an excellent point about the goal of case management: "...[C]ase management presumes a professional orientation that is geared toward empowering families..." (p. 284).

Gerhart (1990) describes the principles of service coordination as individualized, comprehensive, and coordinated services that promote autonomy. Throughout this chapter the importance of empowerment has been emphasized. Empowerment involves collaboration between families and professionals, with an underlying view of families, and the formal and informal networks, as competent and capable. This view supports the philosophy of this book, that parents and their children must be greeted with "open arms" by all service providers (Lowenthal, 1992).

Although children with special needs may frequently require service coordination for extended periods of time, a competent service coordinator should ultimately impart the necessary skills to the families that would allow them to be their own service coordinators. After all, where will the children learn service coordination skills to ultimately become self-sufficient if they do not learn them from their families? This skill is crucial because as children with disabilities strive for independence, a significant aspect of that independence will be the ability to advocate for oneself.

The next chapter continues the discussion of the importance of parents and professionals working in an effective partnership. It also provides a description of attitudes and expectations parents and professions may have about each other, components of effective communication, and conflicts that may arise between parents and professionals.

CHAPTER SUMMARY

- The purpose of service coordination is to foster knowledge and develop abilities within the family regarding how to effectively use social services and supports and to develop self-reliance skills. It also includes coordination of services for children and their families.
- Assessment activities of the service coordinator include defining issues, gathering information from other professionals, and working with children and their families to determine the types of services needed.
- Service coordinators develop service plans that often include transdisciplinary, multidisciplinary, and/or interdisciplinary teams providing services to children and their families.
- Direct intervention involves working with the families to strengthen their ability to help themselves. Indirect intervention involves gaining access to other services that are needed by families.
- Service coordinators monitor and evaluate service plans to ensure that plans are being followed and children are achieving set goals.

REVIEW QUESTIONS

1. What are the major tasks of service coordinators? Why are these tasks important?

2. Why are social networks important? Why are different types of networks needed?
3. What is the "snow dome effect"? How is it useful in understanding the needs of families who have children with special needs?
4. What are direct and indirect interventions? Why are both important?
5. Why is empowerment important?

SUGGESTED STUDENT ACTIVITIES

1. Contact a social worker and discuss the role of the service coordinator and services this person provides.
2. Read the works of Kübler–Ross and consider how her work might be helpful in understanding the grief process of parents who have children with special needs.
3. With a group of your classmates, role-play how a service coordinator might work with other professionals to help family members teach a child to tie shoes.

ADDITIONAL READINGS

Friesen, B. J. & Poetner, J. (1995). *From case management to service coordination for children with emotional, behavioral, or mental disorders: Building family strengths.* Baltimore, MD: Paul Brooks.

Swallow, R., & Huebner, K. M. (Eds.). (1987). *How to thrive and not just survive.* New York: American Foundation for the Blind.

Krementz, J. (1992). *How it feels to live with a physical disability.* New York: Simon & Schuster.

Rothman, J. (1994). Practice with highly vulnerable clients: Case management and community-based services. Englewood Cliffs, NJ: Prentice Hall.

ADDITIONAL RESOURCES

National Association of Social Workers
750 1st Street, N.E., Suite 700
Washington, DC 20002–4241

REFERENCES

Able–Boone, H., Sandall, S., Stevens, E., & Frederick, L. L. (1992). Family support resources and needs:

How early intervention can make a difference. *Infant–Toddler Intervention, 2*(2), 93–102.

Alexander, R., & Tompkins–McGill, P. (1987). Notes to the experts from the parent of a handicapped child. *Social Work, 32,* 361.

Appleby, E. T. (1994). *The relationship between self-advocacy and self-concept.* Ann Arbor: University Microfilms International, No. 9411230).

Biale, R. (1989). Counseling families of disabled twins. *Social Work, 34,* 531–535.

Bishop, K. K., Rounds, K., & Weil, M. (1993). PL 99–457: Preparation for social work practice with infants and toddlers with disabilities and their families. *Journal of Social Work Education, 29,* 36–45.

Brill, N. I. (1976). *Teamwork: Working together in human services.* Philadelphia: J. B. Lippincott.

Buckley, J. J. (1983). Roles of the professionals. In R. K. Mulliken & J. J. Buckley (Eds.), *Assessment of multihandicapped and developmentally disabled children* (pp. 63–73). Rockville, MD: Aspen.

Collins, B., & Collins, T. (1990). Parent–professional relationships in the treatment of seriously emotionally disturbed children and adolescents. *Social Work, 35,* 522–527.

Cone, J. D., Delawyer, D. D., & Wolfe, V. V. (1985). Assessing parent participation: The parent/family involvement index. *Exceptional Children, 51,* 417–424.

Dane, E. (1985). Professional and lay advocacy in the education of handicapped children. *Social Work, 30,* 505–510.

Daniels, S. M. (1982, August). From parent-advocacy to self-advocacy: A problem of transition. *Exceptional Education Quarterly, 6,* 25–32.

Davis, B. H. (1987). Disability and grief. *Social Casework, 68,* 352–357.

DeMyer, M. K. (1979). *Parents and children in autism.* New York: Wiley.

Dennis, R. E., Williams, W., Giangreco, M. F., & Cloninger, C. J. (1993). Quality of life as context for planning and evaluation of services for people with disabilities. *Exceptional Children, 59*(6), 499–512.

DiMichele, L. (1993). The role of the school social worker in early childhood special education. *School Social Work Journal, 18,* 9–16.

DuBois, B., & Miley, K. K. (1992). *Social work: An empowering profession.* Boston: Allyn and Bacon.

Dudley, J. R. (1987). Speaking for themselves: People who are labeled as mentally retarded. *Social Work, 32,* 80–82.

Duwa, S. M., Wells, C., & Lalinde, P. (1993). Creating family-centered programs and policies. In D. M. Bryant & M. A. Graham (Eds.), *Implementing early intervention* (pp. 92–123). New York: Guilford Press.

Early, T. J., & Poertner, J. (1993). Families with children with emotional disorders: A review of the literature. *Social Work, 38,* 743–764.

Featherstone, H. (1981). *A difference in the family.* New York: Penguin Books.

Ferris, P. A., & Marshall, C. A. (1987). A model project for families of the chronically mentally ill. *Social Work, 32,* 110–114.

Fiene, J. I., & Taylor, P. A. (1991). Serving rural families of developmentally disabled children: A case management model. *Social Work 36,* 323–327.

Freedman, S. A., & Clarke, L. L. (1991). Financing care for medically complex children. In N. J. Hochstadt & D. M. Yost (Eds.), *The medically complex child: The transition to home care* (pp. 259–286).

Friesen, B. J. (1989). National study of parents whose children have serious emotional disorders. In A. Algarin, R. Friedman, A. Duchnowski, A. Kutash, S. Silver, & M. Johnson (Eds.), *Second annual conference proceedings—children's mental health services and policy: Building a research base* (pp. 36–52). Tampa, FL: Research and Training Center for Children's Mental Health, University of South Florida.

Gerhart, U. C. (1990). *Caring for the chronic mentally ill.* Itasca, IL: Peacock.

Hanson, M. J., & Lynch, E. W. (1992). Family diversity: Implications for policy and practice. *Topics in Early Childhood Special Education, 12*(3), 283–306.

Harris, S. L. (1983). *Families of the developmentally disabled: A guide to behavioral intervention.* New York: Pergamon Press.

Hughes, R. C., & Rycus, J. S. (1983). *Child welfare services for children with developmental disabilities.* New York: Child Welfare League of America.

Kirst–Ashman, K. K., & Hull, Jr., G. H. (1993). Brokering and case management. In K. K. Kirst–Ashman & G. H. Hull, *Understanding generalist practice* (pp. 492–520). Chicago: Nelson-Hall Publishers.

Kratochvil, M. S., & Devereux, S. A. (1988). Counseling needs of parents of handicapped children. *Social Casework, 69,* 420–426.

Kübler–Ross, E. (1969). *On death and dying.* New York: Macmillan.

Lendrum S., & Syme, G. (1992). *Gift of tears: A practical approach to loss and bereavement counseling.* New York: Routledge.

Lowenthal, B. (1992). Interagency collaboration in early intervention: Rationale, barriers, and implementation. *Infant–Toddler Intervention, 2*(2), 103–111.

Moore, S. T. (1990). A social work practice model of case management: A case management grid. *Social Work, 35,* 444–448.

Morales, A. T., & Sheafor, B. W. (1995). *Social work: A profession of many faces* (7th ed.). Boston: Allyn and Bacon.

Moxley, R. (1989). *The practice of case management.* Newbury Park, CA: Sage.

Mulliken, R. K. (1983). The child in the environment. In R. K. Mulliken & J. J. Buckley (Eds.), *Assessment of multihandicapped and developmentally disabled children* (pp. 37–62). Rockville, MD: Aspen.

Petr, C. G., & Barney, D. D. (1993). Reasonable efforts for children with disabilities: The parents' perspective. *Social Work, 38,* 247–254.

Popple, P. R., & Leighninger, L. (1993). *Social work, social welfare, and American society* (2nd ed.). Boston: Allyn and Bacon.

Rolland, J. S. (1994). *Families, illness, and disability.* New York: Basic Books.

Seligman, M., & Darling, R. B. (1989). *Ordinary families, special children: A systems approach to childhood disability.* New York: Guilford Press.

Sheehan, R. (1988). Involvement of parents in early childhood assessment. In R. D. Wachs & R. Sheehan (Eds.), *Assessment of young developmentally disabled children* (pp. 75–90). New York: Plenum Press.

Smith, J. C. (1992). Parenting seriously disturbed children. *Social Work, 37,* 293–294.

Summers, J. A., Dell'Oliver, C., Turnbull, A. P., Benson, H. A., Santelli, E., Campbell, M., & Siegel–Causey, E. (1990). Examining the individualized family service plan process: What are family and practitioner preferences? *Topics in Early Childhood Education, 10*(1), 78–99.

Thomas, C. C., Correa, V., & Morsink, C. V. (1995). *Interactive teaming: Consultation and collaboration in special programs* (2nd ed.). Columbus, OH: Merrill.

Turnbull, A. P. (1983). Parental participation in the IEP process. In J. A. Mulick & S. M. Pueschel (Eds.), *Parent–professional partnerships in developmental disability services* (pp. 107–122). Cambridge, MA: Ware Press.

Wikler, L., Wasow, M., & Hatfield, E. (1983). Seeking strengths in families of developmentally disabled children. *Exceptional Children, 51*(5), 417–424.

Willner, S. K., & Crane, R. (1979). A parental dilemma: The child with a marginal handicap. *Social Casework, 60,* 30–35.

Woody, R. H., Woody, J. D., & Greenberg, D. B. (1991). Case management for the individualized family service plan under Public Law 99–457. *American Journal of Family Therapy, 19,* 67–76.

CHAPTER 6

PARENTS AND PROFESSIONALS
WORKING TOGETHER

LORRAINE HEDRICK, M.A.

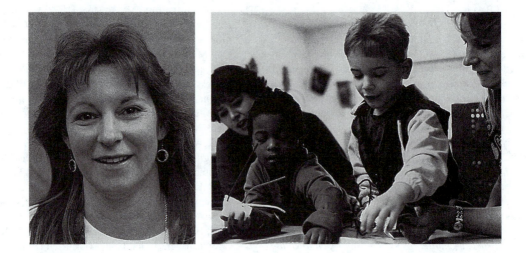

ABOUT THE AUTHOR

Lorraine Hedrick received her master's degree in education in 1985 from the College of Saint Rose, in Albany, New York. She received an associate's degree in childcare from Dutchess Community College, in Poughkeepsie, New York, and in 1978 and in 1980 a bachelor's degree in education from the State University of New York at Geneseo. Ms. Hedrick has New York State permanent certifications in reading, special education, and preschool through grade six elementary education. Her own experiences make her uniquely qualified to write this chapter. She is presently a special education teacher of preschool-aged infants and children with special needs. In 1987, she gave birth three-and-a-half months prematurely to her son, Ernie. Ernie required early intervention services through his preschool years. Ms. Hedrick also has a daughter, Chrissy.

CHAPTER KEY POINTS

- A positive relationship between parents and professionals helps children with special needs develop to their fullest potential.
- Parents' and professionals' attitudes toward and expectations of each other affect relationships between the two groups.
- Parents and professionals use nonverbal and verbal communication to indicate their expectations.

- Conflicts between parents and professionals occur and must be resolved to provide a supportive educational environment for the child.
- Adequately preparing for meetings is necessary to help ensure successful communication between parents and professionals.

The previous chapter discussed the importance of **service coordination** including a focus on the needs of the family. Parents and professionals, including special education teachers, speech and language pathologists, and occupational and physical therapists, must effectively collaborate to help ensure that young children with special needs receive appropriate services (McConkey, 1985). Although professionals know a great deal about the intervention services geared toward specific disabilities, parents typically know their children best. When parents and professionals combine knowledge about services and the child, a plan of action may be developed that supports the child's overall growth and development (Berger, 1995). Professionals have the information and resources that are useful for parents while parents have specific knowledge about their child that professionals can use to guide their decision-making.

PARENT–PROFESSIONAL COLLABORATION

Parents or primary child care providers play a key role in early intervention for children. Without the active involvement of parents, the effects of early intervention are not as positive. Unless parents learn how to work effectively with their child, the gains that are accomplished while the child is in an early intervention program may not be maintained throughout the child's development (Turnbull & Turnbull, 1996).

Parents can contribute valuable information about their child and about the family. They know many things about their child that others do not know, including their child's strengths and weaknesses, likes and dislikes, and medical history. Parents often play important roles in the programs in which their children are enrolled, including serving as voluntary aids, preparing materials and newsletters, fund-raising, and providing support to other parents (Klass, 1996).

When parents and professionals work together to address the individual needs of children in a cooperative rather than adversarial manner, children benefit. Professionals must take responsibility to determine how best to develop this "cooperative partnership" (Mittler, 1979). It is often difficult for parents to feel part of "the team" when they are surrounded by professionals, each with distinct opinions, expertise, vocabulary, and suggestions. Good partnerships do not just happen; they require ongoing communication, conflict resolution, and mutual respect (Bathshaw, 1991).

As mentioned in the previous chapter, all individuals working in a team must feel they are an important part of the team. Each member must view the others as equal partners. Their mutual goal should be to remain focused on finding the most effective method of providing services for the child (McConkey, 1985). Box 6.1 provides an example of the importance of partnerships between parents and professionals. This example is based on the personal experience and reactions of this chapter's author.

CHANGING PERCEPTIONS

Parents and professionals have a very significant similarity—they are people first. Although this fact is obvious, perceptions often change when people play various roles. Because parents typically know their children best, professionals must consider the parents' perceptions of a child. Parents are often

Box 6.1

Ernie

The importance of parent and professional partnerships became very real for my husband and me as we spent most of our time for three-and-a-half months in a neonatal unit with our son, Ernie.

Before Ernie was born, our obstetrician spent seven hours telling us he thought my pregnancy would end in a miscarriage. He told us there was very little chance for survival because our baby was too young to survive outside the womb. Much to the surprise of the doctor, Ernie was born alive. Fortunately, he was also born just as a medical emergency team arrived at the hospital to transport another sick infant to Albany Medical Center, in Albany, New York.

The transport team was asked to provide assistance to Ernie because he was fighting to stay alive. While the arrangements were being made for his transport, I was being consoled by a nurse who thought Ernie would not survive. She explained it was good to begin the mourning process and eventually get on with my life. I held my baby and was shocked to find that he was still fighting for life. I gratefully signed a permission form allowing the transport team to administer an experimental drug that might help Ernie breathe more easily.

The team explained that Ernie had a little less than a 50 percent chance of survival. With teary eyes and shaking hands, I signed a paper giving the team directions not to take extraordinary means to keep our baby alive. I looked down into a special incubator that would take my child in a helicopter to Albany Medical Center. That day ended my partnership with the doctor who delivered Ernie. I could not understand why he did not know Ernie had a chance to live.

The next morning, I began a new chapter in my life. I had no idea of what was in store for my son or what it would be like to sit with my husband at the hospital day after day, willing this child to live. This experience taught me a great deal about partnerships.

My husband and I were treated as very special people when we arrived at Albany Medical Center.

The medical staff provided explanations about what was being done for our baby and what we could expect to happen next. The nurse who helped during the transport brought me to see Ernie. She showed me how I could safely touch him. As the tears of joy rolled down my cheeks, she hugged me and said, "Crying is allowed." Each day, nurses, residents, and doctors helped my husband and me to become involved as much as possible in the care of our baby. Most importantly, they told us to talk to, sing to, and touch our baby. They taught us how to greet him "with open arms."

As any parent who has been through the neonatal unit knows all too well, at times things do not go smoothly. The neonatal unit staff reminded us that for each step forward we should expect two steps backward. These steps backward were very difficult. It was during one of these steps that the primary doctor at the medical center pulled us aside and told us how important we were to the team. He said, "You may not have the medical background or the expertise to understand why certain procedures are done, but you hold a very important key. You know your baby. For over a month, you have sat by your child's side. You know what he likes and what upsets him. You know the body positions in which he functions the best." As it turned out, avoiding body positions that upset our baby and using the positions he preferred made a positive difference in Ernie's oxygen levels, which was key to his continued development.

The doctor also told us that he had used us as an example to the resident physicians of how to work with parents. He explained, "The resident doctors must understand how important parents are in the process. They need to listen to parents. If they do not, they may miss vital pieces of information."

The doctor's words have stayed with me, and I often reflect on them as I work as a teacher with families of children who have special needs. Parents are a vital part of a team. They hold a very important key because they know their child best.

the first to sense that their child has a developmental delay in some area (McConkey, 1985). When parents first bring their child to a professional for help, their hope is often that the professional can "fix" their child's problem (Mittler, 1979).

Professionals in the field of special education are generally very caring individuals who sincerely want to help children and their families (Leviton, Mueller, & Kauffman, 1992). They provide suggestions, guidance, support, and opinions for the parents. Professionals often lead parents to believe that professionals have all the answers and always know what is best for the child (Tizard, Mortimore, & Burchell, 1988). Professionals, however, are responsible for ensuring that parents understand that professionals do *not* have all the answers.

Professionals are responsible for providing a variety of information at a level parents can readily understand. Parents ideally will take an active role in the education process of their child because they are typically the most influential people in the child's life (Davie, Butler, & Goldstein, 1972). Professionals will come and go but parents are parents throughout the child's life.

Professionals must make sure that parents know their own feelings and ideas are important. As discussed in Chapter 5, professionals should encourage parents to be advocates for their children (Brudoff & Orenstein, 1984). They also assist parents in understanding parents are ultimately responsible for the child. Parents are guaranteed the right to be a part of the educational decision-making process because, if they do not participate, it is more likely the child will get "lost in the educational system" and not receive appropriate services.

When parents do not actively participate in their children's education, it is often because they cannot. Parents sometimes are too overloaded with work, for instance, to attend meetings or school events. Professionals, on the other hand, often find it frustrating when parents or guardians do not fully participate in a child's education (Glidden, 1993). Sometimes, suggestions sent home are not followed and meetings are cancelled. Professionals must avoid viewing parents

as uncaring. Professionals have a tendency to interpret a lack of parental involvement to mean that family members do not care about the child. This conclusion is often inaccurate. Many parents have an excessive number of demands placed on their time, and asking them to do one more thing, such as attend a workshop or do a special homework assignment, is enough to shatter the fragile balance in their lives (Turnbull & Turnbull, 1990).

Professionals often focus on the child rather than on the needs of the whole family. They are trained in methods to assist in a child's development. They often become frustrated when parental involvement is not at the level they believe is appropriate. Instead of becoming frustrated or developing a negative attitude toward the parents, professionals must realize that if a parent or guardian is not as involved as the professional would like, it is because the parent simply cannot give more time at that particular point. Professionals must accept the level at which parents become involved, take into account the individual needs of all family members, and avoid placing demands on parents that are likely to add more stress to a stressful life. Parents who are overstressed cannot effectively help their child (Mittler, 1979).

Conversely, parental concerns are naturally focused on their own children rather than the needs of other children with whom professionals work (Hanson & Hanline, 1990; Mittler, 1979). Professionals, however, must be concerned for *all* the children who receive their services. This focus often conflicts with the parents' focus, which is on their individual child (Shea & Bauer, 1991; Turnbull & Turnbull, 1990).

"The squeaky wheel gets the grease" is often true for parents who attempt to acquire services for their child. Parents who make demands on behalf of a child do generally get more attention from professional team members than those who do not (Vaugh, Bos, Harrell, & Lasky, 1988). Professionals often tell parents that they must be advocates for their child. Yet, a parent who *does* argue or plead for a child is frequently labeled as the "difficult parent" or "overdemanding parent."

Most parents do not want to be perceived as difficult or unreasonable. They do not want to cause tension and generally do not intend to make unreasonable demands (Bailey, Palsha, & Simeonsson, 1991). This often leads parents not to act assertively on behalf of the child.

Parents often benefit from guidance on how to be assertive without appearing unreasonable (Bailey & Simeonsson, 1988a). Learning good communication skills, such as reflective listening (i.e., restating the thoughts of the speaker), providing feedback, and being assertive assists parents in effectively "navigating" the educational system with their child. Parent training programs on effective communication are often a valuable addition to early childhood special education programs. Reading books or attending workshops or college classes on developing communication skills are often worthwhile for parents *and* professionals. Table 6.1 provides a list of modes of interaction that parents and professionals find beneficial.

TABLE 6.1 Methods To Help Parents and Professionals Effectively Communicate

- Be honest.
- Remember that it is difficult to anticipate or understand all circumstances.
- It is not reasonable to expect the other to have all the answers, and it is difficult to stay knowledgeable about all the new educational and therapeutic trends that may be beneficial for a child.
- Remember that services are often limited by rules and procedures.
- Whenever possible provide all the information requested.
- Remember that each individual has many responsibilities that often limit their time and focus.
- Share encouraging observations with the other; be positive.
- Show appreciation for the other in words and actions.
- When in disagreement, talk with the other before talking to others about it.

Assertive parents who are active participants in their children's education are the reason that many children receive the required services. When therapists are in short supply, it is usually the assertive parent with an understanding of the laws that pertain to special education who gets services for the child (Dunst, Trivette, & Deal, 1988). Professionals need to consider that when parents complain about or question the services being offered, they usually do so because they believe it is in their child's best interest. Parents who are actively involved in their children's educational programs must be encouraged, not discouraged, to do so (Mittler, 1979).

Professionals often spend much of their personal time thinking about the children in their care, or spend it working on projects designed to help children and their families. This ultimately contributes to professional burnout (Gargiulo, 1985). Burnout does not necessarily lead to professionals leaving their field but contributes to a loss of energy, energy required to be effective on the job. Professionals must remember that they are entitled to personal time and cannot "fix" all the problems children and their families experience. This lesson is often very difficult but is one *all* professionals who wish to last in the field of early childhood special education must learn (Buscaglia, 1975).

"People unfold as they have been folded." This statement was shared at a professional workshop. Every person has a unique set of life experiences. These experiences influence how people deal with difficulties and challenges presented to them. Professionals must remember that parents deal with a child who has developmental delays in their own way. Dealing with these "folds" (individual differences) builds character, provides a person with something to hide behind, or leads to a better understanding of the situation. A child with special needs is just one of the parent's folds. It is not the professional's job to try to smooth out or fix all of the folds in a parent's life. Ideally, professionals provide support while allowing time for the parents to "unfold" themselves (Buscaglia, 1975).

Box 6.2 describes a situation in which the perceptions of this chapter's author changed as she experienced the role of teacher and parent at two similar meetings.

In addition, professionals must keep in mind that parents must be allowed to accept their children without accepting their children's developmental disabilities. Parents who have children with similar disabilities often, however, have nothing in common, any more than, say, parents who have children without disabilities (Westling & Koorland, 1989). As discussed in the previous chapter, one parent may quickly appear to accept a child's disability and readily become involved in the child's education, while another parent appears to be so overwhelmed with the normal responses of grief and anger, that this parent is barely able get through the day.

The goal is to help parents reach an **adaptation phase** in which they are fully aware of their child's needs and learn to compensate for these needs as well as enhance the child's development. A sense of sadness may remain but this is normal if the parents do not let it interfere with their effort to make their child's life the best it can be.

A parent's primary role is to love and encourage a child and create a caring and safe environment in which the child may grow (Darling, 1983). Professionals sometimes focus on helping parents

learn to accept a child's disability. The professional might tell parents that they are in "denial," or that, in order to help their child, they must first "accept" the fact that the child has a disability. This is often not helpful for a parent to hear.

Parents must be allowed to love their child yet at the same time be "allowed" to hate the disability. Again, it is *not* the professional's responsibility to make parents accept a child's disability (Bathshaw, 1991). Rather than being told how to feel, parents benefit most when professionals provide encouragement and specific information on how they can assist their child (Brinkerhoff & Vincent, 1987).

Parents do not need to be lectured to or have their hopes and dreams dashed. They do need:

- To receive their child's diagnosis from professionals with empathy, sensitivity, and openness in a private place where they will not be interrupted;
- To be given plenty of time to ask questions;
- To understand their child's disability, including the known causes and limitations it may create and to develop a realistic outlook;
- To learn how to find and use support services;
- To learn how to cope with other people's reactions to their child's special needs;
- To become familiar with the rights of children with special needs;

Box 6.2 _____

Meeting as a Parent

I have attended many school district Committee for Preschool Special Education (CPSE) and Committee for Special Education (CSE) meetings. At one of the CPSE meetings, I sat on one side of the table as a teacher. I was there to discuss a student's progress and give recommendations for classroom placement that would best match the child's developmental level and educational goals for the following year. The meeting went smoothly and the parent was very happy with the recommendations.

The next meeting was about my son, so I sat on the other side of the table as a parent. In my pro-

fessional role, I knew this was a straightforward meeting. As I sat there knowing all of Ernie's struggles and achievements during the past year, my emotions took over and I suddenly became very choked up and had difficulty talking. The chair even joked a bit and said, "What happened to you?" What did happen? They were telling me Ernie was making great progress and they were going to continue with the support he needed. In the role as parent, I was unable to separate the educational assessment and planning from the personal struggles and emotions.

- To learn how to balance their own needs, other family members' needs, and the needs of their child who has a developmental delay.

Box 6.3 provides some of the author's experiences with her own child when receiving information about him.

ATTITUDES AND EXPECTATIONS OF PARENTS AND PROFESSIONALS

At a parent and professional joint workshop, a set of words, which included *judgmental, anxious, helpful, demeaning, hopeful, self-centered, respect-*

ful, and *intense,* was presented to the audience. Participants were asked to decide whether the words most accurately described a parent or professional. The workshop participants discovered that the words were often used to describe parents and professionals, depending on the situation. In fact, these are words parents and professionals often use to describe each other. Parents and professionals are *people* first and they do have many characteristics in common (Bailey, 1987).

Attitudes and expectations are very important when trying to establish a cooperative partnership. The words mentioned above reflect some of the feelings and ideas that often enter into

---

Box 6.3 _____

Evaluation Dilemma

I remember, all too well, the day my husband and I were told that our baby was profoundly deaf. We sat in a little room waiting for the audiologist to return to discuss the results of the Brain Stem Evoked Potential Test. (See Chapter 9 for a description of the test.) He quickly told us that our son, Ernie, had a "flat line," which meant he was either severely neurologically impaired or profoundly deaf. He went on to tell us that Ernie did not act like most infants who are severely neurologically impaired; therefore, he must be profoundly deaf. At that point, I was no longer listening to what the doctor was saying. I only remember the doctor walking out a few minutes later saying something about how sorry he was.

My husband and I spent the next year going to several different audiologists trying to find out what could be done for Ernie. We believed that Ernie could hear—we had spent so much time in the neonatal unit talking and singing to him and winding up his musical toys and mobiles. He seemed to respond to those sounds. Perhaps because I am a special education teacher, I constantly questioned myself asking, "Am I just shopping around for a doctor who will say what I want to hear? Is it that I cannot accept I have a child who is deaf?"

Finally, at the Clarke School in Massachusetts, which specializes in screening for hearing impair-

ments, our hope was confirmed. Ernie had a moderate to severe high-frequency hearing loss, but he was not deaf. He could hear most of what was said to him. They told us that he would learn how to talk and hearing aids would allow him to hear almost everything.

We brought Ernie back to the original audiologist to retest him. We showed the audiologist the results of the audiological evaluations done at the Clarke School and in our hometown hospital. Both of these hearing tests indicated that Ernie was *not* deaf. We wanted to show him that the testing he had done was inaccurate. We also wanted to let him know that he had caused us almost a year of heartache. We did this in the hope that he would not rely so heavily on the test he had used on Ernie when testing other infants. The audiologist tested Ernie's hearing again. Ernie's hearing test again produced a flat line. The audiologist was confused. Additional testing by the audiologist, though, showed Ernie was not profoundly deaf.

I learned a valuable lesson from this experience. I learned that professionals need to remember that their tests are just one part of the picture. One test should never be the basis on which decisions are made. No matter how the child is diagnosed, parents should never give up on their child's ability to develop.

parent–professional interactions. Teaching children is only part of a professional's responsibility. Another crucial part is working with the key people in a child's life, the parents. Professionals cannot effectively deal with children's needs unless they work effectively with parents or other primary care givers (Bailey, McWilliams, & Simeonsson, 1991). Professionals and parents ideally enter into a partnership in which there is an atmosphere of respect and optimism.

Parents often have difficulty understanding that, although professionals assist parents and their child, the professional cannot "fix" their child. Often, parents' frustrations with their child's developmental delays are directed as anger toward the professional (Gordon, 1988). Parents often seem to have an "attitude" suggesting that they believe, "If only the professional would work harder, my child would be doing better." In some cases this is true, but most often it is not. Instead of blaming each other, parents and professionals must acknowledge and praise what has been achieved and move toward developing appropriate goals for the next level of accomplishment.

Professionals must understand that people are who they are and do *not* readily change. In fact, it is probably easier to change the weather than a person's attitude and behavior. It is important to remember this so that precious time is focused on the child and not wasted attempting to change people. Professionals must accept parents as they are. They should not focus on changing or questioning parents' values (Heisler, 1972).

An area professionals and parents often disagree about is **discipline.** (See Chapter 14 for more information on behavior management.) Sometimes, parents tell professionals about their method of disciplining a child that is contrary to a method the professional believes is best. Professionals must listen to parents and not judge or condemn their methods of interacting with their own children (Harry, 1992). Different cultural groups have different values regarding disciplinary techniques and it is crucial that professionals become sensitive to cultural differences (Boyce,

Behl, Mortensen, & Akers, 1991). When professionals react in a negative way to a disciplinary situation involving a child, the parent may be unwilling to talk at all with the professional about the situation.

A more effective strategy for professionals to use, when they disagree with something a parent says or does, is to listen to and reflect on the parents' actions and responses (Hamlin, 1988). This approach allows parents to realize that their needs and feelings are being valued. After the professional listens and acknowledges the parents' feelings, the parents are often more accepting of suggestions about how to deal with a child's behavior. Professionals often must be patient while parents struggle to understand and follow through on suggestions. Suggestions are much more easily made and agreed on than they are implemented. Suggestions that often seem very clear and obvious to professionals often are not clear and obvious to a parent (Guardini, 1990).

Parents expect a great deal from professionals (Darling, 1983). Parents expect professionals to be knowledgeable, understanding, supportive, enthusiastic, cooperative, kind, and organized. Parents also expect professionals to work with them to plan and implement the best program for the child. Parents expect professionals to be available to discuss their concerns about their child through ongoing communication and conferences (Smith, 1984). These expectations are reasonable as long as they are kept in perspective. Professionals must find a way to make sure that parents recognize that the professional has many obligations, which limits the amount of time the professional spends interacting with any one child (Hildebrand & Phenice, Gray, & Hines, 1996).

Professionals, on the other hand, expect parents to be involved, supportive, enthusiastic, appreciative, and cooperative. Professionals expect parents to understand their busy schedules, time constraints, and limitations. Professionals expect parents to agree with and support their recommendations. When there is a considerable gap between expectations and reality, a breakdown in the parent–professional partnership often occurs. Conflicts are likely to arise. The next section discusses some of these conflicts.

CONFLICTS BETWEEN PARENTS AND PROFESSIONALS

Assumptions concerning Conflict

Conflicts are inevitable. No one passes through life free of conflicts. Conflicts and disagreements are part of nearly all types of partnerships. It is important to understand how these conflicts are resolved and what may be learned from them. This often helps minimize later conflicts. Strategies can be used to prevent conflicts from becoming unmanageable. Some conflicts are unavoidable and cannot be smoothed over but ultimately are resolvable. Finally, and perhaps most importantly, the resolution of a conflict does not have to result in a winner or loser (Bramson, 1988).

Conflict as a Destructive or Constructive Force

Conflict is *destructive* when it diverts energy from more important activities and issues. It often destroys morale and increases the chances of development of negative self-concepts. It often reduces the effectiveness of "inter-group cooperation" (Bramson, 1988). Destructive conflicts are likely to occur when professionals disagree and do not resolve the conflicts.

Conflicts often encourage parents to gather information from all sides systematically, organize it, and begin to push for services they believe their child needs. Many new programs for children with special needs have been developed in part because parents have requested them (Smith, 1980; Webster, 1977).

Conflict is destructive when it emphasizes differences in values and when it produces irresponsible and regrettable behavior such as name-calling or fighting. Being angry consumes a great deal of time and energy. Although feelings must be expressed so that the importance of an issue is

clarified, if too much energy becomes focused on being angry, irreversible damage may occur (Fernsterheim & Baer, 1978). This damage often occurs when name-calling and blaming begin and values are attacked. Instead of focusing on the issue, focus often centers on "saving face" (not being wrong at all costs).

When the focus is on "saving face," little energy is left to solve problems. Creativity is minimized, and the child often suffers when "saving face" becomes the major goal. This is not to say that feelings should not be expressed. Both parties, though, must move beyond their own feelings so that issues are clarified and solving problems begins. The focus must *always* remain on what is best for the child.

Conflict is *constructive* when it opens up important issues and increases the level of involvement. Conflict helps build cohesiveness among people by sharing the conflict, celebrating the settlement, and learning more about each other (Hamlin, 1988). An example of this occurred in the following conflict situation described in Box 6.4.

Three Faces of Conflict

Conflict is most typically handled one of three basic ways: **passively, aggressively,** or **assertively.** In any given situation, a person may use one of these responses. The response chosen often relates to the importance of the conflict and the confidence of the person choosing the response (Bramson, 1988). For example, if a parent feels that the professionals working with their child are not providing enough feedback about the child's daily progress, the parent has several options. The parent could choose to accept the situation the way it is. Although unhappy, the parent offers no resistance and does not display frustration. This is an example of a passive response. This method does *not* enhance a partnership between a parent and professional (Shields, 1987).

As an alternative, the parent could become hostile and verbally attack the teaching staff, calling staff members by telephone, writing letters, or

Box 6.4 _____

An Example of Cooperation Between Parents and Professionals

Conflict resulting in cooperation occurred when the parents of John, a four-year-old in a special education preschool program, received a note from his teacher. John had a history of frequent aggressive temper tantrums. His parents and teacher had been working together for several weeks to try to find a method that would decrease the number of temper tantrums.

The content of the note to his parents explained that John could quickly regain control of his aggressive temper tantrums (hitting, kicking, and throwing objects at staff and peers) after he was placed in a chair in a quiet corner of the room for **time-out.** The teacher further explained in the note that John quickly calmed down and could rejoin the class in less than five minutes. Staff members felt they had finally found a way to reduce the number of his frequent temper tantrums. After reading the note, the parents were outraged and immediately contacted the teacher to request a meeting. A conflict appeared to have arisen between the boy's parents and his teacher.

The teaching team met with the parents. Feelings were intense on both sides. The teaching team could not imagine why John' s parents were upset. "They were clearly confused," one team member thought. The meeting began with the teacher stating the obvious, "It appears you are not in agreement with how we decided to handle John's temper tantrums." The teaching team then listened intently to the parents' comments.

The father explained, "We adopted John after he was taken from his biological parents because they abused and neglected him." He further explained that they did not know all the details about the abuse, but the parents knew he had been strapped to a chair and left for periods of time when he misbehaved. They stated, "We feel that the classroom time-out may trigger very bad memories and push him 'over the edge.' If you use this method again, we will take our son out of this school!"

The teacher responded by reflecting on what was said. She stated, "John has had some terrible experiences you do not want him to relive. Given the circumstances, we understand that using the time-out in an area away from others is *not* an ap-

propriate option. We are sorry that we chose that method of attempting to control John's temper tantrums." The parents quickly agreed.

Until that day, the staff only knew that the child was adopted. The information shared by the parents at this meeting helped the teaching team better understand why the child might be having such intense temper tantrums. The teaching team agreed not to use time-out for John's temper tantrums.

Although the staff had gained a new perspective, the question of what to do with the severe temper tantrums remained. What could be done? The child's emotional difficulties were understandable, but it was unsafe and unfair for classmates to be the targets on whom he acted out his frustrations. The teacher explained the dilemma to John's parents. "We can understand that John has good reasons to feel a great deal of anger. We need to find a way for our classroom to be a safe environment for all the children." The parents agreed.

The teacher then suggested that they list as many ways as possible that might be used to help John. Together, the professionals and parents listed all the techniques that had been used with John at home and school to deal with his temper tantrums. Additional suggestions were obtained when the staff sought out the assistance of the program's psychologist.

Each solution or technique was discussed while attempting to anticipate possible consequences. Finally, it was determined that John responded best when an adult could remove him from a particular situation before the temper tantrum escalated. This approach required the teaching team to agree to provide John with almost constant adult support throughout the day. When John displayed signs of frustration and anger, the teacher who was designated as his supporting adult for the day would quickly but calmly walk with him to a quiet place outside the classroom. He would remain there with the teacher until he was calm and ready to rejoin the group, or the teacher would find another activity in which he could participate.

The teaching staff also discussed another intervention strategy designed to focus on the boy's

continued

BOX 6.4   continued

strengths. John was very creative and enjoyed art activities. It was decided that he would go to the art room and receive one-on-one adult attention once or twice a week. John was also allowed to assist the teaching staff by being designated "special helper." For example, he could hold the items needed during circle time and hand them to the teacher or another student as they were needed. In addition, a psychology intern engaged in "play therapy" with John in the classroom, as well as in a private office. This interaction focused on assisting him in developing coping strategies and expressing feelings through play.

Over the next few months, changes in his ability to cope with conflict became evident. The tantrums diminished in intensity and frequency. The parents and teaching staff frequently communicated through written notes and telephone conversations. The conflict was resolved and everyone won, most importantly, John.

Due to the effort and determination of the parents and teaching staff, John began having many "good" days at school. In addition, the parents and professionals gained new skills that may be useful in future situations.

---

complaining about them to supervisors. Parents may resort to accusations such as, "The teaching staff is lazy, incompetent, and uncaring." These types of reactions are aggressive responses and usually result in major conflicts and negative attitudes developing between parents and professionals. This method is not likely to create an effective partnership (Bailey, 1987).

The most productive response to conflict is an assertive response. This requires a person to state his or her needs clearly but in a nonhostile fashion. A parent using an assertive response might call a teaching staff member or write a note. In the note or conversation the parent might state, "I would like more information about my child's daily progress. Could we set up a regular time to talk on the telephone or could we send a journal between home and school so that written communication is received daily?"

Teaching staff will respond to these types of assertive requests. Teachers of young children who have developmental delays generally understand the importance of ongoing communication. When parents clearly state their needs, most professionals will respond positively (Roberts, Wasik, Casto, & Ramey, 1991). Communication will most likely increase. Sometimes, professionals benefit from reminders or encouragement to keep them attentive. Professionals often spend hours writing notes to parents. Occasionally, these notes receive no response. It is probably unreasonable to write notes to the parent of every child in a class. When, however, parents let the staff know they are interested and appreciate the information provided, most professionals will attempt to find a method to keep the lines of communications open (Guardini, 1990).

A person's response to a particular situation cannot be predicted. A person could be assertive in one situation yet in another become passive or aggressive. There are many reasons people find it difficult to be assertive. Some people fear others will not like them or think they are selfish if they act assertively. Some individuals feel if they ask people for something, those people will expect something in return. Other people are shy, embarrassed, or simply afraid they will hurt someone else's feelings if they act assertively. All of these possible reasons create barriers that must be overcome (Darling, 1983). To be effective advocates for children, parents and professionals must overcome these barriers. It is through conflict resolution, assertiveness, and effective communication that doors are opened and opportunities emerge.

EFFECTIVE COMMUNICATION

Communication between professionals and parents is vital for successful programs to be implemented for children with special needs. The power of effective communication cannot be under-estimated. Effective communication is vital for successful partnerships. Several components of effective verbal and nonverbal communication are discussed below.

Components of Communication

Most people use a variety of **nonverbal** and **verbal** forms of communication. Nonverbal communication includes clothing, physical distance, eye contact, facial expressions, and gestures. Verbal communication includes oral, written, and sign language (DePaulo, Rosenthal, Green, & Rosenkrantz, 1982).

Nonverbal Communication

When communicating, professionals and parents must be conscious of the nonverbal messages they are sending. One example of nonverbal communication in a school setting is the clothing worn during a meeting. A person's choice of clothing is frequently interpreted as an indicator of the importance the person places on the meeting. Preschool staff typically wear comfortable but neat clothing. Professionals who work directly with young children know their clothes are likely to get dirty during art activities, science and cooking projects, playing outdoors, and snack time.

When meetings occur at the preschool site during the day, attire usually remains casual. When professionals meet with parents after regular school hours in a special meeting or during the day at school district special education meetings, they usually dress in more formal attire. This does not mean suits and ties are necessary for meetings between parents and professionals, but attention to mode of dress and grooming may be viewed by another as important (Deutch, 1973). Nonverbal factors also affect the level of effective communication.

Eye contact, facial expressions, physical space between people, and gestures send important messages. Placing hands in a pocket, looking down, or avoiding eye contact often indicate insecurity or dislike. Turning away so that the back is partially toward others suggests a lack of interest or desire to end a conversation (Aiello, 1987). Leaning toward the speaker suggests interest. Sitting an unusual distance away from a person often indicates annoyance, anxiety, or disinterest. Friends generally stand closer together than do strangers or people who do not like each other. Facial expressions also send many messages. A squint or frown often indicates uncertainty or disagreement. A smile often indicates comfort, happiness, or relief (DePaulo et al., 1982).

Some researchers suggest that body language sends an even more powerful message than speaking. If this is true, professionals and parents must try to understand the messages they are sending when they communicate with each other. When meetings between parents and professionals are spent shuffling papers and body language is ignored, communication unnecessarily diminishes (DiMatteo, Friedman, & Taranta, 1979).

Verbal Communication

Verbal communication refers to spoken and written language. The words used are important but the context and the way they are spoken or written often are more important. Parents and professionals must pay attention to the words selected and the tone in which they are presented. This is especially important when sharing information with team members not present at the meeting. Words are easily repeated, but if the tone is changed the meaning is also changed. Tone of voice is very important and affects how messages are interpreted. Table 6.2 lists several verbal communication styles people often use. Communication between parents and professionals is generally most effective when the "caring style" is used.

Written communication plays an important role in most early childhood special education programs. Because of the necessity to document services provided to children with special needs, all communication that occurs must be written

TABLE 6.2   Summary of Communication Styles

Styles that provide little information:

- Superficial—playful, sociable, happy-go-lucky
- Commanding—accusing, dictating, manipulating, blaming

Styles that provide more information:

- Knowledge-based—information at the level of the listener, elaboration
- Caring—concern, sharing, feeling, open, authentic

down. It is important to remember that, although written communication has its purpose, it is not always the best way to develop or maintain ongoing communication between parents and professionals. When the most important thing becomes what is written down about the child, meaningful information is often lost. It is very difficult to get a true picture of children by relying solely on what is written about them.

Written communication's drawback is it is missing body language and tone of voice. Written communication is easy to misinterpret. When used it must be carefully written. For example, faulty communication could occur when classroom staff write home to parents or when parents write to staff. The words might be clear, but the message is not because written words often leave out feelings. The parent may perceive them as cold or misleading.

Written notes often are confusing because they lack sufficient detail, which leads to misinterpretations. In most cases, written notes should be followed by telephone or face-to-face conversations to clarify the meaning of the note. For instance, a teacher sent this note home to a parent: "Joey did not eat his snack." The words were clear but the message was not. Was the teacher indicating that Joey was being disobedient? Did the teacher think Joey was sick? Was the teacher concerned because Joey did not try different types of food? The message was unclear. It was unclear

whether the teacher thought Joey's behavior was typical or atypical.

Language barriers also lead to a source of misunderstanding. Written information must be prepared in the parents' primary language. During meetings with parents, it is often necessary to have a translator present. When professionals talk during the meeting, they should look at the parents, not at the translator. Different cultural groups have different meanings associated with different behaviors. It is important for professionals to be aware of cultural differences in mode of communication and the meanings associated with methods of communication (Vincent, 1992; Hanson, Lynch, & Wayman, 1990).

Listening

The quality of friendships, cohesiveness of family relationships, and effectiveness at work depend in large measure on a person's ability to listen. Research suggests that as much as 75 percent of spoken communication is ignored, misunderstood, or quickly forgotten (Hamlin, 1988). Well-developed listening skills are necessary for effective parent–professional partnerships. Listening involves more than just hearing words. Listening is an activity of the ears, eyes, mind, and heart. Listening is an active process, for which few people have been adequately trained (Fernsterheim & Baer, 1978).

Active listening involves attending, observing, and labeling nonverbal cues, inviting a speaker to say more, and reflective listening. A good listener is actively attentive to the speaker. This attentiveness involves directing eyes and body toward the speaker. Positioning oneself at a comfortable distance from the speaker, maintaining an open posture, and leaning slightly toward the speaker send the nonverbal message that the listener is interested in the speaker's words. The listener must concentrate on the factual information and feelings being expressed to determine what the speaker is trying to convey. To provide adequate concentration, noise from environmental factors, such as radios, televisions, and telephones, should be eliminated as much as possible (Shields, 1987).

Another important aspect of listening includes the ability to interpret nonverbal cues such as body language and facial expressions. For example, a mother who walks with her head down and slumps down into a seat for a meeting with a classroom teacher most likely would benefit from someone listening to her. A comment made by the teacher, such as "You seem down today" or "It doesn't look like you are having a good day," may serve as an invitation to this mother to discuss her feelings freely (Bailey & Simeonsson, 1988b).

An effective listener will use words and phrases encouraging a speaker to continue to share thoughts and feelings. Remarks such as "Really?" "Oh?" "Go on," and "Tell me more." all convey to the speaker that what has been said is important and encourages the speaker to continue sharing information. These phrases, however, become routine or seem insincere if overused.

Active listening also involves responding to the speaker reflectively. An effective listener restates what has been said, clarifying the content and feelings. When reflective listening is effective, the speaker is assured that the listener has really heard and understands what was said (Hamlin, 1988). Active listening lets others know that their thoughts and feelings have been recognized. The benefits of active listening are numerous. It promotes a relationship of understanding and trust. It clarifies what is being said. Active listening also facilitates problem-solving (Apple & Hecht, 1982).

Communication skills are vital to any partnership (Bailey, 1987), so it is important for parents and professionals to develop good listening skills. There are books and video tapes available to assist people in developing good communication skills. Community colleges, universities, parent organizations, and adult education courses in local school districts often offer courses designed to enhance communication skills. It is well worth the time for parents and professionals to learn more about effective communication.

PREPARING FOR A MEETING

Meetings to discuss services for children with special needs often require extra planning (Bailey, 1987). When parents enter meetings to discuss their child, they often are overwhelmed by several different professionals who are giving opinions and recommendations. To feel like a part of the team, it is important that parents also prepare for such meetings. (See Chapter 5 for more discussion of effective team collaboration.)

Preparing for a meeting requires that parents and professionals spend time thinking about and writing down questions, concerns, feelings, and expectations to be discussed at the meeting. Before the meeting, parents and professionals should generate meeting goals. Goals must be realistic and listed in order of importance. Possible barriers that prevent achievement of these goals should also be listed. The lists of goals and barriers should be brought to the meeting (McConkey, 1985).

During the meeting, parents should carefully listen and repeat what they believe was said by each professional. This assists in clarifying concerns, opinions, and goals. At the meeting, parents should state, read, or provide a written summary expressing their goals for the child (Mittler, 1979). See Table 6.3 for information on maximizing the value of meetings.

Some parents bring an **advocate,** a friend or another family member, with them to meetings with professionals. This person helps them gain information by asking questions or expressing concerns the parent has difficulty conveying. The advocate may also take notes for the parent during the meeting.

Soon after the meeting, parents and professionals should write down what was discussed while the meeting is still fresh in their memory. Excessive note-taking during a meeting, however, should be avoided because it limits the ability to

TABLE 6.3   Ways to Help Ensure a Positive Parent–Teacher Conference

Parents' Roles

- Find out who will be attending the conference;
- Inform any other potential attendees of who will be attending the meeting;
- Make a list of ideas about goals for the child;
- Make a list of questions in advance of the meeting;
- Be calm, assertive, and nonjudgmental;
- Bring some of the child's work (e.g., drawings) that may be relevant to the conference;
- Share information about the child's interests and experiences;
- Make the teacher aware of any significant current situations in the child's life (e.g., family stress, a new sibling);
- Ask for suggestions for at-home goals;
- Take notes;
- Get copies of any evaluations or reports;
- Ask for another meeting if time runs out;
- Before ending the meeting, leave time to summarize the major issues discussed;

Teachers' Roles

- Tell parents who will be at the meeting;
- Start the meeting on time;
- Begin and end the meeting on a positive note;
- Be a good listener;
- Be calm and nonjudgmental;
- Avoid making comparisons with other children;
- Allow time for questions;
- Have samples of the child's work;
- Keep language descriptive and nonjudgmental;
- Avoid professional jargon;
- Ask for suggestions for school goals (i.e., find out what the parents' expectations for the child are);
- Take notes;
- Before ending the meeting, leave time to summarize the major issues discussed.

listen. A summary of the meeting should include information about the frequency and types of services a child will be receiving, where they will be provided, when they will begin, and who will be providing each service (Marshall & Herbert, 1981). Parents may also want to include a statement of their own responsibilities.

Usually, the agency involved in providing the majority of services for a child sends the parents a written plan. When parents receive the plan from the agency, they should be encouraged to compare the information with their own meeting notes. If there is any discrepancy or misunderstanding, the parents should be directed to call or write to the service provider indicating the concerns. If necessary, another meeting should be scheduled to resolve the parents' concerns (Masterson, Swirbul, & Noble, 1990).

Parents should be encouraged to keep a **home file** that includes all correspondence with agencies providing services for the child. Many parents keep notebooks with dividers for each area of development in which their child receives reports (e.g., cognitive or special education, speech, physical therapy, occupational therapy, or counseling). It is helpful when parents file each new report on top of the old so that the most current information is readily available. See Table 6.4 for a list of items that might be included in a home file.

The usefulness of keeping a home file was demonstrated when a family relocated out of state and went to meet with the new school district staff. The family was prepared to provide all the information the school district requested. The family had developed a notebook containing several years of documentation about the child's strengths, needs, and progress. There was documentation of the child's triumphs, which the family helped make possible because of a partnership with professionals involved in the education of the child (Tizard, et al., 1988).

CONCLUSION

Children with special needs and their parents have broken through many barriers in our society. A great number of schools are including children with special needs in "regular" classrooms. Children with or without special educational needs are learning together using the inclusion model.

TABLE 6.4   Information to Be Included in a Home File

Information about the child that should be included in a home file:

- Medical records
- School records
- Observations of the child at home
- Observations of the child at school
- Comparisons between the child's home and school behavior
- Test and evaluation results
- Copies of sample work and projects the child produced
- Statements about how the child best learns (i.e., through sight, sound, touch)
- Areas of progress
- Rate of progress
- Successful and unsuccessful methods of intervention used with the child
- Areas that need more intervention
- Self-concept
- Attitude toward teachers, school, and peers

Professionals, parents, and children are working through differences that initially appear very great, and finding a common ground that will help them feel accepted and worthwhile. To assure that this common goal is met, parents and professionals must work in successful collaboration. The world is full of possibilities for children with special needs. Many of these possibilities came about because of the collaboration of parents and professionals.

The next chapter discusses the needs of children who have developmental delays and the role of the special education teacher. Subsequent chapters discuss the need of children with speech, hearing, and motor delays and the roles of professionals trained to meet those needs in collaboration with other professionals and parents.

CHAPTER SUMMARY

- A cooperative partnership between professionals and parents is necessary to best aid a child with special needs.

- Professionals and parents must develop an understanding of the other's point of view.
- Conflicts between parents and professionals may be destructive or constructive. Destructive conflict destroys morale and reinforces poor self-concepts. Constructive conflict opens up important issues and increases an individual's involvement.
- The three faces of conflict are passive, aggressive, and assertive.
- The two major types of communication are nonverbal and verbal.
- Listening carefully is as important as communicating effectively.
- Preparing for a meeting involves writing down questions, concerns, feelings, expectations, and realistic goals.
- Parents should keep a home file on all aspects of a child's development.

REVIEW QUESTIONS

1. Why is it important for parents and professionals to work together?
2. Describe how parents and professionals are similar and different.
3. How might prior positive and negative experiences affect how parents and professionals view each other?
4. Why are active listening skills important for parent–professional relationships?

SUGGESTED STUDENT ACTIVITIES

1. With a partner, role-play an effective and ineffective meeting between a parent and professional.
2. In a small group, discuss the case involving John and suggest other possible solutions.
3. Practice varying your tone of voice and listen carefully. Repeat a poem such as "Mary had a Little Lamb," using different tones and expressions and note the effect on the meaning of the message.

ADDITIONAL READINGS

Bricker, D. D., & Widerstrom, A. H. (1996). *Preparing personnel to work with infants and young children and their families.* Baltimore, MD: Paul H. Brookes.

Cutler, B. C. (1993). *You, your child, and "special" education: A guide to making the system work.* Baltimore, MD: Paul H. Brookes.

Webster, E. J., & Ward, L. M. (1993). *Working with parents of young children with disabilities.* San Diego, CA: Singular Publishing Group.

ADDITIONAL RESOURCES

Children with Special Needs
96 Berkeley Street
Boston, MA 02116

Child Welfare League of America
67 Irving Place
New York, NY 10003

Exceptional Parent
605 Commonwealth Avenue
Boston, MA 02215

High Scope Educational Research Foundation
Family Programs Department
600 N. River Street
Ypsilanti, MI 48197

National Information Center for Children and Youth with Disabilities
P.O. Box 1492
Washington, DC 20013–1492

National Parent Network on Disabilities
1600 Prince Street, Suite 115
Alexandria, VA 22314

Office of Special Education and Rehabilitation Services
U.S. Department of Education
Room 3132, Switzer Building
Washington, DC 20202–2524

Parents Helping Parents
535 Race Street, Suite 220
San Jose, CA 95126

REFERENCES

Aiello, J. (1987). Human spatial behavior. In D. Stokols & I. Altman (Eds.), *Handbook of environmental psychology.* New York: Wiley.

Apple, W., & Hecht, K. (1982). Speaking emotionally: The relationship between verbal and vocal communication of affect. *Journal of Personality and Social Psychology, 37,* 715–727.

Bailey, D. B. (1987). Collaborative goal-setting with families: Resolving differences in values and priorities for services. *Topics in Early Childhood Special Education, 7,* 59–71.

Bailey, D. B., McWilliams, P., & Simeonsson, R. J. (1991). *Implementing family-centered services in early intervention: A team-based model for change.* Chapel Hill, NC: Carolina Institute for Research on Infant Personnel Preparation, University of North Carolina.

Bailey, D. B., Palsha, S. A., & Simeonsson, R. J. (1991). Professional skills concerns and perceived importance of work with families in early intervention. *Exceptional Children, 58*(2), 156–165.

Bailey, D. B., & Simeonsson, R. J. (1988a). Assessing the needs of families with handicapped infants. *Journal of Special Education, 22*(1), 117–126.

Bailey, D. B., & Simeonsson, R. J. (1988b). *Family assessment in early intervention.* Columbus, OH: Merrill.

Bathshaw, M. L. (1991). *Your child has a disability: A complete sourcebook of daily and medical care.* Boston: Little, Brown.

Berger, E. H. (1995). *Parents as partners in education: Families and schools working together* (4th ed.). Columbus, OH: Merrill.

Boyce, G. C., Behl, D., Mortensen, L., & Akers, J. (1991). Child characteristics, family demographics, and family process: What are the effects on the stress of families of children with disabilities? *Counseling Psychology Quarterly, 4,* 273–288.

Bramson, R. (1988). *Coping with difficult people.* New York: Dell.

Brinkerhoff, J., & Vincent, L. (1987). Increasing parental decision-making at the individualized program meeting. *Journal of the Division of Early Childhood, 11,* 46–58.

Brudoff, M., & Orenstein, A. (1984). *Due process in special education: On going to a hearing.* Cambridge, MA: Brookline Books.

rents: A
arles B.
Slack.

Darling, R. B. (1983). *Families against society: A study of reactions to children with birth defects.* Beverly Hills, CA: Sage.

Davie, R., Butler, N., & Goldstein, N. (1972). *From birth to seven: A report of the National Child Development study.* Highlands, NJ: Humanities Press.

DePaulo, B. M., Rosenthal, R., Green, C. R., & Rosenkrantz, J. (1982). Diagnosing deceptive and mixed messages from verbal and nonverbal cues. *Journal of Personality and Social Psychology, 18,* 433–446.

Deutch, M. (1973). *The resolution of conflict: Constructive and destructive processes.* New Haven, CT: Yale University Press.

DiMatteo, M. R., Friedman, H. S., & Taranta, A. (1979). Sensitivity to bodily nonverbal communications as a factor in practitioner–patient rapport. *Journal of Nonverbal Behavior, 4,* 18–26.

Dunst, C. J., Trivette, C. M., & Deal, A. (1988). *Enabling and empowering families.* Cambridge, MA: Brookline Books.

Fernsterheim, H., & Baer, J. (1978). *Don't say yes when you want to say no.* New York: Dell.

Gargiulo, R. (1985). *Working with parents of exceptional children.* Boston: Houghton Mifflin.

Glidden, L. M. (1993). What we do not know about families with children who have developmental disabilities: Questionnaire on resources and stress as a case study. *American Journal of Mental Retardation, 97,* 315–332.

Gordon, S. (1988). *When living hurts.* New York: Dell.

Guardini, R. (1990). *Back to the family.* New York: Random House.

Hamlin, S. (1988). *How to talk so people listen.* New York: Harper and Row.

Hanson, J. J., & Hanline, M. F. (1990). Parenting a child with a disability: A longitudinal study of parental stress and adaption. *Journal of Early Intervention, 14,* 234–248.

Hanson, J. J., Lynch, E. W., & Wayman, K. I. (1990). Honoring the cultural diversity of families when gathering data. *Topics in Early Childhood Special Education, 10*(1), 112–131.

Harry, B. (1992). *Cultural diversity, families, and the special education system: Communication and empowerment.* New York: Teachers College Press.

Heisler, V. (1972). *A handicapped child in the family: A guide for parents.* New York: Grune and Stratton.

Hildebrand, V., Phenice, L. A., Gray, M. M., & Hines, R. P. (1996). *Knowing and serving diverse families.* Columbus, OH: Merrill.

Klass, C. S. (1996). *Home visiting: Promoting healthy parent and child development.* Baltimore, MD: Paul H. Brookes.

Leviton, A., Mueller, M., & Kauffman, C. (1992). The family-centered consultation model: Practical applications for professionals. *Infants and Young Children, 4*(3), 1–8.

Marshall, G., & Herbert, M. (1981). Recorded telephone messages: A way to link teacher and parents. An evaluation report prepared for CEMREL, Washington, DC.

Masterson, J., Swirbul, T., & Noble, D. (1990). Computer generated information packets for parents. *Language, Speech, and Hearing Services in Schools, 21,* 114–115.

McConkey, R. (1985). *Working with parents: A practical guide to teachers and therapists.* Cambridge, MA: Brookline Books.

Mittler, P. (1979). *Parents as partners in the education of their handicapped children.* Paper commissioned by UNESCO, ED/79/conf. 606/7 (UNESCO, Paris).

Roberts, R., Wasik, B. H., Casto, C., & Ramey, C. T. (1991). Family support in the home: Programs, policy, and social change. *American Psychologist, 46,* 131–137.

Shea, T. M., & Bauer, A. M. (1991). *Parents and teachers of children with exceptionalities: A handbook for collaboration* (2nd ed.). Boston: Allyn and Bacon.

Shields, C. V. (1987). *Strategies: A practical guide for dealing with professionals and human service professionals.* Baltimore, MD: Paul H. Brookes.

Smith, P. (1984). *You are not alone: For parents when they learn that their child has a handicap.* Washington, DC: National Information Center for Children and Youth.

Smith, T. (1980). *Parent and preschool.* Ypsilanti, MI: High Scope.

Tizard, B., Mortimore, J., & Burchell, B. (1988). *Involving parents in nursery and infant school.* Ypsilanti, MI: High Scope.

Turnbull, A. P., & Turnbull, H. R. (1996). *Families, professionals, and exceptionality: A special partnership* (3rd ed.). Columbus, OH: Merrill.

Turnbull, A. P., & Turnbull, H. R. (1990). *Families, professionals, and exceptionality: A special partnership* (2nd ed.). Columbus, OH: Merrill.

Vaugh, S., Bos, C., Harrell, J., & Lasky, B. (1988). Parent participation in the initial/IMP conference 10 years after mandated involvement. *Journal of Learning Disabilities, 21*(2), 82–84.

Vincer̲ ̲ ̲, ̲ ̲. ̲. (̲ ̲ ̲ ̲). Families and early intervention: ̲ ̲ ̲ ̲ ̲ ̲ ̲ ̲ ̲. *Journal of Early Intervention,* ̲ ̲ ̲ ̲ ̲ ̲ ̲ ̲ ̲.

Webster, E. J. (1977). Counseling ̲ ̲ ̲ ̲ ̲ ̲ ̲ ̲ ̲ *capped children: Guidelines for improving communication.* New York: Grune and Stratton.

Westling, D. L., & Koorland, M. A. (1989). *The special educator's handbook.* Boston: Allyn and Bacon.

CHAPTER 7

SPECIAL EDUCATION SERVICES

KATHLEEN RYAN, M.S. ED.
MARJORIE DELFORNO, A.S.

ABOUT THE AUTHORS

Kathleen Ryan received her bachelor's degree from Empire State College and State University of New York at Geneseo, New York, and a master's from the State University of New York at New Paltz, New York, in special education. She has a permanent certification from the State of New York in Elementary (preschool through sixth grade) and Special Education (kindergarten through twelfth grade). Ms. Ryan has taught in regular and special education settings. She is a special education teacher at the Saint Francis Preschool Program in Poughkeepsie, New York. She is married and the mother of three young children.

Marjorie DelForno received two associate's degrees, one in early childhood education and the other in child care from Dutchess Community College in Poughkeepsie, New York. She has more than ten years experience as an early childhood educator in regular and special education settings. She also teaches at the Saint Francis Preschool Program. In addition, Ms. DelForno serves as director of a summer day camp for children ages three to eight years old. She is the mother of two children. Ms. DelForno has worked with Ms. Ryan in team-teaching situations at Rainbow's End Child Development Center in Salt Point, New York, and at the Saint Francis Preschool Program in Poughkeepsie, New York. They participated in the National Association for the Education of Young Children (NAEYC) accreditation process and training at Rainbow's End Child Development Center.

CHAPTER KEY POINTS

- Providing young children the least restrictive environment (LRE) may include integrating children with and without special needs for all or part of the day.
- The special education teacher serves many roles within an early childhood special education setting.
- It is crucial for the special education teacher to create environments specifically designed to enhance development in all areas.
- The special education teacher uses the best practices from regular and special education to provide individualized learning opportunities for each child.

Earlier chapters describe several types of children and professionals that are found in an early childhood special education program. This chapter focuses on one type of professional, the special education teacher, who is often part of a team of individuals who work together to provide intervention services for young children. This chapter discusses the value of mainstreaming and inclusion practices and integrating the best practices of regular early childhood education, and various roles the special education teacher plays when attempting to meet the needs of young children who have developmental delays or are at risk of having delays (Salisbury & Vincent, 1990).

PHILOSOPHY OF EARLY CHILDHOOD SPECIAL EDUCATION

The philosophy of most early childhood special education programs is to acknowledge each child at his or her present level of development, to create **developmentally appropriate practices (DAP),** and to help each child move to a greater level of competency (Kostelnick, 1992; Jipson, 1991; Walsh, 1991). For example, if children enrolled in a special education program are functioning at a two-year-old level even though they are four, the staff would provide activities appropriate for children at a two-year-old level. Children enrolled in a special education preschool

are delayed in one area or several areas, or one type of delay may cause delays in other areas (e.g., language delays often affect social and cognitive skills areas) (Graham & Bryant, 1993). Activities and therapies must be developed with a focus on each child's specific area(s) of need (Mahoney, Robinson, & Powell, 1992; Carta, Schwartz, Atwater, & McConnell, 1991; Norris, 1991).

SPECIAL EDUCATION TEACHERS

Training for the **special education teacher** typically involves coursework in several areas, including information about specific disabilities, human development, curriculum strategies, measurement and evaluation, reading and mathematics instructional methods, behavior management techniques, and prescriptive teaching techniques (suggestions for intervention). In most cases, though, coursework in early childhood special education is offered as electives rather than required courses. Many special education teachers have a bachelor's or master's degree in special education, which allows them to teach in preschool and kindergarten through twelfth-grade programs.

Odom and McEvoy (1990) believe that college and university programs should include required coursework in general and special early childhood education for certification as an early childhood special education teacher. Some states are moving toward changing certification requirements for special education by requiring this type of specialized training (Association of Teacher Educators and the National Association for the Education of Young Children, 1991; Burton, Hains, Hanline, McLean, & McCormick, 1992).

Special education teachers must remain updated on new research in education and related fields. Updated information is useful for better understanding specific disabilities, as well as learning about new and effective teaching strategies. As an advocate for children and parents, the special education teacher shares this information with parents and other staff members. It is important for the teacher to remain open to new opinions and ideas and willing to try new approaches (Wolock, 1990).

OVERVIEW OF EARLY CHILDHOOD SPECIAL EDUCATION

Intervention Service Location

Special education teachers who work at early intervention programs are often responsible for coordinating educational services provided to children. They may provide services to a child at the child's home, a clinic, or in a regular or special education preschool classroom.

When working with infants, special education teachers typically work individually with parents or primary care providers, focusing on interactions that enhance the child's overall development. Services provided at the child's home allow for one-to-one interactions focused solely on the child's specific needs within a natural learning environment. Services provided by a special education teacher within the home are often designed to emphasize a parent's role as teacher. Parents are taught techniques that can be used to help their children learn. These services help parents develop a positive attitude toward their child and a sense of competency (Bredekamp, 1987).

Toddlers and preschoolers may also be provided services individually within their home or in a therapy room at a clinic. Services are more typically provided to groups of children in a special education **1:12:1 classroom** (a class with no more than twelve children, one special education teacher, one education assistant, and therapists as needed). These classrooms are often called center-based classes. Classrooms with a smaller student–teacher ratio (e.g., **1:6:1**) might be provided for children with more intensive needs, including children with moderate to severe levels of delays, such as children confined to a wheelchair or who are very aggressive (Odom, 1994).

Center-based classrooms create an environment more like regular preschools and elementary schools by requiring children to focus attention, follow directions and a schedule, wait their turn, and complete tasks. When children receive services outside of their home, parents must break from care providing responsibilities. It also allows parents to develop a social network with other parents of children with special needs. For special education teachers to successfully meet a wide range of needs it is necessary for them to perform many different tasks.

Attending a Regular Preschool Program

Often, children with special needs attend regular preschool programs even though they have developmental delays in one or more areas. They may function well in regular early childhood programs because within a typical classroom there is often a wide range of abilities between children. Teachers at each age level (two-, three-, and four-year-olds) attempt to orient the curriculum toward expectations associated with a particular age (Bruder, 1993; Bailey & McWilliam, 1990).

In regular preschool programs, children are typically grouped according to chronological age. In some cases, children with special needs have difficulty succeeding in a classroom in which activities are designed for children at a particular chronological age. These children benefit from classrooms that select a curriculum focused on developmental levels rather than chronological age.

Most regular preschool programs typically gear services toward the particular age of the children enrolled in the program and have a common set of goals for all children. In contrast, special education preschools focus services on a child's as well as the family's specific needs. Federal laws require family involvement in decisions about the education of their child and family services must be provided for families of children from birth to three years old who have special needs. Family services are not typically a focus of regular preschool education programs.

VARIED RESPONSIBILITIES OF THE SPECIAL EDUCATION TEACHER

The responsibilities of special education teachers described below are specifically geared toward early childhood special education teachers but are applicable for special educators who work with children regardless of their age. Examples provided concentrate on teachers working with children in group settings but are relevant to teachers working in individual home settings or clinics as well.

Using Knowledge about Typical Rates of Development

It is essential for the special education teacher to have a good understanding of the typical stages of child development. The special education teacher uses this knowledge during assessments when determining curriculum and establishing appropriate expectations for each child. Possessing the knowledge about typical stages of development helps teachers understand the sequence of steps necessary to reach the desired educational outcomes for a particular child (Kostelnick, Soderman, & Whiren, 1993).

Being aware of education practices for typically developing children is also relevant when creating a **least restrictive** (normal or typical) **environment (LRE)** for children. Children must learn to function in a variety of environments. It is important to know what types of expectations are common in regular preschool programs, as

well as in early elementary school (kindergarten and first grade), to help prepare them to meet these expectations.

Knowledge of typical development is particularly important when working in **mainstreaming** and **inclusion** settings called integrated settings. **Mainstreaming** requires that children with special needs be taught within a special education classroom for part of the day and in regular education settings for the remainder. In contrast, inclusion involves children with and without developmental disabilities being in the same classroom throughout the day. When attending an inclusion program, a child with special needs may be **pulled out** (taken to another room) to receive therapy services for a limited portion of the day. Carta (1994) describes integration as "the process by which physical, social, and academic opportunities are created for a child with a disability to participate with others in typical school or community environments."

Integrated experiences must be provided whenever possible because they help prepare children to deal with a variety of environments and are required by federal law. Having children with a variety of developmental delays interact together allows special education teachers, parents, and children to understand typical expectations for other children. Integration experiences are valuable for children with and without developmental delays because it provides them with the experience of interacting with many types of people. Children and adults are typically more comfortable and positive toward individuals with developmental delays after integration experiences (Carta, 1994).

Full inclusion may not provide the least restrictive environment (LRE) for all children (Wang, Reynolds, & Walberg, 1994). Proponents for "inclusion as part of a continuum" state educators are obligated to make inclusion work for children for whom it is appropriate, but it is a mistake to have only one type of placement in which "one size fits all" (O'Neil, 1994–1995; Shanker, 1994; Fuchs & Fuchs 1994–1995).

Research on childhood integration indicates that an increasing number of early childhood programs are modifying philosophies and curricula to incorporate education practices effective for children with and without developmental disabilities (Odom & McEvoy, 1990; Peck, Odom, & Bricker, 1993; Wolery, Holcombe, Venn, Brookfield, Huffman, Schroeder, etc., 1993). Professionals and parents involved in these integrated programs perceive many benefits (e.g., children developing greater understanding for individual differences) and report that classroom activities are relatively easily adapted to meet the needs of children with and without developmental delays. Some problems still hinder the success of integration in early childhood education programs. These problems include a lack of adequate teacher preparation to work with children who have special needs and consultation opportunities with other professionals, inappropriately large child–teacher ratios, and a lack of adequate funding.

Collaborative communication between professionals is essential for creating successful integrated classrooms. When working in integrated classrooms, special education teachers must use their knowledge about typical development and regular education practices to establish appropriate curriculum practices for all children. They must also develop an understanding and respect for regular and special early childhood education programs, as discussed later in this chapter.

Participating in a Collaborative Team

Providing individualized education is most frequently accomplished by using a **interdisciplinary, multidisciplinary,** or **transdisciplinary team** approach. Regular preschools often have individuals trained in early childhood education as the only professional staff members. Research indicates that no discipline in and of itself adequately prepares its members to meet the needs of all children who have disabilities (Wolery, Strain, & Bailey, 1992; Odom & McEvoy, 1990). Therefore, special education programs generally have a wide variety of individuals involved in program planning and delivery.

A transdisciplinary, multidisciplinary, and/ or interdisciplinary team approach may be used

for services provided at children's homes, clinics, center-based programs, and inclusion classrooms. As a member of a child's collaborative team, the special education teacher focuses on developing the whole child by attending to all areas of development. This is in contrast to focusing on a single area of development, such as fine motor development, which is the focus of an occupational therapist.

Speech and language, and occupational and physical therapists frequently work with the special education teacher and suggest specific types of classroom activities that are useful for developing abilities in their area of focus. Many therapists also work directly with a child or group of children within the classroom and suggest model strategies the special education teachers may find useful when they work with children.

To be an effective team member the special education teacher must recognize the limits of his or her own knowledge. Special education teachers should develop good listening skills to take advantage of ideas and expertise from other professionals. For example, a special education teacher who is trying to help a child develop a proper method of grasping pencils, crayons, or paintbrushes might ask for guidance from an occupational therapist to develop a task analysis to break each skill down into small steps. The teacher would then provide the child with many opportunities to practice grasping.

An **occupational therapist (OTR)** might also provide the special education teacher with specific suggestions for activities that enhance fine motor skills. For example, the OTR might suggest putting a rubber band on a pencil as a visual cue for where the child should hold the pencil and suggest activities that promote hand strength. The special education teacher should also find ways to incorporate suggestions from other professionals into the daily classroom activities.

Service Coordination

According to Cook, Tessier, and Klein (1992), **service coordination** involves an active, ongoing process that includes helping parents gain access to services identified in their child's **individualized family service plan (IFSP)** or **individualized education program (IEP),** coordinating these services, and facilitating timely delivery of appropriate services throughout the duration of the child's eligibility. As discussed in Chapter 5, social workers frequently serve as service coordinators when the child requires services other than those directly related to education, including medical and social services, and financial support.

Within a preschool setting, the special education teacher is typically responsible for coordinating each child's overall education program and may be thought of as the "umbrella" who covers all areas of development. As service coordinator, the special education teacher often schedules services provided by other team members and arranges meetings at which professionals and parents work together to plan and implement programs designed to meet a child's needs (Wortham, 1996).

Assessing a Child's Strengths and Needs

As mentioned in earlier chapters, **assessment** plays an important role in understanding the developmental levels of a child and determining whether significant developmental delays exist. Special education teachers often conduct initial screenings to evaluate children's overall development and may conduct more detailed assessments when delays are detected.

To conduct assessments, special education teachers must know about typical and atypical development, and have well-developed skills to accurately observe and record behavior and recognize signs of specific disabilities. Special education teachers often request other professionals, who specialize in specific areas of development such as speech and language or motor development, to conduct assessments specific to their areas of expertise (Wolery, Doyle, Gast, Ault, & Simpson, 1993).

At times, discrepancies between **formal** and **informal assessment** may indicate that a child

has acquired certain knowledge or skills but for some reason is not using them in everyday functioning. Sometimes, the opposite occurs and the child displays the abilities in everyday activities but not during formal testing. Formal test scores indicate *only* how a particular child performed on a particular day on a particular test.

It is crucial for special educators to understand that factors other than the child's abilities may play a role in how well a child responds to formal testing. During a formal assessment the child may be tired, hungry, or distracted. Cook, Tessier, and Klein (1992) state, "It is critical that all information, whether derived from formal testing, parental interviews, or informal observations, be integrated and synthesized. It is often the teacher who must assume this responsibility in an effort to see that a comprehensive picture of the child's level of functioning is obtained" (p. 43).

Assessment is a means of documenting a child's growth and ongoing assessment is a necessary part of curriculum planning. It allows the special education teacher to determine patterns of strengths and weaknesses (e.g., cognitive development) and to determine where growth has occurred (Genishi, 1992). Assessment helps teachers and parents create a child's IFSP or IEP for the upcoming year and guides the development of appropriate teaching strategies and learning environments. Special education teachers often use assessment information to develop classroom activities, which may be used to meet each child's needs. (See Table 7.1 for a list of tests, classified as either norm-referenced, criterion-referenced, or curriculum-based, that special education teachers often use.)

Developing and Implementing an IFSP or IEP

Special education teachers are often responsible for developing individualized family service plans (IFSP) or individualized education program (IEP) goals and objectives for each child's needs. These goals and objectives are written once the teacher has completed the child's assessment and has consulted with the child's parents and relevant

TABLE 7.1 Tests that May Be Administered by a Special Education Teacher

Norm-Referenced

- Denver Developmental Screening Test
  Authors: W. K. Frankenburg & J. B. Dodds
  Publisher: Denver Developmental Materials
  Age: birth–6 years

- Bayley's Scales of Infant Development
  Author: N. Bayley
  Publisher: Psychological Corporation
  Age: birth–2½ years

- Developmental Profile II
  Authors: G. Alpern, T. J. Boll, & M. S. Shearer
  Publisher: Western Psychological Services
  Age: birth–9 years

- Boehm Test of Basic Concepts, Preschool Version
  Author: A. E. Boehm
  Publisher: The Psychological Corporation
  Age: 3–5 years

Criterion-Referenced

- Brigance Diagnostic Inventory of Early Development, Revised
  Author: A. H. Brigance
  Publisher: Curriculum Associates
  Age: birth–7 years

- Learning Accomplishment Profile, Diagnostic
  Authors: D. W. LeMay, P. M. Griffen, & A. R. Sanford
  Publisher: Kaplan School Supply Corporation
  Age: 36–72 months

- The Portage Guide to Early Education
  Authors: Portage Preschool Project
  Publisher: CESA 12
  Age: birth–6 years

Curriculum-Based

- Carolina Developmental Profile
  Authors: D. L. Lillie & G. L. Harbin
  Publisher: Kaplan School Supply Corporation
  Age: 2–5 years

- Hawaii Early Learning Profile
  Authors: S. Furuho, K. O'Reilly, T. Inatsuka,
      C. Hosaka, T. Allman, & B. Zeisloft–Falbey
  Publisher: VORT Corporation
  Age: birth–3 years

- Developmental Programming for Infants and Young Children
  Authors: S. J. Rogers & D. B. D'Eugenio
  Publisher: University of Michigan Press
  Age: birth–35 months

- Family Needs Assessment
  The Family Information Preference Inventory
  Authors: Turnbull & Turnbull
  Family Needs Survey
  Authors: Bailey & Simeonsson

Note: To determine which testing materials are most appropriate, potential users should examine test manuals and the Mental Measurements Yearbook (produced by the Buros Institute). Consideration should be given to the test's validity and reliability, characteristics of the normative sample, and factors such as ease in administering the test.

professionals. To develop appropriate IEPs or IF-SPs, the special education teacher must view the child as a child first and then consider the child's special needs. This includes viewing each child as having the potential to grow and change rather than viewing the child as being limited to a certain level of development.

After the long-term goals have been established, the special education teacher must break these goals into small, sequential steps to establish short-term objectives in a process referred to as **task analysis.** This process involves sequencing tasks from the easiest to the most difficult. Generally, the skills needed to complete a task are the important component rather than completion itself. For example, the goal for the task of stringing beads is designed to enhance fine-motor skills, including how to use two hands together, grasp objects, and develop strategies for completing the task. Table 7.2 provides an example of a goal for a child to independently string four beads, broken down into simple tasks.

The type of task analysis outlined in Table 7.2 can be completed for most areas of development including skills needed to use the toilet, sit at large-group activities, build with blocks, and use words to make requests. Another example (provided in

TABLE 7.2   Breaking a Task into Steps

Goal: The child will independently string four beads

1. The child visually notices the string and beads.
2. The child maintains the appropriate posture needed to complete the task (e.g., sits in a chair or on the floor).
3. The child extends one arm and reaches for the string.
4. The child picks up the string using a "pincer" grasp.
5. The child extends the other arm and picks up a bead.
6. The child positions the bead so that the hole is in the proper position.
7. The child uses the hand holding the string to push the string through the hole.
8. The child grabs the string, passes it through the hole using the pincer grasp, and pulls the string through.
9. The child repeats the process for the remainder of the beads.

Table 7.3) of breaking a goal into small steps for developing a child's social skills involves helping the child sit at a large group activity (Bricker & Cripe, 1992).

Developing and Implementing Curricula

Special education teachers are often responsible for establishing classroom lesson plans. It is often helpful if teachers create annual, monthly, weekly, and daily activity plans. Ideally, special education teachers ask other team members, including parents, to collaborate in developing lessons. Plans must be related to a child's goals and objectives. Parents and other team members benefit from receiving outlines of lesson plans so they have the opportunity to use similar activities when interacting with a child. Special education teachers are usually responsible for preparing materials to be used during the day's activities and developing alternate plans if the planned activities are ineffective on a given day (Wolery & Bredekamp, 1994; Kamii & DeVries, 1993/1978).

Guidelines from Professional Early Childhood Organizations.   In 1987, the National Association for the Education of Young Children (NAEYC) and the National Association of Early Childhood Specialists in the Department of Education in various states published a joint position statement discussing appropriate early childhood curriculum and assessment practices (Bredekamp, 1987). Some educators advocated using these guidelines when teaching children with and without disabilities. Other educators have suggested that developmentally appropriate practices are usually suitable guidelines for children with early developmental delays, but some adaptations are also needed (Wolery & Bredekamp, 1994).

The Division for Early Childhood of the Council for Exceptional Children stresses the belief that child-directed activities are the hallmark of all early childhood programs (Odom 1994). Carta (1994) suggested that the appropriateness of any practice may be determined only by evaluating its fit for each child. Wolery and Bredekamp (1994) further suggested that evaluation of the appropriateness of any early childhood practice

TABLE 7.3   An Example of Steps Toward a Long-Term Goal

Goal: Child will sit and attend to a group activity for five minutes on four out of five days per week

1. The child plays quietly during a group activity but is not required to be with the group.
2. The child engages in quiet activities outside the group but remains close by with teacher assistance.
3. The child sits with the group and is allowed to play with a nondistracting object (for example, a book, modeling clay, or small toy).
4. The child participates for three minutes in the group activity with teacher assistance.
5. The child participates for the duration of the activity with minimal teacher assistance.
6. The child participates with the group independently for the full duration of the activity (five minutes).

should result in affirmative responses to the following questions:

1. Does it result in a child's becoming more independent?
2. Does it produce an identified outcome, such as a child's mastery of an IEP objective?
3. Is it more or less efficient than another practice or way of learning?
4. Is it ethically defensible?
5. Does it comply with relevant policies?
6. Is it a practice valued by family members and other consumers?
7. Is it appropriate for a particular child?

Regular early childhood practices are often the starting point for developing curricula for all young children (Beaty, 1996). These practices include enhancing a child's overall development, independence, creativity, self-esteem, and positive socialization through play. These basic practices are often the starting point from which the special education teacher and other early intervention specialists may make adaptations to successfully teach children with special needs (Wolery, Doyle, Gast, Ault, & Simpson, 1993; Wolery, Strain, & Bailey, 1992).

Classrooms for Toddlers. Classrooms for toddlers are set up to allow them to explore freely and interact with the environment (Catron & Allen, 1993). Toddlers learn primarily through their senses and physical movement (Rogers, 1991). Toddlers should, therefore, have many opportunities for a variety of tactile (sensory), movement, and music experiences on a daily basis. Activities should be relevant and memorable to their lives. For example, rather than simply reading a book about fire stations, children might be taken on a field trip to visit a fire station in their neighborhood. If a field trip is not feasible, local fire companies are often willing to bring a truck and equipment to the children.

Group activities must be limited in duration because most toddlers and even older children with special needs have limited attention spans. They should not be expected to pay attention to

any one activity for more than a few minutes. Activities should be presented in a variety of ways, including one-to-one with the teacher and in small and large groups.

Classrooms for Preschoolers. A typical preschool classroom for three-, four-, and five-year-olds includes several learning centers. These include centers for dramatic play, blocks, books, easels for painting and drawing, and manipulatives. Most activities are open-ended (having no particular goal) rather than goal-directed (producing a predetermined "product"). Activities must be presented at a developmentally appropriate level. There should be an area for gross-motor activities within each classroom, including equipment such as a climber with a slide. (Refer to Chapter 12 for further discussion of classroom setup and play materials.)

Use of Themes for Activities. Preschool teachers often plan classroom activities around themes, including seasons of the year, types of vehicles, farm animals, visiting the doctor, and holidays. Teachers must be sensitive to various cultural and religious orientations regarding holidays. Holiday themes provide an excellent opportunity for children to learn about other cultures and religious beliefs. Teachers must also realize, though, that some families do not celebrate holidays, so the teachers must be creative in planning alternative activities for those children (Wolery, Strain, & Bailey, 1992).

Using themes helps to provide a starting point or focus for activities, but children should not be limited to a certain theme during their play. For example, if the classroom theme is "going to the beach," one child might pretend to be swimming while the theme might remind another child about snow. The teacher's role is to facilitate play by asking questions, making suggestions, and describing events in meaningful and interesting ways whether or not they relate to the theme.

Developing Lesson Plans. Ideally, curriculum plans include exposure to books on a daily basis.

Books should be read to children, but children should also be able to look at books independently. Children begin to connect the spoken and written word through exposure to books and other printed materials. Charts, lists, labels, and writing the child's comments on paper encourage preliteracy (pre-reading and writing) skills.

As children mature and their play skills increase, the number of play choices provided should also be increased. It is important to note that, while a special needs class may have fewer play choices available, the activities made available typically remain child-directed. For example, if the teacher's lesson plan calls for making masks and the children start making hats, teachers should be prepared to adjust their plans. Children are frequently more interested in their own ideas, and it is important to encourage their expansion of an activity. With flexibility in activities, teachers must allow sufficient time for children to complete activities without their feeling rushed. There should be some teacher-directed activities as well, since children must begin to learn that by school-age teachers will expect them to complete certain tasks in specific ways (Carta, 1994).

Daily classroom activities must include using self-help skills. Everyday activities such as snack time, using the toilet, washing hands, and putting on outer wear provide opportunities to practice self-help skills (Cantron & Allen, 1993). It may take a little longer for children to be encouraged to attempt or complete these tasks independently, but performing these independently helps build confidence in addition to specific skills (Eliason & Jenkins, 1994).

Balancing between providing children with an appropriate level of support and also encouraging independence often is a difficult task. Most young children struggle between the desire to be independent and need for adult assistance and reassurance. For example, children may want to be able to put on a coat without help but do not want other children to laugh at them if they cannot (Hendrick, 1994).

The next section provides an overview of several general philosophies of curriculum development practiced by early childhood educators. Each section presents a particular philosophy followed by suggestions for how an early childhood special education teacher can modify this practice when working with children who have special needs. The key philosophy of early childhood education is to use strategies that help create a healthy emotional environment for young children (Cook, Tessier, & Klein, 1992; Haywood, Brooks, & Burns, 1990). All teaching styles must support this philosophy.

Helping Children Learn Problem-Solving Skills.
In addition to using appropriate discipline techniques, creating a positive learning environment includes helping children develop skills to solve problems. The goal is to have children stop and think about what is happening, why it is happening, and then attempt to discover solutions independently. **Problem-solving skills** encompass all aspects of children's daily interactions and include using cognitive, motor, and social skills.

Problem-solving skills can be enhanced by teachers asking children guiding questions or making comments encouraging them to analyze a situation. Ideally, teachers encourage children to ask for help in solving problems before children become overly frustrated. For example, a teacher might say, "What can you do about your problem?" or "What do you think will happen if...?" During the early phases of children's learning to solve their own problems adults may suggest possible solutions. When adults provide possible solutions, children should be encouraged to provide suggestions, too. However, adults must gradually encourage children to generate their own solutions.

This technique may be used with toddlers as well as older children. For example, a child who cannot get out of a chair while sitting at a table but has not reached the point of becoming overly frustrated (i.e., has not begun to cry) should be allowed to try to figure out a solution. The teacher might approach the child and comment, "It looks like you are stuck in the chair. What can you do about it?" Even if the child simply uses a gesture indicating that he or she wants to get out of the chair or uses the words "help me," this suggests that the child is beginning to use problem-solving methods. If adults consistently use this approach, children gradually begin to use it on their own.

This method may also be used during conflict situations between children. Consider the following example of conflict resolution using problem-solving techniques. Two children are playing in the sandbox and both want the same shovel. The teacher approaches the sandbox because the children are in a physical struggle over the shovel. Although it may appear obvious, the first thing the teacher might say is, "What is the problem?" The teacher should take possession of the shovel so that the children may be more likely to focus their attention on the conversation with the teacher. Ideally, the teacher avoids asking the children what happened or who was at fault. This is because young children tend to find it very hard to take another person's perspective, referred to as **egocentrism.** (Refer to Chapter 2 for discussion of egocentrism.)

Next, the teacher might then summarize what appears to be the problem by saying, "It looks like you both want the shovel." To encourage the children to solve the problem, the teacher might add, "What should you do?" It is likely that both children will respond, "I want the shovel." At this point, the teacher might be tempted to ask who had it first but should not. It is important for the teacher to realize that, because both children really want the shovel, each is likely to think he or she had it first.

The teacher may attempt to validate their feelings by saying, "I know you both really want the shovel, but we only have one." Ideally, the teacher asks the children for suggestions for how to resolve this conflict. After the children are provided time to suggest solutions, the teacher might suggest trying one of the solutions or say something such as, "One of you may use the shovel for

five minutes, then the other may have a turn." The teacher should restate the solution to ensure that the children heard and understood it. The teacher must monitor the interaction to ensure that the children follow the agreed-on solution. Ideally, the teacher also helps the child waiting to use the shovel become involved in another activity until their turn.

If the teacher were to intervene by taking the shovel away from the children, the teacher would not be helping the children learn problem-solving skills. In addition, both children would probably be angry or upset and the same or a similar incident would be more likely to occur in the future. The children would also not have received "instructions" on how to cope with the conflict. In some cases, a toy must be removed from a play area to resolve or help prevent conflicts. This should occur only after attempts to get the children to resolve the conflict are unsuccessful or if they continue to fight over using the toy.

Some young children or children with special needs are unable to provide suggestions for solutions, but in most cases they can learn to use words rather than physical force when there is a conflict. Most children, even those with limited language skills, can learn to say "No!" As a child's language develops, the teacher can help the child learn more complex communication strategies. The ultimate goal is for children to stop and think and then use words to solve conflicts rather than physical, aggressive behavior or crying.

Problem-solving skills are also necessary during interaction among children. Some children with developmental delays have difficulties developing and maintaining the positive social skills necessary to interact with and learn from their more "socially competent" peers (Kohler & Strain, 1993; Goldstein, 1993). It is often helpful for teachers to model appropriate social problem-solving skills, mediate interactions, and sequentially guide children through various steps of social interactions to help ensure that children experience successful interactions. The goal is for the teacher to gradually reduce the level of intervention.

Providing Choices. Providing children with choices also helps to promote a healthy emotional environment because choices give children some level of control over the environment. Choices must be appropriate for each child's developmental level, and, generally, the younger the child, the fewer the number of choices provided. Too many choices are overwhelming for young children or those who have developmental delays. Choices could be as simple as asking a child, "Do you want to wear your blue or red shirt?" or "Do you want juice or milk?" When adults provide children with choices, they should be willing to accept the children's choices. There will be times when a child is too upset to choose. When this occurs, an adult could comment, "I can see you are not ready to decide. I will decide for you." Once the adult has made the decision it should be carried out.

Another modification that may be needed for children with special needs include limiting the number of choices of activities or play materials rather than allowing freedom to use everything in the classroom. This modification often is necessary because too many choices are overstimulating or overwhelming for some children. For example, children with a limited attention span frequently move from one activity to another without truly exploring any of them. When choices are limited, these children are more likely to attend longer to each activity or more thoroughly explore a particular toy, which is likely to enhance learning.

Encouraging Active Exploration. Children learn through play involving exploration of materials and the environment. One of the most important teacher responsibilities is to create and maintain an environment where children can freely play (Bredekamp 1987; Rogers 1991). (Chapter 12 provides a detailed discussion of play.)

For some children who have special needs, **self-initiated exploratory play** does not spontaneously occur. If this is the case, teacher intervention is necessary. To assist children in developing play skills, a teacher could use **hand-over-hand assistance,** which involves the teacher taking a child's hands and guiding the child through certain actions, or modeling. Hand-over-hand assistance is also frequently useful for children who have motor skills difficulties. Hand-over-hand assistance provides information about appropriate ways to use classroom tools such as crayons or paintbrushes. Using this method helps children with a short attention span stay focused on an activity. This type of assistance provides a touch of encouragement, telling the child, "Let's try this together."

Children with special needs often need direct instruction and individual practice before they attempt a particular play activity independently. **Prescriptive teaching** is a method of working individually with a child on skills development with a clearly defined goal in a sequential manner. Prescriptive teaching is used to enhance play skills by developing a particular skill, such as teaching a child how to string beads, using task analysis. After a particular skill is developed, the goal is then to have the child use the new skills and generalize them during more spontaneous play (Cook, Tessier, & Klein, 1996).

Providing Engaging and Stimulating Environments. Most children benefit from a colorful and stimulating environment including many pictures on the walls, items hanging from the ceiling, and a wide variety of activities. Some children with special needs are easily distracted by visual stimuli, however, and do not learn well in such visually stimulating environments. These children require less visual stimulation to focus and learn. The teacher could accommodate the educational requirements of these children by carefully determining where wall hangings, such as art work, posters, and signs, are placed and deciding whether props (items for children to look at or hold) enhance or distract from learning.

For example, limiting irrelevant stimuli during large group activities might help children who are easily distracted better attend to these activities. For these children, large group activities are frequently most effectively presented in a section of the room where the floor is carpeted in a neutral color and where no objects hang from the ceiling or on the walls. To the observer, this often seems overly plain, but some children benefit from this type of environment because they more easily focus on relevant stimuli.

On the other hand, some children require visual and tactile aids to encourage them to focus their attention on an activity. For example, while singing "The Itsy-Bitsy Spider," children who have difficulty attending who are given pipe cleaner spiders as props may be able to focus on the activity. These children might not focus on the activity without the props. Props also help children focus on other types of activities such as listening to a story. Some children benefit from holding objects because the objects "keep their hands busy." For these children, when their hands are busy their eyes focus on the activity, and when their hands are not busy their eyes constantly scan the environment.

Creating and Promoting a Supportive Classroom Environment.
Another very important role of the special education teacher is to create a classroom environment in which children are respected and guided in a supportive and positive manner. This type of orientation helps children strengthen their confidence and contributes to the development of positive self-esteem.

Adult–child interactions often affect the development of positive self-esteem when adults express respect, acceptance, and support for children. Powell (1991) lists several attributes of positive interaction styles that are used with children, including providing enjoyable activities, encouraging social interaction with peers and encouraging child-initiated activities, sharing control with children, approaching children at their level of understanding, and encouraging children to experience success by providing activities not too easy or difficult.

Powell (1991) describes how adults could provide a give-and-take interaction with children:

"Adults follow the child's lead when talking with a child or entering his or her play activities. Conversations between adults and children are reciprocal exchanges: The adult does not dominate the exchange by asking didactic questions" (p. 102). (See Chapter 15 for further discussion of the importance of helping the child develop positive self-esteem.)

Creating a Language Rich Environment.
In most preschool classrooms the flow of conversation and nonverbal communication is unending. Children are involved in **self-talk** and conversations with peers and teachers. (See Chapters 2 and 8 for discussions on self-talk and other forms of communication.) In most preschool environments, teachers follow children's conversation leads rather than initiating most conversations. Regular preschool teachers typically do not modify their language but talk in extended and relatively complex sentences.

When working with children with special needs adults frequently initiate language. For example, in a classroom for children with special needs there is often less child-initiated language and more teacher-initiated language during play. This is because children who qualify for placement in the special needs preschool class often have language delays.

A teacher may also use grammatically incomplete sentences, which is called **telegraphic speech.** For example, a teacher may say "Open juice?" instead of "Do you want me to open your juice?" Although it is important to provide a model for correct language usage, a teacher frequently use a language stimulation strategy called **parallel talk.** This is a level of speech designed to be at the child's present language ability or one step above the child's level of language rather than at a more complex adult level.

For example, if a child is at the two-word sentence stage, the teacher would use two- or three-word statements because using five- to seven-word sentences may be too complex for the child. Special education teachers are also likely to expand on a child's speech. For example, if a child says, "More cookies," the teacher expands this statement slightly by saying, "Want more cookies." When the child reaches this level the teacher would further expand by saying, "Want more cookies, please," and later, "I want more cookies, please."

In the special education preschool classroom teacher interactions often include the use of **sign language** or **communication boards** (cards or boards with letters, words, symbols, or pictures mounted on them). Sign language and communication boards allow children to express their needs using physical movement. This may ease their frustration at being unable to express needs through verbalizations. For some children, using a communication board or sign language assists in the acquisition of **verbal communication skills.** (See Chapter 8 for a discussion of the use of communication boards and Chapter 9 for a discussion of the use of sign language.)

In contrast, when working with some children who have special needs, a teacher may not respond to some forms of **nonverbal communication,** including gesturing, pointing, or using sign language. To an observer, the teacher may seem unaware or even unresponsive. In most cases, though, teachers are aware of the nonverbal cues the children make but are trying to encourage them to use words to communicate rather than relying solely on nonverbal communication.

For example, during snack time a child may be asked, "Do you want another cookie?" to which the child nods or signs "yes." The teacher may ignore this response if the teacher knows the child can respond by using words. In this case, the teacher might prompt the child by saying, "Use your words to tell me what you want. Do you want another cookie?" and may not give the child a cookie until the child says "yes" or some other developmentally appropriate verbal response.

Process versus Product. Ideally, goals and activities for young children remain focused on the process of "doing" rather than "completing" an activity. At times, adults become too focused on

the child creating a particular object or doing something the "correct way." The process of manipulating objects is generally more important than what is made. Children should, therefore, be provided with many **open-ended activities** that provide materials for manipulating and exploring rather than for creating a specific object. Open-ended activities allow the child to explore materials in a personally relevant manner.

Some children with special needs have limited attending skills and require special strategies to help them stay focused on activities. For these children, the special education teacher may establish specific expectations, making it appear that the focus is on creating a product when in fact the focus is on lengthening attending skills. For example, a child might be told, "I want you to complete this puzzle before you leave." In this case, the goal for requiring the child to finish the puzzle is to enhance attending skills. This is important because a limited attention span often has an effect on other areas of development, such as cognitive, motor, or social skills. Table 7.4 outlines a

TABLE 7.4 Methods for Effective Interactions with Children who Have a Limited Attention Span

When encouraging children with a limited attention span to continue to work at a specific task, it may be helpful to:

- Use physical touch;
- Establish eye contact by having the child look directly at the speaker's face;
- Provide verbal reminders;
- Use verbal prompts for each step of an activity;
- Have the child repeat each verbal prompt back to the speaker before being given the next step in a set of directions;
- Hold the object of discussion directly in front of the child while talking about the object;
- Be in close proximity to the child when communicating with the child;
- Get down to the child's physical height to communicate;
- Use songs or music rather than conversation to communicate.

process of working with children who have a limited attention span.

Children with a limited attention span exhibit behavior that diminishes their own exploration of materials, as well as distracting others. For some children, a special chair, called a **Rifton chair,** helps them more effectively focus on large-group and tabletop activities. This chair has a solid back and sides, wide legs, and may have a "seat belt" to help provide support for children with postural difficulties. It also appears that the chair provides some children with a sense of security that helps them focus on activities for a longer period of time. The seat belt serves as a reminder to continue with a task. It does not serve as a restraint because most children can easily unfasten the belt. Rifton chairs are also more stable than ordinary chairs and help to prevent children from rocking back and forth and tipping over.

Choosing Behavior Management Techniques

Choosing behavior management techniques is often the responsibility of the special education teacher. When choosing **behavior management techniques,** it is essential to focus on the goal of assisting children to develop appropriate social skills. For some children with special needs, a greater variety of behavior management techniques must be used. When implementing a behavior management technique, it is important to try different strategies until one is successful but avoid shifting strategies too quickly. In addition, a child should be allowed to start each day with a clean slate. Once an incident is over, it is over and must not be "harped" on (Graves & Strubank, 1991).

As a part of selecting appropriate behavior management techniques, teachers must create a positive environment by using affirmative and specific terms when communicating with children. It is important to tell children what they should do rather than what they should not. For example, telling a child, "I like the way you shared your cookies with your friend," is better

than saying, "I don't like it when you don't share." Stating expectations in the positive takes practice, but the more it is used the more spontaneous it becomes (Graves & Strubank, 1991).

Betz (1994) discusses the importance of using positive behavior management techniques with young children: "Discipline is not a separate entity from the educational process as a whole. If a goal is to help children develop an internal control and a sense of social values, discipline must be seen as an ongoing, year-long project, one that never ends and is a vital part of the process of growing up" (p. 10). Positive behavior management techniques often used with young children include employing logical consequences (consequences that fit the behavior, such as having the child pick up toys after playing) and redirection strategies (focusing the child on desirable activities). (Chapter 14 provides further discussion of behavior management techniques.)

Working with Family Members

Special education teachers often coordinate parents and professionals working together in order to design and implement programs for children with special needs. Special education teachers must maintain ongoing communication with parents to ensure that parents know their contributions are being considered. A journal sent back and forth on a daily or weekly basis between home and school is one effective means of maintaining contact with parents. Teaching staff visiting the child's home and family members observing class activities are additional ways to maintain contact with family members. These types of visits also allow parents and teachers to directly observe methods of interacting with the child. Regular communication also includes informal and formal meetings, classroom visitations, telephone calls, and written communication. Programs are most effective when parents are encouraged to initiate communication rather than just being passive recipients of information (Carta, 1994).

Because special education teachers are frequently responsible for coordinating the variety of therapy services a child may receive, they often become the primary contact person for family members. Early intervention services are typically designed to support children who are at risk of developmental delays or have special needs and their families. Special education teachers are often responsible for ensuring that services are provided for parents, including training, support, and information. These services usually help develop a positive parent–child relationship, an essential part of the foundation for the child's development.

One of the most important roles of the special education teacher is to help parents understand how important they are in their child's education. (The importance of a parent's role in a child's education is further discussed in Chapters 5 and 6.)

CONCLUSION

Children with and without developmental delays often benefit from many of the early education philosophies described above. As discussed, some modifications are useful or necessary for children with special needs. Integrating good practices from regular and special education is likely to benefit all children.

Although children with special needs typically are identified because they develop at a slower rate than is "typical," they usually benefit from many of the teaching strategies used with children who do not have developmental delays. The overall goal of early intervention is to provide appropriate individualization of services, focusing on a child's current level of functioning rather than chronological age. Early intervention is specifically geared toward increasing each child's strengths and remediating areas of delay. Special education teachers focus on developing the whole child rather than solely on the areas of delay. This helps to ensure that each child will reach his or her full potential.

Special education focuses on the value of each child's uniqueness and on the philosophy that "all children can learn." This belief is shown when children hear adults say, "I knew you could do it!" or "I know you can do it!" and by greeting them with open arms.

The next four chapters discuss the roles and services provided by other professionals who work with young children with special needs. Chapter 8 discusses the role of the speech and language pathologist and enhancing communication skills. Chapter 9 discusses professionals who work with children who have hearing impairments and how these impairments affect development. Chapter 10 focuses on fine motor development and the role of the occupational therapist, and Chapter 11 focuses on gross motor development and the role of the physical therapist.

CHAPTER SUMMARY

Special education teachers may provide services in the child's home, clinic, daycare, or regular or special preschool program. The philosophy of most early childhood special education programs is to acknowledge each child at his or her level of development and create developmentally appropriate practices. Special education teachers use knowledge about typical development to coordinate the student's overall education program by participating in collaborative teams. Special education teachers are responsible for assessing each child's strengths and weakness and taking part in developing IFSPs and IEPs. Special education teachers develop curriculum and lesson plans that encourage children to use problem-solving skills, make choices, and actively explore their environment, focus on process versus product, and create a language rich environment. Special education teachers also create and promote supportive classroom environments, often determine behavior management systems, and frequently are responsible for maintaining ongoing communication with a child's parents. Teaching methods used in regular preschool programs are often effective in programs designed for children with special needs, and all children may benefit from being in integrated classrooms.

CHAPTER REVIEW QUESTIONS

1. Compare and contrast goals at preschools for children with special needs and preschools for children who do not have special needs.
2. What is the difference between a self-contained and an integrated classroom? What are the possible advantages and disadvantages of each?
3. What methods may create a positive classroom environment?
4. What are some of the differences between a classroom designed for toddlers and one designed for preschoolers?
5. What methods may be useful to help gain the attention of a child with a limited attention span?

SUGGESTED STUDENT ACTIVITIES

1. Use task analysis to develop a method for helping a child learn to tie shoes.
2. Visit a special education classroom and observe the roles of the special education teacher and compare these roles to those of a teacher in a regular preschool setting.
3. Imagine that you are a special education teacher working with other professionals. Create an IEP and develop lesson plans for one day that focus on the IEP goals of a student.
4. Review various early childhood special education assessment tools and determine their advantages and limitations.

ADDITIONAL READINGS

Bricker, D. D. (1989). *Early intervention for at-risk and handicapped infants, toddlers and preschool children.* Palo Alto, CA: Vort.

Cook, R. E., Tessier, A., & Klein, M. D. (1992). *Adapting early childhood curricula for children with special needs* (3rd ed.). New York: Macmillan.

Smith, T. E. C., Polloway, E. A., Patton, J. R., & Dowdy, C. A. (1995). *Teaching children with special needs in inclusive settings.* Boston: Allyn and Bacon.

Williams, L. R., & Frombert, D. P. (1992). *Encyclopedia of early childhood education.* New York: Garland.

ADDITIONAL RESOURCES

Center for Innovation in Teaching the Handicapped
2805 E. 10th Street, Room 150
Bloomington, IN 47405

Council for Exceptional Children
1920 Association Drive
Reston, VA 20091

National Association for the Education of Young Children
1834 Connecticut Avenue, N.W.
Washington, DC 20005

Office of Special Education & Rehabilitative Services
U.S. Department of Education
Switzer Building, Room 2123
Washington, DC 20202–2524

Research and Resources for Special Education
1920 Association Drive
Reston, VA 20091

Team of Advocates for Special Kids
1800 E. LaVeta
Orange, CA 92666

REFERENCES

Association of Teacher Educators and the National Association for the Education of Young Children. (1991). Early childhood teacher certification: A position statement. *Young Children, 47*(1), 16–27.

Bailey, D. B., & McWilliam, R. (1990). Normalizing early intervention. *Topics in Early Childhood Special Education, 10*(2), 33–47.

Beaty, J. J. (1996). *Skills for preschool teachers* (5th ed). Columbus, OH: Merrill.

Betz, C. (1994). Beyond time-out: Tips for a teacher. *Young Children, 49*(3), 10–14.

Bredekamp, S. (1987). *Developmentally appropriate practices in early childhood programs serving children from birth to age eight.* Washington, DC: National Association for the Education of Young Children.

Bricker, D. D., & Cripe, J. W. (1992). *An activity-based approach to early intervention.* Baltimore, MD: Paul H. Brookes.

Bruder, M. B. (1993). The provision of early intervention and early childhood special education within community early childhood programs: Characteristics of effective service delivery. *Topics in Early Childhood Special Education, 13*(1), 19–37.

Burton, C. B., Hains, A., Hanline, M. F., McLean, M., & McCormick, K. (1992). Early education policy, practice, and personnel preparation: The urgency of professional unification. *Topics in Early Childhood Special Education, 11*(4), 53–69.

Cantron, C. E., & Allen, J. (1993). *Early childhood curriculum.* Columbus, OH: Merrill.

Carta, J. J. (1994). Developmentally appropriate practices: Shifting the emphasis to individual appropriateness. *Journal of Early Intervention, 18*(4), 242–243.

Carta, J. J., Schwartz, I. S., Atwater, J. B., & McConnell, S. R. (1991). Developmentally appropriate practice: Appraising its usefulness for young children with disabilities. *Topics in Early Childhood Special Education, 11*(1), 1–20.

Cook, R. E., Tessier, A., & Klein, M. D. (1996). *Adapting early childhood curricula for children in inclusive settings* (4th ed.). Columbus, OH: Merrill.

Cook, R. E., Tessier, A., & Klein, M. D. (1992). *Adapting early childhood curricula for children with special needs.* New York: Macmillan.

Eliason, C. F., & Jenkins, L. T. (1994). A practical guide to early *childhood curriculum* (5th ed). Columbus, OH: Merrill.

Fuchs, D., & Fuchs, L. (1994–1995). Sometimes separate is better. *Educational Leadership, 52*(4), 22–26.

Genishi, C. (Ed.). (1992). *Ways of assessing children and curriculum: Stories of early childhood practice.* NY: Teachers College Press.

Goldstein, H. (1993). Use of peers as communication intervention agents. *Teaching Exceptional Children, 25*(2), 37–40.

Graham, M. A., & Bryant, D. M. (1993). Developmentally appropriate activities for children with special needs. *Infants and Young Children, 5*(3), 31–42.

Graves, M., & Strubank, R. (1991). Helping children manage themselves. In M. Brickman & L. Taylor (Eds.), *Supporting young learners: Ideas for preschool and day care providers.* (pp. 145–168). Ypsilanti, MI: High Scope Press.

Haywood, H. C., Brooks, P., & Burns, S. (1990). *Cognitive curriculum for young children* (Experimental Version). Watertown, MA: Charlesbridge Publishing.

Hendrick, J. (1994). Total learning: *Developmental curriculum for the young child* (4th ed). Columbus, OH: Merrill.

Jipson, J. (1991). Developmentally appropriate practice: Culture, curriculum, connections. *Early Education and Development, 2*(2), 120–136.

Kamii, C., & DeVries, R. (1993/1978). *Physical knowledge in preschool education: Implications of Piaget's theory.* New York: Teachers College Press.

Kohler, F., & Strain, P. S. (1993). The early childhood social skills program. *Teaching Exceptional Children, 25*(2), 41–42.

Kostelnick, M. J. (1992). Myths associated with developmentally appropriate practice. *Young Children, 47*(4), 17–23.

Kostelnick, M. J., Soderman, A. K., & Whiren, A. P. (1993). *Developmentally appropriate programs in early childhood education.* Columbus, OH: Merrill.

Mahoney, G. J., Robinson, C., & Powell, A. (1992). Modifying parent–child interaction: Enhancing the development of handicapped children. *Journal of Special Education, 22,* 82–96.

Norris, J. A. (1991). Providing developmentally appropriate intervention to infants and young children with handicaps. *Topics in Early Childhood Special Education, 11*(1), 21–35.

Odom, S. L. (1994). Developmentally appropriate practices, policy and use for young children with disabilities and their families. *Journal of Early Intervention, 18*(4), 346–348.

Odom, S. L., & McEvoy, M. A. (1990). Mainstreaming at the preschool level: Potential barriers and tasks for the field. *Topics in Early Childhood Special Education, 10*(2), 48–61.

O'Neil, J. (1994–1995). Can inclusion work? A conversation with Jim Kauffman and Mara Sapon–Shevin. *Educational Leadership, 52*(4), 7–11.

Peck, C. B., Odom, S. L., & Bricker, D. D. (1993). *Integrating young children with disabilities into community programs: ecological perspectives on research and implementation.* Baltimore, MD: Paul H. Brookes.

Powell, A. (1991). Be responsive. In M. Brickman & L. Taylor (Eds.), *Supporting young learners: Ideas for preschool and day care providers.* (pp. 16–30). Ypsilanti, MI: High Scope Press.

Rogers, A. (1991). Settings for active learning. In M. Brickman & L. Taylor (Eds.), *Supporting young learners: Ideas for preschool and daycare providers.* (pp. 62–89). Ypsilanti, MI: High Scope Press.

Salisbury, C. L., & Vincent, L. J. (1990). Criterion of the next environment and best practice: Mainstreaming and integration 10 years later. *Topics in Early Childhood Special Education, 10*(2), 78–89.

Shanker, A. (1994). Full inclusion is neither free nor appropriate. *Educational Leadership, 52*(4), 18–21.

Walsh, D. J. (1991). Extending the discourse on developmental appropriateness: A developmental perspective. *Early Education and Development, 2*(2), 109–119.

Wang, M., Reynolds, M., & Walberg, H. (1994). Serving students at the margins. *Educational Leadership, 52*(4), 12–17.

Wolery, M., & Bredekamp, S. (1994). Developmentally appropriate practices and young children with disabilities: Contextual issues in discussion. *Journal of Early Intervention, 18*(4), 331–341.

Wolery, M., Doyle, P. M., Gast, D. L., Ault, M. J., & Simpson, S. L. (1993). Comparison of progressive time delay and transition-based teaching with preschoolers who have developmental delays. *Journal of Early Intervention, 17*(2), 160–176.

Wolery, M., Holcombe, A., Venn, M., Brookfield, J., Huffman, K., Schroeder, C., Martin, C., & Fleming, L. A. (1993). Mainstreaming in early childhood programs: Current status and relevant issues. *Young Children, 49*(1), 78–84.

Wolery, M., Strain, P. S., & Bailey, D. B. (1992). Reaching potentials of children with special needs. In S. Bredekamp & T. Rosegrant (Eds.), *Reaching potentials: appropriate curricula and assessment for young children,* Vol. 1 (pp. 92–111). Washington, DC: National Association for the Education of Young Children.

Wolock, E. (1990). *The relationship of teacher interaction style to the engagement of developmentally delayed preschoolers.* Unpublished doctoral dissertation, University of Michigan, Ann Arbor.

Wortham, S. C. (1996). *The integrated classroom: The assessment-curriculum link in early childhood education.* Columbus, OH: Merrill.

CHAPTER 8

SPEECH AND LANGUAGE SERVICES

SUSAN KARNES HECHT, M.S., CCC-SP

ABOUT THE AUTHOR

Susan Karnes Hecht earned her bachelor's degree in foreign language study from the University of Rochester in Rochester, New York, and her master's in communication disorders from the State University of New York College at New Paltz in New Paltz, New York. She is licensed as a speech and language pathologist in New York State and has New York State permanent certification as a teacher of the speech and hearing impaired. She has a Certificate of Clinical Competence in speech and language pathology (CCC-sp) from the American Speech–Language–Hearing Association. Ms. Karnes Hecht is currently employed with the Saint Francis Hospital Preschool program as a senior speech and language pathologist and is a private speech therapist and an adjunct faculty member at SUNY–New Paltz. She is married and has two children.

CHAPTER KEY POINTS

- Speech and language delays are the most frequent type of developmental delay in children who are younger than five years old.
- There are several types of communication skills that develop during the early childhood years.

- Speech and language evaluation include a case history, personal interview, and informal and formal assessment.
- Early intervention is extremely important because language development affects cognitive and social-emotional skills development.
- Speech and language therapy is conducted in individual or group sessions at the child's home, in a clinic, therapy room, or classroom.

As discussed in Chapter 3, the most frequently occurring developmental delays before school age (five years old) are communication delays. These delays frequently negatively affect the development of cognitive and social skills. This chapter focuses on the evaluation of speech and language development and the role of the speech and language pathologist.

THE SPEECH AND LANGUAGE PATHOLOGIST

Speech and language pathologists are typically trained at the bachelor's or master's level (Wilcox, 1989). For example, in New York state, bachelor's level therapists are qualified to practice in schools but must have a master's degree to practice in most other settings or to have a private practice. In most states, speech and language pathologists with a bachelor's degree are required to complete a master's degree to be permanently certified or licensed. Both types of degrees include a specified amount of "student teaching," also called a clinical practicum.

Speech and language pathologists at the master's level may also hold a Certificate of Clinical Competence (CCC-sp) from the American Speech–Language–Hearing Association (ASHA). Speech and language pathologists evaluate and provide therapy for several areas of communication skills discussed below.

OVERVIEW OF COMMUNICATION SKILLS

Newborns reflexively yawn, grunt, burp, sigh, and produce an **"undifferentiated" cry** (Oller &

Eiler, 1988). Over time, however, different needs are signaled by **differentiated crying,** different types of cries. This development suggests that the infant has learned that communicating in this way often lead to the fulfillment of certain needs such as resolving pain, hunger, and fatigue. As infants gradually establish control of breathing and coordination of muscles, they become capable of producing specific sounds.

As general cognitive abilities develop during the first year of life, language abilities also increase. Before speech acquisition, also called **expressive language,** children learn to understand speech, which is called **receptive language** (Wood, 1981). For example, at about six months, most children respond to their own names. They turn and look at a person who says their name. At about nine months, most children appropriately respond to words such as *come* and *up.*

As children begin to increase the number of their vocalizations, the role of adult modeling of language becomes increasingly important. Parents and other care providers model correct language, **semantics** (meaning of words), **syntax** (rules for sentence construction), and **phonology** (sounds) of language. They also provide models for the rules of **conversational speech,** called **pragmatics,** which include taking turns when speaking in a conversation. Adults provide reinforcement by responding to the child after the child vocalizes (Norman & McCormick, 1993).

Care providers and parents frequently use **motherese.** This style of speech uses a simpler, shorter, and more repetitious sentence structure. That is, adults reduce the complexity of their speech when talking to very young children. As a child matures and begins saying words, adults often expand on the child's vocalizations. For example, **expansion** is demonstrated when a child says, "Go car?" and the mother responds, "Yes, daddy went in the car." Motherese and expansion seem to enhance language development (Leonard, 1986).

Around three months, most babies begin **cooing,** which is comprised of soft melodic vowel sounds, including "ooh" and "ahh." Between six and fourteen months old, most babies begin to **babble,** which refers to repeating strings of vowels and consonants (e.g., *bababababa, mamama*). When a child coos or babbles and an adult is present, the adult usually responds to the child in some way (Bloom, 1993). For example, after a child says, *nananana,* the adult may turn toward the child, imitate the child or respond in some other way. When adults respond to children in this manner, it often reinforces vocalizations. Children are more likely to coo or babble if an adult responds (Fey, 1986).

Children typically speak their first word at about twelve months. At this time, most children begin making their needs and desires known through words (Aitchison, 1996). These words are mental symbols that refer to objects, people, and events (Kuczak, 1986). The year-old child typically may say several words. These words are most often names of familiar people or objects such as *mommy, daddy,* and *drink.* These vocal symbols serve as a method for children to **encode** (store in memory) their experiences. They also provide methods for encoding information in **long-term memory** (Clark 1996). Children are likely either to **overextend,** applying a word broadly to a set of stimuli, such as using the word *juice* to refer to any drink, or **underextend,** restricting the use of a word to only one stimulus, such as using the word *dog* to mean only the child's toy dog (Carroll, 1986).

Children's use of art, symbols, and language to represent objects, people, and events is called **symbolic thinking.** The ability to think symbolically is directly related to language development (Gopnik & Meltzoff, 1986). Symbolic thought is evident in preschoolers' dreams, imagery, and play. This form of thought allows children to start fantasizing and creating novel images by manipulating symbols in complex and personal ways. Children's abilities to use symbolic thinking depends on prior development of cognitive abilities that allow them to think about, organize, and process information internally (Norman & McCormick, 1993).

Most toddlers (one to two years old) remember names of objects and pictures. They will imitate and use these names at a later time. They point to toys, pictures in a book, or parts of the body when named. They gradually begin to name objects themselves. In general, children comprehend more language than they can produce (Blank, Rose, & Berlin, 1978). For example, they may be able to respond appropriately to an adult saying, "Give me your shoes," yet be unable to produce the phrase, "Give me your shoes." During the first two years of development, most children without developmental disabilities use single words. Often these words represent a sentence. An example of a one-word sentence, called a holophrase, is when a child says, "juice!" The child is likely to be communicating, "I want a drink of juice!" (Yoder & Warren, 1993; Bloom & Lahey, 1978).

During the second year of life, short sentences begin to be a part of children's language. These sentences are typically composed of a verb and other words. Toddlers typically have acquired a vocabulary consisting of 25 to 300 words (Bloom, 1991). "Me do," "My ball," and "Mine!" are frequent words a two-year-old uses. These two-word utterances are likely to include **telegraphic speech,** which includes core words (key verbs and nouns) and omits less important words. For example, a toddler is likely to say, "more juice," rather than, "I want more juice." Large variations in toddlers' speech often occur. Although rare, some toddlers appear to be very reluctant to speak (selectively mute), but once they do, they typically display a rapid growth of vocabulary (Warren & Kaiser, 1988).

Wide variations in the number of words found in children's sentences are common even for children the same age. One method used by **psycholinguists** (psychologists who study language development) to measure children's language development is **mean length of utterance (MLU).** MLU increases gradually with age. The average sentence length for a child two years old is two words. Children typically use sentences about three to six words in length by three to four years of age (Hoffnung, 1989).

Children two to four years old develop language skills consisting of **communicative** and **noncommunicative language.** Communicative language involves children's ability to tell others what and how they themselves are thinking. Noncommunicative language consists of repetition, **monologue,** and **collective monologue.** Repetition is shown when children repeat what others say (Berko Gleason, 1989). This is frequently observed when children have older siblings or are in a preschool or daycare setting. Children often repeat someone else's statement, acting as if it is their own.

Children's language is referred to as a monologue when they talk out loud to themselves. Children often use this type of noncommunicative language during solitary play (while playing alone) (Berk, 1992). When many children sit together and talk, but not to each other, a collective monologue is being used. This type of language may help guide problem-solving. For example, a child may think aloud and say, "My tower is tall. I'd better be careful or it'll fall down." When preschoolers think aloud in monologues, they are often guiding their own thoughts and actions by communicating with themselves. For example, a four-year-old, while putting toys away might say, "This goes over here." A child who talks out loud also engages in positive **self-talk** such as, "I can do this." Children who use this type of self-talk are more likely to have a positive **self-esteem** than children who use negative self-talk such as, "I can't do this."

Children often control their impulses by **inner speech,** cautioning themselves as their parents would. This speech type may be seen when a child tries to stay out of the cookie jar by thinking or saying, "Wait until after dinner!" Inner speech helps direct children's thinking as they mature. During early childhood, inner speech begins as a whisper or mutter to oneself, and, as the child matures, self-talk (a form of inner speech) becomes silent talking, thinking inside the head (Greene, 1975). Inner speech, however, does not disappear altogether. Most people use it from time to time by saying things like, "I can't believe I did that," "I can't believe how that person is driving," or "I need to be more careful!"

By three or four years old, most children's vocabulary increases rapidly. At this time, children's language typically uses the basic rules of speech and **grammar,** the set of rules that govern how words are used, combined, and altered in a language (Bernstein & Teigerman, 1989). Children use simple sentences that follow a subject-verb-object word order. Children at three-and-a-half years have typically mastered the basic rules of grammar so well they frequently overapply the rules to words that are exceptions, called **overregularization** (Behren, 1988). For example, they may say, "The childs goed to the store." Although this sentence is not grammatically correct, it does indicate that the child understands that plurals are made by adding -s and the past tense is indicated by adding -ed.

Throughout the preschool years, children's communication skills continue to become more effective. They tell others what they want and may use language to manipulate how others perceive a situation. Preschoolers though, frequently cannot describe important features of objects. For example, a three-and-a-half-year-old tells an adult to take down a truck from the closet shelf. If the shelf has several trucks on it, the child may have difficulty clearly communicating the desired truck (Peccei, 1994).

As discussed in Chapter 2, teachers and other professionals often use developmental charts to compare a child's development to the average development of other children the same age. Table 8.1 provides a very general list of language developmental milestones that normally occur between

TABLE 8.1 Overview of Speech and Language Development

AVERAGE AGE	COMPREHENSION SKILLS	EXPRESSIVE SKILLS
0–3 months	• startled response to noise • eye contact • attends to voice	• differentiated cries for various needs
6 months	• localizes voice • responds to name	• cooing and vowel sounds • vocalization after hearing speech • babbling begins • laughing
12 months	• follows simple directions • responds to name and *no* • understands many words, begins to associate words with actions	• first words • gesturing and babbling continue • imitates words • plays peek-a-boo
18 months 24 months	• retrieves a requested object • points to several body parts • answers yes/no questions • distinguishes pronouns	• 20 words • 150 words • word combinations • early grammatical features begin to appear • imitates environmental sounds • refers to self by name • begins to use yes/no questions
30 months	• follows two-part directions • understands *big, little, in, on, one* • understands a few color names	• 350 words • begins to use personal pronouns • begins to use *wh*-questions • recites songs and rhymes
36 months	• identifies objects by their function • understands long or complex sentences	• 700 words • begins complex sentence development • makes up stories • talks about experiences • asks many questions • names a few colors • rote counting • tells own gender
48 months	• follows three-part directions • understands time concepts	• 1500 words • average sentence length of five words
60 months	• understands common opposites • retains information in sequence	• 2000 to 3000 words • defines words • tells attributes of an object • tells sequences of events

birth and five years. The ages represent averages of developmental information found in a wide variety of literature and other resources. It is presented with the caution that children who develop normally vary greatly in their maturation patterns and timetables (Greene, 1975). No single skill should form the basis of any important decisions concerning assessment or treatment. Rather, all areas of development must be considered (Wood, 1981).

INDICATORS OF SPEECH AND LANGUAGE DELAYS

The first indicator of possible speech or language delays often occurs during the first year of life. Infants described as "quiet," who make few vocal sounds other than crying, and appear to be content to be left alone are more likely to be delayed in speech and language skills.

The age at which children begin to speak also can be an indicator of language delays. Most children use one or more words within a few weeks of their first birthday. They often use two-word phrases around eighteen to twenty-four months. Children who do not say single words by eighteen months or are not using two-word phrases by thirty months are likely to be classified as speech or language delayed. Between about three-and-a-half and four-and-a-half years most children begin to experiment with and practice their language skills. They ask many questions and attempt to gain attention by using their verbal skills. If children cannot use language in this way it could indicate a speech or language delay (McReynolds, 1986).

Before children are school-age (less than five years old) speech and language disabilities comprise the largest group of children receiving early intervention services (Nelson, 1993). The pattern changes once children are school-age and those with speech and language delays or disorders make up the second largest group of children receiving special education services from birth through high school. The most common communication disorders involve **articulation** (speech

sound production). Between 5 and 15 percent of all children between birth and twenty years of age demonstrate an articulation problem.

Children learn to produce sounds found within the language of their culture, and these sounds have varying degrees of production difficulty (Stoel–Gammon, 1991). For example, sounds requiring the letters S, R, and L are often difficult for a preschool-age child to pronounce. A child, for instance, may say "thoup" for *soup.* Articulation problems are typically the easiest problems to modify in small children. Many children may speak clearly but have difficulty understanding and effectively using words and sentences, referred to as language rather than speech disorders. Language disorders are often more difficult to modify and typically require longer and more intense therapy.

POSSIBLE CAUSES FOR SPEECH AND LANGUAGE DELAYS

In most cases, the causes of speech and language impairments are unknown. Some known causes, however, include **otitis media** (ear infections), **cleft lip** and **palate,** poor prenatal care, and prenatal exposure to a virus such as rubella or to drugs and alcohol. In addition, some children show overall delays in development as a result of a premature birth, prolonged illness, hospitalization, physical neglect, malnutrition, or abuse. For example, staying in a hospital for extended periods of time often deprive a child of normal interaction with parents and other family members. Such experiences could keep a child from hearing the normal types of sounds typically found at home and negatively affect speech and language development (McKnight–Taylor, 1989).

Language delays are sometimes attributed to cultural differences. In these cases, delays are often not based on a true language disorder but are influenced by styles of communication to which the child is exposed. Cultural variations in styles of communication include the amount of eye contact, physical space between speakers, use of gestures and facial expressions, and amount of speech (Lahey, 1988).

Children who have motor problems such as cerebral palsy or have brain damage frequently have difficulty making intelligible sounds (Love, 1992). Speech requires the brain to coordinate neuromuscular signals to the lungs, larynx (upper portion of the trachea that contains the vocal cords), and mouth, as well as adequate hearing to receive input (sound) and satisfactory ability to comprehend and use signals. Language delays also result from head injuries or illness (Butler, 1991). Brain damage resulting from injury or illness could lead to ineffective muscle control. Difficulty in controlling muscles directly affects speech, swallowing, vision, hearing, gross motor movement, and fine motor skills. (See Chapters 10 and 11 for further discussion on fine and gross motor skills.)

In addition, several conditions such as autism, mental retardation, cerebral palsy, attention deficit hyperactivity disorder (ADHD), and hearing impairments frequently have accompanying speech and language delays (Lindfors, 1987). Children born with **clefts of the lip** and/or **palate** may find it difficult or even impossible to make certain sounds correctly (Nelson, 1993). A cleft of the palate may prevent closure of the nasal cavity resulting in distorted speech. Resonance (quality of voice sounds), phonation (act of producing speech sounds), fluency, grammar, and the ability to understand symbolic concepts are related to these and other anatomical or neurological problems (McCormick & Schiefelbusch, 1990).

OVERVIEW OF SPEECH AND LANGUAGE DELAYS

"My child isn't talking" is a statement parents frequently make when they first become concerned that their child may have a speech or language delay. Parents are often keenly aware of their child's communication abilities because communication is the first interaction between parents and child. Parents bond with children by communicating

nonverbally and verbally. Verbal communication skills are a tangible way for parents to measure the development of their child's skills and compare the child to others the same age (Bernstein & Tiegerman, 1989).

When parents suspect that a child is not communicating at a level in the quantity or quality typically found in other children the same age, it is appropriate for the parents to consult with a speech and language pathologist. The specialist is frequently called a "speech therapist," but this term is misleading because *speech* literally refers to the sounds produced when talking, whereas communication involves many more components. Speech and language pathology is the study of normal, delayed (late), and disordered (different) communication (Koniditsiotis & Hunter, 1993).

SPECIFIC AREAS OF SPEECH AND LANGUAGE DEVELOPMENT

When a young child's communication skills are evaluated, the areas discussed below are generally considered to be important parts of the total picture and are compared to typical developmental patterns. These areas include general behavior and the ability to pay attention, and prelinguistic, receptive language, expressive language, articulation, oral–motor, voice, fluency, hearing, play skills, and problem-solving skills.

General Behavior and Ability to Pay Attention

When evaluating communication skills, it is important to consider a child's general demeanor and activity level. The speech and language pathologist notes how a child reacts to new people and situations and may encourage a brief separation from the parent during the evaluation. The child's ability to make or maintain eye contact with others is also observed. In most cases, when given appropriate toys and materials children exhibit curiosity and interest in touching and playing with them. The child's ability to pay attention to age-appropriate activities is noted as are the activity level, level of distractibility, impulsiveness, or perseverance. The child's frustration level when faced with a challenging task is also evaluated (Creaghead, Newman, & Secord, 1989).

Prelinguistic Skills

A number of **skills prerequisite** for a child to develop language are usually mastered during the first year of life. These skills are considered when assessing very young children or those who exhibit significant language delays. Prelinguistic skills include:

- The ability to pay attention to visual and auditory information;
- The ability to imitate gestures and sounds;
- The development of object permanence (understanding that an object still exists even when it is removed from sight);
- The ability to take turns;
- The ability to understand that objects have intended purposes (understanding of cause-and-effect relationships);
- The use of basic communicative gestures and the ability to associate a word a child hears with its meaning.
    (McCormick & Schiefelbusch, 1990)

A child who has a severe language delay but talks is often found to have inconsistent prelinguistic (also called pre-symbolic) skills (Owens, 1982). "Missing links" in the full set of prelinguistic skills often underlie difficulties with more complex language skills (Cantwell & Baker, 1987).

Receptive Language Skills

Receptive language refers to understanding language, also called comprehension. Receptive language skills include:

- Understanding vocabulary (words);
- Understanding sentences and grammatical structures;
- Following directions;
- Understanding concepts (e.g., prepositions, sizes, colors, numbers);

- Understanding questions (e.g., "What?" "Where?" "Who?").

Children may demonstrate much better skills in some of these areas than in others. They may be able to speak relatively well yet have receptive language deficits.

Expressive Language Skills

Expressive language refers to the language a child produces. A commonly accepted model of expressive language consists of three parts:

- Expressive vocabulary, which refers to the number and type of words a child has acquired;
- Word and sentence formation;
- Pragmatic development, which includes the ability to use language socially (to interact and accomplish an objective).
    (Bloom & Lahey, 1978)

All of these parts working together constitute expressive language. Many children who have a language delay or language disorder exhibit a large discrepancy between their receptive and expressive language skills (Nelson, 1991).

Articulation Skills

Articulation is the production of speech sounds. This means using muscles and other body structures to shape sounds from exhaled air. Children might be able to understand and produce language without being able to speak clearly. When articulation is assessed, the therapist evaluates:

- Whether a child uses the oral structures (muscles, teeth, or tongue) to produce sounds correctly;
- How a child uses sounds to create meaning.

For children with severe articulation disorders, assessment is complex and detailed. Some basic elements that are evaluated include how individual sounds are produced in words and continuous speech, the child's overall speech intelligibility (clarity), and the child's ability to imitate sounds correctly that the child often produces incorrectly when speaking. An ability to imitate sounds indicates that these sounds are more likely to be corrected without direct treatment (Mannix, 1987). Certain error patterns (e.g., difficulty clearly pronouncing "s" or "th" sounds) are normal in development and must be considered in the context of a child's age and language level.

Oral–Motor Skills

Oral–motor skills involve the development of the mouth and surrounding area in terms of its structure and functional ability. Weaknesses in this area often affect articulation development. An important part of assessing oral–motor skills is determining if a child has any problem with eating, drinking, or swallowing. The speech and language pathologist often works on oral–motor and feeding skills in conjunction with other professionals such as the occupational therapist (Mannix, 1987). (See Chapter 10 for further discussion on occupational therapy.)

Voice

The physical health of the **voice,** as well as how it is used to communicate, is within the realm of speech and language pathology. Some aspects of the voice that are assessed formally and informally are the pitch (high or low voice), volume (loud or soft), and quality (such as hoarseness or extreme nasality) (Moore, 1986). The speech pathologist will recommend that a child be evaluated by an **ear, nose, and throat doctor (ENT)** if any aspect of the voice suggests a possible physical problem. This evaluation should be done before providing voice therapy (Lindfors, 1987).

Fluency

Fluency problems, often called stuttering or dysfluency, refer to interruptions in the flow of speech. Dysfluency consists of pauses, prolonged sounds, or repetition of sounds and words. In se-

vere dysfluency secondary characteristics such as jerking motions or blinking often are present. It is important to note that a certain amount of mild dysfluency is normal for many young children. Children whose level of dysfluency interferes with their ability to communicate or the willingness of others to interact with them often require speech therapy services. The speech and language professional assesses dysfluency to determine whether it is a developmental stage or a true disorder (Owens, 1991).

Hearing

For most children, hearing is a primary means of learning to communicate. For this reason, when speech and language development is delayed or disordered, it is essential to find out if the child is hearing adequately (Oyler, Crowe, & Haas, 1987). Assessment takes the form of a screening or full hearing evaluation. If a hearing impairment is found, the speech and language pathologist often works with an audiologist or teacher of the deaf and hearing impaired to provide intervention services. (Chapter 9 provides a more detailed discussion of children with hearing loss.)

Play Skills

Children progress through developmental stages of play. Each of these stages of play relates to speech and language and cognitive milestones. A variety of play experiences should take place for language to develop, especially as the child uses more symbolism (Cheng, 1989). It is important for the speech and language pathologist to engage or observe children during play activities to better understand their level of speech and language development. (Chapter 12 provides more information about the importance of play.)

Problem-Solving Skills

Language assessment also includes consideration of how a child uses language to perform thinking and reasoning tasks appropriate to the child's age. In younger children these skills are manifested in abilities such as matching or naming. As children become older they should be able to analyze things they encounter in more complex ways. They should become able to use language to perform more difficult tasks such as explaining and predicting (Blank, Rose, & Berlin, 1978).

REFERRALS FOR SPEECH AND LANGUAGE EVALUATIONS

Teachers, pediatricians, and speech and language pathologists are often asked, "Should my child be evaluated?" Suspected delays in any of the previously described areas are a legitimate basis for assessment. Most children whose parents ask, "Should my child be evaluated?" benefit from having communication skills evaluated. Parents who show concern about language development may unintentionally change the nature of their interactions with the child, such as talking less with the child or frequently correcting the child's speech. Therefore, a formal speech and language evaluation is often valuable because a child's motivation to talk may be decreased when an adult pays more attention to the details of sound and grammar than to the topic of conversation (Cheng, 1989).

Even if a child is found to be developing within normal ranges, a parents' feeling that their child is "okay" may be very beneficial. Concerned parents should be wary of taking advice from well-intentioned friends or even professionals in fields unrelated to child development who say things such as, "Don't worry, my child started out the same way and he's fine now" or "It's just a stage. He'll grow out of it." Many children do not "grow out of it" without help. In fact, valuable time is lost when speech and language intervention is postponed (Fey, 1986).

If an eighteen-month-old does not seem to understand specific words, such as his or her own name, names of common objects, or simple commands such as "Come here," the child should gen-

erally be referred for a speech and language evaluation. A two-year-old who speaks only a few words, does not use two-word sentences, or seems to have poor comprehension should also be referred for an evaluation (Bloom & Lahey, 1978). Information about obtaining speech and language evaluations may be provided by a variety of individuals or agencies. See Table 8.2 for a list of possible referral sources.

THE SPEECH AND LANGUAGE EVALUATION

As indicated in earlier chapters, evaluation of children with special needs often involves a team of specialists completing evaluations collaboratively. A comprehensive speech and language evaluation begins with gathering **case history** information and conducting a personal interview

TABLE 8.2 List of Referral Sources for Speech and Language Evaluations

Individuals or agencies that may have information about speech and language evaluations include:

1. Pediatricians;
2. Local hospitals or clinics;
3. Local school districts;
4. Local nursery schools and daycare centers;
5. The State Department of Health (DOH);
6. The American Speech–Language–Hearing Association (ASHA) provides information on speech and language development, disorders, and therapy (301) 897-5700 or FAX (301) 571-0457;
7. Other agencies may exist for helping children. For example, New York State has a network of "Early Childhood Direction Centers" that provide assistance in finding a variety of services. Charitable organizations such as United Way may also provide information;
8. Medical insurance plan referral services;
9. A telephone book usually lists speech and language pathologists in the business section;
10. Other parents whose children have communication delays.

with the parents and child before completing a **formal** or **informal assessment.** Case history data includes information about the child's birth, medical, and developmental histories, family members' health and developmental histories, previous assessment or treatment of the child, summaries of school progress, and reasons for the evaluation referral. This information may be acquired during the interview or from a written questionnaire completed by the child's primary care provider. This information is crucial for forming an accurate picture of a child's speech and language development (Fey, 1986).

If a written questionnaire is not provided in advance of the evaluation, it may be helpful for a parent to summarize a child's developmental milestones or bring any written information, such as a baby's record book, in which milestones have been noted. Sometimes, it is very difficult for parents to recall information accurately during the interview, particularly if the child is one of several in the family. Also, parents often experience anxiety during the evaluation, which could limit their ability to remember specific information.

After the case history has been obtained, an assessment of the child's speech and language is completed. Formal, **standardized tests** that provide normative data may be used during the assessment. Some formal tests include specific tasks the child is asked to perform. Other formal assessments are "scales" the clinician fills out based on observations of the child. Many different speech and language standardized tests are available for use with preschoolers (Koniditsiotis & Hunter, 1993). See Table 8.3 for a description of some of the more commonly used tests.

Many young children cannot participate in formal testing for a variety of reasons. For example, the test materials or tasks do not interest them, or they do not have the necessary attention span to complete the test. In this case, the evaluator must rely on informal measures, observation, and interviews. Informal assessment lends itself to a more natural play-type environment. This information is usually considered as useful as information gathered from formal tests. It is important to

remember that, even when using informal measurements, the evaluator is interpreting data and comparing the child's skills to established developmental stages (Lahey, 1988).

The evaluator may request that the parent and child separate for a short time during certain parts of the evaluation. The parent can assist by communicating to the child, "This is okay," and indicating that the parent will return after a short time. If the parent remains present during formal testing, it is important that he or she not coach the child, repeat the clinician's questions, or provide feedback, even nonverbal, regarding the appropriateness of a response.

Depending on where the evaluation takes place, a **hearing screening** or **full audiological evaluation** is often a part of the assessment process. Because hearing is usually a primary method of learning language, it is important to rule out the possibility of a hearing loss for any child demonstrating speech or language delays. This is especially true when there is a history of frequent or severe ear infections. (For more discussion on hearing impairments, see Chapter 9).

A hearing screening simply tests whether a child responds to a small number of sound frequencies (high and low pitches) that are presented at a quiet but audible level. This is accomplished using an instrument called an audiometer, which has earphones, or with an audioscope, which looks like a physician's otoscope (ear scope), but produces the appropriate beeps when placed in the ear. Other screening methods are also available. A screening could be performed by a **speech pathologist, audiologist** (hearing specialist), nurse, or other professional. The screening provides only information about whether a sound is heard.

Frequently, it is difficult to screen very young children because they often have difficulty following directions about how they are to respond to the sounds they hear. A full evaluation may be recommended simply because the required information could not be adequately gathered with a quick screening. If a screening is completed but the child appears unable to hear sounds, a full evaluation should be done (Lahey, 1988).

TABLE 8.3 Formal Tests Commonly Used in Preschool Speech–Language Evaluations

TEST NAME	COMMON NAME	AREA(S) MEASURED
Program for Acquisition of Language with the Severely Impaired	PALS	Prelinguistic Skills
Receptive–Expressive Emergent Language Test	REEL	Early language
Sequenced Inventory of Communication Development	SICD	General language
Preschool Language Scale	PLS	General language
Clinical Evaluation of Language Functions, Preschool	CELF	General language
Test of Early Language Development	TELD	General language
Test of Language Development, Primary	TOLD	General language
Preschool Language Assessment Instrument	PLAI	General language from a pragmatic viewpoint
Token Test for Children	—	Receptive language
Peabody Picture Vocabulary Test	PPVT	Receptive vocabulary
Receptive One-Word Picture Vocabulary Test	ROWPVT	Receptive vocabulary
Test for Auditory Comprehension of Language	TACL	Receptive language
Expressive One-Word Picture Vocabulary Test	EOWPVT	Expressive vocabulary
Boehm Test of Basic Concepts, Preschool	Boehm–Preschool	Understanding of basic concepts
Assessment of Children's Language Development	ACLD	Understanding of directions and syntax
Bankson Language Test	BLT	Psycholinguistic skills
Goldman–Fristoe Test of Articulation	G–FTA	Articulation
Arizona Articulation Proficiency Scale	AAPS	Articulation
Weiss Comprehensive Articulation Test	WCAT	Articulation
Khan–Lewis Phonological Analysis	KLPA	Phonology
Assessment of Phonological Processes	APP	Phonology
Screening Test for Development of Apraxia of Speech	STDAS	Differential diagnosis of apraxia

After the speech and language assessment has been completed, the evaluator will present the parent with diagnostic information and make recommendations based on that information. Questions parents often ask and that a therapist should be prepared to answer include:

- What specific communication areas are affected? How do they relate to each other and to other areas of development? What are the child's strengths and areas of need?
- How delayed is the child and what are typical speech and language abilities for children this age?

- What do ratings such as "mild," "moderate," and "severe" mean?
- Does the child need speech and language therapy? If so, what type and how often? What are some different treatment options or resources?
- Are there any specific strategies that should be used with the child at home?

In a written evaluation, usually following the assessment, the clinician is likely to use a variety of technical terms. These terms are important because they provide an accurate, standard means of communication between professionals (as between the evaluator and treating therapist). The parent, though, has the right to be provided with a clear explanation of all technical terms (Tannock & Girolametto, 1992). Two questions parents frequently ask but which cannot always be answered are discussed below.

Why does my child have this problem? For some children, problems with speech and language development have clear-cut causes such as a congenital cleft palate, disabling childhood syndromes, or demonstrated neurological damage. For many other children, the cause is impossible to identify. There is an enormous number of variables and risk factors within and external to the child that could affect language development. It may be helpful to have a concrete answer to this question, and many parents choose to participate in medical testing to rule out a variety of causes. Frequently, though, there are no answers (Warren & Reichle, 1992).

How long will my child need speech and language treatment, and what will be the results? A therapist cannot, and ethically should not, provide an exact answer to this question. The prognosis (probable outcome) is based on numerous factors. Although an exact answer is impossible, a therapist may predict whether treatment will be short-term (two to three months) or long-term and the degree of improvement that is likely (Wilcox, Kouri, & Caswell, 1991).

THE IMPORTANCE OF EARLY INTERVENTION

In recent years, more emphasis has been placed on the value of early intervention. The benefits for the child are clear—the sooner developmental problems are identified, the sooner they can be addressed. Early intervention often results in more effective and potentially shorter treatment (Theler & Ulrich, 1991). Many parents hope their child will be "cured" by the time the child reaches school age (five years old). In reality, this does not always occur. Many children who receive early intervention services continue to need treatment

during or even beyond the elementary school years. Starting early, however, helps children reach their maximum potential and often prevents the need for more intensive services (Rapin, 1996; Beitchman, Cohen, Konstantareas, & Tannock, 1996).

If developmental problems have a neurological basis, early intervention takes advantage of the immature brain's relative **plasticity** (flexibility and ability to learn) to develop compensatory strategies for learning and communicating. Early intervention also benefits parents. They receive support and education through the often difficult process of accepting a child's disability, which allows them to become more effective in providing for their child's needs. Early intervention is also cost-effective because it has the potential to shorten treatment time (Warren & Reichle, 1992).

SPEECH AND LANGUAGE THERAPY

Speech and language therapy occurs within a wide variety of settings, ranging from an individual session in a clinic or child's home to a group session in a classroom. The evaluator who is making recommendations typically outlines possible approaches and discusses the benefits and disadvantages of each to enable a parent to participate in the decision-making progress (Nelson, 1989).

During individual treatment, a child receives a therapist's undivided attention. Therapy is specifically geared to the objectives set for that child, and may take place in a clinic, home, or school. During individual treatment at school, the child might be pulled out to a separate room or area, or the therapist may go with the child to regular classroom activities, using those activities as a vehicle for treatment. The choice of therapy setting often depends on the particular goal being addressed. For example, a child might need to learn how to produce a particular speech sound such as an "s." Initially, the therapist might use some structured activities such as sitting at a table with a mirror and showing the child where to place his or her tongue to produce the sound. The child might practice using the new sound by working with pictures or objects, using a computer, or playing games. Once the child has mastered the new sound through these methods, the therapist can accompany the child in group activities to monitor and encourage generalization (Langdon, 1989).

Some goals require interacting with other children. For example, if a child needs to learn how to ask for a turn, individual treatment might take place in settings that require sharing materials or equipment during a **child-directed** play period (when children select an activity) or at a playground (McMorrow, Foxx, Faw, & Bittle, 1986). The choice of individual treatment settings also depend on the age and attention span of the child. For example, a very young child or a child with a limited attention span might be unable to work one-on-one for speech therapy but might be able to work for thirty minutes if the therapy is incorporated into classroom activities (Westby, 1980).

Group treatment may consist of structured group activities or informal interaction with a therapist. This treatment could be held in a clinic or school setting where individual treatment occurs. Group treatment in school often consists of **language groups,** in which activities are focused on a limited number of objectives appropriate for all the children in the group. For example, the therapist may plan a cooking activity, making the goal for each child to verbalize a request to have a turn in each step of the process (Girolametto, 1988). This method helps children learn the functional value of language in a highly motivating setting.

The therapist could also lead general class activities, emphasizing individual objectives during interaction with each child. For example, at snack time each child might be required to ask for a snack using the most complex sentence structure feasible for that child. The required response might vary widely between children. One child may provide a one-word request and another a full sentence request. In this way, a group activity takes advantage of more natural settings and peer interactions. There are more opportunities for generalization of new skills during interactions with a variety of people, in a variety of situations. Group treatment results in a high success rate in meeting many kinds of speech and language goals, even those traditionally addressed in structured individual settings. Working in groups encourages conversations as well (Wilcox, et al., 1991).

Conversations are more likely to occur in small groups of three to four children rather than large groups of more than four children (MacDonald, 1985). Many teachers attempt large group conversations during periods such as circle time, when the entire group is brought together, often including twelve to twenty children. If a teacher is spending a great deal of time reminding children that it is not their turn to speak because someone else is speaking, the group is probably too large for effective "two-way conversation" (Kaiser & Warren, 1988).

Conversations are most likely to occur when the topic is of real interest to a child and more likely to be prolonged when adults respond rather than ask questions. Too often, when an adult asks a child a question, the child interprets the situation as a need to figure out the "right" answer. The question becomes a test rather than a method to prolong conversation. Children generally respond well to comments such as, "I never heard about that before," "That's really a funny story," or "That's true." In general, the younger the child, the more the teacher should use small groups and "one-to-one conversations" and avoid too many "one-way conversations" with the entire class (Nelson, 1989).

Research suggests that more statements and requests are made by one child to another when there is no adult in the immediate area (Westby, 1980). On the other hand, more responses to direct questions occur during playtime when an adult is present. The presence of an adult increases the number of verbalizations by the children during more structured group activities. Different types of conversations occur with adults present. Children therefore need opportunities to play when adults are nearby, as well as when adults are not in close proximity (Wilcox, Kouri, & Caswell, 1991).

Early childhood is a critical period for developing communication competence, which includes self-expression, understanding and communicating with others, and verbal reasoning. The development of communicative competence requires that children be engaged in conversation and not simply being passively exposed to language, such as by watching television or hearing a story read.

In recent years, a great deal of speech and language treatment has been provided in the context of **collaboration** between the therapist and classroom teacher (Wilcox, 1989). Collaboration means lessons and activities are jointly planned and executed to fulfill both professionals' objectives. The therapist could use classroom activities as a vehicle for treatment so that speech and language learning is more relevant to a child's typical routines. An example of a typical collaborative activity is an obstacle course that requires a child to perform a variety of fine and gross motor tasks (such as playing with pegboards or jumping). While the child performs these tasks, opportunities occur to teach the appropriate vocabulary and concepts such as "jump," "push," "in," "around," and "next."

Preschool classrooms that promote the development of speech and language skills include interesting materials and activities. Situations that are visually stimulating tend to elicit labeling and questioning by the child. Children communicate more about things that interest them. To maintain interest, it is often necessary to vary the environment frequently and include new activities or materials. One way to do this is to rotate materials, putting some things away and reintroducing them later (McKnight–Taylor, 1989).

In most cases, it is desirable to have materials located where children can have easy access to them. Placing some items out of reach of children but in their view encourages them to communicate by requesting the object. During snack time, children might be given very small portions, so they will need to communicate that they want more. Providing more than one type of snack item could be used to encourage children to choose and communicate the choice. Situations that require children to request assistance, such as helping take a lid off the modeling clay container, also encourage communication.

Children typically are encouraged to communicate when teachers or parents say or do silly things. For example, an adult who puts on a coat upside down and then struggles to use the zipper is likely to encourage children to communicate to them that the teacher is doing something wrong. For example, if the temperature outside is very cold and a teacher says, "I think it would be a good day to go swimming at the beach," children are often motivated to use some form of communication to let the teacher know that this is a silly idea.

Teachers and parents find many ways such as these that encourage the use of speech and language (Roberts, Babinowitch, Bryant, Burchinal, Koch, & Ramey, 1989). Language should be a natural part of a daily routine, and adults should provide a language rich environment that includes naming familiar objects, reading books, singing songs, and conversing with children (McCormick & Schiefelbusch, 1990).

Some children are initially unable to use speech to communicate. In these cases, therapy may include teaching the child sign language for words important to the individual (e.g., *stop, yes,* and *no*) or using a **communication board** as a temporary means of communicating. Children with severe disabilities who are also nonverbal often need to use one of these systems on a long-term basis. Using alternative communication systems (e.g., sign language or communication boards) provides such children a means to communicate when they are unable to produce words and reduces their frustration. Some parents respond negatively to the idea of their child using alternative communication systems, because the parents understand the speech and language goal as learning to speak. Using other types of communication, however, is only one step in the communication process. Using symbols other than spoken words often helps a child learn to speak (Schlosser & Lloyd, 1991).

Communication boards are often used for children with mental or physical disabilities that prevent the effective use of sign language or speech (Love, 1992). Communication boards contain vocabulary that the child needs to answer questions, make requests, direct the actions of others, direct a sequence of events, or make choices. Communication boards could be handmade or expensive computerized devices. In many cases, the less expensive boards are the most effective because they can be easily individualized for each child and several duplicates can be placed at different locations.

A communication board could have pictures of a glass, for instance, or food, and perhaps the words *yes* and *no*. The boards might contain miniature toy objects, photographs, or words. The purpose of the board is to provide a child with a method of communication by pointing to the objects on the board. The child learns that the objects, pictures, or words represent things or people in the environment. They provide the child with a step toward more sophisticated forms of communication, including speech.

One relatively new but controversial form of communication is **facilitated communication.** This method involves a facilitator that provides support to the child's hand and arm, allowing the child to communicate by typing on a keyboard. The actual effectiveness of this method is debated by researchers (Biklen & Crossley, 1992). Facilitated communication using the alphabet symbols is rarely used with children younger than school age because being able to read and write are not considered **developmentally appropriate** tasks for preschool children.

PARENTS' ROLE IN SPEECH AND LANGUAGE THERAPY

Regardless of the setting for treatment, parents can enhance the effectiveness of therapy in a variety of ways. Children, regardless of age or disability, are typically sensitive to their parents' feelings and reactions, and may understand more than parents realize. Parents need to communicate, verbally and nonverbally, that therapy is a positive experience. When parents separate from their child with a smile, for instance, this is one way of communicating confidence (Davis, Stroud, & Green, 1988).

While parents should ask questions and state concerns honestly, some comments are best saved for private discussion, when the child is not present. Parents should try to avoid scheduling treatment at a time of day when the child is usually tired. Parents and classroom staff should support the therapist by following through with homework or record keeping. If these tasks are stressful to the child or appear to make the child unhappy, the therapist should be informed.

Parents should follow through on therapy suggestions, because in most cases parents spend more time with their child than therapists or teachers do. Initially, it may seem overwhelming to parents to try to remember certain methods of talking or working with their child. It is often helpful for them to set aside a particular time during the day to practice therapy skills with the child. In this way, parents may experience opportunities to feel good about helping their child, as well as develop new habits that may gradually become more natural and easier to use. Parents should remain open to receiving training on how to work most effectively with the child (Tannock & Girolametto, 1992). Tables 8.4 and 8.5 contain general suggestions parents and teachers may find helpful for enhancing young children's speech and language development.

CONCLUSION

Communication problems are frequently a parent's first clue that a child is experiencing developmental delays. When communication problems are suspected, a speech and language pathologist should be consulted. A comprehensive speech and

TABLE 8.4   Methods that Encourage Language Development

1. Make talking and conversation a positive experience.
2. Talk, talk, and talk to the child about what he or she is doing and what others are doing.
3. Name objects and give information about these objects (such as their function and characteristics).
4. Encourage conversation by making sure the child receives a turn in family and group conversations (such as at the dinner table).
5. Play pretend and guessing games.
6. Sing songs and use nursery rhymes.
7. Sort and classify things in the child's environment.
8. Be attentive and interested when the child speaks. Periodically, confirm that the child's message has been understood by paraphrasing the essential elements to the child.
9. Try to expand on the child's spontaneous utterances by repeating the child's words in the same order or with added information, for example:
   •Child: "ball" Adult: "ball" (direct imitation)
   •Child: "ball" Adult: "a ball" (expanding grammar)
   •Child: "ball" Adult: "big ball" (adding information)
10. Encourage the child to ask questions to obtain additional information.
11. Encourage the child to imitate nonspeech sounds such as animal or mechanical noises.
12. Use sound-making and voice-activated toys.
13. Encourage games that strengthen the muscles of the mouth such as blowing bubbles or playing musical instruments that require blowing.
14. Read, read, and read to the child. Read everything, not just books: signs, packages, labels. The importance of reading to a child cannot be overemphasized. Talk about stories and pictures while explaining new vocabulary. Encourage the child to fill in words or phrases when you stop reading and predict what will happen next. Let the child retell the story in his or her own words or take a turn reading to you. Use picture stories without words to help the child learn to expand his or her imagination.
15. Provide new and interesting experiences such as field trips and cooking.

TABLE 8.5   Methods that Discourage Language Development

1. Correcting speech or language errors by telling the child "no," implying the child did something wrong, or by insisting that the child repeat a correct model;
2. Discussing any suspected speech or language problems in front of the child or others;
3. Withholding favorite things to encourage the child to speak;
4. Placing unreasonable demands on the child, such as insisting that the child speak or perform in front of others;
5. Interrupting the child;
6. Allowing others to tease or make fun of the child.

language evaluation assesses a variety of areas and may lead to a recommendation for speech and language treatment. Early intervention is important because it typically result in more effective or shorter treatment time.

One of the most supportive things a parent or other care provider can do for a child with a speech and language delay or disorder is to accept the child at his or her developmental level and provide language stimulation appropriate to that level. The effectiveness of therapy is enhanced when parents communicate to the child a positive attitude toward the people and activities involved in therapy and when an honest exchange is maintained between parents and therapist.

Language is an essential tool every child needs to acquire. Without this tool, countless other skills may not emerge. The child who receives speech and language treatment is not only learning how to talk with others but is also placing a key piece into the complicated developmental puzzle.

The next chapter focuses on a group of children that typically need the services of a speech and language pathologist, children with hearing impairments.

CHAPTER SUMMARY

• When parents suspect that their child has a communication delay, they should consult with a speech and language pathologist.

- The different areas of communication skills include the ability to pay attention, prelinguistic (before speech activities), receptive language, expressive language and articulation, oral–motor, voice, fluency, hearing, play skills, and problem-solving skills.
- A speech and language evaluation consists of a case history, interviewing the child and child's parents, and a formal and informal assessment that may include use of a standardized test or scale.
- Speech and language therapy sessions may be conducted in a clinic, child's home, or preschool or daycare setting. The speech and language pathologist provides therapy individually or in a group. Therapy is often most effective when it is integrated into typical daily activities.
- Parents play a crucial role in the development of their child's speech and language skills. Parents need to collaborate with the speech and language pathologist and follow through with the therapist's recommendations.

REVIEW QUESTIONS

1. What are some important prelinguistic skills? Provide examples.
2. What is the difference between receptive and expressive language skills?
3. What are some of the advantages of early intervention?
4. What type of methods encourage communication in a classroom setting?
5. What type of questions might a parent ask a speech and language pathologist?

SUGGESTED STUDENT ACTIVITIES

1. Contact your state Department of Health or Department of Education and ask about the requirements for licensing in Speech and Language Pathology.
2. Obtain copies of one or more of the tests briefly described in this chapter for evaluating speech and language abilities and examine items designed to assess various types of speech and language skills.

3. Interview a speech and language pathologist or observe a speech and language pathologist providing therapy services for a young child and report back to the class or write a summary of your interview.
4. Observe an early intervention classroom and determine how speech and language development is encouraged.

ADDITIONAL READINGS

Fey, M. E., Windsor, J., & Warren, S. R. (1995). *Language intervention: Preschool through the elementary years.* Baltimore, MD: Paul H. Brookes.

Shore, C. M. (1994). *Individual differences in language development.* Thousand Oaks, CA: Sage.

Silverman, F. H. (1995). *Speech, language, and hearing disorders.* Boston: Allyn and Bacon.

Tiegerman–Farber, E. (1994). *Language and communication intervention in preschool children.* Boston: Allyn and Bacon.

ADDITIONAL RESOURCES

American Cleft Palate Association and Education Foundation
University of Pittsburgh
331 Salk Hall
Pittsburgh, PA 15261

American Speech–Language–Hearing Association
10801 Rockville Pike
Rockville, MD 20852

Division for Children with Communication Disorders
The Council for Exceptional Children
1920 Association Drive
Reston, VA 22091

National Institute for Communication Disorders, Hearing and Deafness
National Institutes of Health
Bethesda, MD 20892

Stuttering Foundation of America
5139 Klinge Street, N.W.
Washington, DC 20016–2654

REFERENCES

Aitchison, J. (1996). *The seeds of speech.* NY: Cambridge University Press.

Behren, D. (1988). Overextensions in early language comprehension: Evidence from a signal detection approach. *Journal of Child Language, 15,* 63–75.

Beitchman, J. H., Cohen, N. J., Konstantareas, M. M., & Tannock, R. (1996). (Eds.). *Language, learning, and behavior disorders: Developmental, biological, and clinical perspectives.* NY: Cambridge University Press.

Berk, L. E. (1992). Children's private speech: An overview of theory and the status of research. In R. M. Diaz & L. E. Berk (Eds.), *Private speech: From social interaction to self-regulation* (pp. 17–53). Hillsdale, NJ: Erlbaum.

Berko Gleason, J. (1989). Studying language development. In J. Berko Gleason (Ed.), *The development of language* (pp. 1–34). Columbus, OH: Merrill.

Bernstein, D. K., & Tiegerman, E. (1989). *Language and communication disorders in children* (2nd ed.). Columbus, OH: Merrill.

Biklen, D., & Crossley, R. (Eds.). (1992). Special Issue. Facilitated communication: Implications for people with autism and other developmental disabilities. *Topics in Language Disorders, 12*(4).

Blank, M. S., Rose, S., & Berlin, L. (1978). *The language of learning: The preschool years.* Orlando, FL: Grune and Stratton.

Bloom, L. (1991). *Language development from two to three.* NY: Cambridge University Press.

Bloom, L. (1993). *The transition from infancy to language.* NY: Cambridge University Press.

Bloom, L., & Lahey, M. (1978). *Language development and language disorders.* New York: Wiley.

Butler, K. G. (Ed.). (1991). *Communicating for learning.* Gaithersburg, MD: Aspen.

Cantwell, D. P., & Baker, L. (1987). *Developmental speech and language disorders.* New York: Guilford Press.

Carroll, D. W. (1986). *Psychology of language.* Monterey, CA: Brooks/Cole.

Cheng, L. L. (1989). Intervention strategies: A multidisciplinary approach. *Topics in Language Disorders, 9*(3), 84–91.

Clark, E. V. (Ed.). (1996). *27th annual child language research forum: Proceedings.* NY: Cambridge University Press.

Creaghead, N. A., Newman, P. W., & Secord, W. A. (1989). *Assessment and remediation of articulatory and phonological disorders* (2nd ed.). Columbus, OH: Merrill/Macmillan.

Davis, H., Stroud, A., & Green, L. (1988). Maternal language environment of children with mental retardation. *American Journal of Mental Deficiency, 93,* 144–153.

Fey, M. E. (1986). *Language intervention with young children.* San Diego, CA: College–Hill Press.

Girolametto, L. E. (1988). Developing dialogue skills: The effects of a conversational model of language intervention. In K. Marfo (Ed.), *Parent–child interaction and developmental disabilities* (pp. 145–162). New York: Praeger.

Gopnik, A., & Meltzoff, A. N. (1986). Relations between semantic and cognitive development in the one-word stage: The specificity hypothesis. *Child Development, 57,* 1040–1053.

Greene, J. (1975). *Thinking and language.* London: Methuen.

Hoffnung, A. S. (1989). The nature of language. In P. J. Valletutti, M. McKnight–Taylor, & A. S. Hoffnung (Eds.), *Facilitating communication in young children with handicapping conditions: A guide for special education* (pp. 339–433). Boston: Little, Brown.

Kaiser, A. P., & Warren, S. F. (1988). Pragmatics and generalization. In R. L. Schiefelbusch & L. L. Lloyd (Eds.), *Language perspectives II: Acquisition, assessment, and intervention* (pp. 397–442). Austin, TX: Pro-Ed.

Koniditsiotis, C. Y., & Hunter, T. L. (1993). Speech-pathology-based language intervention within an early childhood education environment. Special issue: Enhancing young children's lives. *Early Childhood Development and Care, 96,* 93–99.

Kuczak, S. A., II. (1986). Thoughts on the intentional basis of early object word extension: Evidence from comprehension and production. In S. Kuczak, II, & M. D. Barrett (Eds.), *The development of word meaning* (pp. 99–120). New York: Springer-Verlag.

Lahey, M. (1988). *Language disorders and language development.* New York: Macmillan.

Langdon, H. W. (1989). Language disorders or difference? Assessing the language skill of Hispanic students. *Exceptional Children, 56,* 160–167.

Leonard, L. (1986). Early language development and language disorders. In G. H. Shames & E. H. Wiig (Eds.), *Human communication disorders* (2nd ed., pp. 291–330). Columbus, OH: Merrill/Macmillan.

Lindfors, J. W. (1987). *Children's language and learning* (2nd ed.). Englewood Cliffs, NJ: Prentice-Hall.

Love, R. J. (1992). *Childhood motor speech disability.* New York: Macmillan.

MacDonald, J. (1985). Language through conversation: A model for intervention with language-delayed persons. In S. Warren & A. Rogers–Warren (Eds.), *Teaching functional language: Generalization and maintenance of language skills* (pp. 89–122). Baltimore, MD: University Park Press.

Mannix, D. (1987). *Oral language activities for special children.* West Nyack, NY: The Center for Applied Research in Education.

McCormick, L., & Schiefelbusch, R. L. (1990). *Early language intervention* (2nd ed.). Columbus, OH: Merrill/Macmillan.

McKnight–Taylor, M. (1989). Stimulating speech and language development of infants and young children. In P. J. Valletutti, M. McKnight–Taylor, & A. S. Hoffnung (Eds.), *Facilitating communication in young children with handicapping conditions: A guide for special educators* (pp. 68–92). Boston: Little, Brown.

McMorrow, M. J., Foxx, R. M., Faw, G. D., & Bittle, R. G. (1986). *Looking for the words: Teaching functional language strategies.* Champaign, IL: Research Press.

McReynolds, L. V. (1986). Functional articulation disorders. In G. H. Shames & E. H. Wiig (Eds.), *Human communication disorders* (2nd ed., pp. 139–182). Columbus, OH: Merrill/Macmillan.

Moore, P. (1986). Voice disorders. In G. H. Shames & E. H. Wiig (Eds.), *Human communication disorders* (2nd ed., pp. 183–229). Columbus, OH: Merrill/Macmillan.

Nelson, D. C. (1991). *Practical procedures for children with language disorders: Preschool–adolescence.* Austin, TX: Pro-Ed.

Nelson, K. E. (1989). Strategies for first language teaching. In M. L. Rice & R. L. Schiefelbusch (Eds.), *The teachability of language* (pp. 263–310). Baltimore, MD: Paul H. Brookes.

Nelson, N. W. (1993). *Childhood language disorders in context: Infancy through adolescence.* Columbus, OH: Merrill/Macmillan.

Norman, M. J., & McCormick, L. (1993). *Early intervention in natural environments.* Pacific Grove, CA: Brooks/Cole.

Oller, D. K., & Eiler, R. E. (1988). The role of coordination in infant babbling. *Child Development, 59,* 441–449.

Owens, R. E. (1982). *Program for acquisition of language with the severely impaired.* Washington, DC: The Psychological Corporation, Harcourt Brace Jovanovich.

Owens, R. E. (1991). *Language disorders: A functional approach to assessment and intervention.* New York: Merrill/Macmillan.

Oyler, H. J., Crowe, B. J., & Haas, W. H. (1987). *Speech, language, and hearing disorders: A guide for the teacher.* Boston: Little, Brown.

Peccei, J. S. (1994). *Child language.* New York: Routledge.

Rapin, I. (Ed.). (1996). *Preschool children with inadequate communication: Developmental language disorder, autism, mental deficiency.* NY: Cambridge University Press.

Roberts, J. E., Babinowitch, S., Bryant, P. M., Burchinal, M. R., Koch, M. A., & Ramey, C. T. (1989). Language skills of children with different preschool experiences. *Journal of Speech and Hearing Research, 32,* 773–786.

Schlosser, R. W., & Lloyd, L. L. (1991). Augmentative and alternative communication: An evolving field. *Augmentative and Alternative Communication, 7,* 154–160.

Stoel–Gammon, C. (1991). Issues in phonological development and disorders. In J. F. Miller (Ed.), *Research on child language disorders: A decade of progress* (pp. 255–265). Austin, TX: Pro-Ed.

Tannock, R., & Girolametto, L. E. (1992). Reassessing parent-focused language intervention programs. In S. Warren & J. Reichle (Eds.), *Communication and language intervention: Vol. 1. Causes and effects in communication and language intervention* (pp. 49–79). Baltimore, MD: Paul H. Brookes.

Theler, E., & Ulrich, B. D. (1991). Hidden skills. *Monograph of the Society for Research in Child Development, 56*(1), Serial No. 223.

Warren, A. R., & Kaiser, A. P. (1988). Research on early language intervention. In S. L. Odom & M. B. Karnes (Eds.), *Early intervention for infants and children with handicaps* (pp. 80–108). Baltimore, MD: Paul H. Brookes.

Warren, S. F., & Reichle, J. (1992). The emerging field of communication and language intervention. In S. Warren & J. Reichle (Eds.), *Communication and language intervention: Vol. 1. Causes and effects in communication and language intervention* (pp. 1–8). Baltimore, MD: Paul H. Brookes.

Westby, C. E. (1980). Language abilities through play. *Language, Speech, and Hearing Services in Schools,* XI, 154–168.

Wilcox, M. J. (1989). Delivering communication-based services to infants, toddlers, and their families: Approaches and models. *Topics in Language Disorders, 10*(1), 68–79.

Wilcox, M. J., Kouri, T. A., & Caswell, S. B. (1991). Early language intervention: A comparison of classroom and individual treatment. *American Journal of Speech-Language Pathology, 1,* 49–62.

Wood, B. S. (1981). *Children and communication: Verbal and nonverbal language development* (2nd ed.). Englewood Cliffs, NJ: Prentice-Hall.

Yoder, P. J., & Warren, S. F. (1993). Can developmentally delayed children's language be enhanced through prelinguistic intervention? In A. P. Kaiser & D. B. Gray (Eds.), *Enhancing children's communication: Research foundations for intervention* (pp. 5–62). Baltimore, MD: Paul H. Brookes.

CHAPTER 9

SERVICES FOR CHILDREN WITH HEARING IMPAIRMENTS

MARY SCALISE–ANNIS, M.A.

ABOUT THE AUTHOR

Mary Scalise–Annis received her bachelor of arts in elementary education in 1974 from the State University of New York at Geneseo, in Geneseo, New York, and her master's in the Education of the Deaf from Teacher's College, Columbia University, in 1975. She is certified in the State of New York as a teacher of the deaf, an elementary education teacher, a teacher of the speech and hearing disabled, and a special education teacher. Mary currently teaches in the Saint Francis Hospital Preschool Program in Poughkeepsie, New York, as a teacher of the deaf, and speech and language pathologist. She is also a teacher of the deaf for the Rhinebeck School District, in Rhinebeck, New York. Ms. Scalise–Annis is married and the mother of two young children.

CHAPTER KEY POINTS

- The three major types of hearing loss are conductive, sensorineural, and mixed.
- Audiologists use several different types of tests to assess hearing levels.
- Hearing losses may be due to genetic causes, prenatal environmental conditions, or illness or injuries after birth.

- The level of hearing loss affects how well a child adjusts to the hearing impairment.
- Various intervention methods may help children who have hearing impairments communicate more effectively.
- Children with hearing impairments behave in much the same way as those who are not hearing impaired.

One reason children have difficulty learning is because they have a hearing loss. Children with **hearing impairments** are often included in regular education preschool programs or preschool programs designed for children who have communication delays. This chapter is designed to describe hearing losses and how they are evaluated and to discuss intervention strategies. Early childhood special education teachers and parents often have many questions about children who are hearing impaired and do not know whom to ask. This chapter is designed to answer some of these questions and provide practical suggestions to aid in coping with the unique learning environments created when young children have hearing losses.

DESCRIBING HEARING LOSS

"Your child has a hearing loss." Those words may cause any number of reactions, ranging from shock and disbelief, to denial or anger, to sadness and confusion. Many images appear in the minds of parents when they learn their child has a hearing impairment. Concern about their child's future and education contribute to the stress with which family members must cope.

To understand hearing lose, it is first necessary to understand how a person hears. Hearing begins when sound enters the external part of the ear and travels into the **ear canal.** Sound then causes **the eardrum** to vibrate. This part of the ear is called the **outer ear.** (See Figure 9.1 for a diagram of the ear.) On the other side of the eardrum is a small space called the **middle ear.** Three tiny bones begin to move in a chain reaction when the eardrum vibrates. These bones connect with the third part of the ear, the **inner ear.** The inner ear includes the **cochlea** and is where nerve impulses are stimulated. Sound is then carried by these nerves to the brain. Hearing loss may be caused when the transmission of a sound is disrupted anywhere within this system.

The three different types of hearing loss are **conductive, sensorineural,** and **mixed,** (Boone, 1987). Hearing professionals, such as **audiologists,** are trained to determine the type of hearing loss of an individual. When sound cannot get through the outer ear or the middle ear, it is considered a conductive hearing loss. When the transmission of sound is disrupted somewhere in the inner ear, such as in the cochlea or **auditory nerve,** it is called a sensorineural hearing loss. When there is a conductive *and* sensorineural problem it is called a mixed loss. Hearing loss does not automatically mean deaf. There are varying **degrees of hearing loss.** In addition, both ears may have a similar loss or one ear may be more affected.

Audiologists measure the amount of hearing loss a person experiences by looking at two dimensions of sound: loudness, measured in **decibels (dB),** and **pitch,** measured in **Hertz (Hz).** Sounds range from high to low pitches. These two dimensions are plotted on a chart called an **audiogram.** Audiologists describe a hearing loss as mild, moderate, severe, or profound (Pappas, 1985). Table 9.1 provides a summary of the generally accepted degrees of hearing loss and their descriptive labels.

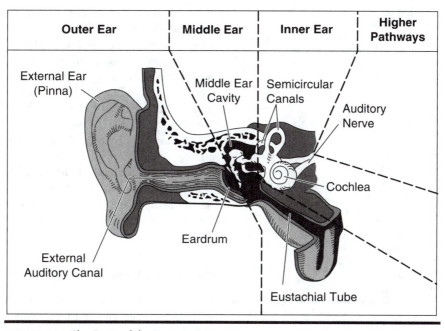

Outer Ear	Middle Ear	Inner Ear	Higher Pathways

External Ear (Pinna)

Middle Ear Cavity

Semicircular Canals

Auditory Nerve

Cochlea

Eardrum

External Auditory Canal

Eustachial Tube

FIGURE 9.1 The Parts of the Ear

The numbers provided by an audiogram tell how loud a sound must be before a person can hear it. For example, if Victoria has a hearing loss of 50 dB, a sound must be louder than 50 dB before she can hear it. Table 9.2 represents Victoria's audiogram. The audiogram shows a significant hearing loss at all frequencies in both ears.

For comparison, Table 9.3 shows the decibel levels of several common sounds found in the environment.

Loudness and pitch are two important factors in sound. **Clarity,** another important factor, is harder to identify. Sounds are sometimes distorted with a hearing loss, resulting in a loss of clarity,

TABLE 9.1 Degrees of Hearing Loss

0–15 dB	Normal hearing
15–30 dB	Mild hearing loss
30–60 dB	Moderate hearing loss
60–90 dB	Severe hearing loss
90+ dB	Profound hearing loss

TABLE 9.2 Victoria's Audiogram

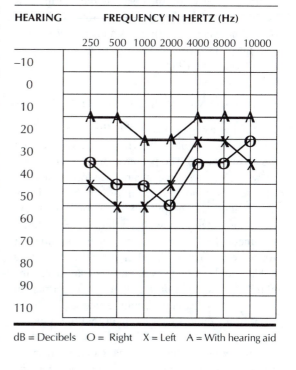

HEARING	FREQUENCY IN HERTZ (Hz)

dB = Decibels   O = Right   X = Left   A = With hearing aid

TABLE 9.3 Decibel Levels of Some Common Sounds

HEARING	EXAMPLE SOUNDS
–10	
0	
10	
20	
30	Soft whisper (10–25)
40	Library sounds
50	Normal conversation (25–50), Living room sounds
60	Crying baby, Air conditioner
70	Vacuum cleaner
80	Ringing telephone, Barking dog
90	Lawn mower, Hair blow dryer
100	Electric razor, Snowmobile
110	Power saw, Jet engine, Helicopter
120	Stereo
130	Rock concert
140	Jet engine (close proximity)

causing one sound to be mistaken for another sound. For example, the word *share* may sound like *chair.* When children experience frequent distortions in everyday conversation, the hearing loss could adversely affect their daily functioning. To determine whether a child has a hearing loss, several different types of hearing tests can be conducted (Pappas, 1985).

EVALUATIONS FOR HEARING LOSS

Pediatricians are usually the first professionals with whom parents talk when a child's hearing loss is suspected. The pediatrician checks for any earwax blocking the ear canals, middle ear fluid or infection, and the condition of the eardrum. The pediatrician removes excess wax or treats existing ear infections with antibiotics. Even after treatment, fluid often remains in the middle ear for three to four weeks after the child has had a cold. Fluid should eventually clear from the child's *eustachian tubes.* If there is no permanent hearing delay, parents should notice an improvement in the child's hearing acuity within a month after the onset of the cold (Quigley & Paul, 1990).

If there is no fluid in the ear canal or other obvious signs of conductive hearing loss and the

child still appears to be having difficulty hearing, the child should be referred to an audiologist or an **ear-nose-and-throat specialist (ENT),** also called an **otolaryngologist** or **otologist.** ENTs examine a child's ears, nose, and throat but typically also arrange for an audiological examination to determine if there is a hearing loss and if so, how much (Northern, & Downs, 1984).

An audiologist tests the child's hearing and middle ear functioning and reports the findings to the referring physician. If **hearing aids** are recommended, approval from a physician is typically required (Bess, 1988). Table 9.4 provides a list of tests an audiologist often uses to assess hearing levels.

IDENTIFICATION OF HEARING LOSS

It is crucial for hearing losses to be identified as early as possible. The first three years of life are a critical time for the development of speech and language (Goldberg, 1993). Far too often, though, children are *not* identified as having a hearing loss until after the age of three. Even when parents suspect there is a hearing loss, they are often told by well-intentioned but less experienced people such as a neighbor or friend, "Your child will probably outgrow these delays." Because of this tendency, a national panel of experts on hearing loss, supported by the National Institutes of Health (NIH), has recommended that all infants be screened for hearing impairments. This screening would be performed nationally with a quick, inexpensive, and noninvasive technique before a newborn leaves the hospital (Goldberg, 1993).

In March 1993, this panel also stated that the newborn screening should *not* replace early childhood hearing tests. The panel further stressed the need for greater public awareness and education of preschool providers and healthcare professionals regarding early signs of hearing impairment. The NIH has set a goal of lowering the average age of identification of hearing loss from three years to six months of age by the year 2000 (Goldberg, 1993).

Because hearing loss occurs in varying degrees, it is often difficult to identify a child with a

TABLE 9.4 Common Hearing Tests

1. Sound-Field Test—A young child, typically with a parent present, sits in a soundproof booth. The audiologist watches how the child reacts to sounds presented through speakers on the right and left sides of the child.
2. Pure-Tone Test—Using headphones, the examiner observes how a child reacts to sounds presented separately to each ear. Play audiometry is a technique often used when evaluating a young child. The child is trained to respond by doing something such as dropping a block into a pail when hearing a sound.
3. Tympanogram—This technique evaluates the way the middle ear functions. It provides information about eardrum mobility, middle ear pressure, existence of fluid in the middle ear, and whether the stapedius reflex is present. This reflex is a further indication of intact hearing. It may also indicate whether the middle ear bones are properly functioning.
4. Acoustic reflexes—This method measures the reaction of tiny ear muscles when a sound is presented. This test is typically conducted at the same time as the tympanogram and may provide information concerning hearing levels in children who are often difficult to test because they often do not understand the instructions regarding how to respond to sounds they hear during the testing.
5. Speech Reception Threshold—This test provides information about the softest speech signal heard and allows a cross-check of pure-tone responses.
6. Speech Discrimination—During this assessment, a child is presented a set of words through earphones at a comfortable loudness. The child is asked to point to pictures that correspond to the spoken words or to repeat the words if able. This test is designed to evaluate the possibility of the ear distorting sounds.
7. Brainstem Response Audiometry (BSRA) or Brainstem Evoked Auditory Response (BEAR)—If a hearing loss is suspected when the child is very young or if a child has other learning difficulties, a specially trained audiologist may perform this test. The child sleeps through this test or is given a mild sedative. Ears are stimulated many times with high frequency clicks and the responses are averaged. This test provides threshold information about high frequency hearing ability. It may also provide information regarding where the disruption of a sound signal occurs.
8. Otoacoustic Emissions Testing (EOAE)—This is a relatively new test procedure that measures cochlear response to sound and provides more specific information than the BEAR.

hearing loss. Naturally, a profound hearing loss is easier to identify because it is much more obvious than lesser degrees of hearing loss. See Table 9.5 for a list of several warning signs that may indicate the presence of a hearing loss.

CAUSES OF HEARING LOSS

Possible causes of sensorineural hearing loss include a family history of congenital sensorineural hearing loss. Also associated with sensorineural hearing losses are complications during pregnancy including **Rh-factor incompatibility,** or intrauterine infection such as **rubella, herpes, cytomegalovirus,** and **syphilis.** Birth complications, including premature delivery with a birth weight of less than 1500 grams, are also related to sensorineural hearing losses.

In addition, syndromes associated with hearing loss may be present at birth, such as **Allport's syndrome, Pendred syndrome, Usher's syndrome, Waardenburg's syndrome,** and **fetal alcohol syndrome.** Prolonged high fever, childhood diseases, such as measles, mumps, small pox, viral infections, including **meningitis** or **encephalitis,** drugs, physical damage to the head or ear, and exposure to a prolonged or sudden intense noise are all known to contribute to sensorineural hearing losses in children (Green, 1976).

Understanding the possible causes of hearing loss may help in preventing and detecting it. Possible causes of conductive hearing loss include blockage of the ear canal with wax or a foreign object, a perforated eardrum or a tear or hole in the eardrum, fluid or infection in the middle ear, loud noises, maternal rubella during pregnancy, meningitis, congenital malformations, such as a sealed ear canal, and bony overgrowth called otosclerosis (Green, 1976).

THE EFFECT OF HEARING IMPAIRMENTS

Many factors influence how well a person copes with a hearing loss. The degree of hearing loss determines how the hearing loss affects other areas, including speech and language, cognitive, and social-emotional development (Green, 1976).

TABLE 9.5 Warning Signs of a Hearing Loss

1. The infant does not react to loud sounds with a startle, blink, widening of the eyes, or crying.
2. At 4 months old, the baby does not turn toward a sound source, such as a parent's voice, just out of the baby's view.
3. At 4 months old, the baby does not become quiet in response to sounds such as voices or soft music or does not smile after hearing a familiar voice.
4. At 7 months old, the baby does not immediately turn toward the source of a voice across a room.
5. At 9 months old, the baby does not babble freely or stops babbling soon after first beginning to babble.
6. The baby at 12 months does not respond to familiar words such as *bye, bye* and *no.*
7. At 18 to 24 months old, the child does not put two words together (e.g., *more juice* or *daddy's car*).
8. The 18-month-old child's speech does not have a "natural" quality to it. When a severe or profound hearing loss is present, a child's speech may be particularly nasal, high-pitched, or monotone with no prosody (sing-song quality) in the voice. The child's voice might also be too loud or quiet.
9. The toddler's speech articulation does not include a variety of vowels and consonants and is relatively incomprehensible.
10. At 18 to 24 months old the child does not appear to be able to hear and follow simple directions. A child with a moderate to severe hearing loss often "mishears" a word, such as, if the child is told, "Go get your shirt," and instead brings back shoes.
11. The child has more difficulty hearing and understanding speech at a distance or in a noisy environment.
12. At 2 years old, the child often turns up the sound on the television or radio.
13. The child does not respond to a statement that excites other children in a group (e.g., "Who wants to go outside?").
14. The child says, "What?" or "Huh?" frequently.
15. The child has more difficulty following instructions when not watching a speaker's face.

Having one or both ears functioning below normal standards also affects the ability to cope with a hearing loss. In addition, the age at which the onset of a hearing loss occurs also affects development. Hearing loss at birth, called a congenital hearing loss, has a greater negative effect on development than does a hearing loss that occurs after a child has developed speech and language at approximately the age of three and beyond (Cole, 1992).

When deafness occurs before the child develops speech, called **prelingual deafness,** it often leads to serious consequences for development of speech and language. Children who never hear language sounds have more difficulty acquiring speech and language skills than a child who had some hearing before the age of two. **Postlingual deafness,** which occurs after the child has acquired some language skills, sometimes called **adventitious deafness,** has a less negative affect on language development (Lane, 1988).

The age at which hearing loss is identified is also important (Bess, 1988). Early **amplification** with hearing aids and early intervention by specialists, such as a teacher of the deaf or a speech and language pathologist, often have a major effect on a child's development. When a hearing aid is worn consistently, the outcomes associated with the hearing impairment, including negative effects on speech and language, cognitive, and social-emotional skills, are typically reduced (Northern & Downs, 1984).

The level of a child's innate intelligence also appears to play a role in the influence of a hearing loss. That is, children who have a hearing loss but are intellectually gifted are generally less negatively affected by a hearing loss than are those who have a hearing loss and are cognitively delayed. If a hearing impairment is the only type of developmental disability a child has, this loss typically has less of an effect on development (McArthur, 1982).

The way in which a child's family reacts to the hearing loss can have a major effect on the child's development. Family members must reach a level of acceptance that allows them to commit to the development of the whole child rather than focusing on the disability (McArthur, 1982). Careful coordination of the type of communication method used at home with the language used at school may lessen the negative affect of a hearing loss (Ling, 1984).

Children with hearing impairments should be encouraged to use the language skills they have rather than being allowed not to try to communicate. Because communication is often more difficult for them, use of language must be encouraged rather than expected. Children who are hearing impaired are less likely to use language spontaneously but use it when encouraged to do so by others.

If a child has a profound hearing loss *not* identified and amplified until after the child's third birthday, the effect can be very significant. The most obvious effect of a hearing loss is difficulty in communicating (Boothroyd, 1978). Loss of hearing within two octaves of the normal range of human speech has a more negative effect on speech and language development than when hearing losses are at higher or lower frequencies.

Language Development

Communication is basic to human interaction and begins the day a child is born. A baby begins to learn at six months that vocalizations have meaning, people take turns when they communicate with each other, direct eye contact is used during communication, and many words are repeated. After listening to the repeated vocabulary and sentence forms, the baby begins to acknowledge a pattern and recognizes the meaning of some words. Within just three months after birth, the baby also begins to understand short sentences and communicates by babbling and using **vocal play** (Calvert, 1984).

A mother who hears her baby say, "da," is likely to exclaim, "She said Daddy!" The baby is likely to enjoy the mother's reaction and, therefore, repeats "da" several times. In turn, the mother remains excited. Through this exchange, the

baby learned that something that occurred was valued by the mother. This type of interaction lays the groundwork for the development of one-word, then two-word combinations, and then more complex combinations of words (Martin, 1987a).

Young children with impaired hearing also begin to babble just as do children who do not have a hearing loss. Over time, if they do not hear their own "melodious" voice, they stop babbling. This interrupts a critical period of speech practice. If babies do not continue to babble, the voice loses its **prosody,** or "sing-song" effect (Stoel–Gammon & Otomo, 1986). Typically, the less babies babble, the less attention they get. This results in fewer episodes of verbal communication, which decreases the opportunities for babies to develop language (Calvert, 1984).

Generally, by the time babies with hearing impairments reach their first birthday, they are already behind in receptive language development (the ability to understand language). Without early intervention, the gap usually becomes even wider (Schildroth, Rawlings, & Allen, 1989; Schildroth & Hotto, 1991). Language is everywhere but children who are hearing impaired have limited access to it. These children miss everyday conversations, hearing questions from siblings, and responses made by parents and other adults.

It is not unusual to see individuals who are hearing impaired or deaf using sign language. Sign language is only one of several methods of communication available to those who are hearing impaired (Naiman & Schein, 1978). The four most prevalent communication systems are **oral-aural, cued speech, total communication,** and **American Sign Language (ASL)** (Stewart, 1990).

The first method, oral-aural, includes the use of hearing aids. These help provide optimum listening with **residual** (remaining) **hearing.** The oral-aural method also uses **speech reading** and visual aids, such as pictures, real objects, and printed words.

The second method, cued speech, includes all of the components of oral-aural. In addition, this method uses special hand shapes that, when placed near the speaker's mouth, represent letters that would be too difficult to read on the lips.

The third method is referred to as **total communication.** This method includes using any and all means available to the learner who is hearing impaired to understand the message. This method includes using sign language, hearing aids or other sound amplification methods, speech reading, visuals, and natural gestures.

American Sign Language (ASL), the fourth major communication method, is a language system that follows a strict set of linguistic rules using **hand signs** to represent letters, words, and phrases. This method is frequently referred to as **manual communication** (Stewart, 1990).

Speech Development

Children with severe to profound hearing loss often develop unique voice patterns (Bess, 1988). Their voices are sometimes too loud or soft. Their voices often lack prosody and sound monotonous or are too high pitched. Such children often do not support longer sentences with proper breathing and have incorrect patterns of syllable stress and phrasing. They often make numerous articulation errors. For example, the word *baby* may sound like *maybe* or the word *school* like *cool.*

With early amplification through the use of hearing aids and intensive speech training, many of these speech patterns are prevented or corrected. If, however, the hearing loss is identified after a child is six to twelve months old, years of speech therapy frequently are needed (Simmons–Martin, 1976). About 25 percent of children with profound hearing loss and 45 percent of children classified as deaf have **unintelligible speech** even with extensive speech therapy intervention.

Cognitive Development

Having a hearing loss does not determine a child's intelligence. **Language deprivation,** however, contributes to a delay in the development of a child's knowledge base. Language enhances understanding and organizing information. Language facilitates many cognitive skills, such as storing and remembering information, discussing how things are similar or different, classifying things, defining and describing, reasoning, inventing, and solving problems. Academic achievement is very dependent on the comprehension of language. If language is delayed, it is likely that cognitive skills, including pre-reading abilities, will also be delayed (Martin, 1987b).

A great deal of information comes from having simple conversations and hearing books read. Children with hearing loss frequently do *not* have the benefit of experiencing enough conversation. Parents of children who are hearing impaired often avoid reading to their children because they believe the children can not benefit from the experience. As a result, a gap between the cognitive abilities of children who are hearing impaired and those who are not frequently develop (Luterman, 1970).

Adults should increase communication with children who are hearing impaired, which includes frequently reading to them. Reading means including specific methods to fill the communication gap, such as using ASL or acting out a story. Parents and preschool teachers should also attempt to increase the knowledge base of children who are hearing impaired by providing firsthand experiences, such as a trip to a farm, riding on a train, including the child in family discussions, and patiently repeating communication as often as necessary (Calvert, 1984).

Parents must fully commit to supporting the educational program developed for each child by consistently using the method themselves and encouraging others who interact with their child to use it as well. If parents refuse to learn sign language, for example, it becomes even more crucial that the child learns to speak. Parents must then commit to having the child learn to speak by encouraging a consistent use of hearing aids and requiring the child to speak when making requests. If parents believe only signing should be learned, they must then be willing to use ASL consistently when communicating with their child (Cole, 1992).

Parents and teachers often must find different methods to increase concept development for a child with a hearing impairment (Ross, 1981). Children without hearing impairments can be told, "This is a dog." Children with hearing impairments typically benefit from having information presented in ways other than just verbal instruction. Children who are hearing impaired acquire a great deal of information through the use of visual (pictures) and concrete props (actual objects). For example, if a speech and language pathologist attempts to teach a hearing impaired child the word *apple* it would be best if the therapist has a real apple to show the child as the word is being presented. As the word *apple* is said the teacher could also show a picture of an apple and other pictures with different colors and sizes of apples. Firsthand experiences are usually the most meaningful for the child.

The following scenario demonstrates the special needs of a child who is hearing impaired. Four-year-old Megan, who is hearing-impaired, asks, "Where is mommy?" Daddy answers, "She went to the circus with Matthew." Megan asks, "What?" Daddy responds, "She'll be home soon." Megan's father did not say more because he decided it would be hard to describe where her mother had gone. Megan's mother did not take her to the circus because she cannot hear well. Megan's mother did not consider that the circus is full of images, colors, movement, and flashing lights and is certainly not limited to sounds. Megan's mother may find it frustrating to explain all that is going on at the circus and may have avoided taking Megan because it is difficult to communicate with her.

Megan's father could enhance the communication process by showing Megan pictures of a circus. He could draw or show her pictures of clowns, tents, circus animals, and trapeze artists. Megan's mother could also help Megan by bringing home a program from the circus to help explain what she saw and did at the circus. Adults

should not simply ignore difficult to explain questions by saying, "Never mind."

Megan needs to be provided experiences such as going to circuses. She would be able to learn a great deal from the experience even though she could not hear announcements and other sounds. All too often adults assume that children with hearing impairments should *not* be taken to activities in which sounds are a major part because they might not fully understand or benefit from all aspects of the experience. Megan is likely to notice things visually and tactilally that her mother does *not*. In fact, after the circus clown has performed the silent pantomime, Megan is likely to have understood the clown's message better than her mother.

Parents and teachers should provide opportunities for children who are hearing impaired to "think things through." For example, allowing a child to bring snow inside to discover what happens might help explain to a child why it melts. Adults also need to resist doing things for children who are hearing impaired that they can do for themselves. Children learn about sorting and classifying when allowed to participate in putting away their toys. They learn much more about the world and how things work when adults allow them to experience life firsthand (Gatty, 1992). It is often quicker for a teacher or parent to take control and put a coat on a child rather than to try to communicate to the child, "It is time to put on your coat," but it does *not* teach the child how to communicate.

Social-Emotional Development

The effect of a hearing impairment on social skills development is fairly easy to predict. Communication among family members and friends is often delayed in quality (limited to simpler concepts and vocabulary) and quantity (less direct communication). This communication breakdown often leaves children who have hearing impairments feeling inadequate and isolated (Lee & Antia, 1992).

Young children with hearing impairments often express their needs and desires in physical ways, such as by grabbing or pushing, or by having temper tantrums, until they develop more socially acceptable ways to communicate. Once they learn the power of language, most children, whether hearing impaired or not, become enjoyable to be around and develop friendships. In addition, verbal negotiating and reasoning skills are gradually developed during the preschool years. Having a hearing loss, however, may slow down these processes, leaving children socially at risk and their self-esteem and emotional well-being negatively affected (Ling, 1984).

EDUCATIONAL INTERVENTION

Once a child's hearing loss has been identified, several important educational decisions must be made. It is critical for parents and professionals to understand the special needs of a young child with a hearing loss so that appropriate interventions are made available to the child (Lowenbraun, 1988).

Technology

Hearing aids are the most frequently used assistive devices for children with hearing impairments (Zelski & Zelski, 1985). Different types of available hearing aids include:

1. **Behind-the-Ear**—This is the most common type of amplification for children. It works well but amplifies all sounds. If a child has a hearing loss in only a limited range of frequencies, the child's hearing would be amplified in all frequencies, even those that do not need amplification. Therefore, hearing may be distorted.

2. **In-the-Ear**—This type of aid fits inside the ear and is more common for adults. It is less noticeable but needs to be fitted specifically to each person's ears. Since children are still growing this may not be a practical type of aid for them.

3. **Body-worn**—This type of aid is worn on the chest with wires to the ear, connected to a personally-fitted "ear mold." For children who are very active this may not be practical.

4. **Vibro-tactile**—This type of aid is for the profoundly deaf and is worn on the wrist. The aid vibrates slightly, giving the wearer some speech information. Sounds are not distinguishable as specific words. Wearers use this device in conjunction with lip reading.

5. **Bone-conduction**—This type of aid is for people whose ear canal is closed. The bone conduction hearing aid rests on the bone behind the ear and is held in place by a headband. This method allows sound to bypass the blocked ear canal and stimulates the hearing mechanism.

The type of aids sold through mail order catalogs or at local department stores are not effective for most children. Parents should seek an audiologist's advice for proper fitting of hearing aids. Children may qualify for public assistance to pay for a hearing aid if insurance does not cover the cost.

Another form of technological intervention is a wireless **frequency modulated (FM) transmission device.** It is most often used in educational settings (VanTasell, Mallinger, & Crump, 1986). Some parents may also find it useful at home with a child who is hearing impaired. It consists of two parts: a transmitter/microphone worn by a teacher or other adult and a receiver worn by the child who is hearing impaired. It functions like a hearing aid but adds two additional benefits. The listener may receive sound signals from a much further distance, about twenty feet, which gives the teacher freedom to move around the classroom. The listener also receives a strong auditory signal directly from the teacher that overrides most background noise in a classroom, so an FM device may be used in lieu of a hearing aid while the child is in school because personal hearing aids cannot compensate for a noisy environment (Ross, 1981).

An additional form of technological intervention is a **cochlear implant** (Geers & Tobey, 1992). This is a medical intervention that must be combined with educational interventions to be successful. It is also the last option after *all* other attempts to improve auditory functioning have failed. This device is designed to provide sound stimulation to children and adults who are profoundly deaf. It is typically only available to patients for whom using hearing aids or vibro-tactile aids has been of no benefit. It requires major surgery and a long period of rehabilitation (relearning how to process sound) with trained professionals. A cochlear implant is not a cure for deafness. It does *not* fully restore hearing but does provide increased sensitivity to sound for most patients. Even with intensive auditory training, most patients still have some level of hearing impairment (Ross, 1982 Craig, 1992).

Appropriate Preschool Placement

A child with significant hearing loss is eligible for team evaluation. An assessment team meets with the child's parents and evaluates the child's degree of hearing loss and level of development in all major areas. After the evaluation is completed, the team makes recommendations for specific early intervention services. These services might include home visits by a specialist, itinerant services, a specialist travels to the child's daycare or nursery school site, or a center-based preschool program for children with special needs. Federal law mandates that this team must find the **least restrictive environment.** Federal law further requires that the child's progress and program be evaluated annually.

Once the type of hearing loss is determined and appropriate medical interventions (e.g., treatment for ear infection or removal of ear wax) have been implemented, educational interventions are developed by the team. The team members consider many factors, including the degree of hearing loss, age of the child, and the existence of other disabilities. A recommendation is made regarding the types of early intervention services appropriate for a particular child and how those services are to be provided (Ling, 1984).

A child with a mild hearing loss and no other disability usually function well with minimal intervention. Intervention techniques might include teaching parents or care providers to face the child when talking, keeping background noise to a minimum during conversations with the child, and maintaining a hearing aid if one is prescribed. Regular preschool education is often appropriate for a child with a mild or moderate hearing loss (Moores, 1985). The majority of children with mild hearing losses have difficulty hearing whispers or faint sounds. They often need speech therapy to help learn to discriminate between and produce certain sounds. These children benefit from sitting near to the person speaking and having adequate lighting to allow for lip reading. They may also need some form of sound amplification such as a hearing aid or FM transmission device (Moores, 1985).

Children with moderate hearing losses have difficulty with loud and soft speech and telephone conversations. They frequently have more difficulty understanding the speech of unfamiliar than of familiar people. These children generally function well in a regular education classroom with extra adult support, as well as some form of amplification. They typically need speech and language therapy on a regular basis (Quigley & Paul, 1990).

Children with more severe hearing loss generally require intensive speech and language training. Specialists help to maximize the development of the children's residual hearing (the hearing they do have). These children have difficulty identifying many consonant sounds. They hear only shouts, loud noises, or amplified speech. They typically have difficulty with speech unless they receive ongoing speech therapy. Children with severe hearing impairments frequently attend special classes.

Teaching children who have severe hearing impairments and their peers how to communicate with each other is also critical. The team of professionals and parents should decide as early as possible about the type of communication system to be used. This depends on the child's degree of hearing loss, age, ability levels, and preferences of the parents. Once the decision regarding the method of communication has been made, all participants must make every effort to provide a unified program. Several different types of communication systems can be used (Bess, 1988).

Total communication, a system in which all means of communication are used, might be chosen as the method of communication with a particular child. The child's family should then take every opportunity to learn and use sign language. When total communication is used, teachers should use sign language throughout the day in the classroom. Other children who are *not* hearing impaired should also be given an opportunity to learn sign language. It would be ideal if all the children could sign, but sometimes it is more realistic to teach basic sign language to one or two of the interested peers. Most preschool-aged children are fascinated with sign language and learn very quickly (Quigley & Paul, 1990).

In addition to using sign language, a child should wear hearing aids throughout the day. At school, a child's ability to hear speech should be amplified. Hearing aids, however, also amplify all nearby sounds along with the speaker's voice, and many noise sources are found in a preschool setting. Because of this, an FM transmission device is strongly recommended by many professionals. The transmission device allows a teacher freedom of movement in the classroom and helps ensure that a teacher's voice carries over the classroom noise (Ross, 1981).

With these guidelines in mind, preschool options for a child with hearing loss include attending regular nursery schools, preschool programs designed for children who have speech and language delays or are hearing impaired, and schools for children who are deaf. There has been a major change of focus regarding the placement of children with special needs. Most states are moving toward the goal of **inclusion,** placing the child with special needs in a classroom with "typical" children. Federal laws mandate that each child must be educated in the least restrictive environment. This environment, or placement option, may be different for each child, depending on many factors such as the child's ability to comprehend language (Gatty, 1992).

Children who are hearing impaired may benefit from inclusion, but several issues must be addressed continuously throughout the school year to ensure that inclusion remains the best option. Questions that should be asked to help determine the least restrictive environment include:

- Does the child have access to instruction in sign language if needed?
- Is the teacher prepared for a child who is hearing impaired to be in the class?
- Is the teacher making the appropriate adaptations to the daily program to accommodate the needs of the child?
- Is the teacher using an FM transmission device and is it being used properly?
- Is the child who is hearing impaired progressing in speech and language, and cognitive skills?
- Is the child making friends?

A preschool class in a program designed specifically for the hearing impaired is another placement option. This type of class might be provided within a facility with only hearing impaired students of different ages or be located in a program where some of the classes are for children with hearing impairments, as well as children without hearing impairments. In a program especially designed for children who are hearing impaired, a teacher of the deaf typically establishes the main educational program. The teacher provides coordinated programs designed to ensure that each child who is hearing impaired receives consistent language instruction throughout the school day. In addition, a speech and language pathologist provides speech and listening instruction that is integrated into classroom activities throughout each school day (Stewart, 1990).

Preschool programs that provide special services for children with **communication disorders** offer children with hearing loss the time to interact with children without hearing impairments. In this case, children who are hearing impaired are in an inclusion setting while benefitting from a specially trained team, including a special education teacher, speech and language pathologist, and teacher of the deaf. Children who are not hearing impaired also benefit from inclusive placements because they learn how to interact with peers who are hearing impaired.

In most cases, children with hearing impairments can be educated in regular preschool classes or in classes that focus on speech and language impairments. In some cases, however, preschoolers who have hearing impairments attend a school for the deaf. Most children who are deaf do not attend these schools until they reach school-age (age five).

To attend a school for the deaf, a child must have a profound hearing loss in both ears. Profound hearing loss, or deafness, is a low incident (less than .01 percent) communication disorder. Schools for the deaf provide a peer group with similar needs. Children who are deaf often feel isolated when placed in the "hearing world." There are still a few "oral" schools for the deaf where the oral-aural method of teaching children who are deaf is practiced and sign language is *not* used, but many schools for the deaf have adopted total communication as an educational approach (Evans & Falk, 1986).

There has been a movement toward the use of American Sign Language (ASL), which does not use the voice for instruction or teaching in the belief that this helps preserve the "deaf culture" (Lane, 1988). The philosophical differences on how best to communicate with and educate children who are deaf often cause great controversy among professionals in the field. Many people believe that it is not reasonable to expect children who are deaf to learn two languages, oral and signing. In addition, people who are deaf believe that forcing children who are deaf to learn how to speak suggests that the children are not acceptable unless they can speak. Other individuals believe that we should help children learn to speak the oral language of their community so they are as "normalized" as possible (Parasnis, 1996).

The issue of whether teaching children to speak versus only teaching them signing gained national attention in the fall of 1994 when Heather Whitestone, who is deaf, became the new Miss America. Some members of the deaf community felt she was not an appropriate representative for the deaf because she speaks well and uses ASL. The concern is that, because she can speak well, people may believe that all people who are deaf can and should learn to speak even though children who lose their hearing prior to developing speech typically have a very difficult time learning to speak. Heather lost her hearing after she had begun to speak and was raised in a hearing and speaking environment. She is living proof, as she said, that "anything is possible."

One example of a program that supports inclusion is the Saint Francis Hospital Preschool Program for children with speech and language delays. This program is coordinated by the Saint Francis Hospital Communication Disorders Department, in Poughkeepsie, New York. Several children with varying degrees of hearing loss are placed in the program's preschool classes. The **multidisciplinary** approach in this program is exemplary. The program's staff includes a special education teacher, speech and language pathologist, and teaching assistant. In addition, a teacher of the deaf provides direct services to children who are hearing impaired, teaches in the classrooms, and consults with program staff regarding the adaptation of daily plans necessary to best help each child.

Based on the team's recommendation, each child may also receive occupational, physical, and art therapy, and mental health services. The team of specialists collaborates on setting goals for each child. Whenever possible, each specialist works with the child, providing therapy in the classroom so that the child does not miss valuable classroom experience.

Staff In-Service Training

At the preschool level, there are frequently several staff members, including teachers, therapists, and medical personnel, with whom children interact. These staff members can benefit from learning specific techniques for working with children who are hearing impaired (Gatty, 1992). The three major areas of **in-service training** might include:

1. Special needs of the hearing impaired: Generally, communication methods and required adaptations need to be discussed so that the child who is hearing impaired may be included and can benefit from every activity.
2. Sign language training: If the program's communication philosophy includes sign language, the staff should then be trained to facilitate communication with the child who is hearing impaired.
3. Learning about the purpose and use of an FM transmission device.

Parent Education and Support

Parents are the primary teachers. Because difficulties in communication frequently accompany hearing loss, it is important that parents learn about language development and the special needs of their child (McArthur, 1982). Although children with hearing loss must be helped to develop the senses other than hearing, it is important to continue to encourage the use of whatever level of hearing the children have (Gregory, Bishop, & Sheldon, 1995). Parents and teachers of children who are hearing impaired may benefit from being made aware of the suggestions listed in Table 9.6.

Parents often need help understanding why children who wear hearing aids must wear them consistently (Gregory, Newson, & Newson, 1995). During the day, a child's hearing aid should be turned on as often as possible. The use of an FM transmission device in school settings is also

TABLE 9.6 Suggestions for Working with Children Who Have Hearing Impairments

1. Continue using **motherese/fatherese,** which includes the higher-pitched, melodious voice mothers and fathers naturally use with a baby (even those with hearing impairments). It is highly interesting and novel to a baby and holds the child's attention. This method includes natural repetition and eye contact ("Hello, baby Brittany! I see that smile. Yes, I see that big smile. I'm gonna get you! Here I come. I'm gonna get you!").
2. Stay close to the child so the child can see and hear you.
3. Keep talking to the child, especially when the child is watching. Talking to the child helps develop listening skills, speech-reading, language, and social growth.
4. Keep hearing aids turned on as much as possible throughout the day. (Some children love the benefits of hearing aids so much that they sleep with them at night.)
5. Several times a day check that the hearing aid is turned on and volume is sufficiently loud, and check the battery every morning.
6. If sign language is used, it should be used as much as possible.
7. Get down to eye level with the child to optimize communication.
8. When attempting to communicate with the child, keep room lights turned on so the child can read lips and see facial expressions. Standing in front of a window often reduces a child's ability to lip-read because of glare from the sun.
9. In a school setting, seat the child who is hearing impaired so all the children's faces are visible to that child. Sitting in a circle is one suitable arrangement.
10. Use props such as stuffed or plastic animals whenever possible to help the child understand and develop vocabulary. Pictures also help develop vocabulary.
11. Provide print (word labels) along with new objects or pictures. Label bulletin board pictures and even common objects at home. Explain each printed label or include the child in the labeling process.

12. Talk and listen to the child as often as possible. A child who is hearing impaired will not acquire language in the same way children without hearing losses do. Talk to a child who is hearing impaired about the environment, activities, and his or her feelings.

13. Teach conversational turn-taking skills so the child can learn to listen and monitor his or her own conversational skills.

14. Check to make sure that the child is following the topic of discussion by asking questions related to the discussion.

15. Blink room lights to gain a child's attention and then use words or signs to communicate.

16. During group activities, such as circle time, pass the FM microphone to the hearing children. Most children love to talk into a microphone, and a child who is hearing impaired may benefit from directly hearing other children's questions and answers.

17. When the teacher asks a question, the teacher should indicate which child is answering the question by pointing to the child. This helps the child who is hearing impaired to know which child he or she needs to look at to lip-read.

18. Encourage interactions between the child who is hearing impaired and children who are not. Teach all the children to speak for themselves. Children who are hearing impaired must be taught words or signs to communicate and then be allowed to "negotiate" on their own.

19. Use the same vocabulary and sentence structure with children whether they are hearing impaired or not. If the child who is hearing impaired does *not* understand it is often helpful to:

    - repeat: "Joseph, put the blocks on the shelf. Joseph, put the blocks on the shelf."
    - rephrase: "Joseph, put the blocks away. Put them on the shelf."
    - use props: Hold up a block, point to the shelf, and repeat the sentence.
    - act out: Demonstrate by putting the blocks on the shelf and repeat the sentence.

20. If someone does *not* understand the child, try using the following techniques:

    - Ask the child to repeat the words.
    - Ask the child to physically show what he or she wants.
    - Try to figure out the word from the context.
    - Ask questions such as, "What do you do with it?" and "Tell me more about it."
    - Have the child draw a picture related to the word(s).
    - Ask someone else to attempt to interpret what the child is trying to communicate.

21. Expand on the child's attempts to communicate. An example of this method follows.

    > Keith: "Ball."
    > Adult: "You want the ball?"
    > Keith: "Ball."
    > Adult: "Here comes the ball. The ball is rolling!"

22. Give the child enough time to answer questions. Children need to be allowed to speak for themselves. If a child is becoming overly frustrated while trying to answer a question, model the sentence for the child and then encourage him or her to repeat the model. This allows the child to practice using the appropriate language.

23. Use natural play situations to help develop language.

24. Speak at a normal rate. Do not exaggerate lip movements because children must practice reading lips when mouth movements are not exaggerated.

25. Be careful not to hide behind a book when reading to the child. The child will not be able to lip-read if the reader's face is behind the book.

26. To make lip reading easier, wear lipstick, trim a mustache, and stand still while talking.

27. During a puppet show, the puppeteer's face should be in view so the child who is hearing impaired may lip-read. A sign language interpreter may be used if the child knows sign language.

28. Masks make communication difficult for a child with hearing loss. Masks hide lips and facial expressions, leaving the child who is hearing impaired unable to understand a conversation. Rather than wearing a mask, it is preferable to use a hat or apply make-up to the face as part of a costume.

to be considered. An FM transmission device can help build language and listening skills at home and in public such as when shopping. There should be a sufficient supply of batteries for hearing aids and FM transmission devices.

Learning the effective use of hearing and how to speak require a great deal of effort on the part of children and the adults helping them. During classroom activities, teachers must remember to make listening fun and interesting. Teachers should take advantage of everyday events, for instance pointing out environmental sounds coming from all directions, from almost anything—a jet plane, woodpecker, truck, motorcycle, helicopter, voices (including laughing and crying), telephones, and musical instruments. Adults must often help focus children's attention to the sounds that occur around them by saying such things as, "Here comes the lawn mower. Oh, it's loud. Uh oh, it's getting louder!"

Learning could be made fun and interesting by playing games such as "freeze." This game involves instructing the child to move while music is playing and then to freeze (stop moving) when the music stops. This game includes listening for when the music starts again, as a cue to start moving. Other games such as make-believe also provide enjoyable modes of learning. Pretend someone is sleeping and encourage a child with hearing loss to yell, "Wake up!" By acting surprised, the child learns the power of communication by playing a simple game. Having the child pretend to sleep and then listen for the words, "Wake up!" encourages focused listening and is enjoyable at the same time. Adults should avoid giving the child clues such as moving or touching.

Games such as hide-and-seek may be modified to include the use of sounds (e.g., ringing a bell or hitting a drum). In this way the child who is hearing impaired can use sound to locate the missing person. This game provides the child with opportunities to practice focusing on sounds. This method could be used to enhance children's language abilities.

When a child who is hearing impaired must focus on specific sounds or on a conversation, other noises should be kept to a minimum. To help the child focus on speech, a quiet environment is necessary. Background noises such as from televisions, radios, vacuum cleaners, or lawn mowers should be reduced. It may also be necessary to provide appropriate classroom modifications such as carpeting, curtains, and acoustic tile to help reduce noise.

Children with hearing impairments often need help to enhance social interaction with their peers. Adults should accentuate the strengths of children with hearing difficulties. Adults should let a child shine in front of peers. A comment such as, "Look, Olivia can find her name card!" could do a great deal to enhance a child's status with peers. Children should be empowered with the words needed to negotiate directly with peers.

Adults should explain to the child's peers the difficulties the child faces. Peers should be taught that the child who is hearing impaired needs to hear and see them and often need to have words repeated. Sometimes, peers might need to use sign language to communicate effectively with their classmate who is hearing impaired. This means they need an opportunity to learn sign language. During interactions with other children, the child who has a hearing loss might need to be provided conversation starters such as "Hi, What's your name?" "Wanna play?" "I have a hamster at home," to initiate interaction with other children. Use of the "buddy system" often helps children who are hearing impaired. These children may imitate the "buddy" who is not hearing impaired when it is time for activities such as clapping to music. These buddies could also be partners during a walk or while on a field trip.

Parents should be encouraged to include in family discussions the child who is hearing impaired. This is important because the family is the social environment in which communication and social-emotional development begins. Parents should also be encouraged to provide a child who is hearing impaired many opportunities to play with children who have normal hearing and be ready to assist in facilitating communication between their child and other children (McArthur, 1982).

Children with hearing impairments may need to be provided with strategies to repair communication breakdowns. Such strategies include learning to repeat, rephrase, draw pictures, use gestures, act out, or sign.

Helping children who are hearing impaired develop "appropriate" behavior is a concern of parents and teachers. It is important to remember that a child who is hearing impaired is a child first, and many types of behavior are typical of children who are the same age, and unrelated to hearing loss. Typically, children who are hearing impaired quickly learn to turn away from an adult who attempts to redirect the child's behavior. It is hard work to maintain a behavior management routine for some children who are hearing impaired because an adult needs to walk to or run after a toddler who is hearing impaired, for example, who cannot hear the adult call. It is exhausting but necessary to follow through to help the child acquire appropriate types of behavior (Bess, 1988).

Children who are hearing impaired need to be held to the same behavior expectations as other children. If they "get away with" more, they might *not* develop into desirable playmates, their siblings might resent them for receiving special treatment, and their self-esteem may not flourish. When giving instructions to a child with hearing loss, adults must be sure the child has "heard" and understood them. If the child understands what to do and chooses not to do it, the child must be held responsible for that behavior.

A young child with a hearing loss often needs extra time and attention. It is very easy to fall into a pattern of doing things for the child because this often takes less time than letting the child do things independently. It is important to remember that a child needs the opportunity to build positive self-esteem. Most children delight in their own accomplishments. Children who are hearing im-

paired will become adults who are hearing impaired. They need to become independent and self-sufficient. The foundation laid by parents and preschool providers make it more likely for the child who is hearing impaired to be proud of accomplishments and better equipped to meet the challenges life offers.

CONCLUSION

Early intervention services are vital to the development of children with hearing impairments. Meeting the needs of a child who is hearing impaired often seems overwhelming at first. Most children with hearing impairments benefit from experiencing the same type of daily activities other children experience. Children with hearing impairments also benefit from activities found in most preschool classrooms, although teachers may need to adapt the method in which the information is presented to the children with special needs. Through careful evaluation and team collaboration while developing an educational plan, children who have hearing loss will reach their full potential.

The next two chapters focus on intervention services for children with motor delays. The role of the occupational therapist and services directed toward fine motor delays are discussed in Chapter 10. The role of the physical therapist for the enhancement of gross motor development is discussed in Chapter 11.

CHAPTER SUMMARY

- The three major types of hearing loss are conductive, sensorineural, and mixed. Conductive hearing loss occurs when sound is not transferred through the outer ear or middle ear. Sensorineural hearing loss occurs when the transmission of sound is disrupted somewhere in the inner ear or sensory nerve.

- Hearing loss varies in severity and the level of severity directly affects many aspects of a child's development, including speech and language, general cognitive, and social-emotional development. The development of speech and language is generally the most negatively affected by hearing losses.

- There are several different methods of communication that can be used with children who are hearing impaired. There are also several different types of amplification devices that can be used by individuals with hearing impairments.
- Young children with hearing impairments may receive intervention at home or attend several different types of preschool programs.
- Many of the needs of children with hearing impairments are the same as those of children who do not have hearing impairments.

REVIEW QUESTIONS

1. How are hearing losses measured? What are the four major levels of hearing loss?
2. What methods can parents and professionals use to help a child with hearing impairments acquire cognitive, speech and language, and social-emotional skills most effectively?
3. What are the advantages of using an FM transmission device?
4. How can adults help children with hearing impairments interact successfully with their peers?

SUGGESTED STUDENT ACTIVITIES

1. Learn more about sign language or other augmentative communication methods. Learn the alphabet and a few simple phrases in sign language.
2. Visit a class that includes preschool-aged children with hearing impairments. Observe how teachers and peers adjust their interactions to meet the needs of the children who are hearing impaired.
3. Visit an audiologist or teacher of the hearing impaired. Ask to be shown the different methods used to test hearing abilities. Ask the audiologist to suggest methods to enhance learning for children with varying degrees of hearing loss.

ADDITIONAL READINGS

Bess, F. H. (Ed.). (1988). *Hearing impairment in children.* York, PA: York Press.

Lane, H. (1984). *When the mind hears: A history of the deaf.* New York: Random House.

Padden, C., & Humphries, T. (1988). *Deaf in America: Voices from a culture.* Cambridge, MA: Harvard University Press.

Walker, L. A. (1986). *A loss for words: The story of deafness in a family.* New York: Harper & Row.

ADDITIONAL RESOURCES

Alexander Graham Bell Association for the Deaf, Inc.
3417 Volta Place, N.W.
Washington, DC 20007

American Deafness Rehabilitation Association
P.O. Box 55369
Little Rock, AR 72225

American Hearing Research Foundation
55 E. Washington Street
Chicago, IL 60602

American Speech–Language–Hearing Association
10801 Rockville Pike
Rockville, MD 20852

American Society for Deaf Children
814 Thayer Avenue
Silver Spring, MD 20910

Better Hearing Institute
P.O. Box 1840
Washington, DC 20013

Captioning and Adaption Branch
U.S. Department of Education
330 C Street, S.W.
Washington, DC 20202

Gallaudet Assistive Devices Center
Department of Audiology and Speech-Language Pathology
800 Florida Avenue, N.E.
Washington, DC 20002

National Captioning Institute
5203 Lessburg Pike, Suite 1500
Falls Church, VA 22041

National Information Center on Deafness
Gallaudet University
800 Florida Avenue, N.E.
Washington, DC 20002

Registry of Interpreters for the Deaf
51 Monroe Street, Suite 1107
Rockville, MD 20850

REFERENCES

Bess, F. H. (Ed.). (1988). *Hearing impairment in children.* York, PA: York Press.

Boone, D. R. (1987). *Human communication and its disorders.* Englewood Cliffs, NJ: Prentice-Hall.

Boothroyd, A. (1978). Speech perception and severe hearing loss. In M. Ross & T. G. Giolas (Eds.), *Auditory management of hearing-impaired children* (pp. 117–144). Baltimore, MD: University Park Press.

Calvert, D. (1984). *Parents' guide to speech and deafness.* Washington, DC: Alexander Graham Bell Association.

Cole, E. B. (1992). Promoting emerging speech in birth to 3-year-old hearing-impaired children. *Volta Review, 94,* 63–77.

Craig, B. (1992). Wendy's cochlear implant. *Our kid's magazine,* Fall, p. 3.

Evans, A. D., & Falk, W. W. (1986). *Learning to be deaf.* New York: Moutan de Gruyter.

Gatty, J. C. (1992). Teaching speech to hearing-impaired children. *Volta Review, 94,* 49–61.

Geers, A. E., & Tobey, E. (1992). Effects of cochlear implants and tactile aids on the development of speech production skills in children with profound hearing impairment. *Volta Review, 94,* 135–163.

Goldberg, B. (1993). Universal hearing screening of newborns: An idea whose time has come. *ASHA, 35,* 63–64.

Green, D. M. (1976). *An introduction to hearing.* Hillsdale, NJ: Erlbaum.

Gregory, S., Bishop, J., & Sheldon, L. (1995). *Deaf young people and their families: Developing understanding.* NY: Cambridge University Press.

Gregory, S., Newson, J., & Newson, E. (1995). *Deaf children and their families.* NY: Cambridge University Press.

Lane, H. (1988). Is there a "Psychology of the Deaf?" *Exceptional Children, 55,* 7–19.

Lee, D., & Antia, S. (1992). A sociological approach to the social integration of hearing-impaired and normally hearing students. *Volta Review, 95,* 425–434.

Ling, D. (1984). *Early intervention for hearing-impaired children: Oral options.* San Diego: College Hill.

Lowenbraun, S. (1988). Hearing-impaired. In E. L. Meyen & T. M. Skotric (Eds.), *Exceptional children and youth: An introduction* (3rd ed., pp. 321–350). Denver: Love.

Luterman, D. (1970). *Counseling parents of hearing-impaired children.* Boston: Little, Brown.

Martin, F. M. (Ed.). (1987a). *Hearing disorders in children.* Austin, TX: Pro-Ed.

Martin, F. M. (Ed.). (1987b). *Hearing disorders in children: Pediatric audiology.* Boston: Allyn & Bacon.

McArthur, S. H. (1982). *Raising your hearing-impaired child: Guideline for parents.* Washington, DC: Alexander Graham Bell Association.

Moores, D. F. (1985). Early intervention programs for hearing-impaired children: A longitudinal assessment. In D. Nelson (Ed.), *Children's language* (Vol. V). Hillsdale, NJ: Erlbaum.

Naiman, D., & Schein, J. (1978). *For parents of deaf children.* Silver Springs, MD: National Association for the Deaf.

Northern, J., & Downs, M. (1984). *Hearing in children* (3rd ed.). Baltimore, MD: Williams and Wilkins.

Pappas, D. (1985). *Diagnosis and treatment of hearing impairment in children.* San Diego: College Hill.

Parasnis, I. (1996). *Cultural and language diversity and the deaf experience.* NY: Cambridge University Press.

Quigley, S. P., & Paul, P. V. (1990). *Language and deafness.* San Diego: Singular Publishing.

Ross, M. (1981). Classroom amplification. In W. R. Hodgson & R. H. Skinna (Eds.), *Hearing aid assessment and use in audiologic habilitation* (2nd ed., pp. 234–257). Baltimore, MD: Williams & Wilkins.

Ross, M. (1982). *Hard of hearing children in regular schools.* Englewood Cliffs, NJ: Prentice-Hall.

Schildroth, A. N., & Hotto, S. A. (1991). Hearing-impaired children under age 6: Data from the annual survey of hearing-impaired children and youth. *American Annals of the Deaf, 137*(7), 168–175.

Schildroth, A. N., Rawlings, B. W., & Allen, T. E. (1989). Hearing-impaired children under age 6: A demographic analysis. *American Annals of the Deaf, 134*(2), 63–69.

Simmons–Martin, A. (1976). A demonstration home approach with hearing-impaired children. In E. Webster (Ed.), *Professional approaches with parents of handicapped children.* Springfield, IL: Charles C. Thomas.

Stewart, D. A. (1990). Rationale and strategies for American Sign Language intervention. *American Annals of the Deaf, 135*(3), 205–210.

Stoel–Gammon, C., & Otomo, K. (1986). Babbling development of hearing-impaired and normally hearing subjects. *Journal of Speech and Hearing Disorders, 51,* 33–41.

VanTasell, D. J., Mallinger, C. A., & Crump, E. S. (1986). Functional gain and speech recognition with two types of FM amplification. *Language, Speech and Hearing Services in Schools, 17,* 28–37.

Zelski, R. F. K., & Zelski, T. (1985). What are assistive devices? *Hearing Instruments, 36,* 12.

CHAPTER 10

MOTOR DEVELOPMENT AND OCCUPATIONAL THERAPY SERVICES

ALLYSON BURNS, OTR/L, B.S.
NANCY M. PATE, OTR/L, B.S.

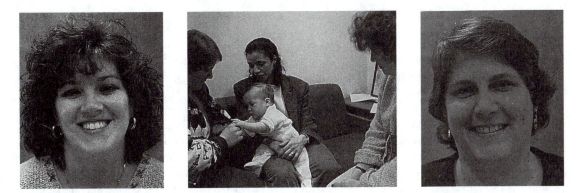

ABOUT THE AUTHORS

Allyson Burns has a bachelor's degree in occupational therapy from Quinnipiac College in New Haven, Connecticut. She has been providing occupational services to children with special needs for more than 5 years. Mrs. Burns is currently employed by a school district as an occupational therapist for school-aged children. She is married and the mother of twins.

Nancy Pate received an associate's degree in occupational therapy from Orange County Community College in Middletown, New York, and a bachelor's degree in occupational therapy from Dominican College in Orangeburg, New York. She also earned a bachelor's degree in social work from West Liberty State College in West Liberty, West Virginia. She has been providing occupational therapy to children for more than twelve years. She currently teaches occupational therapy courses at Orange County Community College in Middletown, New York. She is an occupational therapist for the Rehabilitation Program in Dutchess County, New York, and has a private practice in occupational therapy.

CHAPTER KEY POINTS

- Physical development includes perceptual and fine and gross motor development.
- Occupational therapy focuses on enhancing fine motor skills development.
- There are many types of physical disabilities that may result in the need for occupational therapy, including visual impairments, cerebral palsy, muscular dystrophy, multiple sclerosis, spina bifida, and amputations.

- Occupational therapists evaluate the level of fine motor skills development by using the "clinical observation" method and formal standardized assessment instruments.
- Occupational therapy focuses on upper-extremity, visual-perceptual, cognitive-adaptive, sensory-integration, and self-care skills
- Occupational therapists assess the need for assistive equipment, fabricate the assistive equipment, and train teachers, parents, and children how to use the equipment.
- Proper seating and positioning of the child are also a focus of occupational therapy.

Previous chapters provided a discussion of intervention services that focused on speech and language and cognitive development. This chapter focuses on fine motor skills development and orthopedic needs of young children with special needs. It provides a description of children who have orthopedic developmental disabilities. It also discusses children who are visually impaired because these children frequently benefit from occupational therapy services. The chapter begins with a brief discussion of general and then specific motor skills development.

Special education includes more than the special education teacher attempting to enhance cognitive skills. Because motor development affects all major areas of development special educator must develop a thorough understanding of motor development and occupational therapy. Special educators must integrate activities designed to enhance motor development to most effectively enhance the development of young children with special needs.

OVERVIEW OF MOTOR DEVELOPMENT

During infancy, the neck and back muscles strengthen, allowing the head to become more mobile and hand and arm movements to become more controlled (Harrison & Kositsky, 1983). After two years the rate of physical developmental change gradually slows compared to the rate from birth through two years (Kalverboer, Hopkins, & Geuze, 1993). This slowing is particularly true in the area of weight gain, which is greatest during the first two years. At about two years children begin to lose the "baby-like" look. Their overall body proportions begin to resemble those of an adult. By the time children turn six, about half as much body fat remains as was found at one year. For example, babies' waists are generally about the same size as their hips. By the age of six, children's waists are smaller than their shoulders and hips. **Fine** and **gross motor development** are the two major classifications of **orthopedic development** (bone and muscle growth). In most cases, fine motor movements require the coordination of gross motor muscles (Bigge, 1991).

Gross Motor Development

At birth, babies are not very muscular and peak muscle growth is not reached until adolescence. Good nutrition during these early years of development is particularly important because muscles, bones, and brain grow the most during this period (Keogh & Sugden, 1985). Gross motor skills include learning how to crawl, stand, jump, walk, and run. These types of skills develop as young bodies become less top-heavy and centers of gravity shift downward toward the trunk. Newborns are capable of moving their arms, legs, and heads, and using the muscles in their mouth for sucking.

Gradually, head movement becomes more mobile and controlled as the neck and back muscles become stronger. The infant's hands and arms gradually come under voluntary control (Fraser & Hensinger, 1983).

At birth the head comprises one-quarter of the body. By two years the head comprises one-fifth, and at adulthood about one-tenth of the total body. As body proportions change, balance improves greatly, aiding children in successfully completing tasks that involve large muscle groups. Learning to walk is one of the most significant gross motor accomplishments of infancy. Initially, children walk with a very wide-footed stance and their arms are held out as if walking a tightrope. Gradually, they begin to stand and walk with their feet closer together as they bring their hands closer to their bodies (Connor, Williamson, & Siepp, 1978).

Fine Motor Development

During infancy, children develop the ability to grasp and manipulate objects (Bigge & Burton, 1989). During the preschool years (two to five years old), fine motor development includes the ability to complete puzzles, build structures out of small blocks, color, cut with scissors, and paste. These skills develop as a result of increased muscle control of the hands and fingers. During the preschool years, children's fine motor skills progressively improve in two areas, the ability to care for their own bodies and to draw and write (Rogers, 1982).

In caring for their bodies during the preschool years, children begin to become more self-sufficient at dressing and feeding themselves. Preschoolers enjoy a new sense of independence because they can care for themselves. The typical three-year-old can independently take care of toilet needs. Most four- and five-year-olds can dress and undress with minimal adult aid. When children are tired or in a hurry, though, they often need help. For example, their shirts may be inside out or buttons unfastened. One of the most difficult self-help task for preschoolers is tying shoe-laces and jacket hoods. This task is usually mastered by six-year-olds. The ability to tie shoes requires a longer attention span, greater memory (cognitive) skills, and more advanced sequencing skills to coordinate the detailed hand movements (motor skills) to complete the task (Espenschade & Eckert, 1980).

OVERVIEW OF OCCUPATIONAL THERAPY

Once a child has been identified as needing early intervention services, occupational therapy may be one of the services provided. An **occupational therapist (OTR)** working in an early intervention program delivers services geared toward acquiring normal motor developmental milestones with the greatest focus on fine motor development.

As the importance of **occupational therapy** has become more widely recognized, further clarification of its role has developed. The following definition that may be understood by nonmedical professionals was adopted in 1986 by the American Occupational Therapy Association (Pratt & Allen, 1989):

> Occupational therapy is the therapeutic use of self-care, work, and play activities to increase independent function, enhance development, and prevent disability. It may include adaption of task or environment to achieve maximum independence and to enhance the quality of life (p. 2)

Description of Occupational Therapists

There are two levels of occupational therapy professionals. A **registered occupational therapist (OTR)** has a minimum of a bachelor's degree and has six to nine months of field work in occupational therapy. The bachelor level OTR may also obtain a master's or doctorate in occupational therapy or a related field. A **certified occupational therapy assistant (COTA)** has an associate's degree and field work in occupational therapy. OTRs and COTAs are required to pass a national registration examination to practice occupational therapy, and most states now require licensing as well.

Some states further require licensed therapists to take courses periodically and attend seminars on occupational therapy to continue to qualify for licensing. This chapter refers to all people providing occupational therapy as occupational therapists (OTRs).

Developmental Areas Addressed by Occupational Therapy

OTRs work with a wide variety of populations including but not limited to those of pediatrics, geriatrics, developmentally disabled, and mental health groups. Within these populations, specific locations at which occupational therapists may provide therapy include schools, nursing homes, day treatment centers, hospitals, and private practice. Occupational therapy is a **holistic profession** that focuses on treating the entire person including the physical, social, and emotional needs (Lerner, Mardell–Czudnowski, & Goldenberg, 1987).

After being told that their child needs occupational therapy, parents often think to themselves, "But my child doesn't need a job." The word *occupation* in the professional title may be misleading for many people. *Occupation,* however, in its broadest sense, includes all areas of daily activity. Bathing, dressing, learning, and working are all included in the term *occupation.* Typically, OTRs who work with children younger than school-age rely on play as the principle teaching strategy. Children who have physical limitations or motor delays that require adaptive equipment typically receive therapy services from OTRs (Bailey & Wolery, 1984).

When working with children in a preschool setting, OTRs generally work in teams with other professionals (Clark & Allen, 1985). These teams could include teachers, physical therapists, social workers, speech and language pathologists, and psychologists. Team members work together to address areas of delay as determined through a formal evaluation of the child (Connolly & Russell, 1978). Table 10.1 lists areas in which OTRs may intervene within an educational setting.

TYPES OF DISABILITIES

There are many reasons why a child might receive occupational therapy. Children with **visual impairments** or who are **mentally retarded** typically have difficulty confidently and safely interacting with the environment and often receive support from OTRs (Dennis, 1960). In addition, several disabilities include motor delays as the primary area of impairment, such as **cerebral palsy, muscular dystrophy, multiple sclerosis, spina bifida,** and **amputation** (Clark & Allen, 1985). These physical disabilities are discussed below, beginning with visual impairments.

Visual Impairments

Children who are visually impaired or blind often need special guidance to function effectively day to day. They often need help learning **self-care**

TABLE 10.1 Areas in which Occupational Therapists May Provide Services

1. Upper-extremity skills—joint range or motion, fine motor manipulation of objects, and coordination.
2. Visual perceptual/visual motor skills—the ability to process visual information successfully.
3. Cognitive/adaptive skills—social, emotional, and educational learning.
4. Miscellaneous, which may include:
   a. splinting/orthotics—aids needed for proper body alignment and function.
   b. adaptive equipment—aids needed for independence in daily living activities.
   c. technology—computer, communication devices, and environmental controls.
   d. seating/positioning—proper body alignment for functioning within the school or home.
   e. sensory integration—the ability to process sensory information (external stimuli) for functional use in all areas of daily activity.
   f. feeding/oral motor—assess and enhance the ability of children to chew and swallow properly.

skills and how to move about in the environment. In many cases, special education teachers and occupational and physical therapists who work with children who are visually impaired receive special training on how to provide services to these children (Winner, 1986).

Infants who are blind and receive occupational therapy services are usually provided such services at home. Therapy focuses on training parents and care providers how to help an infant successfully interact with the environment (Barraga & Erin, 1992).

An infant who is blind typically develops in the same sequence as one who can see but often at a slower rate depending on the skill(s). Although infants who cannot see do not lift their heads to look around, they usually roll over, sit up, and assume a crawling position at about the same age as a baby who can see (Bower, 1977). Children who are blind often hesitate to crawl. They initially rely on touch and then begin using sound for information (Progrund, Frazzi, & Schreier, 1993).

As they learn sound cues, babies begin to crawl, stand, and reach out toward sound cues. Their learning to walk typically occurs at about seventeen to twenty months. Children with sight typically learn to walk between twelve and eighteen months of age. Toddlers who are blind tend to be extremely cautious and require a great deal of encouragement from adults to gain confidence walking (Warren, 1994). Typically, after eighteen months toddlers who are blind may be taught to develop self-help skills at about the same rate as children who are not visually impaired (Bower, 1977).

Children who are blind often rock back and forth, head shake, spin, and poke their fingers into their eyes. As children develop interests and abilities, however, many of these behaviors diminish (Harvey, 1975).

Children who are blind lose interest with sitting and looking activities and instead should be provided with touching, smelling, and listening activities. These children typically need more time to get oriented and to explore. They are more likely to bump into and knock over things. They are usually able to learn to function in preschool programs with children who can see. Table 10.2 provides a list of procedures that may help children who are blind function in a preschool classroom (Ferrell, Trief, Dietz, Bonner, Cruz, Ford, & Statton, 1990).

OTRs often help children with low vision (who generally have substantial use of their vision, particularly with correction glasses or contacts) interact most efficiently with the environment (Miller–Wood, Efron, & Wood, 1990). These children use

TABLE 10.2 Methods to Aid a Young Child Who Is Blind

Ways to help a child who is blind:

1. Encouraging the child to use fingertips while pushing in pieces of a puzzle, searching for and picking up small objects, and exploring objects;
2. Helping the child to understand the symbolic "sameness" of a miniature object and a real object by allowing the child to explore and compare as many aspects of the objects as possible (e.g., comparing a miniature dollhouse chair and a real chair);
3. Emphasizing movements from left to right and top to bottom;
4. Helping the child learn to follow motor directions such as left, right, backward, forward, and turn around, and prepositions such as *under, on, in, out, behind, in front of,* and *in back of;*
5. Modeling how to pretend by getting down on the floor and imitating a dog by barking and letting the child explore the body position by touch;
6. Helping the child learn the physical layout of a room by maintaining consistency in the placement of furniture, equipment, and instructional materials;
7. Eliminating auditory distractions (noise) and making sure that the child clearly hears instructions;
8. Using a "buddy system" by assigning a child with sight to be the buddy for a child who is blind.

their vision as a primary method of learning. Young children should be encouraged to use whatever level of vision they have (Bambring & Troster, 1992). They often require training to use their residual vision. Children's vision may vary or stay the same from day to day and vary from one setting to another (Ayers, 1972).

OTRs help evaluate an environment to suggest possible modifications to help a child who is visually impaired. Such modifications include altering the amount of light, distance, contrast, and colors, which affect how well children process visual information. A high contrast color on a low gloss surface (for instance, a bright painted letter on a wooden block) tends to be the easiest for children with visual impairments to see. Children should be seated where they can see and in a place where there is a minimal amount of glare (Palazesi, 1986).

More than half of the children who are visually impaired have an additional disability. Children's abilities to cope with visual impairments are directly related to their overall cognitive abilities. That is, children with higher than average cognitive abilities more readily compensate for their visual disabilities compared to children with average or below average cognitive abilities.

For children with visual disabilities, teachers should provide learning opportunities in modes other than visual. They should provide classroom structure modifications such as larger pictures. Modifying the seating arrangement for children who are visually impaired affects how well they adjust to their visual impairments. Children with visual impairments often benefit from learning to sharpen their listening skills. They must learn to be attentive and how to focus on communication while screening out background noise. Adults should provide exposure to activities designed to sharpen listening skills (Fraiberg, 1977).

Parents and teachers have a tendency to be overprotective of children with visual impairments (Bower, 1977). Children with visual impairments are capable of dealing with most environments and should be allowed to participate in almost all activities. Such children should be encouraged to actively explore their world and not be overly protected (Bambring & Troster, 1992). Initially, infants who are blind may withdraw when adults interact with them and, over time, increase periods of inactivity. In general, infants who are visually impaired need more stimulation. Adults should focus on touch and hearing rather than on interaction through visual means (Palazesi, 1986).

Cerebral Palsy

Cerebral palsy is a lifelong, irreparable, "non-progressive" disorder resulting from brain damage. It may occur before, during, or after birth. Anoxia, the lack of oxygen to the brain before or during birth, is one of the more common causes for cerebral palsy. Childhood diseases, such as **meningitis, encephalitis,** or influenza, could also result in cerebral palsy. Head injuries that occur from accidents, child abuse, poisoning, such as from lead and carbon monoxide, may also result in cerebral palsy. In about 25 percent of all cases of cerebral palsy the causes are unknown (Finnie, 1975).

Cerebral palsy in the **spastic condition** is when one or more limbs of the body are affected, resulting in jerky or uncontrolled movements. These children can move the affected muscles voluntarily, but the movement is slow and erratic. Movements such as walking and facial expressions are often affected. Children with the **athetosis** form of cerebral palsy walk in a lurching and nonrhythmical manner. These children have difficulty controlling their posture and appear to move constantly (Russman & Gage, 1989). They often squirm or grimace as they try to accomplish voluntary muscular activities.

Children who have **ataxic cerebral palsy** are unsteady in their movements. These children "high step" as they walk and often fall. Tremors and rigidity occur in only a small proportion of children with cerebral palsy. These children often have spontaneous, rhythmic movements. Children with rigidity have stiffness of the joints (Hirst, 1989).

Different groups of muscles are affected in cerebral palsy. Muscles may be affected on only one side of the body, in three of the limbs but not the fourth, in the legs more than the arms, or be affected in both legs or all four extremities. The degree of involvement varies from mild—very little limitation of activity—to severe—almost total incapacity. Most people with cerebral palsy have associated disabilities that affect vision, hearing, speech, perception, and behavior (Robinson, 1973). Therapy provided for children with cerebral palsy typically involves a team approach and an occupational therapist, a physical therapist, and speech therapist (Bleck, 1987).

Muscular Dystrophy

Muscular dystrophy is a class of diseases involving the voluntary muscles. **Duchenne's muscular dystrophy,** sometimes referred to as **pseudohypertrophic muscular dystrophy** or **childhood muscular dystrophy,** usually occurs between two and six years old and affects only boys. Early signs include a "waddle-like" walk, "swayback," difficulty climbing stairs and getting up from the floor, and calf muscle enlargement (Dubowitz, 1978).

Muscular dystrophy of any type is a progressive disease; there is usually no pain associated with it, but there is also no cure. Over time, the muscles gradually deteriorate and these children must use a wheelchair. The small muscles of the hand are usually the last to deteriorate. Therapy includes occupational and physical therapy activities including strengthening unaffected muscles and breathing exercises to help keep the lungs healthy. Sometimes, slings, braces, or other special devices are used. Very young children usually have a limited number of symptoms although they are likely to have difficulty climbing stairs. They may also need to do special exercises. Most individuals die ten to fifteen years after the onset (Brooke, 1986).

Multiple Sclerosis

Multiple sclerosis is a rare degenerative nervous system disease leading to the loss of **myelin,** which covers the nerves. The cause of this disorder is unknown. It is *not* infectious and the course

of the disease is unpredictable. It leads to muscle weakness, loss of coordination, and visual impairment, but does *not* affect intellectual functioning. This disease rarely occurs in children (Pratt & Allen, 1989).

Spina Bifida

Another type of physical disability is spina bifida, a condition in which the spine has not completely closed, resulting in some nerves protruding. It is the most common cause of physical disabilities in children (Williamson, 1987). The condition most often occurs in the lower part of the spine. Below this point on the spine children are partially or completely paralyzed, and they may not have bowel or bladder control. Infants with spina bifida might also have hydrocephalus, water on the brain, which results in too much fluid around the brain (Brooke, 1986).

Spina bifida is a very serious condition usually discovered at birth. Typically, the infant undergoes surgery to close the lesion. If the hydrocephalus does not spontaneously stop then an operation to shunt the excess fluid away from the brain to other parts of the body is done. If the shunt should stop working, the child is likely to become lethargic, complain of headaches, and may vomit. This situation requires immediate medical attention.

Children with spina bifida often need a **prosthesis** to walk. A prosthesis could be braces, crutches, or a walker. A wheelchair may be necessary for moving extended distances. Children with spina bifida should be reminded to change positions frequently while sitting to avoid "pressure sores." They learn to use the upper parts of their body quite well. They can learn to be independent in self-help skills, wheelchair skills, and other activities with the help of an occupational therapist (Williamson, 1987).

Amputations

Amputations, **acquired** and **congenital,** are another cause of physical disabilities. Of acquired amputations, almost 70 percent result from some type of injury; the remaining result from disease. Congenital amputation includes complete or partial absence of one or more limbs. Children born without an arm or a leg typically start wearing a prosthesis when they are between three to six months old (Hale, 1979).

Parents and teachers of children with amputations need to help them adapt to various environments. For example, therapy for a child who lost a leg begins with activities designed to enhance balance and then progresses to walking and developing endurance. After the child learns to move well indoors, the child receives training for independence outdoors, including going to a playground.

Most children can learn to control their prosthesis voluntarily by four or five years old. Because extra concentration is often necessary to control a prosthesis, children are likely to tire more quickly. Children who have an amputation often need occupational or physical therapy designed to help them learn to use the artificial limb. Teachers and parents should also help encourage children to use their new limb while working on other areas of development (Tingey–Michaelis, 1983).

REFERRAL FOR OCCUPATIONAL THERAPY

Before, during, or shortly after the birth of a child, it may be determined that the child has a physical delay that requires an OTR's services. In other cases, it is not until a child is a toddler or attending a daycare or preschool program that motor delays are detected. If a child is already enrolled in a preschool program, referrals for OTR services are usually generated by the child's teacher or other professionals working closely and on a regular basis with the child. If a child is not enrolled in a preschool program, referral sources include pediatricians, public health nurses, other health professionals, or parents.

Various offices oversee and approve the distribution of educationally related services within a school setting. For example, in New York, if a child is two to three years old, therapy services

fall under the regulation of the Department of Health (DOH). When children are three to five years old, the process for receiving therapy services typically begins with a "general screening" completed by an OTR. A screening is usually requested by other teachers or professionals working with the child or parents, and is based on concerns about the child's ability to function in daily activities. Some of these areas include social and play skills, activities of daily living such as eating and washing hands, or pre-academic skills such as pre-writing (tracing shapes and letters) and reading readiness.

The screening assesses whether a full, indepth occupational therapy evaluation is warranted (Rogers, 1982). If a full evaluation is deemed necessary, the school district's Committee on Preschool Special Education (CPSE) is petitioned for approval. If approved, the OTR conducts the evaluation, at which time specific goals are generated for any areas in which delays are detected. These recommendations are then taken back to the CPSE for approval before treatment begins. Once committee approval is obtained, in most cases it is the parent's responsibility to obtain a written prescription from a doctor for specific occupational therapy services. OTRs practicing in New York, as well as in many other states, are required by law to have a written medical prescription before treating any child.

ASSESSMENT OF OCCUPATIONAL THERAPY NEEDS

The stated occupational therapy goals and objectives determined during the initial evaluation become part of the child's **individualized family service plan (IFSP)** (for children less than three years old) or **individualized education program (IEP)** (for children three to five years old). Annual reassessment is done to evaluate changes as they occur in the child's growth and development. Any changes, additions, or deletions of goals are done at the time of the annual evaluation (Malina, 1980). Parental input is also an important part of this process. (Refer to Chapters one and seven for additional information on IFSPs and IEPs.)

There are many ways an OTR may assess a child's level of performance. One of the primary sources of information is **clinical observations.** Clinical observations are objective observations of children in their typical environment, at home or school, while engaged in daily activities. It is through these observations that information is gathered in the areas of muscle tone, range of motion, and social and play skills. Information gathered from the child's teachers and parents is also used in the evaluation process. In addition, OTRs may use formal evaluation tools. An OTR's assessment instruments are listed in Table 10.3.

OVERVIEW OF OCCUPATIONAL THERAPY

As mentioned earlier, occupational therapy intervention is applied to a wide variety of populations and in various settings. Within the pediatric framework, OTRs are involved with children as young as **neonates** (newborns) through twenty-one-year-olds. Pediatric intervention, discussed in this section, is broken down into three phases: infants (birth to two years), pre-schoolers (two to five years), and school-aged children (five years and older).

Controversy surrounds the area of early intervention for infants. It is unclear whether children who are less than one year old experience direct and lasting positive effects from occupational therapy. Early intervention, however, is mandated by law at this time for all children birth to two years old who qualify for services. As Hopkins and Smith (1991) stated, "Statistics have shown that, while 1 to 2 percent of neonates are classified with developmental disabilities, the number of children with identified problems increases to 8 to 9 percent by school age and 11 to 12 percent if estimates of preschoolers with significant developmental problems are included" (p. 99).

The main goal of occupational therapy treatment is to enhance a child's daily experiences. This goal is accomplished through direct treatment, fabrication of equipment as needed, such as hand-splinting, and through environmental adaptation if necessary. OTRs focus on enhancing a

TABLE 10.3 Assessment Instruments Used by an OTR

1. Peabody Developmental Scales—These scales provide measurement guidelines for fine and gross motor skills from birth to seven years old. Occupational therapists generally administer only the fine motor component of the assessment. The fine motor component is broken down into the areas of grasp, hand use, eye–hand coordination, and manual dexterity. This information is then compiled to reveal an age equivalence of performance.
2. Motor Free Visual Perception Test (MVPT)—This instrument assesses perceptual skills that do not require hand use on the part of the child. The child is shown various geometric designs and is asked to identify the correct matching response from a set of four choices. Areas of assessment are visual discrimination, visual matching, and visual memory.
3. Developmental Test of Visual Motor Integration (Beery)—This test assesses functioning in the area of visual motor development with a focus on pre-kindergarten to kindergarten-aged children. The child is asked to duplicate on paper various designs presented. Designs progress from copying a simple vertical line to more complex overlapping designs. The areas of visual perception and motor coordination are emphasized.

child's ability to be independent (Fredrick & Fletcher, 1985).

One of the main areas of emphasis of occupational therapy treatment for children is upper-extremity functional skills, such as the ability to hold a rattle or bang two blocks together (Trombly, 1983). Included in the treatment of upper-extremity skills is the enhancement of a child's ability to interact with the environment. **Postural stability** and control, such as remaining upright against the force of gravity when sitting, is another upper-extremity skill that may be strengthened during therapy. In addition, independence in self-care skills, such as bringing objects to the mouth to self-feed, are included in upper-extremity skills therapy (Morris, 1977).

At birth, children have several **primitive reflexes.** These reflexes are movement patterns governing dominating upper-extremity movement. These are called **obligatory** (involuntary) movements and control a child's movement and block the ability to move voluntarily. Between the ages of four and six months, these primitive reflexes begin to become integrated, or become **nonobligatory** (voluntary). At this point, children typically begin to develop purposeful body movements, such as rolling from side to side, reaching, grasping, and releasing objects (Copeland, 1982).

Typically, inborn reflexes such as sucking or grasping gradually disappear from a child's repertoire. If these primitive reflex patterns do not become integrated at an early age, therapeutic intervention may be recommended by the child's pediatrician or another professional (Levy, 1974). Occupational therapy intervention at this time includes assisting or facilitating a child to move through specific motor developmental stages, as well as assisting in educating family members about methods to enhance a child's development through proper positioning and play activities at home (Jaeger, 1987; 1989).

As children mature and begin to learn by exploring the environment, other aspects of development can then be assessed. The refinement of precise prehension (grasp) and manipulation skills may then be monitored. **Bilateral manipulation skills,** meticulously using two hands together, develop and ultimately enable children to perform functional skills, such as passing a toy back and forth between two hands, and more complex skills, such as tying shoes. The preferred use of a dominant hand also begins to emerge between age two to three years.

SPECIFIC GOALS OF OCCUPATIONAL THERAPY INTERVENTION

There are several specific areas in which OTRs provide therapy. They are discussed in the following section and include development of **upper-extremity proximal stability, visual-perceptual, cognitive-adaptive, sensory integration,** and **self-care skills** (Bundy, 1991). OTRs also help evaluate, design, and fabricate **assistive equipment,** determine appropriate seating and positioning, and evaluate the environment to determine the need for possible modifications (Frostig, 1974).

Upper-Extremity Proximal Stability

Upper-extremity proximal stability refers to the level of stability (firmness), ranging from children's trunk and shoulders (proximal) throughout the arms to the hands (distal). Proximal stability is believed to be the foundation on which hand skills may develop. Proximal stability assists children in sitting upright, which allows them to participate in tabletop activities (Frostig, 1974).

Because of the importance of proximal stability, the OTR often places children on various pieces of therapy equipment, such as bolsters or scooter boards, to enhance proximal stability. Working the trunk and upper body through exercises and activities is thought to promote improved proximal stability and distal hand skills (use of fingers for fine motor manipulation) for use in all areas of education and daily life (Larsen & Hammill, 1975).

Visual-Perceptual Motor Skills

Visual-perceptual motor skills are another area of emphasis in occupational therapy. These skills refer to children's physical responses to visual stimulation. Such skills are later used for activities such as reading from left to right or copying from the blackboard. During occupational therapy treatment, the OTR introduces activities that begin to challenge a child's visual-perceptual performance skills. Activities such as finding hidden pictures (figure/ground), bingo and lotto (visual scanning), concentration or memory card games (visual memory and matching), and block design replication (visual-spatial relations) address different aspects within the area of visual-perceptual motor skills.

Cognitive-Adaptive Skills

Cognitive-adaptive skills are another area of focus in occupational therapy. These skills include a child's ability (cognitively, emotionally, and physically) to interact with others and adapt to different environmental situations such as going to a new classroom, adjusting to rearrangement of the classroom, and adjusting to new teachers.

OTRs work with family members and teaching staff to assess skills acquisition and formulate and present activities designed to enhance growth and development in this area. Some of the elements assessed in cognitive-adaptive skills include how children interact with peers and adults in one-to-one or group situations, whether they play or sit with peers or prefer to play alone, how they respond to reinforcement or discipline, and how well they can solve problems and adapt to new people and situations.

Sensory-Integration Skills

Another area of development an OTR addresses is sensory integration. Sensory integration involves a child's ability to incorporate sensory information into purposeful and successful interaction with the environment. Sensory information is interpreted by all the senses including touch (tactile system), sight (visual system), hearing (auditory system), smell (olfactory system), and balance or equilibrium (vestibular system) (Ayers, 1972).

Sensorimotor skills acquisition is based on a child's ability to integrate and process sensory information to elicit a physical response to the environment. Sensory integration and processing is a complex function of the nervous system. Imbalances or dysfunctions in any of these systems may result in sensory integration difficulties (Cherry, 1971). For instance, the impaired ability to visually scan the environment successfully or process tactile information correctly may result in a child lacking the ability to move about safely at home or school.

Children could have sensory integration difficulties for a variety of reasons. Children who have cerebral palsy, are classified as cognitively delayed, and are autistic frequently have sensory integration difficulties. Indicators of sensory integration difficulties include over or undersensitivity to movement or physical contact, abnormally high or low activity levels, difficulty learning new motor tasks, and delays in language acquisition or cognitive abilities (Ayers, 1972).

To enhance **sensory processing,** the OTR structures specific activities needed to address the areas of dysfunction. These activities expose children to sensory tasks they may choose to avoid. Sensory activities include playing in gelatin or with shaving cream and locating objects in rice at the **sensory table.** (See Chapter 12 for a detailed discussion on the use of a sensory table.) During these types of activities, children are not forced to participate but may be encouraged and assisted while attempting the task. Sensory integration enhances the nervous system in organizing and interpreting sensory input to enhance the effectiveness of motor output (Ayers, 1972).

In a therapy setting, the OTR might guide "scissor skills" development by helping children develop an appropriate grasp, which enhances eye–hand coordination. Other activities the OTR uses include blowing bubbles and encouraging children to pop them, playing with puzzles, stringing beads, and stacking blocks. These activities are also designed to enhance eye–hand coordination (Ayers, 1972).

Self-Care Skills

Another area of occupational therapy intervention is self-care skills, such as eating, getting dressed, using the toilet, and bathing. Occupational therapy deals with self-feeding, the hand-to-mouth action of eating. It also deals with eating, including chewing and swallowing, which involves functions and dysfunctions of the oral musculature (muscles). OTRs also focus on the relationship of the swallowing mechanisms to the various textures of food (Hotte, 1979).

Although OTRs often provide treatment in the areas of feeding, in many educational programs or clinics oral motor functioning is an area of specialization for speech and language pathologists. In this case, the OTR and speech and language pathologist address feeding dysfunctions as a team because self-feeding is an area of adaptation rather than remediation. The OTR often plays an active role in obtaining any adaptive equipment that is needed. For example, assistive equipment may include "built-up" utensils (thicker than normal) and spill-proof cups. The OTR focuses on proper positions that help children to function well while sitting. Appropriate positioning is crucial for promoting eating skills and helping to prevent choking. The OTR also provides recommendations about the types of foods that are safe for children to eat without choking.

If a child is experiencing feeding difficulties, the OTR working with the child offers suggestions regarding the mealtime experience based on the individual needs of the child. These recommendations are based on tests that have been completed, as well as clinical observations (Trombly, 1983). The child's OTR often provides a program of therapeutic techniques for the parents or caregivers to use at home. Table 10.4 provides a list of some eating difficulties children with motor impairment may exhibit and for which therapy may be effective (Stern & Gorga, 1990).

An OTR works with parents and staff to help a child develop other self-care skills. Children with disabilities frequently take longer to dress and undress. A therapist may suggest routines and help to establish a time to work on developing self-care skills. Dressing requires a great deal of muscle coordination. It also requires balance and control of muscle tension (Eastman & Safron, 1986). The OTR frequently provides guidance on how to help a child relax and best position a child before dressing the child or helping the child get dressed. The OTR might also provide suggestions

TABLE 10.4 Eating Difficulties that May Be Helped by Therapy

1. Diminished head and trunk control;
2. Oral hyper- or hypo-sensitivity to stimulation;
3. Jaw thrust—a strong protrusion of the lower jaw;
4. Tongue thrust—forceful protrusion of the tongue when sucking, spoon- feeding, chewing, or drinking from a cup;
5. Tonic bite reflex—a forceful closing of the jaw on stimulation to the teeth and gums (hypersensitivity);
6. Lip retraction (called purse string)—extension of the lips into a tight horizontal line;
7. Tongue retraction—a strong pulling back of the tongue into the throat (the pharynx), where it is held against the palate;
8. Jaw retraction—the jaw is pulled back, preventing the alignment of the upper and lower teeth during feeding;
9. Weak or inefficient sucking patterns.
10. Poor lip closure—needed to remove food from a spoon;
11. Poor tongue lateralization—the inability to move food adequately inside the mouth from side to side;
12. Poor chewing technique;
13. Excessive mucus or saliva secretions.

about the type of clothing best suited for self-care (Pratt & Allen, 1989).

USE OF ADAPTIVE EQUIPMENT

The OTR actively observes a child's environment to assess the need for adaptive equipment. This includes anything that might be used to adapt or enhance the ability of the child to be more independent (Fredrick & Fletcher, 1985). Adaptive equipment is sought only after it is determined that the child cannot perform tasks independently without adaptive equipment.

The main focus and goal in using adaptive equipment is to help a child function within the environment. The next section provides a description of some of the types of adaptive equipment available. Because of the vast number of skill areas needed for equipment, it is impossible to list all the equipment commercially available or developed by therapists.

Use of Technology and Switches

For children with special needs who have a limited ability to access their environment independently, many forms of technology are available. For a child with decreased upper-extremity skills, battery-operated toys are now adapted to allow for single switch activation. OTRs often incorporate the use of switches in their treatment sessions. **Switches** are devices that enable a child with physical disabilities to activate battery-operated objects such as equipment, toys, or radios (Esposito & Campbell, 1993; Mistrett, Raimondi, & Barnett, 1990; McMurray, 1986).

A multitude of switch types are available from commercial manufacturers. Also, many switch types may be fabricated by family members or therapists for use with toys. Switch activation has opened up a new world for children who have special needs. These children now have the opportunity to develop more independence in play activities, access computer programs, and have the ability to activate a speech communication system. All of these opportunities allow children with special needs to expand their knowledge, skills, and interaction with others and the environment. For children who have severe physical disabilities, special switches are often used to control power wheelchairs that may allow independence in mobility (Landecker, 1980).

Proper positioning of a child (how the child should sit, stand, or lie) and the need for switches are evaluated by an OTR. Various types of switches can be used so that a child with decreased upper-extremity skills can independently access the same types of toys children without upper-extremity weakness use. Many catalogs are available offering a full range of switches and access devices. Parental input concerning a child's capability to function at home with the various switches may provide the therapist with essential information needed for recommending the appropriate switches (Bleck & Nagel, 1982).

Other Adaptive Equipment

To help children learn to dress independently, adapting the environment may be as simple as changing the type of clothing they wear. For instance, buttons and zippers often are particularly challenging for a child. Therefore, clothes with elastic waist bands, slightly oversized clothes, front rather than back openings or pullover shirts with loosely woven neck openings might be recommended. Velcro closures are particularly useful for facilitating independent dressing. Equipment that helps encourage independent dressing includes button hooks, long-handled extenders, and shoe horns (Bleck, 1987).

Bathing a child is often a concern for parents and caregivers. The OTR may recommend that the bathtub be equipped with a nonslip surface or mat inside and out to help prevent falls. Grab bars secured to the walls might also be recommended for children who require assistance moving in and out of the bathtub (Lazzaro, 1993). Other pieces of equipment could include long-handled sponges, bath mitts (used with children with limited grasp ability), and hand-held shower extensions (Butera & Haywood, 1992).

Using the toilet frequently requires adaptive equipment for children who have motor delays. Many different types of toilet seats are available, for instance. Children who have poor balance and trunk control may require a seat with handle bars on either side to help keep them from falling. For a child in a wheelchair, the height of a toilet seat often needs to be modified. These types of issues are best addressed by having the OTR visit the home or classroom. These visits provide an opportunity for the OTR to determine the most useful adaptive equipment, to demonstrate how to use the equipment, and to give information on how to aid a child without injuring the child or oneself (Cannings & Finkel, 1993).

Feeding skills frequently require the OTR to provide recommendations for adaptive equipment. Many factors may interfere with a child's successful self-feeding. The type of adaptive equipment a therapist chooses depends on the nature of the problem the child demonstrates. For example, a suspension sling, or mobile arm supports, could be used to assist in arm placement during mealtime. Various types of splints can be used to correct the position of the hands or arms. Universal cuffs or utensils with built-up or modified handles might be used to accommodate a weak or absent grasp. Extended handles and swivel spoons can be used for children with limited motion abilities in the arms and hands. A nonslip mat, plate guard, and scoop dishes are often beneficial in assisting children to eat and decreasing the amount of spilled food.

These aids are also helpful for enhancing children's ability to feed themselves using only one hand (Carney, 1983). For children who are severely physically disabled, battery-powered self-feeding devices may be used. Again, the OTR assists in choosing and teaching the proper use of feeding equipment that is needed to enhance a child's ability to become more independent.

The Use of Splints

The terms **orthotics** and **splints** are often used interchangeably, especially in reference to the upper-body extremities. While the professional who is responsible for fabricating children's splints vary among facilities, OTRs are typically responsible for recommendations regarding upper-extremity splinting. Many splints are custom-designed, constructed, fitted, and applied within one to two hours (Meisels & Shonkoff, 1990).

Various types of plastics are usually used to fabricate splints. Two types are high- and low-temperature thermoplastics. The low temperature plastics OTRs normally have access to at a clinic are considered somewhat less durable than the high-temperature laminated plastics professional manufacturers use. There is also a difference in cost. High temperature laminated plastics are usually much more expensive. Splints fabricated by the OTR can also frequently be remolded or adapted to address children's growth and changing needs. Splints are a part of children's overall therapy programs and should be continually monitored (Male, 1994).

The two primary types of splints are **static** (stationary) and **dynamic** (moving). Static splints have no moving parts and hold a portion of the upper extremity in an immobilized (functional) position to prevent contracture (bending). Dynamic splints have moving parts and support the involved portion of the upper extremity in a functional position while allowing a range of motion for the muscles. Reasons for using splints include preventing deformity, supporting, protecting and immobilizing joints, and correcting an existing deformity. Some splints are also fitted with attachments of specialized devices designed to aid in enhancing a child's level of independence.

On receiving a new splint, the OTR formulates specific directions for maintaining and wearing the device. Specific wearing times for a splint should be stated in writing. Written instructions should also include an exercise program for when the splint is *not* worn. General care of the splint should also be explained or stated in writing. It is important that the parents and daycare providers be well educated about the proper use of a splint, and parents and therapists should regularly communicate with each other. As with most forms of treatment, the OTR requires a doctor's prescription to fabricate a splint for a child.

Other Environmental Modifications

An OTR recommends ways to adapt the environment to the child's needs, such as accessible bathrooms, drinking fountains, and play materials to encourage independence. An OTR provides an analysis of rooms to determine if they are set up in a way that allows free movement of children in wheelchairs or who have braces. For children with limited muscle strength, the OTR would make certain that shelves are strong enough for these children to pull up on or lean against. The OTR should help select toys and other equipment designed to encourage exploration and learning that are developmentally appropriate (Ysseldyke, Algozzine, & Thorlow, 1992).

THE IMPORTANCE OF SEATING AND POSITIONING

The proper seating and positioning of children are of prime importance and have a major effect on how well they can interact with the environment. Bergen (1990) suggests that proper seating and positioning have the potential to provide several benefits for children with physical disabilities:

1. Normalize or decrease abnormal neurological influences on the body;
2. Increase range of motion (passive and active), maintain neutral skeletal alignment and control, and prevent muscle contracture;
3. Manage pressure and prevent or decrease the potential for skin sores;
4. Upgrade stability to enhance function;
5. Promote increased tolerance of desired position (comfort);
6. Enhance functioning of the autonomic nervous system;
7. Decrease fatigue;
8. Facilitate components of normal movement in the developmental sequence;
9. Provide maximum function with minimum pathology.

The optimum seating positions for children are a straight trunk (back), hips, knees, and the ankles flexed to 90 degrees, the legs abducted (separated), and the feet supported, not dangling. It is important that the parent or caregiver and therapist work together to develop an appropriate seating system. Physical therapists and speech and language pathologists are involved in the process because proper positioning affects children's speech development. An equipment vendor may also assist by presenting the current seating items

available through commercial manufacturers (Male, 1994).

Funding for assistive equipment is often a critical issue. Families may have insurance that provides coverage for purchased or rented equipment. Funding might also be available through the child's school or an agency providing services for the child. There may also be special funding programs available that a social worker or other personnel can help identify (Male, 1994).

Once a decision has been made regarding a proper seating system, the OTR usually writes a letter of justification that is sent to the funding source. This letter states why the child needs a particular seating system. Seating systems include wheelchairs, other types of chairs or support systems, and positioning aids. A product called a "tri-wall" may be used by the OTR to construct a piece of positioning equipment. Tri-wall is triple thick cardboard that comes in large sheets. It is a more economical way to provide assistive equipment. However, it is usually less durable than manufactured equipment. Because children grow so rapidly, tri-wall is used to keep the cost of changing equipment needs to a minimum. The OTR can fabricate seating aids for strollers, car seats, or other items a child may need (Lazzaro, 1993).

CONCLUSION

For children with motor disabilities, OTRs are often an integral part of a service team in an educational setting. While there is a desirable overlap among professionals, each discipline plays a critical role in the overall treatment of such children. Like physical therapists, OTRs are concerned with sensorimotor development but focus more on fine motor rather than gross motor development. OTRs work with children in a holistic way to enhance function and independence while promoting a positive sense of self through purposeful activity and environmental adaptation.

When working with young children, the trend in method of providing therapy is moving toward the OTR working side-by-side with the teachers in the classroom or parents at home rather than working one-on-one with a child in a therapy room. The goal is to integrate therapy into the daily routine of children, which is often done through play. This method allows parents and staff to learn how to provide activities that enhance motor development. OTRs should be involved in ongoing staff training in the area of fine motor skills development.

The OTR is sensitive to the cognitive skills level of each child and introduces only those activities likely to provide a child with a feeling of success while challenging the child to enhance the child's overall development. The OTR also offers suggestions for carryover (generalization) of these skills by the classroom staff, other therapists, and parents. Carryover is critical for acquiring these skills because repetition helps raise the likelihood of successful skills acquisition and because the OTR is only with a child for a limited amount of time.

The next chapter focuses on motor development as well. Its focus is on gross motor development and the role of the physical therapist who provides early intervention services. Often occupational and physical therapists work in collaboration.

CHAPTER SUMMARY

- Occupational therapy goals include restoring, reinforcing, and enhancing motor performance.
- Types of physical disabilities that often require occupational therapy include visual impairments, cerebral palsy, muscular dystrophy, multiple sclerosis, spina bifida, and amputations.
- The OTR assesses a child's level of functioning by observing the child in typical daily activities and using standardized formal assessment instruments.
- OTRs provide therapy in the upper extremities, perceptual-visual motor-skills, and cognitive-adaptive skills.
- OTRs assess the need for adaptive equipment to help a child who has motor function impairments.

- Proper seating and positioning of the child helps decrease abnormal neurological influences on the body, increase range of motion, manage pressure, decrease fatigue, and enhance autonomic nervous system functioning.

REVIEW QUESTIONS

1. What types of services does the OTR provide?
2. What are common feeding difficulties a child might have? How may an OTR treat these disabilities?
3. What are the various types of assistive equipment OTRs may recommend?
4. Why do OTRs provide therapy within the young child's normal daily environment?

SUGGESTED STUDENT ACTIVITIES

1. Visit a local early childhood special education program and observe an OTR providing therapy services.
2. Review the formal assessment instruments listed in this chapter. Describe their purposes, strengths, and weaknesses.
3. Observe an OTR fabricate a piece of assistive equipment. Ask how it would be used and have the OTR describe how the child and parents would be trained for its proper use.
4. Observe a young child with motor delays and analyze the environment. Determine what environmental adaptation(s) may aid the child.

ADDITIONAL READINGS

Peck, C. B., Odom, S. L., & Bricker, D. D. (1993). *Integrating young children with disabilities into community programs: Ecological perspectives on research and implementation.* Baltimore, MD: Paul H. Brookes.

Rainforth, B., York, J., & Macdonald, C. (1992). *Collaborative teams for students with severe disabilities: Integrating therapy and educational services.* Baltimore, MD: Paul H. Brookes.

Schleickorn, J. (1993). *Coping with cerebral palsy: Answers to questions parents often ask* (2nd ed.). Austin, TX: Pro-Ed.

ADDITIONAL RESOURCES

American Academy of Cerebral Palsy and Developmental Medicine
2315 Westport Avenue
P.O. Box 11083
Richmond, VA 23230

American Council of the Blind
1155 15th Street, N.W., Suite 720
Washington, DC 20005

American Foundation for the Blind
15 W. 16th Street
New York, NY 10011

American Occupational Therapy Association
1383 Piccard Drive, Suite 301
Rockville, MD 20850

American Orthopsychiatric Association
1775 Broadway
New York, NY 10019

Associated Services for the Blind
919 Walnut Street
Philadelphia, PA 19107

Association for Education and Rehabilitation of the Blind and Visually Impaired
206 N. Washington Street, Suite 320
Alexandria, VA 22314

Association for the Severely Handicapped
7010 Roosevelt Way, N.E.
Seattle, WA 98115

Division for the Visually Handicapped
Council for Exceptional Children
1920 Association Drive
Reston, VA 22091

International Institute for the Visually Impaired
1975 Rutgers Street
East Lansing, MI 48823

March of Dimes Birth Defects Foundation
1275 Mamaroneck Avenue
White Plains, NY 10605

Muscular Dystrophy Association
810 Seventh Avenue
New York, NY 10019

National Association for Parents of the Visually Impaired
2180 Linway Drive
Beloit, WI 53511

National Association for the Visually Handicapped
22 W. 21st Street
New York, NY 10017

National Council on Disability
800 Independence Avenue, S.W., Suite 814
Washington, DC 20591

Neurodevelopmental Therapy Association, Inc.
P.O. Box 70
Oak Park, IL 60303

Sensory Integration International
1402 Cravens Avenue
Torrance, CA 90501

Spina Bifida Association of America
3443 S. Dearborn, Suite 317
Chicago, IL 60604

United Cerebral Palsy Association, Inc.
66 E. 34th Street
New York, NY 10016

REFERENCES

Ayers, J. (1972). *Sensory integration and learning disorders.* Los Angeles: Western Psychological Services.

Bailey, D. B., & Wolery, M. (1984). *Teaching infants and preschoolers with handicaps.* Columbus, OH: Merrill.

Bambring, M., & Troster, H. (1992). On the stability of stereotyped behaviors in blind infants and preschoolers. *Journal of Visual Impairments and Blindness, 86*(2), 105–110.

Barraga, N. C., & Erin, J. N. (1992). *Visual handicaps and learning* (3rd ed.). Austin, TX: Pro-Ed.

Bergen, A. F. (1990). *Positioning for function.* Valhalla, NY: Valhalla Rehabilitation Publications.

Bigge, J. L. (1991). *Teaching individuals with physical and multiple disabilities* (3rd ed.). New York: Macmillan.

Bigge, R. A., & Burton, E. C. (1989). *The dynamic infant.* St. Paul, MN: Toys 'n Things.

Bleck, E. (1987). *Orthopedic management in cerebral palsy.* Philadelphia: J. B. Lippincott.

Bleck, E., & Nagel, D. A. (1982). *Physically handicapped children: A medical atlas for teachers* (2nd ed.). New York: Grune and Stratton.

Bower, T. J. P. (1977). Blind babies see with their ears. *New Scientist, 73,* 255–257.

Brooke, M. H. (1986). *A clinician's view of neuromuscular disease* (2nd ed.). Baltimore, MD: Williams and Wilkins.

Bundy, A. C. (1991). Play theory and sensory integration. In A. G. Fisher, E. A. Murray, & A. C. Bundy (Eds.), *Sensory integration: Theory and practice.* (pp. 96–112). Philadelphia: F. A. Davis.

Butera, G., & Haywood, H. C. (1992). A cognitive approach to the education of young children with autism. *Focus on Autistic Behavior, 6*(6), 1–14.

Cannings, T. R., & Finkel, L. (1993). *The technology age classroom.* Wilsonville, OR: Franklin, Beedle & Associates.

Carney, I. H. (1983). Services for families of severely handicapped preschool students: Assumptions and implications. *Journal of the Division for Early Childhood, 7,* 78–85.

Cherry, C. (1971). *Creative movement for the developing child.* Belmont, CA: Lear Sigler/Fearon Pittman.

Clark, P. N., & Allen, A. S. (1985). *O.T. For Children.* St. Louis: C. V. Mosby.

Connolly, B., & Russell, F. (1978). Interdisciplinary early intervention programs. *Physical Therapy, 56,* 155–158.

Connor, F., Williamson, G. G., & Siepp, J. (1978). *Program guide for infants and toddlers with neuromotor and other developmental disabilities.* New York: Teachers College Press.

Copeland, M. E. (1982). Development of motor skills and the management of common problems. In K. E. Allen & E. M. Goetz (Eds.), *Early childhood education: Special problems, special solutions.* (pp. 230–249). Rockville, MD: Aspen.

Dennis, W. (1960). Causes of retardation among institutionalized children: In Iran. *Journal of Genetic Psychology, 96,* 47–59.

Dubowitz, V. (1978). *Muscle disorders in childhood.* Philadelphia: W. B. Saunders.

Eastman, M. K., & Safron, J. S. (1986). Activities to develop your students' motor skills. *Teaching Exceptional Children, 19,* 24–27.

Espenschade, A., & Eckert, H. (1980). Motor development. Columbus, OH: Merrill.

Esposito, L., & Campbell, P. H. (1993). Computers and physically and severely handicapped. In J. Lindsey (Ed.), *Computers and exceptional individuals* (rev. ed., pp. 105–124). Columbus, OH: Merrill/Macmillan.

Ferrell, K. A., Trief, E., Dietz, S. J., Bonner, M. A., Cruz, D., Ford, E., & Statton, J. M. (1990). Visually impaired infants. Research consortium (VII RC): First year results. *Journal of Visual Impairments and Blindness, 84*(10), 404–410.

Finnie, N. R. (1975). *Handling the young cerebral palsied child at home* (2nd ed.). New York: Dutton.

Fraiberg, S. (1977). *Insight from the blind.* New York: Basic Books.

Fraser, B. A., & Hensinger, R. N. (1983). *Managing physical handicaps.* Baltimore, MD: Paul H. Brookes.

Fredrick, J., & Fletcher, D. (1985). Facilitating children's adjustment to orthotic and prosthetic appliances. *Teaching Exceptional Children, 17,* 228–230.

Frostig, M. (1974). *Movement education, its theory and practice.* Workshop presented at the Marianne Frostig Center of Educational Therapy, Los Angeles.

Hale, G. (1979). *The source book for the disabled.* London: Imprint Books.

Harrison, H., & Kositsky, A. (1983). *The premature baby book: A parent's guide to coping and caring in the first years.* New York: St. Martin's Press.

Harvey, B. (1975). Why are they blind? *Sight Saving Review, 45*(1), 3–22.

Hirst, M. (1989). Patterns of impairment and disability related to social handicap in young people with cerebral palsy and spina bifida. *Journal of Biosocial Science, 21,* 1–12.

Hopkins, H., & Smith, H. (Eds.). (1991). Willard and Spackman's occupational therapy. Philadelphia: Lippincott.

Hotte, E. B. (1979). *Self-help clothing for children who have physical disabilities.* Chicago: National Easter Seals Society for Crippled Children and Adults.

Jaeger, D. L. (1987). *Home program instruction sheets for infants and young children.* Tucson, AZ: Communication and Therapy Skill Builders.

Jaeger, D. L. (1989). *Transferring and lifting children and adolescents: Home instruction sheets.* Tucson, AZ: Communication and Therapy Skill Builders.

Kalverboer, A. F., Hopkins, B., & Geuze, R. (1993). *Motor development in early and later childhood.* NY: Cambridge University Press.

Keogh, J., & Sugden, D. (1985). *Movement skill development.* New York: Macmillan.

Landecker, A. W. (1980). Lifting and carrying. In J. Unbreit & P. J. Cardullias (Eds.), *Educating the severely physically handicapped: Basic principles and techniques.* (pp. 33–60). Columbus, OH: Special Press.

Larsen, S., & Hammill, D. (1975). The relationship of selected visual perceptual skills to academic abilities. *Journal of Special Education, 9,* 281–291.

Lazzaro, J. J. (1993). *Adaptive technologies for learning and work environments.* Washington, DC: American Library Association.

Lerner, J., Mardell–Czudnowski, C., & Goldenberg, D. (1987). *Special education for the early childhood years.* Englewood Cliffs, NJ: Prentice-Hall.

Levy, J. (1974). *The baby exercise book.* New York: Pantheon Books.

Male, M. (1994). *Technology for inclusion: Meeting the special needs of all students.* Boston: Allyn & Bacon.

Malina, R. M. (1980). Biological correlates of motor development during infancy and early childhood. In L. S. Green & F. E. Johnstone (Eds.), *Social and biological predictors of nutritional status, physical growth and neurological development.* (pp. 102–139). New York: Academic Press.

McMurray, G. L. (1986). Easing everyday living: Technology for the physically disabled. In A. Gatner & T. Joe (Eds.), *Images of disabled/disabling images.* New York: Praeger.

Meisels, S., & Shonkoff, J. P. (Eds.). (1990). *Handbook of early intervention.* New York: Cambridge University Press.

Miller–Wood, D. J., Efron, M., & Wood, T. A. (1990). Use of closed-circuit television with a severely visually impaired young child. *Journal of Visual Impairment and Blindness, 84*(12), 559–564.

Mistrett, S. G., Raimondi, S. L., & Barnett, M. P. (1990). *The use of technology with preschoolers with handicaps.* Buffalo, NY: Preschool Integration Through Technology Systems.

Morris, S. E. (1977). *Program guidelines for children with feeding problems.* Edison, NJ: Childcraft Education.

Palazesi, M. A. (1986). The need for motor development programs for visually impaired preschoolers. *Journal of Visual Impairment and Blindness, 80,* 573–576.

Pratt, P. N., & Allen, A. S. (1989). *Occupational therapy for children* (2nd ed.). St. Louis: C. V. Mosby.

Progrund, R. L., Frazzi, D. I., & Schreier, F. M. (1993). Development of a preschool "Kiddy Lane." *Journal of Visual Impairment and Blindness, 86,* 52–54.

Robinson, R. O. (1973). The frequency of other handicaps in children with cerebral palsy. *Developmental Medicine and Child Neurology, 15,* 305–312.

Rogers, S. J. (1982). Assessment considerations with the motor-handicapped child. In G. Ulrey & S. Rogers (Eds.), *Psychological assessment of handicapped infants and young children.* (pp. 13–40). New York: Thieme-Stratton.

Russman, B. S., & Gage, J. R. (1989). Cerebral palsy. *Current Problems in Pediatrics, 19,* 65–111.

Stern, F. M., & Gorga, D. G. (1990). Neurodevelopmental treatment (NDT): Therapeutic intervention and its efficacy. *Infants and Young Children, 1*(1), 22–32.

Tingey-Michaelis, C. (1983). *Handicapped infants and children: A handbook for parents and professionals.* Baltimore, MD: University Park Press.

Trombly, C. A. (Ed.). (1983). *Occupational therapy for physical dysfunction* (2nd ed.). Baltimore, MD: Williams and Wilkins.

Warren, D. H. (1994). *Blindness and children: An individual differences approach.* NY: Cambridge University Press.

Williamson, G. G. (1987). *Children with spina bifida: Early intervention and preschool programming.* Baltimore, MD: Paul H. Brookes.

Winner, E. (1986). Where pelicans kiss seals. *Psychology Today, 20*(8), 25–35.

Ysseldyke, J. E., Algozzine, B., & Thorlow, M. (1992). *Critical issues in special education.* Boston: Houghton Mifflin.

CHAPTER 11

PHYSICAL THERAPY SERVICES

SUZANNE J. WARD, P.T., B.S.
LINDA G. SETO, M.S.

ABOUT THE AUTHORS

Suzanne Ward is a licensed physical therapist certified in neuro-developmental treatment techniques. She received her bachelor's degree from Ithaca College, in Ithaca, New York. She has taken extensive continuing education courses specializing in physical therapy for young children. Ms. Ward is presently employed by the Saint Francis Hospital Preschool Program in Poughkeepsie, New York, where she provides physical therapy for children two to five years old. She also works as a consultant for the Dutchess County Department of Health Early Intervention Program, providing services to children from infancy through school age. Ms. Ward also has experience providing physical therapy services to school-age children. She is married and has two boys, Andrew and Daniel.

Linda Seto received a bachelor of arts in psychology and a master's in special education from the State University of New York at Albany, in Albany, New York. She is a special education teacher in the Saint Francis Hospital Preschool Program. She has been a teacher of preschoolers with special needs for more than ten years. She also works as a teacher of adults with special needs attending an adult recreation program. She is married and has a daughter, Rebecca, who has developmental delays.

CHAPTER KEY POINTS

- Physical therapists help develop total body muscle function by treating posture and movement disorders that primarily involve gross motor skills.
- Assessing gross motor skills includes evaluating musculoskeletal status, which includes muscle tone and functional gross motor abilities.

- The two approaches to therapy are developmental (bottom-up) and top-down models.
- Therapy involves physical therapy teachers and childcare providers working together by integrating therapy services into normal daily activities.

As discussed in previous chapters, physical development is one of several areas in which children could have developmental delays. **Physical therapy** focuses intervention on gross motor skills whereas occupational therapy (discussed in Chapter 10) focuses on fine motor skills. Clearly, physical and occupational therapy are closely related, and often therapists within these two disciplines work in collaboration (Beller, 1979). This chapter focuses on gross motor physical development and describes the role of the physical therapist (PT) and methods of intervention for young children, birth through six years old, who have gross motor delays.

Gross motor development affects all other areas of development. Special educators must develop an understanding of gross motor development and should integrate activities designed to enhance gross motor development into the curriculum for young children with special needs.

OVERVIEW OF PHYSICAL THERAPY

Physical therapists (PTs) are health professionals whose goal is to help people develop total body muscle control. PTs receive training in evaluating and treating posture and movement disorders and have a bachelor's or master's degree in physical therapy (Frostig & Maslow, 1970). A PT might also be certified in **neuro-developmental treatment techniques (NDT),** which requires additional training specifically focused on physical therapy for children (Zaichkowsky, Zaichkowsky, & Martinek, 1980).

PTs provide services to help prevent or minimize a disability, relieve pain, develop and improve motor function, control posture deviations (abnormalities), and establish and maintain maximum physical performance within the patient's capabilities (Johnston & Magrab, 1976). They also evaluate the physical environment and assess **gross motor skills.**

Physical therapists make recommendations for how to move a child from one area to another and for selecting appropriate **adaptive equipment,** and provide **movement therapy** (exercise). Within an educational environment, physical therapy services are directed toward helping children with special needs obtain maximal physical independence in all education-related activities (Snell, 1987). Many school districts and preschool programs, for example, use PTs as consultants to work with children with gross motor delays. PTs, however, could also have private practices. PTs are frequently employed by a hospital or rehabilitation center.

PTs may also recommend the best handling procedures for **transfers,** such as moving children from wheelchairs to toilets, and for positioning devices, such as braces designed to improve posture (Maddox, 1987). For example, some children cannot stand on their own and require special support devices such as braces, shoe molds, or walkers to help them stand and, in some cases, move about the school environment independently.

In other cases, children benefit from special chairs designed to support their trunk, which help to improve the use of their hands. These chairs provide needed support so that children do not have to use their hands to support their body weight (Campbell, Green, & Carlson, 1977). (See Chapter 10 for a discussion of physical **assistive devices.**)

Within a school or home, PTs also analyze physical environments to help ensure independent mobility and safety for children with special needs. For example, small curbs become major obstacles to children in wheelchairs. To evaluate the physical environment and make recommendations for modifications, PTs observe how children move within their normal environments during play, indoor and outdoor. During these observations, PTs focus on large muscle movements such as climbing, jumping, running, balancing, and catching and throwing balls (Bobath & Bobath, 1975). In some cases, physical therapy is needed, but before physical therapy can be provided children must be assessed.

USING THE BLUEPRINT FOR GROSS MOTOR DEVELOPMENT

Early motor development lays the foundation for development of later motor skills, as well as skills in other areas (Bayley, 1935). There are no specific ages when **motor milestones** "must" occur. Charts listing the ages at which **developmental milestones** are typically achieved, such as those provided in Chapter 2, can be used as guidelines for understanding the sequences and typical rates of motor development (Johnston & Magrab, 1976).

Even if children cannot perform a particular motor skill within the prescribed age range, this alone does not suggest a significant motor delay. Other factors must be taken into consideration, including overall motor development, ability to function in daily activities, muscle tone, motivation, and whether the delay affects cognitive, language, or social-emotional development (Zaichkowsky, et al.,1980). It is difficult to determine whether children younger than three years old have significant gross motor delays because children's rates of motor development vary greatly. For example, on average children walk at about twelve months old, but a normal range for learning how to walk is between seven and eighteen months old (Berger & Fowlkes, 1980).

Motor delays do not necessarily qualify preschool-age children for access to "free" physical therapy through a public school or clinic. It must be documented that the motor delay or disorder

interferes with learning or that the child's physical safety is at risk. Children who do not exhibit gross motor skills typical of their age range but who function well within a daycare setting and at home are *not* likely to qualify for funding of the therapy (Casto & Mastropieri, 1986). See Box 11.1 for an example of a situation that suggests the need for physical therapy.

Every child is born with a "blueprint" for developing movement. Knowledge of normal movement patterns allows PTs to assess the strengths and weaknesses of children's motor capabilities at home or in the classroom. Treatment strategies based on knowledge of normal movement are often referred to as neuro-developmental techniques (NDT). These involve the physical therapist providing physical support, such as helping the child balance, and facilitation of movement, such as helping the child swing one leg forward to take a step, which aid in developing muscle strength and coordination. Movement patterns required for a specific gross motor skill determine how PTs provide support (Baker & Brightman, 1989).

The blueprint (maturation sequence) is for voluntary control of movement beginning at the head and moving down to the toes, called **cephalocaudal trend** of development. Babies demonstrate this pattern as they develop voluntary control over their neck and head muscles to move their head, which occurs before they gain voluntary control to wiggle their toes. Mothers frequently hold their babies in an upright position, which encourages the baby's development of head control.

Babies also develop control over muscles in the center, or trunk, of their bodies before gaining control over muscles in the arms and legs. This is called the **proximodistal trend** of development. In contrast to muscle control, muscle tone develops first from the feet and then proceeds to the head. This is demonstrated when an adult moves an infant's foot. Moving the foot results in greater resistance than is exhibited when moving an infant's head. At birth, basic underlying muscle tone is greater in the trunk and lower extremities and

Box 11.1 _____

Katie: Evidence of the Need for Gross Motor Screening

A bus driver reported that two-year-old Katie takes a very long time getting on and off the bus. Based on this report to Katie's teacher, combined with the teacher's belief that Katie's motor development appeared to be delayed, the PT was asked to conduct an initial physical therapy screening. The results of the screening indicated that Katie may have motor delays. The PT followed up with a full physical therapy assessment. This evaluation helped explain why Katie was having difficulty getting on and off the bus.

It was determined that Katie had low muscle tone, including limited strength in her legs and difficulty balancing on either leg. Using movement patterns within the normal sequence of develop-

ment, such as kneeling and half-kneeling, the therapist worked on strengthening Katie's hip muscles. As hip muscle strength increased, the therapist added standing activities such as placing one foot on a block and the other foot on the floor while playing at a table. Stepping onto objects of different height while balancing helped prepare Katie for climbing stairs, which may help her getting on and off the school bus.

All of these intervention strategies could be done in Katie's home, at a clinic, regular daycare or preschool, or within a special program for children with developmental delays. Most of the intervention strategies could be integrated into daily activities.

---

less through the shoulder girdle, upper extremities, and face (Bayley, 1935).

Within this blueprint, babies also develop movement control of muscles located on the front and back of the body before they develop control of muscles on the sides of their bodies. Controlling muscles on the sides of the body is shown when babies move their arms and legs out to the side and back and when they roll onto their sides to play. Finally, babies integrate both sides of their body and work on rotation, twisting the body at the waist. At this time, they can cross the **midline** (center of the body) with their arms and use either hand in the opposite work space, meaning they can use their left hand to reach for objects located to the right of their body. Babies learn to respond quickly by using twisting action when off-balance (Adelson & Fraiberg, 1975).

Reflexes are also found within the blueprint for movement (Fiorentino, 1972). A reflex is a specific, automatic (involuntary) movement response elicited by a particular stimulus. For example, a baby is born with a reflex called **physiological flexion,** curling up in a ball-like position. This reflex is demonstrated when newborns are placed on their stomach. In this position, most of the body weight is borne on the side of the head and along

the top of the shoulder, the buttocks are high off the bed, and arms and legs are tucked tightly underneath the body. It is also displayed when infants are laid on their back. In this case, the legs are bent and the head falls to one side. As a result, their vision is limited, as it is directed laterally (off to the side).

Over time, these types of motor reflexes should diminish if muscular and neurological development is normal. Evaluating the level of reflex development is often completed by the child's pediatrician. If a PT is involved in providing therapy for the infant, the therapist typically monitors reflex development (Brooke, 1991).

PHYSICAL THERAPY ASSESSMENT

There are two steps in **physical therapy assessment** (Tingey-Michaelis, 1983). The first step involves a brief and relatively informal assessment of gross motor development, called a physical therapy screening. The second step, called a full formal assessment, occurs only if the screening indicates the likelihood of a gross motor delay. This assessment is more detailed.

During both types of assessment PTs observe how children move from one area to another. For example, a PT might observe how children navigate around furniture and interact with other children in the process of getting ready to go home. This type of observation provides information about children's level of awareness of their body in space. The therapist also observes the posture children assume during play to gain insight into their muscular strengths and weaknesses (Hale, 1979). This evaluation is particularly important because children must coordinate their large muscles to maintain various body positions, as well as coordinate the use of their hands, eyes, tongues, and feet during different tasks.

PTs also watch for signs of fatigue. Children with weak muscles use more energy to accomplish the same tasks than their peers with stronger muscles do. Extra energy needed to accomplish motor tasks limits children's attention span or use of cognitive skills. Fatigue is indicated when children have shortness of breath after minimal physical activity. Some children have spurts of energy followed by frequent rest, which also indicates muscle weaknesses. Other children cannot focus on tasks at the end of the school day, which might indicate they are excessively tired because of weak muscle development (Bathshaw & Perret, 1986).

Physical Therapy Screening

For those children who are enrolled in a daycare facility or preschool program, teachers may be the first to notice motor delays. If a teacher suspects that a child has a motor delay, the teacher should inform a parent and make a referral for the child to have a physical therapy screening (Bleck & Nagel, 1982). When parents are the first to suspect motor delays, they often talk with a pediatrician and discuss these concerns with those who care for their child. If the pediatrician also believes gross motor development is delayed, the pediatrician often recommends a physical therapy screening or full assessment (Wermer, 1987). Box 11.2 provides a description of a child with delays in gross motor development. Children such as Billy, featured in Box 11.2, should be referred for a physical therapy screening.

A physical therapy screening is a relatively simple procedure. The purpose of a screening is to determine if full physical therapy evaluation is warranted. During the screening the therapist receives information from the teacher about how a child performs in the classroom. PTs might also directly observe the child in the classroom to determine the level of gross motor development.

During a gross motor screening the therapist often asks a child to attempt a set of gross motor tasks. This could be done with a child alone or during group gross motor activities, such as playing outdoors or indoors on climbing and riding equipment, dancing to music, or any activity that involves whole body movement. During the screening process, most PTs also request information from the child's parents regarding possible motor difficulties the child may have at home (Baker, Banfied, Killburn, & Shufflebarger, 1991).

PTs provide professional expertise to help understand children, but children's parents often know their children better than anyone. To fully understand a child's needs therapists should ask parents to describe any physical limitations or difficulties the child displays when with the parents. Therapists might ask, "Does your child like the merry-go-round at the playground?" to learn how a child copes with various physical activities (Anastasion, 1978).

PTs may also ask parents to indicate concerns they have regarding their child's physical development. Often, parents notice that their child falls more often or is more fearful of certain physical activities, such as climbing up a ladder to a slide, than most children the same age. Open communication between parents and the therapist is essential for gaining a total picture of the child's needs and strengths, as well as for developing an appropriate physical therapy intervention plan (Williamson, 1987).

Delays That May Be Observed During Assessment

Circle time, when all children in a preschool class are expected to sit on the floor or on chairs, is often

Box 11.2 _____

"Billy," a Child with Gross Motor Delays

Once in the classroom, Billy begins the process of removing his jacket and placing it and his backpack in his cubby. While putting his things away, Billy knocks several other children's belongings onto the floor. After taking longer than all the other children to put his belongings in the cubby, Billy awkwardly walks toward the play area, stepping on coats and bags he knocked down while walking past them. One of the children yells at Billy, telling him not to walk on the coats. Billy does not seem aware that he is walking on these objects.

Billy approaches the other children engaged in an art activity at a large table. Billy stands beside a vacant chair, but it is too near to the table for him to sit on. Billy first tries to sit down without moving the chair by putting his foot in front of the chair and wedging his body between the table and chair. After this fails, Billy struggles but manages to pull the chair awkwardly away from the table. He sits in the chair, which is now misaligned with the table. Billy asks the teacher for some crayons. After handing Billy a box of crayons, the teacher moves Billy's chair into a position more aligned with the table. Billy begins the art activity most of his classmates have nearly completed.

As the art activity concludes, Billy abandons his barely started project and attempts to get up from the chair. He frantically moves about in every direction, appearing not to have a plan for how to get up from the chair. He finally pushes away from the table, knocking the chair over backward. Billy walks over to the area where a group activity (circle time) has already begun. As he joins the class seated on a rug, he "plops" onto the floor and moves immediately into a "W" sitting position (knees together and feet out to the side forming the letter "W").

During the ten-minute group activity, Billy changes positions frequently. He moves from the "W" position to leaning forward on his hands, to lying back on the floor, to leaning against the wall or the teacher who is sitting next to him. He does not stay in any one position for more than a minute. When the teacher asks him a question, Billy is in the middle of changing positions and does not answer. Another adult helps move Billy into an appropriate sitting position, with his legs crossed in front of him. The teacher repeats the question. This time, Billy responds enthusiastically and appropriately.

As circle time ends, the teacher announces that it is free play time (when children choose where they want to play). During free play, Billy quickly moves from playing with a toy train to blocks to playing with cars and trucks. He lies on the floor instead of sitting upright to play with each of the toys. He does not play with any one type of toy for more than two or three minutes. Billy begins wandering around the classroom.

Billy notices another child building a house with blocks. Billy tells this child he wants to help. Billy takes a block and tries to add it to the roof of the house. During the attempt, Billy accidentally knocks over most of the building. The other child cries and says, "I don't want to play with Billy!" This appears to upset Billy and he hides his face.

The teacher approaches the children. The teacher asks Billy to help rebuild the house. Billy tries to fix the house with the teacher's assistance. Again, he accidentally knocks over several blocks. This scenario is typical of the rest of Billy's day. By the time the bus arrives some two hours after Billy first began his morning at school, Billy is exhausted and lying on the floor.

Is Billy a "bad" child who gets into a lot of mischief? Does he need some kind of behavior modification program? Is he lazy? Is he just not careful? The following information suggests why Billy may have the difficulties described above and how he may be helped.

Billy appears to have significant gross motor difficulties that interfere with his ability to pay attention and to learn and use social skills. These gross motor delays are likely to lead to development of negative self-esteem.

Not all children who qualify for physical therapy have all or even many of the characteristics Billy exhibited. Some children have only one or two of the gross motor difficulties described in Billy's case. Any motor difficulty that interferes with a child's educational experiences should be assessed to determine if physical therapy services are needed.

an excellent time to observe a child. Circle time activities generally require trunk muscles to function actively to ensure an upright posture. For children whose muscles are sluggish, the effects of this weakness are often observed while sitting during circle time (Bigge, 1991).

For example, during circle time some children slump forward, which results in rounding of their backs. They may lean forward with their hands on the floor or with their elbows on their knees and hands supporting their head. These postures are part of the normal developmental sequence as children are increasing strength in their back and stomach muscles. These children should not be judged as "lazy" or inattentive (Anderson, Bale, Blackman, & Murphy,1986).

Therapists may also observe children sitting in a **"W" position,** with their knees together and feet out to the side. This position widens the base of support and decreases trunk movement and energy output. This position is believed to be detrimental to the development of good hip alignment and should be discouraged. Children should be asked to sit in a different way, such as cross-legged or with legs straight in front of their bodies. Children with poor hip alignment are more likely to develop walking patterns in which their feet turn inward. An unusual pattern may interfere with balance, as well as the ability to perform other motor tasks (Tyler & Mira, 1993).

Children who have **low muscle tone** in the trunk region often compensate by positioning themselves against a wall, leaning up against another person, or leaning on their own arms. These positions result in additional support for maintaining an upright position. Children who sit away from a group of children and lean against a wall may be viewed as "loners," when instead they may be leaning because of weak muscles. Leaning against an adult may be misinterpreted as a sign of attachment or affection (Schleickorn, 1993).

During free play, children with gross motor delays often lie on the floor rather than sit upright to play with objects. Children may sit on the floor and play in a W sitting position, move to lying on

the stomach, or use **side-sitting** during the entire free play time. When children with motor delays move to more upright positions, such as kneeling or standing, they frequently lean heavily with the body or arms on a support surface such as a table (March of Dimes, 1992). Leaning on furniture may also be observed as these children attempt to step over objects on the floor.

Children with low muscle tone tend to lock their joints to help them control their movement (Robinson, 1973). For example, when children are in standing positions, the knees may be held rigid and they might even appear to be **knock-kneed.** The arches in their feet may also be collapsed. For these children, movements requiring more complex skills, such as jumping, often look rigid or awkward.

When children with low muscle tone bounce a ball or draw a circle with one hand, the other hand often moves in the same manner. While concentrating on these types of activities, **extraneous movements** of the mouth, lips, or tongue may also occur (Hirst, 1989).

Children with gross motor delays often appear to be in perpetual motion and unable to stay more than a few moments at any activity. For these children, movement transitions are often quick and appear impulsive. This might be because children with atypical muscle tone have difficulty moving their muscles gradually (smoothly). They frequently also have problems moving one part of their body in isolation from the other parts, which leads to their unintentionally bumping into things or losing balance (Blackman, 1984).

As a result of motor delays, children's social interactions and play skills are often affected (Bartel & Guskin, 1980). For example, children who adapt to motor delays by playing on the floor rather than sitting or standing at an activity may not have an appropriate level of eye contact with their peers or adults. Children who are constantly in motion frequently are shunned by other children because active children often end up physically stepping on friends or toys during play time.

Ultimately, extremely active children frequently develop negative self-esteem and withdraw. These children could also be inappropriately labeled as having attention deficit hyperactivity disorder.

In addition, some children with gross motor delays act silly or intentionally misbehave to divert attention from awkwardness during gross motor tasks. For example, children who think they cannot perform a motor task might deliberately fall on the floor, anticipating that classmates will laugh. This allows children with gross motor delays to be viewed as "funny" instead of "clumsy" (Baker & Brightman, 1989).

While all behavior problems do not indicate a need for physical therapy, it is important to determine whether there is a behavioral or motor problem (Anastasion, 1978). If children have had a significant motor delay, they need physical therapy to be successful and feel good about themselves. Self-esteem is often lower for children who are uncoordinated (Thompson, Rubin, & Bilenker, 1983). Knowing there is an underlying physical cause for lack of coordination often helps parents and teachers be more responsive and have more patience with the child.

Safety is often a concern for children with gross motor delays. Children with poor balance and coordination often trip over things, bump into other children or objects, or fall. Many children with developmental delays have decreased mobility in their ankles, which causes them to trip and fall because their ankles do not quickly adjust to changes in walking surfaces (Bricker & Bricker, 1976). These children have difficulty lifting their toes off the floor as their legs swing while they walk, which results in their tripping over their own feet. For these children, falling occurs even more frequently outdoors because of varying terrains that constantly require motor adjustment (Adelson & Fraiberg, 1975).

Poor motor coordination often causes preschool-age children to lag behind other children or have difficulty moving through a crowd. Some children also have difficulty standing on a line behind the children in front of them. This becomes a safety concern during a fire drill or other situations when it is important to leave an area quickly and orderly.

Toddlers or preschoolers who are very insecure about their ability to balance or who lack appropriate muscle strength often feel uncomfortable on stairs and choose to crawl up or down (Hanson, 1984). Using this earlier developmental stage for climbing stairs often results in the children lagging behind their peers. Children who have difficulty maneuvering on stairs, however, are typically noticed relatively quickly by teachers and often referred for a physical therapy screening (Orelove & Sosbey, 1987).

Children with **motor planning difficulties** have trouble with something as simple as sitting in a chair without falling off, putting on a coat, or moving smoothly from being on the floor to standing up (Ayer, 1972). They have difficulty planning movements needed to perform everyday activities. Children with motor planning difficulties have trouble playing safely on outdoor equipment. These children are frequently described as awkward or uncoordinated (Orelove & Sosbey, 1987).

Uncoordinated children typically have more bumps and bruises because of a decreased awareness of their own body in space (Mulligan–Ault, Guess, Smith, & Thompson, 1988). In other words, these children often have slower balance responses that contribute to an increased number of bumps and scrapes. Children with motor delays frequently do not demonstrate good judgment when it comes to potential dangers on the playground (Goldfarb, Brotherson, Summers, & Turnbull, 1986). For example, these children may climb too high on the playground equipment and cannot get down without assistance.

Full Formal Assessment

If information collected during the physical therapy screening indicates possible gross motor delays, the PT requests a full physical therapy evaluation. The referral for a physical therapy evaluation includes the reason for the referral, background history of the child, and general observations including the child's responses to movement activities within the home or classroom environment (Bricker & Bricker, 1976). Parents must give permission for a formal physical therapy evaluation to be completed (Berger & Fowlkes, 1980).

In addition to information obtained during the screening, PTs assess together the **muscle tone** and **joint ranges** of children. The PT guides the movement of the child's joints through their normal ranges to evaluate muscle response (Johnston & Magrab, 1976). Muscle tone could be too high or too low. **High tone muscles** feel rigid and low tone muscles feel loose when moving the extremities and trunk. When joint ranges are tight, this could indicate a need for stretching exercises. When joint ranges are too loose, this indicates a need for exercises designed to strengthen the muscles around or near the joint (Zaichowsky, et al., 1980).

Further assessment includes having children move through a developmental sequence during play. The developmental sequence involves placing the child in several positions, including **supine** (lying on the back), **prone** (lying on the stomach), rolling, sitting, **quadruped** (on hands and knees), crawling, kneeling, half-kneeling, transition from floor to standing then to walking, and running.

During the progression through these developmental sequences, PTs analyze quality of movement and transition patterns of children within this sequence. For children who walk fairly well, other more advanced motor skills often are evaluated using stair climbing, jumping, throwing and catching a ball, and balancing (Johnston & Magrab, 1976).

Sometimes, children's motor delays are very obvious, as was shown in Billy's case (Box 11.1), presented earlier in this chapter. Children who cannot do many of the motor activities their peers do frequently have motor delays. For example, some children can ride a tricycle by pushing the pedals while others the same age can only move

the tricycle by pushing off the floor with their feet (Campbell, 1987a).

At other times, behavior indicating a delay in gross motor might be more subtle (Johnston & Magrab, 1976). For example, children may kick or push over a balance beam because they know they cannot walk across it. Table 11.1 provides a list of behavior types children may manifest that can indicate gross motor delays.

Billy, the child discussed in Box 11.1, has many of the characteristics listed in Table 11.1. These delays are likely to interfere with future gross motor, fine motor, cognitive, and social-emotional development.

Sometimes, however, children's motor delays are inaccurately evaluated. Children often be described as having behavioral problems when they do not have the physical control needed to do what is asked (Campbell, 1987b). These children generally are aware of their own limitations and use inappropriate behavior to divert attention from this inability to successfully perform a gross motor task (Fiorentino, 1972). For example, a child

TABLE 11.1 Behavior That May Indicate Gross Motor Delays

Significant gross motor delays may be found in children two years and older who

- Frequently trip, fall, or bump into things or other people;
- Have balance problems;
- Need extra support to maintain basic positions.
- Frequently avoid gross motor activities;
- Tire easily;
- Seem fearful of or avoid playground equipment or certain types of gross motor equipment such as a slide;
- Frequently lag behind other children during transitional activities;
- Use "age-inappropriate" patterns of movement, such as a four-year-old always walking on tiptoes;
- Act "silly" or misbehave when requested to participate in a gross motor activity.

may run around the room to avoid activities the child believes are difficult such as throwing and catching a ball.

A summary statement of all of the PT's observations is developed and includes assessing the effects of motor delays on classroom functioning, social interactions, and, when appropriate, level of self-esteem. Most agencies and schools require standardized assessment and scoring using developmental motor scales as additional evidence of need for physical therapy intervention (Berger & Fowlkes, 1980). If it is determined that a child has a significant gross motor development delay, physical therapy should be provided.

Evaluations and recommendations the PTs make are typically presented to a Committee on Preschool Special Education (CPSE) or Department of Health (DOH). The agencies responsible for approving children to receive agency-funded therapy services varies from state to state. Following the approval for physical therapy treatment, the child's physician must write a prescription authorizing physical therapy. Although evaluations sometimes may be performed without a doctor's prescription, in most states therapy cannot occur without a prescription (Dubowitz, 1990).

COMMON PARENTAL CONCERNS ABOUT PHYSICAL THERAPY

Many parents are concerned when they are told their child should receive physical therapy because they believe therapy is painful. When therapy is done correctly, it does not cause excessive pain. Children might resist therapy because it often makes them tired just as exercise makes most people tired. Therapists must determine children's tolerance for therapy and work within these limits. PTs also vary activities to maintain children's interest. They work toward increasing a child's ability to endure exercises by lengthening the duration of the therapy (Brooke, 1991).

Children are generally eager to participate in **individual therapy** because they receive the undivided attention of the therapist. They also enjoy

participating because equipment and activities used during physical therapy are often novel and attractive. Within the classroom, therapists are generally welcomed by children because therapists help children feel more confident while participating in activities (Fraser & Hensinger 1983).

Parents may be concerned that the child is getting either too much or too little therapy. When children receive therapy paid for by the parents, parents may negotiate a change in the frequency of therapy with the therapist. When children receive therapy paid for by public funding, parents should discuss changes in the frequency of services with the therapist and classroom teacher. Generally, the Committee on Preschool Special Education (CPSE) in the school district in which the child resides must meet to discuss and authorize schedule changes (Orelove & Sosbey, 1987).

Parents often are concerned with a stigma they fear may be attached to children receiving therapy. Children are often sensitive to the attitudes of those around them. If peers, teachers, or parents have a negative view of therapy, children also are more likely to develop a negative attitude. To help children avoid feeling they are being "singled out," therapists might work with two or more children who have gross motor delays at the same time (small group therapy). It is important for parents to realize that it is generally more stigmatizing to appear "clumsy" than to receive therapy (Fraser & Hensinger, 1983). To help children with gross motor delays there are two major models PTs use that guide the choice of physical therapy methods.

PHYSICAL THERAPY SERVICES

Recommendations for physical therapy treatment may include **direct treatment** on an individual basis, ongoing monitoring of the child's gross motor skills when delays are minimal, classroom consultation with the teaching staff to encourage carryover of the physical therapy goals, and gross motor therapy intervention with groups of children (Baker & Brightman, 1989). Practicing gross motor skills is important for building endurance and confidence when engaged in activities involving specific gross motor skills. Group therapy activities are particularly effective for this purpose.

The goal of physical therapy is for children to generalize motor skills performed during therapy to various situations and environments (Crump, 1987). Plans that suggest physical therapy activities to integrate into daily activities at home, called home plans, are crucial to meet the goal of generalizing motor skills. PTs show parents how to integrate therapy activities safely so that parents do not injure the child (Thompson, et al., 1983). Once children begin receiving physical therapy, it is important for parents to maintain regular communication with the therapist to exchange information about the child's progress. It is useful to determine whether the child is using newly acquired skills within the home and school environments and allows parents to ask questions about therapy goals and activities (Tingey–Michaelis, 1983).

If children are receiving physical therapy in school, at a daycare program, or in a clinic, it is often helpful for parents to occasionally observe the therapy sessions. The observations let parents see what occurs during therapy. During the sessions, PTs show parents activities and exercises that should be practiced at home and how best to use toys or other equipment during therapy (Berger & Fowlkes, 1980). Children also need opportunities to practice various types of skills and patient and supportive adults who provide them practice time.

Physical therapy requires a major commitment of time and may be exhausting to therapists, parents, and children. The effort is warranted, though, because physical therapy often results in less energy being needed for custodial activities (e.g., dressing the child) once children are physically more independent. Moving children from little or no self-care to independent self-care in many areas results in less time spent in custodial care (Lifchez & Winslow, 1979). Desired skills are typically acquired more quickly if learning is interesting and fun for children.

It is necessary for parents and professionals to work together to develop a plan that helps children develop gross motor skills. Goals should be set that are appropriate to the child's developmental age. After goals are established, a task analysis is used to break skills to be acquired into small incremental steps (Dubowitz, 1990). These steps are gradually introduced and focused on until mastered. Refer to Figure 11.1 for an example of **task analysis** for kicking a ball. Once skills have been well established, it is necessary to develop a maintenance plan and help children generalize skills learned during therapy to new and varied situations.

In some cases, the focus of therapy may not be on developing skills but on varying muscle tone. Children with high muscle tone have difficulty consciously making their muscles relax. When they get excited or exert effort, their muscles become more tense. In this case, exercises designed

FIGURE 11.1 Sequencing of the Gross Motor Skills for Kicking a Ball

to help children relax decrease muscle tension. Children engaged in enjoyable activities gradually become more relaxed as they experience success. Children with low muscle tone become stronger with practice that occurs in routine daily activities. Exercise helps postpone deformities and proper positioning slows down physical deterioration of the skeletal system, but neither leads to skills development (Beller, 1979). For physical therapy to enhance skills, one of two models of therapy is used.

DEVELOPMENTAL MODELS OF PHYSICAL THERAPY

The two models used to develop physical therapy intervention activities are the **developmental model** and the **top-down model.** The developmental model provides therapy by teaching children skills in the order they appear in the normal developmental sequence. This is also called a **bottom-up model** because it moves a child from low level skills to more complex ones (Casto & Mastropieri, 1986).

For example, an eighteen-month-old whose gross motor development is at a three-month-old level would be taught skills in the same sequence babies normally acquire them, starting at the three-month level. The sequence of therapy would move, for instance, from holding up the head, to rolling from stomach to back, and back to stomach. The bottom-up model stresses the need to master earlier developmental stages before attempting to teach motor skills found later in the developmental sequence (Bayley, 1935).

The target goal of this developmental approach is to let children catch up to the point at which they no longer have significant gross motor delays. Using this model, a PT's primary role is to move each child step by step through the normal developmental sequence of gross motor skills acquisition. For children whose development is three to twelve months delayed or who are less than three or four years old, this model could be helpful. For children who have severe gross motor

delays, it is generally *not* the most effective model to follow for therapy (Jaeger, 1987).

TOP-DOWN MODEL OF PHYSICAL THERAPY

Moving through the normal sequence of skills acquisition is generally not the best therapeutic method for children who are no longer infants or toddlers because they do not have time to practice all the skills found in the normal developmental sequence. It is unlikely that these children will ever catch up using the bottom-up model. Children who have severe or profound motor delays appear to benefit the most from using the top-down model. This model focuses on developing the basic functional motor skills (movements needed to engage in day-to-day activities) needed for adult life (Hale, 1979).

Research by the Kern County School District has indicated that by age seven or eight years, children with severe gross motor delays typically begin a gradual regression on developmental scales. As children's bodies become larger, gravity becomes the enemy. Proper positioning becomes harder, and children are often left in one place because it becomes increasingly difficult to move them around. Bathing and eating, for instance, require one-on-one assistance (Perske, Clifton, McClean, & Ishler Stein, 1986). If children are not toilet trained by seven years, attempts to train are often abandoned. These goals, however, do not need to be abandoned when implementing the top-down model (Snow & Hooper, 1994).

Top-down therapy combines natural body movements with an instructional process. It does *not* focus on normal skills in a set developmental sequence. The focus is on using normal life activities to systematically acquire motor skills (Lifchez & Winslow, 1979). For example, if the goal is to have the child learn how to hold a cup, this skill would then be developed *without* first meeting less complex skills found at earlier stages of development. In the top-down method, the steps needed to hold a cup would be broken down by completing a task analysis. Each step would be taught until mastered, and the child would then be moved to the next step until the target goal of independently holding and drinking from a cup is reached (Gold, 1976).

PTs frequently provide consultation to other team members, including parents, to help the team develop a top-down plan designed to let children practice skills while engaged in other educational and leisure activities (Williamson, 1987). PTs typically consult with children's parents and teachers regarding goals they believe will be useful for each child. Teachers and parents are then instructed on methods of how to integrate activities and appropriate body positioning into daily routines to help children meet specific goals (Finnie, 1975).

For therapy to be effective, practicing skills to become more independent must be performed every day and integrated into daily activities. Appropriate movement rather than static positioning is key to improving bone and muscle health and the development of independent skills. Merely placing children in "good" **static** (fixed, without movement) **positions** does not teach them how to move. Also, using substitutes for motor skills, such as may be provided when using adaptive equipment, does not teach motor skills (Casto & Mastropieri, 1986). To move children toward greater independence, therapy plans must include gradual reductions of physical aid provided to the children. Children should be provided only as much help as they absolutely need to accomplish movement (Cartwright, 1981).

Using a top-down model, a set of skills such as sitting, standing, and walking can be taught simultaneously. In this case, goals for standing correctly can be introduced before sitting skills are mastered. The developmental model, on the other hand, would require that sitting skills be mastered before standing skills are introduced. The top-down approach implies that most people can learn to sit, stand, and walk when given enough physical assistance and improve motor skills if they are taught and practiced systematically (Jaeger, 1987). Using the top-down model, the question is not,

"Can they learn?" but rather, "How long will it take them to learn?"

PHYSICAL THERAPY EARLY INTERVENTION SERVICES

Most children love to explore their environment because it helps satisfy their natural curiosity. Much of what they learn is acquired through movement. Movement is required for nearly all forms of work and play (Bigge, 1991). Climbing, hiding, carrying, hauling, and building are the "work" of children. Through movement they learn about:

- space—Can I play this close to my friend without hurting him?
- size—Will I fit in this space or will this object fit into this space?
- weight—Can I lift this block that high?
- spatial relationships—Can I go up to the top stair?
- speed—Can I walk slowly on the balance beam and not fall off?
- time—Can I complete the activity before it is time to go home?
- sequence—Can I follow this obstacle course in the right order?

Parents, daycare providers, and preschool staff must make sure that all children have daily opportunities for gross motor activities (Dubowitz, 1990). This is especially true for children with gross motor delays. Providing time for gross motor movement helps children with motor delays develop new skills and those without motor delays to continue to develop age-appropriate skills. Gross motor activities also provide children with a positive outlet for their seemingly boundless energy.

Early intervention is very often valuable for children with motor delays. A mild delay could turn into a more severe delay without appropriate intervention (Orelove & Sosbey, 1987). Early intervention also allows PTs to help children more comfortably progress through the development of normal movement patterns before they develop bad habits (Blackman, 1984).

Typically, the earlier children receive intervention, the more positive the outcome for their life-long motor development (Baker & Brightman, 1989). As children grow, gaps between their rate of development and typical rates often increase, making it less likely that they will ever reach average levels of development. In addition, when children have positive experiences with therapy at a young age, they are more likely to be willing to continue therapy, if necessary, as they get older (Bartel & Guskin, 1980).

Children who receive physical therapy as very young children often perceive physical therapy as a "normal" activity. In addition, preschool-age peers, unlike school-age children, typically do not question why other children receive physical therapy or react in a judgmental fashion. When peers do react negatively, however, such as saying, "What's wrong with you?" children in therapy may feel less positive about themselves (Bartel & Guskin, 1980).

Specific Skills Addressed through Physical Therapy

Delays in the development of back muscles frequently are seen during the preschool years. For instance, some children cannot turn their head without moving their whole body. When they turn their head and their body moves as well, they may need to take steps forward to maintain their balance. Stepping forward may cause them to lose focus on the object they turned to look at. A therapist often uses earlier stages of development to help children develop head movements separate from other body movements. When successful, therapy results in improved head control in all positions (Hirst, 1989).

During an activity such as listening to someone reading a book, preschool-age children often show a variety of body positions that help them focus on the story. For instance, some children lie on their stomach with their heads supported in their hands, with legs spread wide apart, to conserve energy while listening. Children with motor disabilities often do *not* spontaneously use energy-conserving positions because their muscles are too weak to allow them to position themselves that way (Fiorentino, 1972). They should be encouraged to assume varied positions that help develop strength rather than being encouraged to sit still. PTs often guide children with low muscle tone into varying positions that aid in strengthening the weaker muscles (Bigge, 1991).

Delayed development of head and neck control may be seen in preschoolers who have difficulty controlling the rate of air flow and tongue movements needed for speech. Good head and trunk control are prerequisites for refining both of these skills. Toddlers and preschoolers who have difficulty producing certain speech sounds benefit from physical therapy that strengthens neck and abdominal muscles. Children are laid on their back in a fully supported position while working on these skills. Good abdominal strength also helps with respiration (Thompson, et al., 1983).

Preschoolers who look up at an object and fall backward probably do so because they do not have adequate strength in their stomach and back muscles. This weakness could be dangerous because falling backward off playground equipment, such as the steps to a slide, could result in serious head injuries. Therefore, preschoolers with weak stomach and back muscles often need physical therapy for safety reasons (Tingey–Michaelis, 1983).

In addition, if preschool-age children experience frequent episodes of falling and receive blows to the face or head, they might have a delay in the development of the protective extension response, also called the high guard response. Children use the **high guard position** of the arms up and out to the side when they first learn to sit, walk, run, climb stairs, and jump. However, frequent use by preschool-age children of the high guard position and a wide base of support (legs spread and toes pointed outward) may indicate a gross motor delay (Bayley, 1935). Delayed motor development might be indicated if preschool-age children generally stand or walk on their toes or when they stand or walk using awkward posture.

After children can walk fairly well, jumping, hopping, and skipping are the basic motor skills that develop. Children continue to refine these motor skills until they are about seven years old (Espenschade & Eckert, 1980). Running, jumping, and climbing are a part of many common childhood games. They are, therefore, important to a child's social-emotional as well as sensorimotor development (Hanson & Harris, 1986).

Beginning at about age seventeen months, most children can jump down from a step. Gross motor development continues in this area through about five years old and includes progress through jumping on the floor with both feet, to jumping off increasingly higher objects, to jumping over objects (Baker, et al., 1991).

Many motor skills require being able to balance on one leg. Kicking a ball, stepping over large obstacles, as well as climbing stairs, require balancing on one foot for brief periods of time (Curtis, 1982). Climbing stairs also follows a particular sequence. Children initially crawl up stairs, turn around, and come down backward. As they move into a more upright position, they walk up and down stairs step-to-step, leading with the same foot while using a railing for support. At about thirty months old, children begin to use alternating feet while climbing stairs (Copeland & Kimmel, 1989). Children may need practice climbing stairs to help develop muscles that allow them to acquire these skills.

Ball skills also follow a developmental sequence (Keogh & Sugden, 1985). Children first learn to track a ball by rolling the ball visually back and forth. At about age two years, most toddlers can throw a small ball while standing. The throw typically is made without control over the direction the ball travels and with little force. As skills improve, children can throw larger balls while standing and purposefully direct the ball toward a target. After the ball is thrown, children often take additional steps forward to maintain their standing position.

Children first learn to catch a ball while holding their arms out straight and then trapping the ball against their chest. They often turn their head away from the ball as it travels toward them to avoid being hit in the face (Molnar, 1982). Children fearful of balls thrown toward them often are more comfortable with soft balls (foam or cloth). Practicing ball catching skills encourages eye-hand coordination. As **visual tracking** skills improve, children can anticipate the path of the oncoming ball (Ayer, 1972). For example, they can catch a ball thrown upward or to the right or left.

Kicking a ball involves visual tracking, motor planning, and balancing skills. Toddlers first walk into a large ball to push it forward. Later in development, children propel balls with a rather stiff leg by swinging the leg backward before kicking. Swinging the leg increases the ball's speed and provides some control over the ball's direction. Children can kick a stationary ball before they can kick a moving ball (Tansley, 1986).

Also providing children with the opportunity to practice balancing skills is use of a balance beam. Initially, the beam should be wide (five inches or more) and placed on or relatively close to the ground so the child avoids injury. As balancing skills develop, children progress from walking with one foot on and one foot off the beam to being able to walk on narrower beams, to walking with both feet on a wide beam, and finally to walking with both feet on a narrower beam.

Children often walk sideways on a balance beam rather than by placing one foot in front of the other. Over time, children gradually progress to mounting the beam and achieving an increasing number of steps with one foot in front of the other before stepping off the beam. The balance beam may provide additional challenges to balancing skills by asking children to walk backward on it or having the balance beam be narrower than five inches or raised off the ground (Nelson, 1977).

Providing Physical Support during Therapy

Teachers can help improve the sitting posture of preschoolers by carefully controlling the method of physically supporting children who sit on their laps or on the floor. PTs can provide guidance to teachers and parents by teaching them where to place their hands to best help the children. Assistance should occur at a level that encourages development of muscle tone. Providing too much support may discourage muscle development (Wolff, 1979).

Some children also benefit from the additional support provided while sitting in a chair. For example, a Rifton chair, which has a solid back and sides and widely spaced legs that prevent rocking the chair, provides support for children to focus more readily on tasks. A Velcro seat belt could be used for preschoolers who need to sit in this type of chair to help support their hips. Feet should be placed flat on the floor to provide additional support. Therapists should advise parents and teachers about the correct size chair for the child (Seamon & Depauw, 1989). (Refer to Chapter 7 for further discussion of the use of a Rifton chair.)

Chair height should allow children to place their feet flat on the floor with the knees below hip level. If the proper height chair is unavailable, a step should be placed in front of the chair at the level where the feet can be placed flat on the step surface. Proper sitting position is crucial for learning because the less energy children use to maintain a position the more energy they have to focus on the activity (Tansley, 1986). Children with gross motor delays often sit on a chair while playing at a table even if the table is at standing height. These children should be encouraged to stand for as long as possible at the table to enhance muscle strength.

It is important, though, to set realistic expectations to avoid frustrating children who have gross motor delays. Expectations vary from child to child, of course, depending on the current level of functioning. One child may be able to walk on a balance beam independently, another may need a hand held, and another may merely want someone close by for additional help, if needed. It is important to acknowledge that children are successful at different levels.

Activities should be geared toward each child's developmental level. For example, most four-year-olds can hop on one foot. If a four-year-old cannot, the child should be offered activities that work on prerequisite skills, such as balancing and strength, which are needed for hopping. If a four-year-old cannot perform motor skills typically mastered by most children of the same age, the teacher should then provide tasks appropriate for this particular child.

Adults should closely monitor a child's movement and serve as "spotters," watching the children as they play. To help further protect children with motor delays, the environment must be evaluated and maintained to ensure safety. Furniture often must be moved and extra supervision may be required to help ensure that children can safely maneuver in their environment.

Physical Therapy during Daily Activities

Physical therapy activities can easily be integrated into classroom and home routines (Jaeger, 1987). Therapy can be provided by working one-on-one or in groups of children in the classroom, outdoors, at home, or in a designated therapy room. In any case, physical therapy activities should always be enjoyable.

Turning activities into games helps ensure that the activities are attractive to children. For instance, most children enjoy climbing and so would also enjoy climbing on large equipment and playing with things such as a very large (more than three feet in diameter) therapy ball (bright and sturdy), for instance. Pretending to go on a camping trip would make children climb over, under, and through various courses while working on balance and coordination and still having fun.

Within the classroom, physical therapy could be provided during transition times. For example, children may pretend to be animals, such as a hopping rabbit or frog or slow-moving turtle, as they move to the table area for an activity. They could pretend to be a bulldozer while picking up toys and putting toys on the shelf during cleanup time. This type of **therapeutic play** incorporates motor activities into daily routines and helps make transitions fun. Often, children do not realize that these activities are a type of work (Tansley, 1986).

Everyday preschool classroom activities are generally more therapeutic when they incorporate a variety of developmental positions (Baker, et al., 1989). For example, rather than having all the children sit at circle time, the children could be told to lie on their stomach. Also, during circle time a therapist might have a child sit on a ball or bolster. This provides the child with extra support and energy that may help the child focus more attention on the activity. For example, using the case mentioned in Box 11.1, the therapist could sit in the circle with Billy, positioning him on a bolster and supporting him so he could more readily focus on an activity.

Another way to work with Billy would be for the therapist to do an activity that involves the whole class. The tasks would be focused on Billy's needs while also allowing the entire class to benefit from and enjoy the activities. Obstacle courses are especially suited for this purpose. Using obstacle courses, therapists can work on developing children's motor skills by asking them to crawl, roll, jump, climb, balance, and catch. Children could be asked to kneel to paint on paper taped to the wall rather than paint while standing at an easel or sitting at a table. Puzzles might be put together while kneeling on all fours, as well as while sitting at a table (Tansley, 1986).

Consulting with PTs helps teachers determine activities that could be beneficial to specific children while also being enjoyed by other children in the class. When the entire class participates no one is singled out. Singling out could make a child feel self-conscious and resist therapy. When group therapy is provided, other children who do not qualify for physical therapy are less likely to feel "cheated" because they are also allowed to participate in what seems to them like a game or learning activity (Rogers–Warren, 1982). Since parents are generally not involved in planning specific lessons, teachers should send them suggestions for gross motor activities their children could be provided at home.

Planning and executing successful group gross motor activities for preschoolers with many different levels of abilities often is a difficult task. Some children, for example, have difficulty waiting their turn. These children should be divided into smaller groups to decrease the amount of time they must wait. One way to reduce waiting time is to have two or more different activities occurring at the same time, but this requires adequate staffing.

During some activities, such as an obstacle course, some children might be afraid to go through the course alone. They may initially require adult guidance or be willing to go with a friend. They could also benefit from previewing the physical therapy room and having a chance to practice moving through the course before all the students enter the room for gross motor time. Practice often helps build self-confidence.

Actions described in a story book could be used to create obstacle courses that are of interest to preschoolers. Any story book can be read with the intent of searching for action verbs, sequences, and spatial relationships described in the story. These words could be used to guide development of a unique obstacle course based on the story. Using a story book theme might help motivate children to follow a specific path in an obstacle course. Creative props relating to the story may spark children's imagination and help focus their attention.

For example, after children have heard a story about a bear, the therapist might say, "Let's go on a camping trip to look for a bear." Children might also be asked to move through an obstacle course representing a path in the woods. They would use different developmental postures, such as rolling as if down a hill or walking as if on an incline down or walking up an incline, crawling through a long cloth tunnel, walking on their knees, and tiptoeing around cones staggered on the floor to find a stuffed bear at the end of the course.

Directions such as front, back, and side can be incorporated into a gross motor group activity. For example, a teacher could say, "Can you follow this same course going backward?" "Can you cross the balance beam while walking sideways?" or "Can you jump through the hoop?" Children need opportunities to develop left and right sides of their bodies to perform smooth and coordinated movements.

In larger group settings (six to twelve) children can also learn concepts related to speed of movement during activities geared toward this size group. As two or more children move along together one after the other, some move more slowly and others more quickly. Each child must adjust to the speed of the child who leads. Activities can also address the concept of speed by asking children to imitate a slow- or a fast-moving animal.

Many schools and home therapy activities do not require special equipment. PTs can teach parents how to incorporate physical exercises into daily activities rather than parents scheduling a special exercise time at home (Anastasion, 1978). For example, rather than handing a child a toothbrush the child may be required to climb onto a stool and balance with one hand holding on the sink to get the toothbrush independently. This sequence of activities could be used to strengthen children's motor skills. An adult should "spot" the child when first learning to use the stool to reach the toothbrush. Before receiving instruction from therapists, parents may have developed the habit of lifting their child onto the stool and getting the toothbrush for the child (Jaeger, 1989). These habits do not provide the child with the needed exercise nor do they encourage the child to develop self-help skills (Thurman & Widerstrom, 1990).

Regular classroom and special therapy equipment may be incorporated into physical therapy. Various pieces of specialized therapy equipment and classroom items can be strategically placed around a classroom to elicit a desired physical response. For example, putting toys on a large foam block encourages children to use a kneeling position to play with the toys. A barrel encourages

children to climb in and out. Large wooden blocks spaced six to twelve inches apart encourage children to practice balancing skills by stepping from one block to another. Therapists should work cooperatively with teachers to share equipment and offer suggestions on how to use the equipment in the best possible way, as well as recommend what types of toys and equipment to use (Lynch, Brekken, Drouin, & Wolfe, 1984). Therapists should also instruct parents on how to use the toys and other objects found at home to stimulate motor development.

While therapeutic equipment is useful, teachers and parents should be creative and use other things to achieve outcomes similar to those achieved by using specifically designed therapeutic equipment. A very large box, for instance such as for a refrigerator, could be made into a club house. While playing in it, children must coordinate their body movements to get in and out of a small door, the box flaps, and move around inside the box.

Landscape borders could be used to practice balancing skills with careful adult supervision. Taking a walk through the park requires a variety of motor skills because it calls for maneuvering over uneven terrain, stepping over branches and large rocks, and moving through small places, such as between two trees. Children will use different muscles to climb up and walk or run down a hill than are required to walk around the level surfaces found in a house or classroom (Rainforth & Salisbury, 1988).

CONCLUSION

Physical therapy is a valuable service, especially at the preschool level. Gross motor delays often can be prevented from occurring or modified. Physical delays often affect children's cognitive and social skills and attention span. These delays may contribute to negative self-esteem and limit children's abilities to function safely within an environment. Early identification and remediation of motor delays is important. Physical therapists, teachers, and parents must work together to identify, evaluate, and provide services for children. The next two chapters discuss the use of play and art in helping children with special needs develop fine and gross motor, cognitive, and social skills.

CHAPTER SUMMARY

- Physical therapists are trained in evaluating and treating posture and movement disorders. Physical therapists often use developmental norms to determine whether children have significant gross motor delays.
- Physical therapists observe how children move to gain insight into their strengths, weaknesses, and level of awareness of their own body in space.
- The goal of physical therapy is for children to generalize motor skills acquired during therapy to everyday situations. Parents, classroom teachers, and other caretakers may help provide the exercise and practice children need to develop these motor skills.
- Early intervention helps prevent mild delays from developing into severe ones and motor delays from negatively affecting other areas of development.
- Parents of children with developmental delays are often concerned about their children receiving physical therapy services because they think physical therapy is painful. They also are concerned their children will be stigmatized if they need physical therapy services.
- Physical therapy services can be provided in a therapy room but are more often integrated into daily activities of young children.
- The developmental and top-down models are frequently used to design physical therapy services.
- Several specific skills can be enhanced using physical therapy.
- Methods of providing support to encourage strength and good posture are also a part of physical therapy services.

REVIEW QUESTIONS

1. What are the major areas of focus for physical therapy?
2. What information is collected during physical therapy screening and full formal assessments?
3. How do gross motor abilities affect other areas of development?
4. What types of behavior indicate children may have gross motor delays?
5. How might a physical therapist alleviate some of the concerns parents often have about their children receiving physical therapy?

SUGGESTED STUDENT ACTIVITIES

1. Observe a physical therapist working with a young child.
2. Using Billy's case (Box 11.1), develop a list of recommendations for Billy's teachers and parents.
3. Create a physical therapy activity for five-year-olds based on an age-appropriate story book.

ADDITIONAL READINGS

Bigge, J. L. (1991). *Teaching individuals with physical and multiple disabilities.* New York: Macmillan.
Jaeger, D. L. (1989). *Transferring and lifting children & adolescents: Home instruction sheets.* Tucson, AZ: Communication & Therapy Skill Builder.
Levy, J. (1974). *The baby exercise book.* New York: Pantheon Books.

ADDITIONAL RESOURCES

American Physical Therapy Association
1111 N. Fairfax Street
Alexandria, VA 22314

Division of the Physically Handicapped
Council for Exceptional Children
1920 Association Drive
Reston, VA 22091–1589

Mobility Opportunities Via Education (M.O.V.E.)
Kern County Superintendent of Schools
5801 Sundale Avenue
Bakersfield, CA 93309–2924

REFERENCES

Adelson, E., & Fraiberg, S. (1975). *Gross motor development in infants blind from birth.* In B. Z. Friedlander, G. M. Sterrit, & E. E. Kirk (Eds.), *Exceptional infant: Assessment intervention* (Vol. 3) (pp. 69–83). New York: Brunner/Mazel.

Anastasion, N. J. (1978). Strategies for models for early childhood intervention of handicapped and non-handicapped children. In M. I. Grualnick (Ed.), *Early intervention and the integration of handicapped and nonhandicapped children.* (pp. 530–549). Baltimore, MD: University Park Press.

Anderson, R. D., Bale, J. F., Blackman, J. A., & Murphy, J. R. (1986). *Infections in children: A source book for educators and child care providers.* Rockville, MD: Aspen.

Ayer, T. (1972). *Sensory integration and learning disorders.* Los Angeles: Western Psychological Services.

Baker, B. L., & Brightman, A. J. (1989). A skills training guide for parents and teachers of children with special needs (2nd ed.). Baltimore: Paul H. Brookes.

Baker, M. J., Banfied, C. S., Killburn, D., & Shufflebarger, K. J. (1991). *Controlling movement: A therapeutic approach to early intervention.* Rockville, MD: Aspen.

Bartel, N. R., & Guskin, S. L. (1980). A handicap as a social phenomenon. In W. M. Cruickshank (Ed.), *Psychology of exceptional children and youth* (4th ed.) (pp. 16–30). Englewood Cliffs, NJ: Prentice-Hall.

Bathshaw, M. L., & Perret, Y. M. (1986). *Children with handicaps: A medical primer* (2nd ed.). Baltimore, MD: Paul H. Brookes.

Bayley, N. (1935). The development of motor abilities during the first three years. *Monographs of the Society for Research in Child Development.* Germantown, NY: Periodical Service Company

Beller, E. K. (1979). *Early intervention programs.* In J. D. Osofsky (Ed.), *Handbook of infancy research.* (pp. 69–83). New York: John Wiley & Sons.

Berger, M., & Fowlkes, M. A. (1980). Family intervention project: A family network model for serving young handicapped children. *Young Children, 35,* 22–32.

Bigge, J. L. (1991). *Teaching individuals with physical and multiple disabilities* (3rd ed.). New York: Macmillan.

Blackman, J. A. (Ed.). (1984). *Medical aspects of developmental disabilities in children birth to three* (Rev. ed.). Rockville, MD: Aspen.

Bleck, E., & Nagel, D. A. (Eds.). (1982). *Physically handicapped children: A medical atlas for teachers* (2nd ed.). New York: Grune and Stratton.

Bobath, B., & Bobath, K. (1975). *Motor development in the different types of cerebral palsy.* London: Heinemann.

Bricker, W. A., & Bricker, D. D. (1976). The infant, toddler, and preschool research and intervention project. In T. D. Tjossem (Ed.), *Intervention strategies with high risk infants and young children.* (pp. 410–439). Baltimore, MD: University Park Press.

Brooke, M. H. (1991). *A clinician's view of neuromuscular disease* (2nd ed.). Baltimore, MD: Williams and Wilkins.

Campbell, P. H. (1987a). Physical management and handling procedures with students with movement dysfunction. In M. E. Shell (Ed.), *Systematic instruction of persons with severe handicaps* (3rd ed., pp. 174–187). Columbus, OH: Merrill.

Campbell, P. H. (1978b). Programming for students with dysfunction in posture and movement. In M. E. Snell (Ed.), *Systematic instruction of persons with severe handicaps* (3rd ed., pp. 188–211). Columbus, OH: Merrill.

Campbell, P. H., Green, K. M., & Carlson, L. M. (1977). Approximating the norm through environmental and child-centered prosthetic and adaptive equipment. In E. Sontag (Ed.), *Educational programming for severely and profoundly handicapped.* (pp. 69–83). Washington, DC: Council for Exceptional Children, Division of Mental Retardation.

Cartwright, C. A. (1981). Effective programs for parents of young handicapped children. *Topics in Early Childhood Special Education, 1,* 1–9.

Casto, G., & Mastropieri, M. A. (1986). The efficacy of early intervention programs: A meta-analysis. *Exceptional Children, 52,* 417–424.

Copeland, M. E., & Kimmel, J. R. (1989). *Evaluation and management of infants and young children with developmental disabilities.* Baltimore, MD: Paul H. Brookes.

Crump. I. (Ed.). (1987). *Nutrition and feeding of the handicapped child.* Boston: College-Hill/Little, Brown.

Curtis, S. (1982). *The joy of movement in early childhood.* New York: Teachers College Press.

Dubowitz, V. (1990). *Muscle disorders in childhood.* Philadelphia, PA: W. B. Saunders.

Espenschade, A., & Eckert, H. (1980). *Motor development.* Columbus, OH: Merrill.

Finnie, N. R. (1975). *Handling the* young cerebral palsied child at home (2nd ed.). New York: Dutton.

Fiorentino, M. (1972). *Normal and abnormal development: The influence of primitive reflexes on motor development.* Springfield, IL: Charles C. Thomas.

Fraser, B. A., & Hensinger, R. N. (1983). *Managing physical handicaps: A practical guide for parents, care providers, and educators.* Baltimore, MD: Paul H. Brookes.

Frostig, M., & Maslow, P. (1970). *Movement education: Theory and practice.* Chicago: Follett.

Gold, M. W. (1976). Task analysis of a complex assembly task by the retarded child. *Exceptional Children, 43,* 78–84.

Goldfarb, L. A., Brotherson, M. J., Summers, J. A., & Turnbull, A. P. (1986). *Meeting the challenge of disability or chronic illness: A family guide.* Baltimore, MD: Paul H. Brookes.

Hale, G. (1979). *The source book for the disabled.* London: Imprint Books.

Hanson, M. J. (1984). *Atypical infant development.* Baltimore, MD: University Park Press.

Hanson, M. J., & Harris, S. R. (1986). *Teaching the young child with motor delays.* Austin, TX: Pro-Ed.

Hirst, M. (1989). Patterns of impairment and disability related to social handicaps in young people with cerebral palsy and spina bifida. *Journal of Biosocial Science, 21,* 1–12.

Jaeger, D. L. (1987). *Home program instruction sheets for infants and young children.* Tuscon, AZ: Communication and Therapy Skill Builders.

Johnston, R. B., & Magrab, P. R. (1976). *Developmental disorders: Assessment, treatment, education.* Baltimore, MD: University Park Press.

Keogh, J., & Sugden, D. (1985). *Movement skill development.* New York: Macmillan.

Lifchez, R., & Winslow, B. (1979). *Design for independent living: The environment and physically disabled people.* Berkeley, CA: University of California Press.

Lynch, E. W., Brekken, L., Drouin, C., & Wolfe, S. (1984). *A resource guide for early childhood special education.* Sacramento, CA: Infant/Preschool Special Education Resource Network.

Maddox, S. (Ed.). (1987). *Spinal networks: The total resource for the wheelchair community.* Boulder, CO: Author.

March of Dimes. (1992). *Spinal bifida: Public health education sheet.* White Plains, NY: Author.

Molnar, G. (1982). Intervention for physically handicapped children. In M. Lewis & L. T. Taft (Eds.), *Developmental disabilities: Theory, assessment and intervention.* (pp. 76–93). New York: SP Medical and Scientific.

Mulligan–Ault, M., Guess, P., Smith, L., & Thompson, B. (1988). The implementation of health-related procedures in classrooms for students with severe multiple impairments. *Journal of the Association for Persons with Severe Handicaps,* 13, 100–109.

Nelson, E. (1977). *Movement games for children of all ages.* New York: Sterling.

Orelove, F. P., & Sosbey, D. C. (1987). *Educating children with multiple disabilities.* Baltimore, MD: Paul H. Brookes.

Perske, R., Clifton, A., McClean, B. M., & Ishler Stein, J. (Eds.). (1986). *Mealtimes for persons with severe handicaps.* Baltimore, MD: Paul H. Brookes.

Rainforth, B., & Salisbury, C. L. (1988). Functional home programs: A model for therapists. *Topics in Early Childhood Special Education, 7*(4), 33–45.

Robinson, R. O. (1973). The frequency of other handicaps in children with cerebral palsy. *Developmental Medicine and Child Neurology, 15,* 305–312.

Rogers–Warren, A. K. (1982). Behavioral ecology in classrooms for young handicapped children. *Topics in Early Childhood Special Education, 2*(1), 21–32.

Schleickorn, J. (1993). *Coping with cerebral palsy: Answers to questions parents often ask* (3rd ed.). Austin, TX: Pro-Ed.

Seaman, J. A., & Depauw, K. P. (1989). *The new adapted physical education: A developmental approach.* Mountain View, CA: Mayfield.

Snell, M. E. (Ed.). (1987). *Systematic instruction of persons with severe handicaps* (3rd ed.). Columbus, OH: Merrill.

Snow, J. H., & Hooper, S. R. (1994). *Pediatric traumatic brain injury.* Thousand Oaks, CA: Sage.

Tansley, A. E. (1986). *Motor education.* Tuscon, AZ: Communication and Therapy Skill Builders.

Thompson, G. H., Rubin, I. L., & Bilenker, R. M. (1983). *Comprehensive management of cerebral palsy.* Orlando, FL: Grune and Statton.

Thurman, S. K., & Widerstrom, A. H. (1990). *Infants and young children with special needs.* Baltimore, MD: Paul H. Brookes.

Tingey–Michaelis, C. (1983). *Handicapped infants and children: A handbook for parents and professionals.* Baltimore, MD: University Park Press.

Tyler, J. S., & Mira, M. P. (1993). Educational modifications for students with head injuries. *Teaching Exceptional Children, 25,* 24–27.

Wermer, D. (1987). *Disabled village children: A guide for community health workers, rehabilitation workers, and families.* Palo Alto, CA: Hesperian Foundation.

Williamson, G. G. (1987). *Children with spina bifida: Early intervention and preschool programming.* Baltimore, MD: Paul H. Brookes.

Wolff, P. (1979). Theoretical issues in the development of motor skills. In L. Taft & M. Lewis (Eds.), *Developmental disabilities in the preschool child.* (pp. 101–137). Symposium presented by Rutgers Medical School, Educational Testing Service, and Johnson & Johnson Baby Products, Chicago.

Zaichkowsky, L. D., Zaichkowsky, L. B., & Martinek, T. J. (1980). *Growth and development: The child and physical activity.* St. Louis, MO: C. V. Mosby.

CHAPTER 12

THE IMPORTANCE OF PLAY

SUSAN M. COVEL, M.ED.

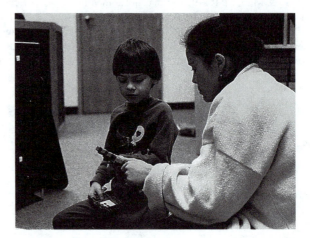

ABOUT THE AUTHOR

Susan M. Covel received her master of education degree in special education from Valdosta State College in Valdosta, Georgia. She received a bachelor of science degree in speech pathology and audiology from Ithica College in Ithica, New York. Ms. Covel has been professionally involved in the field of special education for the past seventeen years, serving as a speech therapist, primary and secondary special education teacher, a program coordinator/administrator, and a volunteer games coordinator and coach for the Special Olympics. She has been employed as a preschool teacher special education teacher/services coordinator for the Saint Francis Hospital Early Intervention Program for the past nine years. In addition, Ms. Covel served as a citizen ambassador with the People to People International Program in the spring of 1993. She traveled with a peer group to Russia, the Czech Republic, and Hungary to exchange ideas pertaining to early childhood special education.

CHAPTER KEY POINTS

- Play, the work of children, affects all major areas of development.
- Play skills develop in five major stages.
- Arrangement of the classroom, types of play materials, and time for play affect children's play.
- Block, house–dramatic play, sensory, art, quiet, and music–movement are the major play spaces in the classroom.

- Children need plenty of time to play at school and home with adults and other children.
- Children with developmental delays may benefit from specific modifications to play activities and the play environment.

Previous chapters have discussed types of developmental delays and specific therapy services available to meet the needs of young children with developmental delays. Several chapters have mentioned the value of using play time as a way to integrate a portion of the therapy services. This chapter is about the importance of play. It elaborates on the developmental stages of play, major areas in the classroom where children play, types of play in which children with specific disabilities engage, and special play modifications that are beneficial to children with special needs (Goldstein, 1994).

Research suggests that the play skills of children with special needs are qualitatively and quantitatively different from the play of children without special needs. It tends to be less organized and complex and there often is ritualistic use of toys and other objects. Children with special needs tend to engage in less group play (Isenberg & Jalongo, 1993). Because play skills are believed to enhance overall growth or development of the young child, the play characteristics of children with special needs could negatively affect other areas of development. This suggests that enhancing play skills can enhance growth. Because play is seen as an enjoyable activity by most children, it may be the most intrinsically motivational form of intervention for children with special needs.

OVERVIEW OF THE IMPORTANCE OF PLAY

Adequate play time is crucial for young children (Bettleheim, 1987). Play is what young children do. They are driven to play. According to Jean Piaget (1971), play is the "work" of childhood. Through play, young children learn about themselves and the world around them. It is a time when children may experiment and have the freedom to express themselves fully without fearing criticism or rejection. It lets them cope with events from the past and present and imagine the future (Isenberg & Jalongo, 1993).

Children often discover how things work during play. Children develop a sense of competency through play. Adults involved in the lives of young children should encourage and support children's play. "Play time" is how young children "prepare for life" (Haller, 1987).

Development Through Play

Although the importance of play time is often a focus during the preschool years, the value of play begins during infancy. For most infants, one of the earliest play times is during feeding. During this time, adults and infants trade smiles and imitate each other, including making sounds and facial expressions. Through these playful interactions, babies learn that their actions affect the people around them. This allows babies to begin to develop a sense of competency (Allen & Marotz, 1989).

Play time also often occurs between babies and adults at other times, including while changing a diaper, bathing and dressing, and undressing the baby. Babies also begin to play with things in the environment; initially, play is limited to looking at objects in the immediate environment. Babies smile at mobiles and stuffed toys within the first few weeks of life. They coo, babble, and laugh when adults shake a rattle. Babies begin reaching for toys as soon as they develop eye–hand coordination. Once they coordinate seeing, grasping, and bringing the objects to their mouths, they explore the objects visually, through touch, and orally (Marino, 1991).

For young children, play often allows them to work through their anxieties. Frequently, children act frightened of a new toy such as a jack-in-the-box, or when a constant in their environment changes, such as when an adult dresses in a costume. They appear to be pleased when they overcome their fears and can enjoy new toys or experiences (Einon, 1985). When adults take time to play with infants or older children, children experience a sense of their own worth (Markun, 1974).

During the preschool years, all areas of development are enhanced through play (Hoorn, Nourot, Scales, & Alward, 1993). Children learn new concepts such as up and down. Physical development is enhanced as they learn to coordinate large and small muscle movements needed in play, as well as in other aspects of life. Children learn that their actions have consequences. They learn how to use their creativity and imagination. Emotional development is enhanced through play as they learn how to express feelings and emotions. During play, children have an opportunity to practice social skills needed for sharing, taking turns, and cooperating as a group (Trawick–Smith, 1994). These varied learning experiences help young children develop a sense of self within the group, as well as help develop positive self-esteem (Hendrick, 1975).

Cognitive Development

Surprising as it may seem, young children learn many academic skills through play. They discover colors, textures, numbers, quantities, locations, descriptions, cause and effect, same and different, relationships between objects, as well as a multitude of vocabulary words that help them make sense of the world (Isaacs, 1972). They learn how to think and solve problems. Children learn at various rates, however. They learn when they are developmentally ready to learn (Caplan & Caplan, 1973). For example, most 2-year-olds are not developmentally ready to name the colors of a rainbow, but many 4-year-olds are able to point to and name colors.

At times, delays are found in children's abilities to acquire academic skills and information. Delays could be mild (several months lag) or severe (more than a year lag). Any delay in acquiring academic skills may necessitate implementing play activities that modify the presentation of information. Modifications vary, though, depending on the needs of the individual child, and might include a slower rate of presenting information or the use of multiple, repetitive presentations of information.

The severity of the delay also determines what information is introduced. It is important that children with delays be presented with information appropriate to their cognitive ability or developmental age rather than information based on their chronological age. This approach increases the chances of a child learning, as well as provides the child with a foundation from which more complex information about the world can be learned. Teachers and parents should recognize the needs of each child and provide a variety of toys, activities, and learning experiences that stimulate every child's desire to learn (Kirk & Gallagher, 1979).

Motor Development

Young children need space to move and the freedom to do so. Running, climbing, riding, jumping, and swinging are favorite activities of most children during the preschool years. These activities help develop large muscles of the body and are called gross motor skills. (See Chapter 11 for more information about gross motor skills.)

Children develop coordination and balance through play (Howes & Matheson, 1992). Sometimes children are observed tripping over people or objects in their path, having difficulty maneuvering around objects, falling down frequently, or falling off toys. Severe gross motor delays lead to safety concerns. The delays also interfere with children's ability to play with peers due to an inability to keep up or fully participate in a game. When parents notice a delay in gross motor skills development, they should discuss their concerns with the child's pediatrician. If the child is in an early intervention program, a physical therapist can be consulted to determine whether therapy is needed and provide the classroom staff with suggestions that facilitate gross motor development. (See Chapter 11 for more information about physical therapy.)

Play also aids in the development of fine motor skills, finger dexterity and eye–hand coordination. Preschool children usually enjoy playing with blocks, toy tools, puzzles, safety scissors, large beads, crayons, paint, and clay. In so doing, they use their fingers and hands to grasp, pinch, squeeze, stack, draw, and cut.

Children with a delay in the ability to coordinate movements needed for such tasks often resist playing with toys or participating in activities that require fine motor control (Eliason & Jenkins, 1977). This deprives these children of social interactions and the opportunity to strengthen fine motor skills. If the child is in an early intervention program, an occupational therapist should be consulted to determine whether therapy is needed and provide classroom staff and parents with suggestions to enhance fine motor skills. (See Chapter 10 for more information about occupational therapy.)

Speech and Language Development

During play activities children use speech and language to communicate with others. The ability to communicate successfully with others is critical. It begins at birth with crying, gazing, and cooing. It progresses to babbling and using gestures and isolated words as children begin to grow. During the toddler and preschool years, children use their words to express wants, needs, and emotions, and communicate with peers and adults. Typically during this time, children learn the names of familiar people and objects in their environment and begin to ask questions. It is important for adults to talk with children about play and daily routines. For example, talking about the bath water being warm or talking about the

color of a toy with which the child is playing may enhance speech and language development (Kennedy, 1991).

Social Development

Children are like sponges: They absorb what is around them. Children do *not* follow the adage, "Do as I say and not as I do." They tend to imitate what they see and hear without fearing the consequences. When children observe sharing, caring, manners, cooperation, and conflict resolution (solving a disagreement, for example, by talking instead of using mean words, yelling, or hitting), they are likely to imitate these types of behavior. Learning these social skills helps children establish and maintain relationships in school, which in turn enhances self-esteem. (Chapter 15 discusses the importance of helping children develop positive self-esteem.)

New social skills also come from paying attention to tasks and people. If a child cannot attend to tasks or wanders from one area to another, it interferes with the ability to learn new information and skills. Sometimes it is necessary to set time limits for activities or play choices, especially when attention to a task is less than several minutes. This may help them focus on the task. For example, the teacher might ask a child to pick a place to play and remind the child to stay at that place until a timer rings (a kitchen timer with a bell). This direction provides children with a better chance to assimilate available information, thus facilitating learning.

Time limits also provide children with the opportunity to finish projects and games, as well as minimize the chance of distracting their peers. This is especially important for children with special needs who participate in inclusion programs. (See Chapter 7 for more information on inclusion programs.) Their disability may draw *negative* attention to them, such as other children making fun of them. The negative attention makes it difficult to form new friendships and may harm self-esteem.

Self-Help Skills Development

Self-help skills are those that allow children to care for their basic needs as independently as possible. Activities generally included in this area of development are eating, dressing, washing, and using the toilet. "Dress-up" is a favorite play activity for many young children. In dress-up, children learn many skills, such as folding, zipping, buttoning, locating the front and back of their clothes, and dressing and undressing themselves.

"Playing house" allows children to practice holding eating utensils to feed themselves. Another example of a self-help skill is washing hands. Arts and crafts and sensory activities often make children's hands dirty. Children involved in these activities have opportunities to wash their hands several times a day. They also learn to use combs and brushes while caring for a doll's hair. Given the chance, most young children will develop a multitude of necessary self-help skills through play.

STAGES OF PLAY

Play skills develop in sequence. Each stage builds on the skills and knowledge previously obtained and takes children's play to a more complex level. The play skills of children with disabilities are often delayed in direct relation to the degree of the disability. Even for children who have developmental delays, however, the sequential order for the stages of play usually remains the same (Sawyers & Rogers, 1988).

In the course of play development, it is important to focus on children's developmental ages rather than on chronological ages. This allows adults to generate appropriate activities that enhance and aid in the development of play skills. Sometimes two stages of play overlap or occur simultaneously. In fact, even children at the most complex stage of play will engage in play characteristic of an earlier stage.

The six major stages of play that occur from birth through the preschool years are exploratory, pretend, solitary, parallel, associative, and cooperative. Understanding stages of play is useful when selecting toys and creating developmentally appropriate play opportunities for children with special needs (Sawyers & Rodgers, 1988).

Exploratory Play (Birth to Twelve Months)

Exploratory play dominates children's active waking time from birth to 12 months. Exploratory play is just what the name suggests: Babies generally explore the world with their senses. They initially use their eyes and ears. As they mature, the other senses become a part of exploration (Gordon, 1970). Once children can grasp small objects, the primary mode of exploration occurs through putting objects in their mouth to taste and feel. It is, therefore, essential that the environment of these crawling "explorers" be clean and safe. Children continue to explore the environment throughout childhood. As children mature and gain more knowledge of the world around them, their way of exploring also matures (Barber & Williams, 1981). For example, preschool children begin to notice and label colors and textures.

Pretend Play (Nine to Eighteen Months)

Pretend play occurs once children have acquired the knowledge and developed the abilities to act out or imitate simple events they have either done themselves or observed someone else doing, such as sleeping or eating. For example, a child sees an adult drink from a cup and then pretends to drink from an empty toy tea cup. Toward the latter part of this stage, children begin to perform these simple actions for others. For example, a child offers mommy, the teacher, or another child some juice from an empty cup.

Children also begin to use one object to represent another during this stage. For example, an orange block may become a carrot. Children also give nonexistent properties to objects. They pretend that toy dishes are wet and so they dry them (Jarrold, Boucher, & Smith, 1993). The knowledge needed for pretend play is based on children's abilities to use real objects in an appropriate manner, such as using a real or toy telephone and pretending to call grandma (Lewis, Boucher, & Astell, 1992).

By observing adults and older children, young children acquire necessary information for pretend play. It is, therefore, important for all children to have opportunities to interact with parents, other adults, older siblings, and other children in school and non-school setting to observe their actions and use of objects. This is called symbolic play and continues to develop through the solitary and parallel stages of play described below (Rescorla & Goossens, 1992).

Solitary Play (Eighteen to Twenty-Four Months)

Children engage in solitary play by playing independently with toys differing from those used by other children within the immediate play area. For example, one child plays with a truck and another with blocks in the same corner of the room. During solitary play, children make no attempt to interact with each other, although they may walk around or step over other children (Rogers & Sawyers, 1988). Solitary play allows a child time to gain understanding of objects and toys within the environment before having to demonstrate that understanding in a group. This stage helps create a sense of security because the children do not have to perform for anyone but themselves.

Although solitary play in young children reflects their inability to participate in more mature forms of play, there are times when older children want or need to engage in solitary play. Some children have a dispositional (personality type) preference for engaging in extended periods of solitary play. It is important to respect each child's unique mode of play.

Without assistance, however, children with disabilities may not be able to resolve how to play with a toy. If this occurs, adults playing with these children should demonstrate how to use the toy. In some cases, adults need to guide the children physically through the movements needed to use the toy. Several repetitions of modeling or guidance may be necessary to help the children learn how to use the toy. Children with motor disabilities, however, often need special toys adapted for

their use. (Chapters 10 and 11 discuss adaptations for children with motor delays.)

Parallel Play (Twenty-Four to Thirty-Six Months)

Imagine the double yellow lines on the road. They run side by side but never touch. Such is the case with parallel play. During parallel play, two or more children engage in an activity or play with similar toys while playing alongside each other. They typically do *not* speak to each other but are comfortable with the proximity of their peers (Gordon, 1972).

Often, children with disabilities engage in parallel play because they do not have the ability or skills to play at the same level as their peers even though they may want to. Teaching staff and parents should recognize this desire and provide ways for children to be included. A teacher might bring out a special toy that can be used simultaneously by several children (Gordon, 1972). The teacher could then take a reluctant child to the area where the other children are playing with this toy while enthusiastically encouraging the child with disabilities to join in playing with the special toy.

Another "substage" of play present during the latter half of the parallel stage is called onlooker behavior; children watch other children play, often talking to them about their play. During the onlooker stage, children might ask questions about play going on around them without actually entering into the activity. It is almost as if children are preparing to enter the play of their peers. This continued observation by the onlooker child, paired with the child's questions, provides the child with an understanding of the rules governing group play.

Associative Play (Thirty-Six to Forty-Eight Months)

During associative play, children play in a group. They play with similar toys or are engaged in a similar activity. They might trade toys and comment on each other's behavior but are not playing or working together for a shared goal (Rogers & Sawyers, 1988). They are together but separate.

Due to varying levels of ability within the classroom, it may sometimes be necessary for a teacher to arrange, or "engineer," situations encouraging children to engage in associative play. This might be done, for example, by having four children sit at a table, each with some blocks and toy cars on a tray. In this example, the children play together with the same toys and have an opportunity to observe and comment on each other's play. This helps set the stage for cooperative play.

Cooperative Play (Forty-Eight to Sixty Months)

Children engaged in cooperative play have a shared goal. It could involve completing a city made of blocks or acting out a dramatic play scene such as pretending to play house. Cooperative play typically includes at least one, sometimes two, leaders in the group. During cooperative play, meaningful communication between peers occurs to help ensure that a common goal is realized (Rogers & Sawyers, 1988).

Adults can elicit higher levels of play by encouraging turn-taking games and modeling turn-taking skills. Adults should also help children orient and maintain attention. When children engage in more complex play, adults must positively respond to this behavior. Play activities provided should integrate all developmental areas with a special emphasis on social communication skills.

USING PLAY TO ASSESS CHILDREN'S DEVELOPMENTAL LEVELS

At times, it is necessary to evaluate children whose developmental age appears to be delayed when compared with their chronological age. Formal, standardized tests for young children often take thirty minutes or more to administer, depending on a child's ability to pay attention. In many cases, it is not realistic to expect children with suspected developmental disabilities to sit at a table for thirty minutes answering questions and performing tasks that in and of themselves have no meaning to them (Brown, 1982).

Standardized tests also typically do not allow examiners to observe how children use information and abilities the children have acquired in daily activities. Formal tests do not allow adjustments for children who "shut down" in the face of structured testing situations (Kennedy, 1991). Formal testing are often stressful for young children if they do not understand what is expected and have limited ways to communicate frustration and confusion (Lewis, 1993).

If the purpose of an assessment is to understand the level at which children function, an ideal way to obtain this information is to observe children playing (Linder, 1990). During play, children spontaneously and authentically demonstrate knowledge and skills. Not all children or all types of skills, though, can be assessed using the less structured play-based assessment. Specific tasks, such as putting together puzzles, may not be spontaneously chosen by children during the evaluation and, therefore, must be set up by the examiner. This should be expected and does not minimize the effectiveness of play-based assessment. It is important to follow a child's lead, which, in addition to revealing strengths, also reveals weaknesses. Play-based assessment is a nonthreatening, reliable way of obtaining an accurate indication of children's current levels of development (Kirk & Gallagher, 1979).

PLAY SKILLS OF CHILDREN WITH SPECIAL NEEDS

As described earlier, the stages of play development follow a specific sequence. Play is developmental, and children with special needs usually follow the typical sequence, although often at a slower rate. Children with special needs also tend to differ in the quality of their play, or how they play (Westby, 1988).

In a special education preschool setting, teachers set up the room to encourage and enhance different types of play with toys appropriate for children at various levels of development (Lieber & Beckman,1991). This allows children to participate at their own level rather than expecting all children to play in the same way (Rogers & Sawyers, 1988). Peer models and "tutors" could be used even at this early age to guide children who have difficulty coping or participating. For example, a teacher could say to a child who does not seem to know how to play with blocks, "Look at the tall block tower Chris is building."

The play skills development of children with special needs is affected by the other areas of development discussed earlier in this chapter. For example, a 4-year-old with the cognitive level of a 2-year-old probably cannot construct an elaborate tunnel of soft blocks through which to drive toy cars. Most 2-year-olds do not play with blocks in this complex way. Additionally, children with communication delays may have difficulty speaking, expressing thoughts, or understanding other children during play. It is the responsibility of the teaching staff to establish an effective communication system for these children. For example, a teacher might develop a picture or communication board for a nonverbal child. If the child wants a car but cannot say, *car,* the child could point to a picture of a car on the communication board (Gowen, 1992).

The home environment of children also affects play skills development. It is essential that children be allowed to explore their surroundings to gain valuable information about how the world works. Children should be allowed to play inside and outside with toys and real objects such as pots and pans. Most children independently find things to play with that they enjoy. The need for adequate play time is especially true for children with special needs (Kennedy, 1991).

Some children who have developmental delays requires play that includes adult-directed activities because it is difficult for them to plan and organize their own play. The child's teacher should provide parents and daycare providers with information and suggestions for appropriate games and activities, as well as ideas for stimulating language, which is necessary for play. Family members must allow children to be independent and creative without the children fearing criticism or rejection. Special ways to use play to aid children with specific developmental disabilities are discussed below.

Autistic or Autistic-Like Characteristics

Children who are autistic or autistic-like (display some autistic behavior, but have not been formally classified as autistic) most often engage in solitary play. These children often appear to be "in a world of their own." They are often involved in activities such as spinning wheels on a toy vehicle while making odd noises (Fay & Schuler, 1980). This type of behavior is self-stimulatory and ritualistic in nature rather than purposeful. Children engaging in autistic behavior frequently line up objects or hold an object in front of their eyes while moving it back and forth. If speech is used by these children during play, it is usually noncommunicative, such as counting objects or repeating dialog from a movie.

Children who are autistic tend to need routines and become upset when routines are changed or when ritualistic play is interrupted. Working with children who are autistic or who exhibit autistic-like behavior requires patience, respect, awareness, and persistence on the part of parents and teachers to help move these children into the play world of their peers (Kirk & Gallagher, 1979).

The language skills of children who are autistic are often delayed, which in turn leads to a significant delay in pretend and symbolic play. In addition to staff helping children play with toys and interact with peers, individual language and play sessions are often beneficial for developing attention and communication skills, prerequisites for certain stages of play. It is unusual for children who are autistic to initiate purposeful play unless it has been previously observed. These children should have frequent modeling of appropriate play with toys and interactions with peers to maximize the probability of those skills and behavior types becoming a part of their spontaneous play (Pushaw, 1976).

Deaf or Hearing Impaired

The inability to hear could interrupt the normal development of play. It often leads to communication barriers and breakdowns with peers as play becomes more social and cooperative and incorporates more rules. Children who are deaf or hearing impaired observe, imitate, and explore during play just like their peers who can hear. Children with varying degrees of hearing loss rely heavily on sight during solitary play and often notice things children who do not have hearing loss might take for granted, such as the intricacies of how a toy functions or a cracked wheel on a toy car. Children with this disability tend to pay attention to details and are more physical during play, including grabbing and pushing to obtain desired toys. Aggressive physical behavior, however, usually diminishes once they learn how to communicate and negotiate (Anitia & Kreimeyer, 1992; Schwartz, 1987).

Symbolic play skills are related to the communication abilities of children who are deaf or hearing impaired, which supports the need for early intervention (Rescorla & Goossens, 1992). Children who are hearing impaired typically develop speech, whereas the majority of children who are deaf do not develop intelligible (understandable) speech. Language delays of these children are often not obvious until speech and language skills are needed for social components of associative and cooperative play. "Reciprocal" games, including taking turns, and "back and forth" games, such as catch, are ideal activities for children who are deaf or hearing impaired because they require eye contact between all participants. (See Chapter 9 for further discussion of the needs of children with hearing impairments.)

Speech and Language Impaired

Children with language impairments often exhibit delays in cognitive development. Play development is frequently delayed as well because the children often do not have the necessary knowledge or familiarity with toys and objects in their play environment. Play skills are likely to develop according to the typical sequential stages but generally at a slower rate. The play of toddlers who are language impaired is often limited and repetitive (Rescorla & Goossens, 1992). This does not imply that these children cannot catch up with their peers. If there are no other significant delays and a structured early intervention program is in place, it is then possible for these children to progress along the "normal" continuum.

Children acquire much of their language through play. Play often takes them from what is familiar to new activities. All of this helps develop and expand language and cognition in young children. Many children with language delays show an inability to spontaneously use the language they have acquired. For example, they can perhaps name the items on the dinner table but cannot "think" to ask for a napkin or say they need a cup at meal time. They have difficulty using their knowledge to obtain or receive information or participate in interactions with peers and adults (Bloom & Lahey, 1978).

It is often necessary to provide verbal cues, or suggestions, during play so that these children can use their knowledge base to expand their play scenes. For example, a teacher might say, "I need a plate to put my food on," and ask the child, "What do you need to put your food on?" Without this cue, children who have a speech or language delay may be unable to correctly answer the question.

Cognitive Delays

Play skills of children with cognitive delays are generally delayed. Their play typically follows the sequence of play stages but at a slower rate. These children tend to prefer toys that are manipulative in nature, such as push–pull toys, pounding toys, and toys with switches and knobs, rather than toys that require them to be more imaginative, such as small figures of people or animals or building blocks (Hellendoorn & Hoekman, 1992). These children generally require great repetition to master object play, such as building with blocks, and social play interacting with peers.

Preschoolers with cognitive delays typically exhibit speech and language delays. The severity of these delays influences play behavior and abilities. Their use of materials for play is often limited as is their repertoire and the sophistication of their play skills. These children appear to lack the creativity, imagination, and knowledge needed to combine toys and other props for more complex or advanced play scenes, as well as for the later stages of play development. In addition, they often lack the cognitive and language skills necessary for rule-governed play and the communication skills necessary for social interactions and dialogue. Children with cognitive delays often have motor delays that also limit their play skills (Gowen, 1992).

Physically Impaired

Children with motor delays often require adaptive equipment or modifications to their environment. For example, children who are in wheelchairs or use crutches or walkers need ample space to move. They need tables to be at a height that allows them to sit and play with objects such as puzzles. Children in wheelchairs need blocks placed on a tabletop rather than on the floor. Children with fine or gross motor delays may require adaptive switches or special knobs in order to play with certain toys. Some equipment is too challenging or unsafe for children with motor delays. Teachers, parents, and peers may be tempted to assume children with motor delays cannot participate in certain activities, so they might need instruction on how to include the children in classroom activities. (Chapters 10 and 11 provide further discussion of adaptations that are needed for children with motor delays.)

Visually Impaired

Children with visual impairments often exhibit delays in the early stages of play due to the inability to see (blind) or difficulty in seeing (partial sight) objects and toys in the play environment. In addition, they may be unable to observe peers and subsequently be unable to imitate their actions. They often are unable to move around the room successfully without assistance.

Exploratory play is essential for children who are visually impaired because it uses the senses other than sight in discovering the shape, size, and function of toys and other objects. The play environment should include toys designed to stimulate senses other than sight.

Children who are visually impaired tend to keep objects close to their body during exploration. If they drop an object, it is more likely to remain close to them and they are more likely to be able to retrieve it. Very young children who are visually impaired often bite and "mouth" objects as well as rub them on their faces. As the children mature, these discovery types of behavior become less socially appropriate, and the children gradually learn new ways to explore toys and objects. (Chapter 10 provides a discussion of the needs of children with visual impairments.)

THE SPECIAL NEEDS PRESCHOOL

The general philosophy underlying most preschools for children with special needs is to provide an environment that encourages and facilitates learning through play experiences. This is the same philosophy found in most regular education preschools. Most special needs preschools have staff members trained in special education, and the number of students in each class is smaller than in most regular education preschool classes.

Several key factors affect the ability to learn, including intellectual function, desire to learn, readiness for learning, and attention span. It is, therefore, important to give children the freedom and support they need to make choices in their daily routine, which promotes self-initiated (self-motivated) activity (Hohmann, Banet, & Weikart, 1979). Children with special needs frequently cannot initiate play without some suggestions from a teacher or parent. It is important for adults to be aware of the interests and developmental levels of children to be able to provide toys and activities that catch the children's interest. Attention to task is more easily achieved when children have a reason to be at the activity, and learning has a better chance of occurring when children can attend to the activity for more than a few minutes.

It is important that the classroom include a variety of toys and materials that allow for individual differences and meet the needs of each child. Children should be able to reach and use the toys in sight. The teacher should *not* place items in play areas if they are not for the children to use. Items such as scissors, glue, and paint generally require teacher supervision but should be accessible to the children on a regular basis because they encourage fine motor skill development, as well as creativity.

Most teachers use daily, weekly, or monthly themes to plan activities. Based on these themes, the classroom is arranged, props brought in, and activities prepared that correspond to the theme and facilitate learning (Brown, 1982). For example, if the theme is "camping," a tent, cooking kit, and sleeping bags could be brought in as props. Fireflies might be made during an art activity and hung from the ceiling, and children encouraged to pretend to roast hot dogs and marshmallows.

Children with more severe delays often spend less time in purposeful play and more time engaged in inappropriate (nonpurposeful) play. Attention span often is a factor, because children who cannot focus for more than a minute or two often wander around the room until something else catches their attention. It is the teacher's responsibility to assist these children in becoming active play participants based on their level of readiness.

A consistent daily routine is an essential component of a successful preschool program for children with special needs. Children need a certain degree of structure and predictability in their lives. Knowing what will happen each day provides a sense of security that can otherwise be absent from their lives. Occasional special events, however, should be integrated into their daily routine.

These variations allow children to adapt to change, but at a gradual rate.

SKILL DEVELOPMENT IN PLAY AREAS

Parents are sometimes dismayed at the thought that their children go to school to play. Parents want to know that their children are learning and what concepts they are learning in preparation for primary school. Play allows children to learn at their own rate and acquire concepts that might otherwise have escaped them if forced to sit at a table and listen to a teacher talk, which often occurs in classrooms not designed for children with special needs. Parents who question whether learning takes place during play should be encouraged to spend time with their child at school to see how productive play time can be. Table 12.1 provides a list of many of the concepts and skills children learn through play activities, including time cleaning up play materials (cleanup time).

ARRANGEMENT OF THE CLASSROOM

The arrangement of the classroom should have well-defined physical spaces that might include blocks, house and dramatic play, sensory, art, quiet, music and movement, and science areas (Hohmann, et. al, 1979). These areas appear consistently in regular and special needs classrooms. The items in each area should be organized, labeled with pictures or words, and stored in plain view so that the children have easy access to them. In addition, the shelves should be labeled with pictures and words so that, when it is time to clean up, the children know where items belong. Area boundaries should be easy to redefine to combine two areas, such as dramatic play and sensory play, to enhance creativity and learning.

Labeling and organizing toys and materials allows for independence and responsibility while putting away the toys and supplies. In addition, classroom organization provides a sense of order and security for children because it allows for a consistent routine for beginning and ending play.

TABLE 12.1   Concepts and Skills Learned Through Play

Cognitive and Language Skills

color	following directions
shape	understanding cause and
size	effect
number	categorizing
location	sequencing
weight	classifying
distance	basic logic
theme-related	sense of time
vocabulary	reading
sorting and matching	

Social Skills (includes attention to task)

perseverance	taking turns
negotiation	resolving conflict
manners	conversational skills
patience	building relationships
empathy	expressing feelings
sharing	nonverbal communication
role-playing	

Self-Help Skills

dressing	washing
buttoning	folding
zipping	napping (fasteners)
eating	drinking

Sensory and Motor Skills

mixing	eye–hand coordination
pouring	touching, smelling, hearing,
pinching	tasting, and seeing
pulling	awareness of their spatial
strength	relation to the
maintaining balance	environment
	stretching
	dexterity
	writing and drawing

Organization also saves time because everything has a specific location, making it is easy to find a particular item. When teachers notice that an area of the room is seldom used, that area should be modified, combined with another area, or other areas temporarily closed off to encourage play in an underused area. Teachers should attempt to facilitate play in this area by familiarizing children with the items found there.

The classroom environment may need to be adapted to accommodate the special needs of children with motor delays. Children in wheelchairs need space to move about and access to toys and tables, for instance, at wheelchair height. Children with motor delays might lean against shelves to move about; therefore shelves must be very stable.

Block Area

The block area is often one of the largest areas in a classroom. The amount of shelf and play space affects the number of toys that can be made available in this area. This area might also be used for large-group activities, generally during circle time when teachers and children meet to plan the day's events, sing songs, and dance or exercise. Items that may be found in this area are shown in Table 12.2.

At home or in school, as adults observe and play with children, they should be aware of how children play with blocks, in particular. According to Hirsch (1984), there are six major stages of building with blocks just as there are stages in the development of play. These stages are outlined in Table 12.3.

Adults should interact and play with children at each child's developmental level. In preschool,

TABLE 12.2   Types of Toys Found in the Block Area

The block area usually contains many of the following objects:

wooden blocks of various sizes and colors	snap-together blocks
cardboard or styrofoam blocks	building sets
a doll house	train tracks
toy garages, farms, and other buildings	road map
cars and trucks of various sizes	traffic signs
toy trains	cardboard
boards	building tiles
carpet squares	puppets
toy people, action figures, or other characters	toy animals

TABLE 12.3 Hirsch's Six Stages of Block Play

Progressing through the six stages of block play, the child will:

- Walk around carrying blocks or pile them up;
- Build towers or lay blocks side by side in rows;
- Bridge space with blocks, using two blocks parallel to each other and a third across the top;
- Build enclosures;
- Build structures that have a particular pattern;
- Use blocks to build and represent structures, buildings, or other things with which the child is familiar and use these structures as props for cars and people.

teachers often take a child's play one step beyond the child's abilities and add to what the child has done. That is, the teacher might build a slightly more complex structure to provide a child with ideas but without forcing the child to build the same thing. The purpose of modeling slightly more advanced play skills is to expose children to different ways of using the blocks to expand their existing repertoire of skills.

House and Dramatic Play Area

The house and dramatic play area is where at any given moment an observer might find a "mommy" (a child pretending to be mommy) cooking dinner for Mickey Mouse (a different child pretending) while Batman (and yet another child pretending) irons his cape. Given an adequate selection of props, young children may become whomever or whatever they wish. Some of the items included in the dramatic play area of the classroom are listed in Table 12.4.

Most young children love to dress up and act out scenes from their daily lives. Typically, boys and girls wear clothes for men and women during role-play and may switch roles several times during a play scene. Sometimes parents feel uncomfortable allowing their sons to wear dresses during play. Parents should be reassured, though, that dress-up is a normal part of play even if boys wear girl's clothing.

Not all children are at the same level of imaginative play or enjoy playing in this area. Teachers

should be aware of each child's level of ability and comfort. The teacher's role in this area might be as a participant in a play scene such as being a patient for the doctor to apply a bandage, or a passenger on a train, or an observer providing dialogue or suggestions if needed. Teachers may read a familiar story during the day and then put the book in the dramatic play area to give children ideas for dramatic play.

Sensory Area

Many classrooms have a sensory area, which could be combined with other areas. Often the sensory area contains a sensory table where children can use their senses to learn. This is a mainstay in most preschool classrooms. A sensory table is large enough for six to eight children to stand around, and has an insert tray about six inches deep. The height of the sensory table should be adapted for children with motor delays, including those in wheelchairs or whose muscle development does not allow them to stand for extended periods of time.

A sensory table has different media (substances or materials) that could be put inside the tray for

TABLE 12.4 Types of Materials Found in a Dramatic Play Area

- toy stove or oven, sink, refrigerator
- toy or real (unbreakable) dishes and utensils, pots, and pans
- iron, broom, dust pan
- telephone
- dress-up clothes and costumes including aprons, scarves, mittens, hats, old plastic glasses frames
- suitcases, wallets, pocketbooks
- baby dolls
- baby bed
- stuffed toy animals
- pillows and blankets
- old jewelry
- keys on a ring
- pretend food, and real food containers and boxes
- baskets and small grocery carts
- pretend money
- brown paper bags

children to smell, taste, touch, see, and listen to during the course of their play, referred to as tactile exploration. Materials put into a sensory table must correspond with the children's developmental level. For example, small objects may be a choking hazard if placed in a child's mouth, and, therefore, would not be appropriate for children who are still mouthing objects. The sensory table is often used for containing messy substances or when the teacher wants to encourage a group of children to be in one area and play together. Storage shelves containing items that can be used in the sensory table are often close to where the sensory table is located. Examples of items that may be used in the sensory table are listed in Table 12.5.

Some children do not like to play with messy materials, get dirty, or explore new sensations. These children should be encouraged to participate at their own comfort level with the teacher carefully increasing their exposure to a substance until they show a more acceptable level of tolerance of it. Many times, children feel uncomfortable interacting with certain items because they have not been exposed to "tactile exploratory" materials at home (Gowen, 1992). Frequent exposure to varying types of materials at school helps children become familiar with them over time. This often results in children returning to the sensory area for play, creating new possibilities for learning at home and school.

TABLE 12.5 *Examples of Sensory Table Materials*

- cups
- funnels
- sponges
- shovels and other containers for dumping and pouring
- sand
- rice and oatmeal (dry and wet)
- dried beans
- shaving cream
- goop (made from corn starch and water)
- snow
- dirt
- cooked macaroni or spaghetti
- dough or clay

Sensory activities could also occur at child-sized tables, especially when precision and/or cutting is involved. A table can be in a central area or in the dramatic play area to encourage children to explore activities such as cooking. Using the utensils in the kitchen, children can "slice" different foods. Depending on the developmental levels of the children, the teacher might provide each child with a tray with some of the material needed to make a particular object, such as a sock puppet. This allows them to explore at their own rate and also encourages the use of their communication skills to obtain items from peers.

Art Area

Art is a creative form of play and this area is often located close to or as part of the sensory area (Atack, 1986). Often, children who avoid the art area need teachers' or parents' support in developing imagination and creativity in the other play areas such as blocks or dramatic play. (See Chapter 13 for a more detailed discussion about the use of art activities to enhance children's abilities.)

Quiet Area

There should be a quiet area in every classroom where the activity and noise levels are less than those found in other areas. This area will usually contain books. It should be a comfortable area that entices children. Most children enjoy looking at books alone but are also just as likely to "read" to one another. Books should be readily accessible and clearly displayed so that they are inviting to children who pass by the area. Books should be made of sturdy materials. The quiet area might also be the location for small toys (manipulatives) that develop fine motor skills. These items include pegs with pegboards, stringing beads, puzzles, nesting cups, and stacking rings. Children can independently and quietly use the toys. Including these items in the quiet area helps limit the distractions that children experience in the larger part of the classroom during play time. Items frequently included in this area are listed in Table 12.6.

TABLE 12.6 Examples of Quiet Area Materials

- books and magazines
- mats
- pillows
- blankets
- carpet squares
- stuffed toy animals
- a small table with chairs around it
- rocking chairs

Depending on the developmental levels of the children in the class, the teacher might have a combined reading and writing area. This area would include paper, individual journals, pencils, markers, tape, perhaps staplers, and stencils. Many older preschoolers ask to be taught how to write their own names. They often like to tell stories and have a teacher write down the stories to be read at a future date.

Movement and Music Areas

It is essential that young children be given time to be physically active during the day. This is especially true for children with special needs because they frequently have delays in their gross motor skills. During movement activities, gross motors skills are developed and enhanced through play.

Movement can be as subtle as a wave or as obvious as jumping up and down. Young children need space to run, jump, climb, and skip. They should be able to swing and go down slides. The playground or gross motor area within the classroom is usually a favorite area in preschool because it provides freedom of movement.

Songs are often used in preschool during transition times. Repetitive tunes are easy for children to learn and can be used to remind them of what time it is, such as during cleanup time. Songs are often sung during circle time. Classical music could be used as background sound or as a soothing agent in an otherwise loud or boisterous room.

Record or cassette players are often found in preschool classrooms. Time for singing or listening to familiar songs with or without accompanying actions is valuable for young children. Toy musical instruments could also be used during music time. Preschool children are not old enough to be self-conscious about their voices and are therefore generally eager to sing regardless of whether they know the words. In addition, many children learn new vocabulary or concepts through music even when they do not grasp the meanings of the same words used in conversation. Teachers and parents should take advantage of this enjoyable way (through music and movement) to promote learning. Table 12.7 lists examples of items to include in the music and movement area.

Science Area

Most children enjoy helping with the care of animals and plants. Children can learn about the needs of other living things by taking responsibility for helping to care for plants or animals. It is not necessary to have a separate science area. A windowsill or sturdy table or shelves, which cannot be knocked over, make excellent locations for most plants or animals. Some children have allergies that would not permit plants and animals in the classroom. As discussed in Chapter 4, children

TABLE 12.7 Examples of Music and Movement Area Materials

Musical supplies
- tape recorder and record player
- tapes and records
- drums
- bells
- sticks to hit together
- cymbals
- triangles

Movement supplies
- tricycles
- balls
- swings
- slide
- climbing apparatus

who are HIV positive should not help care for classroom animals. The science area should also include objects found in nature and other science equipment. See Table 12.8 for a list of items that may be found in this area.

PLAY TIME AT HOME

Children with special needs enrolled in a preschool program need additional time for play at home. Play time should fill most of the child's day. A large space is not required for a child's play area, but it should be an area that is the child's space rather than just a corner next to the television, for example. It should be safe from possible hazards including loose wires or cords. It is also important that young children be able to play outside. If there is no yard adjacent to the child's home, going on walks or to local playgrounds or parks provides excellent opportunities for developing gross motor skills.

Young children should be around other young children. If a child has no siblings, parents should then be encouraged to invite other children of the same age to play. Play partners are important because they provide an opportunity for taking turns, sharing, cooperating, and stimulating dramatic play. Parents should avoid comparing children's abilities and should understand and accept unique developmental needs.

In addition to peer play partners, it is important that parents play with their child and want to do so. Children should know that the adults in their lives want to spend time with them doing what children want to do. Preschoolers enjoy imitating their parents and imitation is one way children learn. When parents play with their child, they should get down to the child's level: if the child is on the floor, the parents should be on the floor.

When children do not want to play with their parents, they often let them know by ignoring the parents, leaving the activity, or telling the parents to leave. Parents should *not* be offended or become upset when children do not want them as play partners. Instead, parents should respect the child's wishes but should remain available if the child later invites them to play or needs them to help resolve a problem or conflict.

It is also important for parents to allow their child to "hang out" with them while they perform daily chores or relax with a good book. Children imitate their parents' actions in play by re-creating them. This allows them to gradually become more advanced and competent in their play skills (Marzollo & Harper, 1972). Parents should let their children help them with chores. This enables children to observe what the parents are doing and learn how to manipulate the tools or necessary utensils. Parents must remember to use their good judgment, however, and make sure children are always safe.

Sometimes, adults do not approve of the way children play. They may take the opportunity to tell children how to use a toy "the right way" or what to draw with the crayons and paper. If adults find themselves doing this, they should find a way to interact with their children that is less judgmental and more supportive of the play. In choosing play items, children learn about making decisions at an early age, which helps to build positive self-esteem.

It is very important to provide children enough time to play. At most preschools, there typically is a

TABLE 12.8 Examples of Science Area Life and Equipment

Animals
mice, gerbils, guinea pigs, turtles, lizards, parakeets, hermit crabs, fish, rabbits

Items found in nature
leaves, acorns, seeds, pine cones, shells, rocks, sticks, dried flowers, bones, feathers, snake skins, insect ectoskeletons

Science equipment
magnifying glass, telescope, binoculars, tweezers, magnets, microscope, clear plastic containers with lids, butterfly nets, small digging tools, child-size work gloves

daily routine allowing ample time for indoor play. Although it is also important for parents to provide their children with ample time to play throughout the day, it does not have to be all at one time. Parents should encourage their children to play throughout the day. Interruptions are inevitable, but parents should try to provide their children with a solid block of time reserved for play time. Parents should understand that time for play is needed just as there must be time for eating and resting. Children with special needs, though, often take longer to become involved in their play and need more time to actually play.

CLEANUP TIME

Children should be actively involved in cleaning up their play materials at home and school. Before cleaning up, there should be at least one warning or a reminder that play time is ending soon. Telling a five-year-old that cleanup time is in five minutes might not be meaningful because most five-year-olds cannot tell time. A timer might be set so that children can see how much time is left. This allows them to finish what they started and lets them know that soon they will need to clean up. If there is no timer, putting on the radio or a favorite record or tape and telling children that, when the song or record is finished, it will be time to put the toys away, can help in the transition.

Cleanup time may result in conflicts when children do not want to put toys away. Parents and teachers should remember that it is important for children to have a specific place for toys. Toy boxes have been popular for years but often become so crowded that it is difficult to find desired toys easily. If possible, parents should reserve shelves or a cabinet so that toys can be organized and readily found. Parents may want to label shelves as is done within a preschool setting. Labeling helps ensure that the toys have a specific location and are easier to find the next time children want to play.

Sometimes, parents and teachers find themselves putting toys away. If that is the case, adults should try to find ways to make cleanup time fun.

If items need to go in a bucket or bin, clean-up could turn into a basketball game by asking children to drop items into the "basket." Most children love to "score points" by making a basket or have someone clap after they score a basket. Adults might try offering their children choices for what to put away first. If children continually take out many toys and then refuse to help clean up, parents should consider limiting the number of toys available for play time. Parents should also teach their children that they need to clean up one set of toys or one area of play before they move on to play in another area or with a different set of toys. It is important not to let cleanup time become a battle that eventually discourages children from wanting to take out and play with toys.

TYPES OF TOYS

There are many different types of toys on the market. Most toys indicate on the box the age range for which they are intended. Adults too often focus on this chronological age and instead should focus on the developmental level of the child. Developmentally inappropriate toys often do not interest and could be a safety hazard to a child even when the child's age corresponds to the age printed on the box (Kaban, 1979). For example, a child who is four years old but developmentally only two may try to taste and accidentally swallow a piece from a toy with many small parts.

When selecting toys, it is important to make sure that the toys, purchased or made, are developmentally appropriate. Safety should, of course, be a primary factor when deciding on a particular toy. To help determine which toy would be developmentally appropriate, children should be observed during play. Children play with objects and toys that interest them. Toys too difficult for them to interact with often frustrate them. For example, a 100-piece jigsaw puzzle would not be appropriate for most four-year-olds.

Educational toys are designed to stimulate children's natural curiosity, as well as to teach certain concepts or skills. It is certainly appropriate to provide children with these types of toys. It is not necessary, however, to demand that children play with these toys only in the way the manufacturer intended. For example, children could use a toy pot for a drum. Children should be allowed to play with toys in the way that most suits or pleases them. Children should be encouraged to play for the enjoyment of play.

Toys do not always need to be purchased to be enjoyable. Many toddlers, for example, love to play with cardboard boxes. They climb in and on them, stack them, and put other items in them to push or pull around the room. Preschool teachers frequently request that parents save and send in "throw away" items, including paper towel tubes or egg cartons. Many projects and toys can be made from items often simply tossed into the garbage or recycling bin.

Parents should be encouraged to ask their child's preschool teacher what type of toys are most appropriate. It is often helpful for parents to spend time in the classroom to observe their child play and play with the child. Parents can benefit from inviting the child's daycare provider to spend time in the preschool class to become more familiar with the child's play style. If everyone involved shares observations and ideas, then greater success is possible with regard to all areas of learning. Table 12.9 provides a guideline for appropriate toys for children birth through preschool, as well as a partial list of types of play for each age group.

CONCLUSION

The importance of play in the lives of young children, especially young children with special needs, cannot be overemphasized. Young children live to play. Play helps develop a positive self-concept. It allows and supports learning at a rate that is developmentally appropriate.

Play is natural and requires minimal props to interest children. Toys can be bought or homemade but should always be developmentally appropriate to avoid frustrating or endangering children using

TABLE 12.9 Toys and Play Activity at Various Ages

Birth to 6 Months

Toys:
- mobiles (suspended in such a way that the child can see the objects)
- music boxes
- stuffed animals (bright colors or black and white)
- rattles
- an unbreakable mirror hung where the child can look into it
- crib play-gym

6 to 12 Months

Toys:
- stacking rings
- stacking cubes and other "nesting" toys
- puppets
- activity box
- balls
- soft blocks
- vinyl books

12 Months to 2 Years

Toys:
- push and pull toys
- surprise box
- bath toys
- toy telephone
- bubbles
- tape recorder
- puzzles
- toy figures
- toy buildings (e.g., houses, garages, farm buildings)

2 to 3 Years

Toys:
- large, brightly colored beads to string on a sturdy cord or pipe cleaner
- push and pull toys
- blocks with rounded corners
- foam blocks (they float and are fun in the tub)
- picture books and books with minimal dialogue
- realistic toys/props for pretend play
- dolls
- toy vehicles
- large pegs and pegboards
- toy animals

continued

TABLE 12.9 continued

- large crayons
- nesting cups or other items (kitchen pots will also do)
- wagon
- riding toys that move when the child moves
- puzzles with pieces that fit in a specific space
- toy lawn mower or vacuum
- containers with lids
- plastic food
- toy dishes and utensils
- pots and pans
- sponges
- broom
- play dough
- nontoxic paint and fingerpaint

Play Activities:
- movement games
- riding on toys
- using puzzles and pegboards
- using scissors to make snips (in modeling clay or paper)
- chanting familiar songs
- using musical instruments
- using hands to explore art and sensory media
- filling and dumping containers
- piling blocks, then stacking and knocking them down
- using realistic props for dramatic play
- running, climbing, jumping
- being messy

3 to 5 Years (include the preceding items)
Toys:
- building blocks with more shapes
- toy action figures or characters to use with blocks and cars
- tricycle
- simple matching games (e.g., shape or bingo-type games)
- balls of various sizes to throw, catch, and kick
- puzzles whose pieces fit together to make a picture
- simple tools
- dress-up clothes, aprons, and costumes
- props for dramatic play (e.g., simple cameras and phones that no longer work)

Play Activities:
- evolving sequences during dramatic play
- making friends

- sharing or taking turns
- using tools to fix things
- climbing
- riding a tricycle
- playing group games such as Duck, Duck, Goose
- throwing and catching balls
- coloring and painting
- cutting and gluing
- stringing beads
- assembling toys that fit together (i.e., plastic bricks)
- using puppets in play
- learning how to roll out dough and using cookie cutters
- using blocks to make a road
- simple cooperative or board games
- building three-dimensional block structures and acting out scenes with toy people and vehicles
- making structures with other toys that fit together
- creating a project or picture without adult supervision in the art area (can assemble items needed and knows how to ask for desired items that are out of sight; can cut out simple picture)
- seeking adult approval for a project completed
- expanded dramatic play including scenes from familiar stories and places visited
- moving and dancing
- playing games with small pieces or moving parts
- performing simple experiments

them. Whenever and wherever possible, it is a good idea to display available toys so children know their choices for play. Toys haphazardly thrown in a toy chest may be difficult to locate and parts often become separated, which leads to frustration.

Although the word *play* implies fun, it also translates into learning and sometimes hard work within a special needs preschool program. Using structured and unstructured settings, the teaching staff can support, enhance, and expand each child's endeavors at learning. It is through these play experiences that the information presented and skills practiced become the learned types of behavior necessary to promote appropriate development.

The next chapter provides a discussion of art, a type of play activity that should be included in the daily activities provided at preschool for children with special needs. Art activities are particularly useful for assessing children's level of development, as well as enhancing all major areas of development.

CHAPTER SUMMARY

- Play provides opportunities for children to learn new concepts such as colors, number, and shape, and enhances other areas including motor, speech and language, and social-emotional development.
- Children with special needs progress through the typical stages of play, including solitary, onlooker, parallel, associative, and cooperative play, but at a slower rate than is found in children without developmental delays.
- Adults can learn a great deal about children's abilities by observing their play and playing with them.
- Classroom arrangements include block, house-dramatic, sensory, art, quiet, music–movement, and science areas, each containing a variety of toys.
- Special intervention often is needed for children with special needs so they can benefit from play time.

REVIEW QUESTIONS

1. How does play enhance each major area of development?
2. What are the names and characteristics of the major stages of play?
3. How can play be used to assess the developmental levels of preschool-age children?
4. What are the major areas of the classroom and why is each important?
5. What type of play occurs in each area?

SUGGESTED STUDENT ACTIVITIES

1. Plan a sensory table activity. What materials did you choose for the table? How will this activity enhance development?
2. Visit a regular and special needs preschool classroom and observe similarities and differences in children's play activities.
3. Look through a toy catalogue and select three toys for children ages 1 through 5 years. Explain why you selected each toy based on how it might enhance development.
4. Develop a drawing that shows how you would arrange a classroom for young children with special needs. Provide an explanation for your classroom design.

ADDITIONAL READINGS

Howard, L. A. (1987). *What to do with a squirt of glue.* Nashville, TN: Incentive Publications.

Jaffke, F. (1988). *Toymaking with children.* Great Britain: Floris Books.

Miller, K. (1985). *Ages and stages.* Marshfield, MA: Telshare Publishing Company.

Mitchell, C. (1989). *Happy hands and feet.* Nashville, TN: Incentive Publications.

Vernon Junior Women's Club. (1974). *Favorite crafts of our children.* Vernon, CT: Vernon Junior Women's Club.

ADDITIONAL RESOURCES

Children's Book Council, Inc.
67 Irving Place
New York, NY 10003

Children's Books in Print
R. R. Bowker
245 W. 17th Street
New York, NY 10011

U.S. Consumer Product Safety Commission
Washington, DC
(800) 628-2772

REFERENCES

Allen, K. E., & Marotz, L. (1989). *Developmental profiles: Birth to six.* New York: Delmar Publishers.

Anita, S. D., & Kreimeyer, K. H. (1992). Social competence intervention for young children with hearing impairments. In S. L. Odom, S. R. McConnell, & M. A. McEvoy (Eds.), *Social competence of young children with disabilities* (pp. 113–134). Baltimore, MD: Paul H. Brookes.

Atack, S. M. (1986). *Art activities for the handicapped.* Englewood Cliffs, NJ: Prentice-Hall.

Barber, L. W., & Williams, H. (1981). *Your baby's first 30 months.* Tucson, AZ: Fisher.

Bettelheim, B. (1987). The importance of play. *The Atlantic,* March, p. 35.

Bloom, L., & Lahey, M. (1978). *Language development and language disorders.* New York: John Wiley and Sons.

Brown, J. F. (Ed.). (1982). *Curriculum planning for young children.* Washington, DC: National Association for the Education of Young Children.

Caplan, F., & Caplan, T. (1973). *The power of play.* Garden City: Anchor Press/Doubleday.

Einon, D. (1985). *Play with a purpose: Learning games for children 6 weeks to 2–3 year olds.* New York: St. Martin's Press.

Eliason, C. F., & Jenkins, T. L. (1977). *A preschool guide to early childhood curriculum.* St. Louis, MO: C. V. Mosby.

Fay, W. H., & Schuler, A. L. (1980). *Emerging language in autistic children.* Baltimore, MD: University Park Press.

Goldstein, J. H. (1994). *Toys, play, and child development.* NY: Cambridge University Press.

Gordon, J. I. (1970). *Baby learning through baby play.* New York: St. Martin's Press.

Gordon, J. I. (1972). *Child learning through child play: Learning activities for 2–3 year olds.* New York: St. Martin's Press.

Gowen, J. W. (1992). Object play and exploration in children with and without disabilities: A longitudinal study. *American Journal on Mental Retardation, 97*(1), 21–37.

Haller, I. (1987). *How children play.* Great Britain: William Collins Sons.

Hellendoorn, J., & Hoekman, J. (1992). Imaginative play in children with mental retardation. *Mental Retardation, 30*(5), 256.

Hendrick, J. (1975). *The whole child: New trends in early education.* St. Louis, MO: C. V. Mosby.

Hirsch, E. S. (Ed.). (1984). *The block book.* Washington, DC: National Association for the Education of Young Children.

Hohmann, M., Banet, B., & Weikart, D. P. (1979). *Young children in action.* Ypsilanti, MI: High Scope Press.

Howes, C., & Matheson, C. C. (1992). Sequences in the development of competent play with peers: Social and social pretend play. *Developmental Psychology, 28,* 961–974.

Isaacs, S. (1972). *Intellectual growth in young children.* New York: Schocken Books.

Isenberg, J. P., & Jalongo, M. R. (1993). *Creative expression and play in the early childhood curriculum.* Columbus, OH: Merrill.

Jarrold, C., Boucher, J., & Smith, P. (1993). Symbolic play in autism: A review. *Journal of Autism and Developmental Disorders, 23*(2), 66–93.

Kaban, B. (1979). *Choosing toys for children from birth to five.* New York: Schocken Books.

Kennedy, M. D. (1991). Play-language relationships in young children with developmental delays: Implications for assessment. *Journal of Speech and Hearing Research, 34,* 112–122.

Kirk, S. A., & Gallagher, J. J. (1979). *Educating exceptional children* (3rd ed.). Boston: Houghton Mifflin.

Lewis, J. M. (1993). Childhood play in normality, pathology and therapy. *American Journal of Orthopsychiatry, 63*(1), 6–15.

Lewis, V., Boucher, J., & Astell, A. (1992). The assessment of symbolic play in young children: A prototype test. *European Journal of Disorders of Communication, 27,* 232–236.

Lieber, J., & Beckman, P. J. (1991). The role of toys in individual and dyadic play among young children with handicaps. *Journal of Applied Developmental Psychology, 22,* 691–700.

Linder, T. W. (1990). *Transdisciplinary play-based assessment.* Baltimore, MD: Paul H. Brookes.

Marino, B. L. (1991). Studying infant and toddler play. *Journal of Pediatric Nursing, 6*(1), 16–20.

Markun, P. M. (1974). *Play: Children's business.* Washington, DC: Association for Childhood Education International.

Marzollo, J., & Harper, J. L. (1972). *Learning through play.* New York: Harper and Row.

Piaget, J. (1971). *Biology and knowledge: An essay on the relation between organic regulation and cognitive process.* Chicago: University of Chicago Press.

Pushaw, D. (1976). *Teach your child to talk.* New York: CEBCO Standard Publishing.

Rescorla, L., & Goossens, M. (1992). Symbolic play development in toddlers with expressive specific language impairment (SLI-E). *Journal of Speech and Hearing Research, 12,* 1292–1298.

Rogers, C. S., & Sawyers, J. K. (1988). *Play in the lives of children.* Washington, DC: National Association for the Education of Young Children.

Sawyers, J. K., & and Rogers, C. S. (1988). *Helping young children develop through play*. Washington, DC: National Association for the Education of Young Children.

Schwartz, S. (Ed.). (1987). *Choices in deafness: A parents' guide*. Kensington, MD: Woodbine House.

Trawick–Smith, J. (1994). *Interactions in the classroom: Facilitating play in the early years*. Columbus, OH: Merrill.

Van Hoorn, J. V., Nourot, P. M., Scales, B. J., & Alward, K. R. (1993). *Play at the center of the curriculum*. Columbus, OH: Merrill.

Westby, C. E. (1988). Children's play: Reflections of social competence. *Seminars in Speech and Language, 9*(1), 2–12.

CHAPTER 13

ART FOR CHILDREN
WITH SPECIAL NEEDS

MARY E. THOMPSON, B.S.

ABOUT THE AUTHOR

Mary E. Thompson received her bachelor's degree in elementary education from the State University of New York at New Paltz, in New Paltz, New York. She is near completion of her master's in special education at SUNY-New Paltz. Ms. Thompson currently serves as a classroom teacher at the Saint Francis Preschool Program. She has more than sixteen years' experience working with preschool-age children with and without special needs. She is the mother of two teenagers.

CHAPTER KEY POINTS

- Art activities can be used to enhance cognitive, speech and language, motor, self-help, and social-emotional development.
- The art area should be a carefully planned section of the classroom.
- Several different factors should be considered when choosing art activities for children with special needs.
- Art activities are often integrated into classroom themes and can be presented to children individually or in small or large groups.
- Art activities can be used to assess children's development and provide art therapy.

Earlier chapters have focused on various types of developmental delays and therapies used to enhance the development of children who have special needs. Chapter 12 discussed how play (including all types of art activities—visual, musical, and movement) is used to enhance all areas of development in young children. This chapter focuses on visual art activities that can also be used to enhance all areas of development. (See Chapter 1 for discussion of the music therapist and the use of music activities.)

Art activities are often a free play option, in which children choose the play activity, a method of therapy, or a means of assessing children's level of development. Art can be used effectively to enhance skills for children with and without special needs. For children with special needs, art is often an effective method to enhance all areas of development.

THE VALUE OF ART ACTIVITIES

The word *art* elicits many different meanings and interpretations. People do not often view art in the same way. Art, however, can tell us many things about a person. The type of art a person likes and creates often is very revealing. For example, pictures found in ancient Egyptian tombs revealed the Egyptians' love of hunting, and pictures preserved on artifacts depicted the lifestyles of the Greeks and Romans (Frankl, 1959). Art, a form of play for young children, often reveals children's lifestyles and preferences as well (Edwards, 1996).

Toddlers' and preschoolers' scribbles gradually become meaningful pictures as their mental abilities expand and they begin to symbolize objects through pictures and other art forms. Children's drawings reveal their thoughts (Coles, 1992). For example, a three-year-old may draw a circular shape with marks that appear to be random and call it a "pizza." See Figure 13.1 for an example of a child's drawing.

Children move logically from making random marks to mastering simple shapes, such as circles and rectangles, to eventually making complex drawings combining several shapes. Children

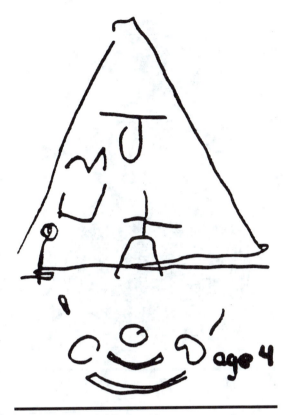

FIGURE 13.1 Child's Drawing

begin using shapes by combining them to form figures such as "stick" people with "circle" heads and "rectangle" bodies. They may label these figures "mom" and "dad." Shapes are also combined to form objects, such as when a child uses a circle and rectangle to make a tree and a square and triangle to make a house (Gardner, 1973).

It is important to honor individuality during art activities. Adults should allow and encourage children to think of their own projects rather than their only being allowed to work on projects designed by the teacher. Allowing children to design their own creations helps to develop independence and imagination (Moon, 1990). Some children, though, enjoy coloring books and pages that require them to stay within the lines, but those drawing activities do not encourage creativity and individuality. These types of activities may be appropriate for

FIGURE 13.2 Child's Drawing

free play choices but should not be considered art activities.

During art activities, children often experiment with different materials and use their imagination to tell stories about their creations. They often seek approval or recognition regarding their creations. It is important for adults not to compare how good one child's work is to another child's (Coles, 1992). See Figure 13.2 for an example of changes in a child's drawing.

Art activities for young children with special needs should be relatively simple. Room furnishings should *not* require elaborate protection from messy art materials such as paint and glue. This allows children and teachers *not* to worry about making a mess or ruining furnishings. An extended amount of time should be allocated for working on art activities. Art time should be considered an important part of the curriculum and not just "stuck in" when there is nothing else to do. Chil-

dren are likely to become frustrated if they are not given plenty of time to complete art activities (Brittain, 1979).

Art activities can be used to enhance skills in all areas including cognitive, speech and language, motor, self-help, and social-emotional development (Rubin, 1984). Art can be readily incorporated into the daily lives of young children at home, in daycare, and regular or special education preschool programs. Art activities include elaborate projects such as building a castle, simple activities such as finger painting, methods for presenting therapies such as physical or occupational therapy, and evaluation procedures (Brittain, 1979).

USING ART TO ENHANCE MAJOR AREAS OF DEVELOPMENT

The focus of art activities used in early childhood special education programs should be on the process rather than product. Art activities naturally enhance all major areas of development (Rubin, 1984).

Cognitive Development

Art activities provide children with a nonverbal way to demonstrate their understanding of certain concepts (Lowenfeld & Brittain, 1969). For example, if the class theme for the week is "big and little," a child might be asked to create big and little objects. A teacher might ask a child to point to a big object and little object in the child's drawing. Children who are nonverbal can often point to something "big" and "little" yet cannot clearly verbally communicate their understanding of these concepts (Beittel, 1974).

Speech and Language Development

Working with children on expressive (ability to communicate) and receptive (ability to understand) language goals can be easily integrated into the art activity of the day. For example, a child's expressive language could be developed by asking the child to talk about what other materials are needed to complete an art project and receptive language could be enhanced by asking the child to put a piece of paper on the table in front of each chair. A child's enthusiasm and interest in art projects, including drawings, paintings, and creating three-dimensional objects, can be used to enhance and elicit language.

A speech and language pathologist may use art activities to encourage children to speak. A therapist could encourage a young child to talk about a drawing by asking questions designed to elicit more than a "yes" or "no" response. For example, a therapist might say, "What color did you paint with today?" Asking children to verbally request different materials or help needed to complete an art activity encourages their use of receptive and expressive language skills (Alkema, 1971).

A speech and language pathologist can design and supervise art activities or assist another teacher or therapist during art activities. The pathologist might tell a child to request the color of paint the child wishes to use. Children who hesitate to communicate verbally are often willing to talk about their art creations. Older preschool children sometimes like to tell stories about their projects and pictures (Anderson, 1978). When this occurs, a child often likes it when a teacher writes down the story and attaches it to the child's picture. To encourage children to talk about their pictures, teachers should say to them, "Tell me about your picture." Teachers should avoid asking children, "What is this?" This type of question might discourage children because it suggests that the teacher cannot tell what the child made.

Motor Development and Self-Help Skills

Art activities can enhancing motor development and self-help skills. Occupational and physical therapists often use art as therapy activities for individual and group therapy (Alkema, 1971). Art activities are used to enhance motor control during activities such as painting with brushes and manipulating clay. Physical therapists use activities such as kneeling or standing while painting to enhance gross motor development. Occupational therapists frequently use art activities when working with children who are **tactically defensive,** a term that refers to not liking the feel of certain things or getting dirty.

Some children hesitate to participate in art activities. One reason is that such children are unfamiliar with certain types of materials being used during the activity. Children are often cautious when interacting in unfamiliar situations and this includes unfamiliar activities. Many children need a gradual introduction to new types of materials (Alkema, 1971). Ways to help encourage hesitant children to participate are listed in Table 13.1.

Children's self-help skills can be enhanced during art activities by involving them in setting up art activities, putting on smocks, and cleaning up after completing the activities. Children should

TABLE 13.1 Methods That May Encourage a Hesitant Child to Participate in Art Activities

- Have the child watch the teacher take out and prepare the material for an activity (e.g., mix paints);
- Let the child help take out and prepare the materials with the teacher supervising (e.g., help mix paint);
- Allow the child to help prepare the art area (e.g., cover the table with old newspapers) while the teacher talks about the upcoming art activity;
- Allow the child to observe the activity without active participation. While the child is observing, encourage the child to ask questions and make suggestions about other children's work on the activity;
- Encourage the child to participate in the activity for a brief time while reassuring the child that he or she can quit at any time.

gradually be encouraged to be more independent in all aspects of art activities.

Social-Emotional Development

Young children not only express themselves through their art work but also exhibit themselves in ways quite innocent yet often quite revealing (Rubin, 1984). For example, a young child might draw a picture of a monster believed to be under the bed. This picture could indicate that the child fears monsters or suggest a more serious social or emotional problem. On the other hand, this might not be the case and adults should avoid overinterpreting (Axline, 1947).

Young children often provide information about their emotions through art activities. Some of these messages illustrate typical daily events, but others could indicate emotional problems. For example, a young child pounding a crayon, tearing or shredding paper, or intensely scribbling on a picture might be indicating anger, unhappiness, or negative **self-esteem.** Unfinished or never-started art projects might be a sign of insecurity or inability to attend to a task for an extended length of

time. Children who have negative self-esteem frequently hesitate to complete tasks because they believe they cannot do a good job (Cohen, 1974).

Teachers should make sure that children do not worry about making their art project look just like the teacher's or other children's. Teachers should talk about the uniqueness of each child's work by saying something like, "You used many different colors," rather than comparing work by saying, "Your picture is the best." Preschool teachers, therapists, and parents should help enhance children's self-esteem by showing interest in children's creativity and productiveness during art activities. Encouragement could be expressed by teachers saying such things as, "All those bright colors remind me of rainbows," followed by smiling at and hugging the child, all of which may enhance self-esteem (Anderson, 1978).

Children who have disabilities often need extra encouragement. When children feel good about what they create during art activities, these feelings are likely to affect behavior positively during other activities. Art activities should provide time for young children to feel free to expand on classroom themes or "do their own thing" while enjoying the comfort and friendship of their classmates. The fun and enjoyment of art activities naturally elicit socialization, including talking and physical gestures such as a smile, which help develop confidence and encourage creativeness (Kellogg, 1969). See Table 13.2 for an outline of art activities that can be used to enhance major areas of development.

THE ART AREA

Location

Whenever possible, it is desirable for the art area to be located near windows because natural light enhances many art creations. If an area of a classroom cannot be set aside for art activities, almost any area in a classroom can be transformed into an art area. Ideally, there should be a sink accessible in the classroom for use during cleanup. If there is no sink, large buckets with soapy and

TABLE 13.2 The Relationship of Art Activities to Developmental Areas

Cognitive
- Experimenting with various colors, shapes, and sizes
- Learning particular relationships such as above, below, on, over, and next to
- Responding to visual and tactile stimuli
- Experiencing textures such as smooth, scratchy, bumpy, rough, soft, wet, dry, slippery, and sticky
- Learning names of objects
- Following instructions, planning, and sequencing

Language
- Asking for supplies
- Describing art projects
- Responding to questions
- Developing conversational skills

Motor
- Enhancing pre-writing skills
- Squeezing and gripping
- Enhancing muscle development and coordination

Self-help
- Opening and closing containers
- Dressing and undressing (when using a smock)
- Organizing supplies
- Washing hands

Social-emotional
- Expressing emotions
- Demonstrating creativity and individuality
- Developing cooperation skills

rinse water can be placed on drop cloths for children and teachers to use for washing hands and art tools (Brittain, 1979).

The art area should be located away from other areas of the classroom that cannot be easily cleaned after messy activities. For example, books, dolls, and stuffed toys should not be next to the art area. The art area should be in a location that allows for projects to be left out to dry without interfering with other activities. Ideally, the art area is in a spot where teachers can monitor who comes and goes to help prevent children from damaging other children's art work or accidentally getting into messy art materials.

Furniture

Furniture often used during art activities includes movable tables, chairs, blackboards, easels, storage cabinets, closets, racks, and shelves. It is generally useful when individual trays are available to provide children with a specific work space or to store unfinished projects.

Art Supplies

An endless variety of materials may be part of preschool classroom art supplies. Many things can be used for protective coverings for floors and furniture, including newspapers, old plastic tablecloths, plastic drop cloths, and old sheets. Ideally, the permanent flooring in an art area should be a hard surface that is easy to clean, rather than carpeting. If necessary, carpeting can be protected with the items listed above. Old, discarded adult-size shirts make ideal smocks if plastic children's smocks are unavailable.

Other supplies that can be used for art activities are listed in Table 13.3. The list of potential art supplies is endless and limited only by a child's, parent's, or teacher's imagination. Children should also be encouraged to participate in collecting art materials such as rocks, shells, leaves, pine cones, twigs, and seed pods. Most children enjoy collecting such "treasures" that can be used during art activities.

Parents could be asked to collect many of these common objects listed above for use in art activities. Items for use in art activities found in most homes are listed in Table 13.4. Again, the potential list of items children and parents can collect is endless, and many items would be thrown away if not used for art activities.

Portable Art Kit

In some cases, it may be desirable to develop a **portable art kit.** This kit would include easily

TABLE 13.3   Materials Needed for the Art Area

Furniture
- large, portable, child-height table and chairs
- easels
- drying racks
- portable cart
- storage cabinets and shelves
- trays

Materials
- finger paint paper
- construction paper
- tissue paper
- large rolls of paper
- large and small sheets of paper
- string and yarn
- washable paints and containers
- painting utensils (e. g., brushes, cotton swabs, sponges, straws, string, and cork)
- washable markers
- colored pencils
- pencils
- crayons
- indoor and outdoor chalk
- nontoxic glue, glue containers, glue brushes, glue sticks
- tape
- staplers
- children's scissors
- plastic cookie cutters
- modeling clay
- glitter
- pipe cleaners
- smocks and table coverings

TABLE 13.4   Common Household Items Useful for Art Projects

ice cream sticks	wood scraps
rubber bands	paper bags
cotton balls	paper scraps
cork	wallpaper scraps
spools from thread	wrapping paper scraps
string, yarn, or ribbon	magazines
metal clothes hangers	newspapers
cardboard tubing	old greeting cards
small stones and sticks	paint color cards
pine cones	plastic silverware
leaves	egg cartons
seed pods	aluminum pie tins
food items (e.g.,	plastic bottles
macaroni, beans)	boxes (all sizes and types)
old jewelry	tin cans/coffee cans
buttons	oatmeal, corn meal, and
fabric scraps	cereal boxes
foam padding	plastic containers

teacher to use art materials outdoors or in a different area.

FACTORS TO CONSIDER WHEN CHOOSING ART ACTIVITIES

Ensuring that furniture and floors are adequately protected from potentially messy activities allows for more spontaneity in the use of art materials. Teachers frequently plan to use one type of material (usually less messy materials), but children often decide they want to do something else (using messy materials). An area adequately protected can accommodate a variety of materials used to complete a project.

Children should be free to explore ways of using materials and be messy (Brittain, 1979). Children quickly become inhibited and respond less creatively when they are constantly being warned to "Be careful!" or told "You are making a mess!" Children should be allowed to "get into" the materials. Experimenting with materials is an important learning experience. This experimentation may include painting with their fingers instead of with the paintbrushes provided.

manipulated materials requiring little preparation or cleanup (Lindsay, 1968). Supplies included in the kit could be crayons, water-based markers, colored pencils, glue sticks, scissors, paper, pieces of scrap paper, modeling clay, chalkboards, colored chalk, a plastic covering, and disposable smocks. These materials can be organized on a portable open-shelved cart or placed in a toolbox type of container. The purpose of a portable art kit is to have materials readily accessible and visible to teachers, therapists, and children to encourage spontaneous art activities. It also allows the

When deciding on what choices will be made available for art activities in a special needs classroom, safety issues must be considered. Art supplies should be easily replaceable and nontoxic because young children explore materials by putting things into their mouth. Breakable containers or sharp objects should not be used. Although it is important to allow flexibility within the art area, children should also be made aware of the boundaries regarding the appropriate use of art materials. Rules might include wearing smocks when painting, keeping art supplies in the art area, and helping with cleanup.

Art activities should encourage children to be creative and "stretch" their imagination, but within certain limits (Brittain, 1979). For example, children might be required to wear smocks when they paint or do other messy activities. If wearing a smock is a classroom rule, but a child chooses not to wear a smock, then the child should not be allowed to paint. If they are told they must keep glue, paint, and glitter in the art area, yet they leave the area and take these materials with them, it may be necessary to have them leave the art area for awhile.

GROUPING FOR ART ACTIVITIES

Amount of time, size of the classroom, number of children in the class, and number of staff in each classroom are likely to play a role in how art activities are presented. Art activities can be presented individually and in small and large groups (Cohen, 1969).

Individual Art Activities

One way of including art activities is to work individually with a child (Crawford, 1962). Interacting one-to-one with a child during an art activity can be very rewarding for the child and adult. The child and teacher can talk with each other, creating a language-rich environment during an activity designed to meet the child's specific needs and interests.

While working individually with a child, a teacher might introduce concepts such as color or shape, or work hand-over-hand (the teacher guiding the child's hands) to help the child develop scissor skills or a mature pencil grip. One-to-one time also allows the teacher to use art time to assess the child's developmental level. Realistically, however, most classroom settings cannot afford the luxury of individual art time on a regular basis. Art activities most often occur in small or large groups (Cohen, 1969).

Small Group Art Activities

Small groups are the most common method of providing art activities. A teacher should be assigned to monitor each small group. Small groups may occur with all the children in the classroom working at a time in groups of three to five children or with one teacher or therapist working with three to five children, while children not in the group engage in other activities. Plans for small group art activities should include consideration of the materials to be used, space, time, and the needs of each child in the small group (Gaitskell & Gaitskell, 1953).

First, the art area should be set up with all the necessary supplies such as scissors, glue sticks, markers, pencils, and paper. There should be ample working space for each child and adequate time allotted for completing the activity. For projects requiring teacher assistance, such as cutting with scissors, it is often helpful to create a group in which most children can use scissors independently and a different group of children who cannot use scissors independently. The latter group may require more time to complete the activity, need a greater amount of teacher support, or require restructuring of the activity so that it does not call for independent scissor skills.

Teachers may find it more effective to have only one or two children in a group of three to five children who cannot use scissors independently. With this grouping model, most of the children work independently while the teacher assists children who need help cutting.

Activities appropriate for small rather than large groups include scissor skills requiring monitoring and guidance, very messy activities (to avoid having many children messy at the same time), or activities where supplies are limited, such as the number of easels. Because there is a small ratio of children to teacher during small group activities, the teacher can provide some level of individual attention. Small groups are also more effective when specific types of art materials are introduced for the first time. For example, the first time children are exposed to finger painting, using watercolors, or glue may require more adult guidance. As children become more familiar with materials and activities, they generally become more independent. Over time, children should be able to set up and clean up the art area relatively independently.

A difficulty that may occur during small group activities is children may complete the project at different rates or not want to participate. This may be because they are just not interested or do not feel comfortable with the activity for some reason. As mentioned earlier, they may not like the feel of the material or getting messy, or doubt that they can successfully complete the activity. Children may not finish an act activity because they are spending the art time in social interaction. Because small group activities are frequently designed to encourage socialization, children may spend more time talking to each other than completing the art activity. Teachers should not be concerned if this occurs because art activities are valuable for the experiences they provide rather than for the product they create.

Large Group Art Activities

When preparing for **large group** art **activities** (the whole class working together), teachers should decide in advance how many adults are needed for adequate supervision, how much time is needed, what equipment and supplies are needed, including tables, easels, chairs, paper, paint, and smocks, and how much time cleanup should take. Materials should be assembled in advance so that time is not lost looking for supplies or equipment.

Most activities appropriate for large groups are not too complex and involve only one or two steps. Large group activities should be designed so that teachers feel confident that the majority of children can complete the task independently or with limited assistance (Nixon, 1969). Just as is the case with small group activities, large group activities can be conducted outdoors or indoors. Outdoor activities may include gathering pebbles or leaves for an art collage, drawing with sidewalk chalk, or painting with feet (putting paint on feet and walking on paper placed on the ground or floor).

It is sometimes difficult to keep the attention of all children in a large group activity. It may also be difficult to incorporate all the children's developmental levels and children who have difficulty working cooperatively. In addition, some children may quickly finish the activity and be ready to move on to another activity while others are slower to complete the activity. Some children grow impatient waiting for the others (Harris, 1963).

An advantage of working in a large group is that everyone has an opportunity to hear the instructions or watch a teacher model the activity at the same time. Using large group activities during the preschool years provides children with practice working together in the types of large groups that are frequently a part of elementary school experiences. Children need practice in learning to share, wait, and work collectively. Large groups provide opportunities to practice these skills (Nixon, 1969).

Art activities requiring an extended period of time (more than twenty to thirty minutes) may need to be presented in parts completed over several days. Large group activities often require longer attending skills than do small group activities. Some children, then, who have special needs that limit their length of attention span, may have difficulty participating in some large group activities (Lowenfeld, 1971).

If an activity requires many steps, such as cutting, gluing, and painting, the teacher might decide to present this activity over a two- or three-day period. Extending the activity over several days provides children an opportunity to experience the need to complete one step before moving to the next step. For example, children may have an activity in which they learn that paint must dry before freshly painted pieces can be glued together. Multi-stepped activities help children develop planning, recall, sequencing, and perseverance skills (Nixon, 1969). Children may be asked to tell what they will do on the project tomorrow or what step they completed the previous day.

An example of an extended activity is drawing a three-foot tree on a piece of heavy poster board, cutting around the edges of the tree, drawing and cutting out red and yellow apples, gluing them on the tree, waiting for the glue to dry, and then mounting the apple tree on a mural on the wall. The activity would involve having the children decide who would work on each part of the activity and recognize the steps needed to complete the project. This type of activity could be completed in small or large groups and be readily related to a classroom theme.

Art activities should be designed so that they accommodate interruptions. Interruptions vary from something as simple as a child asking to go to the bathroom to a fire drill. Activities should be planned anticipating interruptions. Activities that do not readily accommodate interruptions, such as using modeling clay that quickly hardens once exposed to the air, are generally inappropriate for preschool-age children.

Other types of activities that may not be adapted well to interruptions are those that take a long time to set up or complete or are very messy. For example, if a teacher has twelve children finger painting twenty minutes before dismissal time and there is a fire drill, it is unlikely that this activity will be completed before leaving for the day. Teachers should avoid having messy art activities at the end of the day and may want to reconsider having twelve sets of hands all with finger paint on them.

If children begin to use materials in a different way than the teacher envisioned, the teacher should avoid discouraging this type of exploration unless the children are doing something dangerous, making too much of a mess, or distracting the other children. Too often, teachers become dismayed when children deviate from the planned way of doing a project. Teachers should remember that the goal of art activities is to provide an enjoyable learning experience (Nixon, 1969).

INSTRUCTIONAL STRATEGIES FOR ART ACTIVITIES

During art activities, **direct** and **indirect instruction** may be used. The type of instruction selected should be based on the abilities of the children involved, number of children in a group, and type of art materials being used (Rubin, 1984).

Direct Instruction

For the purposes of this discussion direct instruction is defined as telling children what to do and how to do it. This method of presenting art activities is often used when working with children with special needs (Rubin, 1984). Using direct instruction provides the children with an opportunity to have the activity demonstrated by the teacher. Direct instruction is particularly useful the first time children work with a new type of art material or tool, such as scissors.

For example, observing how the teacher puts on a smock or old shirt, covers a table, mixes paint, chooses a brush, demonstrates how to dip the brush into the paint and wipe off the excess are all important learning opportunities for children engaging in an activity for the first time. Modeling these methods often must be repeated over the course of several activities before children with special needs will comfortably perform the task independently (Rubin, 1984).

Over time, however, children should learn to put on smocks, help in covering the table, and mixing paint. A teacher could progress from having the children describe how they plan to complete an activity to asking the children to collect the materials necessary to complete the activity. This helps children learn how to plan activities. Children are more likely to use newly acquired skills spontaneously after they have actively participated in all aspects of the activity.

Children should also learn that **cleanup** is part of the art activity and not a job the teacher does when the children are finished participating. Participating in cleanup helps children learn to take responsibility. When children help clean up, the children and teacher are free to begin a new activity. Children gradually learn that when they clean up together the job is completed much more quickly so that they can move on to another activity. Teachers and parents are often pleasantly surprised by how helpful children are when cleanup is made part of the activity rather than "work" to be done later (Uhlin, 1972).

Children with special needs often require more **teacher-guided instruction** during sensory art activities because they frequently lack confidence, have limited communication skills, have tactile or sensory integration difficulties, fine motor delays, gross motor delays, including difficulty maintaining correct posture, or a limited attention span (Uhlin, 1972). When providing assistance to children with special needs, it is important to follow the children's lead and assist them only when they need assistance.

Many teachers begin the school year using direct instruction for the majority of art activities and gradually move toward greater use of indirect instruction. This allows children more independence and may enhance their self-esteem.

Indirect Instruction

Because children need plenty of opportunities to discover how to use art materials, indirect instruction is often better than direct because the former involves making materials available without providing instructions or models for what should be made (Grozinger, 1955). Indirect instruction provides ready access to materials such as paper, scissors, markers, and crayons as regular free play choices. All children need the opportunity to explore independently using art materials so that they can discover, invent, and achieve on their own. This results in children showing other children and the teacher new ways to use the materials (Goodnow, 1977).

The teacher's role using indirect instruction is to provide access to materials that enhance learning. The teacher should also encourage, question, and help children during activities.

Open-ended activities allow children to explore materials in ways that are personally relevant. Child-initiated (child suggests activity) and child-directed (child decides how activity will be completed) approaches can be used in all learning areas but are particularly appropriate during art activities. The focus should be on what the children experience rather than on what they make. The end product of an art activity does not need to be a recognizable thing. Activities should be designed to accommodate each child's developmental level so that a child needs very little assistance while engaging in a particular art activity (Gardner, 1973).

ART INTEGRATED INTO A THEME

Classroom teachers often adopt a "theme" for the day, week, or even month. Teachers use this approach because themes help provide meaning and purpose for classroom activities. Children should gradually be encouraged to suggest art activities to accompany a particular theme. Over time, children should also be asked to contribute to lesson planning by suggesting theme topics as well.

Typical themes involve seasons of the year and holidays and provide a focus on such things as apples, pumpkins, and turkeys in the fall; snow, valentines, and shamrocks in the winter; bunnies, planting, and farms in the spring; and shells, fishing, and beaches in the summer. However, it is often more fun to have "going to the beach" as the theme in the winter. Topics for themes can also be based on stories in children's books.

Art activities can be integrated into the classroom theme in many ways. Art activities might be used to introduce a theme. For example, at circle time the teacher could demonstrate the intended art activity of the day while all the children are together. This demonstration would be used to set the stage for the theme and could be offered as a free-play activity. Without providing a demonstration of the art activity, children might be less interested in selecting the art area as a free-play choice. Discussing the art activity could also be used to remind the children about the current classroom theme (Nixon, 1969). Having an example of the art project to show children, such as a pre-made macaroni necklace when talking about finding buried treasure or making dinosaurs when reading a book about dinosaurs, also helps motivate students to choose the art area as a free-play activity.

Frequently, teachers ask children to draw a picture relating to the class theme. This type of experience is valuable because elementary school activities typically require children to make or do specific activities without being offered choices. For example, if the classroom theme is birds, the teacher might ask the children to draw a picture of a favorite bird or bird they saw today. This type of activity allows children a choice about what to draw but within the context of a theme. Children are generally more involved when they have choices regarding what they will make and when they make it. They are also more willing to talk about what they have made when they choose the activity.

Teachers should avoid telling children exactly what they must draw. For example, telling children they must draw a red bird on a tree discourages individuality, creativity, and exploration (Lindsay, 1968). To encourage a hesitant child to participate, the teacher could ask the child to ask a friend to draw with the child. Art activities also include a child asking another child or the teacher to draw or make something for him or her. Children should not be expected to participate fully in every activity (Lindsay, 1968).

Some teachers try to integrate art into the classroom theme by asking the children to collect objects and materials from their homes to use during art time. Most children enjoy this type of "homework." Many parents also enjoy participating in this type of activity with their child. This helps involve parents in school activities and provides suggestions and ideas for parents to use at home.

Children may feel bad if they forget to bring in objects or their parents do not allow them to collect objects. If this occurs, the teacher could have a "treasure chest" of objects available for children to select from and contribute to the art project. Teachers should avoid overburdening families with requests, especially for objects for an art project that are hard to find or must be purchased. Parents are often great resources for ideas for art projects. They may also be willing to design or help direct classroom art activities.

Children should be involved in as much of the planning and executing of art projects as possible. Children could be asked to think of things they would like to make relating to a particular theme. The teacher might ask children what materials would be needed to complete an activity (Anderson, 1986). Teachers can also have the children help collect materials for the activity. This provides children some control over the choice of activities and allows practice using more complex levels of thinking and planning (Lindsay, 1968).

ART ACTIVITIES FOR OBSERVATION AND EVALUATION

When developing an art program for young children with special needs, teachers must create art activities designed to incorporate specific goals (e.g., John will use a mature pencil grasp). These types of goals may become part of the daily, weekly, or monthly observation and evaluation process. Observations and evaluations occurring during art activities may be formal and informal (Harris, 1963). Skills used during art activities can help provide information to assess possible delays or document growth in cognitive, speech and language, motor, self-help, and social-emotional areas of development.

Art Activities for Informal Assessment

Informal observations during art activities include the teacher watching a child use scissors. During this observation, the teacher would note the type of grasp the child uses and the level of accuracy of cutting. Informal observation can provide the teacher with insights regarding what activities the child selects and how the child manipulates materials and interacts with adults and peers during art activities. Informal observations provide information about the child's abilities while participating in normal daily activities. This type of assessment is often called **authentic assessment.**

Informal observations during art time can provide the teacher with an understanding of the child's level of cognitive development. For example, the teacher could use art activities as a means of assessing how well the child knows colors, shapes, or other concepts. A child might be asked to pick a large circle from a set of small and large circles and squares to glue on a piece of paper. This activity would assess the child's understanding of the concepts of shape and size, as well as fine motor coordination (gluing).

Other types of fine motor assessment could occur during tracing and drawing activities. The teacher can assess how the child holds a crayon, pencil, or marker. These observations would provide information about fine motor abilities related to pre-writing skills. If it is determined that the child uses an "immature" grasp (uses full hand versus "pencil grasp"), then the teacher could design activities to help the child develop a more appropriate grasp in subsequent activities.

During group art instruction, the teacher can observe how a child shares materials with other children, follows directions, works with others, and how long the child attends to a particular task. These skills are essential for other everyday social interactions. Again, if the child has difficulty with

one or more of these areas, the teacher can specifically design and work on goals to address a particular delay (Gardner, 1973).

The teacher may record these observations in anecdotal form in a written summary of activities or may use a checklist. It would be unnecessary or impractical for the teacher to record information on each child, every day. The teacher could create a running record or checklist of the tasks discussed above. For example, each student's name could be listed on a sheet of paper, along with specific goals. Then, a staff member can simply check off next to each child's name whether the child accomplished the goal. This level of record-keeping, although still informal, provides a more systematic observation of each child than do anecdotal records.

Art portfolios are another method of assessing children and keeping a record of their abilities. An art portfolio provides a summary of a child's developmental level when samples of art work, written anecdotes about the child, and photographs of any three-dimensional work are compiled.

The preschool years are an ideal time to begin putting together an art portfolio. A great deal of information about cognitive, fine motor, and social-emotional development can be obtained by periodically referring to an art portfolio. Samples of art work, signed for the child by a teacher or parent and dated, can become part of each child's personal museum (Salant, 1975). Keeping a portfolio also indicates to the child the art work is valued. This feeling helps contribute to positive self-esteem.

Art Activities for Formal Assessment

In some cases, it is necessary to conduct formal assessments and evaluations. IEP plans require an annual assessment. There are a wide variety of formal assessment instruments (tests) that provide age-appropriate developmental norms for cognitive, fine motor, and social-emotional development. In some cases, these formal tests can be conducted during an art activity (Harris, 1963). Table 13.5 provides a condensed set of reference-guidelines a teacher could use when observing

TABLE 13.5 Guidelines For Assessment during Art

Cognitive
- 2 years—sorts objects by color
- 2½ years—sorts four shapes
- 3 years—points to bigger, smaller, longer, shorter, and taller; sorts objects by (two or three) colors; tells whether objects are the same or different
- 4 years—names four colors
- 5 years—knows basic colors and shapes

Fine Motor
- 1½ years—holds crayon with whole hand (palmer grasp) and scribbles; crumbles and tears paper
- 2 years—holds pencil with whole hand and imitates vertical and circular strokes after the teacher models; attempts to fold paper
- 2½ years—holds pencil with fingers rather than in palm; imitates vertical and circular scribble; can roll, pound, squeeze, and pull clay
- 3 years—uses scissors to nip inaccurately; copies a circle; imitates a horizontal line, vertical line, V-strokes, and a cross (+); spontaneously scribbles in circular motions; displays a dominant hand
- 4 years—copies a cross, square, "V," "H," and "T"; folds and creases paper three times after demonstration; cuts with scissors; makes simple line drawings; cuts following a straight line
- 4½ years—threads a lacing card with running string; copies a square; connects dots; cuts circles
- 5 years—refinement in use of tools (for example, pencils and scissors); uses a crayon or pencil with more precision in small areas; copies a triangle; traces a diamond
- 5½ years—knows left and right; prints some letters and numbers; cuts out pictures with scissors
- 6 years—copies a diamond; uses scissors accurately for straight lines, curves, and angles; hand preference (left or right) generally clearly established; copies printing with left to right progression

Social/Emotional
- 2 years—helps clean up; prefers to be near but not with other children

- 2½ years—works side-by-side with other children during an art activity; makes simple choices during art activities; seeks approval from adults
- 3 years—tells about art activity/project
- 4 years—completes art activities; understands taking turns; recognizes when peers need help
- 4½ years—works with other children in the art area by sharing and taking turns

and evaluating young children during an art activity (Kellogg, 1969).

Teachers can use the developmental guidelines in Table 13.5 to assess the child's developmental level, as well as help guide the development of age-appropriate art activities. A teacher should not expect a 2-year-old to successfully or consistently share a container of paint with two other children. As shown in Table 13.5, it is not until around the time a child is about four and one-half years old that the child would be likely to be successful at sharing a container of paint. A child who is four and one-half years old and has special needs may be unable to successfully share a container of paint because the child's developmental age may be less than four and one-half years.

Assessing children's abilities during art activities is only one of the many methods of assessment discussed in this book. Assessment during art activities adds one more piece to the assessment puzzle. The more comprehensive the assessment, the greater the likelihood of developing a comprehensive plan for intervention.

ART THERAPY

Art therapy is most often used with children older than preschool age but can be useful for children as young as 3 to 4 years old who have social and emotional difficulties or have been battered or sexually abused (Di Leo, 1974). Art therapy encourages children to express their thoughts and experiences through pictures or other creative modes. This method is often useful for children who have delayed communication skills and are too emotionally withdrawn to talk about their experiences. Art activities often provide a safe structure for expressing feelings (Dalley, Case, Schaverien, Weir, Halliday, Hall, & Waller, 1987).

Art therapists who work with children might have degrees in counseling, psychiatry, psychology, social work, teaching, nursing, childcare, or art. Art therapists usually have a master's degree in art therapy, education, or psychology with a concentration in art. The American Art Therapy Association has created education and training guidelines for a master's in art therapy. Recommended coursework for art therapists includes studio art, human growth and development, psychopathology, clinical methods, group and family dynamics, and the history of art therapy. To be certified by the American Art Therapy Association a person must accumulate 1,000 hours of art therapy experience.

Art therapists often work with other professionals including medical doctors, nurses, psychologists, social workers, occupational, physical, and recreational therapists, and educators. Art therapy is based on the philosophy that all children need a variety of modes of expression that will allow them to grow in a healthy way; that is, children have a right to become themselves and to deal with any conflicts they carry inside (Wohl & Kaufman, 1985).

CONCLUSION

Young children should be given many opportunities to explore their environment and learn about the world through art activities. They should be allowed to make choices and experiment with different materials. These opportunities allow them to engage in many active learning experiences that are enjoyable. Parents and teachers should find ways to ensure ample exposure to art activities to maximize the benefits. Art activities should be integrated into a theme or classroom activities rather than merely doing an art project for the sake of making something.

Art activities are enjoyed by most preschool-age children. Rarely do children see art activities as "work," although they may not always be so enthusiastic about cleanup. Discussing a project is an especially good time to practice cognitive, communication, and motor skills. In addition, art activities can be used to better understand a child's level of development.

CHAPTER SUMMARY

- Art therapy enhances development through experience with materials that strengthen cognitive and speech and language skills by encouraging children to talk about their projects, motor skills by encouraging movement, and develops social-emotional skills through opportunities to interact with others.
- Art supplies should be varied and in ample supply to encourage children to participate in art activities.
- Art activities that occur individually allow teachers to provide one-to-one and specialized assistance, as well as to assess the child's developmental level.
- Small group and large group activities provide children with opportunities to share their ideas and learn from others.
- Children should be encouraged to participate in all aspects of art activities, including gathering materials, participating in the activities, and cleaning up.

REVIEW QUESTIONS

1. What type of information can teachers acquire by observing children during art activities?
2. What should the art area look like, including location in the room, furniture, and supplies?
3. What factors should be considered when creating an art activity?
4. What are the advantages and disadvantages of individual and small and large group activities?
5. Explain the difference between direct and indirect art instruction.

SUGGESTED STUDENT ACTIVITIES

1. Design an art activity for one child with special needs. State the child's special needs and list the objectives this art activity is designed to meet. Also list materials needed for the activity.

2. Design an art activity for a small group based on a classroom theme. List the major goals of the activity.

3. Visit preschool classrooms for children who are developmentally delayed and those who are not and compare and contrast the art activities in both classrooms.

ADDITIONAL READINGS

Gardner, H. (1993). *The arts and human development.* New York: John Wiley.

Kellogg, R. (1970). *Understanding children's art.* Palo Alto, CA: Mayfield.

Rubin, J. A. (1984). *Child art therapy* (2nd ed.). New York: Van Nostrand Reinhold.

ADDITIONAL RESOURCES

Very Special Arts
1331 F Street, N.W., Suite 800
Washington, DC 20004

REFERENCES

Alkema, C. J. (1971). *Art for the exceptional child.* Boulder, CO: Pruett.

Anderson, F. (1978). *Art for all the children.* Springfield, IL: Charles C. Thomas.

Anderson, J. P. (1986). Humanism, art educational philosophy in transition. *Art Education, 25*(7), 18–19.

Axline, V. M. (1947). *Play therapy.* New York: Ballantine Books.

Beittel, K. E. (1974). *Alternatives for art education research.* Dubuque, IA: William C. Brown.

Brittain, W. L. (1979). *Creativity, art, and the young child.* New York: Macmillan.

Cohen, H. J. (1974). Learning stimulation. In D. L. Barclay (Ed.), *Art education for the disadvantaged child* (pp. 20–25). Washington, DC: National Art Education Association.

Coles, R. (1992). *Their eyes meeting the world: The drawings and paintings of children.* Boston: Houghton Mifflin.

Crawford, J. W. (1962). Art for the mentally retarded. *Bulletin of Art Therapy, 2*(2), 67–72.

Dalley, T., Case, C., Schaverien, J., Weir, F., Halliday, D., Hall, P., & Waller, D. (1987). *Images of art therapy: New developments in therapy and practice.* New York: Tavistock.

Di Leo, J. H. (1974). *Children's drawings as diagnostic aids.* New York: Brunner/Mazel.

Edwards. L. C. (1996). *The creative arts: A process approach for teachers and children,* (2nd Ed). Columbus, OH: Merrill.

Frankl, V. E. (1959). *Man's search for meaning.* New York: Pocket Books.

Gaitskell, C. D., & Gaitskell, M. R. (1953). *Art education for slow learners.* Peoria, IL: Charles A. Bennett.

Gardner, H. (1973). *The arts and human development.* New York: John Wiley.

Goodnow, J. (1977). *Children drawing.* Cambridge, MA: Harvard University Press.

Grozinger, W. (1955). *Scribbling, drawing, painting: The early forms of the child's pictorial creativeness.* New York: Humanities Press.

Harris, D. B. (1963). *Children's drawings as measures of intellectual maturity.* New York: Harcourt, Brace, and World.

Kellogg, R. (1969). *Analyzing children's art.* Palo Alto, CA: National Press Books.

Lindsay, Z. (1968). *Art is for all: Arts and crafts for less able children.* New York: Taplinger.

Lowenfeld, M. (1971). *Play in childhood* (2nd ed.). New York: John Wiley and Sons.

Lowenfeld, M., & Brittain, W. L. (1969). *Creative and mental growth* (6th ed.). New York: Macmillan.

Moon, B. L. (1990). *Existential art therapy: The Mayvas mirror.* Springfield, IL: Charles C. Thomas.

Nixon, A. (1969). A child's right to expressive arts. *Childhood Education, 6,* 299–310.

Rubin, J. A. (1984). *Child art therapy* (2nd ed.). New York: Van Nostrand Reinhold.

Salant, E. G. (1975). Preventive art therapy with a preschool child. *American Journal of Art Therapy, 14*(3), 67–74.

Uhlin, D. M. (1972). *Art for exceptional children.* Dubuque, IA: William C. Brown.

Wohl, A., & Kaufman, B. (1985). *Silent screams and hidden cries.* New York: Brunner/Mazel.

CHAPTER 14

BEHAVIOR MANAGEMENT

LINDA L. DUNLAP, PH.D.

CHAPTER KEY POINTS

- Behavior management includes developing desirable behavior and eliminating undesirable behavior to enhance children's development.
- The goal of behavior management is to help children develop strategies to manage their own behavior rather than have adults attempt to control children's behavior.
- When forming expectations for their children's behavior, parents must consider each child's developmental level.
- Children with developmental delays respond to behavior management techniques appropriate for children without disabilities including reinforcement, redirection, time-out, extinction, and punishment.

Earlier chapters discussed the special therapeutic needs of children with developmental delays. Willingness to participate in therapy and the ability to comply with requests adults make affect whether therapy interventions are useful. This chapter focuses on the importance of learning how to manage children's behavior effectively to maximize their development. Children with developmental delays have many needs commonly found in most children at a particular developmental level and most often benefit from behavior management techniques that are useful for children without special needs. It is particularly important for those who work with children with special needs to be slow to judge children's behaviors negatively. Their behaviors are often an expression of their uniqueness and attributes associated with a particular special need.

THE IMPORTANCE OF DEVELOPING DESIRED BEHAVIOR

Chapter 12 emphasized the importance of play for enhancing all areas of children's development. During play situations, young children frequently have difficulty successfully interacting with other children their own age (Guralnick, 1990; Sameroff, Seifer, & Zax, 1982). This inability limits learning opportunities and social interactions. For example, children who frequently act aggressively toward other children typically have fewer friends (McEvoy, Odom, & McConnell, 1992; Brandenburg, Friedman, & Silver, 1990). This results in children being less likely to have the opportunity to engage in social interactions (Fields & Boesser, 1994).

"Inappropriate behavior" may result in a child being removed from the learning environment (Strain, et al., 1992). For example, a teacher might tell a child who is bothering other children, "You are not ready to be at this activity." The child can be asked to leave or be led away from the group. If this occurs, the child is no longer present at the activity and, therefore, cannot learn from the experiences (Zirpoli & Melloy, 1996).

An **ecological perspective** suggests the need to create environments that enhance the likelihood of positive behaviors and healthy emotional development rather than focusing on correcting negative behaviors. A positive environment should help prevent the occurrence of problems as well as help resolve conflicts when they occur (Bauer & Sapona, 1991).

Parents and teachers often focus on the importance of developing intellectual skills and fail to acknowledge that social skills are also extremely important (Guralnick, 1993). The focus on social development is perhaps even more important than the development of specific intellectual skills during the preschool years. Research indicates that children who fail to achieve a minimal level of **social competency** by age six are more likely

to have social interaction difficulties as adults (Hildebrand, 1994). These difficulties include a greater likelihood of future mental health problems, marital adjustment difficulties, parenting competence problems, and even occupational adjustment difficulties (Baker, Brightman, Heifetz, & Murphy, 1990).

Social competency includes the capacity to initiate, develop, and maintain satisfying relationships with others. During the preschool years, a child's social skills frequently do not appear to be under the child's conscious control (Blechman, 1985). Research also suggests that those children who are *not* socially accepted because of aggressiveness are more likely to drop out of school and become delinquent (Cordisco & Laus, 1993).

Adults should direct the child through instruction or **coaching** about ways to treat others. Young children frequently need help breaking a negative cycle of interaction (Kaplan, 1991). Adults can help by making specific suggestions. For example, if a child is grabbing toys, the adult might say, "You should ask Jason to share. He does not like it when you grab toys from him."

Preschool environments that enhance social interaction and desirable behavior encourage active exploration and interaction with adults, other children, and materials (Smith & Rivera, 1993). Teachers in this environment avoid highly structured, **teacher-guided activities.** They provide children with opportunities to select their own activities from a variety of opportunities. Teachers also avoid telling children what they must do and when they must do it. Children are physically and mentally active and should *not* be expected simply to sit, watch, and be quiet for long periods of time (Cook, Tessier, & Klein, 1992).

Children need time to work individually or in small, informal groups most of the time rather than in large groups where teacher-guided instruction is often used. Children need direct or hands-on exposure to objects relevant to their lives rather than only indirect exposure through workbooks, photo-copied sheets, or flash cards (Zirpoli & Melloy, 1993). When these needs are adequately met, children are less likely to misbehave.

Teachers should move among the children to facilitate their involvement with materials and each other. Classroom staff may offer suggestions, ask questions, or add more complex material. They should not dominate the environment by telling children what to do. Staff should allow children to discover for themselves that there is more than one way to do things (Allen, 1992; Sainato & Carta, 1992).

Children learn best when they are involved in **self-initiated** problem-solving and experimentation and when they are elaborating on their own topics rather than topics predetermined by an adult (Kazdin, 1995). Rote memorization and drills should be avoided. Parents should also follow these principles at home, because when children are learning, they tend not to misbehave.

Development of children's self-control may be facilitated by using positive guidance techniques, such as modeling and encouraging expected behavior, redirecting children to a more "acceptable" activity and setting clear limits (Dinkmeyer, McKay, & Dinkmeyer, 1993). Teachers must adjust their expectations for children's behavior to match each child's developmental level. Teachers who spend most of the day enforcing rules, punishing unacceptable behavior, making children sit and be quiet, or refereeing disagreements need to modify the classroom activities and re-think expectations (Kagan, Reznick, & Snidman, 1990; Campbell, 1990).

Children should be provided with many opportunities to develop social skills such as cooperating, helping, sharing, showing affection, negotiating, and talking with others to solve interpersonal problems (Landau & Moore, 1991). Adults must talk about, model, and provide activities that encourage these behavior patterns. As prosocial behavior increases, negative behavior, including aggression, tends to decrease (Landau & Milich, 1990). Children who always work individually at desks or spend most of their time listening to a teacher talking to the whole class do not have sufficient opportunities to learn necessary social skills (Langelosi, 1993).

Teachers should help parents select appropriate **behavior management** techniques. The way children act at home often has a direct relationship to how they behave in other settings. In addition, parents who become overly frustrated with their children's behavior often do not create an "optimal environment" for children (Schaefer & Millman, 1981). Therefore, parents often need and benefit from receiving information related to behavior management. Teachers and parents should communicate behavioral expectations to children clearly and consistently. Children easily become confused and frustrated when rules or expectations are not clear or are applied inconsistently (Levin & Nolan, 1991).

GENERAL PRINCIPLES FOR BEHAVIOR MANAGEMENT

Nearly all children demonstrate **behavioral problems** from time to time. Although these problems are relatively common, they are, nonetheless, disruptive. Teachers and parents however, should avoid attempting to **control** children's behavior (Crary, 1984). Control means that someone else takes over and determines what events occur. Parents and teachers need to learn how to respect children and their ability to control their own behavior. When children are in control of their behavior, it makes them more receptive to learning experiences whether at home or at school (Eisenberg, Lennon, & Roth, 1983).

This respect should be demonstrated in language and actions (Honig, 1985). Children should be told what it is that adults like about them, and shown they are valued by receiving smiles and hugs. Showing respect also includes taking time to listen to what they have to say. When children feel they are respected, they are better able to stay in control. Even when children do *not* behave rationally or in control, however, they should still be respected and loved.

Children respond more positively to being told what they can do rather than what they cannot do. Adults would be bewildered if their bosses were to say, "I don't want you to be lazy today." Adults and children prefer and expect to be told what needs to be done. A phrase such as, "Today, we should work together and get this project completed," demonstrates positive expectations.

Whenever possible, children should be given choices rather than told exactly what to do. Adults must be careful, though, not to overwhelm children by providing too many or giving them choices that are "developmentally inappropriate" (Factor & Schilmoeller, 1983). Instead of being told, "Sit down and eat your apple," choices such as, "If you want a snack, you need to sit down. Would you like an apple or an orange?" could be provided.

Children tend to respond positively to a comment such as, "Today, we are going to have fun sharing with our friends," rather than, "Today we are *not* going to grab toys from our friends." Adults should avoid overloading children with negative statements such as *no, don't, stop it, quit that, cut it out,* and *you can't.* Most children gradually stop listening when there are many "no's." Messages of "no" may discourage children and cause them to begin to feel negatively about themselves. Telling children what *not* to do also does not provide them with information about what they *should* be doing.

Children should be continually reassured that they are worth loving and can learn how to do new things. When children sense that other people value them, they are more likely to approach and persevere at tasks they find difficult (McGinnis & Goldstein, 1990). When children sense that adults do not like them or think they cannot be successful, they are more likely to resist participating or to fail when they try.

When children are unsuccessful, they frequently hear comments such as, "That was too hard for you" or "Can't you do anything right?" These messages tell children they are *not* expected to be successful. Messages such as, "That's a really hard job. Let's try again," encourage them (Wyckoff & Unell, 1984).

Adults should *not* attack children's personal worth by using statements such as, "I should have known you'd behave like a monster." Comments that condemn or compare such as, "You'll never amount to anything" and "Why can't you be more like your sister?" may damage a child's self-esteem (Wagonseller & McDowell, 1979). Frequently, when a child is *not* behaving in the desired manner, adults believe the child's behavior must be managed or changed. In some cases, this is true, but in many it may be necessary to change the environment rather than the child (Crary, 1979).

Adults may also need to change their own expectations. Some children intentionally misbehave to get attention. Different children need different levels of attention. Frequently, children with special needs require extra attention because they find it more difficult to succeed (Baumrind, 1977). Therefore, they are likely to respond in ways, positive or negative, to help ensure that people acknowledge them.

Adults too often leave children in situations in which the children have trouble coping due to a lack of sufficient adult supervision. Adults often expect more self-control and mature behavior from children than they can achieve. For example, if a child is constantly taking cookies from a cookie jar, the cookie jar should be put out of sight and reach. If children are fighting over a toy day after day, the toy should be removed. Although attempting to reason with children is admirable, it may not be effective with children less than four or five years old.

Adults must acknowledge *each* child's needs, which means working with rather than against a child. For example, a child who has difficulty sitting for long periods of time should *not* be expected to sit quietly for a ten-minute story. Standing back, observing children, and planning acceptable ways to accomplish certain goals is generally more successful than using a predetermined formula for interacting with children (Izard & Malatesta, 1987). Consistency among care providers is also important. When care providers respond in different ways or respond inconsistently, children cannot learn rules or accomplish goals.

Teachers should establish appropriate classroom expectations. They must be certain that they are not requiring children to engage in activities that they are not mature enough to handle. Teachers should analyze the classroom schedule of activities, physical layout of the room, and level of organization for activities to determine whether these factors are contributing to management problems (Linder, 1983). For example, an overcrowded classroom, too few toys, or tasks that are too difficult may lead to aggression.

Teachers should make sure that they consistently deal with behavior problems. They must take responsibility for supervising children and anticipating problems and preventing them from occurring. They should also analyze whether the environment is one in which children are likely to be successful (Bailey & Wolery, 1984). Teachers often need to seek help from a consultant (e.g., a social worker or psychologist), someone less emotionally involved, to help solve behavior problems. Table 14.1 provides a list of suggestions that facilitate positive classroom interactions.

TABLE 14.1 Strategies for Encouraging Positive Classroom Interactions

- keep classrooms neat and organized
- create classrooms that are attractive and colorful
- create play centers
- establish a special area for disruptive children
- begin activities promptly
- plan ahead and develop routines
- use positive interaction styles
- learn from experience and be willing to change
- ignore undesirable behavior whenever possible
- reinforce desirable behavior
- use nonverbal signals to indicate that inappropriate behavior must stop
- move close to the child who is misbehaving
- remove tempting objects children want or fight over
- follow through on your warnings
- discipline privately whenever possible
- use time-out, but not excessively
- tell children to "stop"

At times, adults will need to attempt to modify or limit children's behavior to ensure their safety. Limits should be communicated clearly, calmly, and consistently. It is important to acknowledge that children see the world differently from adults. Things that are obviously unsafe from an adult's perspective are often not seen as unsafe by children (Berkeley & Ludlow, 1989). For example, adults frequently assume that, because children are taught not to run inside one building, they know the rule and "should know better than to run indoors" anywhere. Children, however, often do not know what adults expect of them. They frequently do not **generalize** expectations from one situation to another (Bredekamp, 1987). In addition, adults often inconsistently respond to children's behavior. For example, they allow children to run down hallways some days but not others.

Rules sometimes help children control **impulsive behavior.** Too many rules, however, lead to their being forgotten and broken (Carta, Schwartz, Atwater, & McConnell, 1991). Rules should be reasonable, enforceable, and appropriate for children's age, health, and developmental level. It is unreasonable to tell a child to sit on a chair until apologizing—the child may never apologize. Rather than saying, "Don't throw the blocks," a child could be told, "Build something with the blocks or we will put them away." If the child throws another block, the blocks should then be put away.

Adults should avoid overloading children with a large numbers of rules. At preschool and daycare centers there should be no more than four or five classroom rules. They should be easy to understand and focus on what children should be doing rather than on what they should *not* be doing (Dunst, 1985). For example, a rule should be stated as "walk in the building" rather than "no running in the building."

When children misbehave, it is generally best to teach them "desired" behavior rather than to use **punishment,** which includes applying a negative consequence or penalty (Dunst, 1986). There are times when using punishment is necessary, although punishing children does *not* teach them proper behavior. Punishment should not model aggressive behavior such as yelling or put the child at physical or emotional risk (Wicks–Nelson & Israel, 1991). It is unethical and illegal for teachers to use aversive behavior management techniques.

Behavior management takes a great deal of time and thought. In fact, it initially takes more time to manage than to than punish children. Punishment only indicates types of behavior that adults find unacceptable. Behavior control tends to emphasize negative aspects of behavior and is generally used after an undesirable behavior has occurred. It includes use of negative comments or punishments and does little to support or encourage desired behavior (Fisher, Hand, Watson, VanParys, & Tucker, 1984). Adults often attempt to change several kinds of negative behavior at once. This is *not* reasonable. It is necessary to determine which behavior should be focused on first.

Behavior management includes what is modeled to the child. Adults need to make sure that they are modeling appropriate behavior (Garwood, 1983), and should ask themselves whether they would want a child to repeat their action and language. One of the major goals of most preschool and daycare programs is to help children acquire socially appropriate behavior (Parker & Asher, 1987). It is best to manage the classroom by creating a positive learning environment that encourages desirable behavior, but sometimes teachers must modify undesirable behavior. It is often difficult, however, to agree on which types of behavior warrant intervention.

DETERMINING BEHAVIOR TO ATTEMPT TO MODIFY

Even though it is *not* appropriate to "go to war" with children, the analogy of "picking battles worth fighting" is useful. Adults should avoid trying to fit children into an ideal mold. It will not work and a child's individuality may be lost.

There are several issues to consider when determining behavior that should be the focus of behavior management. First, it is necessary to collect information about how often the behavior occurs and evaluate the level of intensity and duration (Rosenberg, Wilson, Maheady, & Sindelar, 1992). If children become angry easily and with such intensity that they injure themselves or others, then either the behavior or environment needs modification. See Table 14.2 for guidelines for determining types of behavior that may need modification.

Adults should avoid deciding which behavior must be changed when they are tired or angry (Becker, 1990). A particular behavior may be "the straw that broke the camel's back" and may not be a major or consistent concern. Also, behavior should *not* be modified merely because adults are concerned about "what others may think." A teacher, for instance, should not decide that all children should be made to sit in a chair during a circle time (when children are together in a large group activity) simply because it is expected in another teacher's classroom (Anderson, Hodson, & Jones, 1975). Adults often must be willing to change their own behavior while attempting to modify a child's behavior. For example, if adults tell children that yelling is not allowed, the adult must then *not* yell. Once an adult has decided

TABLE 14.2 Guidelines for Determining Behavior That Warrants Intervention

Intervention should be considered if a child exhibits behavior that is:

- demanding a disproportionate amount of time and attention;
- disrupting other children and preventing learning from occurring;
- becoming more severe;
- more like children of a much younger age;
- leading to a negative self-image;
- being perceived negatively by classmates;
- causing danger to that child or others.

which behavior to attempt to manage, there are several steps that should be used.

BEHAVIOR MANAGEMENT TECHNIQUES

To manage behavior successfully, it is first necessary to state specifically what the child should be doing (Christopherson, 1982). For example, saying to children, "be nice," is too vague a statement. Children should be told what "be nice" means and be given specific directions such as, "You must share the blocks with Chris."

There are several specific techniques used to manage behavior. Several of the most common are discussed below, including **reinforcement, redirection, time-out, extinction,** and punishment. Reinforcement and redirection should be used whenever possible and reduce the need to use the other techniques (Miller, 1980).

Reinforcement

One goal of most teachers and parents is to help children acquire types of behavior they need to function effectively day to day. Using rewards, or reinforcers, often helps to increase "appropriate" behavior (Miller, 1980). Adults often give children reinforcers when they behave in desired ways. For example, when children remember to put away their toys, they might earn a sticker. Adults often **praise** children for sharing their toys. Children usually enjoy receiving reinforcement in the form of a reward such as money, gold stars, blue ribbons, and trophies. A **reward** is something considered nice or valuable (Patterson, 1990).

A reinforcer is defined by its effect on behavior. Not all rewards reinforce all behavior. A reinforcer is a consequence that follows a behavior and increases the likelihood of that behavior occurring again (Anderson, et al., 1975). For example, if children are given a small snack for spending five minutes putting away their toys, they are likely to help put away their toys in the future. The snack is a reinforcer. If, however, children are only given a small snack for spending an

hour cleaning, they may not be willing to help in the future. In both cases the reward was the same; while the snack was a reinforcer for the five minutes of picking up toys, it was not a reinforcer for working an entire hour.

Reinforcers are usually thought of as "nice" things, but a reinforcer could be *any* consequence, such as an event or object that increases the behavior it follows (Harter, 1978). A reinforcer does *not* need to be something pleasant, healthy, or valuable. It is something that increases the number of times a behavior occurs. For example, researchers have found that nagging children for not cleaning up their toys actually increases (reinforces) the chances of their *not* cleaning up in the future (Harter & Zigler, 1974). In this case, nagging, certainly considered unpleasant, is a reinforcer for *not* working.

Just as children are different, different things reinforce them. Also, for any one person, what reinforces one behavior may not reinforce another behavior (Ickes & Kidd, 1976). When selecting a reinforcer it may be helpful to look at a list of rewards that could be used, choose one and then find out if the reward is really a reinforcer for a specific behavior for a specific child. Table 14.3 provides a list of rewards teachers and parents often use.

If teachers or parents are considering using material rewards, it is often helpful to ask children what they want for a reward. If children cannot clearly communicate their preferences, then observing them often provides clues about the types of objects they prefer (Heshusius, 1986). For example, if a child is constantly asking for stickers, it is then likely that providing stickers as rewards will reinforce that child's behavior.

Before attempting, however, to modify behavior using reinforcement, it is first necessary to assess the number of times the behavior selected to be modified occurs over a span of several days (Lepper, 1981). After recording the number of times the behavior occurs, rewarding the desired behavior can begin. Rewards should be given immediately after each occurrence of

TABLE 14.3 Commonly Used Rewards

Verbal Approval and Praise
"Thanks so much for helping me."
"That's right!"
"I really *like* the way you did that."
"That's a good job of painting."
"You're such a hard worker."
"Wow, you've got a good memory!"
"You're playing so nicely together."
"Tell me about your picture."

Nonverbal Approval
Smiling
Nodding
Clapping hands
Looking interested
Laughing
Winking
Looking surprised

Physical Contact
Hugging
Touching
Shaking hands
Holding
Patting
Holding on lap

Activity Rewards
Watching a video
Providing free time
Helping the teacher
Listening to tapes or records
Reading a special story
Being first in line
Having show and tell
Providing sensory play

Material Objects
Toys
Trinkets
Art material
Pennies
Snack
Books
Games
Stickers

Tokens
Stars or points on a chart
Marks on an index card
Play money
Poker chips

the desired behavior. A record of the number of times a behavior occurs during reinforcement should be maintained. If the frequency of the desired behavior increases, then the reward is a reinforcer (Lovaas, 1987). Consider the following example of a use of rewards.

Four-year-old Jesse is having difficulty stacking blocks. For fourteen days, Jesse's teacher recorded the number of times Jesse stacked blocks during free play. The teacher discovered that Jesse rarely played with blocks and *never* attempted stacking blocks. Since the teacher wanted Jesse to learn how to stack blocks, the teacher looked for possible reinforcers. Knowing Jesse loved stickers, she asked Jesse if he wanted a chance to earn some stickers. Jesse nodded affirmatively. The teacher then told Jesse that, if he played in the block area, he could select a sticker to take home. Jesse immediately went to the block area, sat down to play, and asked for a sticker.

The next day, the teacher reminded Jesse about the stickers and he immediately went to play in the block area. Even though Jesse was now playing in the block area, he was not stacking blocks. He made roads with the blocks and played with cars on the "roads." The teacher modified the plan and told Jesse, "I'll give you two stickers if you stack blocks." The teacher demonstrated putting one block on top of another.

The following day, Jesse began lining up blocks. The teacher sat down beside Jesse and modeled stacking blocks. The teacher reminded Jesse about earning stickers for stacking blocks. She walked to her desk, grabbed the box of stickers, returned, and sat beside Jesse. Jesse looked at the box of stickers and began to stack blocks. The teacher held out the box and Jesse chose two stickers. The teacher said, "I knew you could do it!" Over the next few days, Jesse's teacher continued to reward his stacking the blocks. Three weeks after the start of behavior modification Jesse no longer requested stickers for this type of play.

In Jesse's case, it appears the stickers were reinforcing. The stickers alone did not increase block-stacking though, until the teacher modeled the desired behavior. It is possible Jesse would have been reinforced by receiving praise or attention and would not have needed to receive the stickers.

Adults need to decide whether they will use primary or **secondary reinforcers** (Miyake, Campos, Kagan, & Bradshaw, 1986). Primary reinforcers are things people need to live and grow physically and emotionally. Food, air, shelter, sleep, food, water, and physical contact are examples of primary reinforcers. Secondary reinforcers, sometimes called conditioned reinforcers, have been paired with primary reinforcers to acquire their reinforcing value. Praise, tokens, and stickers are examples of secondary reinforcers. Praise is a very useful secondary reinforcer because it is easy to give and the supply is endless. Some children do not initially find praise reinforcing, but if it is paired with a primary reinforcer, it may become reinforcing and the primary reinforcer can gradually be reduced (Peters, Neisworth, & Yawkey, 1985). Consider the following example of a use of primary and secondary reinforcers.

Four-year-old Aaron never sat quietly for more than a few seconds during story time. After keeping a record of Aaron's behavior during story time for one week, Aaron's teacher found that Aaron sat quietly on an average of thirty seconds at a time. The teacher decided to give Aaron his favorite snack, raisins, for every thirty seconds that he sat quietly. After two weeks of consistent reinforcement with raisins, Aaron could sit quietly through story time, which lasted ten minutes.

Next, the teacher decided to pat Aaron on the shoulder and smile at Aaron every time a raisin was given. For the next week, the teacher gave Aaron the raisin only every other time but nodded and smiled after every thirty seconds he listened quietly. The number of raisins was gradually reduced but nodding and smiling continued, however, on an irregular basis. Nodding and patting had become secondary reinforcers. Nearly anything can become a secondary reinforcer (Whitman, 1990). Tokens or money, for instance, could be exchanged for other forms of reinforcement such as earning enough tokens to be allowed to watch a video.

A **token system** can be used almost anywhere. Stickers, points, or plastic chips could be earned when children engage in a specified behavior. These tokens can then be traded for a variety of things or activities that reinforce a child's behavior. See Figure 14.1 for an example of a token reward system.

Reinforcers should be used to motivate appropriate behavior. The relationship between a reward and behavior is called a **contingency.** Reinforcers should be given *only* to achieve the behavior desired. When "desired" and "undesired" behavior are reinforced, it is difficult for children to learn which is the "desired" way to get reinforcers (Whitman, 1990).

For example, a teacher wanted to increase the amount of time a child spent cutting with scissors. For every sixty seconds of cutting, the teacher gave the child a pretzel. The teacher also gave the child a pretzel when the teacher thought the child was about to start cutting because the teacher hoped the pretzel would encourage the child to try harder. The amount of time the child spent cutting did *not* increase. Although the teacher was consistent about reinforcing the cutting, the teacher also gave the child reinforcement when not cutting. This provided the child with inconsistent reinforcement. To make the reinforcement effective the teacher must only reinforce the cutting.

Before starting a reinforcement program it should be explained to the child. The child should be told which behavior is desired and the consequences for the behavior (Lovaas, 1987). At the beginning of each day, or perhaps more frequently, the child should be reminded about the contingencies. Then, each time the behavior is reinforced the contingency should be stated. For example, every time Steven hangs up his jacket he receives a sticker. As the teacher gives him a sticker the teacher says, "I am giving you this sticker because you remembered to hang up your coat." The teacher might also add, "It makes me happy when you remember to hang up your coat." See

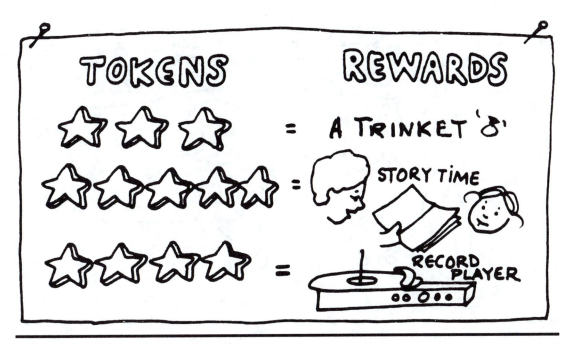

FIGURE 14.1   Example of a Token Reward System

Table 14.4 for a list of actions that help ensure reinforcements will be effective.

Adults should avoid power struggles with children. Using an **if-then** technique may help avoid them. For example, saying, "*If* you finish putting the blocks away, *then* we will have a snack," may help modify a certain type of behavior by establishing a reinforcement contingency.

TABLE 14.4   Effective Use Of Reinforcement

1. Give the reinforcer immediately following the desired behavior.
2. Be consistent by reinforcing the behavior every time it occurs.
3. Be pleasant when presenting the reinforcer.
4. Be specific and clear by telling the child why the reinforcement is being given.
5. Do not try to reinforce and reprimand at the same time by providing a reinforcement, while also stating how the behavior might be improved.

This method requires children to behave appropriately before another activity (reinforcement) can begin. It provides logical and positive consequences rather than negative ones. See Figure 14.2 for an example of the use of a contingency statement.

Although using reinforcement is generally preferred over other behavior management techniques, other methods may be necessary. Reinforcements are used only to develop desired behavior. There are times when the goal of behavior management is to eliminate undesirable behavior. Redirection, time-out, extinction, and punishment are often appropriate techniques to use when children misbehave (Cordisco & Laus, 1993).

Redirection

Redirection involves orienting children to desirable rather than undesirable behavior (Rogers & DeLalla, 1991). For example, a child who begins

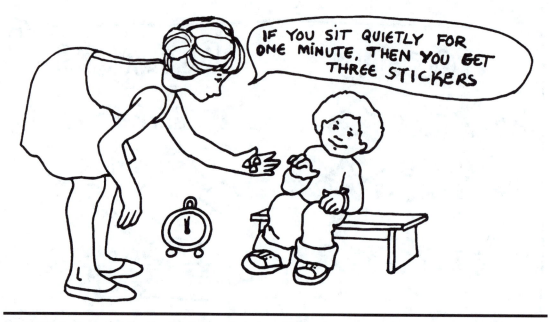

FIGURE 14.2   Example Use of a Contigency Statement (If-Then)

to flip sand out of a sand box might be encouraged to play somewhere else. During redirection, the teacher does *not* reprimand the child but instead asks or tells the child to find a new place to play by saying something like, "You've played a long time in the sand box. Please go play on the slide." Children sometimes get "on the wrong track" and need to be shown the correct direction (Zirpoli, 1995).

Time-Out

Time-out is very similar to redirection. Time-out involves actively removing children from a situation in which they are having difficulty controlling themselves. It is designed to provide children with an opportunity to get back in control, as well as to keep them from disrupting others. Time-out should be used as a calming device rather than as a form of punishment (Strain, et al., 1988). For children under six, about a minute of time-out for each year of age is generally a reasonable duration. For example, time-out should last for about four minutes for most four-year-olds. For children

who are very young or who have attention deficit hyperactivity disorder (ADHD), are autistic, or who have other developmental delays, using a minute or less may be appropriate (Olson, 1989).

The time-out spot should be located in an uninteresting place where a child cannot interact with other people. A consistent location should be used. When adults place children in time-out, they should limit discussion of the event and avoid "emotional reactions" (Kaplan, 1991). Children should be told why they are being sent to time-out (contingency statement). For example, a teacher might say, "Beth, you need to go sit in the time-out area for two minutes because you hit John." Once time-out is over (the time has passed), there should be no or very limited discussion about the incident. It is important *not* to overuse the time-out technique.

Extinction

Extinction is a nonactive way of discouraging undesirable behavior. Children have a tremendous desire to demonstrate their "power," "ability," and influence. When an adult becomes upset with a child's actions, the child's goal of gaining control is accomplished. When a child cries or whines for a snack, it is generally most appropriate to ignore the child, which is called extinction (Kaplan, 1991). Attending to children should occur only after crying has stopped. Children should appropriately ask for a snack before they receive it. Giving children a snack to stop the crying or whining may reinforce the behavior of crying, thereby encouraging them to cry or whine (Polloway & Patton, 1993).

Using extinction involves ignoring undesirable behavior when it occurs. Extinction can be useful when trying to eliminate behavior such as whining. For example, the child who whines should be told that whining is unacceptable and will be ignored. The child should be reminded at the beginning of each day that whining will be ignored. When the child whines, the whining should be ignored. It probably would not be useful to tell the child to stop whining. This type of attention might reinforce whining. When the child is *not* whining the child should then be told something like, "I like it when you talk in such a nice way." It is not always easy or safe to ignore all types of undesirable behavior. Unfortunately, not all behavior can be managed by using reinforcement, redirection, time-out, and extinction. In some cases, it is necessary to use punishment.

Punishment

Dangerous behavior may require using punishment. Punishment is a negative consequence administered in reaction to a child's "undesirable behavior" (Alberto & Troutman, 1990). Punishment involves adding something negative to a child's environment, such as making the child clean up after throwing a cup filled with juice. It could also involve a penalty, taking something positive away. For example, removing a toy used to injure another child is considered a penalty.

When punishment is necessary a **penalty** is generally the preferred form (Rosenberg, O'Shea,

& O'Shea, 1991). Turning off the television when Sally fights with her sister while watching it is an example of a penalty. In this case, Sally lost the right to watch television (something positive) as a penalty for fighting. This penalty is a **logical consequence** of her behavior and is typically more effective than yelling or spanking because it does not model angry or aggressive behavior (Wyckoff & Unell, 1984).

When punishment is used, adults should make sure they are not punishing themselves rather than the child. *Not* going out to dinner because the children were arguing in the car on the way to dinner is a logical consequence, but if the children do *not* care about going out to dinner it is *not* a punishment.

Reinforcement, redirection, time-out, extinction, and punishment all need to be used to help manage children's behavior. A wide variety of behavior must be managed. Discussion of several behavior types follows.

STRATEGIES FOR COMMON BEHAVIORAL PROBLEMS

There are several types of common problems that must be managed. Some types of behavior bother some adults more than others. It is important to remember that it is only appropriate to attempt to change one or two behavior problems at a time.

Temper Tantrums

Throwing **temper tantrums** often is a child's way of expressing anger or getting attention. Behavior displayed during tantrums includes crying, yelling, biting, hitting, and kicking. Young children frequently throw tantrums because they cannot verbally express their feelings. Young children with language delays are more prone to throwing tantrums because of their limited ability to communicate (Wagonseller & McDowell, 1979). Children with motor delays may have tantrums because they cannot perform tasks they would like to or observe other children doing (Goodman, 1992).

Tantrums may also be a response to frustrating situations including limits imposed by adults, lack of time to complete tasks, or in response to another child's actions, such as taking away a toy (Bagnato & Neisworth, 1991). Tantrums are *not* considered abnormal unless they occur frequently and last for a long time. It is important not to overreact to temper tantrums. When a tantrum appears likely, using redirection may prevent it or lessen the intensity (Crary, 1979). Methods used to reduce the likelihood of tantrums include avoiding saying the "no" words.

Removing objects that contribute to tantrums and placing them out of a child's sight and reach also helps reduce tantrums (Bressanutti, Mahoney, & Sachs, 1992). Allowing children to make choices and providing them with advanced warning for impending transitions is also helpful in preventing tantrums (Blechman, 1985). For example, a child who often has a tantrum when asked to help clean up could be told, "It will be time to put away the toys in five minutes. Let's set the timer. After we clean up, we'll have a snack."

Once a tantrum has begun, it is best to ignore it (extinction). During tantrums children may need to be moved to a safe spot that reduces their chances of being hurt. When children appear to be "out of control," it might be necessary to firmly hold them for a few minutes to help them regain control and prevent them from hurting themselves or someone else (Dreikurs & Cassel, 1972).

Adults should *not* yield to demands that lead to the tantrum. For example, if a child began to throw a tantrum because the child was not allowed to have another cookie, the child should *not* be given a cookie during the tantrum or after it stops. Giving the child a cookie might reinforce the child's behavior, leading to even more tantrums in the future. After the tantrum is over, children often need to be comforted because the "loss of control" frequently is frightening and embarrassing. Once the tantrum is over, adults should not focus on the tantrum (Blechman, 1985). An adult might say, "You were very upset. I am glad that you are feeling better," and then continue with the regular activities.

Frequent or very intense tantrums or tantrums that result in children intentionally hurting themselves or someone else are abnormal. In these situations, it is advisable to seek professional help. Pediatricians, social workers, and psychologists are appropriate individuals to contact (Thurman & Widerstrom, 1990).

Aggression

Aggression refers to any behavior that results in injury or discomfort to another person and includes hitting, name-calling, yelling, and damage to property (Saarni & Crowley, 1990). Dealing with aggression at home or school is one of the most difficult challenges adults encounter. It is difficult *not* to feel anger toward children who hurt others. It is difficult *not* to worry that others may reject a child who behaves aggressively.

Acts that result in injury but are unintentional are generally not classified as aggressive behavior (Sherburne, Utley, McConnell, & Gannon, 1988). Children playing closely together frequently experience situations in which another child accidentally gets hurt. Unfortunately, most young children do not distinguish between intentional and unintentional acts. For example, a child who is accidentally hit by a ball thrown by another child might respond by hitting that child. Adults should help young children interpret these situations by saying something like, "Joey didn't mean to hit you with the ball. He was playing catch. Joey should be more careful." Adults should monitor children and create environments that help minimize unintentional injuries (Killen & Turiel, 1991).

Sometimes, children are intentionally aggressive (Sherburne, et al., 1988). For example, a child may push another child aside to be the next to go up a slide. In this case, the child acted aggressively based on the desire to use the slide without waiting. Adults should help children to develop alternative methods to meet their goals and impose logical consequences when they behave aggressively. For example, an adult might respond to the slide situation by saying, "You need to wait your turn to use the slide. Pushing can hurt someone. Because you did not wait your turn you may not use the slide."

Aggression is more likely to occur when children are frustrated. **Frustration** occurs for many reasons, such as when children are unable to obtain a desired goal, when they are involved in activities too difficult for them, are asked to wait, or are not allowed to participate in activities, when the play area is overcrowded, and when they are not adequately supervised (Strain, et al., 1992). Children who are frustrated react in different ways. Some children respond by acting aggressively, having temper tantrums, or crying, while others become very sad, withdrawn, or shy. A child who acts aggressively needs reassurance that, although an adult does not like that behavior, the adult still likes the child (Miller & Sperry, 1987).

When confronted with a frustrating situation, a child often finds helpful an adult's comments that address the child's feelings. For example, an adult might say, "I can tell you are feeling very sad because Shelly took your toy. Sometimes, when I feel sad or angry, I take a walk. Would you like to take a walk with me?" In this example, the adult helped the child understand the anger and frustration, as well as suggested the alternative activity of taking a walk rather than hitting or having a tantrum (redirection).

Sometimes children behave aggressively when there seems to be no logical reason for the aggression (Saarni, 1984). Aggression can occur immediately following an incident or may be deferred to a later time. For instance, Katie might hit Jenny during circle time because Jenny grabbed a car from Katie during free-play time. Children who are frequently aggressive need to be taught to "use their words" and say something like, "Don't take my car!" Adults need to allow children to say "no." This is a much better alternative than aggressive behavior. Saying "no" may seem bossy or even unreasonable to an adult but saying "no" is preferred to aggression. When adults hear a child telling another child "no," the adult should be supportive and say something like, "Claire, I know you really like this car. You

have been playing with it for a long time. In five minutes you will let Beth have a turn. Let's set the timer together."

When aggressive acts occur, adults should avoid asking young children,"What happened?" or "Did you hurt Jill?" Children are not likely to admit they were at fault or that they hit another child (Saarni, 1985). When adults enter situations where children are upset, they need to resist the temptation to guess what happened or expect children to explain what occurred. Too often, children who have behaved aggressively in the past are automatically blamed for causing conflicts (Saarni & Crowley, 1990).

When adults do not see the aggressive incidents, they need to remind *all* children involved in the incident that they should not hurt each other. Children might also be told, "If you are *not* happy playing together, you will *not* be allowed to play together." It is an adult's responsibility to monitor children closely. If conflicts continue, the children should be separated or the environment needs to be changed, such as removing the object over which the children are arguing (Strayer, 1986).

Whining

Whining poses no immediate threat to anyone but can quickly become intolerable. There are many reasons why children whine. They do it to get attention, when they are overtired, or in response to a stressful event, such as the birth of a sibling or going to a new school (Baker, et al., 1990). Given the passage of time alone, most children stop whining without systematic behavior modification (Becker, 1990).

When intervention seems necessary, the best way to help children learn how not to whine is to stop reinforcing whining and teach them more pleasant ways to communicate (Baker, et al., 1990). When children feel they must whine to get attention or get what they desire, they are more likely to continue the whining. Sometimes, adults become so busy they do not pay attention to children unless they whine. The quickest and easiest way to reduce a child's tendency to whine is to pay attention to things the child says without whining.

If a child has been whining over an extended span of time, whining may have become a habit (Kauffman, 1989). Habits often take a long time to change. If children have developed the habit of whining, it will need to be replaced with a new habit of *not* whining. To change the habit, an adult might say, "Whining makes me sad. When you whine I am not going to listen." Adults should not make demeaning comments such as, "Whining is for babies." In addition, children should be expected to talk without whining. If whining continues, it should be ignored and non-whining speech should be reinforced. Children should be reinforced for talking in the preferred, non-whining voice. They should *not* be held, cuddled, or touched while they are whining. If possible, adults should even avoid eye contact or walk away from a child who whines (Campbell, 1990).

Overdependency

Overdependent behavior involves intensely seeking help, affection, or attention from another person, which interferes with the ability to learn. Dependency is normal but not when it prevents children from doing things they can do for themselves. Overdependency results in children being unable to function without adult support (Pader, 1981). Children who are overdependent often whine and cry and may refuse to do things they are capable of doing. They constantly seek an adult's assistance, physical proximity (nearness) to the adult, and say things such as, "watch me," "talk to me," or "look at what I made."

Some children attempt to control their environment by acting overdependent or like the "baby" because this behavior often gets an adult's attention (Gargiulo, 1985). Many adults feel a sense of sadness as their children grow up and reinforce immature overdependent action. They may overprotect children to keep them from harm.

Adults sometimes reinforce overdependency because they feel guilty for not paying enough attention to children (Blechman, 1985).

One method that can help prevent overdependence is to encourage children to make choices, such as deciding what to eat, wear, and play. Adults should avoid dominating children by imposing too many rules or by nagging. These actions produce children who are obedient but often overdependent. They should also avoid doing things for children that they can do for themselves (Seligman & Darling, 1989).

Once an adult has made a reasonable request, such as "Go get your coat and put it on," adults should not help children if they are capable of independently performing the task. Whenever children act overdependent, adults should encourage them to practice their independence by saying, "You need to do this yourself." Adults should remind children how "good" it feels when tasks are completed independently by making comments like, "Wow! You did it yourself!" When adults gradually increase expectations for more independent behavior, most children adjust to the expectations (Hussey–Gardner, 1992).

Intense **separation anxiety** is an especially troubling form of overdependent behavior. Separation anxiety occurs when children become very upset during separation from their parents or other significant people, such as teachers, siblings, and friends. It is normal for children to act nervous, be "clingy," or regress to more "infantile" behavior when adjusting to new school settings, new homes, new babies, or other stressful events (Hussey–Gardner, 1992).

It is *not* normal for children to cry for an excessively long time after separation. To help reduce separation anxiety, adults should allow children to take along something special, such as a favorite toy, during the process of separation. Teachers should greet children as they arrive at school and help them find an activity on which to focus. This helps children feel more comfortable during separation. Making activities readily available and providing lots of "fun" things may help children "separate" more easily (Blechman, 1985).

Fears

Children have many common childhood fears that are not of major concern. Strong and consistent fears, though, results in children being unable to function (Wachs & Gruen, 1982). For example, a child who is extremely afraid of dogs might refuse to leave the house. Extreme fears lead children to exhibit nervous mannerisms such as stuttering, biting their nails, and sucking their thumbs. Deep-rooted fears may lead to shyness and withdrawal or unexpected acts of aggression (Blechman, 1985). Unexpected acts of aggression can also result from reactions to fears, such as turning a child into a bully because the child was afraid of a bully.

Most fears come from experiences children cannot understand that seem threatening or from seeing someone else respond fearfully. Children who lack confidence, are clumsy, or have developmental delays are also likely to have a greater number of fears. In addition, lack of communication skills prevents children from asking questions or understanding explanations and contribute to fears. Children with motor delays more frequently fall, bump into things, or have things hit them. These experiences can contribute to their fears (Miller, 1980).

Children also acquire fears modeled by other people (Becker, 1990). For example, if a child's father is afraid of heights the child may develop such a fear. Children find it comforting, though, to learn that adults are sometimes afraid and that they learned to overcome their fears. The subject matter of television shows and books should be monitored because fears often develop after watching or hearing a scary story (Sherburne, et al., 1988). Children have a very vivid imagination and sometimes believe things are real when they are not. Talking with an adult often helps children separate fantasy from reality.

Family tension, including fighting, separation, divorce, and drug abuse, often contributes to fears and insecurities (Strain, et al., 1992). Also, overanxious adults constantly warning children to be careful contribute to fears. Appropriate levels of fear, however, are useful because they suggest the need to be cautious and can help prevent children from being harmed. Children who are autistic frequently develop intense and unfounded fears and often do *not* develop fears of real dangers, such as jumping into a pool of water or walking along a narrow ledge. Special precautions should be taken to help keep children safe who do not develop appropriate fears.

Although each child is unique, each age tends to brings on characteristic fears. Table 14.5 lists several common fears birth though five years old.

TABLE 14.5   Common Childhood Fears

Birth to 2 Years
Personal—sudden dropping sensation
Auditory—loud noises
Visual—masks and costumes

2 years
Personal—mother's departure, bedtime, going to school or daycare
Auditory—trains, trucks, thunder, flushing toilet, vacuum cleaner, wind
Visual—dark colors, large objects, hats
Spatial—moving objects to new locations, fear of going down the drain
Animals—dogs and wild animals

3 years
Personal—burglars, mom and dad going out at night, death
Visual—older people, masks, monsters, darkness, animals, people in uniforms

4 years
Auditory—fire engines

5 years
General—much less fearful, more visual than auditory fears
Personal—more fears about "bad" people, getting lost, mom not coming home
Spatial—falling
Animal—fewer fears of animals

To help children overcome their fears, they should be encouraged to try new things while adults are close by to provide reassurance. If children will experience something they are likely to fear, such as going to the hospital, they should be given as much information as possible about what to expect. Reducing uncertainty often reduces fear. Children who have fears should be encouraged to deal with these fears gradually (Kaplan, 1991). For example, a child who is afraid of the dark should gradually be encouraged to sleep in the dark rather than shutting the door and making the room completely dark all at once.

Extremely debilitating fears, called **phobias,** are intense irrational fears. Children rarely exhibit phobic behavior but those who do should be referred to a professional counselor (Westling & Koorland, 1989). Children should *not* be ridiculed, scolded, or punished for any type of fear. They should be encouraged to talk about them. Making children pretend they are not afraid, though, is likely to enhance fears (Kaplan, 1991).

Finicky Eaters

Parents and teachers frequently worry when young children eat very little or are very **finicky eaters,** such as those only willing to eat two or three favorite foods. One goal of early childhood education is to provide children with new experiences (Smith & Rivera, 1993). Providing them opportunities to try new foods is frequently part of that goal. One way to encourage a finicky eater to try a new food is to involve the child in preparing and serving the food. Children need opportunities to explore food by touch and smell. Adults should avoid requiring children to be overly neat when eating because this also may discourage them from trying new foods (Johnson, Pugach, & Devlin, 1990).

When children first reject a new food, this does not mean they will never like it. Foods should be reintroduced on a regular basis because a food a child did not like may become a favorite later. Adults should avoid saying things such as, "Don't give them that. They won't eat it." It is often helpful to ask children to sample new foods by taking a spoonful, sometimes called a "no thank you helping," rather than requiring them to eat a full serving. Adults' and other children's reactions to certain foods often affect a young child's preferences. Children are likely to imitate the way others react to new foods (Deiner, 1993).

Because a child's stomach is much smaller than an adult's, children typically need to eat less but more frequently. Even though children need snacks the snacks should be nutritious. Children should be provided choices of food to encourage them to eat, but too many choices can be overwhelming (Westling & Koorland, 1989).

Meal and snack times should be pleasant and relaxed and not include a discussion of stressful events. Children should be allowed to eat at their own pace. If the food is not eaten after a reasonable amount of time, it should be "unemotionally" removed. An adult might comment, "I guess you were not hungry." Children are likely to be hungry the next time food is offered and will probably eat at that time (Kauffman, 1989).

Children who are autistic often have difficulty controlling the muscles required for chewing. This makes it difficult for them to learn how to eat lumpy foods. They may refuse to try new types of food and become agitated when it is presented to them. New food, therefore, should be introduced very slowly.

Short Attention Span

Attention span refers to the length of time an activity is pursued. A child's ability to focus attention is reduced by distracting noises, sights, or personal feelings. Children with a short attention span often shift quickly from one activity to another and are easily sidetracked. Some children, such as those children diagnosed with attention deficit hyperactivity disorder (ADHD), lack adequate screening or filtering mechanisms that aid them efficiently attend to relevant tasks or events (McGee & Share, 1988). (See Chapter 3 for a discussion of children with ADHD.)

Attention span generally increases as developmental age increases. The "average" attention span is approximately seven minutes for two-year-olds, nine minutes for three-year-olds, twelve minutes for four-year-olds, and fourteen minutes for five-year-olds (Campbell, 1985). It is important to remember that a four-year-old performing tasks typical for a two-year-old may also have the attention span of a two-year-old.

Children who are easily distracted may lose belongings, misplace items, not finish tasks, and be drawn from one activity to another. The length of children's attention span often varies, depending on the type of activity presented to them. If a toy is very interesting, even children who are easily distracted can play with it for an extended amount of time (Douglas, 1983). Children who have difficulty focusing attention may watch television for long stretches of time. This misleads some teachers and parents into thinking that these children can attend to other tasks for as long as they attend to television.

An unusually short attention span could be due to delayed neurological development, impaired perceptual skills, including hearing or sight impairments, or cognitive delays. Children who feel anxious or insecure may also have a short attention span. Lacking self-confidence leads children to choose *not* to attend to tasks because they fear they will not be successful even if they try (Richman, Stevenson, & Graham, 1982).

Children are not likely to stay with a task if they are frequently criticized or are unsuccessful. They are likely to move to other tasks that produce less anxiety. Unfortunately, children quickly learn they cannot fail if they do not try. Tasks that are too difficult or easy do not promote a feeling of adequacy or competency (McGee & Share, 1988). Children who believe, "I can do it," are more likely to pay attention and withstand distractions. Children should be praised for attending to tasks for extended periods of time. It is particularly important to acknowledge children who try to attend.

Children who are easily distracted, especially children with ADHD, generally respond positively to environments designed to minimize distractions and maximize the attractiveness of stimuli to which they must attend (Jacob, O'Leary, & Rosenbald,

1978). Cabinets and tables should be organized and uncluttered. When an activity is completed, materials should be put away. Children who are easily distracted need to be allowed to succeed in completing frequent, short, specific tasks.

An adult's expectation of how long a child should remain focused should gradually be lengthened. Children who have difficulty attending to a task for a designated amount of time often benefit from using a timer to help them remember to stay on task. To help children focus their attention, task instructions should be as clear and specific as possible (Jacob, et al., 1978). Children should be asked to look at an adult who is stating the instructions. Adults should model "reflective thought" (thinking aloud) to children by saying something like, "I wonder how we could solve this puzzle. First, I'll turn all the pieces right side up, and then I'll do the easy pieces first. I can do this."

Self-Stimulating Behavior

Self-stimulating behavior, such as rocking back and forth, head-banging, flapping arms, twirling objects in the sunlight, hitting ears, and banging objects together, are often disruptive and prevent children from engaging in other, more beneficial learning experiences. Children often self-stimulate to withdraw from the constantly changing demands of the outside world. Children who are autistic or have ADHD frequently engage in self-stimulating behavior. Children who are autistic appear to cope with the demands of the environment by moving into their own world and locking themselves away into that world (Lovaas, 1977). (See Chapter 3 for descriptions of autism and ADHD.)

Self-stimulating behavior provides physical sensations that are reinforcing, predictable, and give children a sense of mastery. Children often self-stimulate because they lack the play skills that allow them to play in more meaningful ways (Cohen & Donnellen, 1987). One way to attempt to reduce the amount of self-stimulating behavior is to encourage alternative behavior that is incompatible with self-stimulating behavior. For example, a child could be allowed to hold a favorite toy during circle time *only* when *not* engaging in self-stimulatory behavior. Adults must avoid reinforcing self-stimulating behavior through focusing attention on a child. Children should be reinforced when they are *not* using self-stimulating behavior (Kauffman, 1989).

Genital self-stimulation, called **masturbation,** is a common form of self-stimulation. It is normal but should be discouraged if it is excessive or displayed in public. Excessive masturbation prevents children from focusing on other experiences (Kauffman, 1989). It is important *not* to overreact, humiliate, or punish children who masturbate. Teaching children that certain parts of the body are private provides an important safety lesson. Saying, "We don't touch other's private parts, and we don't let anyone touch or see ours," provides a factual nonthreatening lesson. If children are engaging in masturbation in public they could be told, "Touching yourself in front of other people makes them feel uncomfortable. Please stop." It may be helpful for adults to use a signal, such as a hand signal, to remind a child to stop a self-stimulating behavior (Dreikurs & Cassel, 1972).

Of particular concern is self-stimulating behavior in the form of **self-abuse,** including hitting, pinching, scratching, or biting oneself. Children who are autistic frequently engage in self-abusive behavior. It is important to learn the warning signs that precede this type of behavior to attempt to prevent it. When a child begins to engage in self-abusive behavior, saying "no," placing them in time-out, or firmly holding them until they are calm helps to eliminate or reduce self-abusive behavior. If children frequently engage in self-abusive behavior, professional counseling may be needed (Hussey–Gardner, 1992).

Toilet Training

Parents and teachers must work together when training preschool-age children how to use a toilet. Parents should determine when training begins and decide on the method used (Hussey–Gardner,

1992). Preschool staff should support the ongoing efforts to train children once they begin to use the toilet at home. Sending children to preschool or daycare *not* wearing diapers before they are trained is not reasonable. Teachers should *not* spend a large part of their day cleaning up and changing children after toilet accidents. These activities interfere with time for other activities and other children.

Most parents do not attempt training children until they are at least 2 years old. Most children are trained by 5 years of age and daytime trained before they are nighttime trained. Toilet training success primarily depends on the child's level of neurological development. It is also affected by cognitive, speech, and language skills (Seligman & Darling, 1989).

Adults are often pressured to push toilet training by comments such as, "He's three years old. He should already be toilet-trained." Children should be toilet-trained when they indicate they are ready. Table 14.6 lists the most common indicators of readiness for training. Just as some children learn to walk earlier or later than others, children vary in the age that they are ready to learn to use the toilet. Children with developmental delays are often delayed in learning how to use the toilet (Christopherson, 1982). Adults should remain patient and not worry. Table 14.7 lists guidelines that may be useful when attempting to train children.

TABLE 14.6 Indicators of Readiness for Toilet Training

- knows body parts
- knows words or signs relating to using the toilet
- indicates awareness of urges
- announces or acknowledges the "act"
- is cooperative
- can follow multi-stepped instructions
- demonstrates coordination and dexterity
- demonstrates bowel and bladder control
- does not have fears related to using the toilet

TABLE 14.7   Guidelines for Toilet Training

- pick a starting date during a less hectic week
- talk about the beginning of toilet training a few days in advance
- obtain child-sized toilet equipment
- have a set of rewards available (small toys, stickers)
- reward success, do not punish accidents (expect them)
- reward dryness and cleanness
- chart progress
- do not have the child stay on the toilet too long (five minutes maximum)
- ask the child try to use the toilet no more than once an hour
- slowly phase out rewards for successfully using the toilet

CONCLUSION

Teachers and parents must remember that more can be accomplished by keeping a positive approach to behavior management. Adults must remember it is normal for children to misbehave. Children need guidance in developing positive methods of interacting with others. Those children who can manage their own behavior most of the time benefit more from the learning opportunities provided them. Children tend to be more receptive to having their behavior managed when they feel loved, valued, and greeted with open arms.

The final chapter of this book provides a discussion of the importance of helping children with special needs and their family transition from one form of early intervention services to the next. The chapter concludes with a discussion of the importance of enhancing the self-esteem of young children with special needs.

CHAPTER SUMMARY

- Behavior management includes encouraging desirable behavior and discouraging undesirable behavior.
- Undesirable behavior interferes with development. Children with developmental disabili-

ties can be taught how to control their own behavior.
- Children are generally more cooperative when they are told what they can do rather than *only* being told what they cannot do.
- Expectations must be appropriate for a child's developmental age.
- Reinforcement, redirection, time-out, extinction, and punishment are common behavior management techniques.
- Children are more likely to be aggressive when they are frustrated. Adults can reduce a child's frustration by providing the child with alternative ways to express frustrations.
- Specific methods of intervention are appropriate for most young children for common problems, including temper tantrums, aggression, whining, overdependency, fears, short attention span, self-stimulating behavior, and toilet training

REVIEW QUESTIONS

1. What are the major components of effective behavior management?
2. Why is information about a child's behavior at home useful for adults other than the child's parents?
3. What are some common fears children may develop? Why do they develop and how can adults help children deal with them?
4. Why do children engage in self-stimulating behavior and how should adults react?
5. When should teachers intervene in a classroom situation and what methods of behavior management facilitate positive classroom interactions?

SUGGESTED STUDENT ACTIVITIES

1. Visit an early childhood special education classroom and a regular preschool classroom and compare the types of behavior management problems and techniques found in each setting.

2. Observe parents in public settings and notice how they respond to their children's temper tantrums. What methods are most effective for dealing with tantrums?

3. In groups of three or four students, pretend to be two or three years old under the supervision of one adult played by a student. Demonstrate effective and ineffective methods of dealing with children who are fighting over a toy.

ADDITIONAL READINGS

Alberto, P. A., & Troutman, A. C. (1995). *Applied behavior analysis for teachers.* Englewood Cliffs, NJ: Prentice-Hall.

Erickson, M. T. (1992). *Behavior disorders of children and adolescents: Assessment, etiology, and intervention.* Englewood Cliffs, NJ: Prentice-Hall.

Faber, A., & Mazlish, E. (1980). *How to talk so kids will listen and listen so kids will talk.* New York: Avon.

Kerr, M. M., & Nelson, C. M. (1989). *Strategies for managing behavior problems in the classroom* (2nd Ed). Columbus, OH: Merrill.

Marion, M. (1995). *Guidance for young children* (4th ed.). Columbus, OH: Merrill.

ADDITIONAL RESOURCES

Association for the Advancement of Behavior Therapy
15 W. 36th Street
New York, NY 10018

Association for Behavior Analysis
Department of Psychology
Western Michigan University
Kalamazoo, MI 49008

American Psychological Association
1200 17th Street, N.W.
Washington, DC 20036

Parents Anonymous
22330 Hawthorne Blvd., Suite 208
Torrance, CA 90505

REFERENCES

Alberto, P. A., & Troutman, A. C. (1990). *Applied behavior analysis for teachers: Influencing student performance* (3rd ed.). New York: Macmillan.

Allen, K. E. (1992). *The exceptional child: Mainstreaming in early childhood education* (2nd ed.). Albany, NY: Delmar.

Anderson, D. R., Hodson, G. D., & Jones, W. G. (1975). *Instructional programming for the handicapped student.* Springfield, IL: Charles C. Thompson.

Bagnato, S. J., & Neisworth, J. T. (1991). *Assessment for early intervention: Best practices for professionals.* New York: Guilford Press.

Bailey, D. B., Jr., & Wolery, M. (1984). *Teaching infants and preschoolers with handicaps.* Columbus, OH: Merrill.

Baker, B. L., Brightman, A. J., Heifetz, L. J., & Murphy, D. M. (1990). *Behavior problems.* Champaign, IL: Research Press.

Bauer, A. M., & Sapona, R. H. (1991). *Managing classrooms to facilitate learning.* Englewood Cliffs, NJ: Prentice Hall.

Baumrind, D. (1977). Some thoughts about child rearing. In S. Cohen & T. J. Comiskey (Eds.), *Child development: Contemporary perspectives* (pp. 14–36). Itasca, IL: F. E. Peacock.

Becker, W. C. (1990). *Parents are teachers: A child management program.* Champaign, IL: Research Press.

Berkeley, T. R., & Ludlow, B. L. (1989). Toward a reconceptualization of the developmental model. *Topics in Early Childhood Special Education, 9,* 51–66.

Blechman, E. A. (1985). *Solving child behavior problems at home and at school.* Champaign, IL: Research Press.

Brandenburg, N. A., Friedman, R. M., & Silver, S. E. (1990). The epidemiology of childhood psychiatric disorders: Prevalence findings from recent studies. *Journal of the American Association of Child and Adolescent Psychiatry, 29,* 76–83.

Bredekamp, S. (Ed.). (1987). *Developmentally appropriate practice in early childhood programs serving children from birth through age 8* (expanded ed.). Washington, DC: National Association for the Education of Young Children.

Bressanutti, E., Mahoney, G., & Sachs, J. (1992). Predictors of young children's compliance to maternal requests. *International Journal of Cognitive Education and Mediated Learning, 2,* 198–209.

Campbell, S. B. (1985). Hyperactivity in preschoolers: Correlates and prognostic implications. *Clinical Psychology Review, 5,* 405–428.

Campbell, S. B. (1990). *Behavioral problems in preschool children: Clinical and developmental issues.* New York: Guilford.

Cangelosi, J. (1993). *Classroom management strategies: Gaining and maintaining students' cooperation* (2nd Ed.). New York: Longman.

Carta, J. J., Schwartz, I. S., Atwater, J. B., & McConnell, S. R. (1991). Developmentally appropriate practice: Appraising its usefulness for young children with disabilities. *Topics in Early Childhood Special Education, 11,* 1–20.

Christopherson, E. R. (1982). *Little people: Guidelines for common sense child rearing* (2nd ed.). Austin, TX: Pro-Ed.

Cohen, D. J., & Donnellan, A. M. (Eds.). (1987). *Handbook of autism and pervasive developmental disorders.* Silver Springs, MD: Winston.

Cook, R. E., Tessier, A., & Klein, M. D. (1992). *Adapting early childhood curricula for children with special needs.* New York: Merrill.

Cordisco, L. K., & Laus, M. K. (1993). Individualized training in behavioral strategies for parents of preschool children with disabilities. *Teaching Exceptional Children, 25*(2), 43–47.

Crary, E. (1979). *Without spanking or spoiling: A practical approach to toddler and preschool guidance.* Seattle, WA: Parenting Press.

Crary, E. (1984). *Kids can cooperate: A practical guide to teaching problem solving.* Seattle, WA: Parenting Press.

Deiner, P. L. (1993). *Resources for teaching children with diverse abilities.* Ft. Worth, TX: Harcourt Brace Jovanovich.

Dinkmeyer, P., McKay, G. D., & Dinkmeyer, J. S. (1993). *Early childhood STEP.* Pines, MN: AGS.

Douglas, V. I. (1983). Attentional and cognitive problems. In M. Rutter (Ed.), *Developmental Neuropsychiatry* (pp. 280–329). New York: Guilford Press.

Dreikurs, R., & Cassel, P. (1972). *Discipline without tears: What to do with children who misbehave.* New York: Hawthorn/Dutton.

Dunst, C. J. (1985). Rethinking early intervention. *Analysis and Intervention in Developmental Disabilities, 5,* 165–201.

Dunst, C. J. (1986). Overview of the efficacy of early intervention programs. In L. Bickman & D. L. Weatherford (Eds.), *Handbook of special education: Research and practice* (Vol. 3, pp. 259–293). Elmsford, NY: Pergamon.

Eisenberg, N., Lennon, R., & Roth, K. (1983). Prosocial development: A longitudinal study. *Developmental Psychology, 19,* 846–855.

Factor, D., & Schilmoeller, G. L. (1983). Social skill training of preschool children. *Child Study Journal, 13*(1), 41–56.

Fields, M. V., & Boesser, C. (1994). *Constructive guidance and discipline: Preschool and primary education.* Columbus, OH: Merrill.

Fisher, K. W., Hand, H. H., Watson, M. W., VanParys, M. M., & Tucker, J. L. (1984). Putting the child into socialization: The development of social categories in preschool children. In L. G. Katz, P. J. Wagemaker, & K. Steiner (Eds.), *Current topics in early childhood* (Vol. 5, pp. 27–72). Norwood, NJ: Ablex.

Gargiulo, R. M. (1985). *Working with parents of exceptional children: A guide for professionals.* Boston: Houghton Mifflin.

Garwood, S. G. (1983). Special education and child development: A new perspective. In S. G. Garwood (Ed.), *Educating young handicapped children: A developmental approach* (pp. 3–37). Rockville, MD: Aspen.

Goodman, J. F. (1992). *When slow is fast enough: Educating the delayed preschool child.* New York: Guilford Press.

Guralnick, M. J. (1990). Social competence and early intervention. *Journal of Early Intervention, 14,* 3–14.

Guralnick, M. J. (1993). Developmentally appropriate practice in the assessment and intervention of children's peer relations. *Topics in Early Childhood Special Education, 13*(2), 344–371.

Harter, S. (1978). Effectance motivation reconsidered: Toward a developmental model. *Human Development, 21,* 34–64.

Harter, S., & Zigler, E. (1974). The assessment of effectance motivation in normal and retarded children. *Developmental Psychology, 10,* 169–180.

Heshusius, L. (1986). Pedagogy, special education, and the lives of young children: A critical and futuristic perspective. *Journal of Education, 186,* 25–38.

Hildebrand, V. (1994). *Guiding young children* (5th ed.). Columbus, OH: Merrill.

Honig, A. S. (1985). Research in review. Compliance, control, and discipline. Part 1. *Young Children, 40*(2), 50–58.

Hussey–Gardner, B. (1992). *Parenting to make a difference: Your one- to four-year-old child.* Palo Alto, CA: Vort Corporation.

Ickes, W. J., & Kidd, R. F. (1976). An attributional analysis of helping behavior. In J. H. Harvey, W. J. Ickes, & R. F. Kidd (Eds.), *New directions in attribution research* (Vol. 1, pp. 311–334). Hillsdale, NJ: Erlbaum.

Izard, C. E., & Malatesta, C. A. (1987). Perspectives on emotional development I: Differential emotions theory of early emotional development. In J. D. Osofsky (Ed.), *Handbook of infant development* (2nd ed., pp. 494–554). New York: Wiley & Sons.

Jacob, R. B., O'Leary, K. D., & Rosenbald, C. (1978). Formal and informal classroom settings: Effects on hyperactivity. *Journal of Abnormal Child Psychology, 6*(1), 47–59.

Johnson, L. J., Pugach, M. C., & Devlin, S. (1990). Professional collaboration. *Teaching Exceptional Children, 22,* 9–11.

Kagan, J. J., Reznick, J. S., & Snidman, N. (1990). The temperamental qualities of inhibition and lack of inhibition. In M. Lewis & S. M. Miller (Eds.), *Handbook of developmental psychopathology* (pp. 219–226). New York: Plenum Press.

Kaplan, J. S. (1991). *Beyond behavior modification: A cognitive-behavior approach to behavior management in the school.* Austin, TX: Pro-Ed.

Kauffman, J. M. (1989). *Characteristics of behavior disorders of children and youth* (4th ed.). Columbus, OH: Merrill.

Kazdin, A. E. (1995). *Conduct disorders in childhood and adolescence.* Thousand Oaks, CA: Sage.

Killen, M., & Turiel, E. (1991). Conflict resolution in preschool social interactions. *Early Education and Development, 2,* 240–255.

Landau, S., & Milich, R. (1990). Assessment of children's social status and peer relations. In A. M. LaGreca (Ed.), *Through the eyes of the child* (pp. 259–291). Boston: Allyn & Bacon.

Landau, S., & Moore, L. (1991) Social skill deficits in children with attention-deficit hyperactivity disorder. *School Psychology Review, 20*(2), 235–251.

Lepper, M. R. (1981). Intrinsic and extrinsic motivation in children: Detrimental effects of superfluous social controls. In W. A. Collins (Ed.), *Aspects of the development of competence* (pp. 155–214). Hillsdale, NJ: Erlbaum.

Levin, J. & Nolan, J. F. (1991). *Principles of classroom management.* Englewood Cliffs, NJ: Prentice Hall.

Linder, T. W. (1983). *Early childhood special education: Program development and administration.* Baltimore, MD: Paul H. Brookes.

Lovaas, O. I. (1987). Behavioral treatment and normal educational and intellectual functioning in young autistic children. *Journal of Consulting and Clinical Psychology, 55,* 3–9.

McEvoy, M. A., Odom, S. L., & McConnell, S. R. (1992). Peer social competence intervention for young children with disabilities. In S. L. Odom, S. R. McConnell, & M. A. McEvoy (Eds.), *Social competence of young children with disabilities: Issues and strategies for intervention* (pp. 113–133). Baltimore, MD: Paul H. Brookes.

McGee, R., & Share, D. L. (1988). Attention deficit disorder-hyperactivity and academic failure: Which comes first and what should be treated? *Journal of the American Academy of Child and Adolescent Psychiatry, 27,* 318–325.

McGinnis, E., & Goldstein, A. (1990). *Skillstreaming in early childhood: Teaching prosocial skills to the preschool and kindergarten child.* Champaign, IL: Research Press.

Miller, L. K. (1980). Principles of everyday behavior analysis (2nd ed.). Monterey, CA: Brooks-Cole Publishing.

Miller, P. A., & Sperry, L. L. (1987). The socialization of anger and aggression. *Merrill-Palmer Quarterly, 33*(1), 1–31.

Miyake, K., Campos, J. J., Kagan, J., & Bradshaw, D. L. (1986). Issues in socioemotional development. In H. Stevenson, H. Azuma, & K. Kakuta (Eds.), *Child development and education in Japan* (pp. 239–261). New York: Freeman.

Olson, S. L. (1989). Assessment of impulsivity in preschoolers: Cross-measure convergence, longitudinal stability, and relevance to social competence. *Journal of Clinical Child Psychology, 8*(2), 176–183.

Pader, O. F. (1981). *A guide and handbook for parents of mentally retarded children.* Springfield, IL: Charles C. Thompson.

Parker, J. G., & Asher, S. R. (1987). Peer relations and later personal adjustment: Are low-accepted children "at risk"? *Psychological Bulletin, 102,* 357–389.

Patterson, G. R. (1990). *Families: Application of social learning to family life.* Champaign, IL: Research Press.

Peters, D. L., Neisworth, J. T., & Yawkey, T. D. (1985). *Early childhood education: From theory to practice.* Monterey, CA: Brooks/Cole.

Polloway, E. A., & Patton, J. R. (1993). *Strategies for teaching learners with special needs.* Columbus, OH: Merrill.

Richman, N., Stevenson, J., & Graham, J. J. (1982). *Preschool to school: A behavioral study.* London: Academic.

Rogers, S. J., & DeLalla, D. (1991). A comparative study of the effects of a developmentally based instructional model on young children with autism and young children with other disorders of behavior and development. *Topics in Early Childhood Special Education, 11*(2), 29–47.

Rosenberg, M. S., O'Shea, L. J., & O'Shea, D. J. (1991). *Student teacher to master teacher: A handbook of preservice and beginning teachers of students with mild and moderate handicaps.* New York: Macmillan.

Rosenberg, M. S., Wilson, R., Maheady, L., & Sindelar, P. (1992). *Educating students with behavior disorders.* Boston: Allyn & Bacon.

Saarni, C. (1984). An observational study of children's attempts to monitor their expressive behavior. *Child Development, 55*(4), 1504–1513.

Saarni, C. (1985). Indirect processes in affect socialization. In M. Lewis & C. Saarni (Eds.), *The socialization of emotions* (pp. 187–209). New York: Plenum Press.

Saarni, C., & Crowley, M. (1990). The development of emotion regulation: Effects on emotional state and expression. In E. A. Blechman (Ed.), *Emotions and the family: For better or for worse* (pp. 53–73). Hillsdale, NJ: Erlbaum.

Sainato, D. M., & Carta, J. J. (1992). Classroom influences on the development of social competence in young children with disabilities. In S. L. Odom, S. R. McConnell, & M. A. McEvoy (Eds.), *Social competence of young children with disabilities: Issues and strategies for intervention* (pp. 93–109). Baltimore, MD: Paul H. Brookes.

Sameroff, A. J., Seifer, R., & Zax, M. (1982). Early development of children at risk for emotional disorders. *Monographs of the Society for Research in Child Development, 47,* serial no. 199.

Schaefer, C. E., & Millman, H. L. (1981). *How to help children with common problems.* New York: Van Nostrand Reinhold.

Seligman, M., & Darling, R. B. (1989). *Ordinary families, special children: A systems approach to childhood disabilities.* New York: Guilford Press.

Sherburne, S., Utley, B., McConnell, S. R., & Gannon, J. (1988). Decreasing violent and aggressive theme play among preschool children with behavior disorders. *Exceptional Children, 55,* 166–172.

Smith, D. D., & Rivera, D. (1993). *Effective discipline* (2nd ed.). Austin, TX: Pro-Ed.

Strain, P. S., McConnell, S. R., Carta, J. J., Fowler, S. A., Neisworth, J. T., & Wolery, M. (1992). Behaviorism in early intervention. *Topics in Early Childhood Special Education, 12*(1), 121–141.

Strayer, J. (1986). Children's attributions regarding the situational determinants of emotion in self and others. *Developmental Psychology, 22*(5), 649–654.

Thurman, S. K., & Widerstrom, A. H. (1990). *Infants and young children with special needs.* Baltimore, MD: Paul H. Brookes.

Wachs, T. D., & Gruen, G. E. (1982). *Early experiences and human development.* New York: Plenum Press.

Wagonseller, B. R., & McDowell, R. L. (1979). *You and your child: a common sense approach to successful parenting.* Champaign, IL: Research Press.

Westling, D. L., & Koorland, M. A. (1989). *The special educator's handbook.* Boston: Allyn & Bacon.

Whitman, T. L. (1990). Self-regulation and mental retardation. *American Journal of Mental Deficiency, 94,* 347–362.

Wicks–Nelson, R., & Israel, A. C. (1991). *Behavior disorders of childhood.* Englewood Cliffs, NJ: Prentice-Hall.

Wyckoff, J., & Unell, B. C. (1984). *Discipline without shouting or spanking: Practical solutions to the most common preschool behavior problems.* New York: Meadowbrook Books.

Zirpoli, T. J. (1996). *Behavior management: Application for teachers and parents* (2nd Ed.). Columbus, OH: Merrill.

Zirpoli, T. J. (1995). *Understanding and affecting the behavior of young children.* Columbus, OH: Merrill.

Zirpoli, T. J., & Melloy, B. (1993). *Behavior management: Applications for teachers and parents.* Columbus, OH: Merrill.

Chapter 15

TRANSITIONS: PREPARING FOR THE NEXT STEP

LINDA L. DUNLAP, PH.D.

One hundred years from now, it will not matter
What kind of car I drove,
What kind of house I lived in,
How much money I had in my bank account,
What my clothes looked like,
But the world may be a little better,
Because I was important to the life of a child.

Author Unknown

CHAPTER KEY POINTS

- Children with special needs and their parents benefit from being provided specific services during transition from one program to another.
- Transition plans are mandated by federal law for children who are entering special education preschool programs.
- The agency currently providing services and the agency that will be providing services to the child must work together to reduce the stress often associated with change.
- Several specific methods help ease a child's transition into a new program.
- Kindergarten programs may be inappropriate placements for some children.
- Helping children develop positive self-esteem enhances their ability to grow and learn.

Early childhood special education programs are reported to have many positive effects on the development of young children (Guralnick & Bennett, 1987; Mitchell & Brown, 1991). During the time children receive early intervention services, they must often move from one program to the next or from services provided at their homes to early childhood or elementary school settings. This chapter is devoted to discussing methods to help children cope with these types of **transitions.**

DEALING WITH TRANSITIONS

Transitions from one program or type of service delivery, such as home- or site-based or a clinic, to another are often stressful for children as well as parents, teachers, and even the therapists (Hanline & Knowlton, 1988). Many transitions occur for children with special needs and their parents including moving from

- Intensive care units to home care;
- Home care to infant–toddler programs;
- Infant–toddler to preschool programs;
- Preschool to primary school programs;
- Home-based to clinic or site-based (classroom at a preschool site);
- Public to private or private to public programs;
- Segregated (self-contained) to integrated (mainstream or inclusion) programs.

Transitions often involve major changes in routines. Federal laws mandate that there be **transition planning** for children 3 years old entering a special education preschool program. This transition plan must be included in the **individualized family service plan (IFSP)** (see Chapter 1), and must include a statement of the services that will be provided to help the child adjust to and function most effectively at the new placement (for example, home to clinic, clinic to preschool, or preschool to kindergarten).

Public Law (PL) 102–119 requires the agency a child leaves and the new agency that will provide services to work together, which includes meeting with the child's parents ninety days be-

fore the child's third birthday to formally begin the transition process (McGonigel, Kaufmann, & Johnson, 1991). **PL 99–457 Part H** dictates the content of procedures that must be included in the child's IFSP transition plan (Hurley, 1991; Kagan, 1991a). Many states voluntarily use the guidelines for other transitions and include them in an **individualized education program (IEP)** (Rosenkoetter & Shotts, 1992). (See Chapter 1 for more information on IEPs.). The transition plan for 3-year-olds must include a formal statement regarding:

1. How the transition is to be conducted;
2. Who is responsible for coordinating the transition process;
3. Which agency is responsible for costs associated with the transition;
4. Membership of the transition team;
5. Who is responsible for providing access to needed services not provided by the program the child will attend.

Parents must be made aware of all potential placement options. Options for service delivery are generally greater for children less than 3 years old and include family childcare (care provided by an individual), childcare provided in a preschool or daycare setting, preschool programs (special or regular), play groups, private therapists or programs, public programs, pre-kindergarten classes, **respite care** (helping to take care of a child while the parent(s) take a break), and recreational programs (Fowler & Titus, 1996; Bricker, Peck, & Odom, 1993).

Transitions must be carefully planned and individualized for each child based on the child's and family members' unique characteristics. Information must be openly provided to all members of the transition team. Parents must feel comfortable advocating for their child during the transition process (Conn–Powers & Ross–Allen, 1991).

Parents of infants and toddlers who have developmental delays often ask, "Will my child ever be able to attend a daycare or preschool program?" And one of the most frequently asked questions by parents of preschoolers with special needs is, "Will my child be ready for kindergarten?" Most parents hope that their child will be able to enter a "regular" education kindergarten classroom when they are school-age (Fowler, Schwartz, & Atwater, 1991).

Children must be provided opportunities to experience a successful transition into whatever program they are developmentally ready to enter. In some cases, toddlers are unprepared to enter a site-based program or preschoolers are unready to enter regular kindergarten when they reach school age. They may enter when they are older than "typical" or cannot have their needs effectively met within a particular type of education program (Beckoff & Bender, 1989).

The ultimate goal for most parents and early childhood teachers is to find ways to best prepare children for the next step on the educational ladder. Children should not be forced to participate in activities such as counting, practicing writing the alphabet, or responding to flash cards. These types of activities often result in negative side effects, including children disliking learning and school, teachers, or their parents (Barbour & Seefeldt, 1993).

Most children have a natural desire to learn. This desire is reduced if they are expected to perform tasks not developmentally appropriate for them. Children are left believing that learning is boring or hard work, or that they are destined to fail (Diener & Dweck, 1978). Forcing children to engage in tasks for which they are developmentally unprepared results in limited, if any, success.

When children are expected to perform tasks too difficult for them, they begin to perceive themselves as "failures," which leads to developing a strategy of not trying rather than trying and risking failure. This process is frequently referred to as **learned helplessness** (Dweck, 1975).

TRANSITION TO NEW PROGRAMS

Whether children enter a new classroom, program, or school, the transition is often stressful (Bennett, Raab, & Nelson, 1991). The transition involves leaving a familiar and safe environment and moving to a place with many new adults and children. The change involves making friends, adjusting to new teachers, and learning new rules and skills. Many children approach these changes with enthusiasm while others find them very stressful (Caldwell, 1991). They often act timid, have tantrums, toilet accidents, trouble sleeping, complain of stomach aches, or regress to behavior typical of younger children, such as sucking their thumb or using "baby talk."

Children often display separation anxiety during the process of separating from parents when changing to a new classroom environment, old behavior problems resurface, or new ones emerge. For example, when children experience transitions, they may display old patterns of temper tantrums or become aggressive toward others for the first time. Skills a child demonstrates in the old school may not be demonstrated in the new school setting (Balaban, 1985; Bender, 1992). For example, a child who could zip his or her coat at the old school does not do so at the new school, a change that indicates insecurity or lack of generalization of the skill.

When a child's behavior regresses, new teachers or parents often assume that the child is not really ready for the demands of the new classroom. Many children need an extended period of time to adjust to a transition. Ideally, preschool staff or a therapist from the program the child is leaving, along with the parents, must work with the new classroom teacher to help create a positive transition. Children should be provided opportunities well in advance of a transition to gain the prerequisite skills needed for the new classroom (Bricker, et. al, 1993).

The Role of Staff Members in the Child's Current Program

It is important for teachers and therapists of a current program to assess any major differences between that school and the new classroom environment. Teachers and therapists who provide services at the old and new programs should talk with each other and try to visit each other's classrooms. These visits help children and parents during the transition process and help the new teachers develop an understanding of the parents' and present teachers' expectations. It is also helpful for parents to visit the new classroom with and without the child to observe how class activities occur (Epps, 1992).

If major differences are noted, children can be taught routines and skills that will be needed in the new classroom. Children should also be told about differences they are likely to encounter, such as a larger building or fewer teachers and more classmates. Ideally, children will be allowed to visit the new school building, see the classroom, and meet the new teacher(s) before the first day of attending the new class. It is also useful for teachers to note similarities between the programs. Children, as well as parents, find comfort in knowing there are things that are similar or the same (Conn–Powers & Ross–Allen, 1991).

As children become older and move from one program to another, the number of children in each setting or class generally increases. For instance, there are typically more children and fewer teachers per child in a kindergarten classroom. A larger ratio of children to teachers generally results in less attention being given to each child. Children need to be gradually prepared to work and play more independently and expect less one-on-one time with a teacher. They should learn to function effectively with fewer instructions, prompts, praise, and attention.

Preschool teachers help ease the transition into a new program by gradually reducing teacher guidance during activities. Teachers must avoid providing children attention for disruptive behavior unless it puts someone in physical danger, and gradually reduce the number of **secondary reinforcers** designed to develop appropriate behavior as well. For example, if a child is whining for more snack, it would be best to ignore the child until the child asks for more without whining (Fowler, Hains, & Rosenkoetter, 1990).

It is often difficult for a child to adjust to a classroom filled with a large number of children if the child came from a classroom with just a few children. It is helpful for the child to have opportunities to get to know the other children who will be in their new classroom. It is helpful when schools provide these opportunities for children and families to meet each other before entering a new school (Hanline & Knowlton, 1988).

For example, rather than having one visiting day for entering preschoolers or kindergartners, the transition program could be extended to include a movie night, story time, or ice-cream social. Ideally, school districts and agencies that support programs for children with or without special needs will have recreation programs or story hours. These also provide opportunities for families and children to meet before beginning formal classroom experiences if extended to children during transition.

Preschool programs should help children become comfortable with other types of classroom procedures they will need in new classrooms. Children often benefit from learning such things as sitting at assigned seats, raising their hand before talking, and walking in line. Children can be helped to prepare for a transition by providing them exposure to similar classroom activities while at the old school or at home (Graue, 1993).

Preparing a child for something simple such as using a bathroom only for boys or girls helps prevent a child from becoming upset or embarrassed when attending a new program. Having children learn to take care of their own personal needs, such as washing hands and dressing, helps prepare them for experiences in a new classroom. For example, a teacher of twenty-five children most likely cannot provide all of them with as much help getting ready to go home as they probably received in preschool. Therefore, preschool teachers should encourage children to develop a wide array of **self-help** skills as soon as possible (Hains & Rosenkoetter, 1991).

Children who are accustomed to receiving a star when they hang up their coat are often bewildered to discover that coat-hanging behavior does not warrant stars in a new classroom. Children with a history of behavior management problems are often used to receiving frequent and consistent praise for a desired behavior. If the new program does not reward appropriate behavior in the same way, children are more likely to have problems maintaining self-control. Children benefit from preschool teachers reducing praise for the types of behavior other teachers are likely to expect to occur without rewards or reminders. However, teachers in new programs or classes should consider increasing the amount of individual attention and praise with children who are first entering the program (Hains & Rosenkoetter, 1991).

Most preschool children experience free-play time as a major school activity. Free-play time (a time period in which children choose their own activities), is often not a major part of the day's activities in kindergarten classrooms. Children in kindergarten classes typically spend the majority of time in **teacher-guided large group** activities such as singing songs or story time. Therefore, introducing more structure and rules toward the end of the preschool experience and an increased level of teacher-guided large group time helps children better prepare for the transition to kindergarten (Graue, 1993).

Determining the best placement for a preschooler with special needs is a hard task. School districts providing free kindergarten programs are required to provide appropriate educational experiences for all children of kindergarten age even if they are unready for the standard kindergarten curriculum. If the school district cannot provide a **developmentally appropriate** program, the district must often pay for costs associated with sending children to an appropriate program that is not provided by the district. Children are placed in a kindergarten class, **self-contained class** (class for children with special needs), or an **inclusion** class that includes children who have and do not have special needs (Hains, Fowler, Schwartz, Kottwitz, & Rosenkoetter, 1989). Inclusion generally places children with and without special needs in

the same class for all or most of the day. There are cases, though, when a child's needs will be best met in a self-contained classroom. Children who are initially placed in this type of classroom do not necessarily remain in special educational classes in later years (Kagan, 1991a).

Some parents hesitate to allow school districts to receive information regarding their child's enrollment in early intervention programs. Parents are often concerned that their child will be "labeled for life." In most cases, local school districts have provided approval and partial funding for children to receive early intervention services. Therefore, school districts already have information on who has been receiving special education services. Generally, it is helpful for parents to give permission for all records to be released to the new school. Parents need help understanding the potential advantages of providing teachers and therapists who work at the new program with as much information as possible (Conn–Powers & Ross–Allen, 1991).

If parents do not give permission for information to be transmitted from one program to another, agencies cannot legally share that information. New teachers and therapists gain important insights from prior assessments and information taken directly from the child's previous preschool teachers or therapists. In addition, valuable time is consumed collecting data about the child already available in the child's records (Hains & Rosenkoetter, 1991; Hains, Rosenkoetter, & Fowler, 1991).

Even though there are often major differences between many preschool and kindergarten programs, most children adjust well to the changes, often more quickly than their parents do (Golant & Golant, 1990). Parents accustomed to being able to write daily notes, receive daily communication, or call the teacher whenever they have a question find it difficult to adjust to the more hands-off, less communication, less parent involvement philosophy found in many kindergarten programs (Kagan, 1991b). Helping parents adjust to the transition is often as important as directly helping the child adjust. Parents anxious about a transition are likely to display this anxiety when the child is present. The parents' anxiety is ultimately transferred to the child (Kilgo, Richard, & Noonan, 1989).

When a transition to a new program occurs, parents lose relationships with teachers and therapists they have grown to trust and value. Parents often believe that no one else can care for their child as well as the child's current teachers or therapists. Parents are often concerned new teachers will not like their child, the child will not like the new teachers, or other children in the new class will not like their child. Parents are often particularly concerned about these issues when the transition involves their child moving from a segregated classroom to an inclusion setting (O'Brien, 1991).

When children change programs or classes, the parents must develop new relationships and adjust to new ways of doing things. Parents often report feeling a sense of abandonment. In fact, sometimes when parents are told their child no longer has significant developmental delays, the parents are not overjoyed by the news, which is understandable because it means their child will no longer receive services and the parents' support from professionals will not continue (Sainato & Strain, 1993).

Parents often feel a loss when children move from infant and toddler programs to preschool or primary programs because the level of family services often diminishes. Reduction of services occurs because mandated family services are for children less than three years old. Federal laws, however, allow for IFSPs to stay in effect until a child enters primary school if the state, school district, and parents agree (Peterson, 1991). Parents are often dismayed when the variety of services diminishes not only for themselves but also for their child. There is generally a wider variety of program options available for infants and toddlers than for preschool and school-age children.

When a child receives services outside the home, this often affects other members of the family (Stephens & Rous, 1992). Moving from home-based to center-based programs requires special scheduling, coordination of travel, and arrangement for childcare when parents spend time visiting their child's center-based program or meet with a therapist. It is not always appropriate for a child with special needs or other siblings to accompany parents on these visits.

Parents are often concerned that their child is incapable of dealing with the expectations found in the new classroom. Parents are faced with changes in classification terminology when children move from one program to another or when the family moves to a new school district, particularly when the new school district is located in a different state (Sainato & Strain, 1993).

For example, children are often classified as "cognitively delayed" before age 6 and mentally retarded after age 6. Having someone say, "Your child is classified as mentally retarded," is likely to be more unsettling than is, "Your child has a cognitive delay." The term *developmentally delayed* implies that a child has fallen behind in skills development, whereas the label *mentally retarded* suggests that a child has a permanent disability.

Parents frequently become overwhelmed with other concerns, including:

- What their child should wear to school;
- What supplies the child needs;
- What type of food is served at school;
- What safety precautions the bus driver and school administrators take;
- Whether there are appropriate before- and after-school programs;
- Whether the staff is qualified to deal with the child's special needs;
- Whether there are parent support groups;
- Who the parents' advocate or contact at the new program will be.

Teachers at the program the child is leaving help alleviate some of the parents' concerns by developing and using a comprehensive transition plan tailored to the individual child's and family's needs and sharing it with all the people involved in the transition (Peterson, 1991).

Staff members at the child's current placement should research potential receiving programs and identify the contact person at these programs. Teachers should recommend goals and objectives for the child during and after the transition. They should also participate in the child's placement by consulting with the parents on a regular basis before, during, and after the placement in the new program (Peterson, 1991).

Teachers, therapists, and parents should include the child in the transition process as much as possible (Noonan & Ratokolau, 1991). Parents should be encouraged to visit the classroom with the child to see the new classroom and meet the teacher(s). After the visit, parents and teachers should talk about the upcoming change by emphasizing how much the child will enjoy the new school. Children facing transitions should be reminded about all the things they have already learned and be reassured that there are many more fun things to be learned at the new school.

ROLE OF THE NEW PROGRAM IN TRANSITIONS

The program to which the child is moving helps ease the stress of the transition by openly receiving the child, parents, and staff members from the other programs when they visit the classroom (Stephens & Rous, 1992). Teachers and therapists at the new program, with the parents' permission, should carefully review the child's records. They should also help parents arrange transportation and make sure that all special assistive equipment the child needs is available before the transition.

The new classroom teachers should also understand the program philosophy and procedures of the placement the child is leaving. Staff members must make sure they have been properly trained regarding how best to meet the child's special needs. For example, if the child wears arm splints, the teacher must know whether they should be worn during water play. If they must be removed, the teacher must learn how to remove the splints and put them back on properly after the water play.

The staff of the new program should try to accentuate similarities between the new and old programs. Most importantly, teachers and therapists should not claim that other methods of working with the child were inappropriate or that the new program provides services in a "better" way. Teachers and therapists at the new program should frequently communicate with parents during the first few days of the child's transition into their program. They should assist parents in locating services the child or parents need that are not provided through the new program.

DETERMINING WHETHER A CHILD IS READY FOR KINDERGARTEN

Although most parents and teachers hope children are ready to enter a regular kindergarten program, when some children first reach school age they may be unprepared to deal with the curriculum typically found in kindergarten classrooms. Children must be accepted and educated at their current level of development (Benner, 1992). When children are pressured to learn things they are not yet ready to learn, their natural love of learning diminishes. Children must have many opportunities to experience success. This is accomplished when they are provided developmentally appropriate activities and materials. Preparing children for transitions into new types of educational experiences is also crucial for success (Peck, Carlson, Helmstetter, 1992).

Characteristics of Kindergarten Programs

Many kindergarten programs are like the first or second grade of the past. Not all children, whether or not they have special needs, are ready for kindergarten when they are five years old. Typical goals for many kindergarten programs are listed in Table 15.1. This list does not include other higher-level academic goals many kindergarten programs have. Higher-level goals include learning to read and solving simple addition and subtraction problems. Clearly, these types of goals are beyond the

TABLE 15.1 Typical Goals for Kindergarten Programs

Children should be able to

1. Recognize and print their names;
2. State the name of colors and letters;
3. Distinguish between sounds;
4. Tell a picture story in sequence;
5. Name six shapes;
6. Name and count objects 1–10;
7. Sequence the numerals 1–10;
8. Match numerals with objects 1–10;
9. Color within boundaries;
10. Know personal facts (e.g., name, telephone number, address);
11. Independently dress and undress;
12. Use scissors with ease;
13. Express ideas during group discussions;
14. Listen attentively for up to thirty minutes;
15. Recognize likenesses and differences;
16. Work and play cooperatively;
17. Practice self-control;
18. Complete projects promptly, independently, and neatly;
19. Follow directions and obey rules;
20. Practice good health habits (e.g., washing hands);

abilities of many five-year-olds (Kilgo, Richard, & Noonon, 1989).

More than 85 percent of kindergarten programs focus on academic activities, and 70 percent attempt to teach the children how to read. Many kindergarten classrooms use a curriculum considered to be at the first grade level of the 1960s and 1970s (Golant & Golant, 1990). Since a majority of children attend preschool programs before entering elementary school, many kindergarten programs do not emphasize teaching social skills. As many as twenty to thirty-five children are taught by one teacher in a kindergarten class. In many school districts, teaching children how to wait in line, share, and play cooperatively are frequently considered to be skills children should acquire before entering kindergarten (Graue, 1993).

Many of the activities found in kindergarten classrooms involve teachers presenting informa-

tion in a large group format or children sitting quietly at desks working on work sheets. These types of tasks require a longer attention span and well-developed listening skills. These tasks (too long or too difficult) and instruction techniques (primarily teacher-guided) are often incompatible with children's (four to six years old) developmental levels, learning styles, or levels of social maturity (Barbour & Seefeldt, 1993).

Preschool Program's Role

Ideally, one of the major focuses of early intervention programs for children, with or without special needs, would be to provide opportunities to develop social skills. Research indicates that a lack of "social maturity" is the major reason some children are unsuccessful in preschool and kindergarten programs (Rule, Fiechtl, & Innocenti, 1990).

Preschool programs should provide children with opportunities to work cooperatively with adults and other children who are not family members. Research also indicates that children who have developed satisfying relationships with peers are most likely to adjust well to transitions to new programs (Vincent, Salisbury, Walter, Brown, Gruenwald, & Powers, 1980). Interaction with peers provides opportunities to learn social skills such as taking turns, compromising, and interacting with unfamiliar children.

Academic readiness is important for kindergarten success. The single most important academic readiness skill involves the ability to communicate. Parents and teachers who provide children with activities that include exposure to many types of books, storytelling, songs, and other language experiences help prepare the children for academic activities. Most preschool programs provide many opportunities for conversation and **cooperative play** activities (Wolery, 1989). Parents can also extend these opportunities at home as well.

In addition, most preschool programs provide many opportunities to use pencils, paper, crayons, and markers, which help children develop **prewriting skills.** Teachers use books and other print materials that help enhance **pre-reading skills.** Preschools consistently, although often informally, help children learn many important concepts such as colors, numbers, seasons, and classifications. They also provide opportunities that enhance fine and gross motor abilities, attending skills, and levels of independence (O'Brien, 1991).

Children should also learn the importance of being on time and prepared, and methods of organization. For example, they should have opportunities to learn that putting things away where they belong saves time and frustration later. They must have opportunities to practice organizing things they take to school, remembering to take them, finding them at school to bring home, and then remembering to bring them home. Children also must learn what things do and do not belong to them and that they cannot take home items that belong to others or the school without permission (Rule, et al., 1990).

Early childhood special education programs must provide children with encouragement and opportunities to practice newly acquired skills. Teachers must strive to help children develop a sense of accomplishment, which often provides excellent motivation to continue to learn.

Parents' Role

Parents must be encouraged to guide rather than push their preschool-age children. Parents should encourage their children to respond cooperatively to requests adults make. This is aided by providing many opportunities to follow directions (Kagan, 1991a). Parents should gradually increase the number of steps in the directions they give to a child. For example, they should give one-step directions such as, "Go get your socks," and later add another step such as, "Go get your shoes and socks," or "Go get your socks and put them on."

Children must learn to respond to an adult's request at the time the adult makes it. For example, when a parent calls a child to dinner, the child needs to learn to respond promptly. Parents must avoid making the request repeatedly or waiting an unreasonable length of time for the child to respond. These types of expectations are important, because when a teacher announces to twenty-five students that it is time to clean up, it is unreasonable for the twenty-five to dictate their own preferred schedules. Many kindergarten teachers expect children to follow relatively strict classroom schedules (Wasserman, 1990).

Adults should help children learn to take responsibilities by giving them small jobs that help the entire family, such as setting the table and collecting the trash. Children should be encouraged to complete these jobs without supervision. Most young children must be reminded to do these jobs, although parents should gradually reduce the number of directions, prompts, or assistance they provide. It is also desirable to encourage children to engage in activities without expecting to be rewarded. Children should be encouraged to take responsibility and use self-help skills such as washing their hands and dressing and undressing without adult help or supervision (Caldwell, 1991: Ross–Allen & Conn–Powers, 1991; Conn–Powers, Ross–Allen, & Holburn, 1990).

Reading books to children helps develop language skills and strengthens attending skills. Parents should read books that have increasing numbers of words. After reading to the child, parents should encourage their child to retell the story or recall specific details from the story. Parents should be encouraged to read books appropriate for preschool-age children with special needs about going to school or moving to a new place. These stories provide excellent opportunities to discuss an upcoming transition to a new classroom.

Providing opportunities for children to play with children their own age helps them learn how to get along with others. Children should also be encouraged to solve minor arguments with their peers. Young children need some level of adult supervision, but adults frequently intervene too quickly and "fix" problems without allowing children to work through them on their own.

Parents often give children attention when they whine or cry. This behavior will be considered immature and inappropriate by most kindergarten teachers. Children must learn "acceptable" ways to gain attention and ask for help. Parents must create situations in which children ask for help without crying or whining. They must learn to solve problems and know how to ask for help when they cannot solve problems independently (Graue, 1993).

Parents help a child develop **academic readiness skills** while also helping to ensure a child's safety by teaching a child personal information. Children benefit from learning their first and last names, parents' first and last names, street address, city, and telephone number. They should be taught how to use a telephone to call home, and learn to recognize their printed name. Some children are also ready to learn to print their own name (Graue, 1993).

Parents must avoid last-minute "cramming" sessions designed to force children to acquire new skills. Cramming often does not result in learning and presents learning as unenjoyable (Fowler, et al., 1991). Parents must take advantage of everyday activities that promote **concept development.** Folding laundry can include a discussion of such things as colors, ownership, size, shape, number, one-to-one correspondence while putting socks together in pairs, and organizational skills while putting clothes away (Chandler, 1992). Cooking activities can incorporate measuring, counting, estimating, time concepts, and estimating. Taking walks can include conversations about changes in the environment and discussions about what will be seen next. There is an endless number of daily activities to provide learning opportunities.

HELPING CHILDREN BELIEVE IN THEMSELVES

This book has discussed attributes and needs of children who have developmental delays and the types of services available to them. Throughout this book, the importance of valuing each child as a unique individual has been emphasized. It is appropriate to conclude this book with an additional emphasis on providing children with a sense of **unconditional positive regard.** Adults must interact with children in ways that help encourage positive **self-esteem.**

Providing Unconditional Positive Regard

Children must feel they are valued just as they are. Children must not think they are "broken" and therefore "must be fixed." All children inherit different characteristics, among them learning aptitudes and physical attributes. Children must be assured that teachers, therapists, parents, and daycare providers value them as individuals even though certain aspects of their development are delayed (Mahoney, Robinson, & Powell, 1992).

Acceptance and approval must be unconditional, with "no strings attached," frequently referred to as unconditional positive regard. Children should not have to be well-behaved to know they are loved and accepted. Adults should separate the deed from the doer; they may dislike the child's actions without rejecting the child (Barrett & Campos, 1987). Children must be encouraged to like themselves.

Development of Positive Self-Esteem

Self-concept or self-image involves perceptions, feelings, and attitudes one has about one's self. Self-esteem is one dimension of self-concept. It refers to self-evaluation, or judgment of one's own worth. Positive self-esteem includes knowing and accepting one's self without feeling ashamed of limitations or differences.

Listening to children, getting down to their eye level, and praising them even when they are less than perfect helps develop positive self-esteem. This helps reduce a child's level of anxiety, allowing for easier transitions into new situations and a greater willingness to approach new tasks (Lewis, Sullivan, Stanger, & Weiss, 1989).

Children with positive self-esteem are more likely to try new tasks with enthusiasm and approach peers and adults with confidence. They are more likely to explore the environment and assume some control over events in their lives. They frequently say, "I can." This makes them more open to new ideas, willing to face challenges, enjoy success, and cope with disappointment. Children with positive self-esteem also tend to have greater levels of creativity, are more assertive and vigorous in social interactions (participants rather than listeners), and have more friends (Marsh, 1989).

Adults must help children develop positive self-esteem without the children becoming self-centered. Self-esteem develops through experiencing positive interactions with others. It is strengthened by undertaking challenging tasks, overcoming obstacles, and helping others. If a task is too easy it will not boost self-esteem. If a task is too difficult it is likely to lead to a sense of failure and have a negative effect on a child's self-esteem (Marsh, 1986).

Adults must avoid being overprotective. Adults often shelter children with special needs so that they will not get hurt, but all children must experience as many so-called "normal" activities as possible. Adults must help children build on their strengths and must bolster their weaknesses. Even very young children develop "defeatist attitudes" and give up when things appear too difficult or puzzling (Mahoney, et al., 1992).

Children with less positive self-esteem often react as if they believe they are incapable of succeeding in most situations. Negative self-esteem is related to decreased mental health and impaired academic achievement. Children with negative self-esteem are more likely to make comments such as, "I can't." This orientation often interferes with the ability to learn. Feelings of inadequacy often result in children being bossy and aggressive or submissive and unsure. Children with negative self-esteem often appear withdrawn or self-conscious and tend to focus on themselves. Table 15.2 lists some principles that help children feel they are valued and develop positive self-esteem.

Children learn that they are unique or special and are valued by hearing what others say about

TABLE 15.2 Principles to Promote Positive Self-Esteem

Adults should:

- Listen attentively to children and ask them for suggestions;
- Help children learn to identify their own positive attributes;
- Provide many experiences in which children are likely to feel successful;
- Allow children to carry out and complete tasks independently;
- Help children learn to evaluate their own accomplishments and work for improvement rather than perfection;
- Give children responsibilities, such as jobs around the house or school;
- Avoid comparisons and competition between children;
- Create an atmosphere of trust and love;
- Be available to children (make time for them);
- Stimulate and lead but do not push;
- Make sure children know that they are unique and special.

them and seeing how others act toward them. Children who are told, "I am glad you are here," tend to feel valued. When adults take time to stop and listen or give them a hug, children sense they are valued (Nottelmann, 1987). Children need plenty of affirmation. When they are treated with concern and approval, they are more likely to develop positive self-esteem. Children, however, who are rejected or frequently criticized are likely to develop negative self-esteem. See Table 15.3 for a list of statements of affirmation.

In addition, when children finish tasks, such as buttoning their coat unassisted, they have a reason to feel good about themselves. Adults must make certain children have these types of experiences.

When children are taught new skills, there must be plenty of opportunities to feel successful. "Positive feedback" must be provided at different points in the process of learning a task. For example, a teacher could say, "I really like how hard you are working on your picture. You are using so

TABLE 15.3 Statements of Affirmation

A child's self-esteem can be enhanced by statements of affirmation such as:

- I am glad you are you;
- You can grow at your own pace;
- I value you just the way you are;
- You can make mistakes and I will see them as mistakes and not failures;
- When I feel I must discipline you I will try to do so in private;
- I will teach you what I want you to do as well as what I don't want you to do;
- You can express your feelings;
- You can explore and experiment while I support you;
- I like to watch you initiate activities and grow and learn;
- I love and care for you willingly;
- I love you whether you are active or quiet;
- Even when you are not with me, I love you.

many colors." In this example, the adult does not say, "It's a beautiful picture" or "You made the best picture." Often, children's pictures are not particularly beautiful and only one child draws the "best" picture. Stating facts about their pictures such as saying, "You used many colors," is not judgmental or comparative but does tell children that their work is important and someone took time to notice the uniqueness of their picture.

"False praise" or "comparative praise" such as, "You are the best," is often misleading, and a child realizes when the same compliments are also used for other children. Adults too frequently repeat the same praise to all children. When adults respond uniformly, children learn that praise is not directed at them but is just something adults say without really meaning it. Adults should always acknowledge the completion of tasks, whatever they are. Saying something like, "Wow! You're done. You worked for a very long time," avoids comparative evaluation yet acknowledges perseverance.

Just as a plant needs sun and water, children need encouragement. Children who need encouragement most get it least. This leads them to be-

have in ways that contribute to adults' negative reactions and make the children feel discouraged or even rebellious. See Box 15.1 for a method adults use that provides children with information about their value and enhances positive self-esteem.

Setting Realistic Expectations

Children with special needs are especially vulnerable to adults' unrealistic expectations. Comments such as, "Isn't he ready for regular kindergarten?" or "I hope my child will outgrow this delay by the time he is five years old," suggest to children that they are not "good enough" the way they are. These types of comments place pressure on children to try to attain unrealistic goals. Attempting to reach developmentally inappropriate goals leads children to a sense of failure (Stipek, Gralinski, & Kopp, 1990). Lack of success often results in less positive self-esteem, which results in children avoiding certain tasks. Avoiding tasks is likely to further increase the level of delay. These failures create a vicious cycle of more inappropriate expectations, frustrations, and failures.

Children with special needs must adapt to being different. These children often feel guilty about the inconvenience they perceive they have caused. They hear comments such as, "All these doctor

BOX 15.1

The "Have I Told You?" Game

Try playing the game, "Have I told you today?" This game helps make sure children are told at least once a day that they are valued and loved. Parents should sincerely tell their child, "I love you." It should not only be said but shown everyday. At some point every day or even several times a day, ask the child, "Have I told you today?" The child should always be able to say, "Yes!" Teachers can play the same game by saying, "Have I told you how much I like having you in my class?"

bills prevent us from taking a nice vacation," "She requires all of my time," or "Will she ever be able to write her name?"

Children with special needs also become aware of their brothers' and sisters' feelings of frustration because they overhear such things as, "Mom, it isn't fair that you spend all your time with Billy." Individuals involved with children with special needs at times feel frustrated, overwhelmed, and even angry when things are difficult and when their dreams for their child do not come true.

Children with special needs sense others' frustrations, anger, and depression, which leads to their developing these same feelings (Mahoney, et al., 1992). When children sense that others feel good about them, they are more likely to succeed (Bullock & Lütkenhaus, 1988). When adults spend time with children, children come to believe they are valued. When adults indicate confidence in children, children are more likely to attempt ever more difficult tasks.

There is perhaps no other area of development more important than children's self-esteem. Because self-esteem is primarily composed of successes and how they interact with expectations, adults must help children develop appropriate expectations. Children must be taught to value differences in themselves and other people (Marsh, 1986).

CONCLUSION

Professionally designed early intervention programs are crucial for children with special needs. The quality of interaction is important but children also need a great deal of time interacting with caring adults. Parents are children's lifelong teachers and must work with professionals on behalf of their own children. As children move from one program or service delivery method to another, it is crucial that transition plans are created. These plans must be collaboratively developed and must consider each child's and family member's specific needs.

It is often easier to love children than to like their behavior or accept their level of abilities. Adults must provide unconditional positive regard by using kind words, smiling, and always greeting children with open arms.

CHAPTER SUMMARY

- Transitions to new programs are often stressful for children, parents, teachers, and therapists.
- Transition plans must be included in the child's IFSP and should be a part of the IEP as well. These plans must include a timetable and procedures for the transition and be developed cooperatively by parents and all professionals who are a part of the transition team.
- There are several actions a child's current program and new program can take to help ease the transition process for the child and its family.
- Some children are not ready to enter kindergarten programs when they are five years old because many programs expect high levels of social maturity and cognitive skills.
- There are several readiness activities preschool teachers and parents should provide for children.
- Children should be provided unconditional positive regard, which promotes positive self-esteem.
- Children with positive self-esteem are likely to try new things and have the confidence to interact with peers and adults in new situations.
- All adults who work with children who have special needs must approach these children with open arms.

REVIEW QUESTIONS

1. What might teachers and therapists do to help ease the stress of the transition process for children and their families?
2. What requirements for transition planning are found in early childhood education federal laws?

3. What might teachers and parents do to help develop kindergarten readiness skills?
4. What is unconditional positive regard and how might it affect self-esteem?
5. Why are children with special needs at risk of developing negative self-esteem?
6. What might parents and teachers do to enhance positive self-esteem in children?

SUGGESTED STUDENT ACTIVITIES

1. Visit and compare and contrast preschool and kindergarten programs.
2. Ask preschool teachers in a regular and special education preschool how they prepare children for kindergarten.
3. Ask a kindergarten teacher how he or she prepares for the inclusion of a child with special needs.
4. Assume the role of a professional who has been asked to give a parent–teacher workshop on developing positive self-esteem in children. What would you include in your workshop presentation?

ADDITIONAL READINGS

Cook, R. R., Tessier, A., & Klein, M. D. (1996). *Adapting early childhood curricula for children in inclusive settings* (1996). Columbus, OH: Merrill.

Maxim, G. W. (1997). *The very young: Guiding children from infancy through the Early Years* (5th Ed.) Columbus, OH: Merrill.

Peck, C. B., Odom, S. A., & Bricker, D. D. (Eds.). (1993). *Integrating young children with disabilities into community programs: Ecological perspectives on research and implementation.* Baltimore, MD: Paul H. Brookes.

Rosenkoetter, S. E., & Hains, A. H. (1994). *Bridging early services for children with special needs and their families: A practical guide for transition planning.* Baltimore, MD: Paul H. Brookes.

ADDITIONAL RESOURCES

Bridging Early Services Transition Project—Outreach
Associated Colleges of Central Kansas
105 E. Kansas Avenue
McPherson, KS 67460

Portage Multi-State Outreach Project
CESA 5 626 E. Slifer Street
Portage, WI 53901

Preschool Preparation and Transition Outreach Project
Department of Special Education
University of Hawaii
1776 University Avenue, UAA-7
Honolulu, HI 96822

Project STEPS
Child Development Centers of the Bluegrass, Inc.
465 Springhill Drive
Lexington, KY 40503

The Community Integration Project
Department of Teacher Preparation & Special Education
The George Washington University
2201 G. Street, N.W., No. 524
Washington, DC 20052

REFERENCES

Balaban, N. (1985). *Starting school: From separation to independence.* New York: Teachers College Press.

Barbour, N. H., & Seefeldt, C. A. (1993). *Developmental continuity across preschool and primary grades: Implications for teachers.* Wheaton, MD: Association for Childhood Education International.

Barrett, K., & Campos, J. (1987). Perspectives on emotional development: A functionalist approach to emotions. In J. Osofsky (Ed.), *Handbook of infant development* (2nd ed., pp. 555–578). New York: Wiley & Sons.

Beckoff, A. G., & Bender, W. N. (1989). Programming for mainstream kindergarten success in preschool: Teachers' perceptions of necessary prerequisite skills. *Journal of Early Intervention, 13*(3), 269–280.

Bender, S. M. (1992). *Assessing young children with special needs. An ecological perspective.* White Plains, NY: Longman Publishing Group.

Bennett, T., Raab, M., & Nelson, D. C. (1991). The transition process for toddlers with special needs and their families. *Zero to Three, 11*(3), 17–21.

Bricker, D. D., Peck, C. B., & Odom, S. L. (1993). Integration: Campaign for the new century. In C. B. Peck, S. L. Odom, & D. D. Bricker (Eds.), *Integrating young children with disabilities into community programs* (pp. 271–276). Balltimore, MD: Paul H. Brookes.

Bullock, M., & Lütkenhaus, P. (1988). The development of volitional behavior in the toddler years. *Child Development, 59,* 664–674.

Caldwell, B. M. (1991). Continuity in the early years: Transitions between grades and systems. In S. L. Kagan (Ed.), *The care and education of America's young children: Obstacles and opportunities: Nineteenth Yearbook of the National Society for the Study of Education* (pp. 69–89). Chicago: University of Chicago Press.

Chandler, L. K. (1992). Promoting children's social/survival skills as a strategy for transition to mainstreamed kindergarten programs. In S. L. Odom, S. R. McConnell, & M. A. McEvoy (Eds.), *Social competence of young children with disabilities: Issues and strategies for intervention* (pp. 245–267). Baltimore, MD: Paul H. Brookes.

Conn–Powers, M. C., & Ross–Allen, J. (1991). *TEEM: A manual to support the transition of young children with special needs and their families from preschool into kindergarten and other regular education environments.* Burlington, VT: University of Vermont, University Affiliated Program, Center for Developmental Disabilities.

Conn–Powers, M. C., Ross–Allen, J., & Holburn, S. (1990). Transition of young children into the elementary mainstreamed kindergarten programs. *Topics in Early Childhood Special Education, 9*(4), 91–105.

Diener, C., & Dweck, C. (1978). An analysis of learned helplessness: Continuous changes in performance, strategy, and achievement cognitions following failure. *Journal of Personality and Social Psychology, 36,* 451–462.

Dweck, C. (1975). The role of expectations and attribution in the alleviation of learned helplessness. *Journal of Personality and Social Psychology, 31,* 674–685.

Epps, W. J. (1992). Program coordination and other real-world issues in strengthening linkages. In U.S. Department of Education, *Sticking together: Strengthening linkages and the transition between early childhood education and early elementary school—Summary of a national policy forum.* Washington, DC: Office of Educational Research and Improvement.

Fowler, S. A., Hains, A. H., & Rosenkoetter, S. E. (1990). The transition between early intervention services and preschool services: Administrative and policy issues. *Topics in Early Childhood Special Education, 9*(4), 55–65.

Fowler, S. A., & Titus, P. E. (1996). Managing transitions. In P. Beckman & G. B. Boyce (Eds.), *Deciphering the system: A guide for families of young children with disabilities.* Boston: Brookline Books.

Fowler, S. A., Schwartz, I. S., & Atwater, J. B. (1991). Perspectives on the transition from preschool to kindergarten for children with disabilities and their families. *Exceptional Children, 58*(2), 136–145.

Golant, S., & Golant, M. (1990). *Kindergarten: It isn't what it used to be.* Los Angeles: Lowell House.

Graue, M. E. (1993). *Ready for what? Constructing meanings of readiness for kindergarten.* Albany, NY: State University of New York Press.

Guralnick, M. J., & Bennett, F. C. (1987). *The effectiveness of early intervention for at-risk and handicapped children.* New York: Academic Press.

Hains, A. H., Fowler, S. A., Schwartz, I. S., Kottwitz, E., & Rosenkoetter, S. E. (1989). A comparison of preschool and kindergarten teacher expectations for school readiness. *Early Childhood Research Quarterly, 4,* 75–88.

Hains, A. H., & Rosenkoetter, S. E. (1991). *Planning transitions for young children with special needs and their families: Wisconsin manual.* McPherson, KS: Associated Colleges of Central Kansas, Bridging Early Services Transition Project.

Hains, A. H., Rosenkoetter, S. E., & Fowler, S. A. (1991). Transition planning with families in early intervention programs. *Infants and Young Children, 3,* 38–47.

Hanline, M. F., & Knowlton, A. (1988). A collaborative model for providing support to parents during their child's transition from infant intervention to preschool special education public school programs. *Journal of the Division for Early Childhood, 12(2), 116–125.*

Hurley, O. L. (1991). Implications of P. L. 99–457 for preparation of preschool personnel. In J. J. Gallagher, P. L. Trohanis, & R. M. Clifford (Eds.), *Policy implementation and P.L. 99–457: Planning for young children with special needs* (pp. 133–146). Baltimore, MD: Paul H. Brookes.

Kagan, S. L. (1991a). The strategic importance of linkages and the transition between early childhood programs and early elementary school. In U.S. Department of Education, *Sticking together: Strengthening linkages and the transition between early childhood education and early elementary school—Summary of a national policy forum.* Washington, DC: Office of Educational Research and Improvement.

Kagan, S. L. (1991b). Moving from here to there: Rethinking continuity and transitions in early care and education. In B. Spodek & O. N. Saracho (Eds.), *Yearbook in early childhood education of America's young children: Obstacles and opportunities* (pp. 50–68). Chicago: University of Chicago Press.

Kilgo, J. L., Richard, N., & Noonan, M. J. (1989). Teaming for the future: Integrating transition planning with early intervention services for young children with special needs and their families. *Infants and Young Children, 2,* 37–48.

Lewis, J. M., Sullivan, M. W., Stanger, C., & Weiss, M. (1989). Self-development and self-conscious emotions. *Child Development, 60,* 146–156.

Mahoney, G., Robinson, C., & Powell, A. (1992). Focusing on parent-child interactions: The bridge to developmentally appropriate practices. *Topics in Early Childhood Education, 12*(1), 105–120.

Marsh, H. (1986). Global self-esteem: Its relation to specific facets of self-concept and their importance. *Journal of Personality and Social Psychology, 51,* 1224–1236.

Marsh, H. (1989). Age and sex effects in multiple dimensions of self-concept: Preadolescence to early adulthood. *Journal of Educational Psychology, 81,* 417–430.

McGonigel, M. J., Kaufmann, R. K., & Johnson, B. H. (Eds.). (1991). *Guidelines and recommended practices for the individualized family service plan* (2nd ed.). Bethesda, MD: Association for the Care of Children's Health.

Mitchell, D., & Brown, R. I. (Eds.). (1991). *Early intervention studies for young children with special needs.* New York: Chapman and Hale.

Noonan, M. J., & Ratokolau, N. B. (1991). Project profile—PPT: The Preschool Preparation and Transition Project. *Journal of Early Intervention, 15*(4), 390–398.

Nottelmann, E. (1987). Competence and self-esteem during transition from childhood to adolescence. *Developmental Psychology, 23,* 441–450.

O'Brien, M. (1991). *Promoting successful transition into school: A review of current intervention practices.* Lawrence, KS: University of Kansas, Kansas Early Childhood Research Institute.

Peck, C. B., Carlson, P., & Helmstetter, E. (1992). Parent and teacher perceptions of outcome for typically developing children enrolled in integrated early childhood programs: A statewide survey. *Journal of Early Intervention, 16*(1), 53–63.

Peterson, N. L. (1991). Interagency collaboration under Part H: The key to comprehensive multidisciplinary, coordinated infant/toddler intervention services. *Journal of Early Intervention, 15,* 89–105.

Rosenkoetter, S. E., & Shotts, C. (1992). *Bridging early services: Interagency transition planning.* McPherson, KS: Associated Colleges of Central Kansas, Bridging Early Services Transition Project.

Ross–Allen, J., & Conn–Powers, M. (1991). *TEEM: A manual to support the transition of young children with special needs and their families from preschool into kindergarten and other regular education environments.* Burlington, VT: University of Vermont, University Affiliated Program, Center for Developmental Disabilities.

Rule, S., Fiechtl, B. J., & Innocenti, M. S. (1990). Preparation for transition to mainstreamed post-preschool environments: Development of a survival skills curriculum. *Topics in Early Childhood Education, 9,* 78–90.

Sainato, D. M., & Strain, P. S. (1993). Integration success for preschoolers with disabilities. *Teaching Exceptional Children, 25*(2), 36–37.

Stipek, D., Gralinski, H., & Kopp, C. B. (1990). Self-concept development in the toddler years. *Developmental Psychology, 26,* 972–977.

Stephens, P., & Rous, B. (1992). *Facilitation packet for the development of a system for the transition of young children and families.* Lexington, KY: Child Development Centers of the Blue Grass.

Vincent, L. J., Salisbury, C. L., Walter, G., Brown, P., Gruenwald, L., & Powers, M. (1980). Program evaluation and curricular development in early childhood/special education: Criteria for the next environment. In W. Sailor, B. Wilcox, & L. Brown (Eds.), *Methods of instruction for severely handicapped students* (pp. 303–328). Baltimore, MD: Paul H. Brookes.

Wasserman, S. (1990). *Serious players in the primary grades: Empowering children through active learning experiences.* New York: Teachers College Press.

Wolery, M. (1989). Transitions in early childhood special education: Issues and procedures. *Focus on Exceptional Children, 22,* 1–16.

1:6:1 classroom—Special education classroom consisting of one teacher, six students, and one teacher's aide.

1:12:1 classroom—Special education classroom consisting of one teacher, twelve students, and one teacher's aide.

academic readiness skills—Abilities needed for school-related activities including reading, writing, and mathematics.

academic skills—Skills needed to achieve within a school setting, including reading, writing, mathematics, and problem-solving.

acquired disabilities—Disabilities caused by accident, illness, or child abuse.

acquired immunodeficiency syndrome (AIDS)—A viral disease, for which there is no cure, in which the body's immune system breaks down. It is caused by the human immunodeficiency virus (HIV).

active learning—Being involved in learning situations by asking questions, seeking help, and initiating activities.

active listening—Focusing attention on the speaker and asking questions or responding to what the speaker said to demonstrate understanding.

activity-based instruction—Instruction that is integrated in the daily activities or play rather than given as a separrate lesson or instruction activity.

acute health problems—Crisis point of disease is rapidly reached.

adaptation phase—The transition period of adjustment many parents experience after first learning that their child has a developmental delay.

adaptive devices (assistive devices or equipment)—Equipment, such as a hearing aid, designed to improve body functioning.

adaptive equipment—Equipment that has been modified, such as a wheelchair, to meet the needs of persons with special needs.

ADD—(See attention deficit disorder.)

addiction—The quality of being physically dependent on a habit-forming drug.

ADHD—(See attention deficit hyperactivity disorder.)

adult-directed activities—(See teacher-guided instruction.)

adventitious—A handicap that develops from disease or trauma any time after birth.

adventitiously blind—A profound or severe visual impairment that occurs after the age of two years.

adventitious deafness—(See postlingual deafness.)

adventitious visual impairment—Any visual problem that develops after birth.

advocate—An individual such as a parent, neighbor, or professional who speaks on behalf of a person or group having developmental disabilities.

age-out—No longer qualify for certain services because of age.

aggression—Forceful action intended to do physical harm, dominate, or intimidate.

AIDS—(See acquired immunodeficiency syndrome.)

AIDS-related dementia—Generalized cognitive and behavioral deterioration due to brain dysfunction caused by AIDS.

alcohol abuse—(See alcoholic.)

alcoholic—Someone who consumes alcohol habitually.

Allport's syndrome—A genetic condition that affects hearing ability and kidney functioning.

alternate feet step climbing—Climbing stairs by using alternating feet.

American Sign Language (ASL) (Ameslan)—A visual gestural language with its own rules of syntax, semantics, and pragmatics.

American Speech–Language–Hearing Association (ASHA)—A professional organization concerned with communication disorders.

amplification—Increasing the volume of sound.

amputation—The severing of a limb from the body because of a birth defect, disease, or accident.

animism—Belief that inanimate objects are alive that is common in children who are pre-conceptual at about age two to six.

anoxia—Inadequate supply of oxygen to the body and brain.

anterior/posterior positions—Front and back body orientation.

antibodies—Biochemical substances produced by the body's immune system that attack foreign cells or proteins that enter the body.

anxiety disorder—Disorder characterized by painful uneasiness, emotional tension, or confusion.

aphasia—The loss or impairment of the power to use words

appropriate education—A standard required by Individuals with Disabilities Education Act (IDEA) that guarantees that students with disabilities will receive educational programs tailored to their abilities and needs.

aptitude tests—Tests designed to measure an individual's potential for acquiring various skills.

arena assessment—One form of ecological assessment used by transdisciplinary teams where one or more team members conducts the evaluation while other team members observe.

art portfolio—A method of retaining art work that can be used for informal or formal assessment.

art therapy—Therapy that uses art to help children's development and expression.

articulation—Producing speech sounds (phonemes).

articulation disorders—Abnormal production of speech sounds (phonemes).

assertive—Using bold or confident interactions.

assessment—Process of determining students' current functioning levels.

assisted ventilation—Method of aiding respiration.

assistive devices—(See assistive technology.)

assistive technology (adaptive devices)—Devices that help with functioning in daily activities, including hearing aids, FM auditory trainers, canes, wheelchairs, walkers, and augmentive communication devices.

associative play—A form of social play in which children sometimes share toys, but each child plays independently without mutually accepted goals or rules.

asthma—A chronic condition causing difficulty breathing that includes wheezing, coughing, and difficulty exhaling.

asymptomatic—Living without symptoms, as in the case for children who are more than fifteen months old and test positive for HIV antibodies but do not show the clinical symptoms of AIDS.

ataxic cerebral palsy—A form of cerebral palsy that includes lack of coordination because of a poor sense of balance and body position.

athetosis cerebral palsy—A form of cerebral palsy that includes involuntary, jerky movements of the head, tongue, and extremities.

at risk—Phrase used to describe children who are not classified as disabled but considered to have a greater than usual chance of developing a disability.

attention—The ability to focus on specific stimuli.

attention deficit disorder (ADD)—A condition characterized by hyperactivity, inability to control one's own behavior, and constant movement, which is now formally referred to as ADHD.

attention deficit hyperactivity disorder (ADHD)—A diagnostic category of the American Psychiatric Association DSM-IV describing children who exhibit developmentally inappropriate behavior including inattention, impulsivity, and hyperactivity.

attention span—The length of time a person attends to a task.

audiological evaluation—The method of determining the degree of hearing loss.

audiogram—A chart that plots level of hearing ability measured in terms of loudness, decibels (dB), and pitch in Hertz (Hz).

audiologist—A professional who specializes in evaluating hearing ability and treating impaired hearing.

auditory abilities—A person's hearing abilities.

auditory canal (external acoustic meatus)—Amplifies and transports sound waves from the external to the middle ear.

auditory discrimination—Ability to differentiate between various sounds.

auditory nerve—Either of the eighth pair of cranial nerves connecting the inner ear with the brain, which transmit hearing and balance impulses.

auditory training—A training method that focuses on enhancing the use of residual hearing abilities.

auricle—External part of the ear that carries sound waves to the auditory canal.

authentic assessment—An approach to assessment where information about abilities is obtained by observing children during daily activities.

autism—A disorder characterized by extreme withdrawal, limited or no speech or other communication skills, lack of display of emotions, self-stimulation, self-abuse, and aggressive behavior.

autonomy—A level of independence.

AZT (zidovudine/azidothymidine)—Medical drug used to treat AIDS (also called retrovir).

babbling—Prelinguistic stage beginning at around 6 months characterized by a repetition of consonant–vowel combinations such as *bababa* or *mamama*.

back and forth interaction—Communication between two individuals in which both respond and reciprocate emotions and thoughts.

bargaining—Stage of bereavement, sometimes used to describe a reaction by parents of children with special needs.

basic interpersonal communications (BICS)—The language of face-to-face conversation skills that is normally acquired at about two years.

behavioral goals and objectives—Statement of desired outcomes for a child.

behavior control—Method of modifying behavior that often includes using negative comments or punishment after "undesirable" behavior has occurred.

behavior disorder—A handicapping condition characterized by behavior that differs markedly and chronically from current social and cultural norms and adversely affects educational performance. Sometimes called seriously emotionally disturbed.

behaviorism—Theory of learning concerned primarily with observable components of behavior, including classical and operant conditioning.

behavior management—Techniques used to help children learn to use more appropriate behavior and less inappropriate behavior.

behavior modification—The systematic application of procedures to achieve desired changes in behavior.

behavior problems—Types of actions or responses that are considered inappropriate.

behind-the-ear hearing aid—A small amplifying device worn behind the ear, the most common type of hearing aid worn by children.

bilateral amplification—Amplification of sound in both ears.

bilateral manipulation skills—The ability to coordinate the use of both hands.

bilingual—Ability to read, write, and speak two languages fluently.

biological causes—Changes in physiological fuunctioning due to genetic or environmental factors.

blind—Having either no vision or only light perception; incapable of reading conventional printed material.

blueprint for movement—Predetermined sequence of muscular growth and ability to move.

body-worn hearing aid—Amplification device worn on the chest with wires to the ear, connected to individually fitted ear mold.

bolsters—Covered foam cushions of various shapes often used during occupational or physical therapy.

bone-conduction hearing aid—Amplification device for a person whose ear canal is closed, which allows sound to bypass the blocked ear canal and stimulate the hearing mechanism. It rests on the bone behind the ear and is held in place by a headband.

bottom-up model—(See developmental model.)

brain injury—Any damage to the brain caused by accident, illness, or drug use.

broker role—One role of a social worker that involves linking a family with services.

case coordinator (case manager)—(See service coordinator.)

case history—Background information on a child that may include educational and psychological testing and family history.

catheter—A tube that is inserted into the urethra to drain urine from the bladder.

center-based classrooms—See center-based programs.

center-based programs—Intervention services provided in a segregated classroom or therapy room.

Centers for Disease Control (CDC)—Agency that monitors the incident rates of various diseases.

central auditory dysfunction—A hearing impairment, sometimes called central hearing loss, that interferes with sound transmission.

central hearing loss—(See central auditory dysfunction.)

centration—Tendency to focus on one aspect of a situation and neglect other important features, a thinking process found in Piaget's preoperational stage (ages 2 to 6 years).

cephalocaudal trend—An organized pattern of physical growth that proceeds from head to toe.

cerebral palsy—Motor impairment caused by brain damage usually occurring during the prenatal period or birth process that is not curable or progressive.

certified occuupational assistant (COTA)—Individual who has an associate's degree and occupational therapy field work experience.

chemical messenger system—The pathway a neurotransmitter travels to transmit information between neurons.

child development—A field of study devoted to understanding human growth from conception through adolescence.

child-directed (-initiated) activities—Play or work events a child chooses or develops.

childhood muscular dystrophy—Another name for Duchenne's muscuular dystrophy.

chromosomal abnormality—A defect in chromosome structure that may affect development.

chronic health problems—Prolonged or lingering medical conditions.

chronic mourning context—Orientation that uses the stages of bereavement to describe the emotions parents of children with special needs may experience (see bargaining as one example).

chronic user—A person who uses drugs for an extended period of time, usually connoting an addiction, distinguished from someone who must have medicine for health-related conditions.

chronological age—How old a child is.

circle time—Time in which children gather to engage in large group activities such as singing, movement activity, or discussing the day's activities.

clarity of sound—Clearness of sound.

classical conditioning—A form of learning that involves associating a neutral stimulus with a stimulus that automatically leads to a reflexive response, such as learning to answer the telephone when it rings.

classroom management—Manipulating the classroom environment to facilitate positive interactions.

cleanup time—The time spent cleaning up at the close of an activity at home or in school, for example.

cleft lip—A congenital condition characterized by incomplete closure of the upper lip that may affect speech and can be closed with surgery.

cleft palate—A congenital split in the palate that results in an excessive nasal quality of the voice and can be repaired by surgery or a dental appliance.

client empowerment—Creating an emotional sense of personal control and involvement with social issues such as legal rights.

clinical observation—Data collected in a child's natural environment.

coaching—Directing family members to talk to team members about their concerns or observations.

cocaine—A drug that induces a feeling of euphoria and self-confidence in users and is usually inhaled (through the nasal cavity).

cochlea—Main receptor organ for hearing located in the inner ear that contains tiny hairs that transform mechanical energy into neural impulses that travel through the auditory nerve to the brain.

cochlear implants—Microprocessors that replace the cochlea and may allow some people who are deaf to process sounds.

cognitive adaptive skills—Terms referring to thinking and problem-solving abilities and ability to interact with others in a variety of situations.

cognitive delays—Intellectual (thinking) skills developing later than is typical for a particular chronological age.

cognitive development—Changes in behavior related to perceiving, thinking, remembering, and problem-solving.

cognitive processes—Basic components of thinking and problem-solving that include perception, attention, reasoning, and memory.

cognitive skills—The ability to solve problems, perceive, think, and remember.

cognitive theories—An approach that views children as actively building thinking skills in stages.

collaboration—Cooperation among professionals and parents to provide services to students with disabilities.

collective monologue—See monologue.

communication—Transfer of knowledge, ideas, or opinions either verbally or nonverbally.

communication board—A device containing words, pictures, or other symbols to facilitate the communication of an individual with limited vocal abilities.

communication disorders—An impaired ability to function using speech or language.

communication signal—Gesture, social formality, or voiced message that announces a current event, person, action, or emotion.

communication skills—Ability to share and provide information effectively, verbally or nonverbally, with another person.

communication symbols—Spoken words or utterances, letters of the alphabet, pictures, or gestures used to relay a message related to present, past, or future events.

communicative competence—How well an individual can communicate with others.

communicative language—A child's ability to tell others it's desires and thoughts.

community-based approach—Services provided to children with special needs in a community rather than residential setting.

comprehensive service plan—A plan that includes social, financial, and medical care, mental health, recreation, employment, and housing. (See service plan.)

compulsive reaction—The need to do something in a particular way.

concept development—The development of a thought, notion, or abstract idea (e.g., up, down, two, and dog).

concrete operational stage—Third stage of Piaget's stages (ages seven to ten) characterized by an understanding of conservation (understanding that the amount of an object does not change unless something is added or taken away) and readiness for other mental operations involving concrete objects.

conduct disorder—A type of behavioral disorder in which persistent, negative, hostile, and anti-social behavior impairs daily life functioning that includes disobedience, disruptiveness, fighting, and temper tantrums.

conductive hearing loss—Hearing loss caused by an obstruction in the outer or middle ear that interferes with the conduction of sound waves to the inner ear.

conflict—Disagreement between two or more people.

congenital—Any condition that is present at birth.

congenital anomalies—Abnormalities of the body that are present at birth.

congenital disability—A disability present at birth

congenital heart defects—Heart problems present at birth.

congenital rubella syndrome—German measles contracted prenatally.

congenital visual impairment—Visual impairment present at birth.

constructivist perspective—A viewpoint that suggests children construct their own understanding of the world by actively seeking understanding of their environment through exploration.

contingency—Part of a contract or agreement in behavior management (e.g., "If you pick up your toys, then you can play.").

continuous perspective—View that regards development as a cumulative process of adding more of the same types of skills (children can remember a greater number of items as they grow older).

control—The exercise of direct authority over someone.

conventional stage—Kohlberg's second level of moral reasoning that focuses on a desire to establish and maintain good relations with others, sometimes called the law and order stage.

conversational speech—The everyday speech used between two or more people.

convulsions—A violent sequence of uncontrollable muscular movements caused by a seizure.

convulsive disorder—Condition that produces convulsions or seizures.

cooing—Vowel-like sounds infants make beginning around two months old.

cooperative play—Form of play in which children share toys and use mutually accepted goals and rules.

crack—A form of cocaine that can be smoked.

crisis group—A support group for families to help resolve issues.

criterion-referenced test—An evaluation method in which an individual's performance is interpreted relative to specific curricular objectives.

critical period—The period during which an appropriate stimulus must be presented for learning to occur.

cued speech—A method of supplementing oral communication by adding hand signals made near the chin.

cultural–familial mental retardation—Any case of mental retardation for which an organic cause cannot be found.

culturally diverse—Distinct world views, values, styles, and language among people.

curriculum-based assessment (CBA)—A method of evaluating a child's learning and instructional procedures by collecting data on the student's daily progress on instructional tasks.

cystic fibrosis—A chronic lung infection and malabsorption of food resulting in digestive and respiratory problems.

cytomegalovirus (CMV)—A common herpes virus that usually causes few if any symptoms in an adult but may cause severe brain damage in a developing fetus.

daycare provider—A person who supervises children younger than school-age (less than five or six years old).

deafness—A profound hearing disability preventing a person who is deaf from processing sounds in the environment.

decibel (dB)—The unit of measure of sound intensity on a scale beginning at zero, which is the faintest sound a person with normal hearing can detect.

deductive reasoning—Form of thinking in which one draws a conclusion that logically follows two or more statements.

degrees of hearing loss—Levels of hearing loss including mild, moderate, severe, and profound.

delusions—Characteristic of a psychotic disorder involving beliefs opposed to reality but firmly held despite evidence of their falsity.

depth perception—A sense of how far away objects are or appear to be.

deterministic perspective—Belief that human development is primarily based on genetic endowment.

developmental age—Age stated in terms of ability level as compared to other children (e.g., if a seven-year-old functions as a five-year-old socially, then the developmental age is five years old.)

developmental charts—Method of tracking the developmental progress of children.

developmental delay—Physical or psychological changes occurring at a slower than typical rate (i.e., discrepancy between actual skills level and chronological age).

developmentalist—A professional whose interests focus on human development.

developmental learning disability—A term used to describe children younger than school age who have difficulty acquiring the prerequisite skill needed for later academic tasks.

developmental level—The level at which a child functions in regard to cognitive, social-emotional, or motor skills.

developmentally appropriate activities—Activities designed to match the developmental needs of students.

developmentally appropriate practices—Method of instruction and philosophy of creating an environment that provides activities based on each child's skill level. Also known as developmentally appropriate activities.

developmental milestones—Acquisition of significant or major behaviors.

developmental model—A method of physical therapy, sometimes called the bottom-up model, used to teach children the skills needed in the sequence of normal development.

developmental psychology—The branch of psychology devoted to the study of changes in behavior and abilities over the course of life.

developmental readiness—The level at which a child has the prerequisite skills to perform certain tasks.

developmental screening—Evaluation that discovers the child's level of functioning to determine whether the child has a developmental delay.

diabetes—A disease that results from insufficient production of insulin.

diabetic coma—Unconscious state that occurs due to an excessive amount of blood sugar.

diagnosis—The process of identifying the nature of a disability by using standardized tests and observations.

Diagnostic and Statistical Manual (4th ed.) (DSM-IV)—Manual published by the American Psychiatric Association that therapists use to classify psychological disorders.

diagnostic testing—Testing used to determine areas of weakness.

differentiated cry—Differing cries of a child that signal different needs (e.g., a tired cry sounds different from an angry cry).

direct instruction (treatment)—Therapist or teacher providing instruction to a child or group of children.

direct intervention—Services that include teaching parents problem-solving skills and providing direct counseling.

disability—A measurable dysfunction or impairment.

discipline—Training expected to produce a specified character or pattern of behavior that will result in moral or mental improvement.

discontinuous perspective—A view in which new and different modes of interpreting and responding to the world emerge at particular stages.

discovery learning—Teaching method that uses minimal teacher guidance and maximum student exploration, including trial-and-error learning.

diverse background—Coming from a different heritage or culture than the majority.

dominant language—The language the child reads, writes, and speaks most fluently.

Dopamine—A neurotransmitter in the brain.

Down syndrome—A chromosomal abnormality that often causes moderate to severe mental retardation along with physical characteristics such as a large tongue, heart problems, poor muscle tone, and a broad, flat bridge of the nose.

dramatic play—Pretend play which includes taking the roles of others.

Duchenne's muscular dystrophy—Most common form of muscular dystrophy, also called progressive muscular dystrophy or pseudohypertrophic muscular dystrophy.

due process—Set of legal steps guaranteed in federal law PL 94–142, designed to protect an individual's constitutional and legal rights.

dynamic splints—Adaptive or assistive devices designed to support or position the body to allow for more productive movement.

dysfluency—(See stuttering.)

dysfunctional family—A family that demonstrates impaired or abnormal functioning over a period of time in areas such as economic responsibility for dependents, socialization of the young, or provision of emotional support.

dyslexia—A learning disability related to the ability to read or of learning to read.

ear canal—Tube between the outer ear and the eardrum.

eardrum—Another name for the tympanic membrane, which is the boundary between the outer and middle ear that vibrates to sound.

early childhood educator—A teacher at a preschool, daycare, or early infant school program.

early childhood intervention programs—Preschool, daycare, and early infant school programs that include children with developmental delays and their families.

ear, nose, and throat specialist (ENT)—Medical doctor who specializes in the functioning of the ears, nose, and throat and may be called an otolaryngologist or otologist.

EBD—(See emotional behavior disorder.)

echolalia—The repetition of what other people say, as if echoing them, that is characteristic of some children with delayed cognitive development, autism, and communication disorders.

ecological assessment—Evaluation that considers all dimensions of the individual's environment.

ecological context—Sociocultural view of development that ranges from direct interactions with social agents to indirect impact of the culture.

ecological perspective—Viewpoint that incorporates the impact of environmental influences on the pattern of human development.

ED—(See emotionally disturbed.)

educational placement—The location or type of classroom program in which the child receives educational services.

Education for All Handicapped Children's Act of 1975—(See Public Law 94–142.)

Education for All Handicapped Children Ammendment of 1986—PL 99-457, Part H, now referred to as Individuals with Disabilities Act (IDEA).

egocentrism—Term Piaget used to describe a young child's inability to distinguish viewpoints of others from one's own.

elective mutism—Refraining from speaking that is not the result of physical problems with the muscles or organs of speech production and is believed to be due to emotional causes.

emotional behavior disorder (EBD)—(See emotional disturbance.)

emotional disturbance—A term, used interchangeably with behavioral disorders, that includes lack of control, difficulty in interpersonal relationships, depression, lack of contact with reality, and unexplained physical problems.

emotionally disturbed (ED)—The inability to maintain satisfactory relationships with peers that interferes with educational performance for an extended length of time.

emotions—The feelings or affective component of human behavior.

empathy—A sympathetic response to the thoughts and feelings of another person.

empowerment—To turn over control to someone else.

encephalitis—A virus that causes inflammation of the brain that may result in cognitive and language disabilities (encephalopathy) if left untreated.

encephalopathy—A progressive infection of the brain.

encode—The conversion of information into a system capable of being conveyed in a communication channel.

encoding information—Attending to and forming internal relationships of certain features of the environment.

ENT—(See ear, nose, and throat specialist.)

environment—A person's surroundings or experiences.

environmental influences—Factors from a person's experiences that contribute to behavior.

environmentalist—Person who believes that behavior is based primarily on a person's environment and learning experience.

epilepsy—A disorder of the central nervous system characterized by recurrent seizures.

eustachian tubes—Bony tubes connecting the middle ear with the nasopharynx that provide for equalization of air pressure on both sides of the tympanic membrane.

evaluation—Assessment of special characteristics such as intelligence, physical abilities, sensory abilities, preferences, and achievement.

expansion—Responses that elaborate on a child's utterance by increasing its complexity.

exploratory play—Play that uses discovery learning to help develop concepts and involves the use of trial and error.

expressive language—Language a child uses appropriately during conversations.

extended family—A family group consisting of parents, children, grandparents, and occasionally uncles, aunts, and cousins.

external auditory canal—(See outer ear.)

extinction—A behavior modification procedure in which reinforcement for a previously reinforced behavior is withheld (e.g., a teacher ignoring a child's disruptive behavior instead of responding to it).

extraneous movements—Movements of the mouth, lips, and tongue while concentrating on a movement activity such as coloring or building with blocks.

extrinsic rewards—Rewards created by external factors, teachers, or other students.

facilitated communication—A form of augmentative communication that involves supporting an individual's arm and hand while typing messages.

FAE—(See fetal alcohol effects.)

failure to thrive—Failure to gain weight or develop at a normal rate for no apparent reason.

family assessment—Process by which family members and case coordinator define the characteristics, source, progression, and possible consequences of and solutions for a problem.

family-centered approach—Focus on the family as a unit that benefits the individual members and assumes a family is competent and has strengths.

family-centered programming—Includes families as decision, policy, and program participants, as well as recipients of support.

family counseling—Procedure used by social workers and other therapists to help family members learn to communicate and respond to different members of the family.

family-systems oriented—Child-centered and parent-centered services where the entire family system is provided intervention services.

FAPE—(See free appropriate public education.)

FAS—(See fetal alcohol syndrome.)

fears—Feelings of alarm caused by the expectation of pain, danger, disaster, or apprehension.

feedback—Positive or negative reaction to one person's behavior by another.

feeding oral motor skills—Abilities needed to allow children to chew and swallow properly.

feeding tube—Method to provide food that bypasses the esophagus.

fetal alcohol effects (FAE)—A disabling condition in which full fetal alcohol syndrome cannot be documented.

fetal alcohol syndrome (FAS)—A condition sometimes found in infants of alcoholic mothers that may result in low birth weight, developmental delays, and cardiac, limb, and other physical defects.

fetus—The unborn child from the eighth week of pregnancy to the time of birth.

fine motor development—Small-muscle development used for activities such as drawing, cutting, and writing.

finicky eater—Person who eats very limited type of foods.

fluency—The rate and smoothness of speech.

fluency problems—Delays related to oral speech.

FM transmission devices—(See frequency modulated transmission devices.)

follow-up—Later monitoring, evaluation, diagnosis, or treatment after the initial diagnosis or treatment of a condition.

foot alignment—The foot's position in relation to the other parts of the body.

formal operational stage—Fourth of Piaget's stages of cognitive development that describes the abilities of children older than eleven years as being characterized by abstract thinking and hypothetical deductive reasoning.

formal support systems—Includes social service agencies, medical services, educational services, and other service providers.

formal testing (assessment/evaluation)—A systematic method of evaluating the child using tests.

fragile-X syndrome—A chromosomal abnormality that occurs more often in males than females and is associated with mild to severe mental retardation; it is believed to be the most common cause of inherited mental retardation.

free appropriate public education (FAPE)—A standard set forth in PL 94–142, now called the Individuals with Disabilities Education Act (IDEA), that entitles students with disabilities to a free appropriate public education, including supportive services and highly individualized educational programs.

frequency modulated (FM) transmission devices—Equipment used in many classrooms for students with severe hearing impairments that allows direct oral transmission from the teacher to each student individually.

frequency of sound—The number of vibrations per second of molecules through some medium such as air, water, or wires.

frustration—The feeling of being prevented from completing a task.

generalization—The use of newly acquired skills in a variety of situations.

general practitioner—A physician who does not limit practice to a specialty.

genetic endowment—Another term for inherited attributes passed from biological parents to offspring.

genetic influences—Biological factors that are a result of heredity (come from genes).

gestational age—The chronological age of an embryo or fetus dating from conception.

goals—Expected and desired learning outcomes for students.

good practices—Methods considered developmentally appropriate and effective.

grammar—A set of rules that determines how sounds are combined to make words and how words are combined to make sentences.

grand mal seizure—A severe seizure resulting in loss of consciousness and convulsions.

gross motor development—large-muscle development of the arms, legs, and torso needed for activities such as running or climbing.

growth (or development)—Changes in emotional stability, intellectual maturity, social competence, and physical growth.

half-kneeling position—Kneeling on one knee and foot.

hallucinations—Sensory perception (e.g., hearing a noise or seeing an object) that occurs in the apparent absence of an environmental stimulus.

hand-over-hand assistance—Method of assisting a child by physically guiding a child through an activity.

hand signs—(See manual communication.)

hard-of-hearing—Level of hearing loss that makes it difficult although not impossible to comprehend speech through the sense of hearing alone.

health impairment—Physical health problems limiting an individual's strength, including chronic illness or weakened condition that requires ongoing medical treatment and interferes with everyday functioning.

hearing aids—Electronic devices that amplify sound before it reaches the receptor organ.

hearing impairment—Describes the condition of anyone who has a hearing loss significant enough to require special education, training, or adaptation, including the deaf and hard-of-hearing.

hearing screening—Simple method to assess hearing quickly to determine if more extensive testing is necessary.

heart condition—Any disorder of the heart that limits performance.

hemophilia—A hereditary plasmacoagulation disorder principally affecting males but transmitted by females, characterized by excessive, spontaneous bleeding.

hepatitis B—Strain of hepatitis resulting from infectious or toxic agents that results in inflammation of the liver and often leads to jaundice and fever.

heredity—Transmission of physical and personality characteristics from parent to offspring.

heredity influences (hereditary information)—That portion of development that can be attributed to characteristics passed from parent to offspring.

herpes simplex B—A virus that normally causes cold sores near the lips but can also cause brain damage.

hertz (Hz)—A unit of sound frequency used to measure pitch, equal to one cycle per second.

high guard position—Walking position with arms up and out to the side that suggests abnormal physical development or balance problems if this position is typically used beyond the toddler years.

high muscle tone—Muscles are very rigid and tense.

high risk—(See at risk.)

High Scope model—Focuses on active learning, which includes children participating in the planning and preparing of activities and then reviewing the process at completion.

HIV—(See human immunodeficiency virus.)

holistic profession—Focuses on treating the entire person including cognitive, physical, and social-emotional needs.

holophrases—One-word sentences or "whole phrases" that express a complete thought, typical of eighteen-month-olds.

home file—A record system parents maintain about their child's medical and educational history.

human immunodeficiency virus (HIV)—The virus that causes acquired immune deficiency syndrome (AIDS).

hydrocephalus—A condition present at birth or developing soon afterward, characterized by an enlarged head caused by cerebral spinal fluid accumulating in the cranial cavity, which often results in brain damage and mental and physical retardation.

hyperactive—Describes excessive motor activity or restlessness.

hyperactivity—A level of activity that is distracting to others and self. (See ADD and ADHD.)

hypertonia—Muscle tone that is too high, resulting in tense, contracted muscles.

IDEA—(See individuals with disabilities education act.)

identification—To seek out and classify children with disabilities within special education categories.

IEP—(See individualized education program.)

if–then technique—Behavior management technique based on contingencies (e.g., "If you put away your toys, then we can have our snack time.").

IFSP—(See individualized family service plan.)

imitation—Learning by watching and copying the behaviors of others (also called modeling or observational learning).

immunizations—Injections given to children to help prevent certain types of diseases such as polio and measles.

immunodeficiency—A breakdown of the immune system.

impaired articulation—Difficulty saying specific sounds.

impairment—Damage, defect, or deterioration that may result in a disability.

impulse control—Ability to think before acting.

impulsive behavior—Acting without thinking about consequences.

impulsiveness—Behaving in a disruptive manner or unable to delay gratification.

incidental learning—Gaining skill as a result of experiences not specifically designed to teach that skill.

inclusion—Providing special education services to students with special needs in regular education classrooms for most of the day.

inclusion classroom—A setting with children who have special needs and those who do not.

incubation period—The development of an infection from the time of entry into an organism up to the time of the first appearance of symptoms.

indeterminate infection status—Classification of infants born to mothers who are HIV-infected but show no symptoms of HIV infection.

indirect instruction (intervention)—Involves a service coordinator locating and acquiring the services needed for a family.

individual differences—Abilities, traits, and qualities that distinguish one person from another.

individualized education—Education tailored to address the strengths and weaknesses of each student.

individualized education program (IEP)—Written document required by Public Law 94–142 (IDEA) for every child with a disability, which includes statements of individual strengths and weaknesses, performance levels, annual goals, short-term instructional objectives, specific educational service needs, relevant dates, level of regular education participation, and evaluation procedures signed by parent or guardian and education personnel.

individualized family services plan (IFSP)—A portion of Public Law 99–457, Education of the Handicapped Act Amendment of 1986, that requires coordination of early intervention services for infants and children who are handicapped up to the age of three, similar to the IEP requirement for children three years and older who have special needs.

Individuals with Disabilities Education Act (IDEA)—Formally referred to as the Education for All Handicapped Children. (See PL 94–142.)

inductive reasoning—Reasoning in which a conclusion is made about the probability of some state of affairs based on available evidence (e.g., it must be cold outside because it is snowing).

infancy—From birth to one year of age.

inflection—Changes in pitch or loudness of the voice to indicate mood or emphasis.

informal assessment—Using observations and conversations with the child as a method of evaluation during daily activities such as play, art, eating, and dressing.

informal observation—(See informal assessment.)

informal support system—Includes nuclear and extended family, neighbors, friends, and work colleagues.

information processing theory—Suggestion that learning disabilities occur due to an inability to organize thinking, approach learning tasks systematically, and store information effectively.

inner ear—Internal part of the ear consisting of the vestibular system and the cochlea; essential organ of hearing and equilibrium in the temporal lobe, which connects to the auditory nerve.

inner speech—The final stage in the development of speech that occurs about age seven and includes silent self-talk, which guides thinking.

in-service training—Any educational program designed to provide professionals or parents with additional knowledge and skills.

insomnia—Prolonged inability to sleep.

instructional goals—A plan for learning that includes a statement of results to be achieved after specific instruction.

instructional objectives—Statements about learning that relate to an overall goal, which includes a description of the student's behavior, the conditions under which the behavior occurs, and criteria for acceptable performance.

insulin reaction—A diabetic condition caused by low blood sugar that often results in dizziness, fatigue, and drowsiness.

integrated classes—Regular education classes in which students with special needs learn alongside students without disabilities.

intellectual functioning—The actual performance of tasks believed to represent intelligence, such as observing, problem-solving, and communication.

intelligence—A person's ability to think and apply information, often measured using standardized tests.

intelligence quotient (IQ)—The numerical figure, with the score of 100 being average, obtained from standardized tests and used to express mental development ability.

intelligibility—The capacity of speech to be understood.

interactionists—Individuals who believe that environmental and genetic factors contribute to development.

interdisciplinary team—Group of professionals from different disciplines (e.g., education, psychology, speech and language, and medicine) who work together to formulate and implement an educational plan (i.e., an IEP or IFSP) of a child with a developmental disability.

intervention—All the efforts made on behalf of children and adults with disabilities designed to prevent, remediate, or compensate for the disability.

in-the-ear hearing aid—Aid that fits inside the ear, most commonly worn by adults.

intrauterine—Growth that occurs within the uterus.

intravenous—Entering by way of a vein.

involuntary action (movements)—Automatic reflexive actions.

itinerant specialists—Specialists from various disciplines, such as special education and speech, occupational and physical therapy, who provide services on a scheduled basis rather than as part of day-to-day educational services.

jargon—Specialized vocabulary of a group.

jaundice—A disease or abnormal condition that causes yellowish discoloration of the skin and body fluids caused by deposits of bile pigments.

jaw retraction—The jaw is pulled back, preventing the alignment of the upper and lower teeth during eating.

jaw thrust—A strong protrusion of the lower jaw.

joint ranges—Degree of flexibility in the joints.

judicial hearing—A hearing before a judge in a court.

kinesics—The study of body movements.

Klinefelter syndrome—Results from the presence of an extra X chromosome in a male child, marked by the presence of both male and female secondary sexual characteristics.

knock-kneed—Knees touch together as the child stands or walks, with feet in a wide stance and sometimes turned inward.

labeling—Assigning an individual to a group (e.g, Latinos) or marking names on objects (e.g., toy car).

language—A system of vocal symbols (sounds) that provide people who understand the language a method of communication.

language acquisition device (LAD)—Proposed biologically based mental structure that many believe plays a major role in children's learning language and comprehending and producing speech.

language delay (disability)—Classification for children who do not develop language skills as quickly as their peers.

language deprivation—Being denied exposure to language-oriented experiences such as conversation, radio, or television.

language disorder—Difficulty or inability to master language systems, their rules, or applications, which interferes with communication (also referred to as language delay, or disability).

language group—Group therapy for language and speech problems.

large group activities—Interactions that occur in groups larger than four to five children.

law and order stage—(See conventional stage.)

lead poisoning—Acute or chronic poisoning by lead or any of its salts that may result in severe stomach problems, anemia, constipation, partial paralysis, or mental retardation.

learned helplessness—A situation that occurs when an individual expects to fail, becomes afraid of taking risks or attempting tasks, and often does not engage in learning activities.

learning disability—Specific learning disorder that results in lower academic achievement than a child's aptitude would predict.

least restrictive environment (LRE)—The educational setting in which a child with disabilities can receive an appropriate education that is, as much as possible, most like a regular classroom.

legally blind—Visual acuity measured as 20/200 or worse in the better eye with correction or peripheral vision no greater than 20 degrees.

licensed practical nurse (LPN)—A person who has undergone training and obtained a license conferring authorization to provide care for the sick.

lip retraction (purse string)—Extension of the lips into a tight horizontal line.

logical consequence—Ensuring that a punishment or penalty is logically related to the inappropriate behavior (e.g., a child is required to clean the wall after drawing on it).

long-term memory—Memory ability with potentially unlimited capacity and duration.

loudness—One of the two aspects of voice, referring to the intensity of sound produced while speaking.

low muscle tone—Loose or weak muscles.

low vision—A mild to moderate visual impairment with visual acuity between 20/70 and 20/200.

LPN—(See licensed practical nurse.)

LRE—(See least restrictive environment.)

mainstream classroom—Classroom in which students with special needs attend on a part-time basis with children without special needs.

mainstreaming—The return to the regular education classroom for all or part of the school day of children with disabilities who were previously educated exclusively in segregated settings.

malnourished—Suffering from improper nutrition.

manual communication—Any formal or established system of hand gestures used for communication, such as fingerspelling or American Sign Language.

mastery—Competency, clear-cut understanding of a complete skill or knowledge.

masturbation—Genital self-stimulation.

maternal deprivation—Process of being denied access to bonding with one's mother.

maturation—The biologically controlled process by which each child "unfolds" according to the child's individual timetable.

mean length of utterances (MLU)—The average length of a child's sentence, which usually increases with age.

mechanistic model—Orientation based on the belief it is useful to view human beings in terms of their reactive, machine-like characteristics.

memory—Mental capacity to store and later recognize or recall previously experienced events.

meningitis—Inflammation of the membranes covering the brain and spinal cord, which can affect vision, hearing, and intelligence.

mental age—An estimate of mental ability expressed as the average chronological age of a child who can ordinarily correctly answer questions in a test.

mental retardation—Subaverage general intellectual functioning resulting in or associated with deficits in adaptive behavior and manifested during the developmental period.

mental symbols—Thoughts or ideas children have in their minds that represent objects.

metabolic disorders—The inability to correctly utilize nutrients.

microcephaly—A condition characterized by an abnormally small skull with resulting brain damage and mental retardation.

microorganisms—An animal or plant of microscopic size, especially a bacterium.

middle ear—A small membrane-lined cavity, separated from the outer ear by the eardrum, that transmits sound waves from the eardrum to the partition between the middle ear and inner ear through a chain of tiny bones.

midline position—In the middle or center of the body.

milestones—Significant developmental events (e.g., first words).

minimal brain dysfunction—A once popular term used to describe the learning disability of children with no actual evidence of brain damage.

mixed hearing loss—A hearing loss resulting from a combination of conductive and sensorineural hearing losses.

MLU—(See mean length of utterances.)

mobility—The ability to move safely and efficiently from one point to another.

modeling—An instructional technique by which one person demonstrates how to do a task or solve a problem.

model program—A program that implements and evaluates new procedures or techniques to serve as a basis for the development of other programs.

monologue—When children speak out loud to themselves.

morality—The ethical aspect of human behavior bound to the development of an awareness of acceptable and unacceptable behavior.

motherese (fatherese)—Form of language adults adopt when speaking to infants and toddlers, made up of short sentences with high-pitched exaggerated intonation, clear pronunciation, and distinct pauses.

motor delays—Area of disabilities that involve muscle and skeletal movement.

motor planning difficulties—Lack of ability to plan and carry out movements, frequently resulting in awkward or uncoordinated movements.

movement therapy—Exercise therapy under the direct care of a physical therapist.

multi-cultural education—An educational approach in which the curriculum and instructional methods for all children instill an awareness, acceptance, and appreciation of cultural diversity.

multidisciplinary team—A team in which professionals act as consultants but do not provide hands-on treatment.

multifactored evaluation (MFE)—An assessment of a student's abilities that combines several sources of data.

multiple disabilities—Having more than one disabling condition.

multiple sclerosis—A disease that includes patches of hardened tissue in the brain or spinal cord, associated with partial or complete paralysis and jerking muscle tremors.

muscle tone—Either a tense or relaxed state that affects the ability to flex or extend a muscle smoothly.

muscular dystrophy—A group of diseases that gradually weakens muscle tissues and usually becomes evident by age four or five.

music therapist—Individual trained in an approved music therapy program who uses music to enhance development.

myelin—Tissue that covers the nerves to enhance conductivity of nerve impulses.

National Association of Social Workers (NASW)—Professional organization of social workers.

native language—The first language a child learns to speak fluently.

nativist—Theorists who believe that skills are innate and naturally occur as a child matures.

neuro-developmental treatment (NDT)—Specific training a physical therapist may receive, specifically focused on providing physical therapy for children.

neurological impairment—Any physical disability caused by damage to the central nervous system (i.e., brain, spinal cord, ganglia, or nerves).

neuromuscular impairment—A neurological problem that affects the muscles, such as muscular dystrophy.

neurosis—Any of a group of nonpsychotic disorders characterized by unusual levels of anxiety and associated problems.

neutral stimulus—Something that initially does not elicit a particular response.

newborns—Babies less than two weeks old.

noncommunicative language—Speech that does not convey meaning to a listener.

nonobligatory movement—Muscular movement once involuntary that has become voluntary.

nonverbal behavior—Physical or gestural communication or actions.

nonverbal communication—Method of transmitting messages to another person using gestures or physical action, including smiling and body languages, that does not use oral communication.

normalization—Allowing each person's life to be as normal as possible in all aspects, including residence, schooling, work, recreational activities, and overall independence.

normative approach—An approach in which age-related averages are computed to represent a child's typical rate of development.

norm-referenced test—A standardized test in which the performance of an individual is interpreted relative to the performance of a group of others at the same age or grade level.

nuclear family—Family membership consisting of a mother, father, and the offspring.

nurse—A person trained to care for the sick or disabled under the supervision of a physician. (See registered nurse and licensed practical nurse.)

nutritionist—A person trained and specializing in the study of proper dietary habits.

objectives—Statements of desired behaviors to be acquired.

object permanence—A Piagetian term describing the understanding that objects continue to exist when they are out of sight.

obligatory movement—Primitive reflexes a child is born with that are involuntary.

observational learning—Acquiring skills by watching someone else.

obsessive reactions—Prolonged concern, thought, emotion, or impulse even when it is unreasonable.

occupational therapist—A professional who programs or delivers instructional activities and materials that help children and adults with motor-related disabilities participate in activities.

ODD—(See oppositional defiant disorder.)

ongoing assessment—Assessment of a child during typical daily activities.

on-looker behavior—A substage of parallel play in which children watch each other play.

open-ended activities—Activities that do not have a specific end or goal.

operant conditioning—Learning that occurs as a result of stimuli that strengthen (reinforce) or weaken (punish) a given behavioral response.

ophthalmologist—A physician specializing in the treatment of eye diseases.

opportunistic infections—Infections that occur in people with weakened immune systems.

oppositional defiant disorder (ODD)—Developmental disorder characterized by non-compliance and excessive anger.

optometrist—A nonmedical professional who specializes in examining, measuring, and treating visual defects by means of corrective lenses or other methods.

oral approach (method)—An educational approach used with children who are deaf that stresses learning to speak as the essential element for integration into the hearing world.

oral–aural—One communication method available to those who are hearing impaired that includes the use of hearing aids, speech-reading, and visual aids.

oral–motor skills—Ability to use information obtained through oral cues to regulate a pattern of motor responses needed for speech, chewing, and swallowing.

organismic model—Orientation with the assumption that people are active rather than simply reactive or machine-like.

orthopedic development—The development of bone and muscle tissue.

orthopedic impairment—Any disability caused by disorders of the musculoskeletal system.

orthotics—Aids needed for proper body alignment and function, including braces and splints.

ossicle—Three small bones (hammer, anvil, and stirrup) that transmit sound energy from the middle to the inner ear.

other health impaired—A category in IDEA of children who have limited strength due to health problems.

otitis media—An infection or inflammation of the middle ear that can cause a conductive hearing loss.

otolaryngologist—(See ear, nose, and throat specialist.)

otologist—(See ear, nose, and throat specialist.)

OTR—(See occupational therapist.)

outer ear—Consists of the auricle and external auditory canal.

overdependence—A child's inability or unwillingness to participate in activities without the aid of an adult.

overextension—An early vocabulary error in which words are applied too broadly to a wider collection of objects and events than is appropriate.

overregularization—Grammatical error, usually appearing during early language development, in which rules of the language are applied too widely, resulting in incorrect linguistic forms (e.g., "childs" and "goed").

parallel play—A form of play in which children are side by side but do not interact.

parallel talk—At a child's present level of speech or one step above the child's speech rather than at an adult level.

Parents Needs Survey (PNS)—Instrument used to assess the needs of families of young children with disabilities.

partially sighted—Having low vision.

partnership—Relationship between two or more people working together to reach a common goal.

passive—Lacking in energy or will to express oneself.

passive learning—Characterized by a lack of asking questions, seeking help, or initiating learning.

pathogen—Any agent that causes disease, especially a microorganism such as a bacterium or fungus.

PDD—See pervasive developmental disorder.

pediatric AIDS—AIDS that occurs in infants or young children, often contracted by unborn fetuses from the blood of the mother through the placenta or blood transfusions. It results in a variety of physical and mental disorders and is thought to be the fastest growing infectious cause of mental retardation.

pediatrician—A doctor who specializes in the field of medicine that deals with the care of children.

penalty—A form of punishment that involves the loss of something desirable.

Pendred syndrome—A genetic disorder that affects hearing abilities and causes thyroid problems.

perception—The ability to sense a stimulus.

perceptual development—The development of a child's sensorimotor skills.

perceptual disability—Visual and auditory disabilities.

perceptual-motor training activities—The training of motor, visual, or auditory skill to improve academic performance.

perinatal—Occurring at or immediately following birth.

perinatal factors—Conditions that occur during birth, labor, or delivery.

perseverance—Ability to attend to a task for an extended period of time.

personality disorder—A group of behavior disorders including social withdrawal, anxiety, depression, feeling of inferiority, guilt, and unhappiness.

personality type—The enduring characteristics and dispositions that provide some degree of coherence across the various ways in which a person behaves.

pervasive developmental disorder (PDD)—Severe disorder characterized by abnormal social relations, including bizarre mannerisms, inappropriate social behavior, and unusual or delayed speech and language.

petit mal seizure—Epileptic seizure characterized by mild convulsions with transient consciousness.

phenylketonuria (PKU)—An inherited metabolic disease that can cause severe retardation; it can be detected at birth and the detrimental effects prevented with a special diet.

phobia—An irrational fear of something that interferes with one's life.

phonology—The rules within a language used to govern the combination of speech sounds to form words and sentences.

physical delays—Delays in areas of perceptual or motor development, including fine and gross motor development.

physical disability—A problem with the body that interferes with functioning.

physical therapist (PT)—A professional trained to help people with disabilities develop and maintain muscular and orthopedic capability and make correct and useful movements.

physical therapy—The treatment of disorders of movement.

physiological causes—See biological causes.

pitch—An aspect of voice referring to the high or low sound quality.

PKU—(See phenylketonuria.)

PL 90–538—(See Public Law 90–538.)

PL 91–230—(See Public Law 91–230.)

PL 92–424—(See Public Law 92–424.)

PL 93–380—(See Public Law 93–380.)

PL 94–142—(See Public Law 94–142.)

PL 99–457—(See Public Law 99–457.)

PL 101–476—(See Public Law 101–476.)

PL 102–119—(See Public Law 102–119.)

placenta—A structure that develops in the uterus following conception through which nutrients and wastes are exchanged between the mother and the fetus.

plasticity of the brain—The ability of one part of the brain to perform the function typically performed by another part.

play-based assessment—An informal approach of evaluating a child using the child's natural curiosity and imagination to determine skill level.

play therapy—A therapeutic technique in which a child and therapist communicate through make-believe, using dolls and other props.

PNS—(See Parents Needs Survey.)

polio—An infectious viral disease occurring mainly in children that may attack the central nervous system and produce paralysis, muscular atrophy, and deformity.

portable art kit—A set of art supplies that can be moved outside the classroom art area to other areas, including outdoors.

positioning—Proper body alignment for functioning within the school or home.

positive reinforcement—Presentation of a stimulus or event immediately after a behavior has been expressed that increases the occurrence of that behavior in the future.

post-conventional—Kohlberg's third level of morality, characterized by reflecting on an understanding of the social contract and more individualistic principles of morality.

postlingual—Occurring after a person learns to speak.

postlingual deafness—Deafness that occurs after a child has acquired some language skills.

postnatal—Occurring after birth.

postnatal factors—Conditions that occur after birth.

postural stability—The ability to remain upright while sitting or standing.

pragmatics—The component of language concerned with how to engage in effective and appropriate communication with others.

praise—An expression of warm approval or admiration, often used as a reinforcer for appropriate behavior.

pre-academic skills—Abilities needed for success in school.

preconventional—The first of Kohlberg's three levels of moral development that is based on hedonistic or obedience-oriented judgments.

prehension—Taking hold, seizing, or grasping.

prejudices—Adverse judgments or preconceived opinions or biases formed without knowledge or examination of the facts.

pre-kindergarten—A learning environment for children who will be eligible for kindergarten by a school district's entrance date, but who are judged developmentally unready for kindergarten.

prelingual—Occurs before a child has acquired speech and language.

prelingual deafness—Deafness occurring before a child has acquired language skills.

prelinguistic skills—Skills such as cooing and babbling that are needed for acquiring speech skills.

premature delivery—Birth that occurs before prenatal development is complete.

prenatal—Occurring before birth.

prenatal asphyxia—A lack of oxygen during the birth process, usually caused by an interruption of respiration that may cause brain damage.

prenatal care—The care taken by a mother before the birth of her child, including diet, nutrition, medical services, and monitoring the intake of toxic substances.

prenatal factors—Conditions that affect fetal development.

preoperational stage—Second of Piaget's stages, characterized by centrism, discovery of qualitative identity, increased use of symbols, and continued dependence on appearances.

pre-reading skills—Abilities needed for reading, including letter recognition and left-right discrimination.

prescriptive teaching—Methods of working individually to help a child develop skills by using clearly defined goals in a sequential manner.

pretend play—Activities that include make-believe games, daydreaming, imaginary playmates, and other forms of pretending.

prevalence—The number of people who have a certain condition at any given time.

pre-writing skills—Abilities needed for writing, including prehension, mature grasp, and eye–hand coordination.

primary literature—Original research studies or writings by a theorist or researcher.

primary reinforcer—Things people need to grow physically and emotionally, including food, shelter, air, and physical contact; can be paired with a secondary reinforcer.

primitive reflexes—Involuntary actions that control a child's movements.

problem-solving skills—The process of searching out, analyzing, and evaluating facts using various reasoning and thinking skills to develop appropriate and effective solutions.

prognosis—Prospect of recovery as anticipated from the usual course of a disease.

progressive infection—An infection that gradually becomes more severe.

prompting—Giving cues to help students arrive at a correct solution.

prompts—Cues or suggestions to help students arrive at a correct solution.

prone—Lying on the stomach.

prosocial behavior—Positive social contacts or actions that benefit others.

prosody—The melodic quality of speech.

prosthesis—Any device used to replace a missing or impaired portion of the body.

proximal stability—Ability to sit upright to participate in tabletop activities.

proximodistal trend—An organized pattern of physical growth that proceeds outward from the center of the body.

pseudohypertrophic muscular dystrophy—Another name for Duchenne's muscular dystrophy.

psycholinguist—Person who studies the relationship between language (linguistics) and developmental thinking, learning, and behaving (psychology).

psychologist—Person trained to perform psychological analysis, therapy, or research.

psychosis—A generic term for a severe departure from normal actions, thinking, and feelings that interferes with everyday activities, often characterized by delusions and hallucination.

psychosocial—Area of development concerned primarily with personality, social knowledge and skills, and emotions.

psychosocial disadvantage—Category of causation for mental retardation that requires evidence of subnormal intellectual functioning in at least one parent and one or more siblings, often associated with impoverished environments involving poor housing, inadequate diet, and inadequate medical care. (May be called cultural–familial retardation.)

psychotic disorders—A loss of contact with reality (e.g., schizophrenia).

PT—(See physical therapist.)

Public Law 90–538—The Handicapped Children's Early Education Assistance Act, passed in 1968, that provided grants for the development and implementation of experimental programs for early education for children with special needs birth to age six.

Public Law 91–230—In 1969, this act consolidated all other special education laws into the Education of the Handicapped law.

Public Law 92–424—In 1972, this act, the Economic Opportunity Amendment, required that not less than 10 percent of Head Start enrollment opportunities be available to children with handicaps.

Public Law 93–380—In 1974, this law required states to establish the goal of providing full educational opportunities for all children with special needs birth to age twenty-one.

Public Law 94–142—In 1975, this act, the Education for All Handicapped Children Act, mandated that, to receive funds under the act, every school system must make provisions for a free, appropriate public education (FAPE) for every child between the ages of three and twenty-one regardless of the type or level of disability.

Public Law 99–457—In 1986, this law extended the requirements of PL 94–142 to include children birth to three years old.

Public Law 101–476—The Individuals with Disabilities Education Act of 1990, which changed the terminology from *handicap* to *disability,* added autism and traumatic brain injury as categories, required transition services, emphasized the role of parents, and recognized the importance of assistive devices.

Public Law 102–119—A reauthorization of IDEA, which included changing case management to service coordination.

pullout therapy—Therapy that involves removing students from a regular classroom to receive specific services.

punishment—Involves either the presentation of an unpleasant stimulus or withdrawal of a pleasant stimulus as a consequence of inappropriate behavior.

pure sounds—Sound waves of specific frequencies used to test an individual's hearing ability.

quadruped position—On hands and knees.

qualitative assessment—A method of assessment that uses observations and other methods that do not focus on providing numerical data.

quantitative assessment—A method of assessment that uses numerical values or quantities to describe skills levels.

rate of behavior—A measure of how often a particular action occurs.

raw scores—The score a student receives on a test before it is converted to a standard score.

reasoning—Process of realistic thinking in which conclusions are drawn from a set of facts.

reasoning ability—(See reasoning.)

receptive language—Ability to comprehend language.

redirection—Involves orienting children to desirable rather than undesirable behavior.

reflective listening—Summarizing what is heard after listening.

reflexive responses—Inborn (automatic) responses to a particular stimulus.

registered nurse (RN)—A nurse licensed by a state after passing qualifying examinations.

registered occupational therapist (OTR)—Professional who has a minimum of a bachelor's degree and occupational therapy field work experience. (See occupational therapist.)

regular education classroom—A typical classroom designed to serve students who do not have disabilities.

regular education teacher—Teacher of a classroom without children who have special needs.

rehabilitation—A social service program designed to teach a person newly disabled the basic skills necessary for independence.

rehearsal—A strategy of repeating information to enhance memory.

reinforcement—A reinforcement increases the probability of a recurring response.

reinforcer—In operant conditioning, a stimulus that increases the occurrence of a response.

remediation—A program designed to teach a person to overcome a disability through training and education.

residual hearing—The remaining hearing, however slight, of a person who is hearing impaired.

residual vision—The amount and degree of vision of which one has functional use despite a visual handicap.

respite services—Care provided for children that allows parents to rest from the stress of caring for a child.

reversibility—The mental ability to complete a series of steps in a problem and then reverse the process.

reward—Reinforcement given for correctly performing a task.

Rh blood type—Blood type containing an extra protein.

Rh factor incompatibility—A protein, when present in the fetus's blood but not the mother's, that can cause the mother to build up antibodies that could destroy red blood cells, reducing the oxygen supply to the fetus's organs and tissues.

rhythms—Regularly occurring events.

Rifton chair—A chair with a solid back and sides, wide legs, and seat belt.

ring sitting—Feet together in a wide base.

RN—(See registered nurse.)

role-playing—Action of practicing assuming various roles to aid in the development of skills.

rotational position—Turning position.

rote learning—Learning by memorization and repetition without necessarily understanding the meaning of the information.

rubella—German measles; when contracted by a woman during the first trimester of pregnancy, may cause visual impairments, hearing impairments, mental retardation, and other birth defects in the child.

salmonella infection—Infection caused by a rod-shaped bacterium of the genus pathogen.

schizophrenia—A severe behavior disorder characterized by loss of contact with one's surroundings and inappropriate affect.

school readiness—Ability to cope physically, socially, emotionally, and academically with a school environment.

screening—A procedure in which children are examined or tested to identify the high-risk children, who are then referred for more intensive assessment.

secondary reinforcer—Sometimes called a conditioned reinforcer because it has been paired with a primary reinforcer to acquire reinforcing value (e.g., stickers, tokens, and praise).

segregated classes—Classes used exclusively for students who have special needs.

seizure—A spontaneous, abnormal discharge of the electrical impulses of the brain.

seizure disorder—Sudden alteration of consciousness resulting in involuntary motor or sensory responses caused by abnormal brain activity.

selective attention—Ability to attend to the critical features of a task.

selective listening—Focusing only on one sound in an environment, such as a teacher's voice.

self-abuse—Form of self-stimulation including hitting, pinching, scratching, or biting oneself.

self-care skills—Ability to take care of one's basic needs including using the toilet, bathing, dressing, and eating.

self-concept—A sense of self or an idea about oneself.

self-contained class—A special classroom, usually located within a large educational setting, that provides intensive, specialized instruction.

self-esteem—An individual's sense of self worth, importance, and competency.

self-fulfilling prophecy—Positive or negative beliefs and expectations that society may have about a child or that a child has about himself or herself that affect the child's behavior.

self-handicapping strategy—Process of intentionally interfering with one's own best performance.

self-initiated activities—Activities the child selects or creates.

self-stimulating—An action or behavior in which the child engages for self-pleasure; characteristic of autism.

self-talk—Guiding one's own behavior by talking to oneself.

semantics—The study of meaning in language including content, intent, and meaning of the spoken and written language.

sensorimotor stage—First stage of Piaget's cognitive development theory, in which a child develops sensory and motor abilities, such as the coordination of sensorimotor abilities, development of object permanence, and the beginning of internal symbolic representation.

sensorineural hearing loss—A hearing loss caused by damage to the auditory nerve or inner ear.

sensory area—Portion of the classroom where children use their senses to learn (e.g., sensory table or science corner).

sensory delays—See sensory impairments.

sensory impairment—Inability to perceive or understand information.

sensory integration skills—The ability to process sensory information for functional use in all areas of daily activities.

sensory table—Table designed to allow children to use tactile and visual senses to learn.

separation anxiety—A fear of being separated from a caregiver that usually manifests itself in children between seven and thirty months.

seriously emotionally disturbed—Classification of U.S. Department of Education referring to social-emotional disabilities.

service coordinator—Person who organizes, coordinates, and sustains a network of formal and informal support and activities to maximize the functioning of people with special needs.

service plan—A plan for intervention services that will be provided for a child.

SES—(See socioeconomic status.)

shaping—Reinforcing each small step of progress toward a desired goal or behavior.

short-term memory—Memory processes associated with the recall of a limited number of recent events or experiences that will be forgotten unless rehearsal occurs.

siblings—Offspring (brothers or sisters) of the same biological parents.

sickle cell anemia—A usually fatal genetic disorder of the red blood cells that reduces their ability to carry oxygen properly, most commonly found among the African American population.

side-sitting—Position in which the knees are bent and both legs are to one side.

sign language—A system of hand gestures used for communication.

SLP—(See speech and language pathologist.)

small group activities—Interactions that occur in groups of two to five children.

snow dome effect—Used to describe the emotional "ups and downs" of families with children who have special needs.

social competency—Ability to function effectively with other people.

social-emotional disorders—(See personality disorders.)

social experiences—Events occurring in the presence of other people.

social initiative—Eliciting an interaction with another person.

social network—A wide range of individuals and institutions with whom the family connects and maintains relationships.

social play—Activity that involves interaction between two or more children that frequently takes the form of games with more or less clearly defined rules.

social services—Support systems society organizes to contribute to solving or preventing social problems.

social work—Profession that coordinates the acquisition of social services and involves a service coordinator.

social workers—Helping professionals who have a degree in social work.

socioeconomic status (SES)—Economic level of the family (i.e., upper, middle, or lower classes); determined by occupation, level of education, and disposable income.

special education—Interventions designed to help students with special needs achieve the greatest possible self-sufficiency and success in school and the community.

special education teacher—Person trained to teach children who have special needs.

special services committee—A multidisciplinary team that follows the process of identifying and planning services, developing an IEP or IFSP, and evaluating the child's progress throughout the year.

speech—A system of using breath and muscles to create specific sounds for communication.

speech aids—Visual aids such as pictures, real objects, and printed words.

speech and language disorder—An impaired ability to communicate effectively.

speech and language pathologist (SLP)—A professional who works in a variety of roles and settings with children who have communicative disorders.

speech disorder—Abnormal speech that is unintelligible, unpleasant, or interferes with communication and includes problems of voice, speech clarity, or fluency (stuttering).

speech mechanisms—The various parts of the body used during oral speech, including tongue, lips, teeth, mandible, and palate.

speech reading—Process of understanding a spoken message by observing the speaker's lips in combination with information gained from facial expressions, gestures, and the context.

spina bifida—A developmental defect in which the spinal column fails to close properly.

splints—(See orthotics.)

stages—Identifiable phases in the development of human beings.

standardized assessment—Method oof evaluating ability level using a fixed methodology and normative data.

standardized test—Uniform test that can be used for classifying children with special needs that involves comparing scores to those of children of the same age or grade level.

standard score—Derived scores that have been transformed to produce a distribution with a predetermined mean and standard deviation.

state education agency (SEA)—Typically a state's department of education or division of special education.

static positioning—Placing a child in a fixed position.

static splints—Stationary assistive devices that hold a part of the body in an immobile position.

stereotype—An overgeneralization of behaviors attributed to members of a particular group based on common characteristics such as age, sex, race, or disability.

stereotypic behavior—Repetitive nonfunctional movements (e.g., hand-flapping, rocking) characteristic of autism or other severe disabilities.

stimulus—Environmental condition that elicits responses from an individual.

stuttering—A complex fluency disorder of speech affecting the smooth flow of words, which may involve repetition of sounds or words, prolonged sounds, facial grimaces, muscle tension, and other involuntary physical movements.

successive approximation—Rewarding students for learning a simple behavior, which when combined with other simple behavior patterns creates a more complex behavior.

supine—Lying on the back.

switches—Devices children with physical disabilities use to activate battery-operated toys or adaptive equipment.

symbolic concept—Understanding that a word or symbol can stand for an object or idea.

symbolic play skills—The ability to use objects in play to represent other objects.

symbolic thinking—Cognitive thought in which one object or action stands for another.

syntactic structure—The part of grammar dealing with the way words are put together to form phrases, clauses, and sentences.

syntax—The system of rules governing the meaningful arrangement of words in a sentence.

syphilis—One form of veneral disease associated with sensorineural hearing loss.

tactically defensive—Responding to physical contact with an unusual level of resistance (e.g., a child who will not finger-paint because it is messy).

tactile exploration—Using the sense of touch to learn more about the environment.

tactile stimulation—Response using the sense of touch.

task analysis—Process of breaking down a complex skill or chain of behavior patterns into smaller, teachable units.

Tay-Sachs disease—A progressive genetic disorder that affects the nervous system causing profound mental retardation, deafness, blindness, paralysis, and seizures; it is usually fatal by five years of age.

TBI—(See traumatic brain injury.)

TDD—(See teletypewriter.)

teacher aide—Parent or full-time staff member who assists the teacher in a classroom.

teacher-guided instruction—Person who teaches by demonstrating or lecturing.

teacher of deaf and hearing impaired—A teacher with special training in methods of working with children who are hearing impaired.

technology—Using machines and devices to aid in instruction, development, and independence of individuals with disabilities.

Technology-Related Assistance for Individuals with Disabilities Act (1988)—federal act that provides funding and allows for technical assistance to people with disabilities as they select and use assistive technology.

telecommunication devices—Devices that use sight and hearing to improve communication, such as captions.

telegraphic speech—Early utterances that leave out most articles, prepositions, and conjunctions.

teletypewriter (Telecommunications Device for the Deaf [TDD])—A device that enables those who are deaf to make and receive telephone calls by using typewritten messages.

temper tantrum—An outburst of anger, rage, or irritability.

theory—An organized, systematic explanation of observations useful for analyzing and predicting behavior.

therapeutic play—Using typical play activities as therapy time.

time-out—A behavior management technique that involves removing the opportunity for reinforcement for a specific period of time following an inappropriate behavior.

toddler—A child one to three years old.

token system—Using a sticker, token, or any other item that can be exchanged for other forms of reward and given to a child after the child has displayed a particular behavior.

top-down method of physical therapy—A method of physical therapy focusing on teaching everyday skills a child will need as an adult.

total communication—An approach to education for students who are deaf that combines oral speech, sign language, and fingerspelling.

toxemia—Presence of toxic substances in the body.

toxic substances—Foreign substance that can be harmful or destructive to the body (e.g., alcohol, nicotine, and narcotics).

transdisciplinary team—A team whose members plan and provide services within and across discipline boundaries to provide integrated services.

transductive reasoning—Characteristic of thinking during Piaget's pre-operational stage, the process of reasoning from one particular event to another.

transfer—How a person is physically moved from one position to another.

transient behavioral disabilities—Social-emotional disturbances that come and go.

transition—A period when a person makes a change from one setting to another.

transition plan—A statement of the process to help a child move from one type of program to another.

traumatic brain injury (TBI)—A category of disability in IDEA referring to an injury to the brain that impairs learning or motor functions.

trial and error—(See discovery learning.)

tuberculosis—An infectious disease usually affecting the lungs.

Turner syndrome—A sex chromosome abnormality found in females resulting in sterility and characterized by short stature, distinctive facial features, webbing of the neck, a broad shieldlike chest, and heart conditions.

unconditional positive regard—Acceptance or love given without conditions that involves feeling good about or valuing a child no matter what the child does.

underextend—Early vocabulary error in which words are applied narrowly to a smaller number of objects and events than is appropriate.

undifferentiated cry—Crying that expresses discomfort but is not specific to any particular stimulus.

unintelligible speech—Speech that cannot be understood by most listeners.

universal—Common to children of all cultures.

universal norms—Average or standard performance level of children of a particular age.

upper-extremity proximal stability—Includes joint range or motion and fine motor manipulation of objects and coordination.

Usher's syndrome—Genetic disorder that causes gradual loss of vision and hearing.

verbal communication—Use of written or oral communication.

vibro-tactile hearing aid—An aid for the profoundly deaf worn on the wrist and vibrating slightly, giving the wearer additional speech information.

viral infections—Infections caused by a virus that can be fatal to children with deficient immune systems (e.g., pediatric AIDS).

visual acuity—Sharpness and clarity of vision.

visual efficiency—How well a person can use sight, influenced by acuity and peripheral vision.

visual impairments—All levels of visual loss.

visual-perceptual motor skills—The ability to process visual information that allows for successful movement.

visual-perceptual skills—Physical response to visual stimulation that will be needed for such skills as reading and writing from right to left.

visually track—Watch or follow an object using the eyes.

vocal play—Parent and infant imitating each others' sounds.

vocal symbols—Words children use to express themselves.

vocalization—Utterances and sounds children make as they learn to speak.

voice—A sound described in terms of quality, pitch, loudness, resonance, and duration produced by vibrations of the lungs, larynx, or pharynx.

voice disorder—Abnormal spoken language production characterized by unusual pitch, loudness, or quality of sounds.

voluntary responses—Intentional movements.

Waardentburg's syndrome—Genetic disorder that causes hearing impairments and is often characterized by eyes of two different colors and changes in skin and hair pigmentation.

weight-bearing—Supporting his or her own weight in different positions.

W sitting—Sitting with knees together and feet out to the side.

SUBJECT INDEX

DATE DUE

3/2/03			
ILL # 3369573			
5608059 11			
9.27.09			